11072   25⁰⁰

11072   25⁰⁰

Melvin Ricks'

Alaska Bibliography

The *Alaska Bibliography* of Melvin Byron Ricks, under the editorship of Stephen and Betty Haycox, is a unique research tool for understanding the Great Land's historiography. The result of over twenty-five years of research, it assists both the casual reader and the specialist in northern studies.

Unlike most bibliographies, the Ricks' is annotated and encyclopedic. Many entries are cross-referenced within the volume and keyed to other bibliographical sources. In compiling and organizing his material, Ricks presents information with special concern for the reader who might not be aware of important historical relationships. Thus, this work provides an uncommon foundation for an understanding of the Alaskan past. No other available bibliography offers this. Its reasonable price is made possible through private and public funding.

While the members of the Alaska Historical Commission are intent upon generating income which can be used for financing other writing projects, their goal is also to assure wide distribution and public access to works produced. The publication of this volume constitutes a research milestone in the history of the Alaska Territory and the 49th State.

Melvin Ricks'
Alaska Bibliography:

An Introductory Guide to Alaskan Historical Literature

Melvin B. Ricks

Melvin Ricks'

Alaska Bibliography:

An Introductory Guide to Alaskan Historical Literature

Edited by

Stephen W. and Betty J. Haycox
University of Alaska, Anchorage

Published by

Binford & Mort

2536 S.E. Eleventh • Portland, Oregon 97202

for the

Alaska Historical Commission

Foreword

The goal of the Alaska Historical Commission is to assure accurate, inclusive, and comprehensive data about the Great Land. Efforts at achieving this are four-fold: information retrieval and dissemination; education in historical methodology and interpretation; research; and publication. From May, 1973, when its office was first established, through statute, the Commission envisioned research and publication directed at producing references, chronicles, and narratives. Initial emphasis has been upon research tools and the development of an historical methodology series to encourage citizen participation in researching community history and biography.

Melvin Ricks' *Alaska Bibliography: An Introductory Guide to Alaskan Historical Literature* is the second hardbound publication produced by the Commission. It is a reference of major importance in Alaskan historiography, updating, complementing, and supplementing James Wickersham's *A Bibliography of Alaskan Literature* (1927); *The Arctic Bibliography* (Arctic Institute of North America); Valarian Lada-Mocarski's *Bibliography of Books on Alaska Before 1868* (1969); and Elsie Tourville's *Alaska: A Bibliography, 1570-1970* (1975).

For over a quarter-century, Melvin Ricks gathered historical material. This *Bibliography* is the result of his love affair with the Great Land. His quest into her past and present produced a collection of Alaskan books of over 1,000 titles; 84 volumes of pamphlets and occasional literature; 16,000 notecards; a four-volume typescript of Alaskan historical data, "Gleanings From My Notebooks"; a postal history of the 49th State; and the translation of three early Russian journals (published by the Cook Inlet Historical Society) under the title, *The Earliest History of Alaska* (1970).

Following his retirement from federal and state service, Melvin Ricks returned to Alaska, where for the last six months of his life he was the first full-time paid curator of the Cook Inlet Historical Society's Museum. Following Ricks' death, his children, Mrs. Thomas L. Wright and Mr. Leon J. Ricks, presented the Alaskana collection to Alaska Methodist University with the proviso that the Cook Inlet Historical Society would have publication rights to his manuscripts until 1969, whence they would be transferred to AMU.

For ten years the typescript of this bibliography (in several forms) received little attention. Then in 1974, Professor Stephen Haycox became interested in editing it. He presented his plan to the members of the Alaska Historical Commission, who agreed to coordinate funding for preparation and publication. During 1975 and 1976 Stephen and Betty Haycox edited and updated the manuscript.

This volume was made possible through a partnership of public and private institutions committed to the production of quality materials on Alaska's past and present. The University of Alaska, Anchorage, encouraged the editors to undertake the project. It also has provided office space to the Historical Commission. The Board of Trustees of Alaska Methodist University granted publication rights to the State of Alaska.

The Rasmuson Foundation presented the Commission with two handsome grants, the first for manuscript preparation and the second for publication. The Cook Inlet Historical Society, so instrumental in bringing Melvin Ricks back to Alaska, greatly aided the editing with two annual grants. The State of Alaska supplied major funding for the production of this book. Since the support of this historical work bridges two administrations, it is appropriate to acknowledge the Commission's indebtedness to Governor William A. Egan and Governor Jay Hammond and their staffs and departments for encouragement and assistance. We also wish to express appreciation to the members of the Eighth, Ninth, and Tenth Alaska Legislatures for continued philosophic commitment and fiscal provision.

Finally, because each chairman and member of the Commission has contributed to the development of this research tool since 1974, acknowledgment of their valuable counsel is affirmed in a roster of appointment and service carried in these introductory pages.

The State of Alaska and its Historical Commission are most grateful for the private and public partnership which has made possible the printing of Melvin Byron Ricks' *Alaska Bibliography*. The partnership considers itself fortunate to have been favored with the personal attention, professional care, and technical excellence of Thomas Binford and his colleagues at Binford and Mort, Publishers, as well as the historical knowledge, editing skills, and scholarly dedication of Stephen and Betty Haycox.

Robert A. Frederick
Executive Director
Alaska Historical Commission

Contents

Acknowledgments

The
ALASKA HISTORICAL COMMISSION

wishes to express its appreciation to this partnership
of public and private institutions. Publication was
made possible through generous grants from

THE RASMUSON FOUNDATION

THE COOK INLET HISTORICAL SOCIETY

THE STATE OF ALASKA

and with the support of

THE UNIVERSITY OF ALASKA, ANCHORAGE

and

ALASKA METHODIST UNIVERSITY

Roster of Appointment and Service

THE ALASKA HISTORICAL COMMISSION

Chairman
Lieutenant Governor H.A. Boucher
1973-1975

Chairman
Lieutenant Governor Lowell Thomas, Jr.
1975-

Members
Nominated by the Alaska Historical Society;
Appointed by the Governor

Evangeline Atwood, Anchorage
1973-1974

Emily Ivanoff Brown, Fairbanks and Unalakleet
1973-1975

Robert N. De Armond, Juneau
1973-1976

Richard W. Montague, Anchorage
1973-1974

Patricia McCollom, Anchorage
1975-1976

Patricia Roppel, Ketchikan
1975-

Martha Larson, Bethel and Kongiganak
1976-

Herbert Hilscher, Anchorage
1976-

William B. Workman, Anchorage
1977-

Introduction

This bibliography was compiled and written by Melvin B. Ricks, 1896-1964. Ricks was educated at several universities, including Stanford, DePauw (A.B., 1922) and Missouri (M.A., 1923). His majors were Spanish language and literature. He worked on the Panama Canal project, taught school and college, and spent the largest portion of his adult life as a probation officer for Los Angeles County. He came to Alaska as a probation officer in 1957. Retiring in 1959, he came to Anchorage in 1963 where he continued his researches into Alaska bibliography, contributing as well to the work of the Cook Inlet Historical Society.

Throughout his career Mel Ricks made Alaska bibliography and history an avocation, collecting books, noting articles, and generally familiarizing himself with Alaska literature. Initially interested in Spanish exploration of the Northwest coast, he expanded his labors first to the Russian period, learning the language well enough to produce several translations of significant documents, including Shelikhov's account of his journey across Siberia, and Khlebnikov's biography of Baranov. Later, he worked on the American period. Mel Ricks died of a heart attack in Anchorage in June, 1964.

Ricks began work on his bibliography in 1959, and produced a preliminary version by the end of 1960. Copies of this were bound, and are housed in the Alaska State Historical Library, and the Alaska Methodist University Alaskana Collection. There is as well a copy available on microfilm at the University of Alaska's Rasmuson Library in College. Between 1960 and 1964 Ricks continued to work on the bibliography, expanding it significantly. He died, however, before completing his revision.

Mel Ricks' heirs made a gift of his notes and materials to the Alaskana Collection of the Alaska Methodist University in Anchorage. With the exception of a postal history of Alaska, and translations of three Russian works, all publication rights to Mel Ricks' work were deeded to AMU.

With the generous assistance of Miss Elizabeth Carroll of the AMU Library, I began editing Ricks' materials, with the assistance of my wife Betty, in 1971. Because of the need for a single, comprehensive, introductory bibliography to cover the years since the Wickersham bibliography (1926), we determined to prepare the unfinished Ricks revision for publication. Our work was greatly aided by the encouragement and aid of Prof. Robert Frederick of the Alaska Historical Commission, who encouraged support of the project by many, and made all of the facilities of his office available to us. We were assisted also by the University of Alaska, particularly Dean Wendell Wolfe of the Anchorage Senior College. The work would not have been possible, also, without generous grants from the Cook Inlet Historical Society, and the Rasmuson Foundation. The editors hereby gratefully acknowledge the generous and necessary aid and support they have had in this work from these persons and agencies, and from all others who have contributed, most particularly Miss Jo Antonson, whose meticulous reading of the manuscript has saved us from many a foolish and unintended error. The editors also take full responsibility for errors of fact contained in the work. Users are encouraged to call these to our attention by writing to the Department of History, University of Alaska, Anchorage.

Stephen W. Haycox

Guide to Use

This bibliography lists introductory sources on most personalities and aspects of Alaska history and literature. Unlike many other bibliographies, it contains not only a listing of books, but also articles and government publications. It contains annotations as well, where the original compiler (Melvin B. Ricks) and the editors have felt they would be useful.

The work is intended primarily for those unfamiliar with Alaska historical sources, rather than for the professional scholar. However, it is the experience of the editors that much material listed in this work is not listed elsewhere. It is also felt the annotations constitute a useful contribution to Alaska historical studies. Researchers interested in pursuing further any author or topic listed in this bibliography are cautioned that this work is not intended to be exhaustive. Students should consult the following bibliographies, available at most major libraries within, and outside, Alaska:

1. The *Arctic Bibliography*, published by the Arctic Institute of North America; it is the most comprehensive and complete bibliography dealing with Alaska subjects, literature and authors.

2. Wickersham's *A Bibliography of Alaskan Literature*, published at the University of Alaska (Alaska Agricultural College and School of Mines) in 1927, containing as well a complete list of newspapers.

3. Elsie Tourville's *Alaska: A Bibliography, 1570-1970* published by G.K. Hall Company at Boston in 1975. This comprehensive work unfortunately does not include periodical literature or government publications. It also does not include much secondary material listed in this (Ricks') work. It is particularly useful, however, for Russian materials.

These bibliographies are referred to in many entries in this work. AB-2245 refers the reader to item number 2245 in the *Arctic Bibliography*. The notation "See the *Arctic Bibliography*" following any entry in this work (Ricks) indicates the reader should find the same entry in the Arctic Bibliography under which he is reading in this work.

W-9937 refers to item number 9937 in Wickersham's *Bibliography*.

T-3865 refers the reader to item number 3865 in the Tourville *Bibliography*.

S-1902 refers the reader to item number 1902 in Smith's *Pacific Northwest Americana*.

In each case the reader should consult the bibliographies indicated for additional materials bearing on the subject of his investigation.

This bibliography contains topical entries under which are listed a variety of sources containing material about the topical entry. The reader should consult the entries listed under any given topic, or personality or author or place, first in this bibliography, and then in the other bibliographies indicated. Many of the works listed in this bibliography contain specific bibliographies on the subject of the work within the volume, either as footnotes to the text, or as a separate appendix or section. The researcher is cautioned not to overlook these specific bibliographies, for they are often the most useful.

Most of the materials listed in this bibliography are available at the Alaska State Historical Library, at the Rasmuson Library of the University of Alaska, College, or the Library of the University of Alaska, Anchorage. Most are available to local municipal or university and college libraries through the national interlibrary loan system. Primary materials for Alaska history are deposited in a variety of collections in and outside Alaska. There are significant collections at the Alaska State Historical Library and the Alaska State Archive in Juneau, the Rasmuson Library of the University of Alaska in College, the Suzzallo Library at the University of Washington, the Bancroft Library at the University of California, the National Archives of the U.S. at Washington, D.C., and the National Archives and Federal Records Center, Region Ten, Seattle, Washington, among other places. Some of these have been microfilmed, and are available on loan; most have not been filmed and are therefore not available on loan. Consult the bibliographies in secondary works on the subject of interest, Robert A. Frederick's "Caches of Alaskana," and the individual libraries with Alaska holdings for further information.

Melvin Ricks'
Alaska Bibliography:

An Introductory Guide to
Alaskan Historical Literature

A

ABALONE

Alaska Life, Apr., '40; *Alaska Sportsman*, Apr., '40 (found on west coast, southeast Alaska); May, '42; Feb., '43; Aug., '51 (Prince of Wales Island); Dec., '57; *Alaska Weekly*, Sept., '51 (Fish & Wildlife Service survey); Nov. '51 (commercially infeasible); *Alaska Magazine*, July '72.

ABASA, SERGEI S. (Chief, Asiatic Division Western Union Overland Telegraph Expedition; cp.)

Shiels; St. Petersburg *Vied* (in Russian), 1867; W-6010

ABBE, CLEVELAND, Jr.

See Brooks, Alfred H.

ABERCROMBIE CANYON

Allen (descr.); Baker ("there is no canyon, one bank being flat"); *Alaska Sportsman*, Nov., '61.

ABERCROMBIE RAPIDS

Alaska-Yukon Magazine, Aug., '09 (photo by Hegg); Baker (in Copper River above Miles Glacier, named by Mendenhall and Schrader, 1903); Whiting.

ABERCROMBIE, THOMAS J.

"Nomad in Alaska's Outback," *National Geographic*, April, 1969.

ABERCROMBIE, WILLIAM RALPH (b. 1857) (US Army officer)

"Supplementary Expedition in the Copper River Valley," in *Compilation of Narratives* (see US Congress, Senate, Committee on Military Affairs, 1900). Report of unsuccessful ascent of Copper River, 1884; information on navigation, topography, and natives.

"Report of Captain W.R. Abercrombie on Explorations in Alaska (a military reconnaissance of the Copper River Valley), 1898," *Compilation of Narratives*. Crossing of Valdez Glacier, ascent of Copper River, and return. See also the Arctic Bibliography, and Wickersham's Bibliography.

US Copper River Exploring Expedition, 1899. Wn.DC: GPO, 1900 (US Army). Expedition constructed 80 miles of pack trail from Valdez to the Klutina River headwaters. This report contains numerous sub-reports of tangential reconnaissances in the Copper and Matanuska River areas by the expedition.

"The Copper River Country, Alaska," *Journal of the Franklin Institute*, 1904. Summary of the expeditions of 1884, 1898, and 1899. On the 1899 ex-

pedition Abercrombie rescued several hundred miners at Valdez and as far inland as Copper Center who had struck overland to reach the gold fields in the Klondike, having underestimated the distance, conditions and supplies needed.

see the following:
Alaska Sportsman, Jan., '41; Allen, Lt. H.; Andrews, C.; Baker, M.; Bikert-Smith and de Laguna (unpublished Abercrombie manuscripts used); Brooks, A.; Colby; Higginson; Hulley; Sherwood, M. (analysis of Abercrombie's role); Tompkins (description of Valdez prospectors rescued by Abercrombie).

ABORIGINAL RIGHTS

Alaska Life, Dec., '44; June, '45; Jan., '48; *Alaska Sportsman*, Jan., '54; May, '54 ("Unalakleet Eskimos do not claim 'rights' "); Dec., '56; *Alaska Weekly*, Aug., '51 (Knik Indians and the Matanuska valley); Alaska Chamber of Commerce, misc. corresp. and resolution, 1944-45 (in Alaska State Historical Library); Bigjim, F.S. and James Ito-Adler, *Letters to Howard* (Anchorage: Alaska Methodist University, 1974) ("anonymous" letters to the editor of the *Tundra Times*, native newspaper published at Fairbanks, during the debate over the Alaska Native Claims Settlement Act in the US Congress, 1970-71); Buynitzky, S.N., "Land Rights of Natives in Alaska," trans. of memo to Sec. St. William Seward, Aug., 1867 (Buynitzky was minister of foreign affairs at St. Petersburg) (in Alaska State Historical Library); Cohen, Felix, *Handbook of Federal Indian Law* (Wn.DC: GPO, 1940) (this significant compendium of American Indian law was reissued in 1956 by the Dept. of Interior under the editorship of Frank B. Horne); see also several articles by Felix Cohen in Lucy Kramer Cohen, ed., *The Legal Conscience: Selected Papers of Felix S. Cohen* (New Haven: Yale University Press, 1960); Dall, William, *Alaska and Its Resources* (Sampson, Low, Son and Marston, 1870); Federal Field Commission for Development Planning in Alaska, *Alaska Natives and the Land* (Wn.DC: GPO, 1968) (landmark study of conditions of Alaska natives, utilized in the settlement act debate); Fedorova, Svetlana, *The Population of Russian America*, trans. and ed., Richard Pierce (Kingston, Ontario: Limestone Press, 1972); Gruening, Ernest, *State of Alaska*; Gsovski, Vladimir, *Russian Administration of Alaska, and the Status of Alaska Natives* (Wn.DC: GPO, 1950) (prepared for the US Congress); M.G. Levin, "Ethnographic and Anthropological Materials as Historic Sources," *Arctic Anthropology* 1 (1962: 51-57); Nancy Lurie, "Indian Cultural Adjustment to European Civilization," in *17th Century America: Essays in Colonial History*, ed. James M. Smith (Chapel Hill: University of North Carolina Press, 1959); US Dept. of the Interior, *Hearings on the Claims of Natives of Hydaburg, Kake, Klawock, etc. held in Alaska in 1944* (copy in Alaska State Historical Library); US Senate, Committee on Interior and Insular Affairs, *Hearings on the Conditions on Natives in Alaska, 1935* (Wn. DC: GPO, 1935); Monroe Price, *Law and the American Indian: Readings, Notes and Cases* (Indianapolis: Bobbs-Merrill, 1973); George Rogers, *Alaska in Transition* (Baltimore: Johns Hopkins Press, 1960); James Van Stone, "Annotated Ethnographical Bibliography of the Nushagak River Drainage," *Fieldana Anthropology*, 54 (1968): 148-189; Wilcomb Washburne, *Red Man's Land, White Man's Law* (New York: Charles Scribner's Sons, 1971), and "The Moral and Legal Justification for Dispossessing the Indians," in *17th Century America*, ed. Smith. See also *Collection of Documents and Copies of Documents Pertaining to the Transfer of Alaska and the Formation of a Committee to Report on Aboriginal Rights of Indians in Alaska, 1867-92*, Alaska State Historical Library, and *Report of Claims Attorneys to Tlingit and Haida Indians of Alaska* (1959), Alaska State Historical Library, both in manuscript. See also Arnold, R., *Alaska Native Claims Act*.

ABRUZZI, DUKE OF
See Filippi, de Filippo

ABSENTEE OWNERSHIP
Nichols, *Alaska;* Sundborg; Tompkins; Wickersham, *Tales and Trails*. See Alaska Steamship Co., Alaska Syndicate, Ballinger-Pinchot Controversy, Guggenheim Brothers. See also Gruening, *State of Alaska*.

ACKERMAN, ROBERT
T-1

A'COURT, H. HOLMES (British Naval officer)
Andrews, C.; Brooks, A.; Clark, H.W.; Gruening; Hulley; Nichols; Scidmore; Tompkins; see also *HMS Osprey* (the vessel, under A'Court's command, responded to a plea from Sitka in 1879 for an authority to impose order when no American authority seemed to respond); see Sherwood.

ADAK ISLAND (Aleutians, Andreanov group)
Alaska Sportsman, July, '39; Dec., '43 (naval installations); Jan., '55; Aug., '55; Feb., '66; *Alaska Life*, Oct., '43 (photos); *Alaska Weekly*, June, '50; July, '50 (ratless until '45, now thousands); Baker (sighted in 1761; Aleut word means crab or father); Bancroft (probably sighted by Chirikov; Tolstykh there in 1761; Drushinnin, Glottov there in 1763); cp. Berkh (*Chronological Sketch of the Discovery and Settlement of the Aleutian Islands*); Dall (volcano smoking in 1760); Denison (photos; FDR there; village destroyed by Japanese); Gruening (possible Orient refueling stop); Hulley (Chirikov probably took on water); *National Geographic Magazine*, Aug., '43 (color plates); March, '49 (eclipse equipment); Tewkesbury (Attu and Kiska bombed by Japanese from Adak airfield); Tompkins (natives fought Russians under Bashmakov in 1752). See also Brian Garfield, *Thousand Mile War*.

ADAMOV, ARKADII GRIGOREVICH (b. 1920)
Russian, historian of the Russian period in Alaska; numerous publications, all in Russian, dealing with Baranov, Khlebnikov, Kashevarov, Zagoskin, Shelikhov and Serebrennikov and exploration generally. See the following: AB-43487, 20035, 38419, 49110, and 27645; also 27644 and 27646. See also T-4 ff.

ADAMOV, E.A.
"Russia and the United States at the Time of the Civil War," *Journal of Modern History*, II (1930): 602 ff. (discussion of the Russian fleets which visited New York and San Francisco during the war, bearing on the Alaska purchase). See Adams, John Quincy for further references on Alaskan diplomacy. See also various United States diplomatic histories, and histories of the Secretaries of State; see Jensen.

ADAMS (steamer, US Navy)
See the following:
Andrews, C. (under Commander Merriman at Sitka); Bancroft (Capt. Merriman used *Corwin* to shell Angoon in 1882, as *Adams* was too large); Scidmore; Willard (succeeded *Wachusett*, Oct., 1882; trouble at Killisnoo and Angoon); see also references discussing the period between 1879 and 1884 when the US Navy was the primary government authority in Alaska).

ADAMS, ANSEL
The Great Land (with 12 photos). Sierra Club Bulletin, June, 1950.

ADAMS, BEN (journalist)
Alaska, the Big Land: the 49th State in Pictures. New York: Hill and Wang, 1959. See review, *Daily Alaska Empire* (Juneau), June 24, 1959. 213 pp.

The Last Frontier: A Short History of Alaska. Illus. George Ahgupuk. New York: Hill and Wang, 1961. 181 pp.

ADAMS, EPHRAIM DOUGLASS
Great Britain and the American Civil War. New York and London: Oxford University Press, 1925. 2v. (discussion of the purchase of Alaska)

ADAMS, JAMES TRUSLOW
The Adams Family. Boston: Little, Brown & Co., 1930. (discussion of the role of John Quincy Adams in the Russo-American treaty of 1824 and the Russo-British treaty of 1825). See also the Adams Family papers edited by Lyman Butterfield, and diplomatic histories of the United States and also histories of the American Secretaries of State.

ADAMS, JOHN QUINCY (1767-1848) (President, Secretary of State)
See the following:
Adams, J.T.; Greenhow (Adams as minister to Russia); Hulley (claims of Russia in the Pacific Northwest); Thomas; Tompkins (re: Rumyantsev and American rights in Russian-American waters); see also Nichols, I.C., and Buzanski, P.M. See as well references to the world diplomatic situation as background to the Russian-American treaties in works by Dexter Perkins (the Monroe Doctrine) and Bradford Perkins. See esp. Bagot, and also Thomas A. Bailey, and Ronald Jensen.

ADAMS, RUTH
"Alaska: Again our Stepchild Outpost Enjoys a Boom Born of Crisis," *Life Magazine*, Oct. 2, 1950.

ADAMSON, HANS CHRISTIAN
Keepers of the Lights. New York: Greenberg, 1955 430 pp. (section on Arctic lightkeepers).

ADDINGTON, CAPE (west of Craig on Noyes Island)

Baker (named by Vancouver for Speaker of the House of Commons); Hadman (description, plates); Vancouver (v. 3).

ADKINS, JOHN N.

"The Alaskan Earthquake of July 22, 1937," *Bulletin of the Seismological Society of America*, 1940 (Berkeley).

ADMIRALTY BAY (Arctic coast, east of Barrow)

Baker (forms the head of Dease Inlet; named for British Admiralty, 1856).

ADMIRALTY BAY (same as Yakutat Bay)

Baker (named by Portlock, 1786; Spaniards adopted Portlock's name); Vancouver ("I have adopted the name of Beering's Bay, instead of that of Admiralty Bay, so named by Mr. Dixon."); Dall (called Admiralty Bay by Dixon; in 1798 Khvostov explored Admiralty Bay).

ADMIRALTY ISLAND

Alaska Sportsman, Jan., '39; Dec., '41 (bears); Sept., '43; Jan., '54 (retirement of Allen Hasselborg, 56 years at Mole Harbor); Oct., '55 (Hasselborg's return to Pioneer Home; Lake Hasselborg named); *Alaska Magazine*, Sept., '70; Baker (named by Vancouver, 1794; shown as Khutsnoi (bear) Island by Tebenkov); Becker; Burchard and Chapin (*Marble Deposits of Southwestern Alaska* [Wn.DC: GPO, 1920]); Colby; Denison; Dufresne; Grinnell (*Birds and Mammals of the 1907 Alexander Expedition to Southeastern Alaska* [Univ. Calif. Publ. in Zoology, v. 15, No. 2]); Gruening (on controversy over creation of national monument status); Heintzleman; Higginson, Holzworth; Howard (Indians cultivated potatoes and vegetables); Scidmore (Indian troubles at Angoon, Killisnoo); Sheldon; Sundborg (area 1664 sq. miles); Vancouver (on tobacco cultivation; on general east coast survey; "making the intermediate land, which had hitherto been considered as part of the continent, one extensive island, which I called Admiralty Island"); Williams; Wright (USGS reconnaissance, Bull. 287, 1906); see also numerous references in the Arctic Bibliography.

ADNEY, TAPPAN (b. 1868) (*Harper's Weekly* Klondike corresp.)

The Klondike Stampede of 1897-98. New York: Harper and Brothers, 1900. See Klondike.

AFOGNAK ISLAND (and village)

Alaska Sportsman, Feb., '45; Sept., '45; Jan., '55 (road with covered bridge abandoned; elk thrive); *Alaska-Yukon Magazine*, Oct., '08 (descr. of village life; pop. are Aleut and Creole); Bancroft (fortified station est. by Shelikhov; village desc.); Baker (village est. by Russians here in first quarter of 19th century for pensioned employees of Russian-American Co., called Rubertz, Rubtzovskaia, or possibly Rutkovsky; present village distinct from Litnik, 5 miles north); Colby; Couch (post office 1888-95, 1899-1900 and since 1904); Denison (Roosevelt elk est. on island in 1927); Higginson; Sundborg (elk from Olympic Pen.); Tewkesbury (natives are mixed Russian, Indian, Eskimo, Aleut); Vancouver ("the land to the westward of St. Her-

mogenes Island, which land the Russians call "Fogniak"); see also Wickersham Bibliography (W-6951) (by Pres. Harrison's proclamation of 1892 Afognak was reserved as a Forest and Fish Culture Reservation).

AGATHON, OSHIN and JOHN GUILDAY

"Glacier Bear," *Carnegie Magazine*, June, 1958.

AGATTU ISLAND

Baker (called Krugloi [Round] by the Russians, said to have been called St. Abraham by Bering; one of the Near [Far] Island group); Bancroft (here Russians first fired on natives); Coxe (exclusive of children, Attu, Agattu and Shemya support 60 males); Garfield; Gruening (Attu islanders captured by Japanese in World War II were returned to Agattu Island following their return in 1945).

AGHILEEN PINNACLES

Baker (a remarkable row or series of black castellated rocks west of Pavlov Volcano on the Alaska Peninsula); Hubbard (like the Dolomites of South Tyrol, but larger; photo); *National Geographic Magazine*, Jan., '29 (notes, photo).

AGNEW, EDITH J. (b. 1897)

My Alaska Picture Story Book. New York: Friendship Press, 1948. 56 pp. See T-16

AGRANAT, GREGORII ABRAMOVICH, et al.

Several works in Russian on the development of the American North. See T-18 ff.

AGRICULTURE

The following is a select listing of references. See the following categories in this bibliography, and in other bibliographies and works on Alaska: Agricultural Experiment Station; G.W. Glasser; C.C. Georgeson; Matanuska Valley, Tanana Valley, U.S. National Resources Planning Board, University of Alaska, Institute of Agricultural Sciences, Alaska Rural Rehabilitation Corporation. See the following:

Alaska Life, July, '43 (Heintzleman); Aug., '42 (Sundborg); Nov., '43; Jan., '44; Jan., '45; May, '45; May, '46 (Siberian grains); Oct., '46; *Alaska Sportsman*, Aug., '37; Sept., '39; Apr., '41; Oct., '54 (internat'l farm youth exchange programs); Jan., '57; Feb., '57; June, '57; Sept., '57 (military consume 3/4ths Alaska produce); May, '58; Alaska Territory, Department of Agriculture (see listing in Alaska State Historical Library, Juneau); *Alaska-Yukon Magazine*, May, '09; Feb., '12 (Alaska exhibits at shows in New York and St. Paul, Minn.); Alberts (*The Potato* [Alaska Agri. Exp. Sta. Bull. No. 9, 1931]); Andrews, R.A. and H.A. Johnson (*Farming in Alaska* [AAES Bull. No. 20, 1956], an extensive review); same authors, (*The Potato in Alaska* [AAES Misc. Circ. No. 6, 1952]); Arctic Bibliography (numerous entries); Bancroft (Ross Colony); Brooks; Clard; Colby; Bennett, H.H. and T.D. Rice (*Reconnaissance of Soils and Agriculture, Kenai Peninsula* [Report 16, US Bureau of Soils, 1914]); Buswell; Chamberlin, J.C.; Cosby (*Capability and Need of Alaska Agricultural Land* [Proc. Alaska Science Conf., 1951]; Day, Thomas (*The Soil Conservation Service* [Proc. Alaska Science Conf., 1953]); Dearborn; Denison; Dickson; Fahnestock, C.R.; Fohn-Hansen; Francis; Greeley; Gruening;

Hedla, L. (*Agriculture in Alaska* [AAES, College, 1956]) (reprint of original 1917 edition); Hilscher; Hodgson; Hulley; Irwin, Don L. (see Arctic Bibliography); Jacobin; Laughlin; Litzenberger, S.C. (*Recommended Varieties of Farm Crops for Alaska* [AAES, Palmer, Circ. No. 11, 1950]); Logsdon, Charles (*Diseases of Economic Crops in Alaska* [University AES, Bull. 900, 1956]); Mick, Allan (*Arctic and Sub-arctic Agriculture in Alaska* [18th Biology Colloquium, 1957]) (See Arctic Bibliography); Miller, Orlando (*The Matanuska Valley and the Alaska Frontier* [New Haven; Yale University Press, 1975]); Morris (agriculture in 1877); Moore, Clarence (*Alaska Farms* [AAES, Palmer, Misc. Circ. No. 1, 1951]); *National Geographic Magazine*, various articles (check index), incl. Smith, Middleton (July, 1909), Gannett (Sept., 1903), Georgeson, C.C.; Nuttonson, M.Y. (*Wheat-Climate Relationships and the Use of Phenology in Ascertaining the Thermal and Photothermal Requirements of Wheat* [Wn.DC: Amer. Inst. of Crop Ecology, 1955]) (388 pp bibliography; incl. data for Tanana and Matanuska Valleys); Piper, C.V. (*Grasslands of Southeast Alaska* [Wn.DC: GPO, 1905]); Rockie, W.A. ("Pitting on Alaska Farm Lands: A New Erosion Problem," *Geographic Review* [Jan., '42]); same author ("What of Alaska?" [*Soil Conservation*, Jan., '46], farm lands in 17 basic land resource areas in Alaska); Scidmore (1805-1890); Sherwood (*Cook Inlet Collection*); Sprague, R.; Stuck; Sundborg (North Pacific Planning Project); Sweetman, Wm. J. (three bulletins issued at the AES, Palmer: *Better Forage* [1950], *Raising Dairy Calves* [1951], *Getting a Start in Dairying* [with Branton, C.I., 1955]); same author (*Tips on Making Silage* [Univ. AES, Circ. No. 23, 1954]); Taylor, Roscoe and J.C. Brinmade (*Gasser Wheat: A New Grain for Alaska* [AAES, Cir. 21, 1955]); same author (two circulars issued by the University AES in 1958: *Field Crops* and *Weeds in Alaska*); Tewkesbury; Underwood; US Aricultural Research Administration (exploratory investigations); US Bureau of Land Management (agricultural lands); US Bureau of Land Management (Papers presented at the Seminars in Alaska, Feb. 2-3, 6-7, 1950: see AB-32610); US Bureau of Reclamation, Alaska District Office (*Report on the Water Resources of the Territory* [Wn.DC: GPO, 1952]); US Bureau of the Census (agriculture in Alaska); US Congress, House, Committee on Public Lands (veterans's homesteading act); US Dept. of Agriculture; US Dept. of the Interior (mid-century Alaska); US National Resources Planning Board (biblio., abstracts, re: agriculture); University of Alaska Extension Service (various pamphlets); Washburn, Richard (circulars issued by the Univ. AAES. *Bad News for Bugs: Insect Control* [1958], *Root Maggots* [1957]); Wilson, Charles W. (*Land Clearing in Alaska* [Univ. AES, 1951]). See also in the Wickersham Bibliography, W-127 through 182, particularly for early articles by C.C. Georgeson, E.S. Harrison and J.J. Underwood.

AHGUPUK, GEORGE ADEN (b. 1911) (Eskimo artist)
Alaska Sportsman, June, '41 (skin etchings); Aug., '56 (showing in Calif.); Apr., '57 (born Shishmaref, began drawing in Kotzebue hospital in 1935, res. Anchorage); Oct., '57 (Rockwell Kent "discovered" Ahgupuk in late '30's and spread fame); *Alaska*

Weekly, Aug., '51 (moves from Nome to Anchorage); Colby; Denison; Hayes; Hulley; Keithahn (Ahgupuk illustrations); Russell, Lillian (in Alaska State Historical Library); Tewkesbury (biography; served as postmaster at Shishmaref in 1946).

AHMAOGAK, ROY and DONALD H. WEBSTER
Inupiam Ukaluni, 3 v. (Eskimo Readers, No. 1, 2, and 3). Fairbanks: Summer Linguistics Institute, 1963.

AH-TEN-OW-RAH (or AT-TUN-GOW-RAH) (shaman at Point Hope)
Aldrich (had five wives in 1887); Brower (descr. death); Stuck ("the drunken, despotic, polygamous chief at Point Hope"); Stuck (*Missions:* manner of death).

AKADEMIIA NAUK (Naval Academy, St. Petersburg)
See Berkh, *Chronological Sketch*.

AKIAK (Village)
Baker (Eskimo village on Kuskokwim River 30 miles above Bethel); Couch (post office 1916-1920, and since 1926).

AKIFEV, IVAN NIKOLAEVICH (1872-1906) (surgeon with the Russian-American-English Expedition, 1900)
To the Far North for Gold (in Russian). St. Petersburg: Kommerch, Skoropech, Tile, 1902. (descriptions from diary of a journey from London to Washington, San Francisco, Alaska and the Chukotsk Peninsula, eastern Siberia, where the expedition hoped to find gold. Information on Chukchis).

AKLAVIK (Eskimo village in Mackenzie River delta, Yukon)
Alaska Sportsman, May, '42; Feb., '47 (on Peel Channel, fur trading center, natives are wealthy); Dec., '56; Ederer; Hutchinson; Lindberg, Anne (stopover); Sundborg (lignite mined here).

AKNIK
See Green, Paul

AKULURAK (mission station in the Yukon delta)
Baker (pass or slough connecting Kwikluak with Kwemeluk pass, spelled also Akularak and Akulurok, root meaning "in between"); Couch (post office here 1924-1951, mission school moved to Andreafski [(St. Mary's] 1951); Llorente (descr. life in Catholic boarding school); O'Connor (priest's story of school life); Santos (priests moved here from Tununak in 1893).

AKUN ISLAND (Fox group, Aleutians, east of Unalaska)
Alaska Sportsman, Dec., '45 (sulphur mine here '25); Baker (native name, by Krenitzin, 1768, Aleut for "distant", northern point is Akun head, Akun Strait separates island from Akutan Island); Bancroft (two villages on the island caught in small-pox epidemic of 1838); Dall (slight volcanic activity, 1828, 1865); Oliver (sulphur mine in crater of volcano, Alaska Sulphur Mining Co. had base at lost harbor); Petrov (settlement of sea-otter hunters); Sundborg (good harbor).

AKUTAN ISLAND (east of Unalaska, 4,100 feet)

Alaska Sportsman, Feb., '47 (whaling station closed during war); Apr., '47 (red hot lava flowing from Akutan Volcano Jan., '47); Aug., '49 (major eruption April 29-May 10, 1949, ashes fell on Akutan village, 8 miles distant); June, '61; Baker (largest island, Krenitzin [now Fox] group, native name reported by Krenitzin and Levashev in 1768); Bancroft (Russian hunters [28] under Poloskov here in 1767, Aleuts attacked and killed 4); Berkh; Birkeland (whaling); Colby (descr. whaling); Couch (post office 1909-11, since 1914); Hubbard (volcano, area "cradle of storms"); Sundborg (whaling site); Tewkesbury (settlement still extant in 1949); Winchell (descr. whaling station); also Oliver; *National Geographic Magazine*, Dec., '42 (photo, whaling activity); July, '52 (whaling station closed in 1938, notes on villages).

ALAGANIK (Indian village at mouth of Copper River)

Alaska Sportsman, Aug., '39 (photo of old Russian trading post); Abercrombie (summer village of Eyaks); Allen (Serebrenikov here in 1847, Russian redoubt built few miles south in 1788, photo); Baker (in 1885 natives settled at Skatalis, thought by Allen to have been original redoubt site, Alaganik most westerly slough of Copper); Koehler.

ALASKA (on origin of name)

Baker (This word is a corruption of some native word or phrase of uncertain origin); Colby (the Aleut name al-ay-ek-sha is supposed to mean 'mainland', and is used today [1930's] in that way by natives of Shumagins); Cook ("I have already observed that the American continent is here called by the Russians as well as the islanders, Alaschka, which name, though it probably belongs only to the country adjoining to Oonemak, is used by them in speaking of the American continent in general, which they know perfectly well to be a great land." [by the phrase "great land" Cook means continent, as opposed to island or peninsula]); Coxe ("They then sailed to the most remote island Alaksu, or Alachshak" [Alaxa on Krenitzin's chart?], "Few of the islands produce wood. . .Unalga and Alaxa contain the most." "Alaksu, or Alachshak, one of the most remote Eastern islands." [from this discussion is confirmed the notion that the Russians initially supposed what is now the Alaska Peninsula to be an island lying east of Unimak; the above remarks are in Coxe's 1780 edition]); Coxe [1787 edition] ("Alaxa, called sometimes Alaxsu, Alachshak and Alashka. . .supposed to be a great island in the vicinity of America, was found by Cook to be a promontory of that Continent."); Coxe [1803 edition] ("Directing their course due west they discovered that land in 56° latitude which is now called Alaska."); Dall ("We have, then, Alaska for the territory, Aliaska for the peninsula, and Unalaska for the island, all derived from the same root, meaning great land [in the sense of continent, or large land mass]; the island now known as Unalaska was called "Na-gun-alayeksa, or land near Alayeksa."); Dole (Sumner's peroration cited, in which the name Alaska is suggested for the newly acquired possession); Geoghegan ("It is commonly stated that Alaska is an Aleut word meaning 'great country'. This is incorrect. The Aleut name Alaxsxaq refers

only to the Alaska Peninsula, and cannot be translated as 'great country.' " [There are apparently no words in the Aleut language which could be combined to mean "great country", and still resemble Alaxsxaq]); Halleck, Gen. H.W., commander of the Military Division of the Pacific (See his letter of May 22, 1867 [40th Cong., 2nd session, House Document 117, pp. 57-58], to Brevet Major Gen. E.D. Townsend, in which recommendation is made that the name Alaska be applied to the new territory, since Col. Bulkley had assured Halleck that Russians and natives in the territory were already using the term to denote most of the territory.); James ("Senator Sumner seems to have been the first to suggest. . ." the name Alaska. "It has been stated also that Secretary Seward originated the name, Alaska." [See Seward, Frederick W., *Reminiscences of a War Time Statesman and Diplomat* [New York: Harper and Row, 1916]); Neue Nachrichten ("Alaeksu" is described and located as the large island north of Kadjak); Pilgrim ([a common misrepresentation] "The name Alaska is commonly believed to be the English pronunciation of the native word 'Al-ay-ek-sa', meaning 'the Great Land' or 'mainland'."); Ransom (in Aleut the word Alaska means mainland); Seward, F.W. (see James above; Stewart doubts the validity of F. Seward's claim that his father suggested the name Alaska); Shiels (Sumner's speech fully quoted); Staehlin (author's map shows Alaska as large island extending east and west through 56° latitude); Stewart (excellent analysis of the origin of the name Alaska); Sumner (see his speech suggesting the name Alaska for the new territory); Wagner (v. 2 on map 772—Bodega y Quadra, 1791—there is shown the words *Provincia de Alaska* at the lower end of the Alaska Peninsula, "taken no doubt from the accounts of the Martinez expedition of 1788, or of Cook's voyage.").

ALASKA

Monthly magazine published at Juneau from May, 1917, to November, 1918, edited by Sydney D. Charles. W-4984

ALASKA (US Naval vessel)

Gruening (at Sitka April 3 to June 14, 1879); other vessels have borne the name, including one christened in 1943 at Camden, New Jersey, a cruiser (*Alaska Sportsman*, Nov., '43), which was deactivated after World War II (*Alaska Sportsman*, Dec., '57); The *Alaska* of the Alaska Steamship Company is pictured in *Alaska Sportsman* (Nov., '38), a ship which probably went around near Prince Rupert on October 28, 1940 (*Alaska Sportsman*, Sept., '41).

ALASKA AGRICULTURAL COLLEGE AND SCHOOL OF MINES

See University of Alaska

ALASKA ALMANAC

Published annually 1905-09 by the Arctic Club of Seattle, compiled by W.M. Sheffield (1905-07) and Edward S. Harrison (1908-09). Information on industrial development, resources, geography, history, government, ethnology, distances, mail services, etc., with a directory of territorial officials. Some issues were known as *Alaska Club's Almanac*. Complete file at University of Washington Library. See also Harrison. Sheffield wrote an article, "Work of the Arctic Club" for the *Alaska-Yukon Magazine*, October, 1906.

ALASKA BAR ASSOCIATION
See T-31

THE ALASKA BOOK
The Alaska Book: Story of our Northern Treasure-land. Chicago: J.G. Ferguson, 1960. 320 pp. 56 articles from *Alaska Sportsman*.

ALASKA BOUNDARY TRIBUNAL
The tribunal was created by a convention signed at Washington, D.C., in 1903, to settle the boundary between Alaska and Canada. The cases and arguments of both parties are printed in full; see W-893-7. The principal argument concerned definition of the word "coast." The Canadians interpreted the coast as following the general direction of the shore, while the Americans interpreted the term more literally, no matter how far inland it might follow inlets, bays, channels and estuaries. The Canadians, for example, claimed Skagway, at the head of Lynn Canal, far inland from the coast by their way of reasoning. The Americans claimed it as well, reasoning that it was actually on the coast. The Russo-British treaty of 1825, the first delineation of the border between Alaska and Canada, defined the boundary as the crests of the mountains which lay parallel to the coast, at no point removed from the coast more than ten marine leagues, about 35 miles. The crests proved difficult to locate with precision, so in the 19th century were generally presumed to be the span between highest peaks reasonably close to the coast. Generally speaking, the award favored US contentions. Following the award the actual boundary was marked along its entire distance, save the more rugged portion of the St. Elias range. See the following:
Alaska Sportsman, July, '44; Aug., '45 (boundary cleared every six years, alternately by Canadians [1944] and Americans. See also Cole, D; Harper; Penlington; see also International Boundary Commission. See also John Munro, ed., *The Alaska Boundary Dispute* (Toronto: Copp Clark Publ. Co., 1970). See Boundary Issue.

ALASKA CENTRAL RAILROAD
Alaska Central Railroad Co., Official Prospectus. Seattle: Yerkes Printing Co., 1902; *Alaska-Yukon Magazine*, Sept., '09 (sold by receiver in 1909 for a tenth the investment); Davis (Seward founded, intent to tap Matanuska coal fields, then Yukon, 70 miles of track laid); Seward (General Manager Dickinson approved name "Vetuska" [now Seward] for terminal city); Dole (to tap Tanana Valley, 53 miles of track laid); Underwood (US bought 72 miles of track for one-sixth cost). See also Alaska Northern Railway, Alaska Railroad.

ALASKA CHAMBER OF COMMERCE
Numerous circulars and brochures, including *Glimpses of Alaska: As it Was and Is* (Juneau, 1935; reissued, 1937), and *Alaska: Its Needs for National Defense and Air Mail Service* (Juneau, 1934).

ALASKA COMMERCIAL COMPANY (1868-1901)
A select listing of references: *Alaska-Yukon Gold Book* (early history); Anti-Monopoly League; Bancroft; Clark; Elliott; Hulley; Johnston (company history to 1940); Kitchener (defense); Gruening (quotes Swineford, enormous initial profits, fought progress in Alaska); Morris (accused of opposing development of Alaska, Elliott wrote articles for the company); Nichols; Ogilvie; Schwatka; Scidmore (organization, control of fur trade); Swineford (critical of company in his governor's reports); Tompkins (Alaska a "company possession," as in Russian days); US Congress (Fur Seals and Other Fisheries); Wickersham (Old Yukon); Young (fought political progress in Alaska, employed writers to "talk down" the territory); see also Alaska Commercial Company manuscripts in the Jackson Library, Stanford University (Palo Alto); see also Fur Trade, Pribilof Islands, Alaska Exploration Company; see also T-49 ff.

ALASKA COMMUNICATIONS SYSTEM
Alaska Life, Aug., '48; *Alaska Sportsman*, Apr., '37 (23 regular stations with 98 summer [cannery] stations); Apr., '55 (opened in 1903 as WAMCATS [Washington Alaska Military Communication and Telegraph System]); Brice; Gruening (federal agency, operated by US Army Signal Corps); Nichols, Edwin C.; Sundborg (rates, service); US Army (*Building Alaska with the US Army*). The WAMCATS line was the first telegraph connection with the lower 48 states. It utilized the right-of-way surveyed by the Russian-American Overland Telegraph Expedition in the 1860's, and a line cut from Valdez to the Copper River, and through Mentasta Pass to Eagle on the Yukon, the first 80 miles of which was cut by Abercrombie in 1899. The Valdez-Eagle telegraph trail was cut by Greely and Mitchell in 1901-03. Its purpose was to provide an all-American communications route to the Klondike gold fields and related gold mining activity in Alaska. The Richardson Highway would eventually be laid over the same route, changing direction for Fairbanks at Gulkana after the discovery of gold in that place in 1903. Copper Center was the primary interior station on the line. See Mitchell (*Memoirs*), *Richardson Highway*, Alaska Fund, Alaska Road Commission.

ALASKA CONSTITUTIONAL CONVENTION
The Alaska Constitution. Fairbanks: Alaska Constitutional Convention, 1956. See Alaska Statehood AB-43539. *Alaska Sportsman*, May, '56 75 days) see Naske; Spicer; see also *Proceedings of the Alaska Constitutional Convention* (bound typescript, Alaska State Historical Library). See also Victor Fischer, *Alaska's Constitutional Convention* (Fairbanks: U of A Press, 1975).

ALASKA CONSTRUCTION
Periodical, published at Anchorage.

ALASKA COOPERATIVE WILDLIFE RESEARCH UNIT (College Alaska)
Published a quarterly report from 1951 into the 1960's. The unit represented the cooperative activities of the Alaska Game Commission, the University of Alaska, and other territorial and federal, as

well as some private agencies interested in wildlife conservation. Research projects were concerned with, among others, beaver preservation, muskrat, migratory water fowl, peregrine falcons, wildlife economics, and the bison herd at Big Delta.

ALASKA "COTTON"
Alaska Sportsman, July, '37; March, '41; Sept., '51 (Steese Highway); Anderson, J.P. (cotton grass, ten varieties, Eriophorum angustifolium Roth descr., common throughout Alaska, drawings); Colby; Sharples.

ALASKA CRIPPLED CHILDREN'S ASSOCIA-TION (Anchorage)
Eskimo Cook Book (Anchorage, 1952, 1958) (re-issued with the title *Out of Alaska's Kitchens*). A small mimeographed booklet containing recipes brought to the Shishmaref Day School by Eskimo children. See *Alaska Sportsman*, March, '55. The association was formed at Anchorage in 1946.

ALASKA DAILY EMPIRE (more recently *Daily Alaska Empire* and *Southeast Alaska Empire*)
Founded at Juneau, November 2, 1912; first editors were J.F.A. Strong and John W. Troy, both later territorial governors of Alaska. See Gruening (the paper opposed statehood after Troy's death).

ALASKA DAY (commemoration of 1867 purchase, October 18)
Alaska Weekly, Oct., '51; *Alaska-Yukon Magazine*, Jan., '09 (original celebration originated by attorney Cecil H. Clegg [b. 1873], later a federal judge); Tewkesbury (Clegg biography); see also T-58 ff

ALASKA DEVELOPMENT BOARD (see Alaska, Territory, Development Board)

ALASKA DIPLOMACY (see John Q. Adams, Alaska Boundary Tribunal, etc.)

ALASKA DIRECTORY AND GAZETTEER
Seattle, 1932-33 (Alaska Directory Company). Contains alphabetical and geographical listings of all residents and businesses, with territorial information and statistics. An edition in 1934-35 (bi-ennial) was also published. Cp. Dynes' Directory.

ALASKA EARTHQUAKE
Alaska Department of Fish and Game (Post-earth-quake fisheries evaluation [Juneau, 1965]); Carder (earthquakes in the western US); Clark and Groff, Engineers (environmental health); Davis, N.Y. (role of Russian Orthodox church); Eckel, E.B. (Dept. Interior); Engle (general narrative); Hansen (field investigations); Kachadoorian (Kodiak, USGS); Kirby (Montague Island USGS); National Research Council (Committee on the Alaska Earthquake); Roberts, M. (photo history); Stanley, K.W. (regional effects); US Alaskan Command (its role); US Coast and Geodetic Survey (descr. [Fergus Wood, gen. ed.]); US Coast and Geodetic Survey (tsunami); US Geological Survey (7v., effects on communities); USGS (effects on hydrologic regimen); US Office of Emergency Planning (its role); Vorhis, R. (hydrologic effects outside Alaska). See also T-3273.

ALASKA EDUCATION ASSOCIATION
Alaska chapter, National Education Association, a professional organization of teachers. Publishers of *NEA Alaska*, a successor of *The Alaska Teacher*, at Anchorage, monthly during the school year.

ALASKA ENGINEERING COMMISSION
See Alaskan Engineering Commission

ALASKA FACTS
Alaska Facts: What is Alaska Today? (Seattle, 1945 [compiled by "a group of Alaska businessmen in the interests of the Territory of Alaska]).

ALASKA FEDERATION OF NATIVES
Statewide organization of Alaska natives, founded at Anchorage, 1966. Initial board included Emil Notti and Nick Gray. Very active in representation of native viewpoint during the land claims settlement debate in Congress, 1968-71. See Alaska Native Claims Settlement Act.

ALASKA FISHERIES POLICY
Arlon Tussing, et al (ISEGR, University of Alaska, 1972). See Fisheries.

ALASKA FISHERMAN'S ALMANAC
Ed. Bailard Hadman. Issued at Ketchikan, 1946-47. See *Alaska Sportsman*, Aug., '47. See T-1152.

ALASKA FORUM
Mimeographed weekly from Sept., 1900 to Aug., '06, at Rampart. Underwood says copies were issued in 1898. Contributors included Rex Beach, and Erastus Brainard, later long time editor of the *Seattle Post-Intelligencer*.

ALASKA FRIENDS
Alaska Sportsman, Dec., '57 (home dedicated at 6741 Beacon Street, Seattle, 300 members; begun in 1947 by eight former Alaskans).

ALASKA FUND
See US Congress, Senate, Committee on Territories, *Compilation of Alaska Statutes* (1913). The fund was established by the Nelson Act of 1905, out of the sale of business and liquor licenses for businesses outside incorporated towns, Congress providing an initial capitalization of $25,000. Its monies were used for education, care of the insane, and for the construction of roads and trails. The US Army, Alaska Road Commission, was created to expend the construction funds, and its first effort was a wagon road from Valdez to Copper Center, and later on to Fairbanks, with a spur to Chitina to meet the Copper River & NW RR. This was the beginning of the Richardson Highway. Initially expended by the US Bureau of Education, the education funds later were handled by the territorial Commission of Education. Care of the insane was handled by contract with Oregon hospitals, there being no adequate facility in the territory. Interestingly, funds for this purpose were charged directly to the Department of Interior (see Thomas Smith). See the following:
Gruening (abolished by 1949 territorial legislature); Henderson (schools received 25% of the fund 1905-09, then 30%); Hulley (on establishment); Nichols (full notes); Tompkins.

ALASKA GAME COMMISSION
See Alaska, Territory, Game Commission, and Alaska, State, Board of Fish and Game

ALASKA GASTINEAU GOLD MINING COMPANY
Alaska Sportsman, June, '41 (abandoned buildings at Thane); *National Geographic Magazine*, Sept., '42 (plate, mine abandoned July, 1921); see also Spray, Lafe E. in *Mining and Scientific Press* (April 17, 1915). W-4849. See also Thane; see also Brooks.

ALASKA HERALD (San Francisco)
Founded March 1, 1868 by Agapius Honcharenko, published semi-monthly in Russian and English in parallel columns. Edited and published 1872-1876 by A.A. Stickney. Apparently, neither editor ever visited Alaska. W-5002. See the following:
Bolser (*Pacific Northwest Quarterly*); Kitchener (Honcharenko also composed grammar lessons for schools on the Pribilof Islands [operated by the Alaska Commercial Company]; Honcharenko's charges against the ACC were reprinted from the *Herald* as a *History of the Wrongs of Alaska*.); Petrof (H. sowed discord and dissatisfaction among Russian-speaking citizens of the US). See also Hutchinson and Kohl, Alaska Commercial Company. See also *Alaska Herald-Free Press* (reprint) (Saratoga, Calif.: R & E Research Associates, 1967; 4v).

ALASKA HIGHWAY ("Alcan" for Alaska-Canada) (opened Nov. 20, '42)
The following is a select listing of references. As the highway continues as a novelty because of its length and the long stretches of undeveloped land along it, countless popular articles continue to be written about it. *Alaska Life*, Jan., '43 ("A [coastal] route); Feb., '43 (R.L. Neuberger); Feb., '43 (E.L. Bartlett); Apr., '43; Jan., '44 ("B" [interior] route); July, '44 (construction); Sept., '44 (poem); Dec., '44; April, '45 (on the Hazelton route); July, '46; *Alaska Sportsman*, Jan., '39 (editorial opposing inland route); Nov., '42; Aug., '45; Dec., '45 (breakthrough at Beaver Creek); Apr., '46 (Canadians take over); Dec., '46; May, '47; Aug., '47 (bus trip); Nov., '47 (300 ft. on either side of road not open to homesteading); May, '48; Sept., '48 (road conditions); March, '49 (truck mail service over road to Fairbanks); Oct., '49; Aug., '50; Jan., '51; Aug., '51; Aug., '52; Sept., '52; Jan., '54; Dec., '54; Oct., '55 (elephant and hippo at Pelly River); Jan., '57; July, '57; Dec., '57; March, '60; *Alaska Weekly*, Oct., '51 (McDonald says road bad decision); American Automobile Association (*Alaska and the Alaska Highway* [Washington, 1949]); *American Journal of International Law* ("Exchange of Notes between the Secretary of State of External Affairs of Canada, and the American minister concerning a military highway to Alaska" [July, 1942]); Atwood, G. (the road in 1942); Baker, R. (mammals); Barger; Baskine; Berton; Bright; Burpee; Canada, B.C.-Yukon-Alaska Highway Commission (*Rept. on Proposed Highway through B.C. and the Y.T. to Alaska* [Ottawa, 1941; 2v]); *Canadian Army Journal* (May, '52; Oct., '54); Coe (construction); Correll (botanical-geological survey); Davies, R.A. (*Arctic Eldorado* [Toronto: Ryerson, 1944]); Dawson; Denison; Eager and Pryor ("Ice formation on

the Alaska Highway" [*Public Roads*, 24 (1945): 55-74]); Ells (economic); Emerson; Finnie (Canol); Fisher and Franklin ("Alaska and the Alaska Highway" [*Journal of Geography*, Oct., '50]); Flint (winter road maintenance); *Forest and Outdoor Magazine*, 39 (1949): 297 ff (stringing 1600 miles of telephone line); Gilman; Godsell; Goodman (*Roads and Bridges*, Feb., '45 [on Liard River bridge piers]); Grant (gospel tour); Greenwood; Grennan; Griffin; Gruening; Haglund; Harrington; Harris; Hart; Herron; Hewetson; Hilscher; Himes (geologist); Hinton and Godsell (historical); Holmes (*Forest and Outdoor Magazine*, Jan., '47); Honigman (Indians); Hulley; Huntley and Royall (construction in detail); Illingworth; Jackson, Alexander Young (*A Painter's Country* [autobiographical] [Toronto: Clarke and Irwin, 1958]); Jaillite, W. Marks (*Military Engineering*, Nov., '44 [flight strips, built 1943-44]); Johnson, F. (archaeological survey); Jacobin; Kursh; Lane, Albert ("The Alcan Highway: Road Location and Construction Methods" [*Military Engineering*, Oct., '42]; [*Civil Engineering*, March, '43]); Lanks; Lee (poems); Leechman (prehistoric sites); *Love* (maintenance); McMillon (history of highway proposals); Magee (*Mineralogist*, Jan., '57 [ecological concern]); Melin; Menzies; *National Geographic Magazine*, Feb., '43; Norman; North Pacific Planning Project; Noyes; Paneth; Perkins; Potter, *Alaska Under Arms* (chapter on road); Pryor (*Public Roads*, Jan.,-March, '47 [road planning from aerial photography]); Puhr; Purdue University (*Joint Highway Research Project*, 2v. mimeographed, 1953); Rand; Raup (vegetation); *Reader's Digest* (Feb., '51); Remington (butterflies); Richardson, P.S. (construction); Roberts, L.; Remley, D.A.; Rossiter; Spindler (*Highway Magazine*, special issue, Nov.-Dec., '43); Steward; Sturdevant; Sundborg; Sutherland-Brown; Taber; Taylor (Canadian towns described); Tewkesbury (descr., homesteading); Thomas, L.O. ("Alcan Highway; A Potential Aid to Prospecting" [*Engineering and Mining Journal*, Aug., '44]); Thomsen (*Roads and Engineering Construction*, Apr., '57 [muskeg]); *Travel Magazine*, June, '50; US Alaskan International Highway Commission (*Report*, 1940); US Bureau of Land Management (land settlement); US Commission to Study the Proposed Highway to Alaska (*Report*, 1933); US Congress, Commission on Roads (fundamental sources); US Dept. of the Interior (*Mid-century Alaska*); US National Park Service (recreation); Wardle ("The Alaska Highway" [*Engineering Journal*, March, '42] [history of the idea of a highway]); Wechsberg, ("Alaska; Springboard of Attack" [*Canadian Geographical Journal*, Apr., '43]); Whishaw; Williams, F.; Winslow; Wright, William Preston (*The Alaska Highway: How We Put it To Peacetime Use* [Gr. Falls: *Great Falls Tribune*, 1945]); Yates ("Maintaining the Alaska Highway [*Royal Engineers Journal*, March, '54]); see also Milepost, Highways and Trails, Yukon Territory; see also T-66 ff. See also David Remley, *The Crooked Road* (New York: McGraw-Hill, 1976).

ALASKA HISTORICAL ASSOCIATION See T-68.

ALASKA HISTORICAL COMMISSION See Alaska, State, Off. of Governor

ALASKA HISTORICAL LIBRARY AND MUSEUM (created by US Congress 1900)
Alaska Historical Museum, Juneau: Alaska Historical Association, 1922 (descr. booklet on museum); published by Fr. A.P. Kashevaroff, then museum director. There have been several subsequent editions.

Biennial report, 1923-24 to 1957-58. See also:
Alaska Sportsman, June, '41 (after Kashevaroff's death, Mrs. E.J. White placed in charge of museum); Chase; Kitchener.

ALASKA HISTORICAL SOCIETY (Sitka)
Alaska Life, Jan., '46 (an annual meeting took place in the spring of 1890, officers listed).

ALASKA HISTORICAL SOCIETY
Organized in 1967 as part of the Alaska Centennial celebration, at Anchorage; annual meetings; occasional publications.

ALASKA HISTORY RESEARCH PROJECT (University of Alaska)
Alaska History Documents (also sometimes titled *Documents Relating to the History of the Orthodox Church in Alaska*, and classified in the archives of the Rasmuson Library, University of Alaska, College, as Alaska Church History), 15v typescript. Select excerpts, translated, from records of the Russian Orthodox Church in Alaska and other documents in the Library of Congress, Manuscripts Division (900 boxes). The selections and translations were made by Cecil Robe of the University's History Department, and Tikhon Lavrischev, of the Language Department, through a Rockefeller Foundation grant in 1936-37. See Russian-Orthodox Church, T. Lavrishev; see also Basov (article on the collection); Smith (survey of Alaska archive of the church); see also *Orthodox Alaska*, periodical published intermittently from 1969 by the Orthodox Diocese of Sitka and Alaska.

ALASKA HOME RAILWAY (Valdez)
Alaska-Yukon Magazine, Oct., '07 (on beginnings, photos); Gruening (promoted by H.B. Reynolds, supported by John Brady); Hulley (Keystone Canyon murder); Nichols (Brady criticized at time; workman killed); Whiting (Reynolds "slick" promoter).

ALASKA-JUNEAU GOLD MINING COMPANY (San Francisco)
Annual Reports, 1915-1923 (n.p., n.d.), 9v; *Alaska Sportsman*, May, '36 (net profit in 1935 of $1,563,798); May, '40 (recovery 90 cents per ton, operating costs 66 cents per ton); June, '41 (operations, 900 employees); Oct., '45 (silver and lead; total recovery to '44 $80,843,000); Bradley, Philip ("Estimation of Ore Reserve and Mining Methods in Alaska-Juneau Mine" [*Transactions of the American Institute of Mining and Metallurgical Engineers*, 1922-25]); Colby (company began surface mining in 1897, caving system in 1913); Davis (Harding visit); *Daily Alaska Empire* [Apr., 14, '53] (mine closed since '44, may make pulp); Denison (adjusted differences with miners' union in '46, re-opened production; local capital invested); *Engineering and Mining Journal*, Sept., '32 (entire

issue [AB-503, 4629]); Franck (operations descr.); Hellenthal ("not able to realize profit until quite recently," only skilled engineering made mining profitable); *National Geographic Magazine*, June, '47 (total metal recovered worth $80,962,000); Sundborg (all gold mining ordered closed in 1942 as non-essential to war effort, A-J continued operation under arrangement to process chrome from Kenai Peninsula which never arrived, actually closed in 1944 when miners demanded 14 cents hr increase); US Congress, House, Committee on Judiciary ([*Rept.* No. 48, 81st Cong., 1st sess.] favorable to company's claim for crushed rock).

ALASKA LEGIONAIRE
Periodical, published at Juneau. (Bound volumes, 1922-1942, in Alaska State Historical Library).

ALASKA LIFE (the Territorial Magazine)
Periodical (monthly), published at Seattle by Alaska Life Publishing Company, Jan., '38 to Aug., '49. Known as *Alaska Radio Guide*, Jan.-March, '38, *Alaskan and Alaska Radio Guide*, April, 1938.

ALASKA LITERARY DIRECTORY
See T-628

ALASKA MAGAZINE (Juneau)
Issued Jan. to May, 1927 by Alaska Magazine, Inc., edited by John Edward Meals. The January issue, reportedly quite scarce, contains a Tlingit fairy story, articles on Lisiansky, LaPerouse, and Cook, with a table of Alaska mountain peaks. The February issue is devoted to Veniaminov, written by Fr. Kashevaroff (Alaska Historical Association, Alaska Territorial Museum). There are also articles on Skagway and on glaciers by Wickersham, and Tlingit mythology.

ALASKA MAGAZINE (Anchorage)
See Alaska Northwest Publishing Company.

ALASKA MAGAZINE PUBLISHING COMPANY
See T-80 ff.

"ALASKA MARY"
See "China Mary".

ALASKA MEXICAN GOLD MINING COMPANY
See T-85. See also Treadwell Mines.

ALASKA MINING AND ENGINEERING SOCIETY
See T-86 ff.

ALASKA MINING LAW
See T-88 ff.

ALASKA MONTHLY MAGAZINE
Published at Juneau, 1906-07, edited by C.W. Taylor. See *Alaska-Yukon Magazine*, Apr., '07 (editor E.S. Harrison states his A-Y Mag. was not a successor to *Alaska Monthly*).

ALASKA NATIVE BROTHERHOOD
Founded 1912 at Juneau, representing primarily southeast Alaska natives. See the following:
Davis (abolish all fish traps); Denison (Gruening addresses 31st annual convention on alcohol); Drucker (history; founded by 10 Presbyterian In-

dians); Hayes (purposes, inspired by missionaries); Tewkesbury (political power in 1920's, Peratrovich faction and Paul faction); *Alaska Sportsman*, Dec., '55 (editorial). See Alaska Federation of Natives, Arctic Native Brotherhood, Alaska Native Foundation, Alaska Native Claims Act, Alaska Natives and the Land.

ALASKA NATIVE CLAIMS SETTLEMENT ACT (1971)

The act capitalizes 12 native regional development corporations with $500 million from the US Treasury over a 20 year period, and $425 in federal mineral royalties. It also makes a federal grant of approximately 40 million acres of land in Alaska to the regional corporations and village corporations, commensurate with federal withdrawals and land already in private ownership. Philosophically, the act attempts to insure the integrity of native cultures and land use patterns, particularly subsistence living, as well as provide the means to economic stability and social justice. The grant of land extinguishes any further native claims. Historically, the act accomplishes the settlement of native ownership rights provided for in the 1867 purchase treaty with Russia, but never acted on by the US Congress. See the following:

Alaska Native Foundation (*A Technical Analysis*); Berry, M. (*The Alaska Pipeline*); Bigjim and Ito-Adler (*Letters to Howard*); Cohen (*Handbook of Federal Indian Law*); Daugherty ("Political Power Struggle"); Ely, Guess and Rudd (*Summary and Analysis*); Federal Field Commission (*Alaska Natives and the Land*); Galligher (*Etok*); Gsovski (*Russian Administration*); Morgan, L. (*And the Land Provides*); Nathan, R.R. (*Implementing the Alaska Native Land Claims Settlement Act*); Pierce, N. (*The Pacific States*); *The Tundra Times*; US Congress, House (Report No. 746, 92nd Cong., 1st sess. [the act]); Washburne (*Red Man's Land*). See Robert Arnold, et alii, *Alaska Native Claims Act*; see also those materials listed under Aboriginal Rights. See U.S. Congress, Senate (92nd Cong., 1st Sess.), Report No. 92-405, *Alaska Native Claims Settlement Act*. See also Aboriginal Rights.

ALASKA NATIVE FOUNDATION

A research organization founded at Anchorage in 1972, primarily with Ford Foundation funding, to provide technical and other assistance in the implementation of the Alaska Native Claims Settlement Act of 1971, particularly to the several regional development corporations. See Arnold.

ALASKA NATIVES

Alaska Natives: A Survey of Their Sociological and Educational Status (Stanford: Stanford University Press, 1935), Anderson, H. Dewey and Walter Crosby Eells. This study was undertaken at the behest of the US Commissioner of Education, William John Cooper, financed by the Carnegie Foundation. The 472 page study was commended to the US Congress by the Alaska Territorial Legislature, and contributed to the reorganization of the Alaska Native Service, which was transferred from the Office of Education to the Office of Indian Affairs in 1931. Available in a Krauss reprint (Millwood, New York: 1973).

ALASKA NATIVES AND THE LAND

Alaska Natives and the Land (Wn.DC: GPO, 1968). Final report of the Federal Field Commission for Development Planning in Alaska. The Commission was established in 1964 by President Lyndon B. Johnson to survey all aspects of native life and culture in Alaska, preliminary to a settlement of Alaska native claims. The massive study provided the basic statistical data and overall notion of Alaska native conditions, needs and aspirations for the Congressional debate on settlement of Alaska native claims.

ALASKA NELLIE

See Lawing, Nellie (Trosper) Neal.

ALASKA NORTHERN RAILWAY

Gruening (took over Alaska Central Railroad, failed after 71 miles were built from Seward); Lipke (trip over uncompleted right-of-way), see W-9416. Line completed to Kern Creek.

ALASKA NORTHWEST PUBLISHING COMPANY

Publishes *Alaska Magazine* (successor to *Alaska Sportsman*), *Alaska Journal*, a quarterly journal of history and the arts for popular audiences (from 1971), *The Milepost*, an annual annotated guide to the Alaska Highway and all Alaska and connecting highways (including the "Alaska marine highway"), *Alaska Geographic*, a quarterly devoted to photographic and literary materials on regions of Alaska, an index to *Alaska Sportsman* and *Alaska Magazine*, and numerous special and monograph publications on Alaska subjects. A bibliography of all titles published is available from the publisher.

ALASKA NORTHWESTERN RAILROAD

Prospectus, New York, n.d., 15 pp.

ALASKA OIL AND GUANO COMPANY

Statement in relationship to Alaska fisheries; n.p., 1910, 23 pp. by Carl Spuhn, president.

ALASKA PACIFIC CONSOLIDATED MINING COMPANY

See T-98.

ALASKA PACKERS ASSOCIATION

Influenza epidemic in Bristol Bay (Naknek, Nushagak, Kvichak), 1919: "Service," the true measure of any institution lies in the service it renders (San Francisco, 1919) (typewritten copy, including photos of natives in groups, in Alaska State Historical Library); see also the following:

Clark ("one of the earliest and largest fish trusts of Alaska," packed half the total of Alaska production, established market prices); Glenn (local agent raised foxes on Fox Island near Orca in Prince William Sound); Gruening (operated hatcheries at Karluk and Loring, fought taxation, APA formed in 1893, largely controlled by former owners of Alaska Commercial Company, Sloss and Liebes organized the first great Alaska salmon trust, also Capt. J.F. Moser); Hulley (one of the outside corporations in control of the salmon industry); Nichols (Moser an advocate of salmon conservation until association with APA); US Congress, Committee on Merchant Marine and Fisheries (Rept. 9528, 64th Cong., 1st sess.); Wead (APA "Star" fleet); Wickersham—3095. See also T-99-101.

ALASKA PENINSULA

Baker (excellent summary citing Cook, Lutke, Veniaminov, Berkh, Dall and Grewingk); Brooks; AB-numerous references; see also US Dept. of Interior, Alaska Planning Group, Alaska Task Force (US Bureau of Land Management, US Fish and Wildlife Service) *Illiamna National Resource Range, Final Environmental Statement* (Alaska Task Force, 1974), 620 pp. The Alaska Task Force is a combined effort of the US Bureau of Land Management and the US Fish and Wildlife Service, compiling environmental impact statements on all areas of Alaska. On Alaska Peninsula see also Alaska (origin of name), Hubbard, and Bernard.

ALASKA PERSEVERANCE MINING COMPANY
(Silver Bow Basin)

Alaska-Yukon Magazine, Sept., '07 (mill photo).

ALASKA PIONEER

Issued irregularly by Alaska Pioneers, Igloo No. 1. .

ALASKA PIONEER'S ASSOCIATION (1887)

Alaska-Yukon Magazine, Dec., '08 (primarily founded to return the body of R.T. Harris to Juneau, association of long-time Alaska residents [initially, anyone in Alaska prior to 1886, the year of significant gold discoveries along the Forty-mile River]); see also Pioneers of Alaska.

ALASKA PIONEER'S HOME (Sitka)

Bi-ennial reports from 1917, annual reports 1913-16.

ALASKA PLANNING COUNCIL

General information regarding Juneau, 1941. Alaska Development Plan, 1941. Preliminary economic survey, Seward Peninsula (Juneau, 1940); *Alaska Life*, Apr., '41 (Council organized by L.R. Huber, authorized by 1937 territorial legislature, issued two reports on taxation, and the development plan); Sundborg (mentions study of agricultural development).

ALASKA PURCHASE

See Purchase of Alaska; see also Seward.

ALASKA RAILROAD

Alaskan Engineering Commission, Message from the President of the United States, transmitting reports of the Alaskan Engineering Commission, together with maps, charts and profiles (Wn.DC: GPO, 1916), 2v, 210 pp.

Alaska, Railroad Records, 1915-24. 3 ft. Manuscript Division, Library of Congress. Progress reports, correspondence, etc.

Resources of Alaska (ARR, 192?).

Alaska, the Newest Homeland (Anchorage: ARR, 1930).

Alaska Railroad Record, issued weekly, Nov. 14, 1916 to June 29, 1920, at Anchorage by the Alaskan Engineering Commission, during construction of the Alaska Railroad from Seward to Fairbanks.

Alaska Railroad Commission. Railway routes in Alaska, Message from the President (Taft) transmitting report of the Alaska Railroad Commission (Wn.DC: GPO, 1913), 172pp. (US Congress, House, Exec. Doc. 1346, 62nd Cong., 3rd sess.). The Alaska Railroad Commission was appointed to study the feasibility of railroad construction in Alaska, and to assess the role of the federal government. In the report cited here the Commission commented on possible rail routes between the following points: Whitehorse-Yukon (Dawson), Haines-Fairbanks, Katalla-Controller Bay, Cordova-Fairbanks, Valdez-Fairbanks, Seward-Fairbanks, Iliamna-Kuskokwim. President Wilson made the final decision for the Seward-Fairbanks route, and recommended legislation creating the Alaskan Engineeing Commission, the builder of the rail line.

Prospectus of the Rehabilitation Program, Anchorage, 1946.

See the following:

Alaska Life, Nov., '41; July, '42 (Ohlson [general manager from 1928] photo); Sept., '43; Feb., '44; Dec., '44 (Whittier, US Army port of entry); Nov., '48 ("loop" on Kenai Peninsula); *Alaska Sportsman*, Jan., '43 (Whittier); Feb., '43 (Nenana bridge); March, '45 (first serious accident); Jan., '47; Aug., '47; Feb., '48 ("Aurora"); Oct., '48; Apr., '49; Aug., '49; Nov., '49; Feb., '50 (survey for route to Canada); May, '50; March, '51 (back overtime paid, $2 million); Apr., '51 (million dollar fire at Anchorage); Sept., '51; Nov., '51; Jan., '52 ("loop" abandoned); Aug., '52 (125 Eskimos employed); March, '54; July, '55; Sept., '55 (Harding coach sold); Feb., '56; March, '57; July, '57; Feb., '58; June, '58; etc.; *Alaska Weekly*, Dec., '50 (Johnson as general manager); *Alaska-Yukon Magazine*, July, '12 (original equipment from Panama Canal RR); Anderson, Anton ("Construction and Maintenance Problems on the Alaska Railroad," *Proc. Alaska Science Conf.*, 1951 [historical account of construction]); Andrews (effect of construction); Ballaine (millions wasted); Bernhardt (AEC history); Cameron (former Panama man at Nenana); Carpenter (first spike photo); Capps (geology); Chase ("loop"); Clark (on Ballaine); Colby; Denison; Franck (on Ohlson); Gruening ("scrap the railroad," Richardson Highway toll, G. Parks' analysis of construction); Fitch (narrative history); Grupp (diesels); Hellenthal ("very little to haul except Bureau officials"); Hulley (rehabilitation); Kitchener (Ruby's attempt to get terminal, role of NC Co.); Kola (on construction of Whittier tunnels); Lane, Franklin K. (three articles on constr. in *Railway Age* [March 7, Dec. 19, 1919, Nov. 13, 1913]); *National Geographic Magazine*, Dec. '15; Sept., '42; Oct., '49; Noyes, John R. ("Transportation in Alaska," *Military Engineer*, 45 (1953): 99-103 [review of Alaska Railroad, Richardson Highway and White Pass and Yukon Railway]); Potter (rate controversy, first profit in 1938); Prince (pictorial history); Smith, P.S., et. al. (*Investigations in the Alaska Railroad Belt* [Wn.DC: GPO, 1933] [mineral resource survey]); Sundborg; Tewkesbury; Tompkins (both Richardson Highway and Alaska Railroad completed in 1923); Underwood; US Congress, House, Committee on Interstate and Foreign Commerce (*Transportation in Alaska* [Rept. 1272, 80th Cong., 2nd sess.]); US Congress, House, Document No. 176, 87th Cong., 1st sess. [Batelle Report, 3v, on transportation and growth]); US Congress, Senate, Committee on Interior and Insular Affairs, (Alaska Coal Lands [84th Cong., 1st sess.] [on need for spur to Cripple Creek coal mine, Healy area]); US Congress, Senate, Committee on Territories and Insular Affairs (Settlement and Development of Alaska

[Hearings on S. 3577, 76th Cong., 3rd sess.] [ARR considered incidental to development]); US Dept. of Interior, Office of Territories (*Mid-Century Alaska*, 1951, 1952, 1957, 155 pp. [Wn.DC: GPO] [general information summary]); Wahrhaftig (USGS Professional Papers, Engineering and Geology, ARR [1958], 1947 earthquake [1948]); Wilson, William. See also W-5450-5580, and the Arctic Bibliography.

ALASKA RANGE (Mts)
See Washburn. Dall suggested name at meeting of the Boston Society of Natural History, Nov. 4, 1868. Grewingk had already written *"Gebirge von Alaeksa"* on the first of three maps in his *Beitrag zur Kenntniss*.

ALASKA RESOURCES DEVELOPMENT BOARD
See Alaska, Territory, Development Board.

ALASKA REVIEW
Intermittent quarterly published by Alaska Methodist University, Anchorage. See also Frederick, Robert A.

ALASKA RURAL REHABILITATION CORPORATION (US)
Questions and Answers about the Matanuska Colonization Project in Alaska, Wn.DC: GPO, 1936.

The ARRC came into existence on April 12, 1935, as the non-profit benevolent corporation intended to rehabilitate the Matanuska Valley colonists. Although initially administration of the colony was carried out by the FERA and then the Dept. of Interior, the ARRC emerged in 1936 as the primary administration agency. The ARRC should not be confused with the Matanuska Valley Farmers Cooperating Association (the valley cooperative).

See the following:

Alaska Weekly, Sept., '51 (financial history); Atwood, (*We Shall Be Remembered*); Colby; Denison ("not much more than a real estate agency and bank", controls leases and sales of land, rents machinery for land clearing); Hulley (in 1940 MVFCA purchased ARRC holdings including creamery, hatchery, cannery, garage, trading post, power plant, hospital, dormitory, and staff houses, control of these facilities being transferred in 1941); Miller, O. (excellent history of the management of the colony and analysis of the concept of rural rehabilitation); Sundborg; see also the collection of colony deeds and manuscript materials in the Alaska Methodist University Alaska Archive. See the bibliography in O. Miller's *The Frontier in Alaska and the Matanuska Colony*.

ALASKA SCHOOL SERVICE
Medical Handbook, Krulish, Emil, M.D. and Daniel S. Neuman, M.D.; see US Bureau of Education.

ALASKA SCIENCE CONFERENCE
See Alaskan Science Conference.

ALASKA SEARCHLIGHT (Juneau)
Weekly tabloid issued at Juneau 1894-1898; contains considerable material on travel routes from southeast Alaska to the Yukon gold fields.

ALASKA SHORT LINE RAILWAY AND NAVIGATION COMPANY
See T-108.

ALASKA SLED-DOG AND RACING ASSOCIATION
See T-2705.

ALASKA SMELTING AND DEVELOPMENT COMPANY
See T-110.

ALASKA, STATE (Government)
Commission on Human Rights, *Laws Against Discrimination*, Juneau, 1965.

Court System. The Alaska State Court System has published manuals of procedure and administration on all court levels, Municipal, Superior, District and Supreme Court. See also *Alaska Reporter*, *Alaska Digest*, Judicial Council, Alaska Constitution.

Criminal Justice Planning Agency, *Alaska Comprehensive Criminal Justice Plan*, Juneau, 1971.

Department of Administration, various reports and annual budget information; see *Improving the Budget Process in Alaska*, Juneau, 1971.

Department of Commerce, various reports and annual register of corporations, *Corporate Directory*, Juneau, also annual *Directory of Manufacturers*.

Department of Community and Regional Affairs, various reports.

Department of Economic Development, annual reports and various other reports; see *Promise of Power* (on mineral resource development of southeast Alaska), Juneau, 1972 (by Rush McNair Hoag); the department earlier was named Economic Development and Planning.

Department of Education, numerous reports and handbooks, and curricular material from the Division of Instruction; see the following: *Administrative Handbook for Rural Education* (1966), *Adopted Textbooks for Elementary Schools* (1968), *Alaska Department of Education and Education in Alaska, 1785-1966* (1966), *Alaska's Transportation Systems* (1966), *Alcohol Education in Alaska's Classrooms* (1967), *Compiled School Laws* (1965), *Alaska History Time-Line* (1970), *Elementary Course of Study* (1959), *Resource Unit for Teaching Alaska History, Geography and Government* (1961), *Tips for Teachers* (1961).

Department of Environmental Conservation, *State of Alaska Air Quality Control Plan*, Juneau, 1972.

Department of Fish and Game, numerous reports and studies, see the following: *Alaska Commercial Fishery Operators* (annual), *Alaska's Wildlife and Habitat* (1973), *Catalog of Rivers, Lakes and Streams that are important for the spawning or migration of anadromous fish* (1968), *Guide Register* (annual), *Post-earthquake Fisheries Evaluation* (1965), *Review of Literature on Lake Trout Life History* (1967), *Revised Annotated Bibliography on the Dolly Varden* (1969 [Resource Report No. 7]).

Department of Health, *Plan for Hospital and Medical Facilities* (annual), *Current Investigations in Alaska* (1968), various other reports.

Department of Health and Social Services (previously Department of Health and Welfare); as Department of Health.

Department of Highways (Department of Transportation), various reports and papers, and

Long-range Highway Program (annual).

Department of Labor, various reports and *Directory of Labor Unions and Employee Groups* (annual).

Department of Law, *Manual for Police Departments* (1964), *Comments on the Proposed Trans-Alaska Pipeline* (1971), *Opinions of the Attorney-General* (annual).

Department of Military Affairs, various reports.

Department of Natural Resources, *Land Use and Alaska's Past* (1972), numerous specific studies.

Department of Public Safety, various reports.

Department of Revenue, numerous handbooks, regulations and reports; see *What's Happening to Alaska's Money* (1971).

Division of Aviation, numerous regulations, reports and guides.

Division of Commercial Fisheries, annual forecasts of fish runs, etc.

Division of Community Planning, various census data and *Selected 1970 Census Data* (1974).

Division of Economic Enterprise, *Alaska Statistical Review*.

Division of Finance, various reports, annual budget information.

Division of Game, numerous regulations and forecasts.

Division of Geological and Geophysical Surveys, numerous specific surveys, and *Bibliography of Alaska Geology, 1831-1918* (1971).

Division of Highways, numerous reports and projection studies.

Division of Insurance, numerous regulations and directories.

Division of Lands, numerous reports and surveys, regulations. See also Federal-State Lane Use Planning Commission.

Division of Libraries, *Long-range Program, 1972-77* (1972), *Guide to Alaska Packers Association Papers* (1972), *Guide to Russian Holdings in the Alaska State Historical Library* (1971), *Education in Russian Alaska* (1972), *Map Index, Alaska State Historical Library* (1972), *List of Publications, Manuscripts and Reference Data of the Federal Field Commission* (1972), and others.

Division of Mental Health, numerous reports.

Division of Mines, surveys and reports.

Division of Occupational Licensing, numerous directories, state examinations.

Division of Parks, various reports and miscellaneous publications, including *Alaska Archaeology, A Bibliography* (1972), *Alaska's Abandoned Towns* (1972), *Alaska Roadhouses* (1973), *Aids to Navigation in Alaska History* (1974), *Lower Copper and Chitina Rivers: An Historic Resource Study* (1974).

Division of Plannning and Research, numerous studies, and *This is Alaska* (1962), and *Tuberculosis Report*, annual.

Division of Sport Fisheries, regulations and forecasts.

Division of State Planning, *Alaska's Population and Economy* (1962 [George Rogers]), *Economic Potential of Alaska's Military Surplus* (1970).

Division of State Troopers, *Motor Vehicle Laws*, annual.

Division of Tourism and Economic Development, various reports.

Division of Vocational and Adult Education, numerous reports and guides.

Housing Authority, *Bibliography of Informational Materials in the ASHA Library* (1972), *Housing the Alaska Native* (1967), *Native Housing in Alaska* (1968).

Industrial Development Division, *Alaska Native Artists and Craftsmen* (1968), *Japanese Investment in Alaska* (1971).

Judicial Council, annual reports.

Legislature, annual journals, House and Senate, summary of legislation, bills and bills introduced, and reports of bills; *Joint Pipeline Impact Committee Report* (1972).

Legislative Affairs Agency, *Conference on the Future of Alaska* (Brookings Institute, 1970) (4v), *Economic Considerations Bearing on Valuation of Alaska Crude Oil and State Policy on Pipelines* (1970), *Making of Alaska Law* (1973), *Legislative Manual* (annual), *Minutes of the Proceedings of the Alaska Constitutional Convention* (1965), *Public Land in Alaska* (1966), *Summary of Alaska Legislation* (annual), and others.

Local Affairs Agency, various reports and guides.

Office of the Governor, Alaska Historical Commission, *Writing Alaska's Past* (1974).

Public Service Commission, various reports.

Public Utilities Commission, various reports.

Secretary of State's Office, annual official election returns.

State Centennial Commission, annual reports, 1964-67.

State Council on the Arts, annual and other reports.

State Geographical Board, annual report.

Transportation Commission, annual report.

ALASKA STATEHOOD

Enactment official, January 3, 1959. See the following: Alaska Statehood Committee, manuscript material in Alaska State Historical Library; Atwood, E. (*Alaska's Struggle*); Atwood, R. (in *State Government*); Bartholomew (in *Southwest Social Science Quarterly*); Egan, William; Gruening (*State of Alaska, Battle for Alaska's Statehood, Many Battles*); Hilscher (*Alaska Now*); McCutcheon; Moberg (in *Western Political Quarterly*); Naske (*An Interpretive History*); Rogers (*Alaska in Transition*); Ross (*Gruening*); Shannon, G. (in *Public Management*); Sherwood (*Alaska and Its History*); Spicer; Stewart, T. (in *State Government*); Sundborg (*Statehood*); Swanson; Swap. See the excellent bibliography in Naske's *An Interpretive History*. See also Alaska Constitution.

ALASKA STEAMSHIP COMPANY

Alaska Life, March, '42 (protest of 45% increase in rates); *Alaska Sportsman*, May, '36 (19 vessels in service); Aug., '39; July, '50; Sept., '50 (whistles); Dec., '51 (freight increases as passenger traffic decreases); May, '53; Oct., '54; Nov., '54 (passenger service closed); Dec., '54; June, '55 (60th anniversary); July, '56 (on two vessels); *Alaska Weekly*, June, '50 (notes on vessels); Jan., '51; Feb., '51; March, '51 (old steamers, Kuskokwim service); Apr., '51 (fares); Apr., '51 ("Duchess" Lysbeth Rawsthorne; *Alaska-Yukon Magazine*, May, '08 (vessels, routes); Nov., '09 (operating vessels); Clark (Alaska Syndicate purchased Alaska Steam in 1902, transportation monopoly a menace); *Daily Alaska Empire*, Feb., '59 (history of company, organized 1895,

70 ships operating during WW II, containerization);
Franck (to Siberia); Gruening (owned by Morgan-
Guggenheim, preferential rates for Syndicate's
copper, reported only half profits, merged with
Northland Transportation, trucks to Fairbanks);
Hulley (Guggenheim group "merged Pacific and
Alaska Steamship companies with its own line and
obtained control of ocean transportation between
Alaska and the US," company "never paid any
worthwhile tax to the Territory," fought general
taxation though deriving its entire revenue from
Alaska); Morgan (narrative of 28 years with the
company as steward, clerk, agent, purser, Ketchikan
general agent); Nichols (Syndicate's steamer interests
merged with Alaska steam in 1908); Rickard; Wickersham; see also T-112 ff; see Alaska Syndicate.

ALASKA SYNDICATE

Clark (J.P. Morgan-Guggenheim); Colby (primarily copper, but holdings in salmon and steamship
lines); Gruening (right-of-way struggle near
Cordova); Nichols (history); Pilgrim (interests included Bonanza Mine [Chitina district], Northwestern Commercial Co., Northwest Steamship Co.
[merged with Alaska Steam], Northwest Fisheries
Co., Copper River & Northwestern Railroad [built
1906-11], Northwest Development and Lighterage
Cos.); Slotnik; Young (had grip on Bering and
Matanuska coal fields, withdrawal of coal fields
from entry curbed Syndicate power); see also Wickersham (Old Yukon) for his criticism of the Syndicate,
from which he failed to get a position he sought.

ALASKA, TERRITORY

The most complete collection of material on the
Territory is in the Alaska State Historical Library
and the Alaska State Archive. See the records of the
Office of the Governor, a microfilm of portions of
which has been made by the Federal Records
Center, Seattle. See also material in the various
federal agency records which operated in the Territory, e.g., Department of Interior, Committee on
Territories, Bureau of Education, Bureau of Indian
Affairs, US Army, Alaska Road Commisson, etc. See
also records of the US Congress for debates and
reports and hearings, National Archives and Library
of Congress. At the time of transfer from territorial
to state status the following Territorial agencies were
in operation. The researcher should take care to dis-
tinguish between federal and territorial agencies:

Alaska Department of Agriculture
Alaska Visitors' Association (semi-official)
Alaska Department of Aviation (and Division of
Aeronautics)
Civil Defense Districts
Communications, Terr. Dept. of (and Aeronautics
and Communications Commission)
Development Board (Alaska Resource Develop-
ment Board)
Education, Terr. Dept. of (and Commissioner of
Educ.)
Employment Security Commission
Finance, Dept. of
Fish and Game, Alaska Dept. of (and Fish and
Game Commission, and Commission on Commercial
Fisheries, and Sport Fisheries, and Fur and Game)
Fisheries Products Laboratory (joint federal-
territorial)

Governor's Office (a federal appointee)
Health, Alaska Dept. of (and Board of Health)
Highways and Public Works, Alaska Dept. of (and
Alaska Highway Commissioner)
Historical Library and Museum
Housing Authority (and Territorial Planning
Agency)
Insurance Dept. (and Insurance Commissioner)
Juvenile Institutions, Board of
Labor, Terr. Dept. of (and Commissioner of
Labor)
Land, Alaska Dept. of Public
Legislature, Territorial
Library Service, Dept. of
Mines, Terr. Dept. of
National Guard, Alaska (Territorial Militia)
Police, Territorial
Pioneers' Home
Rural Development Board
Taxation, Dept. of
Towns, Incorporated (31)
Treasurer, Territorial
University of Alaska (Board of Regents)
Veterans' Affairs Commission
Vocational Education, Board of
Vocational Rehabilitation, Alaska Office of
Welfare, Alaska Dept. of Public

ALASKA, TERRITORY, AERONAUTICS AND COMMUNICATIONS COMMISSION
Alaskan Aircraft Operations, bi-ennial summary
report.

ALASKA, TERRITORY, AGRICULTURAL COL-LEGE AND SCHOOL OF MINES
(subsequently, University of Alaska)
Address by James Wickersham at laying of corner-
stone, July 4, 1915
Bi-ennial Reports, Board of Trustees, from 1921
Bulletins, from 1922
Catalogs, from 1923
Farthest North Collegian, student magazine, from
1923
See Cashen, *Farthest North College President*; see
University of Alaska.

ALASKA, TERRITORY, AGRICULTURAL EX-PERIMENT STATIONS
The following is a select listing of publications.
*List and Analytical Index of Publications of Alaska
Experiment Stations, 1898-1931* (Elizabeth Lang-
dale, GPO, 1932)
Annual Reports, 1897-1933. From 1933 these
reports were issued from the Alaska Agricultural Ex-
periment Station, College, Alaska
Suggestions to Pioneer Farmers, C.C. Georgeson,
1902
Vegetable Growing, C.C. Georgeson, 1905
Hay Making (Kenai Peninsula), GPO, 1907
Information for Prospective Settlers, C.C. George-
son, 1916 (same, revised, 1917, 1923; by H.W.
Alberts, 1930; again revised, 1948)
Improved Hardy Strawberries, C.C. Georgeson,
1922
The Potato in Alaska, H.W. Alberts, 1931
Oat Production, F.L. Higgins, 1932
Cereal Growing in Alaska, C.C. Georgeson and
G.W. Glasser, 1926
Vegetable Gardening in Alaska, GPO, 1928

Bulb Growing in Alaska, C.C. Georgeson, 1928
Brief History of Cattle Breeding in Alaska, GPO, 1929
Forage Crops for Interior Alaska, H.W. Alberts, 1933
Feeding Dairy Cows in the Matanuska Region, W.T. White, 1933
Field Crops for Interior Alaska, F.L. Higgins, 1933
Agricultural Land Use in Alaska, Palmer 1954
Buildings for Alaska (homes and farms), College, 1955
Matanuska Valley Memoir, Palmer, 1955
Land Occupancy, Ownership and Use on Home-steads in Kenai Peninsula, Palmer, 1956
Alaska Farm Facts (a general compilation of agricultural statistics for the years 1953-57), AEC, University of Alaska, 1961
Growing Vegetables in Alaska, Fairbanks, 1947
Livestock in Alaska, Fairbanks, 1947 (rev. ed.)
Information for Prospective Settlers, Fairbanks, 1948 (rev. ed.) (n: author given where known, author only indicates published at Wn.DC by the Government Printing Office, as does GPO).
See O. Miller, *The Frontier in Alaska and the Matanuska Colony* for fuller bibliography on Alaska agriculture, the experiment stations, and the Territorial Department of Agriculture.

ALASKA, TERRITORY, ATTORNEY GENERAL
Bi-ennial Reports, from 1917.

ALASKA, TERRITORY, AUDITOR, OFFICE OF
Bi-ennial Reports, from 1929.

ALASKA, TERRITORY, AVIATION, DEPT. OF
Alaska Airport Directory. Diagrams of all airports.

ALASKA, TERRITORY, BANKING BOARD
Report, bi-ennial from 1913.

ALASKA, TERRITORY, BUDGET, BOARD OF
Report, bi-ennial from 1931.

ALASKA, TERRITORY, CIVIL DEFENSE, DEPT. OF
Civil Defense Plan, Juneau, 1952
Civil Defense Planning, Juneau, 1950

ALASKA, TERRITORY, DEVELOPMENT BOARD
(later Resource Development Board)
Report, bi-ennial from 1945.
Alaska's Recreational Resources, Juneau, 1946
Alaska Agriculture (4 reports by Glasser), 1946 (on general information for settlers, Tanana Valley, Matanuska Valley, livestock)
Anchorage: Analysis of Growth and Possibilities, 1953
Estimate of Alaska Population, annual from 1956 (?)
Fairbanks: A Survey of Progress, 1954 (Richard Cooley)
Fur Farming Opportunities, 1947 (Richard Gorman)
Juneau: A Study of the Gastineau Channel Area, 1956 (Juan Munoz)
An Economic Study of Haines, 1953 (Richard Cooley)
Northwestern Alaska, 1949

Trade and Industry Now in Alaska, 1946 (rev. 1949)
The Cordova District, *1951 (Ralph Browne)*
Report: Gubik Gas Field, 1954
Klukwan: New "Mesabi", 1953 (Ralph Browne)
Valdez Industrial Report, 1955 (Sundborg)
Ketchikan: Problems and Opportunities, 1951 (Ralph Browne)
Seeing Alaska, 1950
Alaska's Dollar Shortage, 1951 (Sundborg)
Alaska Passenger Traffic Survey, annual, from 1951
Financial Data, Towns and Cities, annual, from 1951(?)
The Sitka District, 1950

ALASKA, TERRITORY, EDUCATION, BOARD OF, COMMISSIONERS OF, DEPT. OF
Historical Sketch of Alaska, 1932 (Lester Henderson)
Report of the Commissioner, bi-ennial from 1917
Alaska School Bulletin, 1918-1941
School Laws, Compiled, 1949 (rev. 1953)
Educational Directory, annual
General Instructions (for schools outside incorporated towns), 1956
Course of Study for Elementary Schools, 1939 (A.E. Karnes)
Books About Alaska, 1942
Administrative Manual, 1958
A Manual for Board Members, 1958

ALASKA, TERRITORY, EMPLOYMENT SECURITY COMMISSION
Financing Alaska's Employment Security Program, 1958

ALASKA, TERRITORY, FINANCE, DEPT. OF
Corporations on Record, 1956

ALASKA, TERRITORY, FISH COMMISSION
Report, 1919-1925 (bi-ennial); special report, 1923
Conservation of the Fisheries, 1923 (contains speech by Pres. Harding and Sec. of Commerce Hoover
The Alaska Salmon, 1921 (A.J. Sprague)

ALASKA, TERRITORY, FISHERIES PRODUCTS LABORATORY (Ketchikan)
Alaska Seafood Recipes, 1951 (Charlotte Speegle and Marjorie Bassett)

ALASKA, TERRITORY, GAME COMMISSION
Regulations, 1925, annual or bi-ennial thereafter; in 1925 in cooperation with the Bureau of Biological Survey, Dept. of Agriculture; from 1940, with Dept. of Interior, US Fish and Wildlife Service. See also:
Alaska Sportsman, Nov., '38; Feb., '40; May, '46 (statistics); Aug., '49 (laws); Nov., '51; Jan., '52; *Alaska Life*, March, '41; Gruening (first act [1902] inadequate; second act [1925] created commission); Higginson (1902 act).

ALASKA, TERRITORY, OFFICE OF THE GOVERNOR
Messages, miscellaneous reports
Alaska: Outline of its History and Summary of its Resources (Scott Bone), 1924 (?)

Alaska: Its Past, Present and Future (Scott Bone), 1925

Glimpses of Alaska from 1728 (George Parks), 1926

Annual report, 1884-1958 (essential survey for the researcher)

Handbook of Alaska Regionalism (for Constitutional Convention (George Rogers), 1955 (bibliography)

ALASKA, TERRITORY, HEALTH DEPARTMENT
Bi-ennial Reports

First Five Years of the Alaska Board of Health, 1945-50, 1950

Other reports were issued periodically, including regulations governing the control of contagious diseases, and also a monthly journal on health matters.

ALASKA, TERRITORY, HIGHWAY ENGINEER
Bi-ennial Reports, from 1933

ALASKA, TERRITORY, HISTORICAL LIBRARY AND MUSEUM
Historical and Descriptive Booklet, A.P. Kashevaroff, various editions

Annual Report of the Secretary of the Alaska Historical Association and the Librarian and Curator of the Alaska Historical Library and Museum, from 1923

Report of Progress and Condition, 1923 (Kashevaroff)

Descriptive Booklet, Edward Keithahn

ALASKA, TERRITORY, COMMISSIONER OF LABOR
Bi-ennial report, from 1919

Report on Industrial Accidents, 1927 (B.D. Stewart).

ALASKA, TERRITORY, LAWS AND STATUTES
Various compilations, and session laws from 1913.

ALASKA, TERRITORY, LEGISLATIVE COUNCIL
Various reports and handbooks; staff memoranda.

Final Report on Workmen's Compensation, 1956

Memorandum on Blue Sky Legislation, 1952

Preliminary Report on Reorganization of Territorial Government, 1959

ALASKA, TERRITORY, TERRITORIAL LEGISLATURE
Session laws, House and Senate Journals, Reports of Committees and Joint Committees, Manuals.

ALASKA, TERRITORY, TERRITORIAL MINE INSPECTOR
Annual reports, 1915-1927 (except 1918-19)
(Office susp. 1927)

ALASKA, TERRITORY, DEPARTMENT OF MINES
Report of the Commissioner, biennial from 1935; continues the report of the Inspector of Mines, 1912-1933.

Prospecting in Alaska, 1944. (R.L. Stewart)

Industrial Minerals as a Field for Prospecting in Alaska, 1946 (A.E. Glover).

ALASKA, TERRITORY, TERRITORIAL BOARD OF PHARMACY
Laws Regulating the Practice of Pharmacy, three issues, 1914, 1917, 1918.

ALASKA, TERRITORY, PIONEERS' HOME (Sitka)
Biennial Report, from 1914; early superintendents were A.G. Shoup, Harry F. Morton and Theodore Kettleson.

Report of the Pioneers' Home Building Commission, 1937.

ALASKA, TERRITORY, PLANNING COUNCIL
Preliminary Survey of Taxation in Alaska, 1938 (James C. Rettle)

Graphical Survey of Territorial Administration and of Basic Industries, 1939 (mimeograph)

Preliminary Economic Survey of the Seward Peninsula Area, 1940 (mimeograph)

Alaska Development Plan, 1941

General Information Regarding Alaska, 1941; earlier editions of this work were issued by the Department of Interior under the title General Information Regarding the Territory of Alaska.

ALASKA, TERRITORY, BUREAU OF PUBLICITY
Monthly Bulletin, 1919-1921, except became bimonthly in October, 1919.

Miscellaneous reports, bulletins, circulars concerning southeast and southwestern Alaska.

ALASKA, TERRITORY, BOARD OF ROAD COMMISSIONERS
Biennial Report, from 1921. The Territorial Road Commission is often confused with the Alaska Road Commission of the US Army, and also with the Bureau of Public Roads of the Forest Service of the Department of Agriculture. All three agencies constructed roads in Alaska, the Alaska Road Commission constructing the bulk, and the Bureau of Public Roads working only on Forest Service land.

ALASKA, TERRITORY, TERRITORIAL RURAL DEVELOPMENT BOARD
Kotzebue and the Noatak-Kobuk Region, 1925

The Silver Fleece (economic survey of the Bristol Bay region), 1958 (James Hawkins and Elizabeth Daugherty.)

Village reports, 14v, 1958-59 (Andreafski, Angoon, Arctic Village, Gambell, Hamilton, Holy Cross, Kaltag, Kivalina, Mountain Village, Noatak, Noorvik, Savoonga, Tenakee, Venetie). (Paul L. Gagnon)

The Beaver Report, 1959 (voluntary community housing project in the village of Beaver) (Paul L. Gagnon)

ALASKA, TERRITORY, SECRETARY OF ALASKA
Reports, biennial, from 1917

Bulletins, to 1924 (concern elections, embalming practice, leasing school lands, procedures for foreign corporations, list of domestic corporations, etc.). After 1924 with the expansion of territorial government many of the responsibilities of the Secretary were delegated to other territorial agencies.

ALASKA, TERRITORY, TERRITORIAL SHIPPING BOARD
Report, 1920

ALASKA, TERRITORY, STATEHOOD COMMITTEE OF THE TERRITORIAL GOVERNMENT
Facts About Alaska Statehood, 1949; manuscript material. See Naske.

ALASKA, TERRITORY, TERRITORIAL TREASURER
Report of the Treasurer, biennial from 1913

ALASKA, TERRITORY, UNEMPLOYMENT COMPENSATION COMMISSION
Report, biennial from 1937

ALASKA, TERRITORY, UNIVERSITY OF ALASKA
See University of Alaska

ALASKA, TERRITORY, OFFICE OF VOCATIONAL EDUCATION
Territorial Plan for Vocational Education, 1956
Statement of Policies, 1956

ALASKA, TERRITORY, OFFICE OF VOCATIONAL REHABILITATION
Alaska Rehabilitation, 1946-57, 1957

ALASKA TIMES (Sitka)
Weekly newspaper established at Sitka May 1, 1868 by W.S. Dodge (according to Petrof), and continued by Thomas G. Murphy, a tailor, until 1870. Andrews says the *Alaska Times* was established on April 23, 1869, issuing editions until October 1, 1870. See also Ted C. Hinckley, *Americanization of Alaska*. Nichols lists a handwritten copy dated September 19, 1868 in the Alaska Historical Library, and numerous other copies to 1871. Wickersham (in his bibliography [W-5023]) doubts all dates, stating no original copies of the paper can be found (1924) in Alaska libraries.

ALASKA TRADE COMMITTEE
See T-131

ALASKA TRANSPORTATION, TRADING AND MINING COMPANY
See T-132

ALASKA TREADWELL GOLD MINING COMPANY
See Treadwell Mines; see also T-134 ff.

ALASKA UNITED COPPER EXPLORATION COMPANY
See T-135 ff.

ALASKA UNITED GOLD MINING COMPANY
See T-138 ff.

ALASKA UNIVERSITY
See University of Alaska

ALASKA UTILITIES DEVELOPMENT COMPANY
See T-139

ALASKA WEEKLY
Weekly newspaper published at Seattle from May 1, 1923 to October, 1956. During most of this time Earle W. Knight was editor. The paper began as the *Juneau City Mining Record* (weekly) in 1888; it became the *Alaska Mining Record* in 1894, the *Alaska Daily Dispatch* in 1899, the *Sunday Alaska Dispatch* in 1919, when it was moved to Seattle, becoming the *Alaska Weekly* in 1923. The paper was not successful after Knight's death. Its circulation was primarily in Seattle. Lulu M. Fairbanks was assistant editor for years.

ALASKA WOMAN
Magazine published at Juneau, 1941-43, Mary B. Poole, editor.

ALASKA WRITERS WORKSHOP
See T-141

ALASKA YEARBOOK
Published annually 1926-28 at Seattle by *Alaska Weekly*.

ALASKA YOUTH, INC. (Port Chikoot-Haines)
Articles of Incorporation, 1957

ALASKAN
Monthly magazine published at Anchorage by W.W. and Jacquelene Vickroy from March, 1958.

ALASKAN AGRICULTURALIST
Quarterly magazine published at Anchorage by E. Baldwin, "in the interests of Alaska's modern pioneers." Merged into *Alaska Quarterly*, 1954. See also T-238

ALASKAN ALPINE CLUB
Formed September, 1951; see descr. article in *Appalachia*, December, 1955 by Keith Hart.

ALASKAN BOUNDARY SURVEY
See Alaska Boundary Tribunal; see also J.E. McGrath; see also T-1815

ALASKAN CHURCHMAN
Quarterly journal of the Episcopal Church in Alaska, est. 1906. From 1899 to 1906 a diocesan paper, *Cross Bearer*, was published at Skagway.

ALASKAN COLLECTOR
See *Alaskan Philatelist*

ALASKAN ENGINEERING COMMISSION
Alaska Railroad, 2v, Wn.DC: GPO, 1916; Bernhardt (history of the Commission); Denison (Anchorage site selected in 1915 [but surveyed in 1914] Fitch; Gruening (members' names, coal mining); Hulley (governed Anchorage through Mgr. Coffey); US Dept. of Interior (*Mid-Century Alaska* [appointed 1914, abolished 1923]); see also Alaska Railroad. See also Anchorage.

ALASKAN MAGAZINE
Quarterly magazine published at Haines by Mildred Young, 1948-49, continued at Haines by H.R. and Mary B. Barrer; last issue 1953.

ALASKAN MAGAZINE: THE OCCIDENT AND ORIENT
Magazine published at Tacoma, Washington, then Chicago, by P. deW. Whitehead, March-November,

1900 (except April). E.S. Meany edited the March and May issues. Original name was *Alaskan Magazine and Canadian Yukoner*.

ALASKAN PHILATELIST
Official organ of the Alaska Collectors' Club; superseded *Alaskan Collector* in 1959. Initially published at Stillwater, Minnesota, Bill Rolke.

ALASKAN QUARTERLY
Published at Anchorage by Alaska Enterprise, 1954; est, by merger of *Alaskan Agriculturist* and *Alaskan Record*, and later (1955), the *Alaskan Reporter*.

ALASKAN REPORTER
Magazine published at Anchorage (by the *Anchorage Times*) by Herb and Marilyn Rhodes, from January, 1952. Merged with *Alaska Quarterly*, 1955.

ALASKAN SCIENCE CONFERENCE
Alaskan Science Conference of the National Academy of Sciences and the National Research Council, an annual conference held in Washington, DC and different Alaska locations, from 1950. See Arctic Bibliography for complete list of papers and publication of abstracts. See also discussion of the conference in *Science*, Feb., 1955, by Troy Lewis Pewe.

ALASKAN-CANADIAN BOUNDARY COMMISSION
Joint Report of the United States and British Commissioners on the Alaskan-Canadian Boundary, Wn.DC: GPO, 1898. William Ward Duffield represented the US, William Frederick King represented Great Britain. See also Alaska Boundary Tribunal.

ALASKA'S HEALTH
Bi-monthly report published by the Territorial Department of Health (after statehood name changed to Alaska's Health and Welfare).

ALASKA-YUKON MAGAZINE
Monthly magazine established at Juneau, 1906, by Mrs. Edna Jones. It moved to Seattle in 1907 under the editorship of Edward Sanford Harrison until his death in 1910. Although continued intermittently, it last appeared in 1912.

ALASKA-YUKON-PACIFIC EXPOSITION
At Seattle, opened June 1, 1909. Alaska exhibits were all in a single building designed for them. Visitors included President Taft and Governor Hoggatt. See the following:
The Argus (Seattle), special edition, Feb. 20, 1909
Butler Hotel Annex (Seattle), *History of the Exposition*, 1909
Chicago Illustrated Review, special edition, March 13, 1909
Edgren, Adolph, *Songs for Sweden Day*, S-1685
Hartman, John P. Address, S-4132
Hill, James J. Address, S-4465
McLean, Henry, A. Address, S-6416
Martz, Henry *A-Y-P Exposition*, 110 pp. S-6573
National Magazine, September, 1909
US Congress, Senate Document No. 671 (61st Cong., 3rd sess.) Participation in the A-Y-P Exposition.

See also T-145 ff. See also *Alaska Weekly*, June, '50 (expo originally planned for Alaska alone); *Alaska-Yukon Magazine*, March, '07; June, '07 (chronology of development); Apr., '08; March, '09 (E.S. Harrison); July, '09 (complete coverage); Gruening (Taft's disappointing speech re: Alaska); Hulley; Nichols (Taft episode in full); see also W-2818 ff, and W-3224.

ALASKINDIA
Post office, 1938-45 at Wrangell Institute

ALATNA (village and river)
Baker (Eskimo name is Alashuk [Alatna is Indian]); Couch (post office from 1925, name changed to Allakaket in 1938); Stuck.

ALBATROSS (US Fish Commission steamer)
Alaska Life, Jan., '45 (in Alaskan waters 20 years from 1888); Gruening (J. Moser, captain 1896-1901); see also Wickersham's bibliography. An older *Albatross*, a Boston trader, operated in Alaskan waters circa. 1813; see Dall, and Chevigny, *Lord of Alaska*.

ALBEE, RUTH SUTTON and WILLIAM H. (b. 1907)
Alaska Challenge (with Lyman Anson), Dodd, Mead & Co., 1940. 366 pp. Autobiographical: recounts travel to Dawson from Prince Rupert in 1930, followed by float trip on the Yukon to Eagle. Child born at Fairbanks. School teaching (one year) at Wales (Alaska Native Service); second child born.
"Family Afoot in the Yukon Wilds," *National Geographic Magazine*, May, '42.
"Farthest West," *Sat. Eve. Post*, Feb., '38.

ALBEE, WILLIAM H.
"New Frontier," *Popular Mechanics*, Jan., '39.
Kanguk: A Boy of Bering Strait, Boston: Little, Brown, 1939. 116 pp. Juvenile, collected from Eskimo of Wales.

ALBRECHT, CONRAD EARL (b. 1905) (physician, Health Commission)
Alaska Weekly, Feb., '51 (biography, U of A Regent); Denison (campaigned against tuberculosis, medical officer at Fort Richardson, WW II); Herron (first Commissioner of Health, 1945); Tewkesbury.

ALBRIGHT, HORACE M.
Oh Ranger: A Book About the National Parks, Stanford: Stanford University Press, 1928. 178 pp.
"Mt. McKinley, Park of the North, *Home Geographic Monthly*, October, 1932

ALCOCK, FREDERICK JAMES (b. 1888)
"Past and Present Trade Routes to the Canadian Northwest," *Geographical Review*, August, 1920

ALCOHOL IN ALASKA
The literature on alcohol in the North is extensive. The following is only selective, and deals primarily with literature before statehood. The researcher should see the Arctic Bibliography, and should contact the various agencies dealing with alcohol problems, e.g. the National Council on Alcoholism and Alcohol Abuse and the Center for Alcoholism Studies of the University of Alaska. See the following:

Alaska Sportsman, July, '41 (effects on Eskimos); August, '42 (effects of no winter supply at Nulato); Aug., '47 (1946 Alaska per capita consumption was over 17 gallons); Apr., '51, March, '53 (floating saloon at St. Michael); July, '54 (consumption figures); Aldrich (whalemen and Eskimos); Andrews (British-Russian agreement, smuggling, "hootch"); Bancroft (Gov. Kinkead, scurvy); Arctander (Metlakatla); Caldwell (conditions generally); Cameron (prohibition); Clark (prohibition); Dall (Golovin's recommendations); Denison (consumption); Franck (on natives); Glenn (effects on Indians); Gruening (importation, sale, smuggling); Hayes (Hoonah dry in 1939); Henderson (starvation); Hulley (Brady advocated legal sale, high license); Kitchener (AC Co. paid $27,000 in liquor tax in one year); Morris (destruction of stills, "hootch" recipe); Nichols (saloons); Ray and Richardson (steamers); Savage (natives, Diamond Jennes); Stuck (felony offense, dry election of 1916); Sundborg (distribution at Fairbanks); Walden (never on trail); Wead (role of *Bear*); Wickersham (sold everywhere despite Congress). See also Sherwood.

ALDRICH, HERBERT L.
Arctic Alaska and Siberia, Chicago: Rand, McNally, 1889. 234 pp. Author was observer of 1887 whaling fleet, transferring freely between nine vessels. Route lay northeast along Siberia to East Cape, then to Barrow. Aldrich lived in New Bedford, Massachusetts, claimed to be first writer of the then 40 year whaling industry to experience hardships first-hand. Also New Bedford: Reynolds Print Co., 1937.

ALEKNAGIK (village)
Baker (name *Lake* Aleknagik dates from 1826 [Sarychev]); Couch (post office since 1937); Doward (name is Eskimo for "wrong way home," settlement inundated by influenza in 1918); Dall; Sundborg (Seventh Day Adventists); Tewkesbury (Bristol Bay Mission School).

ALEKSEEV, ALEKSANDR IVANOVICH
See T-0168 (*Okhotsk: Cradle of Russian Pacific Fleet*)

ALERT BAY (village off NE coast of Vancouver Island)
Alaska Sportsman, Aug., '38 (photo of grave totems); Cameron; Colby; Higginson (young girls sold at potlatches); *National Geographic Magazine*, July, '33 (photos); Scidmore (Kwakiutl); Willoughby.

ALEUTIAN ISLANDS
The following is selective: see Grace Hadley Fuller for fuller bibliography. *Alaska Life*, March, '41 (by teachers at Umnak); Aug., Sept., Oct., '42 (3 part series); Feb., '44 (on soldiers); June, '44 (Seabees); July, '44; Nov., '45; Apr., '46 (soldier lost); Apr., '48; *Alaska Sportsman*, Dec., '44; Apr., '47 (mail service); May, '47 (ships); Oct., '51 (mental health of soldiers in Aleutians); Apr., '53; Allen, E.W.; Baker (name apparently derived from Aleut "Allik" meaning "what"); Bancroft (name); Bank; Berkh (*Chronological Sketch of the Discovery and Settlement of the Aleutian Islands*, 1823); Borden; Campbell; Chevigny; Collins; Clark, Walker; Cook;

Coxe; Dall; Denison; Dole; Elliott; Ford; Golder; Greely; Griffin; Hall; Handleman; Harriman (Dall); Herron; Higginson; Hrdlicka; Hubbard; Hudson; Hulley; Hutchinson; Jochelson; Krenitzen; McCracken; Masterson; Brower; Morgan; Murie; Oliver; Pallas; Paneth; Ranson; Sauer; Scidmore; Shelikhov; Thorburn; Tompkins; Veniaminov; Wardman; Waxell; Wheaton; Wickersham; Winchell; Yarmolinsky; Zubkova; of more recent literature, see Fedorova and Garfield, B. See also Aleuts, and names of individual islands. All accounts of Russian-America necessarily deal extensively with the Aleutian Islands since most of the fur gathering activity was carried out there, as do accounts of WW II in Alaska since the most significant activity of the war occurred in the Aleutians.

ALEUTS
On name origin see Dall in Harriman, and Baker and Bancroft. *Alaska Life*, March, '44 (Burnett Inlet); June, '43; *Alaska Sportsman*, Dec., '4 (on death customs); Dec., '42; Apr., '43 (WW II evacuees); May, '45 (Ward Cove, Ketchikan); May, '48; Feb., '64; Alexander, Fred ("Medical Survey of the Aleutian Islands," *New England Journal of Medicine*, June, 1949); Andrews (Aleut rebellion of 1762); Anderson, Eells; Bancroft (*Native Races*); Bank; Barbeau; Bigelow; Chevigny; Clark; Colby; Cook; Dall; Denison; Dole; Driscoll (Pribilof Islanders at Funter Bay, Atkans at Killisnoo); Elliott; Greely; Grinnell; Harriman (less than 2000 in 1899); Hellenthal; Higginson; Hrdlicka; Hulley; Jochelson; Kitchener (troubles at St. Paul Island); Martin, Geoghegan (language); Miller, M. (population); Morgan (bibliography); Morris (population c. 4000 in 1869); Muir; Petrof (cites Veniaminov); Pilgrim; Quimby; Ranson; Reclus; Scidmore (pop. 900 in 1890); Sundborg (evacuation to SE Alaska); Swineford (700 Aleuts, 300 Creoles 1898); Thalbitzer (language); Tompkins (rebellion); US Dept. of Interior (*Mid-century Alaska*); Veniaminov; Wheaton.

ALEXANDER I (1801-1825)
Bancroft (Krusenstern); Chevigny; Clark; Hulley; see also Lobanov-Rostovsky, A.A. (*Russia and Europe, 1789-1825* [Durham: Duke University Press,1947]) and Riasanovsky, N. (*A History of Russia* [New York; A. Knopf, 1963]).

ALEXANDER II (1855-1881)
Hulley (sale of Alaska); Pares, B. (*A History of Russia* [New York: Random House, 1960]); Tompkins (friendly to US); see also Purchase of Alaska.

ALEXANDER ARCHIPELAGO
Baker (named by US Coast Survey in 1867 for Alexander II); Dall (14,143 sq. mi.); Denison; Scidmore (name suggested by Davidson, earlier Prince of Wales Archipelago, King George III Archipelago [Vancouver], and Sitka Archipelago); Scidmore; Vancouver.

ALEXANDER, BENNO
"In the Wonder Realm of Alaska's Glaciers," *Alaska-Yukon Magazine*, Apr., '09. Alexander spent two summers at Yakutat, 1905 and 1906, and ascended Mt. St. Elias with the Duke of Abruzzi.

ALEXANDER, GEORGE FORREST (US District Judge, Juneau, 1943-47)
Gruening (denied aboriginal right in land).

ALEXANDROVSK (two Russian trading posts)
Andrews (Nushagak post built by Korsakov); Baker (est. by Delarov at entrance to Cook Inlet [Port Graham]; post est. by Russians 1718 now called Nushagak); Bancroft; Chevigny; Dixon (no fort at Port Graham in 1786); Hulley (Port Graham post attached by Lebedev-Lastochkin Co.); Kitchener (Shelikhov-Lebedev-Lastochkin rivalry); Okun (Baranov descr. of rivalries); Petrof (trade at Nushagak); Portlock; Sherwood; Swineford (Alaska Commercial Co. at Port Graham); Tikhmenev.

ALEXIS (Bishop of Sitka and Alaska)
"Nushagak," *Russian Orthodox American Messenger*, Oct., '37.

ALGARDI, FILIPPO
"Il Centenario di un Pioniere, Padre Pasuale Tosi," *Vie D'Italia e del Mondo* (Milan) 3 (1935): 745-69. Fr. Tosi (1837-98) was a prominent Yukon missionary from 1886.

ALICE ISLAND (off Mt. Edgecumbe Island in Sitka Sound)
Baker (named by US Naval officers in 1880)

ALITAK (village, cape, bay, south Kodiak Island)
Baker (called Kashuvagmiut on 1849 Russian map); Couch (post office in village 1933-45); Colby (Aleut fishing village); Hulley (here Glottov first met Kodiak Islanders, who were not Aleut; *Alaska Sportsman*, Nov., '40 (cannery).

ALLAKAKET (mission village at mouth of Alatna, 1906)
Alaska Sportsman, Aug., '44; Apr., '53; Allen (1885); Baker; Colby; Couch (post office since 1925 [named Alatna 1925-38]); Hayes (mission); Steward (Allen); Stuck (descr.).

ALL-ALASKA REVIEW
Monthly, published at Seward, 1915-16, and at Juneau, 1917, by J.J. McGrath. See also T-1076.

ALL-ALASKA SWEEPSTAKES (dog races, Nome, 1908-17)
Alaska Sportsman, Dec., '37; *Alaska-Yukon Magazine*, March, '09; Apr., '09; June, '10; Allan, "Scotty"; Clark; Colby; Darling; Garst; Hines; Ricker (Leonhard Seppala); Seppala; Underwood; Willoughby. See also T-172.

ALLAN, ALLAN ALEXANDER (1867-1941) (Nome musher)
Gold, Men and Dogs. New York: G.P. Putman's Sons, 1931. 337 pp. Known as "Scotty," Allan achieved fame in the All-Alaska Sweepstakes as a musher and trainer. He was a superior trainer, and was hired by the French government in the First World War, collecting 450 dogs for wartime service. A Scot, he came to the Klondike in 1897, and went to Nome where he worked variously as a prospector, freighter and bookkeeper. Barrett Willoughby wrote a novel based on Allan's career.
"Bravest Dogs in the World," *Sunset*, April, 1925

"Gold Lust," *Collier's Magazine*, January, 1929
"On Dog Sense," *Good Housekeeping*, April, 1929
See the following:
Alaska Sportsman, Dec., '37 (dog races); Cameron; Clark; Colby; Darling; Garst (Allan biography); Underwood; Willoughby.

ALLEN, A. JAMES (d. 1944) (Arctic coast trader)
Alaska Sportsman, June, '37 (took 32 whales from canoes); Aug., '37; May, '40 (at Wainwright); Andrews; Poor; Richards (buried at Wainwright, earlier at Point Hope); Stuck (*Winter Circuit*, "flaw whaling"); Van Valin.

ALLEN, ARTHUR A.
"The Curlew's Secret," *National Geographic Magazine*, Dec., 1948.
"The Bird's Year," *National Geographic Magazine*, June, 1951.

ALLEN, EDWARD WEBER (b. 1885) (Seattle attorney)
Jean Francois Galaup de Laperouse: A Checklist. San Francisco: L. Kennedy, 1941 (reprint from *Cal. Hist. Quarterly*). *North Pacific: Japan, Siberia, Alaska, Canada.* New York: Professional and Technical Press, 1936. 282 pp. A brief history of the beginnings of Pacific coast fishing industries.
The Halibut Commission: Its Legal Powers. Seattle, 1936. (International Fisheries Comm. Circular)
The Vanishing Frenchman: The Mysterious Disappearance of Laperouse. Rutland: Charles Tuttle, 1959. 321 pp. A biography in the form of imaginary conversations among personnel aboard the two ships used on Laperouse's last voyage.
"Beyond Three Miles," *Alaska Life*, July, 1939 (Japanese encroachment).
"The Fishtrap Question," April, 1946 (a defense)
"Trouble in the Bering," July, 1938 (conservation efforts)
Allen was a member of the International Pacific Salmon Fisheries Commission and the International Fisheries Comm. See the following:
Alaska Weekly, Jan., 59 (on proposed Japanese-American fisheries treaty); Sept., '59 (resignation from Comm.); Gruening (cites Allen's testimony in defense of traps).

ALLEN, EUGENE C. (b. ca. 1870) (journalist)
Published the *Klondike Nugget* at Dawson, 1898-99; edited the *Teller News*, 1901-02. He bequeathed his newspaper files to the University of Washington. See Bankson; Denison, Mahoney.

ALLEN, E. J.
"Life-line to Alaska," *Blackwood*, 288 (1960): 216-222.

ALLEN, HENRY TUREMAN (1859-1930) (US Army officer)
Report of an Expedition to the Copper, Tanana and Koyukuk Rivers. . .in the Year 1885. US Army (Wn.DC: GPO, 1887). 172 pp. Included in *Compilation of Narratives*.
"Atnatanas: Natives of the Copper River, Alaska," in *Annual Report, Smithsonian Institution*, 1886.
Allen's was the first successful reconnaissance of the Copper River, and the report is a seminal work

for geographic, geologic and social data. The party traveled from Sitka to Nuchek on Hinchinbrook. The narrative of the expedition up the Copper, across Mentasta Pass, down the Tanana and later, up the Koyukuk, is one of the best written and complete of all the military exploratory narratives. At the mouth of the Copper (Alaganik) Allen met the Copper River trader John Bremner who became a member of the expedition. See the following:

Andrews; Baker; Brooks (high praise); Davis; Sherwood (extensive); Stuck (*Voyages*, praise); Underwood, Wickersham (*Old Yukon*).

ALLEN, JOEL ASAPH (1838-1921) (naturalist)
History of North American Pinnipeds. Wn.DC: GPO, 1880. 785 pp. On walrus, sea lion, sea bear and seal. See also T-181 ff.

ALLEN, ROSEMARY A.
"Patterns of Preferential Marriage Among the Alaskan Haidas," *Anthroplogical Papers*, University of Alaska, 1954
"Changing Social Organization and Kinship Among the Alaskan Haidas," *Anthropological Papers*, University of Alaska, 1955.

ALLEN, WILLIS BOYD (b. 1855)
Gulf, and Glacier, or the Percivals in Alaska. Boston: D. Lathrop, 1892.
Red Mountain of Alaska. Boston: Estes and Lauriat, 1889.

ALLISON, WILLIAM L.
See Samuel M. Smucker

ALLMAN, JACK (1892-1953)
Edited *Matanuska Valley Pioneer*, 1935-38.
"Alaska's White Death," *Police Gazette*, March, 1951.
See *Alaska Life*, July, 1938.

ALMALCOLM P.O. See Smith, Alexander Malcolm.

ALPINE CLUB OF CANADA
"The Mount Logan Expedition," *Canadian Alpine Journal*, 15 (1925): 1-126. Discussion by eight writers.

ALPINE JOURNAL (London)
Articles or notes on Mt. McKinley as follows: Feb., '03 (1902 Brooks expedition); Aug., '04 (1903 Cook expedition); Aug., '11 (altitude measurement); Nov., '43 (1913 Stuck expedition); Nov., '42 (Army Test expedition of 1942).

ALSEK RIVER (valley and glacier)
Alaska-Yukon Magazine, Aug., '10 (photos); Baker (in St. Elias region between Lituya and Yakutat Bays); Dall (flows into Dry Bay); Hansen (in *Coast*, March, '06); Robson ("The Conquest of the Alsek," *Alaska-Yukon Magazine*, Aug., '10).

ALTHOFF, JOHN (priest, Wrangell, 1879-1895)
Alaska Searchlight, Feb., '95 (full resume); Santos; Young.

ALTSHELER, WILLIAM BRENT
Natural History Index-Guide: An Index to 3,365 Books and Periodicals. New York: H.W. Wilson, 1940 583 pp.

Maladministration Through the Alaska Syndicate. Louisville, 1910. 25 pp. On the Ballinger-Pinchot controversy.

ALUMINUM COMPANY OF AMERICA
A Collection of Notes and Comments about the Taiya Hydroelectric Project. Pittsburgh, 1952. See also:
Alaska Sportsman, Oct., '57 (Canada kills project); *Alaska Weekly*, Feb., '51; Apr., '51; June, '51 (Skagway or Kitimat?).

AMBROSSY, RIGHT REVEREND BISHOP
Alaska Sportsman, Oct., '57 (Bishop at Sitka, re: 1917, Church separated from mother church in Russia).

AMCHITKA ISLAND
See Arctic Bibliography for information on the atomic test explosions (AEC) on Amchitka (Millrow, 1969) (Cannikin, 1971).
See the following:
Alaska Sportsman, Sept., '47 (Attu, Shemya and Amchitka to be abandoned); Jan., '49 (photo); *Alaska Weekly*, July, '50 (numerous rats spread 12 miles along beach from Army dump); Baker (elev. 1,281, called St. Makarius by Bering); Bancroft (Benyovski, Billings); Dall (coal and kaolin); *National Geographic*, March, '49 (photo, air base); Scidmore (on Vancouver-Yokohama steamer route); Tompkins (Bering possibly visited); also Hrdlicka.

AMEIGH, GEORGE C., JR. and YULE M. CHAFFIN
Alaska's Kodiak Island. Anchorage: Anchorage Printing, 1962. 180 pp.

AMERICAN ALPINE JOURNAL (New York)
Numerous material on Alaska mountains and climbing; see index, and also see Washburn.

AMERICAN AUTOMOBILE ASSOCIATION
Numerous travel publications. Contact the association, and see T-192.

AMERICAN BAR ASSOCIATION (section on judicial administration)
Alaska Grand Jury Handbook. Juneau, 1960

AMERICAN BIBLE SOCIETY
See T-193 ff.

AMERICAN COMMITTEE ON INTERNATIONAL WILDLIFE PROTECTION
See T-197

AMERICAN GEOGRAPHICAL SOCIETY
See T-199

AMERICAN GEOPHYSICAL UNION
Transactions, 1926, National Research Council. Symposium on scientific cooperation in the Aleutians. See also the Arctic Bibliography.

AMERICAN HISTORICAL ASSOCIATION
What has Alaska to Offer Post-war Pioneers? Madison, Wisc.: US Armed Forces Institute, 1944. 38pp Biblio.

AMERICAN HISTORICAL REVIEW
Numerous articles; see index.

AMERICAN MINING CONGRESS
Alaskan Problems. Reprint from *Proceedings*, 14th Annual Session, Wn.DC: GPO, 1912

AMERICAN MUSEUM OF NATURAL HISTORY
(New York)
The Andrew J. Stone explorations in Arctic and sub-Arctic America. New York: 1905. See also *Alaska Sportsman*, May, '39 (Clark-Kissel expedition, fall 1937); Dec., '50 (George F. Mason).

AMERICAN ORNITHOLOGIST'S UNION
See T-207

AMERICAN ORTHODOX MESSENGER
See T-211; see also Smith, Barbara.

AMERICAN-RUSSIAN COMMERCIAL COMPANY (San Francisco)
By-laws. Organized May, 1853. San Francisco: O'Meara and Painter, 1855.
The Alaska Fur Seal Bill. San Francisco, 1869.
See the following:
Bancroft (withdrawal of bid on fur seal harvest); Kitchener (bid on Pribilof furs); Petrof (commercial operations).

AMERICAN-RUSSIAN COMPANY (fictitious)
Clark (proposed sale of Alaska); see also Purchase of Alaska.

AMERICAN STATE PAPERS
Class I, Foreign Relations, Vols. IV and V. Wn.DC: GPO, 1858 (re: Russian monopoly on the Northwest coast).

AMERICAN UNITED COMPANY (Russian)
Usually known as the Russian-American Company. See Tompkins (formed August 3, 1798 by union of Shelikhov-Golikov Co. and the Myluikov group; became Russian-American Co. on July 8, 1799).

AMERIKANSKII SEVER (The American North)
A collection of translated articles, ed. N.M. Baranskii. Moscow, 1950. Authors translated include Walker, E.P. and Sundborg.

AMERIKANSKII PRAVOSLAVNYI VIESTNIK
The Holy Apostles in the Aleutian-Fox Dialect. See Smith, B. (*Preliminary Survey*).

AMES, ROBERT ANDREW
See T-212

AMUNDSEN, ROALD ENGELBREGT GRAVNING (1872-1928) (explorer)
The Northwest Passage. London: Constable, 1908, 2v. Record of a voyage of exploration in the ship *Gjoa* in 1903-07. It is claimed Amundsen was the first to visit both poles, and the first to make both the northeast and northwest passages.
My Life as an Explorer. Garden City: Doubleday, 1927. 282 pp. Contains accounts of the *Gjoa* expedition through the northwest passage, the *Maud* expedition of 1918-25 along the Siberian coast, the

attempted polar flight in 1925 with Lincoln Ellsworth, the Amundsen-Ellsworth-Nobile polar flight to Alaska in 1926.
First Polar Crossing. New York: Doran, 1927. Story of the flight of the *Norge* from Spitzbergen to Teller, Alaska, in 1926.
Our Polar Flight: the Amundsen-Ellsworth Polar Flight. New York: Dodd, Mead, 1925. 373 pp. Two flying boats flew from Spitzbergen to latitude 87°44' N where they were forced down. They succeeded in getting back to Spitzbergen safely.
Nordostpassagen (Northwest Passage). Christiania, 1921. Popular narrative of the first two years of the *Maud* expedition of 1918-25, leaving Norway and drifting eastward in waters north of Siberia to Cape Chelyuskin, where the party wintered. Contains a description of Sverdrup's sojourn among the Chuchi natives. See also T-213 ff. See the following:
Alaska Sportsman, Aug., '49 (souvenirs taken from *Gjoa* at Nome); Dec., '49 (*Gjoa* photo); May, '50 (*Norge*; chair given museum at Juneau); Jan., '57 (Amundsen at Eagle); June, '57 (Amundsen photo); see also *Alaska Journal*, '74 (Alaska Historical Society placed plaque at Teller); *Alaska Weekly*, Dec., '50 (*Norge* landed May 13, 1926; Historical Museum has numerous artifacts); see also Colby; Davis (Eagle); Darling (dog "Oolik Lomen" born on *Gjoa*); Kitchener (news); Mirsky; Stuck (*Voyages*, Amundsen describes Indian chief John Herbert); Underwood (failed to find Stefansson's "blond" Eskimos); Wead (*Maud* at Nome).

AMUR RIVER (Historic Siberian river)
Chevigny (Russian capture of valley); Dall (Collins at mouth); Collins (voyage down Amur); Golder; Henderson; Tompkins (Russian policy, 1844); Whymper (town, Nicolaevski).

AMYROSSY, Bishop
"Alaska Needs Priests," *Russian Orthodox Journal*, February, 1957.

ANABLE, EDMUND A. (b. 1903) (Jesuit missionary)
Alaska Weekly, Dec., '50; *Jesuit Missions*, Apr., '45; Santos (arrived in Alaska 1938).

ANADYR RIVER (northeast Siberia)
Bancroft; Brooks (town Anadyrsk founded 1650); Chevigny; Bush (history of region); Dall; Golder; Henderson (village of Anadyrsk, Baranov's post plundered); Hulley (Dezhnev's trip, Billings); Kennan; Potter (airfield and air line); Tompkins; Whymper; see the Arctic Bibliography for works in Russian.

ANAKTUVUK PASS (village, pass)
Alaska Sportsman, Apr., '64; May, '61; Dec., '65; Apr., '69; Nov., '72; *Alaska Weekly*, Dec., '50 (Homer Mekiana, first postmaster); Jan., '51 (anthropologists discover culture in pass similar to Denbigh); Baker (crossed by Peters and Schrader in 1901, divides Yukon and Arctic drainages); Couch (post office from 1951); Ingstad; Irving (birds); Stuck. Abandoned through most of the 20th century, villagers related to those who once lived at Anaktuvuk Pass returned there in the 1950's, forsaking the coastal (Barrow) culture which had drawn them to the Arctic in the time of the whalers.

ANATOLII, Archimandrit
Indiane Aliaski (Indians of Alaska). Odessa: Tjp.
E. I. Fesenko, 1907 (?). 139 pp.
Indianskoe plemia Thlingit (The Thlingit Indian
Tribes). New York: Press of the Orthodox Messenger, 1899. 88 pp.

ANCHOR POINT (Kenai Peninsula)
Baker (named by Cook, Russian names Laidennoi
[Icy] and Jakorny [Anchor]; native name Kasnachin); Cook; Couch (post office from 1949);
Petrof (coal); Sherwood.

ANCHORAGE (city)
Popular literature on Alaska's most populous and
"urban" center abounds. The city began in 1915 as
the headquarters of the Alaska Engineering Commission, administrative agency charged with construction of the Alaska Railroad. By the end of the
year the federal government had auctioned off lots
south of Ship Creek, and 2000 or more residents had
established a tent city and frame buildings were
under construction for Commission personnel (by the
government) and for future townspeople. The Commission erected a hospital, and numerous buildings
for the railroad. By the 1920's Anchorage had surpassed Valdez and Cordova as the primary service
and transportation center of southcentral Alaska,
supplying the interior, and the seat of the judicial
district was transferred there. After a brief loss due
to WWI, population stabilized in the 1920's and
1930's. WW II brought a significant population increase to Anchorage with Fort Richardson and later
Elmendorf AFB. After the war numerous federal
agencies (BIA, BLM, FAA, USFS, USFWS, etc)
established district headquarters there, adding to the
population. The international airport grew in importance with increased and jet international air
travel in the 1960's, and communications and transportation became the primary economic mainstay of
the city. Tourism also plays a significant role, and in
the late 1960's major oil companies established
district offices in the city for exploration and production. Almost forgotten in the urban activity of the
modern era are the Tanaina who inhabited the area
in Russian times, and the gold prospecting which
took place on the upper Kenai Peninsula before
1915. The gold mining north of the city in the
Talkeetna Mountains, coal mining east of the city,
and the Matanuska Valley agricultural region also
have contributed to the city's growth. Anchorage is
an all-year warm water port. Early history is documented in AEC records and Land Office records.
Little work has been done in the city archives, which
date from 1925. Researchers should examine the
Alaska Sportsman Index published by the Alaska
Northwest Publishing Co., and also the following:
Anchorage Times, Anchorage News (dailies); *Alaska
Life*, Apr., '40 (20,000 pop. predicted in 50 years);
Apr., '42; June, '44; March '45 (special issue on Anchorage); Oct., '45 (cost of living); Dec., '45 (air
photo); Jan., '46 (photos); Apr., '46; Feb., '47;
June, '47 (air photo); *Alaska Weekly*, May, '50
(typhoid); May, '50 (14 story apt. bldg. at 1200 L);
June, '50 (146 teachers); aug., '50 (housing); Sept.,
'50 (evacuation drill); Nov., '50 (National Bank of
Alaska); Jan., '51 (weather summary); Feb., '51
(pop.); March, '51; Apr., '51 (earthquake ins.);
May, '51 (housing); June, '51 (sales tax); July, '51

(mail); Aug., '51; Sept., '51 (record rain); Sept., '51
(PNA scheduled Seattle service, DC-4, 7-1/2 hrs.,
$75); *Alaska's Health*, Feb., '54 (ANS hospital);
American City, June, '54 (annexation); July, '54
(parking); Atwood, E. (*All-America City*); Brooks
(in Sherwood, *Cook Inlet Collection*); Browne, R.;
Caldwell; Chambers ("Some properties of the
Community Air Supply [after 1953 Mt. Spurr eruption which spread ash on the city], *Proc. Alaska
Science Conference*, 1957); Colby; Couch (post
office since 1914); Dachnowski-Stokes ("Peat
Resources of Alaska," circ., US Dept. Agri., 1941);
Davis; Denison; Dobrovolny (USGS, 1950); Eldridge (*Proc. Alaska Science Conf.*, 1952); Elliott, L.
(*Reader's Digest*, Dec., 1960); Foster, W.S. (in
American City, Nov., '54, Aug., '54); Fournelle
(*Public Health Reports*, March, '57); Gruening
(*News* against statehood until failure of Eisenhower
to endorse); Gustafson (*Our Public Lands*, Oct.,
'54); Hall; Helmericks; Herron; Hilscher; Hyland
and Reece (*Jrnl of New Eng. Water Works Assn*,
March, '51); Jeffrey (Z.J. Loussac provides library);
Jenkins (*Mosquito News*, Dec., '48 [results of Alaska
Insect Control Project]); Kederick (*Explosives Engineer*, Nov. '53 [Eklutna power]); Kellogg and Nygard (*Soils*); Kitchener (merchandising); Kuehnelt-
Liddihn; Lawing; *Life Magazine*, Oct., '50, Nov.,
'52 (photos); Lipke; Mitchell, J.M.; *Newsweek
Magazine*, Aug., '50 (night view); Poor (wartime);
Potter; Romig; Roose (*Alaska's Health*, Oct., '50);
Scott and Weiss (*Public Health Reports*, May, '53
[food]); Stone, K.H. (*Geographic Review*, July, '48
[aerial photography]); Stuck (*Missions*); Sundborg;
Tewkesbury; *Time Magazine*, June, 1958 (air
photo); Underwood (original townsite); US Bureau
of Reclamation (*Eklutna Dam and Power Plant*,
Denver: 1958); Vancouver (Inlet survey); Young
(first sermon); see also Anchorage City Directories
(privately published) for various years; see also
reports and records of various federal agencies. See
also T-232 ff. See also Wm. Wilson.

ANCHORAGE DAILY NEWS
Founded at Anchorage, 1946 by Norman C.
Brown. *Flood*. Anchorage, 1967 (Fairbanks flood
photos) *The Village People*. Anchorage, 1966
(photo).

ANCHORAGE DAILY TIMES
Founded at Anchorage, 1916, as the *Cook Inlet
Pioneer*. *Alaska's Struggle for Statehood* (Mrs. Robert
B. Atwood [Evangeline Atwood]). Anchorage, 1950
The *Times* played an active role in the debate over
statehood; editor Robert Atwood was chairman of
the Alaska Statehood Committee.

ANCHORAGE FUR RENDEZVOUS (annual winter
carnival from 1935)
Annual illus. magazine published by Greater
Anchorage, Inc.

ANCON (sidewheel steamer)
Alaska Life, Jan., '46 (history, operated between
Seattle and southeast Alaska ports, numerous
wrecks); *Alaska Sportsman*, Aug., '41 (photo);
Sept., '41 (wrecked at Loring cannery, 1890); Sept.,
'49 (boilers still visible); Baker (steamer named for
Panama "mountain," Ancon Peak [3300 ft] on

Woronkofski Island named for steamer); Franck (only *Ancon* and *Bruno* were running to Alaska in 1886); Scidmore (1885).

ANDERSON, ALEXANDER CAULFIELD
See T-241

ANDERSON, BERN (Rear Admiral, USN)
Surveyor of the Sea: The Life and Voyages of Captain George Vancouver. Seattle: University of Washington Press, 1960. 247 pp.

ANDERSON, CHARLIE ("Lucky Swede," Klondike miner) (d. 1939)
Alaska Sportsman, Jan., '52 (his "strike"); Bankson (story of his lucky purchase); Berton; Morgan; O'Connor; Winslow.

ANDERSON, ESKIL
Asbestos and Jade Occurrences in the Kobuk River Region, Juneau, 1945.

ANDERSON, EVA GREENSLIT (Washington State legislator)
Dog-team Doctor. Caldwell, Idaho: Caxton Printers, 1940. 298 pp. A biography of Dr. Joseph Herman Romig (1872-1951) who came to Alaska as a Moravian medical missionary about 1896 on the Kuskokwim River. He later served as a school superintendent, and general physician. Later still he was a US Commissioner, surgeon for the Alaska Railroad, and chief of staff at the Anchorage railroad hospital. He retired in 1942 to Colorado Springs. This work portrays interestingly native life on the Kuskokwim.

ANDERSON, HOBSON DEWEY and WALTER CROSBY EELLS
Alaska Natives: A Survey of Their Sociological and Educational Status. Stanford: Stanford University Press, 1935. 472 pp. This major study was urged by William John Cooper, US Commissioner of Education, 1929-1933, and funded by the Carnegie Foundation. The study is based on field work conducted by the Stanford University School of Education and concern primarily (but not exclusively) the Eskimos and Aleuts of western Alaska.

ANDERSON, ISABEL W.P. (Mrs. Larz Anderson) (b. 1876)
Odd Corners. New York: Dodd, Mead, 1917. 368 pp.

ANDERSON, JACOB PETER (1874-1953) (botanist)
Flora of Alaska and Adjacent Parts of Canada. Ames: Iowa State University Press, 1959. 543 pp. illus. "A Comparison of the Flora of Iowa with that of Alaska and the Yukon," *Proceedings,* Iowa Academy of Science, 1949.
Anderson was a long-time Alaska resident and began publication of numerous botanical studies in 1916. See the Arctic Bibliography.

ANDERSON, JIM
Boating on the Yukon River. Juneau: Alaska Publishing Company, 1930. 48 pp.

ANDERSON, LAURA DAVID
See T-249

ANDERSON, R. M. and B. B. ROSWIG
See T-250

ANDERSON, ROBERTA
"Alaskan Libraries in 1945," *Quarterly,* Northwest Library Association, July, 1945.

ANDERSON, WILLIAM R. (Captain, USN)
Nautilus: 90°N. Cleveland: World Publishing Co., 1959. 251 pp.
First Under the North Pole. Cleveland: World Publishing Co., 1959. 64 pp.
"The Arctic as a Sea Route of the Future," *National Geographic,* January, 1959.

ANDREAFSKY (lower Yukon, two sites)
Alaska Weekly, Apr., '50 (Spils to move mission school from Akulurak to Andreafsky); Baker (on right bank, Clear River, 2 miles above Yukon, and 5 miles above Old Andreafsky, No. Comm. Co. winter headquarters); Cameron (Old Andreafsky founded 1853, Russian traders killed there in 1855, very small in 1919); Colby (notes on both); Couch (post office at Andreafsky from 1913, named changed to Andreafski in 1951, post office moved to St. Mary's 1955); Dall (descr. fort, killing of traders, revenge by Kogenikov and Ivanohov); Henderson (descr. Indians); Kitchener (NC Co.); Moore; Schwatka (Kerchinikov) Stuck (*Voyages,* history, steamers, abandonment); Underwood (Kerchinikov); Walden (Yukon 6 miles wide); Wiedemann.

ANDREANOF ISLANDS
Baker (middle Aleutians, east of Seguam Pass, explored by Andreian Tolstyk in the *Andreian and Natalia* in 1761, islands named for Tolstyk or his ship); see also Berkh.

ANDREE, SALOMON AUGUST (1854-1897) (scientist)
Andree's Story: the complete record of his Polar Flight. New York: Viking Press, 1930. 389 pp. Trans. 1897 attempt to drift over the pole by balloon, the *Eagle.* From Spitzbergen, forced down over White Island after 64 hours. Though they carried homing pigeons the fate of the party (including Nils Strindberg and Knut Fraenkel) remained a mystery for 33 years. When found, dramatically, the bodies were well preserved and the diaries and notes legible. For Andree's works see the Arctic Bibliography; see also the following:
Bankson (rumor of 1898 discovery of body [actually found in 1930]); Mirsky (complete story); Wead (polar flight).

ANDREEV, ALEKSANDR IGNATEVICH (b. 1887)
Russian Discoveries in the Pacific Ocean and North America in the 18th Century. Trans. Carl Ginsburg. Ann Arbor: American Council of Learned Societies, 1952. Contains previously unpublished documents, including a report by Ponomarev and Golikov of the discovery of Umnak and Unalaska Islands in 1758-59, the discovery of the Andreanof Islands in 1764, reported by Lazarev and Vasiutinskii, Shelikhov's relations with the government, and the travels of N.I. Korobitsyn, 1795-1807.
See also an untranslated work, *Russkie Otkrytiia v Tikhom Okeane i Severnoi Amerike v XVIII Veke* (Moscow: OGIZ Gosudarstvennoe izd-vo. Geo-

grafichestoi Literatury, 1948) which includes the texts of 40 historical documents, 1733-1792, including the voyages to Bolshaya Zemlya, apparently to Alaska in 1732, a description of Chukchi area in 1742, reports of I. Korovin, I. Soloviev, and materials on the trading companies of I.I. Golikov and G.I. Shelikhov in the Aleutians and America. See Berkh, and cp. Tikhmenev.

ANDREWS, CLARENCE LEROY (1862-1948)
The Story of Sitka. Seattle: Lowman and Hanford, 1922. 108 pp.
Sitka. Caldwell, Idaho: Caxton Printers, 1945. 145 pp. Historical guide to Sitka with photos and 1867 map.
The Story of Alaska. Seattle: Lowman and Hanford, 1931. 258 pp. (second edition, 1938, Caxton Printers)
Wrangell and the Gold of the Cassiar. Seattle: Luke Tinker, Commercial Printer, 1937. 61 pp. paper. Map and historical notes, photos.
The Pioneers and Nuggets of Verse. Seattle: Clarence Andrews, 1937. 55 pp. paper.
The Eskimo and His Reindeer in Alaska. Caldwell, Idaho: Caxton Printers, 1939. 253 pp. Based primarily on Andrews' experiences as a teacher on the Seward Peninsula, 1923-29. The work attacks the Lomen Brothers of Nome for consolidation of the reindeer industry in the 1920's, arguing their activity deprived the Eskimos of certain grazing lands and marketing privileges. See Lomen for a rebuttal to the argument.
The Eskimo, a quarterly journal published at Seattle by Clarence Andrews, Feb., 1936 to January, 1938.
Andrews published numerous articles in the *Washington Historical Quarterly* (now the *Pacific Northwest Historical quarterly*), among them the following:
"Research in Alaska," October, 1915
"Marine Disasters (over 400)," January, 1916
"Russian Alaska: Baranof," July, 1916
"Russian Alaska: Industry, Trade, Social Life," October, 1916
"Alaska Whaling," January, 1918
"Salmon in Alaska," October, 1918
"Russian Plans for American Dominion," April, 1927
"Wreck of the St. Nicholas," January, 1922
  "Wreck of the St. Nicholas," January, 1922
"Biography of Captain William Moore," July, 1930, January, 1931, April, 1931
"Russian Shipbuilding in America," January, 1934
"Driving Reindeer in Alaska," April, 1935
"Some Notes on the Yukon by Stewart Menzies," April, 1941
Andrews' contribution to Alaska literature was significant. His research was thorough and the accuracy of his material is seldom in doubt. His writing, however, tended toward hyperbole and romanticism. He died at 85 in Eugene, Oregon. Much of his personal library became the property of Sheldon Jackson College. See the following:
Alaska Life, Apr., '42; July, '42 (at Skagway customs office); May, '49 (obituary, photo); *Alaska Sportsman,* Sept., '45; July, '48 (obituary); *Alaska-Yukon Magazine,* July, '09 (as special agent at Alaska-Yukon-Pacific Exposition); *Alaska Weekly;* Apr., '48 (obituary); Davis; Meany; Nichols (newspaper collection).

ANDREWS, RALPH WARREN
Various books of photographs. See T-259 ff.
Alaska's Trophy Sport Fisheries. Alaska State Department of Fish and Game, 1969.

ANDREWS, ROY C.
"Shore-whaling: A World Industry," *National Geographic,* May, 1911. See also W-6696 ff.

ANDREYEV, A. I.
See Andreev, A.I.

ANDRIASHEV, ANATOLII P.
A Contribution to Knowledge of the Fishes from the Bering and Chukchi Seas. Trans. L. Lanz and N.J. Wilimovsky. Wn.DC: US Fish and Wildlife Service, 1955. 81 pp.

ANGOON (village, Admiralty Island)
Alaska Sportsman, Feb., '41 (photo); Oct., '55 (photo); Sept., '57 (witchcraft); Apr., '51 (village to move); *Alaska Weekly,* Nov. '50 (vote to move); Andrews (shelling by *USS Adams*); Baker (north of Killisnoo); Colby; Couch (Killisnoo destroyed by fire, 1928, Killisnoo post office [est. 1882] moved to Angoon 1930); DeLaguna (anthropology); Dole (on 1882 bombardment); Scidmore (bombing by Capt. Merriman); Rogers (witch hunting); Young (beginnings of mission work).

ANGUS, HENRY FORBES (b. 1891)
British Columbia and the United States, with F.W. Howay and W.N. Sage. Toronto: Ryerson, for the Carnegie Endowment for International Peace, 1942. 408 pp. History

ANIAK (village, Kuskokwim)
Alaska Sportsman, Feb., '53 (photo); Jan., '56 (medical fund); Colby (Lukeen here in 1832); Couch (post office 1914-32 and from 1936); Dall; Kitchener (small NC Co. post).

ANIAKCHAK (bay and crater, Alaska Peninsula)
Baker (on southern shore, written Aniakshak by Russians); Colby (crater 6 miles diameter, discovered and named by R.H. Sargent, USGS, 1923, exploded May 1, 1931); Hubbard (exploration, photos).

ANIAN, STRAIT or STRAITS (mythical northeast passage)
Brooks (on Zaltieri's 1566 map); Clark; Goldson, William (Observations on the Passage between the Atlantic and Pacific, Portsmouth: W. Mowbray, 1793); Golder; Greenhow (named by Gaspar Cortereal, 1500, literary history); Nunn (origin of concept); Ruge; Sykes (in *Bulletin,* Am. Geog. Soc. [1915]); Wagner (varying concepts explained); Wytfliet. See Wickersham's Bibliography.

ANNABEL, RUSSELL (naturalist)
Hunting and Fishing in Alaska. New York: A. Knopf, 1948. 341 pp. Personal, anecdotal.
Alaskan Tales. New York: A.S. Barnes, 1953. 137 pp.
Tales of a Big-Game Guide. New York: Derrydale Press, 1938. 198 pp.
"Indestructible Sourdough," *Sat. Eve. Post,* October, 1950.

A resident of Valdez from six months, Annabel ran away from home to fish, hunt and mine. A well known guide and steamboater on the Yukon, he served as a correspondent in the Pacific in WW II.

ANNAHOOTZ, ALEXIS (d. 1890)
Alaska-Yukon Magazine, Oct., '07 ("White Man's Friend'"); *Alaskan* (Sitka), Feb., '90 (white man's friend, chief of the Kog-wan-tans at Sitka); Andrews (photo); Howard (speech favoring peace); Morris (attended religious service dressed in old officers clothing, opposed importation of Chinese); Scidmore (pine doorplate); Willard (wife's death); Wright (war chief).

ANNETTE ISLAND
Alaska Sportsman, Apr., '51 ("Chinatown"); July, '52 (photo); Feb., '53 (village by wartime airstrip); Apr., '54 (wind); *Alaska Weekly*, Jan., '51; Baker (named by Dall in 1879 for his wife, Annette Whitney Dall, Tsimshian Reserve by act of 1891); Colby (reserve conveys exclusive fishing right); Couch (post office at airport since 1947); Denison; Gruening; Higginson; Hulley; *National Geographic*, Oct., '40 (CCC builds airport); Scidmore (Gravina island group discovered and named by Camano); Sundborg (Metlakatlans); Vancouver (named Point Davison); see also Metlakatla, William Duncan.

ANTHROPOLOGY
See Aleut, Eskimo, Indian, Bibliography and individual authors.

ANTI-MONOPOLY ASSOCIATION OF THE PACIFIC COAST
History of the Wrongs of Alaska, San Francisco, 1875, 43 pp. Attack on Alaska Commercial Company by unsuccessful bidders for fur seal contract. See *Alaska Herald*.

ANTISARLUK, CHARLIE
Alaska-Yukon Magazine, July, '07 (left 200 deer at death); Brevig (leading man); Brower (deer driver); Dole (to Pt. Barrow with Jarvis); Harrison (one of first to receive reindeer); Stewart (with Jarvis); US Cutter Service (*Bear*); Wead (lent 133 reindeer).

ANTISARLUK, MARY (d. 1949)
Alaska-Yukon Magazine, July, '07 ("Queen of Reindeer"); Cameron (largest herd); Carrighar ("Sinuk Mary"); Harrison (richest Eskimo); Jackson.

ANVIK (Yukon village)
Bancroft; Chapman (was there 1887-1930); Colby; Couch (post office since 1897); Helmericks; Hrdicka; Schwatka; also *Alaska Sportsman*, Dec., '40.

ANVIK RIVER
Baker (explored by Glazunov, 1833); Dall; Davis; Henderson; Hulley; Judge; Raymond.

ANVIL CITY (and Creek, Mountain, Peak, Rock)
Andrews (strike); Baker (creek 4 miles NW of Nome, Peak 5 miles N of Nome, 1050'); Brooks ("Discovery" claim, Sept. 22, 1898); Cameron (Beach had cabin near summit of Anvil Rock); Clark (Alexander McKenzie jumped claims); Colby; Harrison; Hulley, Kitchener (Anvil City [Nome] a

tent town, NC Co. arrived with first shipping in 1899); Tompkins (250 pop. in 1899); see also Nome.

ANZER, RICHARD C. (b. ca. 1878) (journalist)
Klondike Gold Rush. New York: Pageant Press, 1959. 236 pp.

APHOON (mouth of Yukon)
Alaska-Yukon Magazine, March, '07 (slough connecting St. Michael with Aphoon to be dredged to eliminate hazards of Bering Sea); Baker (also "Apoon," cites Tebenkov, Coast Survey, Fr. Barnum, Wm. Hamilton); Higginson (one of three principal outlets); Raymond (northernmost); Schwatka; Stuck (*Voyages*, Kwishluak is the largest mouth, steamboat exit is by the north or Aphoon mouth); *US Coast Pilot* ("Aphoon Pass," [channels and banks subject to rapid changes from erosion and deposit]); Walden ("by hugging the right bank we struck the Aphoon channel").

APPEAL OF YUKON MINERS
See T-272

APPEL, BENJAMIN
See T-273

APPLETON, LeROY
See T-274

ARAI, TSUGUO
Alaska and Japan, Anchorage: Alaska Methodist University Press, 1972.

ARCHAEOLOGY
See Anthropology, see Arctic Bibliography and individual authors. See also the *Alaskan Sportsman* Index. See the following:
Alaska Life, July, '44; *Alaska-Yukon Magazine*, March, '07 (entire mammoth, in ice, found on Cleary Creek); Jan., '08 (Smithsonian has petrified stump with steel axe cuts); July, '12 (mummified humans on King Island); *Alaska Weekly*, Nov., '50 (Giddings artifacts at Cape Denbigh, old flints, USGS findings Anuktuvuk Pass); Bankson (3000 lbs skull and horns found on Klondike claim, March, 1899); Bogoras; Colby (tusks and bones at Mammoth Creek, Elephant Point mammals); DeLaguna; Dufresne (27 Pleistocene animals); Franck (University museum, Barrow, Unimak sites); Geist; Giddings; Hrdlicka; Jenness; Larsen; Lipke (at Seldovia); *National Geographic*, May, '39 (Bering Strait fragments by H.B. Collins); Oct., '49 (15,000 year old baby elephant near Fairbanks); Sept., '42 (Rainey on Point Hope); Oliver (village excavation on Akun Island); Rainey; Rickard (mammoth parts found in Alaska, intact mammoth found on Lena in Siberia prepared and exhibited); Rowe (Pt. Hope, Ipiutak culture); Scidmore (problem with artifact hunters; Willoughby exhibited supposed pterodactyl collarbone at Juneau); Skarland (Denali highway); Stuck (Eschscholtz Bay, Point Hope); Walden (sales by Indians); Wickersham (mammoth); Wiedemann (Woodchopper Creek).

ARCHER, S. A.
A Heroine of the North. Toronto: Macmillan, 1929. 187 pp. Memoir of Charlotte Selina Bompas (1830-1917), wife of first Bishop of Selkirk. Life at

Forts Simpson, Norman and Resolution, and at Fortymile in the Yukon.

ARCHIMANDRITOV, Captain
See Baker, list of manuscript maps, 1848-50.

ARCTANDER, JOHN WILLIAM (1849-1920)
The Apostle of Alaska: the Story of William Duncan of Metlakahtla. New York: Fleming H. Revell, 1909. 395 pp. (Written at Metlakahtla during the summer of 1908.)
The Lady in Blue: A Sitka Romance. Seattle: Lowman and Hanford, 1911. 63 pp.
Arctander spent the summers of 1904-1908 with Duncan at Metlakahtla. L.R. Huber writes in *Alaska Sportsman*, Aug., '45, that when *Apostle* was published, Duncan was incensed to find that Arctander referred to the Tsimshians as savages. Duncan bought the copyright on the book, and had all unsold copies recalled. A Mr. James Wallace had supplied Arctander with 50 or 60 Tsimshian legends recorded during the winters, 15 of which appeared in *Apostle*.

ARCTIC
Journal of the Arctic Institute of North America, Montreal.

ARCTIC (Yukon steamer)
Cameron (70', between St. Michael and Nome, 1919, notorious for discomfort); Curtin (built at St. Michael, 1889, first to Dawson, 1896); Kitchener; Ogilvie (built by AC Co.).

ARCTIC AND ARCTIC COAST
See Arctic Bibliography.

ARCTIC BIBLIOGRAPHY
Prepared for and in cooperation with the Department of Defense (US), under the direction of the Arctic Institute of North America. Initial volumes under the directorship of Dr. Henry B. Collins, Jr., Chairman of the Directing Committee. Wn.DC: GPO, from 1953.
Each volume contains 1200-1600 double column pages. Books are listed alphabetically by author, with a subject index in volume 3 and at the end of each succeeding volume. Experts were engaged to review materials in the Library of Congress and in other cooperating libraries, including the Stefansson Arctic Library at Dartmouth. Entries include description, review and indication of location. Material tends toward technical and scientific. Generally available material is listed in the first three volumes which were issued as a unit.

ARCTIC BROTHERHOOD
International (Alaskans) fraternal order organized at Skagway, February, 1899. In 1905 there were chapters (camps) in 18 communities (including Nome), and a membership of 5000. It lapsed with the decrease of prospecting activitiy. See T-278 for souvenir publications, and minutes of annual meetings. See also the following:
Alaska Sportsman, Aug., '38 (factor in development); Jan., '56; Dec., '56 (Robert Service); *Alaska-Yukon Magazine*, Sept., '06; Apr., '07; Dec., '07; May, '08 (Alaska-Yukon-Pacific Exposition); Dec.,

'08; Feb., '12 (Portland, Ore.); Alaska-Yukon Gold Book (organized on *City of Seattle* enroute to Skagway); Cameron (est. as protection against lawlessness); Chase (photo); Chealander and White (official history); Clark (Wm. Connell); Colby; Davidson (history); Davis; Dole (speech by Dr. J. Moore, Univ. Washington, 1909 to 7000); Harrison (Nome); Hines (Hannum); Mahoney (initially had to be "North" before 1897, later relaxed to require only a winter); Nichols (on civil government); Underwood (protection, mascot); Wickersham (initiation); Wilcoxen (history).

ARCTIC CIRCLE
Alaska Sportsman, Nov., '51 (Fort Yukon); Denison (1/4th of Alaska north of the circle); Franck; Mirsky (on Greek origin of concept [astronomy]); Rickard (Fort Yukon); Sundborg; Wickersham.

ARCTIC CITY
Baker (mining camp on Koyukuk near Arctic circle, named by miners, 1899); Chase (1893 origin); Stuck (*Missions*) (roadhouse and store changed named from Moses City).

ARCTIC CLUB (Seattle)
Alaska-Yukon Magazine, Feb., '08 (organization); March, '08 (building); Apr., '08 (absorbed Alaska Club); Jan., '09; Feb., '09; Aug., '09; Feb., '12; March, '12; July, '12; Nichols (Alaska Club formed Sept., '03, Arctic Club, '08, for the benefit of investors in Alaska development, some formed Alaska Home Rule Club).

ARCTIC INSTITUTE OF NORTH AMERICA (Montreal)
Founded in 1945 to study problems common to Alaska, Canada and Greenland, financed by the United States and Canada. Scientific studies and conferences, working in close association with the defense establishments of both countries, and with universities, including the University of Alaska. The Institute, with the National Academy of Sciences and the University of Alaska has sponsored annually an Alaskan Science Conference, the papers of which are published, from 1950. The Institute also publishes the scientific journal *Arctic*. See the following, in addition:
Alaska Sportsman, Dec., '49 (Yakutat study); June, '50; May, '53; *Alaska Weekly*, Feb., '50 (on founding); May, '50 (on funding by US); June, '50 (on field studies); Hulley; US Dept. of Interior (*Mid-Century Alaska*).

ARCTIC VILLAGE
Alaska Sportsman, June, '57 (on the Chandalar River); Couch (post office, 1909-1910); Kitchener (photo with natives); US Bureau of Census (pop. 24 in 1939).

ARGUELLO, CONCEPCION DE (San Francisco)
Andrews (daughter of Commandant at Yerba Buena, 1805); Atherton; Bancroft (Rezanov romance); Chevigny; Dall (Luis de Arguello mollified by romance); Langsdorff; *Life Magazine*, June, '59 (heirs in California); Russell (Rezanov translation).

ARMAGNAC, ALDEN P.
"Six Months Miracle: Canadian-Alaskan Military Highway," *Popular Science*, Feb., 1943.

ARMSTRONG, ALEXANDER
See T-304

ARMSTRONG, NEVILL ALEXANDER DRUMMOND
Yukon Yesterdays. London: J. Long, 1936. 287 pp. Personal memoir of Klondike rush.

ARMSTRONG, TERRENCE EDWARD
The Northern Sea Route. Cambridge: Scott Polar Research Institute, 1952. 162 pp.
The Russians in the Arctic, 1937-57. Fair Lawn: Essential Books, 1958. 182 pp.
Russian Settlement in the North. London: Cambridge University Press, 1965.
Soviet Northern Development. Fairbanks: University of Alaska Press, 1970.

ARNOLD, ROBERT, et alii.
Alaska Native Land Claims. Anchorage: Alaska Native Foundation, 1976. xii & 348 pp. *Teacher's Guide*, Lydia Hays. *Student's Workbook*, Lydia Hays. Collaborators: Janet Archibald, Margie Bauman, Nancy Yaw Davis, Robert A. Frederick, Paul Gaskin, John Havelock, Gary Holthaus, Chris McNeil, Thomas Richards, Jr., Howard Rock, Rosita Worl.
Secondary school history and explanation of the Alaska Native Claims Settlement Act of 1971, in three sections: History of natives and native claims in Alaska; background of the design and passage of the act; explanation of the entities established by the act and their implications for native life in Alaska. Although written as a secondary school textbook, this is the most useful and comprehensive history of natives in Alaska which is readily available and easily read. Its explanation of the workings of the claims act is clear and thorough.

ARONSON, JOSEPH DAVIS (b. 1889)
"The History of Disease Among the Natives of Alaska," *Alaska Health*, July, 1947. Aronson concludes from a study of Russian material that while food deficiencies were common before white contact, smallpox, tuberculosis and syphilis probably were not. Smallpox has apparently caused the greatest decimation (1947).

ARRON, WALTER JACK
"Aspects of the Epic in Eskimo Folklore," University of Alaska Anthropological Papers, 1957.

ART and ARTISTS
The following is only suggestive and is primarily historical. See the articles by McCollom and Frederick in the *Alaska Journal*. See the following:
Ahgupuk, George Aden (see Ahgupuk); *Alaska Life*, Nov., '39 (T.R. Lambert); *Alaska Sportsman*, Sept., '37 (WPA artists); Oct., '43 (Frank Towle); March, '55 (R. Takilnok); June, '55 (Heurlin); Sept., '55; Oct., '56; Alaska Native Arts and Crafts (a marketing agency); *Alaska Weekly*, July, '51 (Ziegler, Lambert, Crumrine, Heurlin); June, '51; Aug., '51; Nov., '51; see information at the various Alaska museums and universities; see also the Alaska

Music Festival (annual, Anchorage); Davis (Sidney Laurence [Anchorage], Jan Van Emple [Seward], Eustace Ziegler [Cordova], Rockwell Kent); Denison (Ahgupuk, Simon Oliver [Anchorage], Ziegler, Ted Lambert); Gruening (WPA); Hadman; Hellenthal (Laurence, Ziegler); Hulley (Laurence, Crumarine, Lambert, Machetanz, Ziegler, Heurlin, Ahgupuk, Dahlager, Kehoe, Gil Smith; Eudora Preston, Goodales); Jaques; Jeffery (Lucas); Kent (Machetanz); Poor (descr. of Alaska by wartime artist); Whymper (artist with Western Union); Ziegler (see Ziegler).

ASBESTOS
Alaska Sportsman, October, '49 (commercial shipments, '44).

ASHBROOK, FRANK GETZ and E. P. WALKER
Blue Fox Farming in Alaska. Wn.DC: GPO, 1925. 33 pp.

ASHTON, JAMES M.
Ice-Bound: A Trader's Adventure in the Siberian Arctic. New York: G.P. Putnam's Sons, 1928. 235 pp. Investigations voyage of the Phoenix Northern Trading Co. posts in 1922.

ASMOUS, VLADIMIR C. (b. 1891)
Numerous articles in the periodical *Russia* (English language) on Dezhnev, Bering, Wrangel, Khostov and Davydov, and on Kasilov, oldest Russian settlement in America (?), the Aleutians, Wrangel Island, etc. See also the Arctic Bibliography.

ASSEMBLIES OF GOD
Alaska Sportsman, Nov., '42, and Feb., '43 (appeal for missions in Anchorage, Fairbanks, Fort Yukon, Juneau, Ketchikan and Wrangell); Tewkesbury (in 1946 missions were located at Anchorage, Craig, Fairbanks, Fort Yukon, Juneau, Ketchikan, McGrath, Nome, Saxman, Seward and Wrangell).

ASTOR, JOHN JACOB (1763-1848)
Andrews (Baranov bought cargo of the *Enterprise*, opposed by Golovnin; Wilson Hunt at Sitka on the *Beaver*); Bancroft; Chevigny (Hunt at Pribilovs); Dall (Hunt founded Astoria in 1811; Alexander I approved Baranov's dealings with Astor); Hoy, Calvin (*John Jacob Astor*, Boston: Meador, 1936); Hulley; Irving (*Astoria*); Paxton; Porter, K.W. (2v. authoritative history); Ross; Speck; Tompkins.

ATAHUALPA (Boston trader)
Alaska Sportsman, June, '53 (1805 attack by Bella Bella Indians at Dryad Point); *Alaska-Yukon Magazine*, Jan., '11 (ship's journal); Chevigny (purchased by Baranov, renamed *Bering*); Dall (discovered mouth of the Stikine in 1802); Greenhow (attacked in Millbank Sound, 1805; heard of but did not discover the Stikine).

ATHAPASCANS (also Athabaskans)
See literature and bibliography on North American Indians. See also Indians; see the following: Allen (Ahtanatnas); Bancroft (*Native Races*); Colby (Tagish not Athabaskan); De Laguna (Ahtna); Denison (Denali); Dall; Farb; Hulley; Josephy; Mason; Petrof; Stuck; Sundborg; Washburn; Wickersham (Yako). See also Alaska Natives, Alaska Native Land Claims, etc.

ATHERN, ROBERT G.
"An Army Officer's Trip to Alaska in 1869," *Pacific Northwest Quarterly*, January, 1949.

ATHERTON, GERTRUDE FRANKLIN (1857-1948)
Rezanov. New York: Authors and Newspapers Association, 1906. 320 pp. Fictionalized account of the Rezanov-Arguello romance.
Rezanov and Dona Concha. New York: Stokes, 1937. 218 pp.

ATKA ISLAND
Alaska Sportsman, June, '40 (photo); Aug., '40 (Hodiakof suicide); Nov., '42 (Japanese); Oct., '43; Apr., '45 (prewar photo); Aug., '46 (animals reintroduced by ANS); Oct., '57 (reindeer); Baker (4,988', Coxe and Cook); Bancroft (Trapeznikov probably on 1749-53 voyage, Shevyrin winter of 1759-60, killed by natives; Rezanov punishment of trader Kulikalov for beating Atka woman and child); Berkh; Chevigny (fur station 1790); Colby; Couch (post office from 1940); Dall; Driscoll (evacuation to Killisnoo, WW II); Fedorova; Hrdlicka; Kitchener (AC Co.); Petrof (village of Nazan [pop. 230] moved from Korovinsky Bay where first church built in 1826); Sundborg; Wheaton.

ATKINS, BARTON
Modern Antiquities. Buffalo: Courier Co., 1898. 190 pp. Early sketches of Alaska.

ATKINSON, THOMAS H.
Alaska Petroleum Directory. Anchorage: Petroleum Publications, 1962 and others.

ATLIN (village, lake, British Columbia)
Alaska Sportsman, Apr., '43 (gold routes); Apr., '53; July, '57; *Alaska Weekly*, Aug., '50; Anzer; Baker; Cameron; Colby; Garland; Whiting.

ATWOOD, EVANGELINE
Alaska's Struggle for Self-government: 83 Years of Neglect. Anchorage: *Anchorage Times*, 1950. Reprint of *Times* editorials on statehood.
Anchorage: All-American City. Portland: Binfords and Mort, 1957. 118 pp.
We Shall Be Remembered. Anchorage: Alaska Methodist University Press, 1966. 191 pp. Matanuska colony

Who's Who in Alaskan Politics: A Biographical Dictionary of Alaskan Political Personalities, 1884-1974. Portland: Binford & Mort, 1977. With Robert DeArmond.

ATWOOD, FRED N.
Alaska-Yukon Gold Book. Seattle: Sourdough Stampede Association, 1930. 146 pp. Sub-title reads: A roster of the progressive men and women who were the argonauts of the Klondike gold stampede and those who are identified with the pioneer days and subsequent development of Alaska and the Yukon Territory.
"Dawson Night Life Wasn't So Tough," *Alaska Life*, December, 1941.

ATWOOD, GEORGE H.
Along the Alcan. New York: Pageant Press, 1960. 212 pp. Construction

ATWOOD, ROBERT BRUCE
"Alaska's Struggle for Statehood," *State Government*, 31 (1958): 202-208.
"Anchorage," *Alaska Life*, January, 1944
See also:
"Thanks to Winnetka," by Charles Barker in *Alaska Life*, May, 1942; ; Gruening; Pierce, N. (*Pacific States*); Tewkesbury. See also *Anchorage Times*, Alaska Statehood.

AUER, HARRY ANTON
Camp Fires in the Yukon. Cincinnati: Stewart & Kidd, 1916. 204 pp. Big-game hunting

AUGUR, HELEN
Passage to Glory: John Ledyard's America. Garden City: Doubleday, 1946. 310 pp. Ledyard is supposed the first white American to set foot on Alaskan soil. He accompanied Cook on the 1778 voyage.

AUGUSTINE (island, mountain, Kamishak Bay, Cook Inlet)
Alaska Sportsman, Apr., '38; July, '52; Baker (named by Cook, called Chernoburi or Chernabura [black-brown] by Russians); Dall; Sherwood (eruptions); US *Coast Pilot*; Vancouver (detailed descr.).

AUKE BAY (village, lake)
Alaska Sportsman, Feb., '36; Nov., '38; July, '41; Apr., '42; Apr., '58; *Alaska Weekly*, May, '51; June, '51 (Alaska Cellulose); Baker (north end Stephens Passage); Colby; Couch (post office since 1946); Denison (recreation site at old Indian village); Tewkesbury (cemetery); US *Coast Pilot*.

AUKE COVE, AUKE CREEK
Baker (northern shore, Admiralty Island, named by Meade for Auke Indians); Broaddus (shown as Admiralty Cove and Creek).

AUKE INDIANS
Alaska Sportsman, March, '55 (Keithahn); Chevigny (Baranov); Colby; Denison (at Sitka, wore gold ornaments); Hulley; Scidmore (two villages; pop. 1869 800, 1880 640, 1890 277; Vancouver's visit); Young (two villages, nearly all villagers moved to Juneau).

ATTU ISLAND
Alaska Life, Nov., '42 (wartime notes by Andrews); Aug., '43 (Attu attack, photos); Sept., '43; Oct., '43 (war photos); Nov., '43 (post-battle); Feb., '44; Jan., '45; Dec., '45; *Alaska Sportsman*, Oct., '43 (native photos); Feb., '44 (battle); Nov., '45 (Etta Jones); Jan., '46 (23 Aleuts returned from Japan, 17 died of TB while captive); Feb., '46 (air photo); March, '46 (prisoners); June, '46 (battle); July, '46 (342 Americans killed in battle, all Japanese save few); March, '47 (photo of village in '34); Sept., '47 (20 meteorologists left at Attu); May, '48 (prisoners' experience in Japan); July, '48; Dec., '48; Aug., '49; July, '51; Apr., '52 (11,000 American troops landed, 500 Japanese committed suicide); Nov., '64; Dec., '66; June, '72; Baker (westernmost large island, 3,034', may have been Bering's St. Abraham or St. Etienne, or Chirikov's St. Theodore); Bancroft; Berkh; Colby; Dall (discovered by Basov in 1745, Ingenstrom here in 1829); Denison;

Hulley (paleo-Aleuts); Garfield; Oliver (photo Hodikov); Petrof (Nevodohikov first to land in 1747); Scidmore; Sundborg (42 taken by Japanese); Tewkesbury; Tompkins (15 natives massacred by Belaev in 1745). See also Sherman (*Alaska Cavalcade*) (1942 battle photos).

AULT, J. P.
"Sailing the Seven Seas in the Interest of Science," *National Geographic Magazine*, December, 1922.

AUMACK, THOMAS M. (b. 1920)
Rivers of Rain. Portland: Binfords and Mort, 1948. 216 pp. See also Jewitt, Garst.

AURORA BOREALIS ("northern lights")
See Arctic Bibliography

AURORA BOREALIS
Mimeographed newspaper published at St. Michael, 1897-98.

AUSTIN, BASIL
See T-325

AUSTIN, H. T. and WILLIAM PERRY
See T-326

AUTHORS (Alaskan Books)
See Alaska Literary Directory; see also *Dictionary of North American Authors* (who died before 1950), Toronto: Ryerson Press, 1950, and *Who's Who Among North American Authors*, Los Angeles: Golden Syndicate. See also Northwest Books. See also Bibliography.

AUZIAS DE TURRENNE, RAYMOND (b. 1861)
See T-327 ff.

AVACHA BAY (Siberia)
Andrews (Bering founded Petropavlovsk in 1740); Bancroft; Dall; Tompkins; see also Bering.

AVERKIEVA, Iu. P.
See T-329 ff.

AVERY, MARY
"The Mart A. Howard Klondike Collection," *Pacific Northwest Quarterly*, April, 1959.

AVIATION IN ALASKA
Numerous popular material continues to be produced on Alaska aviation. See the *Alaska Sportsman* Index and the index in Tourville. See also the following:
Alaska Life, Nov., '42; Jan., '43; May, '43; March, '44 (AAC rescue); Oct., '44 (by R. Neuberger); Apr., '45; Alaska, Territory, Department of Aviation (also State); Amundsen; Baidukov; Balchen; Carlson, W.S.; Clark; Chase (St. Clair Street, 1920); Day (Reeve); Greiner; Helmricks; Herron; Lindbergh, A.; McDonald (Whaley); Harkey (Wien); Mills, J.; Mills, S.E.; Mitchell (1930); Potter; Rengstrom; Satterfield; Stark (Blount); Streett (1920 flight); Thomas, L.; US CAA (accident reports [superseded by FAA and CAB]; Wambheim (Eielson); Washburn; Wilkins; Willoughby. See also the names of individual fliers, particularly the following:

Crosson, Eielson, Gillam, Merrill, Mitchell, Sampson, Wien and Winchell.

AYER, ANN S.
"Life was Free and Easy up There," *Alaska Sportsman*, January to June, 1946 (Life in Nome)
"Moose Hunt," *Alaska Life*, September, 1945
"Steel Creek Farming," *Alaska Life*, August, 1945
"Uses of Oil Drums," *Alaska Life*, June, 1945

AYER, N. W. and Son
Directory of Newspapers and Periodicals. Philadelphia, 1943. 1341 pp. section on Alaska papers

B

BABCOCK, JOHN PEASE et. al.
Investigations of the International Fisheries Commission to December, 1930. Seattle, 1930. 29 pp. (International Fisheries Commission Report No. 7) also W.A. Found, Miller Freeman and Henry O'Malley.

BACK, Sir GEORGE (1796-1878)
Narrative of the Arctic Land Expedition, 1833-35. London: J. Murray, 1836. 663 pp. To the Great Fish River (now the Back River), north central Canada, previously known as the Thleweechodezeth. The expedition's objective was aid to members of the Second Ross Expedition.
Narrative of an Expedition in HMS Terror, 1836-37. London: J. Murray, 1838. 450 pp. Objective was more complete charting of the coast between Prince Regent's Inlet and Turnagain Point in Canada.

BACK, H. S.
See T-333.

BACON, Sir FRANCIS (1561-1626)
See the following entry in Greenhow: "The Northwest Coast was 'terra incognitissima;' there Bacon placed his 'Atlantis.'" (p. 97). Bacon is significant in the history of western thought for his reliance on inductive reasoning as a method of investigation, rather than *a priori* scholasticism. Among his writings was *The New Atlantis*, a scientific utopia, founded on an ancient myth, and partially realized in the creation of the Royal Society in 1660. First mention of Atlantis, supposedly a lost civilization, occurs in Plato's *Timaeus*. Many writers have tried to prove the state's existence (usually perceived as an island), and societies for the discovery of Atlantis are still active today.

BADE, WILLIAM FREDERIC (1871-1936)
The Life and Letters of John Muir. 2v. Boston: Houghton, Mifflin, 1924. See also T-3226 ff. See John Muir.

BADLAM, ALEXANDER
The Wonders of Alaska. San Francisco: Bancroft Co., 1890. 152 pp. Primarily glaciers, though additional data on southeast Indians, salmon, mining, phantom cities and education. Badlam was treasurer of the California-Russian Fur Co.

BAEDEKER, KARL
The Dominion of Canada. New York: Scribner's Sons, 1907. 254 pp. Includes Alaska
The United States, With Excursions to Mexico, Cuba Porto Rico and Alaska. New York: Scribner's Sons, 1909.

BAER, KARL ERNST VON (1792-1876)
Avtobiografiia (Autobiography), ed. E.N. Pavlovskogo. Leningrad, 1950. 544 pp.
Ueber das Klima von Sitcha (On the Climate of Sitka). St. Petersburg, 1889.
Untersuchungen uber von Stellerbeobachteten nordischen Seekuh (Rytina illiger) (Investigation of Steller's norther Sea Cow. St. Petersburg, 1840.
With Count von Helmersen. *Beitrage zur Kenntniss des Russischen Reiches, etc.* (Contribution to Knowledge of the Russian Empire). 44v. St. Petersburg, 1839-1900.
Peters des Grossen und Geographischen Kenntnisse. (Peter the Great and Geographical Knowledge). V. 16 of the above work.
There are also works on Krusenstern and Wrangel; see T-338 ff. See also Glazunov.

BAETS, MAURICE de
See de Baets, Maurice.

BAGLEY, CLARENCE BOOTH
Indian Myths of the Northwest Coast. Seattle: Lowman and Hanford, 1930. 145 pp.

BAGOT, Sir CHARLES
Bagot Papers, Mss. Russian Correspondence. Transcripts of letters between Sir Charles Bagot in St. Petersburg to Sir George Canning, British Foreign Secretary, 1822-1825. Ottawa: Canada Archives. See also John Quincy Aams. The correspondence concerns, among other things, the Russo-American treaty of 1824, and the Russo-British treaty of 1825, establishing the Canada-Alaska boundary.

BAGOT, JOSCELINE
George Canning and His Friends. 2 v. London and New York, 1909. See also Perkins, Bradford, and Perkins, Dexter. In the negotiations, first Bagot, and then Stratford Channing (a cousin of Sir George) represented Great Britain at St. Petersburg. Pierre Poletika and Count Nesselrode represented Russia, and Ambassador Henry Middleton the United States. Adams had represented the US in Russia before becoming Secretary of State. The Russians, accepting the concept of limitation of their Pacific claims, pushed for 51°N (approx. the northern end of Vancouver Island). The Americans and British had in 1818 signed a convention for joint occupation of the Pacific Northwest, and in 1819, by the Adams-Onis Treaty, Spanish claims were extinguished north of 42°N. The British wanted the Russians to stay north of 61°N, and west of 139°W (in the St. Elias range, south of Kluane Lake). The present BC-Yukon Terri-

tory border is 60°N. At one time the US had claimed north to 54°40' (Dixon Entrance, the current Alaska-Canada boundary). The British yielded to 57°50' (Cross Sound), and then, with American persuasion, to 54°40', provided the Russians would yield to 141°W (the current Alaska-Canada boundary). During these negotiatons the United States unilaterally announced a hemispheric policy (the Monroe Doctrine) prejudicial to any further colonial activity. See also Alaskan Boundary Tribunal. See also Bailey, Thomas.

BAIDAR, BAIDARA, BAIDARKA (Aleut fishing boat)
See Andrews; Chevigny (open skin boats, require 48 hours drying every 4 days); Colby; Higginson; Schwatka (Russians call the single-opening boat a bidarka [kyak], a large open skin boat, a baidara); Scidmore.

BAIDUKOV, GEORGII FILIPOVICH
See T-344 ff.

BAILEY, ALFRED MARSHALL (b. 1894)
Birds of Arctic Alaska. Denver: Colorado Museum of Natural History, 1948. 317 pp. The Museum sponsored the author and R.W. Hendee for a 15 month survey in 1921-22. The area surveyed included Cape Prince of Wales north and east to Demarcation Point.
The Birds of Cape Prince of Wales, Alaska. Denver: Colorado Museum of Natural History, 1943. 113 pp.
"Cruise of the *Bear*," *Natural History* (New York), September, 1943.
"Report on Birds of Northwestern Alaska," *Condor* (Berkeley), January and November, 1925.

BAILEY, BERNADINE (b. 1901)
Picture Book of Alaska. Chicago: A. Whitman, 1959.

BAILEY, KENFIELD
"On the Dotted Line: Some Episodes in Early Alaskan History," *National Historical Magazine*, August, 1938.

BAILEY, THOMAS A.
A Diplomatic History of the American People. New York: Appleton-Century-Crofts, 1950. 896 pp.
America Faces Russia: Russian-American Relations from Earliest Times to Our Day. Ithaca: Cornell University Press, 1950. 375 pp.
"The North Pacific Sealing Convention of 1911," *Pacific Historical Review*, 14 (1935).
"Russian-American Relations: Legend and Fact," *Pacific Spectator*, Winter, 1949.
"The Russian Fleet Myth Re-examined," *Mississippi Valley Historical Review*, June, 1951.
"Theodore Roosevelt and the Alaska Boundary Settlement," *Canadian Historical Review*, June, 1937.
"Why the United States Purchased Alaska," *Pacific Historical Review*, March, 1934.

BAILLIE-GROHMAN, WILLIAM ADOLPH
See T-352.

BAIN, J. ARTHUR
Life and Explorations of Fridtjof Nansen. London: Scott, 1897. 449 pp.

BAINES, THOMAS
See T-353.

BAIRD, ANDREW
See T-354.

BAITY, ELIZABETH CHESLEY
See T-356.

BAKER, A. J.
"Fray Benito de la Sierra's Account of the Hezeta Expedition to the Northwest Coast in 1775," *California Historical Quarterly*, September, 1930.

BAKER, GEORGE E.
The LIfe of William H. Seward. New York: J.S. Redfield, 1855. See also Seward.

BAKER, JOHN CLAPP
See T-359.

BAKER, MARCUS (1849-1903)
Geographic Dictionary of Alaska. Wn.DC: GPO, 1902. 446 pp. Second edition prepared by James McCormick, 1906. 690 pp. A long introduction to the second edition recounts the history of exploration in Alaska, with bibliographical notes. Baker's was a significant work in early mapping and charting of Alaska. Most of his work was with the Coast and Geodetic Survey, although in 1880 he accompanied Beardslee of the US Navy on an expedition over Chilkoot Pass to open it for miners. He worked with Dall on a revision of the *Coast Pilot*, published in 1879. His is the first significant geographical dictionary of Alaska, and still reliable. See William Dall, "Marcus Baker, 1849-1903," *Bulletin of the Philosophical Society of Washington*, 14 (1900-1904): 280. See also Sherwood. Mt. Marcus Baker in the Chugach Mountains between Prince William Sound and the upper Matanuska River is named for him. See also the Arctic Bibliography.

BAKER, WILLIAM L. (journalist)
Metlakatla, Alaska and the Annette Community. Mimeographed, Ketchikan, 1962. 60 pp. For the diamond anniversary of the village.

BALBI, A.
See T-360.

BALCH, EDWIN SWIFT (1856-1927) (editor)
Letters and Papers relating to the Alaska Frontier. Philadelphia: Allen, Lane and Scott, 1904. 134 pp. Material relating to the boundary dispute between the US and Canada supplied by the editor's brother, Thomas W. Balch.
Mount McKinley and Mountain Climbers' Proofs. Philadelphia: Campion, 1914. 142 pp. Favors Cook's claim. Balch also favored Cook's claim to the North Pole.
The North Pole and Bradley Land. Philadelphia: Campion and Co., 1913.

BALCH, THOMAS WILLING (1866-1927)
The Alaska Frontier. Philadelphia: Allen, Lane and Scott, 1903. 198 pp.
The Alasko-Canadian Frontier. Philadelphia: Allen, Lane and Scott, 1902.

Balch Mss. are in the Library of the Pennsylvania Historical Society. See *Alaska Sportsman*, July, '50, May, '53.

BALCHEN, BERNT (b. 1899)
Come North with Me. New York: Dutton, 1958. 318 pp. Relief pilot for Byrd on the Atlantic flight of 1927, and a member of the Byrd Antarctic Expedition. Autobiographical.

BALCOM, MARY GILMORE
Creek Street. Chicago: Adams Press, 1963. 115 pp.
Ghost Towns of Alaska. Chicago: Adams Press, 1965. 80 pp.
Ketchikan, Alaska's Totem Land. Chicago: Adams Press, 1961. A discussion of all totem poles in the area.

BALDWIN, "LUCKY"
Alaska Weekly, June, '50 (Nome, 1900-04); Fitz (phone line, Nome to Council); Hines.

BALL, GEORGE B. (d. 1955)
Alaska Sportsman, July, '42; July, '55; Jan., '57; Nov., '57; guest ranch operator on the Stikine River.

BALL, MOTTRONE DULANY (1835-1887)
Alaska LIfe, Jan., '46 (manager, *Sitka Alaskan*); Delaney (Collector of Customs, Sitka, 1878-1881, US Atty., Sitka, 1885-1887); Nichols; Gruening (delegate to Washington from Harrisburg district convention, Juneau); Tompkins.

BALLAINE, JOHN EDMUND (b. 1868)
Strangling of the Alaska Railroad. Seattle: 1923. "Seward, Its Beginning and Growth," *Alaska-Yukon Magazine*, July, 1911.

BALLANTYNE, ROBERT MICHAEL (1825-1894)
Hudson's Bay, or Everyday Life in the Wilds. Edinburgh: Blackwood, 1848. 328 pp. Ballantyne was a company clerk from 1841 to 1847. See also S-480.

BALLINGER-PINCHOT CONTROVERSY
Alaska-Yukon Magazine, Sept., '09; Ballinger; Clark; Glavis; Gruening; Hellenthal; Hulley; Ickes; Mathews, John L. ("Pinchot-Ballinger Controversy," *Hampton's Magazine*, Nov., '09); Nichols; Smyth; Slotnik; Tompkins. Clarence Cunningham and other individuals filed on coal claims in southcentral Alaska after 1900, when the Morgan-Guggenheim combine was building the Kennecott copper industry. Gifford Pinchot, Chief Forester under Theodore Roosevelt, and his agent L.R. Glavis, believed the claims were fraudulent in the sense that a monopoly was being organized. Commissioner of Public Lands, Richard A. Ballinger of Seattle, supported the validity of the claims. Ballinger resigned his post, and became counsel for the Cunningham claimants. Later Taft appointed him Secretary of Interior. By so doing, Taft opened way for a charge of collusion. In the 1930's Secretary of Interior Harold Ickes made an official inquiry, pronouncing Ballinger innocent. At the time, Alaskans were in a difficult position, not wanting to support Pinchot who was an extreme conservationist, but not

wanting either to support monopolistic exploitation of Alaska's resources by non-Alaska business interests, and a cartel as well.

BALLINGER, RICHARD A. (Secretary of Interior)
"A Portrayal of Bureaucratic Government in Alaska," *Alaska-Yukon Magazine*, Nov., '11; see also statement of R.A. Ballinger before the Committee on HR 18198, March 3, 1908 (60th Cong., 1st sess.); see also *Outlook*, April, 1910 and May, 1910.

BALLOU, MATURIN MURRAY (1820-1895)
The New Eldorado: A Summer Journey to Alaska. Boston: Houghton, Mifflin, 1889. 355 pp.

BALTO (Nome sled-dog)
Ricker (serum race to Nome, 1925); Savage (statue in Central Park); *Alaska Sportsman*, December, 1956. See also Leonard Seppala.

BALUSHIN, AMOS
Bancroft (with Konovolov, founded St. Nicholas Redoubt at mouth of Kenai); Chevigny (Ft. Nicholas terrorized by Indians); Vancouver (who spelled it Ballusian). Balushin was an agent of the Lebedev-Lastochkin Company, competitors with Shelikhov-Golikov. See Sherwood (*Cook Inlet Collection*) for description of Kenai by Vancouver.

BANCROFT, FREDERIC
The Life of William Seward. New York: Harper and Brothers, 1900. 2v.

BANCROFT, HUBERT HOWE (1832-1918)
History of Alaska, 1730-1885. San Francisco: A.L. Bancroft and Co., 1886. 775 pp. Bancroft "wrote" 39 volumes on the history of the west by hiring researchers and writers and publishing their work under his name, often with only the most cursory editing. The first comprehensive history of Alaska, this volume of Bancroft's was written by Alfred Bates, Ivan Petrof and William Nemos (See William Morris in the *Oregon Historical Quarterly*, December, 1903). On Petrof see Richard Pierce. Although the work is not without merit, its shortcomings are significant in many areas, and it is at least as significant as a period piece of history. This generally acknowledged, the work continues to be widely circulated.
History of the Northwest Coast. San Francisco: A.L. Bancroft, 1884. 2v. This work deals with the early exploration of the coast, before the opening of the Oregon country.
History of British Columbia, 1792-1887. San Francisco: The History Company, 1887. 792 pp.
Native Races of the Pacific States of North America. New York: Appleton, 1874. 5v. Written by H.L. Oak, T.A. Harcourt, Albert Goldschmidt, W.M. Fisher and William Nemos. Volume I deals with "Wild Tribes," including the Tlingit and Haida.
Literary Industries. San Francisco: The History Company, 1890. 808 pp. Autobiographical. See also Hunt, Morris, Oak and Caughey. See also Sherwood.

BANDI, HANS-GEORG
Eskimo Prehistory. Trans. Ann E. Keep. College: University of Alaska Press, 1969. 226 pp.

BANK, THEODORE II (Ted) (b. 1923)
Birthplace of the Winds. New York: Crowell, 1956. 274 pp.
University of Michigan Expedition to the Aleutian Islands, 1948-49, Preliminary Report. Ann Arbor, 1950. 220 pp.
"Ecology of Prehistorical Aleutian Village Sites," *Ecology*, April, 1953.
"Wild Flowers Deck the Aleutians," *Nature*, May, 1953.
"Cultural Succession in the Aleutians," *American Antiquity*, July, 1953.
"Biological Succession in the Aleutians," *Pacific Science Quarterly*, October, 1953.

BANKS, DELLA MURRAY (1864-1950)
Six articles on Homer in the *Alaska Sportsman*, Jan., Feb., Oct., Nov., and Dec., '45, and Jan., '46. Pioneer resident of Homer who traveled the Klondike Trail in 1898.

BANKO, WINSTON E.
The Trumpeter Swan. Wn.DC: GPO, 1960. USF&WS. Copper River breeding ground.

BANKSON, RUSSELL ARDEN (b. 1889)
The Klondike Nugget. Caldwell, Idaho: Caxton Printers, 1935. 349 pp. Written from the only extant files of the gold rush newspaper, edited by Eugene C. Allen, who lent the author his files for this work.

BANNISTER, HENRY MARTYN (1884-1920)
"Journal," published in *The First Scientific Exploration of Russian America and the Purchase of Alaska*, by James Alton James. The journal was kept largely at St. Michael, Russian America, where the author was a weather observer and naturalist with the Western Union Telegraph Expedition. He was of considerable aid to Charles Sumner in compiling information on Alaska prior to the purchase. See Sherwood (*Explorations*).

BAPTIST MISSIONS
See the Wickersham Bibliography. The first Baptist missionary was appointed to Alaska in 1886. An orphanage was established at Wood Island (Kodiak) in 1938. In 1948 a vessel, the *Evangel*, was placed in service around Kodiak. See also Baker, John (history to 1912); Dye, Higginson (beginnings of Kodiak mission).

BARANOF CASTLE (Sitka)
Alaska Sportsman, Oct., '55 (agricultural bldg. to be razed); *Alaska-Yukon Magazine*, Oct., '07 (photo); Andrews (*Story of Sitka*); Ballou (ivy-covered, plain; "haunted room"); Belcher (1837 visit); Chevigny (built by Kushov for Baranov); Colby (3 or 4 bldgs. on site, house now owned by Dept. of Agriculture); Collis (not castle-like); Clark (new castle begun 1836); Davis; Dole (Lisiansky helped with the castle, which has burned, and been twice destroyed by earthquake); Elliott (illustration of 1809-1827 building, unlike the usual representation); Hayes (present building from 1894); Higginson; Hulley; Lisiansky; Lutke; Pierce, R. ("Russian Governors"); Rezanov; Scidmore (Baranov initially occupied a leaky, two room cabin at the foot of Katleen's Rock, later built a blockhouse on the height; Kupreanov built a mansion, destroyed by the great

earthquake of 1847, rebuilt on the same plan); Sessions (built high on Katleen's Rock, of logs covered with boards, and riveted to the rock); Swineford (Baranov found here an Indian house surrounded by a stockade); Whymper (photo).

BARANOV, ALEKSANDR ANDREEVICH (1746-1819)
Ode, or Song, Chanted by Baranov at the Establishment of Fort New Archangel on Sitka Bay, August, 1799. Recovered by Zagoskin, printed in the Russian periodical, *Moski-vitjanin*, March, 1849. Trans. Henry Elliott and Richard Geoghegan. Fairbanks, 1925.

See the following:
Adamov; Andrews; Cheney; Chevigny; Irving; Khlebnikov; Jones, Rbt. (*Alaska-Yukon Magazine,* Oct., '07); McNeilly; Manning; Ricks; Simpson; White, S.

All accounts of Russian America deal with the central role of Baranov. Khlebnikov's is apparently the first biography (1835), and significant documents appear in Tikhmenev and in Andreyev; see also Barsukov, and Fedorova.

BARANOV, MAKARY ANDREW (b. ca. 1883) (Orthodox cleric)
Alaska Life, May, '43 (on St. Paul and southeast Alaska); *Alaska Sportsman*, March, '55 (Pribilofs and Unalaska from 1936).

BARANSKII, N. N.
See T-388.

BARBEAU, CHARLES MARIUS (b. 1883)
Alaska Beckons. Caldwell: Caxton Printers, 1947. 343 pp. Dene, Tsimshian and Tlingit legend and mythology.
Haida Myths Illustrated in Argillite. Ottawa: Queen's Printer, 1953. 417 pp. Argillite is a blue or dark slate which can be worked like hardwood. In the 1820's prospectors found a deposit of the material in the Queen Charlotte Islands which proved to be the primary source of the material.
Medicine Men on the North Pacific Coast. Ottawa: Queen's Printer, 1958. 95 pp. Shamanism and Haida carvers.
Pathfinders in the North Pacific. Ottawa: Queen's Printer and Toronto, Ryerson Press, 1958. 235 pp. Historical: Russian period, fur trade, Klondike.
The Indian Speaks. Caldwell: Caxton Printers, 1943. 117 pp.
Totem Poles. Ottawa: Queen's Printer, 1964. 2v. Full history of totemism among southeast Alaska native groups and others.
Tsimsyan Myths, Illustrated. Ottawa: Queen's Printers, 1961. 97 pp.
The Tsimshean: Their Arts and Music. New York: J.J. Augustine, 1952. 290 pp.
Totem Poles of the Gitksan, Upper Skeena River, B.C. Ottawa: Queen's Printers, 1929. 275 pp.
"The Modern Growth of the Totem Pole on the Northwest Coast," Smithsonian Institution, *Annual Report*, 1939.
"Totem Poles, A Recent Native Art of the Northwest Coast," Smithsonian Institution, *Annual Report*, 1931.
"Old Fort Simpson in 1859-66," *Beaver*, September, 1940.

"Siren of the Seas: History of the Fur Business on the Pacific Coast and the Trade with China and Russia," *Beaver*, December, 1944.
"How Asia Used to Drip at the Spout into America," *Washington Historical Quarterly*, July, 1933.
"The Gold Rush of 1898," *Canadian Geographical Journal*, July, 1934.
"North Pacific Coast: Its Human Mosaic," *Canadian Geographical Journal*, March, 1940.

BARBER, OLIVE
Lady and the Lumberjack. New York: Crowell, 1952. 250 pp.
Meet Me in Juneau. Portland: Binfords and Mort, 1960. 175 pp.

BARKDULL, CALVIN H.
"I Saw Soapy Killed," *Alaska Sportsman*, June, '52. See also *Alaska Sportsman*, Dec., '51 (freighting over White Pass, daughter first white child born in Skagway); Aug., '52.

BARNARD, EDWARD CHESTER (topographer)
See Marcus Baker, *Geographic Dictionary*, p. 18 (maps and charts).

BARNARD, JOHN
See T-1826.

BARNARD, J. J. (British naval officer)
Allen (medicine man "Red Shirt" involved); Bancroft (massacre at Nulato, 1851); Brooks (account of death); Cameron; Dall (Barnard shot in bed); Henderson (heir imposter); Ogilvie (Barnard was investigating Franklin); Petrof (full account of massacre); Schwatka; Stuck; Whymper; Wickersham.

BARNES, CLIFFORD A.
See T-401.

BARNES, FARREL F.
See *Landscapes of Alaska*, ed. Howel Williams, Berkeley: University of California Press, 1958.

BARNES, KATHLEEN and HOMER E. GREGORY
'Alaska Salmon in World Politics," *Far Eastern Survey*, March, 1938.
North Pacific Fisheries. New York: American Council, Institute of Pacific Fisheries, 1939. 322 pp.

BARNETT, H. G.
"The Southern Extent of Totem Pole Carving," *Pacific Northwest Quarterly*, October, 1942.

BARNETTE, ELBRIDGE T. (founder of Fairbanks)
Alaska Sportsman, Aug., '39 (town named after Fairbanks to please his friend Wickersham); Chase (established trading post, winter of 1901-02); Couch (post office from 1903); Davis (Barnette's boy, Wada, started the stampede); Hulley (first mayor); Kitchener (NC Co. from 1903); Rickard; Stuck; Tompkins; Wickersham.

BARNUM, FRANCIS S. J.
Grammatical Fundamental of the Innuit Language. Boston: Ginn, 1901. 384 pp. A non-scientific compilation of linguistic roots.

Life on the Alaska Mission. Woodstock, Md.: College Press, 1893. 39 pp.

"Catholic Missions in Alaska," *Historical Studies*, May, 1900.

See also *Alaska-Yukon Magazine*, Jan., '08 (descr. Yukon delta); and Nov., '09 (northern Eskimo language); Said to be a nephew of P.T. Barnum, Francis Barnum was a well respected Catholic missionary.

BARONOVICH, CHARLES VINCENT (d. ca. 1880)
Alaska Life, Feb., '41 (first mining claim under American rule in Alaska, quartz, near Sitka, 1867); Andrews (Austrian smuggler); Morris (badly crippled in 1876, formerly owned fishery, copper mine and steamer [*Pioneer*]); Scidmore (Russian trader and pelagic sealer, married Chief Skowi's daughter).

BARRACK, JAMES EDWARDS (b. 1883)
See Down's Encyclopedia. Barrack was manager of both the Alaska Machinery Company and Sampson Hardware Store in Fairbanks.

BARRELL, GEORGE
See T-405.

BARRETT, "Chief George"
See *Sunset*, June, 1916. Barrett was an Indian scout and northern coal prospector.

BARRETT-HAMILTON, GERALD
See T-406.

BARRINGTON, DAINES (1727-1800)
Miscellanies. London: J. Nichols, 1781. Has Journal of the 1775 voyage of F.A. Maurelle, translated. The Journal was pirated from Spain and published at a time when no information concerning Spanish exploration on the Northwest coast was available.

BARRINGTON, SIDNEY C.
Alaska Life, Feb., '42 (boatman, on the Yukon to 1916, then the Stikine); Apr., '48; *Alaska Sportsman*; *Alaska Weekly*, May, '51 (piloted *Judith Ann*) on first trip up Telegraph Creek); Kitchener (Northern Navigation Co., from Dawson to Whitehorse, 1913); Willoughby.

BARROW (village)
Alaska Sportsman, Oct., '40 (whaling); May to Sept., '44; Nov., '44; Apr., '47; Apr., '48; March, '53 (Naval Petroleum Reserve); July, '53; July, '54 (Will Rogers monument); Oct., '55; Aldrich; Baker (Point Barrow named by Beechey in 1826 for Sir John Barrow; the post office at Utkiavik is called Barrow); Brower; Caswell (Ray Expedition); Colby; Denison; Hutchison; International Polar Expedition; Leffingwell; Mikkelsen; Murcoch; Okakok; Ray; Poor; *Sat. Eve. Post*, June, '52 (white women at Barrow); Scidmore (NY yachtsman chartered Japanese steamer in 1891, 3 months for $25,000); Stuck; Van Valin; Wead (the *Bear*); Wickersham. The local Eskimo name for Barrow is Utkiavik. There is also a small settlement known as (Browerville), or Cape Smyth Settlement. Seven miles north is a sand spit on which is located the small village of Nuwuk (the Point). See references relating to Alaska aviation, Arctic exploration,

northern whaling, and petroleum development. See also information dealing with native claims, the North Slope Borough, and Eban Hobson.

BARROW, HENRY D. (b. ca. 1890)
Paradise North: An Alaskan Year. New York: Dial Press, 1956. 242 pp. Marine study near Wrangell.

BARROW, Sir JOHN (1764-1848)
Voyages of Discovery and Research within the Arctic Region. New York: Harper and Brothers, 1846. 359 pp. From 1818 to 1846.

A Chronological History of Voyages into the Arctic Regions. London: J. Murray, 1818. 379 pp.

See also T-409 ff. Barrow was for 40 years England's Secretary of the Admiralty, and for his encouragement, financing and support, has been called the father of Arctic exploration.

BARROW POINT (northernmost inhabited point in North American continent)
Aldrich (descr., 7 miles above Cape Smyth, low, sandy); Swineford.

BARSUKOV, IVAN PLATOVICH
A series of works on Veniaminov (Innocent), written in the 1880's, in Russian. See T-414 ff.

BARTER ISLAND (village)
Alaska Sportsman, Jan., '55; May, '56; Aug., '56; Aldrich; Colby; Couch (post office, called Kaktovik, from 1955); *Sat. Eve. Post*, June, '52; Stuck.

BARTLETT, EDWARD LEWIS (b. 1904) ("Bob" Bartlett, Alaska delegate)
Alaska Life, Apr., '45 (by R. Neuberger); Jeffrey; Potter; Tewkesbury; see also Denison and Gruening. "Bob" Bartlett was born in Seattle, Washington and attended Fairbanks High School, the University of Washington (1922-24) and the University of Alaska (1924-25). He was a reporter for the Fairbanks *News-Miner*, 1925-33. In 1933 and 1934 he was secretary to Alaska delegate Anthony J. Dimond. After mining gold for a few years in Alaska he became chairman of the Alaska Unemployment Compensation Commission, and in 1939 was appointed secretary of Alaska by Franklin Roosevelt, in which position he served until resignation in early 1944. He was a member of the Alaska War Council, 1942-44, and was himself elected delegate to Congress in 1945, serving until statehood, 1959. He drew the two year term for US Senate from Alaska in 1959, having been handily elected. Re-elected in 1960 and 1966, he served as US Senator until his death in 1968. "Bob" Bartlett was active in the Alaska statehood movement, and in the preliminary work on Alaska native claims. Popular articles about him are numerous. See material on Alaska statehood, Alaska constitution, and mss. sources on the Territory of Alaska. An annual lecture series at the University of Alaska is named in Bartlett's honor. See also T-421 ff.

BARTLETT, ROBERT ABRAM (1875-1946)
Sails over Ice. New York: Scribner's Sons, 1934. 301 pp.

The Last Voyage of the Karluk. Boston: Small, Maynard, 1916. 329 pp. Bartlett was the master of the *Karluk*, flagship of Vilhjalmur Stefansson's

Canadian Arctic Expedition of 1913-16. The *Karluk* drifted with ice across the Bequfort and Chukchi Seas, and in January, 1914, was crushed in the ice. The crew dog-sledged to Wrangell Island, and then the Siberian coast, but only nine of 20 men survived. Stefansson had left the ship at Point Barrow.

The Log of Bob Bartlett. New York: G.P. Putman's Sons, 1928. 352 pp. Autobiographical. Bartlett came from a family which had lived a century and a half. This work includes accounts of the *Karluk*, a voyage with Peary, and the *Morrissey*. See also Fitzhugh; Putnam; Streeter; Mirsky; Wead.

BARTZ, FRITZ
Alaska. Stuttgart: K.F. Koehler, Verlag, 1950. 384 pp. See also T-424. Scientific observation.

BASKETRY
There are numerous sources on basketry; the following is selective. See the Arctic Bibliography and the following:
Alaska Life, Feb., '41; *Alaska Sportsman*, July, '43 (baleen); *Alaska-Yukon Magazine*, Sept., '07; Apr., '08; Burkher, Howard ("Behind Baleen Baskets," BIA Mss. in Historical Library, Juneau); Cameron; Cavana, Violet (*Alaska Basketry*, Oregon Beaver Club, 1917 [49 pp.]); Colby; Corser; Emmons (The Basketry of the Thlingit," in *Memoirs* [publication of the American Museum of Natural History], 1903); Hayes; Higginson; James, George W. (*Indian Basketry*, Pasadena, 1912); McDowell; Mason, Otis T. ("Indian Basketry," *Report*, US National Museum, 1902); Meany, Edmund S. ("Attu and Yakutat Basketry," *Pacific Monthly*, October, 1903); Montgomery, Ethel ("Weaving," *Daily Empire*, January, 1923); O'Connor; Paul, Frances; *Provincial Museum* [Victoria] (Attu Baskets); Wardle, H.N. ("Certain Rare West Coast Baskets," *American Anthropology*, April, 1912); Wharton, James George (*How to Make Indian and Other Baskets*, New York: Malkan, 1903); Willoughby.

BASKINE, GERTRUDE
Hitch-hiking the Alaska Highway. Toronto: Macmillan, 1944. 317 pp.

BATCHELOR, GEORGE
See T-426.

BATES, EMILY KATHARINE
Kaleidoscope: Shifting Scenes from East to West. London: Ward and Downey, 1889. 275 pp.

BATES RAPIDS (Tanana River)
Allen (no difficulty in passing); Baker (named by Allen for an Englishman who descended the Tanana with Harper); Rickard (stopped Barnette in the *Lavelle Young*); Stuck (descr.); Schwatka.

BATES, ROBERT H.
"Mt. McKinley in War-time," *Harvard Mountaineering*, Cambridge, April, 1943 (the US Army Test Expedition of 1942-43). See as well "Mt. McKinley, 1942," *American Alpine Journal* by the deputy commander of the project.

BATES, RUSSELL S.
The Man on the Dump. Seattle: O. Patten, 1909. 67 pp. Poetry. Alaska-Yukon-Pacific Exposition souvenir edition.

BATH, MARKUS
See T-429.

BATTELLE REPORT
See US Congress, House, Committee on Interior and Insular Affairs, House Document No. 176, 87th Congress, 1st session (Wn.DC: GPO, 1961).

BATTEN, E. STANLEY
See T-430.

BAUER, H.
See T-431.

BAUMGARTNER, R. E.
"Organization and Administration of Justice in Alaska," *American Bar Association Journal*, January, 1934.

BAXTER, DON VAWTER and F. H. WADSWORTH
See T-432, and others.

BAYLY, GEORGE
Sea-life Sixty Years Ago. New York: Harper, 1886. 191 pp. Sub-title: A Record of the Adventures Which Led up to the Discovery of the Long-Missing Expedition Commanded by the Comte de La Perouse.

BAYOU, KATHERINE (b. 1924)
Alaska Sportsman, a series beginning March, 1943 and ending May, 1947, based largely on the experiences of Chris Spillum, a Seldovia sourdough, and Katherine Bayou, a Seldovia Indian girl.

BEACH, REX ELLINGWOOD (1877-1949) (novelist)
Pardners. New York: McClure, Phillips, 1905. 278 pp.

The Spoilers. New York: Harper, 1906. 314 pp. Illus. by Clarence F. Underwood.

The most powerful of Beach's novels, the plot is based on incidents at Nome during the gold rush there. The "spoilers" plot to "jump" the rich claims of an early miner, using force when necessary. Should the matter reach court, a judge sympathetic to the plotters will appoint one of their number "receiver" of the claim until the litigation can be settled, during which interval the "spoilers" will rapidly work off the claim. The scheme fails.

In actuality the "receiver" was Alexander McKenzie, politician and attorney for the claim jumpers. He successfully sought appointments at Nome for his friends, Arthur H. Noyes (US District Judge), C.L. Vawter (US Marshal), and Joseph K. Wood (US District Attorney). Upon arrival in Nome on July 19, 1900 Noyes appointed McKenzie receiver for all jumped claims. Noyes later refused to recognize writs obtained by the legitimate claimants who sent attorneys to the US Court of Appeals at San Francisco. The Court appointed James Wickersham to evaluate the opposing claims, however, and eventually all three of McKenzie's cronies were arrested and tried in San Francisco. Noyes paid a fine of one thousand dollars, and the others served jail sentences.

Many classic elements of the romantic western novel appear in Beach's novels: the brave, strong hero who is bashful toward women, easily identified evil overcome by the virtue of law and the hero, the undoing of villains by their own corruptibility and by acts of fate, and the starry-eyed young woman overwhelmed by the hero's combination of strength, determination and goodness.

In life Beach himself identified somewhat with this heroic model. He was a large, strong man, an "outdoorsman," who mined some in Alaska, and traveled to many of the gold camps as journalist and adventurer.

The Spoilers, a play in four acts, which Beach wrote with James McArthur, is in the Library of Congress (n.p., n.d.). Several film versions of the story have been produced.

The Looting of Alaska. ("The True Story of a Robbery by Law.") *Appleton's Booklover's Magazine*, serially, January to May, 1906.

The Barrier: A Novel. New York: Harper, 1908. 309 pp. The setting for this novel is Rampart, on the Yukon, in the story, "Flambeau." The plot, romantic and western, involves an army officer (Lt. Barrell), several villains, one of whose daughter is pursued by a collection of men, including the officer. Several one-to-one physical battles resolve the plot, which includes gold discoveries and river boats.

Beach lived at Rampart the winters of 1898-99 and 1899-1900. See *Alaska-Yukon Magazine*, June, 1907, and *Canadian Magazine* (Toronto), October, 1899, for material concerning the identity of some of the characters in this novel.

The Silver Horde: A Novel. New York: Harper, 1909. 389 pp. This novel is set in the Bristol Bay salmon canning area, and Seattle and Chicago. Less successful than other Beach novels, the plot involves competing financial interests and a four-cornered romance. It is carried by successive contrived situations which overstrain credulity. Again, the characters and nuances of the plot are typical of the romantic novel with a western setting.

The Iron Trail: An Alaskan Romance. New York: Harper, 1913. 390 pp. This most famous of Beach's novels is set in Prince William Sound, and is taken from the competition to construct a railroad from the coast to the copper deposit country on the Chitina River. The setting and cast of characters correspond in many respects to the reality of the time, 1905-08: Valdez (Cortez), Katalla (Kyak), Orca (Omar), Ellamar (Hope), Guggenheim Brothers (Heidlemans), Michael J. Heney (O'Neil), J.P. Morgan (Herman Heidleman), Dr. Whiting (Dr. Gray), Stikine Bill Robinson (Tom Slater, Superintendent of Transportation), Alaska Reynolds Company (Cortez Home Railway), Keystone Canyon (Beaver Canyon), Copper River (Salmon River), etc. With several romantic angles, and Beach's familiar idealization of good and evil, the story concludes with the construction of the "million dollar bridge" over the Copper River between Miles and Childs Glaciers, the bridge which Heney built for the Guggenheim's Copper River and Northwestern Railway. See Lone Jansen.

Winds of Change. New York: Harper, 1918. 521 pp. The setting for this novel is the Klondike gold rush of 1898, with Dawson, the trail from Dyea, and the Yukon River.

Alaskan Adventures: Omnibus. New York: Harper, 1937. Collection includes *The Spoilers*, *The Barrier*, and *The Silver Horde*.

Valley of Thunder. New York: Farrar and Rinehart, 1939. 326 pp. This novel set in Juneau and involving fish canneries, is the first in which Beach introduces serious political nuances. Communism ultimately loses out to free capitalist enterprise, and the novel is marred by incredulous feats of battle by the hero.

The World in His Arms. New York: Putnam's, 1945. This last Beach novel is set in Russian America, before the Alaska purchase.

Rex Beach also penned numerous articles and short stories for several popular magazines. For examples, see the representative analysis of Alaska in the Great Depression era, "Gold in Them Hills: Prospecting in Alaska as a Government-financed Project for American Youth," *Reader's Digest*, Dec., 1936. "Gold is Where You Find It: Tale of Alaska in the Days of the Gold Rush," *Reader's Digest*, May, 1941. "Alaska's Flying Frontiersmen," *American Magazine*, April, 1936. On Rex Beach see the following:

Alaska Sportsman, May, '55 (prospected Minook Creek); Nov., '57 (modeled hero of *Valley of Thunder* on Bob Reeve); *Alaska-Yukon Magazine*, Apr., '09; Franck (1898 Rampart cabin, *Iron Trail*); Gruening (on the *Spoilers*); Harrison (photo); Hines (played mandolin at Golovin); Davis (Al Mayo a *Barrier* character? photo of Rampart cabin); Whiting (spent two months with Heney getting material for *Iron Trail*). See also "How Rex Beach Got His Start in Alaska," *Alaska-Yukon Magazine*, September, 1906.

BEACH, W. W.
The Indian Miscellany. Albany: J. Munsell, 1877. 490 pp. Contains *Alaskan Mummies* by Dall.

BEACH, WILLIAM NICHOLAS
In the Shadow of Mount McKinley. New York: Derrydale Press, 1931. 289 pp. Four trips in the Alaska Range.

BEAGLEHOLE, JOHN CAWTE
Captain James Cook. Stanford: Stanford Univ. Press, 1974.

The Exploration of the Pacific. London: A.C. Black, 1934.

The Journals of Captain James Cook. 3v. Cambridge: Cambridge University Press, 1955-56.

BEAN, EDMUND
Brooks (led party to Chilkoot Pass and returned, 1880); Colby; Ogilvie (first gold party over Chilkoot, first non-native ascent of Chilkoot in 1875).

BEAN, JAMES M.
Andrews (Mrs. Bean killed in Tanana Valley, first reported by Capt. Bailey, 1880); Brooks (wife killed at Harper's Bend, 1878); Bur. of Educ., 1896 *Report;* Allen (murder scene 48 miles above Tanana mouth, 20 below Toklat River); Schwatka (descr.); Wickersham (saw trader at St. Michael from 1869, went to Harper's Bend 1878).

BEAN, MARGARET
"The Old Alaskan Outpost of the Czar," *Travel*, May, 1928.

BEAN, TARLETON H.
See Wickersham Bibliography and Arctic Bibliography.

BEAR (US Revenue Cutter, Alaska patrol)
Alaska Life, Nov., '44; March, '48 (sold as surplus, for sealing); *Alaska Sportsman*, Nov., '41; Dec., '41 (photo); Aug., '53; Aldrich (service to whalers, rescue of James Vincent); Cochran, C.S. ("The *Bear*: Most Famous of All Ships in the Arctic Service," *Proceedings*, US Naval Institute, May, 1929); Gray, W.C.; Henderson; Hrdlicka (on *Bear* Nome to Barrow, 1926); *National Geographic* (by Sheldon Jackson, Jan., 1896); Shiels (cruise of 1897-98); Wead (excellent); Wickersham (see the Bibliography); see also US Revenue Cutter Service, *Report*, Cruise of 1897-98 and others. The *Bear* was built in Scotland for sealing in Newfoundland; there were sister ships *Wolf*, *Lion*, *Leopard*, and *Tiger*. She was bought by the US in 1883 for use in the rescue of Greely, and was assigned to the US Revenue Marine for Alaska duty in 1885. She made 34 sailings for Barrow, arriving 28 times, the last voyage in 1926. Her service was primarily customs inspection and collection, but she served in rescue and communication, and carried many government officials and guests. After six years in Oakland (three as a marine museum), she sailed to Boston and the Antarctic in 1932-33, and returned under Byrd in 1935, and in 1939. In 1941-44 she was used in war patrol off Greenland, and in 1948 was sold as surplus ironically, for sealing in Newfoundland.

BEARDSLEE, LESTER ANTHONY (1836-1903) (US Naval officer)
See reports while Jamestown commander, US Navy Department; see also the following:
Andrews; Baker; Dole; Bancroft; Gruening; Hinckley; Nichols; Scidmore; Underwood; Wickersham. Beardslee was the effective authority of the United States in Alaska from 1879 to 1884. Alaska was not created a territory of the US in 1867, but only a military and a customs distict. The US Army was the effective authority until its removal in 1877 to fight the Nez Perce Indians in Idaho. A unique incident occurred in 1879 when an appeal was sent from Sitka to "any of His Majesty's ships at Nootka Sound" to maintain order, should hostilities between the natives and non-natives occur. *HMS Osprey* under Capt. A'Court responded, and remained on station until the arrival of the *Jamestown* under Beardslee.

BEATTIE, KIM
Brother, Here's a Man. New York: Macmillan, 1940. 309 pp. Klondike novel.

BEATTIE, WILLIAM GILBERT (b. ca. 1880)
Marsden of Alaska. New York: Vantage Press, 1955. 246 pp. Biography of Edward Marsden, Tsimshian Indian minister opposed by Duncan. Marsden was born in British Columbia in 1869, went to Metlakatla with Duncan, and died in Ketchikan in 1932. At the time of his death he was minister of the Presbyterian church at Metlakatla.

BEAUFORT SEA
Baker (named by Franklin in 1826 for his friend Capt. Francis Beaufort, R.N.); Stuck (Franklin named Beaufort Bay and Beechey named Cape Beaufort, both for the Admiralty hydrographer, Francis Beaufort. The Bay has been enlarged in con-

cept to Beaufort Sea); *Encyclopedia of Canada* (that part of the Arctic Ocean which lies between Alaska and the Canadian Archipelago).

BEAVER
Periodical, published quarterly by Hudson's Bay Company from 1920. Popular.

BEAVER (Yukon village)
Alaska Sportsman, June and Sept., 57 (photo, new homes); Colby (52 miles below Fort Yukon, northeast bank); Gagnon (est. by Frank Yasuda and a group of Eskimos about 1909; Yasuda who died in 1958 had with him some Japanese men who mated with Eskimo women from Anaktuvuk Pass; name taken from Beaver Creek [name Beaver Creek published by the Coast Survey in 1897]); Stuck (Alaska Road Comm. had trail out from the Chandalar mining district, striking the Yukon where Beaver was founded); Waller, Roger (USGS *Report*, 1957); Williams, John R. ("Observations of Freeze-up and Break-up at Beaver," *Journal of Glaciology*, April, 1955).

BEAVER, C. MASTEN
Fort Yukon Trader. New York: Exposition Press, 1955. 185 pp. By a Port Angeles man who went to Fort Yukon for three years, 1943-46 where he was a trader, and US Commissioner and agent for Wien Alaska Airlines. Despite trivial content the work gives a vivid account of life in Fort Yukon. Beaver was a trader for Northern Commercial Company.

BEAVERS
Alaska Sportsman, Nov., '38 (abundant in Cook Inlet); May, '39 (by Steve McCutcheon); June, '41; Jan., '42 (Stikine); June, '42 (Susitna); Oct., '42; May, '43; Sept., '43; Sept., '44; Feb., '46; June, '57; and others; Dufresne; Williams, Jay; see also Gene Coghlan, a series in the *Alaska Sportsman*, July to December, 1952.

BECHERVAISE, JOHN [?]
See F.W. Beechey.

BECK, GEORGE
See T-461.

BECK, LARRY
See T-4048, 4057; see Robert Service.

BECKER, ETHEL ANDERSON (b. ca. 1890)
Klondike '98: Hegg's Album. Portland: Binfords and Mort, 1949. 127 pp.
Treasury of Alaskana. Seattle: Superior, 1969. 183 pp.

BECKER, GEORGE FERDINAND (1847-1919)
Reconnaissance of the Gold Fields. USGS Annual Report, 1896-97.

BECKWITH, EDWARD P.
"The Mt. McKinley Cosmic Bay Expedition, 1932," *American Alpine Journal*, II (1933): 45-68. A complete account of the Carpé-Koven tragedy.

BEE, JAMES W., and EUGENE RAYMOND HALL (b. 1902)
Mammals of Northern Alaska. Lawrence, Kansas:

University of Kansas Museum of Natural History, 1956. 309 pp. Shrews to whales, with 57 pp. on lemmings.

BEEBE, BURDETTA FAYE
See T-465.

BEEBE, IOLA
The Life Story of Swiftwater Bill Gates. 1st ed., n.p., 1908; 2nd ed. Seattle; Lumberman's Printing Co., 1915. 139 pp. In the Klondike Gates rose from dishwasher to millionaire. This story, by his mother-in-law, recounts an irresponsible career of adventure and women.

BEECHEY, FREDERICK WILLIAM (1796-1856)
(British naval officer)
Narrative of the Voyage to the Pacific and Bering's Strait. London: Henry Colborn and Richard Bently, 1831. 2v. (for other editions see T-467). Subtitle: in support and to co-operate with the polar expeditions performed by His Majesty's ship *Blossom* under the command of Captain F.W. Beechey in the years 1825, 26, 27, 28. In 1826 Sir John Franklin traversed the Arctic coast westward from the Mackenzie River, reaching as far as Return Reef in Alaska. Beechey was to meet Franklin coming along the coast from the west in the *Blossom*. Beechey did not reach Point Barrow, but one of his small boats did, commanded by his mate Elson. The gap between Point Barrow and Return Reef was not traversed (of record) until 1837, by Thomas Simpson, coming from the Mackenzie River.
The Zoology of Captain Beechey's Voyage. London: 1839. 180 pp. 44 colored plates.
See also the following:
Analysis of a Narrative and Travels of Captain Beechey. London: Royal Geographic Society, 1832, by Wm. Ainsworth.
A Narrative of the Voyages and Travels of Captain Beechey. London: 1936 by Robert Huish; this volume also contains the "Travels of Captain Back."
A Voyage of Discovery Towards the North Pole. London: 1843. 351 pp. In the ships *Dorothea* and *Trent* under the command of Captain David Buchan. Beechey took part in this voyage under Capt. John Franklin (*Trent*), the object of which was the discovery of a passage (northwest) to the Pacific. See also Baker, and Huish; see as well T-2173 and 2219.

BEGG, ALEXANDER (1825-1905)
History of British Columbia. Toronto: Briggs, 1894. 568 pp.
A Sketch of the Successful Missionary Work of William Duncan. Victoria: 1901.
Report Relative to the Alaskan Boundary Question. Victoria: R. Wolfendon, 1896. 17 pp.
Review of the Alaskan Boundary Question. Victoria: T.R. Cussack, 1900. 32 pp.

BEHM CANAL
Alaska Sportsman, June, '51; Oct., '57; Baker (named by Vancouver in 1793 for Major Magnus Carl von Behm, commander in Kamchatka in 1799); Bancroft (Behm appointed to Kamchatka in 1772, took charge in 1793; Ismailov reported to Behm on Cook's Alaska voyage); Cook (on Behm re: Clerke's visit to Kamchatka in 1779); Scidmore (descr.;

Commander Newell was among first to transit canal in a steamer); Vancouver (to commemorate the "weighty obligations conferred by Major Behm on the officers and crews of the *Resolution* and *Discovery*").

BEHOVIC, GRACE MARIE
"Alaskan Lady," *Ebony*, December, 1948. Rock collecting on Baranof Island.

BEHRENDS, BERNARD M. (1862-1936)
Alaska Monthly, Oct., '07 ("A great mercantile institution"); *Alaska-Yukon Magazine*, Sept., '07 (came to Alaska 1887); DeArmond (concise biography); Downs.

BEKLEMISHEV, K. V. and E. A. LUBNY-GERTSYK
See T-473.

BEL, JEAN-MARC
See T-474.

BELCHER, Sir EDWARD
Narrative of a Voyage. London: H. Colburn, 1843. 2v. In the *Sulphur*, 1836-42, including details of naval operations in China from Dec., 1840 to Nov., 1841. On this little discussed voyage Belcher visited Sitka in 1837, and visited other Alaska ports including Kodiak, Nuchek and others.
See the Arctic Bibliography for other reference to Belcher, including his expedition in the *Assistance* in search of John Franklin, 1852, 53, and 54. There were five ships in the expedition under Belcher's command. After spending two winters in the Canadian Arctic, Belcher refused to spend a third, and abandoned four sound ships to return to England in *North Star*. One of the abandoned ships floated out into Baffin Bay and was commandeered by American whalers. In England Belcher demanded a court-martial to clear his name. Although acquitted, Belcher's sword was returned him in silence. In the Arctic ind 1826-27 on *Blossom* under Bechey, Belcher had lost a barge, and with it the lives of two men and a boy, off Choris Peninsula.
See the following:
Brooks (descr. Nuchek); Dall (descr. Ross colony); Mirsky ("a mediocrity"); Scidmore (entertained by Kupreanov at Sitka); Wickersham; see also R.B. Hinds (*The Zoology of the Voyage of HMS Sulphur*).

BELDEN, A. L.
See T-477.

BELIAKOV, ALEKSANDR VASIL'EVICH
See T-478.

BELKOFSKI (south coast, Alaska Peninsula)
Alaska Life, July, '44; *Alaska Sportsman,* Feb., '38; Feb., '39; March, '39; Colby (name means "squirrel"); Couch (post office 1888-91, and 1921-51); Baker; Gruening (descr. from 11th census); Higginson (old center of sea-otter trade); Jackson (1880 pop. 11 whites, 257 Aleuts and Creoles, sell annually $100,000 sea otter pelts); Petrof (pop. 300, new church); Swineford (75 frame houses, finest church [save interior] in Alaska); see also Hotovitzki (d. ca. 1952).

BELL, BAILEY E.
Alaska Snowtrapped. New York: Vantage, 1960.
194 pp. Novel.

BELL, E. MOBERLY
See T-480.

BELL, F. H.
See T-4513 ff.

BELL, JOHN (1799-1868)
Brooks (built Fort McPherson on the Mackenzie in
1840); Colby (floated down Porcupine to the Yukon
in 1846); Stuck; it is presumably for John Bell that
the Bell River is named which flows into the
Porcupine.

BELL, MARGARET ELIZABETH (b. 1898)
A series of books for girls, published by William
Morrow and Co., New York (for a complete listing
see T-481). Born at Thorn Bay, Prince of Wales
Island, Margaret Bell was the daughter of salmon
cannery pioneers. She was educated in Seattle and
Tacoma, lived in Portland and San Francisco, and
did war work in Canada and the Aleutians.
See the following:
Alaska Life, Apr., '48; *Alaska Sportsman*, June,
'48 (*Tall White Sail* biography); *Alaska Weekly*,
March, '51; Brinsmade; Tewkesbury (Margaret Bell
Howard).

BELL, WILLIAM HEMPHILL (1834-1906)
The Quiddities of an Alaska Trip. Portland: C.A.
Steel, 1873. 67 pp. Humor.

BELL ISLAND
Alaska Life, Jan., '48; *Alaska Sportsman*, July,
'37; Aug., '38; Aug., '54 (replacement of $60,000
fire damaged resort bldgs.); Baker (named by Vancouver, in Behm Canal north of Revillagigedo
Island); Couch (post office 1932-54); Vancouver
(after one of the gentlemen in *Chatham*).

BELLAH, JAMES WARNER
Alaska. Reprinted from *Holiday*, August, 1959.

BELLARD, WALTER
See T-491.

BELLESSORT, ANDRE
See T-492 (re: La Perouse).

BELLIN, JACQUES NICOLAS
See T-493 ff; see also Wagner. Bellin was a
French geographer whose opinions carried considerable weight with the early explorers (his works
were published in 1755 and 1766). In particular he
refused to accept the stories of de Fuca and de Fonte
on the northwest passage.

BELLINGHAUSEN,   FADDEI   FADEEVICH
(1799-1852)
*Dvukratnyia Izyskaniya v Iuzhnom Ledevitom
Okeanie in Plavanie Vokry Sveta v Prodolzhanii.* St.
Petersburg: I. Glazunov, 1831. 2v. Bellinghausen
commanded the *Vostok*, accompanied by M.P. Lazarev in *Mirnyi*, in this voyage across the Pacific in
1819-21, and subsequently around the world. See
Dall; Ivanshinstov.

BELOV, MIKHAIL I.
Semen   Dezhnev. Moskva: Izd-vo "Morskoi
transport," 1955. 155 pp.
"Istoricheskogo plavaniye Semena Dezhneva (The
Historic Voyage of Semen Dezhnev)," *Izvestiya Vse.
Geog. Obshchestva*, 81(1949); 459-472.
The Sale of Alaska. Los Angeles: Mankind Pub-
lishing Company, 1967.

BELYAVIN, VASILI IVANOVICH
See T-4538.

BELUGA (small white whale)
Alaska Sportsman, May, '40 (photo); Nov., '56
(gorging on salmon at Nushagak); May, '57; *Alaska-
Yukon Magazine*, May, '08 (photo); *National Geographic*, Oct., '49; Dufresne; Schwatka (easily
captured).

BENDELEBEN, OTTO von
Brooks (reported placers while constructing telegraph line near Port Clarence, Seward Peninsula);
Dall (at Port Clarence 1865); Dole (found gold on
Niukluk River); James (mentioned by Bannister,
read funeral service for Robert Kennicott); Underwood.

BENEDICT, NEAL DOW
The Valdez and Copper River Trail. Hastings,
Fla.: 1899. 178 pp. typescript. 158 photos by the
author. See also Western Union Overland Telegraph
Expedition.

BENHAM, DANIEL
See T-498.

BENIOWSKI, MORIZ AUGUST
See T-499.

BENNETT, LAKE (British Columbia)
Davis (connected to Lake Lindeman by a mile of
rapids and cascades, photo showing tents); Becker;
Garland (gold rush descr.); Schwatka (named for
James Gordon Bennett, American patron of geographical research [apparently named by Schwat-
ka]); Winslow (named for James Gordon Bennett,
owner of the *New York Herald*).

BEN-MY CREEK (on Taku Arm of Tagish Lake)
Alaska Sportsman, Feb., '43 (A.L. Swanson, Otto
Partridge); *Alaska Weekly* (A.W. McKinely); Franck
(descr., 80 miles from Carcross).

BENSIN, BASIL M. (b. 1881)
*History of the Greek Orthodox Catholic Church in
North America.* New York: 1941. No mention of the
Church in Alaska after 1867, not based on sources.
Russian Orthodox Church in Alaska, 1794-1967.
Toms River, N.J.: *Ocean County Sun*, 1966. 80 pp.
For the 1967 purchase centennial.

BENSON, BENNY (1913-1975)
Alaska Sportsman, March, '50 (13 yr. old schoolboy at Jesse Lee Home, Seward, won design competition for the Alaska flag, 1926); *Alaska Weekly*,
March, '51 (met sister, Mrs. John Allen, at Anchorage after 33 years); Chase; Franck; Krasilovsky.

BENT, ARTHUR C.
"Note on Birds in Alaska [Aleutians and Bering Sea], 1911," *Report*, Smithsonian Institution, 1912.

BENT, SILAS
See T-507.

BENTLEY, JOHN BOYD (b. 1896)
"Annual Report of the Bishop," *Alaska Churchman*, Feb., 1946. See also Tewkesbury (at Anvik, 1921-25; Archdeacon of the Yukon, 1930-31).

BENYOVSKI, Count de MAURITIUS AUGUSTUS
Memoirs and Travels. London: 1790. 2v. Benyovski was a Polish castaway in Siberia in the 18th century. From Yakutsk he went eastward, appearing in Kamchatka at Bolsheretsk in the 1770's where he apparently fomented rebellion, and assumed the governorship. He seized a ship there and sailed to the Aleutians, landing, by his own account, at Kodiak and Amchitka, and at Bering Island and on the Siberian coast at 64° where he spoke to the Chukchi natives. When King visited Kamchatka in 1779, the population there feared his vessel might be a pirated ship bent on destruction.

BERG, LEV SEMENOVICH (1876-1950)
Otkrytie Kamchatki i Ekspeditsii Beringa, 1725-42 (The Discovery of Katchatka and the Bering Expeditions). Petrograd, 1924. 379 pp. Berg published numerous books and articles on early Russian exploration. See the Arctic Bibliography, and T-512 ff. Few of his works were written in English, and none have been translated. See the *Proceedings*, Pacific Science Conference, Toronto, 1933.

BERGEN, HANS von
Jagdfahrten im Kanada und Alaska. Neudamm: J. Neumann, 1928. 264 pp. Hunting trips in Alaska.

BERGER, ANDRE
Dans Les Neiges de l'Alaska. Paris: Berdardin-Bechet, 1930. 140 pp.

BERGSLAND, KNUT
See T-522.

BERING RIVER COALFIELDS
Alaska-Yukon Magazine, March, '08 (photos); May, '10; Sundborg; Whiting (proposed railway spur); Young (Morgan-Guggenheim).

BERING SEA
Alaska Life, July, '38 (fish conservation); *Alaska Sportsman*, March, '41 (Coast Guard patrol); Allen; *Bering Sea and Strait Pilot*; Goodhue; Hudson; Miller; *National Geographic*, Dec., '42 (photo showing differing colors in waters of sea where Pacific Ocean might be said to meet the Bering Sea); Niedieck; Shepard; US Coast Guard (*Report*, Oceanographic cruise, cutter *Chelan*, 2v.); Wead; Wickersham; Winchell. See also D. Ray.

BERING SEA CONTROVERSY
Behring Sea Arbitration (letters to the *Times* by its special correspondent [London: Clowes, 1893]); Bering Sea Tribunal; Eward; Hart; Shiels; Stanton; Wishart.

BERING SEA TRIBUNAL
Bering Sea Tribunal of Arbitration. Fur Seal Arbitration. Proceedings (convened at Paris under a treaty concluded between the United States and Great Britain, Washington, 1892, for the determination of questions between the two governments concerning the jurisdictional rights of the U.S. in the waters of the Bering Sea). Wn.DC: GPO, 1895. 16v. See also the Wickersham Bibliography.

The Alaska Commercial Company, by terms of its lease with the US government, had exclusive rights to the fur seal harvest in the Pribilof Islands. Serious inroads were made on the seal population, however, by pelagic sealing by other nations, killing seals in open water during their migration to the islands. Acting on the theory that it had exclusive jurisdiction in the waters of the Bering Sea, the US boarded numerous vessels and took them as prizes to Sitka. A study of the habits of the fur seal constituted a part of the material on which a determination of jurisdiction was made. The US lost on four of five points submitted for arbitration, and by terms of the Bering Sea Claims Commission, $425,000 was paid by the US. See Tompkins.

BERING STRAIT
Alaska Sportsman, May, '58; *National Geographic*, May, '39; Scidmore. See the Arctic Bibliography for technical data, and the Wickersham Bibliography.

BERING, VITUS JONASSEN (1680-1741)
"Logbooks Compiled on Voyages to America," in Golder's *Bering's Voyages*. See the bibliography in Vol. I. See also the following:

Akademiia Nauk; Andreev; Baker; Bancroft; Barbeau; Berg; Berkh; Chaplin; Coxe; Dall; Davidson; Denton; DuHalde; Ford; Gmelin; Golder; Goodhue; Granberg; Henderson; Kruber; Lauridsen; Laut; McDonald; Masterson; Muller; Murphy; Pallas; Pedersen; Pekarskii; Pokrovskii; Rasmussen; Speck; Stejneger; Staehlin; Steller; Sumner; Tompkins; Waxell; Wendt; Wolff; Yarmolinsky; and others. See also T-524 ff.

BERKH, VASILII NIKOLAEVICH (1781-1834)
Khronologicheskaia Istoriya Otkrytiya Aleutskikh Ostrovov (Chronological History of the Discovery of the Aleutian Islands). St. Petersburg, 1823. 169 pp. This work was translated by Dmitri Krenov as a WPA Federal Writers Project in 1938, the typescript deposited in the Library of Congress and never published. Melvin Ricks translated the work which was published in a limited edition with two other works (Khlebinikov's biography of Baranov and Shelikhov's account of his journey through Siberia) by the Cook Inlet Historical Society in 1970. Richard Pierce translated the work and published it through his Limestone Press in 1975. The account describes briefly 130 voyages made between 1743 and 1822 with statistics on the cargoes of fur returned to Siberia. Berkh also published several other accounts of Russian marine activity in the 18th century, including material on Bering's voyages (from the geographical point of view), a chronology of all vessels sailing to polar lands, biographies of the first Russian admirals and the account of the wreck of the *Neva* near Sitka (published in 1817). He also translated

into Russian the account of the voyage of Hearne and MacKenzie. For information on these see T-527 ff, and the Arctic Bibliography.

BERLIN KONIGLICHEN MUSEEN
See T-534 ff.

BERNHARDI, CHARLOTTE
See Kruzenshtern.

BERNHARDT, JOSHUA (b. 1893)
The Alaska Engineering Commission. New York: Appleton, 1922. 124 pp. History, activities, organization.

BERNHEIM, BEATRICE B.
America's Great Northwest. New York: Jaques & Co., 1919. 93 pp. Poetry.

BERRIES, ALASKAN
Alaska Sportsman, Jan., '54; Sept., '57; *Alaska-Yukon Magazine,* June, '07; Dall (14 varieties); Leonard; Morris; Rearden; Sundborg; University of Alaska Extension Service; White, Helen (excellent); Willard. See also Cranberries.

BERRY (Ester Creek mining camp)
Colby (named for Clarence Berry, prehistoric bones uncovered by hydraulic mining); Couch (post office from 1902 [save 1912]); Kitchener (store here supplied by NC Co.).

BERRY, CLARENCE J.
Brooks (1898 devised method of steam thawing); Bankston (photo of No. 4, Eldorado, Klondike); Couch (operated trading post at Berry); Colby; Henderson (family history); Kitchener (claim at Eagle, and on Mammoth Creek).

BERRY, EDWARD W.
"Former Land Connection between Asia and North America as Indicated by the Distribution of Fossil Trees," *Proceedings,* Pacific Science Conference, Victoria and Vancouver, 1933. Toronto: University of Toronto, 1934.

BERRY, ERICK
Mr. Arctic. New York: David McKay, 1966. Stefansson.

BERRY, M. P.
Gruening (practiced law at Sitka); Morris (collector of Customs, ill in Victoria in 1877, resigned post); Nichols (defeated Ball in contest for Alaska delegate, 1881); see also Andrews (Major M.P. Berry appointed by Commander Glass at Sitka to command defense forces against drunken Indians).

BERRY, MARY
A History of Mining on the Kenai Peninsula. Anchorage: Alaska Northwest Publishing Co., 1973.
The Alaska Pipeline: The Politics of Oil and Native Land Claims. Bloomington: Indiana University Press, 1974.

BERRY, WILLIAM
See T-540.

BERTHOLF, ELLSWORTH P.
The Rescue of the Whalers. Reprinted from *Harper's Magazine,* June, 1899. See also Golder. A herd of reindeer were driven from Kotzebue Sound to Point Barrow, 1600 miles, between November, 1897 and September, 1898. See also US Revenue Cutter *Bear,* and *Alaska-Yukon Magazine,* Dec., '08.

BERTON, LAURA BEATRICE (b. ca. 1878)
I Married the Klondike. Boston: Little, Brown, 1954. 269 pp. The author went to the Klondike in 1907, and lived across the street from Robert Service in Dawson. This entertaining account of Dawson in that period contains notes about Belinda Mulroney, Mr. and Mrs. George Black, Alex McDonald, Archdeacon McDonald, Robert Service, Grant Henderson, Diamond Tooth Gertie, and Frank Berton.

BERTON, PIERRE (b. 1920)
A Klondike Biography. Kleinsburg, Ontario, 1958.
The Stampede for Gold. New York: Alfred A. Knopf, 1955. Juvenile.
The Klondike. Toronto: McClelland and Stewart, 1958. This is the same as Klondike Fever.
The Klondike Feer: Life and Death of the Last Great Gold Rush. New York: Alfred A. Knopf, 1958. 457 pp.
The Mysterious North. New York: Alfred A. Knopf, 1956.
Pierre Berton was a schoolboy in Dawson in the dying days of the gold rush; his mother was Laura Berton, his father was Frank Berton. As he says, he grew up there not realizing his was a queer town with a queer history. In *Klondike Fever* Berton has produced the best single work on the history of the Klondike so far published, quite favorably reviewed and very thorough.

BESANT, Sir WALTER
Captain Cook. London: Macmillan, 1894.

BETHEL (Kuskokwim village)
Alaska Life, March, '42 (hospital); June, '42 (Oliver Anderson, NC Co. manager); July, '42; *Alaska Sportsman,* July, '40 (largest govt. hospital); Aug., '41 (moving river); July, '43 (muskrat hunt); Aug., '55; *Alaska Weekly,* Oct., '51 (old hospital burned 1950); *Alaska-Yukon Magazine,* Sept., '09 (photo); Nov., '10 and Jan., '11 (photos); *American Journal of Physical Anthropology,* 28 (1941): 331-41 (measurements of Eskimo children, comments by Hrdlicka); Anderson; Bethel Chamber of Commerce (*Bethel,* 1959); Franck; Gapp; Hamilton; Kitchener; Hulley (named by Moravian missionaries); Couch (post office since 1905); Schwalbe; see also Moravian Church.

BETTICHER, CHARLES EUGENE, Jr. (pioneer missionary)
Alaska-Yukon Magazine, Jan., '09 (photo); Jenkins (founded *Alaska Churchman*); Stuck (arr. Fairbanks 1905, founded mission at Tanana Crossing); see also Wickersham Bibliography.

BETTLES (village, Koyukuk River)
Alaska Sportsman, Aug., '44; May, '55 (photo); Baker (at head of navigation on the Koyukuk, named for trading post owners); Couch (post office from 1901, Gordon C. Bettles first post-master);

Kitchener (boomed in 1901); Stuck; Underwood Bettles est. at head of navigation in 1898; mine at Coldfoot in 1892). Bettles Field, 18 miles north of Bettles, now has the post office and a community of FAA employees. Before jet aircraft, Bettles Field was a regular refueling stop on the Fairbanks to Barrow route.

BETTLES, GORDON CHARLES (1864-1945)

Alaska Life, Feb., '42 (articles by Bettles' second wife who married him at Bettles, and who was a BIA employee at Akiak, Quinhagak, Goodnews Bay, Koyukuk and Chanega Island); July, '45 (Bettles relates starting *Yukon Press* with Rev. Prevost at Ft. Adams in 1894); *Alaska Weekly*, Aug., '51; Atwood (*Gold Book*); Chase (partnership with Billie Moore); Downs (Detroit printer, Treadwell in 1886, Fortymile in 1887, founded Bettles, 1896, married Sophie Kokrines in 1900); Franck; Kitchener; Wickersham.

BETTON ISLAND (near head of Behm Canal)

Alaska Sportsman, Apr., '53 (wolf thief); Vancouver (named for a crewman who had been wounded in the thigh by an Indian's spear in a fight near Traitor's Creek).

BEYNON, WILLIAM

"Tsimshians of Metlakatla," *Amer. Anthropologist*, January, 1941.

BIBLIOGRAPHY OF ALASKA

Alaska Div. of Libraries, *Guide to Papers of the Alaska Packer's Association* (in the Alaska State Historical Library), Juneau, 1966 (rev.).

Alaska Division of Libraries, *Guide to Russian Holdings* (in the Alaska State Historical Library), Juneau, 1965.

Alaska Division of Libraries, *Some Books on Alaska*, Juneau, annual from 1971.

Alaska Northwest Publishing Company, *Bibliography of Books on Alaska*, Anchorage, 1974.

Alaska Northwest Publishing Company, *Subject Index to Alaska Magazine* (formerly *Alaska Sportsman*), *1935-1972*, Anchorage, 1972.

Arctic Bibliography, 15v., Arctic Institute of North America (in cooperation with the US Department of Defense), Washington: Government Printing Office, from 1953.

Barbeau, Charles Marius. *Totem Poles*, 2v. (Vol. I: Totem Poles according to crests and topics; Vol. II: Totem Poles according to location). Ottawa: Queen's Printers, 1964.

Barrow, John. *Voyages of Discovery* (and research within the Arctic regions from the year 1818 to the present time. . .abridged and arranged from official naratives, with occasional remarks). London: J. Murray, 1846. 530 pp.

Basanoff, V. "Archives of the Russian Church in Alaska in the Library and Congress," *P.H.R.* II, No. 1 (1933): 72-84.

Bee, James W. and Eugene Raymond Hall, *Mammals of Northern Alaska on the Arctic Slope*, Lawrence, Kansas: Museum of Natural History of the University of Kansas, 1956. 309 pp.

Bemis, Samuel F. and Grace G. Griffin, *Guide to the Diplomatic History of the, United States, 1775-1921*. Cambridge: Harvard University Press, 1935. 970 pp.

Bibliography of Alaskana, Rasmuson Library; see

University of Alaska.

Bolton, Herbert, *Guide to Materials for the History of the United States in the Principal Archives of Mexico*. Washington: National Archives, 1913.

Brinsmade, Ellen Martin. *Books on Alaska for Young People, Annotated Bibliography*. Sitka: Sitka Printing Co., 1961.

Brinsmade, Ellen Martin. *Children's Books on Alaska: An Annotated List*. Sitka: Sitka Printing Co., 1956. 32 pp.

Bromberg, Erik. "A Bibliography of Theses and Dissertations Concerning the Pacific Northwest and Alaska," *Pacific Northwest Quarterly*, July, 1949.

Bromberg, Erik. "A Further Bibliography of Theses Concerning the Pacific Northwest and Alaska," *Pacific Northwest Quarterly*, April, 1951.

Bromberg, Erik. "A Bibliography of Theses and Dissertations Concerning the Pacific Northwest and Alaska," *Pacific Northwest Quarterly*, March, 1958.

Bureau of Indian Affairs; see US Bureau of Indian Affairs.

Caswell, John E. *Arctic Frontiers: United States Explorations in the Far North*. Norman: University of Oklahoma Press, 1956. 232 pp.

Catalogue of the Everett D. Graff Collection; see Graff.

Chevigny, Hector. *Lord of Alaska: Baranov and the Russian Adventure*. New York: Viking Press, 1942. 320 pp.

Chapman, Charles E. *Catalogue of Materials in Archivo General de Indias*. Berkeley, 1919.

Colby, Merle Estes. *Guide to Alaska: The Last American Frontier*. New York: Macmillan, 1939. 427 pp.

Compilation of Sources; see Works Progress Administration.

Dall, William H. *Alaska and Its Resources*. Boston: Lee and Shepard, 1870. 627 pp.

Dall, William H. and Marcus Baker. "Partial List of Books, Pamphlets, Papers in Several Journals, and Other Publications on Alaska and Adjacent Regions," *Pacific Coast Pilot: Coasts and Islands of Alaska*, 2nd Series.

Decker, Peter. *Priced and Descriptive Checklist Together with Short Title Index* (describing almost 7,500 items of Western Americana comprising books, maps, and pamphlets of the important library [in four parts] formed by George W. Soliday, Seattle, Washington). New York: Peter Decker, 1940-45. Corrected Edition, compiled with notes by Peter Decker, New York: Antiquarian Press, 1960. (Note: Corrected Edition omits *Priced and* from the title).

Eberstadt, Edward and Sons. *The Northwest Coast: Personal Narratives of Discovery, Conquest and Exploration, 1741-1841*. A Book Catalogue (No. 119). New York: Eberstadt Booksellers, 1941. 127 pp. Bibliography and historical notes.

Farquhar, Francis P. and Mildred P. Ashley. *A List of Publications Relating to the Mountains of Alaska*. New York: The American Alpine Club, 1934. 37 pp.

Fisher, Raymond H. *Records of the Russian-American Company, 1802, 1817-1867*. Wn.DC: GPO, 1971. (National Achives).

Franklin, Burt; see W.H. Ifould (Bibliography of Cook).

Frederick, Robert A. "Caches of Alaskana," *Alaska Review* (published by Alaska Methodist University) II (Fall-Winter, 1966): No. 3, 39-79. A listing of secondary and manuscript sources in government, university and private libraries in the United States.

Fritts, Crawford E. and Mildred E. Brown. *Bibliography of Alaskan Geology*, 3v. (Vol. I, 1831-1918; Vol. II, 1919-1949; Vol. III, 1950-1959). Wn.DC: GPO, 1971 (USGS).

Fuller, Grace H. *Alaska: A Selected List of References*. Wn.DC: GPO, 1943 (Library of Congress, Division of Bibliography, available in mimeograph).

Fuller, Grace H. *Aleutian Islands: A List of References*. Wn.DC: GPO, 1943 (Library of Congress, Division of Bibliography, limited edition).

Gabrielson, Ira N. and Frederick C. Lincoln. *The Birds of Alaska*. Harrisburg: Stackpole, 1959. 922 pp.

Glenbow-Alberta Institute. *Royal Canadian Mounted Police*, Glenbow Achives Series No. 5. Edmonton, 1973. Bibliography of Resource Material.

Glenbow-Alberta Institute. *Lomen Brothers' Photographic Collection* (Nome, Alaska, 1900-1935). Glenbow Archives Series No. 3. Edmonton, n.d. An Inventory.

Glenbow-Alberta Institute. *Western Stock Growers' Association, 1896-1963*. Glenbow Archives Series No. 1. Edmonton, n.d. Papers inventory.

Golder, Frank A. *Guide to Materials for American History in Russian Archives*. 2v. (Vol. I, 1917; Vol. II, 1937). Washington, DC, Carnegie Institute. Available on microfilm from the University of Washington Library.

Golder, Frank A. *Golder Collection of Photostat Copies of Documents in the Russian Archives*. Microfilm A2908. University of Washington Library.

Catalogue of the Everett D. Graff Collection of Western Americana. Compiled by Colton Storm. Chicago: University of Chicago Press, 1968. Published for the Newberry Library.

Gsovski, Vladimir. *Russian Administration of Alaska and the Status of Natives*. Wn.DC: GPO, 1950 (81st Congress, 2nd Session, Senate Document No. 152).

Guide to Holdings; see Alaska, Division of Libraries.

Haywood, Charles. *A Bibliography of North American Folklore and Folksong*. New York: Greenberg, 1951. 1292 pp.

Hrdlicka, Ales. "Anthropological Survey of Alaska," in *Annual Report*, 1928-29, Bureau of American Ethnology. Wn.DC: GPO, 1930. pp. 19-374.

Hulley, Clarence. *Alaska: 1741-1953*. Portland: Binfords & Mort, 1953. 406 pp. More recent edition, *Alaska: Past and Present*, 1958.

Hulten, Erik. *Flora of Alaska*, Parts I-X. Lund (Sweden): Universitet, Arsskrift, 1941-50. 1902 pp.

Hunt, William R. "Northwest Bibliography from Dall to Lada-Mocarski," *Pacific Northwest Quarterly*, July, 1971.

Ifould, W.H. *Bibliography of Captain James Cook, R.N., F.R.S., Circumnavigator*. New York: Burt Franklin, 1968. Originally published at Sydney, 1928.

James Bushrod Washington. *Alaska: Its Neglected Past, Its Brilliant Future*. Philadelphia: Sunshine Publishers, 1897. 444 pp.

Judson, Katherine Berry. *Subject Index to the History of the Pacific Northwest and Alaska* (as Found in the United States Government Documents, Congressional Series, in the American State Papers,

and in other documents, 1798-1881). Olympia, Washington: 1913. Prepared for the Seattle Public Library.

Keithahn, Edward L. *Totem: Monuments in Cedar*. Ketchikan: Robert Anderson, 1945. 160 pp.

Kelly, J.S. and J.M. Denman. *Geological Literature on the Alaska Peninsula and Adjacent Areas*. Wn.DC: GPO, 1971 (USGS).

Kerner, Robert. "Russian Expansion to America: Its Bibliographic Foundations," *Papers of the Bibliographic Society of America*, XXV: 111-129.

Lada-Mocarski, Valerian. *Bibliography of Books on Alaska Published before 1868*, with an introduction by Archibald Hanna, Jr. New Haven: Yale University Press, 1969. 567 pp. Index. Cyrillic index.

Lawrence Lande Collection of Canadiana in the Redpath Library of McGill University: A Bibliography Collected, Arranged and Annotated. Lawrence Lande, with an introduction by Edgar Arnold Collard. Montreal: Lawrence Lande Foundation for Historical Research, 1965.

Lantis, Margaret. *Alaskan Eskimo Ceremonialism*. New York: J.J. Augustin, 1947. 127 pp.

Larson, S.M. *Fire in Far Northern Regions: A Bibliography*. Wn.DC: GPO, 1969 (Bureau of Land Management).

Lawrence Lande Collection; see Lande.

Levin, M.G. "Ethnographic and Anthropological Materials as Historic Sources," *Arctic Anthropology*, I (1962): 51-57.

Lowther, Barbara J. *Bibliography of British Columbia: Laying the Foundations, 1849-1899*, with the assistance of Muriel Lang, prepared under the auspices of the Social Sciences Research Centre, University of Victoria. Victoria: University of Victoria Press, 1968.

McKennan, Robert A. *The Upper Tanana Indians*. New Haven: Yale University Department of Anthropology, 1959.

Mezhov, Vladimir I. *The Siberian Bibliography: An Index of Books and Articles on Siberia in the Russian Language* (and books [only] in foreign languages, for the period since the beginning of printing [in the Russian language]). St. Petersburg: Tip. I.N. Skorokhodova, 1891-92. 3v.

Miller, Orlando W. *The Frontier in Alaska and the Matanuska Colony*. New Haven: Yale University Press, 1975.

Mirsky, Jeannette. *To the Arctic*. New York: Viking Press, 1934. Story of Northern Exploration from Earliest Times to the Present.

National Archives; see US National Archives.

National Museum of Canada. *Publications*. Ottawa: Queen's Printers, 1972 (list of publications from early 20th century through 1970).

Nichols, Jeannette Paddock. *Alaska: A History of its Administration, Exploitation and Industrial Development* (through its first half century under the rule of the United States). Cleveland: Arthur H. Clark, 1924.

Olsen, Michael L. *A Preliminary List of References for the History of Agriculture in the Pacific Northwest and Alaska*. Davis, California: University of California, 1968. A cooperative project by the Agricultural History Branch, Economic Research Service, US Dept. of Agriculture, and the Agricultural History Center. 58 pp.

Oswalt, Wendell H. "The Kuskokwim River Drainage: An Annotated Bibliography," *Anthro-*

pological Papers, University of Alaska, 13 (1965): 53-77.

Overland Monthy. "Alaskan Articles that Have Appeared in the *Overland*," *Overland Monthly*, October, 1897.

Priced and Descriptive Checklist; see Peter Decker.

Reid, Virginia H. *The Purchase of Alaska: Contemporary Opinion.* Long Beach, California: *Press-Telegram*, 1939.

Robertson, J.A. *List of Documents in Spanish Archives Relating to the United States.* Wn.DC: GPO, 1910 (Library of Congress).

Sabin, Joseph, et. al. *A Dictionary of Books Relating to America.* 29v. New York: 1868-1937. Rare books.

Sarafian, Winston L. and James W. VanStone. "The Records of the Russian-American Company as a Source for the Ethnohistory of the Nushagak River Region, Alaska," *Anthropological Papers*, University of Alaska, 15 (1972): 53-77.

Shepard, W.R. *Guide to the Materials for the History of the United States in Spanish Archives.* Wn.DC: GPO, 1907.

Smith, Barbara S. *Preliminary Survey of Documents in the Archives of the Russian Orthodox Church in Alaska.* Boulder, Colorado: Western Interstate Commission on Higher Education [for the University of Alaska, Anchorage], 1974.

Smith, Charles W. *Pacific Northwest Americana.* Third Edition, revised and extended by Isabel Mayhew. Portland: Binfords and Mort, 1950 (Checklist of Books and Pamphlets Relating to the History of the Pacific Northwest). This was originally published for the Washington State Library in Olympia in 1909.

Smithsonian Institution. *Preliminary Guide to the Smithsonian Archives.* Archives and Special Collections of the Smithsonian Institution, No. 1. Wn.DC: GPO, 1971.

Some Books Received; see Alaska, Division of Libraries.

Stemple, Ruth. *Smithsonian Institutions Annual Reports* (Indexes). Wn.DC: GPO, 1963. 1849-1961.

Spencer, Robert F. *The North American Eskimo.* Wn.DC: GPO, 1959. Smithsonian Institution.

Stejneger, Leonhard H. *Georg Wilhelm Steller.* Cambridge: Harvard University Press, 1936. 623 pp.

Storm, Colton; see Edward Graff.

Thomas Winthrop Streeter Collection of Americana, Volume 6, The Pacific West: Oregon, British Columbia, Alaska, Canada, Hawaii. New York: Parke-Bernet Galleries, 1969.

Stockbridge; see US Army.

Tarsaidze, Alexandre. *Czars and Presidents.* New York: McDowell Obolensky, 1958. 383 pp.

Thomas, Benjamin P. *Russo-American Relations, 1815-1867.* Baltimore: Johns-Hopkins University, 1930. 185 pp.

Todd, Ronald. "Theses Related to the Pacific Northwest: University of Washington Checklist," *Pacific Northwest Quarterly*, XXXV (1944): 55-64.

Todd, Ronald. "Theses Related to the Pacific Northwest: University of Washington Checklist," *Pacific Northwest Quarterly*, XL (1949): 65-69.

Tompkins, Stuart R. *Promyshlennik and Sourdough.* Norman: University of Oklahoma Press, 1945. 350 pp.

US Army, Alaskan Command. *Annotated Reading List of Alaska.* Seattle: Alaskan Command, 1966. Truman R. Stockbridge.

US Bureau of Indian Affairs. *Annotated Bibliography of Alaska.* Juneau, 1960.

US National Archives. *Guide to Cartographic Records.* Wn.DC: GPO, 1971. 444 pp.

US National Archives and Federal Records Center, Region 10 (Seattle). *List of Manuscript Holdings.* Mimeograph, 1974.

US National Museum. *List of Publications, 1875-1946.* US National Museum Bulletin No. 193. WN.DC: GPO, 1947.

US Navy, Naval History Division. *United States Naval History, A Bibliography.* 5th ed. Wn.DC: GPO, 1969. 33 pp.

University of Alaska, Department of Education. *A Bibliography of Alaskana*, by students of the Department. College, n.d. (poetry, children's literature, etc.)

University of Alaska, Department of Reader Services. *Bibliography of Alaskana* (intermittent). College. Articles pertaining to Alaska in periodicals received by the Library.

University of Alaska, Extension Service. Numerous pamphlets and other literature, including some bibliographies.

University of Alaska, Institute of Social, Economic, and Governmental Research, *List of Publications* (intermittent). College.

University of Alaska, Library, Archive. Calendars of Papers in the Archive.

University of Alaska, Anchorage. *Bibliography of Historical Resource Material Available in the Anchorage Area.* Boulder, Colorado: Western Interstate Commission on Higher Education, 1973 [for the University of Alaska, Anchorage]. Janis Burke.

VanStone, James W. "Annotated Ethnohistorical Bibliography of the Nushagak River Drainiage," *Fieldana Anthropology*, 54 (1968): 148-190.

Wagner, Henry R. *The Plains and the Rockies.* San Francisco: John Howell, 1921. Revised and extended by Charles L. Camp, 1937, 3rd edition revised by Charles L. Camp, Columbus: Long's College Book Company, 1953. A Bibliography of Original Narratives of Travel and Adventure, 1800-1865.

Wickersham, James. *Bibliography of Alaskan Literature, 1724-1924.* Fairbanks: University of Alaska [Alaska Agricultural College and School of Mines], 1927. 635 pp.

Workman, Karen W. *Alaskan Archaeology: A Bibliography.* Anchorage: Alaska Division of Parks, 1972.

Workman, William B. and Karen W. "Some Perspectives on the Anthropology of the North Pacific Rim," in *Alaska and Japan* (Anchorage: Alaska Methodist University, 1972), ed. Tsuguo Arai.

Wroth, Lawrence C. "The Early Cartography of the Pacific," *Papers*, Bibliographic Society of America, 32 (1944): 85-268. See also the listing in the topic section of the Tourville Bibliography.

BIELKOV, Z. and I. NETSVIETOV
See T-554, and B. Smith.

BIEMILLER, CARL L.
"Alaska, Seward's Folly to Last Frontier," *Holiday*, June, 1948.

BIG DELTA (village, Tanana River)
Alaska Sportsman, Apr., '56 (residence center for Army Arctic Training and Testing Center [Fort Greeley]); July, '56 (buffalo range south to Donnelly Dome, buffalo brought from US in 1920's); Colby; Couch (post office from 1925); Dennison; Sundborg; contemporary maps show Delta or Delta Junction.

BIGELOW, MARVIN JAY
Urdag the Aleut. New York: Vantage Press, 1955. 161 pp.

BIGJIM, FREDERICK and JAMES ITO-ADLER
Letters to Howard: An Interpretation of the Alaska Native Claims Settlement Act. Anchorage: Alaska Methodist University Press, 1974.

BILLINGS, JOSEPH (1758-1806)
See Sauer, and Sarychev. Billings was an English naval officer in the service of Russia under Catherine II. He made two voyages from Russia in 1790 and 1791. Although shown as author in some bibliographies, accounts of his voyages were written by his secretary (Sauer) and a lieutenant (Sarychev). See Brooks (Billings sailed with Cook in 1778).

BINGHAM, JOSEPH W.
Report on the International Law of Pacific Coastal Fisheries. Stanford: Stanford University Press, 1938.

BINDLOSS, HAROLD (b. 1866)
Delilah of the Snows. New York: Stokes, 1907. 339 pp.
Thrice Armed. New York: Stokes, 1908. 377 pp.

BINNS, ARCHIE (B. 1899)
Northwest Gateway. Garden City: Doubleday, 1941. 313 pp.

BIOGRAPHY
See under subject's name, and also the following: *Alaska-Yukon Magazine*, numerous issues; Harrison (miners and businessmen of early Nome); Jeffery (500 Alaskans); Pioneer Igloo (numerous brief notices); Tewkesbury (sketches); see also the Wickersham and Tourville bibliographies. See the following authors:

Anderson, B.	George Vancouver
Anderson, E.	Dr. Joseph Romig
Arctander, J.	Fr. William Duncan
Arneson, O.	Roald Amundsen
Bade, W.	John Muir
Bancroft, F.	William Seward
Barsukov, I.	Innokenti (Veniaminov)
Bauer, H.	Knud Rasmussen
Beaglehole, J.	James Cook
Beattie, K.	Klondike Boyle
Beattie, W.	Gilbert Marsden
Bellesort, A.	Jean LaPerouse
Belov, M.	Semen Dezhnev
Benham, D.	Jan A. Miert
Bernhardi, C.	Adam Krusenstern
Besant, W.	James Cook
Burkholder, M.	James Cook
Carrington, H.	James Cook
Carruthers, J.	James Cook
Caughey, J.	Hubert H. Bancroft
Chase, W.	Capt. Billie Moore

Chukovskii, N.	Vitus Bering
Cody, H.	Fr. William Bompas
Connelly, J.	Amasa Delano
Conrad, E.	William Seward
Dafoe, J.	Clifford Sifton
Dalby, M.	Johnny O'Brien
Davis, M.	Dr. J. Scott
Davydov, I.	John Franklin
Day, B.	Bob Reeve
deBaets, M.	Archbishop Charles Seghers
Denison, M.	Klondike Mike
Divin, V.	A.I. Chirikov
Divin, V.	M. Golovnin
Eaton, J.	Sheldon Jackson
Engstrom, E.	John Engstrom
Fletcher, I.	Vilhjalmur Stefansson
Ford, C.	Georg Steller
Fradkin, N.	S.P. Krasheninnikov
Fraerman, R.	V.M. Golovnin
Gleaves, A.	William Emory
Glody, R.	William Walsh
Godwin, G.	George Vancouver
Golder, F.	Fr. Herman
Goodhue, C.	Vitus Bering
Gould, R.	James Cook
Graham, A.	George Mitchell
Grech, N.	V.M. Golovnin
Green, F.	Robert Bartlett
Greiner, J.	Don Sheldon
Grierson, J.	Sir Hubert Wilkins
Hale, C.	Innocent (Veniaminov)
Hanson, E.	Vilhjalmur Stefansson
Hanssen, H.	Roald Amundsen
Headley, P.	Rev. Edward Hammond
Hill, E.	Rev. Aaron Lindsley
Hofmann, C.	Frances Densmore
Hooker, W.	David Douglas
Howay, F.	George Vancouver
Hulbert, W.	Sheldon Jackson
Jenkins, T.	Peter Rowe
Johnshoy, W.	Rev. Tollef Brevig
Jones, H.	Sydney Laurence
Kashevaroff, A.	Father Herman
Keim, C.	Otto Geist
Kennan, G.	E.H. Harriman
Kennedy, K.	Wien brothers
Khlebnikov, K.	A.A. Baranov
Kingston, W.	James Cook
Kippis, A.	James Cook
Kitson, A.	James Cook
Knight, C.	Bernt Balchen
Kohlstedt, E.	William Duncan
Lane, A.	Franklin Lane
Lang, J.	James Cook
Lauridsen, P.	Vitus Bering
Lawing, N.	Alaska Nellie Lawing
Lazell, J.	Sheldon Jackson
LeBourdais, D.	Vilhjalmur Stefansson
London, Joan	Jack London
Loring, C.	William Sturgis
Low, C.	James Cook
Lucia, E.	Klondike Kate Rockwell
Luciw, W.	Ahapius Honcharenko
McIlraith, J.	Sir John Richardson
Mack, G.	Lewis and Hannah Gerstle
McKeown, M.	Mont Hawthorne
Manwaring, G.	Admiral James Burney
Marich, M.	Fedora Litke
Martinsen, E.	Edward Lung

Meany, E.	George Vancouver
Menshutkin, B.	M.V. Lomonosova
Miller, M.	Soapy Smith
Mitchell, W.	Gen. A.W. Greeley
Montgomery, R.	Lorne Knight
Morenus, R.	Slim Williams
Muir, J.R.	James Cook
Murphy, E.	William Bompas
Noice, H.	Vilhjalmur Stefansson
O'Connor, R.	Jack London
Ordaz, L.	Jack London
Ordin, A.	V.P. Chkalov
Owens, F.	Harold Wood
Page, E.	Kansas Gilbert
Partridge, B.	Roald Amundsen
Pasetskii, V.	Vitus Bering
Peary, R.	Vilhjalmur Stefansson
Peisson, E.	Roald Amundsen
Peterson, M.	Joaquin Miller
Pierce, E.	Charles Sumner
Pierce, R.	D.P. Maksutov
Pollak, G.	Michael Heilprin
Porter, K.	John Jacob Astor
Putnam, G.	Robert Bartlett
Rickard, M.	Tex Rickard
Roberts, L.	Samuel Hearne
Robertson, R.	Soapy Smith
Romano, V.	Jack London
Ross, E.	Aaron Lindsley
Ross, S.	Ernest Gruening
Russell, T.	Warren G. Harding
Samoilov, V.	Semen Dezhnev
Samuels, C.	Tex Rickard
Seward, F.	William Seward
Shenitz, H.	Veniaminov
Shteinberg, E.	Krusenstern, Lisianski
Simpson, A.	Thomas Simpson
Sparks, J.	John Ledyard
Speck, G.	Samuel Hearne
Stark, C.	H.L. Blunt
Stejneger, L.	Georg Steller
Stewart, R.	Sheldon Jackson
Stone, I.	Jack London
Storey, M.	Charles Sumner
Sullivan, E.	Wilson Mizner
Thiery, M.	James Cook
Vaeth, J.	Roald Amundsen
Van Deusen, G.	William Seward
Villiers, A.	James Cook
Wachel, P.	Oscar Winchell
Walcutt, C.	Jack London
Walker, R.	Jack London
Weems, C.	Peter Rowe
Wentworth, E.	William Duncan
White, S.	A.A. Baranov
Whiting, F.	M.J. Heney
Wisting, O.	Roald Amundsen
Wrangell, F.	S.O. Makarov
Young, S.	John Muir

See also Atwood and DeArmond, *Who's Who in Alaskan Politics: A Biographical Dictionary of Alaskan Political Personalities, 1884-1974* (Portland: Binford & Mort, 1977).

BIRCH CREEK (near Yukon at Fort Yukon)
Alaska Sportsman, Jan., '53 (parallels Yukon); Aug., '53 (photo); *Alaska-Yukon Magazine*, Sept., '08 (Rev. McDonald discovered gold); Brooks (gold discovered by two half-breeds, biggest producer,

1893-96); Baker (12 miles from Yukon at Circle); Kitchener (McQuesten outfitted Pitka and Siroski who found gold there in 1893); Ogilvie; Stuck (entitled to name "river"; Preacher's Creek was probably Mastodon); Walden; Wickersham; Winslow (many important tributaries).

BIRCH, STEPHEN (b. ca. 1870)
Alaska-Yukon Magazine, Apr., '10 ("Pioneering Capital"); May, '10 (photo); Colby (copper holdings; was president of Kennecott Copper); Couch (was last postmaster at Kennecott, 1938); Davis; Hulley (bought holdings in 1900); Morgan (refused London and Beach permission to write his biography); Wickersham (Smith and Warner); see Kennecott Copper, Guggenheims, etc.

BIRDS
Alaska Sportsman, see index; see the Arctic Bibliography; Bailey, Brandt; Dixon; Gabrielson and Lincoln; Harriman (Keeler); Nelson; Taverner.

BIRKELAND, KNUD BERGESEN (1857-1925)
The Whalers of Akutan. New Haven: Yale University Press, 1926. 171 pp. Account of whaling in the Aleutians, North Pacific Sea Products.

BIRKET-SMITH KAJ (b. 1893)
The Eskimos. New York: Dutton, 1935. Trans. W.E. Calvert. Includes materials on the Aleuts.
The Eyak Indians of the Copper River Delta, Alaska, with Frederica de Laguna. Copenhagen: Levin, 1938. 591 pp.
The Chugach Eskimo. Copenhagen: Nationalmuseet, 1953. 261 pp.

BISHOP, ERNEST FRANKLIN
The Timber Wolf of the Yukon. Chicago: Digest Press, 1925. 278 pp. See also play by same author.

BISHOP'S MOUNTAIN
Alaska Sportsman, Apr., '57 (whirlpool above Koyukuk); Brooks (Bishop Rock, murder of Archbishop Seghers near here, 1886); Cameron (large cross on high promontory); Helmericks; Stuck (photo).

BISON, AMERICAN
Alaska Sportsman, Jan., '52 (six buffalo released at Delta); March, '56 (four bison released on Popoff Island, Gulf of Alaska); March, '58 (photo, notes); see also index; *Alaska Weekly*, Sept., '50 (seven to upper Copper River); Oct., '50; Colby (arrival Fairbanks 1927); Denison; Dufresne.

BLACK, GEORGE
Alaska Weekly, July, '51 (30 years at Ottawa representing Yukon Territory); Berton; Cameron; O'Connor (appt. Commissioner of Y.T. 1912).

BLACK, MARTHA LOUISE (1866-1957)
My Seventy Years. New York: Thomas Nelson, 1938. Early figure at Dawson as wife of Commissioner Black. Appears in many Dawson accounts. See *Alaska Sportsman*, May, '58.
Yukon Wild Flowers. Vancouver: Price Templeton, 1940.

BLACK, ROBERT F.
"Wrangell Mountains," in Howel Williams. Geology.
"Lowlands and Plains of Interior and Western Alaska," in Howell Williams.

BLACK RAPIDS (glacier, stream)
Alaska Sportsman (photo); Colby (sudden movement 1936); Hayes (endangered roadhouse).

BLACKBERRY, ALVA W. and LINN A. FORREST
Tale of an Alaska Whale. Portland: Binfords and Mort, 1955. Thlingit (Wrangell) legend of the origin of the killer whale.

BLACKBURN, MT.
Alaska Sportsman, Dec., '38; Nov., '41; Jan., '51 (visible from Chitina); Sept., '52 (alt. 16,523); Allen (named in honor of J.C.S. Blackburn of Kentucky); Colby; Rohn; Washburn (first ascent by Dora Keen); Wickersham (on eradication of native name).

BLAKE, EUPHEMIA (1817-1904)
Arctic Experiences. New York: Harper, 1874. 486 pp. Notes on Capt. George Tyson's drift on an icefloe, a history of the Polaris Expedition, cruise of the *Tigress*.

BLAKE, H. L.
History of the Discovery of Gold at Cape Nome. 56th Cong., 1st sess., Sen. Doc. No. 441. See also Brooks; Kitchener; Tompkins.

BLAKE, S. F.
Guide to Popular Floras of the United States and Alaska. A bibliography. Wn.DC: GPO, 1954. 56 pp. Department of Agriculture.

BLAKE, THEODORE A.
"Topographical and geographical features of the Northwest Coast of America," *American Journal of Science*, July, 1867.
"General topographical and geological features of the Northwestern Coast of America, from the Straits of Juan de Fuca to 60°N Lat.," in *Report*, 1867, US Coast and Geodetic Survey (George Davidson). In his report, William P. Blake, brother of Theodore Blake, refers to Theodore as the geologist of the 1867 expedition; see William Blake.

BLAKE, WILLIAM P. (1826-1910)
"The Glaciers of Alaska, Russian America," *American Journal of Science*, July, 1867. Blake was a guest on the Russian corvette *Rynda* on a reconnaissance of the Stikine River in 1863. His notes are contained in President Johnson's message to Congress in February, 1868, and were later printed in California and in Russian at St. Petersburg. Morris discusses Blake's theories on gold in southeast Alaska, and Brooks calls Blake the first geologist to examine any part of Alaska.

BLANKE, JOHN H. D.
"Engineers Trailblaze the Alaska Highway," *International Engineer*, February, 1943.

BLANKET TOSS ("Nelakatuk")
Alaska Sportsman, March, '57; Apr., '57; Brower; Forrest; Richards; Van Valin.

BLASCHKE, EDUARD L.
"Some Remarks on a Voyage in Baidarkas, and on the Fox Island Aleuts (in Russian)," in *Moroskoi Sbornik*. Blaschke was a surgeon employed by the Russian-American Company. He published a work in Latin describing some of his work at Sitka. Bancroft discusses his battle with a smallpox epidemic, 1836-38. This is the same epidemic in which many Thlingit first consented innoculation, due partly to the work of the Orthodox priest, Veniaminov.

BLAUCH, LLOYD E.
Educational Service for Indians. US Advisory Committee on Education. Wn.DC: GPO, 1939. 137 pp.
Public Education in the Territories. US Advisory Committee on Education. Wn.DC: GPO, 1939. 243 pp.

BLOCH, ADAM (d. 1914)
Lipke (agent of AC Co.; perhaps the soldier who caught the flag on the day of transfer, at Sitka, 1867).

BLOMKVIST, E. E.
"A Russian Scientific Expedition to California and Alaska, 1839-1849," *Oregon Historical Quarterly*, LXXIII (1972): 101-161.

BLOND, GEORGES
The Plunderers. New York: Macmillan, 1951. 243 pp. Novel.
The Great Story of the Whales. Trans. Garden City: Hanover House, 1955. 251 pp.

BLOSSOM
Dall; Beechey; Hulley; Stuck; see also Baker: Cape Blossom, Blossom Island, Point Blossom, Blossom Shoals.

BLOUNT, ELLEN S.
North of '53: An Alaska Journey. London: Humphries, 1925. 128 pp. 1914 trip to Dawson, Skagway, Tanana, and St. Michael.

BLUE, GEORGE VERNE
"Vessels Trading on the Northwest Coast of America, 1804-1814," *Washington Historical Quarterly*, October, 1928.

"BLUE PARKA BANDIT"
Alaska Sportsman, Dec., '54 (notes, 1905-06); Jan., '56 (a member of Bishop Rowe's church); Hulley (waylaid Bishop Rowe); Jenkins.

"BLUE TICKET SYSTEM"
Alaska Sportsman, Dec., '56 (at Dawson); Beach (blue ticket means leave town within 24 hours; pink ticket means leave by the earliest safe conveyance); Hines; Whiting.

BLUFF (Nome mining camp area)
Alaska Sportsman, Oct., '40 (beach gold); *Alaska-Yukon Magazine*, March, '09 (photo); Baker (also Bluff City); Couch (post office 1901-09); Cameron; Harrison; Kitchener; Tewkesbury.

BLUNT, HARRY L.
Alaska Sportsman, July, '57 (bush pilot); Hubbard; Stark.

BLYTHE, A. D.
The Arctic Sheba. Kansas City: Burton Publishing Co., 1948.

BOAS, FRANZ (1858-1942)
Primitive Art. Oslo: Aschehoug: also Cambridge: Harvard University Press, 1927.
Handbook of the American Indian Languages, Wn.DC: GPO, 1911-13. The Smithsonian Institution. 3v.
Grammatical Notes on the Language of the Tlingit Indians. Philadelphia: University Museum, 1917. 179 pp.
"The Decorative Art of the Indians of the North Pacific Coast," *Bulletin*, American Museum of Natural History, 1897.
"Vocabularies of the Tlingit, Haida, and Tsimshian Languages," *Proceedings*, American Philosophical Society, 1892.
"Vocabularies from the Northwest Coast of America," *Proceedings*, American Antiquarian Society, 1916.
The American Aborigines. Ten Papers Presented at the 5th Pacific Science Congress, Canada, 1933. Toronto: University of Toronto Press, 1933. 396 pp. Includes Boas' "Relationships Between Northwest America and Northeast Asia."
See other listings in the Arctic Bibliography and in Tourville.
Boas concentrated his interests on Northeastern Canada (Cumberland Sound, Baffin Island) and British Columbia, though he touched briefly on Indian and Eskimo cultures in Alaska. As a young man he spent a year (1883-84) among Eskimos at Baffin Island. He spent much time studying museum exhibits, and he collaborated with other ethnologists in the compilation of native vocabularies, folk lore and songs. In his work on decorative art Boas discusses the process of conventionalization of design as exemplified in Haida, Tsimshian and Tlingit objects, including Chilkat blankets.

BOCA de QUADRA INLET
Alaska Sportsman, May, '41 (photo); Baker (means "Quadra's Channel; apparently named by Camaano); Potter (Gillam crashed here with 5 passengers); Schwatka (also known as Bouquet Inlet, Cape Fox Salmon Cannery here 1883); Vancouver (deduced from Camaanos chart that he was in Boca de Quadra).

BODEGA Y QUADRA, JUAN FRANCISCO de la (1743-1794)
Account of a Voyage from San Blas, Mexico, to the Alaskan coast (about 58°N. Lat.) in 1775. Mss. in the Archivo General de la Nacion, Mexico City. Bodega was highly respected by other explorers of the north, especially Vancouver, who with him named the large island north of Juan de Fuca Strait Bodega and Vancouver's Island; in the course of time it has become shortened to the single name. Bodega has named the mountain on Kruzov Island "San Jacinto," but Cook changed it by calling it Mt. Edgecumbe. On Bodega y Quadra see the following:
Baker; Bancroft; Greenhow (Bodega Bay, at first thought to be San Francisco Bay, was discovered by Bodega on the 1775 voyage). On Bodega Bay see Greenhow; and Wagner (Drake may have entered the bay); see also Dall (Ross colony), and Hulley.

BODFISH, HARTSON HARTLETT
Chasing the Bowhead. Cambridge: Harvard University Press, 1936. 281 pp. Bodfish hunted whales in the north for 31 years. He was one of the first to winter in the north, and to introduce fresh food into the diet of his men.

BOER, FRIEDRICH
Igloos, Yurts, and Totem Poles. New York: Pantheon, 1957. 124 pp.

BOGORAZ, VLADIMIR GERMANOVICH (1865-1936)
"Folklore of Northeastern Asia," *American Anthropologist*, October, 1902.

BOGOSLOF ISLAND
Alaska Life, Apr., '43; Aug., '48 *Alaska Sportsman*, May, '36; March, '54; Burroughs; Cantwell; Dall (Baranov's story of origin); Harriman; Higginson; Hubbard; Miller; Morris, G. (*Field Engineer's Bulletin*, USC&GS, 1936); Powers, S. ("recent changes" in *Geographic Review* [1916]); Scidmore; Swineford (history); Underwood; Whymper.
Bogoslof Island lies about 60 miles west of Unalaska Island. It is said to have risen from the sea as a single peak on May 1, 1796. It is now several peaks joined by lowlands. It has been called the "Jack in the Box" and the "Theologian", having been named by the Russians for St. John the Theologian (Joanna Bogoslova). It is called by the Aleuts "Agashagok."

BOHN, DAVID
See T-595 ff.

BOIT, JOHN
"Log of the *Columbia*," *Proceedings*, Massachusetts Historical Society, Vol. 53, 1919. This is the ship of Robert Gray for which he named the Columbia River. Excerpts of the log were printed in the *Washington Historical Quarterly*, January, 1921.

BOLANZ, MARIA
"Whalers of Murder Cove," *Alaska Journal*, Spring, 1971. Thlingit art.

BOLLES, T. DIX
"Chinese Relics in Alaska," *Proceedings*, US National Museum, 1892.

BOLLING, PATRICIA and ANNE D. HARDINGS
Bibliography of Articles and Papers on North American Indian Art. US Dept. of Interior, Indian Arts and Crafts Board. Wn.DC: GPO, n.d.

BOLSHAKOFF, SERGE
The Foreign Missions of the Russian Orthodox Church. New York: Macmillan, 1943.

BOLTON, HERBERT EUGENE (b. 1870)
Guide to Materials; see bibliography.

BOLYAN, HELEN (1896-1959)
See pseudonym, Martha Martin.

BOMPAS, CHARLOTTE SELINA (1830-1917)
See Archer, S. Memoirs.

BOMPAS, WILLIAM CARPENTER (1834-1906)
See T-602 ff. See also the following:
Alaska Sportsman, July, '55 (slept on wharf at

Seattle); *Alaska-Yukon Magazine*, Sept., '08 (photo); Brooks (at Ft. Yukon 1869); Henderson; Smith; Stuck; see as well Cody (Memoirs); Faris, J. (*Apostle to the North*); Grahame; Jenkins (at Forty-mile).

BONCH-OSMOLOVSKII, A. F.
"Tsarist Alaska: American Alaska," *Sovitskoe Draevedenie*, September, 1936.

BOND, JAMES H. (b. 1906)
From Out of the Yukon. Portland: Binfords and Mort, 1948. 220 pp. Big game hunting areas.

BONE, J. H. A.
"Russian America," *Atlantic Monthly*, June, 1867.

BONE, SCOTT CARDELLE (1860-1936) (Governor of Alaska, 1921-25)
Alaska: Its Past, Present, Future. Juneau: Governor's Office, 1925. Collected speeches and addresses.
Alaska: Outline of its History and Summary of its Resources. Juneau: Governor's Office, 1924.
Chechahco and Sourdough: A Story of Alaska. California: Western Publishers, 1926. 281 pp. Fiction.

BOONE and CROCKETT CLUB
See T-608 ff.

BOONE, LALLA ROOKH (b. 1890)
"Captain George Vancouver and His Work on the Northwest Coast," unpublished doctoral dissertation, University of California (Berkeley), 1939.

BOOTH, ERNEST SHELDON (b. 1915)
Birds of the West (including Alaska, Western Canada, and Hawaii). Escondido, California: Outdoor Pictures, 1960. 413 pp.

BORDEN, CHARLES E.
"Facts and Problems of North Coast Pre-history," *Anthropology in British Columbia*, 1951. Supports the assumption of de Laguna and H.B. Collins that Eskimo stratum underlies Indian cultures in the southcentral Alaska area.

BORDEN, LOUISE
The Cruise of the Northern Light. New York: Macmillan, 1928. 317 pp. Account of the Borden Field Museum Alaska-Arctic Expedition of 1927.

BORIGO, EDNA E.
Shades of Joe Juneau. Juneau: Totem Press, 1953. 39 pp.

BORIS, Hieramonk
"The Holy Eastern Orthodox Catholic and Apostolic Church in North America," *Orthodox Catholic Review*, January, 1927.

BORLAND, EARL (d. 1929)
Alaska Sportsman, Nov., '57 (killed with Ben Eielson in 1929); Chase (photo with Eielson); Hulley (Eielson's mechanic).

BORODIN, D. N.
"Russian Paper Money, Postage Stamps, and Cancellations in Alaska," *Stamp Collector's Magazine*, n.d.

BOSCO, ANTOINETTE
Charles John Seghers. New York: P.J. Kenedy, 1960. 191 pp. Juvenile.

BOSTON-ALASKAN SOCIETY (Boston)
Boston Alaskan, official monthly publication, from 1906. Four issues, dated 1906-1907, are in the Alaska State Historical Library. The society was founded by ex-Alaskans.

BOUNDARY ISSUE (Alaska-Canada)
Alaska Boundary Tribunal; Bailey; Baker; Balch; Begg; Davidson; Eward; Hodgins; International Boundary Commission; Mills, *National Geographic*, 1893, 1899, 1903, 1904, 1908, 1909, 1912; Stuck; Tansill; Tompkins; see also the Wickersham Bibliography.

BOVET, LOUIS A., Jr.
Moose Hunting. Philadelphia: Dorrance, 1933. Alaska and Canada.

BOWEN, ROBERT O.
An Alaskan Dictionary. Spenard, Alaska: Nooshnik Press, 1965. 35 pp.

BOWEN, ROBERT O. and R. A. CHARLES
Alaskan Literary Directory. Anchorage: Alaska Methodist University Press, 1964.

BOWEN, ROBERT SIDNEY (b. 1900)
Red Randall in the Aleutians. Juvenile. New York: Grosset and Dunlap, 1945. 214 pp.

BOXER (US Bureau of Education vessel)
Alaska Life, Nov., '44 (succeeded by *North Star* in 1932); *Alaska Sportsman*, Jan., '36 (ports); March, '41 (frozen in at Bethel); Dec., '49 (photo); Aug., '51; Brower (rescue of *Lady Kimberly* Crew); Pilgrim; Richards (cruise of 1924); see also US bureau of Education records.

BRACKETT TOLL ROAD
Alaska Sportsman, June, '52 (C.H. Barkdull took four wagons over the road from Skagway in July, 1898, then by pack train from White Pass City [9 miles from summit] to Lake Bennett); Brooks (George A. Brackett built 15 miles of wagon road, completed in the spring of 1898, charged $20 per ton as toll); Franck (Brackett from Minneapolis, sold the road to the White Pass and Yukon Railway when overtaken by their construction crews); Higginson; Jenkins; Mahoney; Rickard; Winslow (toll road became impassable in spring).

BRADFORD, GAMALIEL
Union Portraits. Boston: Houghton, Mifflin, 1916. Includes William Seward.

BRADY, ELIZABETH PATTON (d. 1951)
Two pamphlets published by the Women's Board of Missions of the Presbyterian Church, New York, 1911 and 1912: *Sheldon Jackson*; *First Alaska Missionary* (Mrs. A.R. McFarlane). See obituary in *Alaska Sportsman*, May, 1951.

BRADY, JOHN GREEN (1848-1918) (Governor of Alaska, 1897-1906)
Alaska Sportsman, Oct., '57 (by son, Hugh Brady, of Seattle); *Alaska-Yukon Magazine*, Oct., '07 (Alaska Home Railway); Andrews (founded Sitka mission, 1878); Brooks (probably found competition with Russian Orthodox Church at Sitka distasteful);

Clark (came as missionary in 1878, ousted by T. Roosevelt [from Alaska governorship] in 1906 for unfortunate connections with promoters, Sheldon Jackson losing office at the same time); Colby (with Miss Kellogg opened school at Sitka, later resigned to manage Sitka Trading Company); Higginson; Gruening; Hinckley; Morris; Nichols (political troubles); Tompkins (missionary work at his own expense); Wright (gave his 160 acre claim to mission); Young (did not take his missionary work too seriously).

BRADLEY, C. B.
"A Reference List to John Muir's Newspaper Articles," *Sierra Club Bulletin*, 10 (1960); 53-59.

BRAINARD, ERASTUS (1855-1922)
"Alaska and the Klondyke." 13 volumes of clippings, letters, etc., compiled 1897-98, at Seattle. In the Library of Congress.

BRAMBLE, CHARLES A.
Klondike: A Manual for Goldseekers. New York: Fenno, 1897. 313 pp.

BRAMHALL, ERVIN H.
"The Central Alaska Earthquake of 1937," *Bulletin*, Seismological Society of America, 1938.

BRANDON PRINTING COMPANY
Alaska and the Yukon Valley. Nashville: Press of the Brandon Printing Company, 1897. 124 pp. How to Get There.

BRANDT, HERBERT
Alaska Bird Trails. Cleveland: Bird Research Foundation, 1943. 464 pp. Account of the Hooper Bay Expedition of 1924 by the US Biological Survey and the Bird Research Foundation.

"BREAK-UP"
See the *Alaska Sportsman* index, and the Arctic Bibliography (Ice). See examples of break-up literature in the following:
Davis (descr.); Heller (descr. Fairbanks); Judge (at Holy Cross, Nulato, Fortymile, 1892-94); Mahoney (at Dawson, 1898); *National Geographic*, May, 1906; Wickersham; Wiedemann (Nunabislogarth); Walden; Young.

BREBNER, J. B.
The Explorers of North America. New York: Macmillan, 1933.

BREETVELD, JIM
Getting to Know Alaska. New York: Coward-McCann, 1958.

BREITFUS, LEONID L'VOVICH
See T-651 ff.

BREMNER, JOHN
See his journal (Copper River trader) in Seton-Karr's *Shores and Alps of Alaska*. See also the following:
Allen (at Taral, had scurvy, hardships affected mind); Chase (murdered at Koyukuk River, Indian hanged); Heller; Kitchener; Stuck (John River named for him); Tompkins (advised Abercrombie); Wickersham.

BREVIG, TOLLEF LARSON (1857-1935) (Lutheran missionary)
Apaurak in Alaska. Philadelphia: Dorrance, 1944. 325 pp. Brevig's records compiled and translated by Walter Johnshoy. Apaurak is said to mean "father of all" in the Eskimo dialect in the vicinity of Teller.

BREWER, CHARLES
Reminiscences. Boston: n.p., 1884.

BREWER, WILLIAM H.
See the Arctic Bibliography and Wickersham's Bibliography. See "The Alaska Atmosphere" in the Harriman Expedition accounts, a description of sky color, clouds, fog, mirages, etc. on the 1899 cruise. Brewer was a member of the expedition.

BRICE, HOWARD
"The story of Mrs. Etta Jones, captured on Attu," *Alaska Life*, December, 1945. Three years as a prisoner.

BRIDAL VEIL FALLS
Alaska Sportsman, Oct., '37 (photo); July, '56 (near Valdez); Colby.

BRIGGS, HORACE W.
"The Story of Metlakatla," *Alaskan* (Sitka), May, 1889.

BRIGHT, ELIZABETH
Alaska: Treasure Trove of Tomorrow. New York: Exposition Press, 1956. 203 pp.

BRIGHT, NORMAN
"Billy Taylor, Sourdough," *American Alpine Journal*, 1939.

BRILES, E. A.
"Traveling with the National Editorial Association." In the Alaska State Historical Library.

BRINDZE, RUTH
Story of the Totem Pole. New York: Vanguard Press, 1951. 64 pp. Juvenile.

BRINSMADE, ELLEN MARTIN
Children's Books on Alaska. Sitka: Sitka Printing Company, 1961. 32 pp.
Books on Alaska for Young People. Sitka: Sitka Printing Company, 1961. 24 pp.

BRISTOL BAY
Alaska Sportsman, Jan., '39 (trapping); Feb., '39 (salmon run); Apr., '54 (fishing); Baker (named for Cook by the Earl of Bristol); Bancroft; Chevigny; Colby; Cook (named for Admiral Earl of Bristol); Dall; Denison; Higginson; Hulley; Sundborg; see also Fedorova and Hawkins.

BRITISH COLUMBIA
Alaska Sportsman, June, July, 1948 (Cariboo Highway); Sept., '48 (flying); *Alaska-Yukon Magazine*, July, 1910 (entire issue); Bancroft; Barbeau; Begg; *British Columbia Pilot*; Gosnell; Howay; Large; Morice (history, missions); Sage; Scholefield (history); Taverner; Scidmore; Woodcock; see also Bulkley; Russian-American Telegraph Expedition; Cassiar; Telegraph Creek; Stikine River; Inside Passage; Kitimat; Alaska Highway.

BRITISH COLUMBIA, PROVINCE OF
Nootka. In series, Our Native Peoples. Department of Education, Victoria. 1952.
Queen Charlotte Islands. In series, Our Pioneers. Department of Education, Victoria, 1953.
Porcupine-Chilkat District. Reports under the Porcupine District Commission Act of 1900, by Hon. Archer Martin. Victoria: R. Wolfenden, 1901. Related to Boundary dispute.
British Columbia Historical Quarterly, published by the Provincial Archives, Victoria.

BRITISH COLUMBIA-YUKON-ALASKA HIGHWAY COMMISSION
See T-672.

BRITT, WILLIAM (1863-1932)
See *Stroller's Weekly*, April, 1932.

BROAD PASS
Baker (between Chulitna and Cantwell Rivers, named by Muldrow, called Caribou Pass by Glenn, 1898); Colby (lowest railway pass in the Rocky Mountains); Couch (post office 1951-54); Franck; Rickard (watershed between Tanana and Susitna Rivers); Underwood; Yanert (descr. first exploration of pass in 1898). From Broad Pass flow the head-waters of streams flowing to the Tanana and the Bering Sea through the Yukon, to the Susitna and the Pacific through Cook Inlet, and to the Gakona and Prince William Sound through the Copper River.

BROADUS, JOHN PRICHARD
"Gazetteer of Alaska," unpublished master's thesis, Arizona State Teacher's College (Flagstaff), 1944. 292 pp.

BROBDIGNAG
Greenhow (must have been situated near the Strait of Juan de Fuca).

BROCEE, MYRTLE
Bankson (full story of suicide).

BROKE, HORATIO GEORGE
With Sack and Stock in Alaska. London: Long-mans, 1891. 150 pp. Attempted climb of St. Elias.

BROMBERG, ERIK
See Bibliography.

BROOKE, JOHN
Two items in Circular No. 8, Surgeon General's Office, *Report*, Hygiene in the US Army, Wn.DC: GPO, 1875: "Baranoff Castle"; "Sitka, a Brief History."

BROOKE, ROBERT
See T-679.

BROOKFIELD, R. M.
"Expedition across Valdez Glacier," see Abercrombie and USGS Professional Papers.

BROOKS, ALFRED HULSE (1871-1924)
The Geography and Geology of Alaska. Wn.DC: GPO, 1906. 327 pp. A summary of existing knowledge, with a section on climate by Cleveland Abbe, Jr., and a topographic map and description by R.U. Goode. Issued also as US congress, House Document No. 20, 59th Congress, 1st Session. Note: Abbe's Climate of Alaska was also issued separately as a USGS Professional Paper, No. 45, 1906.
"An Exploration of Mount McKinley," *Annual Report*, Smithsonian Institution, 1903.
"History of Mining in Alaska," *Alaska-Yukon Magazine*, May, 1909.
"The Value of Alaska," *Geographical Review*, January, 1925. Natural resource summary.
"A Reconnaissance of the Tanana and White River Valleys in 1898," *Annual Report*, USGS, 1898-99.
The Mineral Resources of Alaska. Brooks produced volumes of this title nearly annually from 1902 to 1925 in which he, or subordinates, summarized all mining activity in the territory, often by reprinting the physical reconnaissance of a mining district, and then reporting mining activity in the district since the previous year's survey. Since he included company names, and where known, their owners, the volumes collectively form a significant historical source for the history of mining in Alaska.
The Mount McKinley Region, Alaska. Wn.DC: GPO, 1911.

Blazing Alaska's Trails. Caldwell, Idaho: Caxton Printers, 1953. 528 pp. Published posthumously by Burton L. Fryxell of the University of Alaska. The volume contains 27 essays by Brooks between 1914 and 1922. Brooks made 24 trips to Alaska, beginning in 1898. The volume was published in cooperation with the Arctic Institute of North America.
National Geographic, seven articles: Oct., '02 (Brooks Expedition); May, '04 (geography); Feb., '06; May 1900 (White River); Jan., '03 (Mt. McKinley); Apr., '02 (USGS surveys in Alaska); March, '07 (Alaska railways).
See also the following:
Alaska-Yukon Magazine, July, '09 (photo); Baker (summary of work); Dole; Nichols; Smith, Philip S. ("Memorial of Alfred Hulse Brooks," Geological Society of America, *Bulletin*, 1926); Sherwood (*Exploration*); Underwood (work of USGS in Alaska); Wickersham.
See the Arctic Bibliography for the technical works of Brooks, and see also the Tourville bibliography, T-680 ff.

BROOKS, ALICE M. and WILLIETTA E. KUPPLER
The Clenched Fist. Philadelphia: Dorrance, 1948. 206 pp. A narrative on life in Kenai between 1911 and 1914 from the diary of a school teacher in the government school. Russian influence still predominated. The teacher later married the US Commissioner for the village.

BROOKS, CHARLES WOLCOTT
Japanese Wrecks. San Francisco; California Academy of Sciences, 1876. 23 pp. See T-685.

BROUGH, CLAYTON S.
The Thrill of Seeing Alaska. Toledo: n.p., 1950. 52 pp.

BROUGHTON, WILLIAM ROBERT (1762-1821)
A Voyage of Discovery. London: T. Cadell and W. Davies, 1804. 394 pp. Broughton commanded the *Chatham* under Vancouver in 1795-98.

BROWER, CHARLES DeWITT (1863-1945)
Fifty Years Below Zero. New York: Dodd, Mead, 1942. 310 pp. Written by Charles Anson and Philip Farrelly from Brower's diary before they had ever met Brower. Born in New York, Brower spent 50 years in the Arctic where he entertained such notables as Amundsen, Wilkins, Bartlett, Rasmussen and Stefansson. He was at Barrow during the famous rescue reindeer drive under William Lopp and Lieutenants Jarvis and Bertholf, and he is critical of the enterprise, arguing that the animals were not needed, and were useless from the toll taken by the trek anyway. See also the following:
Alaska Sportsman, Apr., '45; Dec., '49; *Alaska-Yukon Magazine*, Dec., '08; Denison; Miller; Poor; Stuck; Wead.

BROWN, EMILY IVANOFF
See T-4534 ff.

BROWN, EVERETT S.
The Territorial Delegate to Congress and Other Essays. Ann Arbor: George Wahr, Publishes, 1950.

BROWN, J. N. E.
The Evolution of Law and Government in the Yukon Territory. Toronto: University of Toronto, 1907.

BROWN, JOHN W.
An Abridged History of Alaska. Seattle: Gateway Printing Co., 1909. 96 pp.

BROWN, MELVILLE C. (US District Judge)
Delaney (photo); Shiels (Judge, 1st Division, 1900-04); Wickersham (met Brown at Skagway).

BROWN, T. GRAHAM
Mt. Foraker, Alaska. Reprinted from *Alpine Journal* (London), 1935. First ascent, 1934.

BROWN, TOM
Oil on Ice. San Francisco: Sierra Club, 1972.

BROWNE, BELMORE (1880-1954)
The Conquest of Mount McKinley. New York: Putnam's, 1913. 381 pp. Expedition of 1906, and 1910, 1911.
The Frozen Barrier. New York: Putnam's, 1921. 267 pp.
The Quest of the Golden Valley. New York: Putnam's, 1916. 276 pp.
The White Blanket. New York: Putnam's, 1917. 317 pp.
See the Wickersham bibliography for further references, including Browne's testimony favoring the establishment of Mt. McKinley National Park.

BROWNE, RALPH
Alaska's Largest City. Juneau: Alaska Development Board, 1953. 90 pp.
Klukwan, New Mesabi. Juneau: Alaska Development Board, 91 pp.
Problems and Opportunities Facing Ketchikan. Juneau: Alaska Development Board, 1951. 27 pp.
The Cordova District. Juneau: Alaska Development Board, 1951. 81 pp.
The Sitka District. Juneau: Alaska Development Board, 1950. 81 pp.
Northwestern Alaska. Juneau: Alaska Development Board, 1949. 66 pp.

BROWNELL, DON CARLOS (1882-1952)
Alaska Weekly, July, '52 (career at Seward); *Alaska Life,* June, '47 (at Juneau, first elected Senator in 1941).

BROWNING, ROBERT J.
"Fisheries of the North Pacific," *Alaska Geographic,* I (1971): 1-121.

BRUCE, MASON B.
"National Forests in Alaska," *Journal of Forestry,* June, 1960.

BRUCE, MINER WALT
Alaska: Its History and Resources. Seattle: Lowman and Hanford, 1895. 128 pp. Descr. of steamer route, story of "Silent City" hoax. See also the following:
Alaska-Yukon Magazine, July, '07 (first reindeer Superintendent in Alaska); Gruening (in Juneau, 1889, elected Republican National Committeeman); Harrison (reindeer Superintendent at Teller, elected to Nome school board 1901); Nichols (in political activity); Rickard (with Willoughby created "Silent City" hoax); Robins (Nome, 1900); Young (had warehouse in Nome).

BRUET, EDMOND
L'Alaska. Paris: Payot, 1945. 451 pp. Descriptive. This was published after the author's works on Labrador and New Quebec.

BRUMMIT, STELLA
Looking Backward, Thinking Forward. Cincinnati: Women's Home Mission Society, 1930. 278 pp. Jubilee history of the Women's Home Mission Society of the Methodist Episcopal Church. Alaska Methodist missions at Unalaska, Unga, Nome and Seward. Jesse Lee Home, Seward.

BRYANT, CHARLOTTE KRUGER
See T-708 ff.

BRYCE, GEORGE (1844-1931)
Remarkable History of the Hudson's Bay Co. London: Low and Company, 1900. 501 pp.
The Siege and Conquest of the North Pole. London: Gibbings, 1910. 334 pp.
History of Arctic Expeditions. London: Gibbings, 1907-09.

BRYNTESON, JOHN
"Discovery of Anvil Creek," *Alaska Pioneer,* I (1913): No. 4.

BUACHE, PHILLIPPE
See T-712 ff.

BUCARELI BAY (Prince of Wales Island)
Baker (discovered 1775 by Bodega in *Sonara,* named for Antonio Maria de Bucareli y Ursua, 45th Viceroy of Mexico); Dall (Bodega, Arteaga and Maurelle re-visited in 1779); Bancroft; Wagner.

BUCHAN, LAURA and JERRY ALLEN
Hearth in the Snow. New York: Wilfred Funk, 1952. 306 pp. Narrative of life of a village school teacher, Alaska Peninsula.
Tundra Tales. Fairbanks: Soroptimists Club, 1959. Nine tales told by native children.

BUCHANAN, GEORGE
See Smith, A.M.

BUCHANAN, JAMES (1791-1868) (President, 1857-1860)
Clark (Senator Gwinn and the proposed Alaska purchase); Gruening (Gwinn interviews Russian ambassador); Tompkins (conversation with von Stoeckl about Mormons); see also Alaska purchase.

BUCHANAN, JOHN R., S. J.
Alaska Sportsman, March, '57 (founded Copper Valley School; formerly at Holy Cross); see also Copper Valley School.

BUCKLEY, JOHN LEO (b. 1920)
"Animal Population Fluctuations in Alaska," *Transactions,* North American Wildlife Conference, March 1954.
Wildlife in the Economy of Alaska. College: University of Alaska, 1955. 44 pp.
Research and Reports, with Wilbur L. Libby. Ladd Air Force Base, Arctic Aeromedical Laboratory, 1957. 105 pp. Terrestial bioenvironments and faunal population, as related to survival in air crashes.
Distribution of Alaska Plant and Animal Life. Ladd Air Force Base, Arctic Aeromedical Laboratory, 1959. 43 pp.

BUCKNER, ADELE
"Notes of an Alaska Vagabond," *Alaska Life,* December, 1941.

BUCKNER, SIMON BOLIVAR, Jr. (US Army officer) (d. 1945)
"Cannery That Wasn't There: Camouflaged Airfields Guard Dutch Harbor," *Scholastic* (Dayton), April, 1943. See the following:
Alaska Life, December, 1941 (photos); March, '42 June, '44; June, '45; *Alaska Sportsman,* Aug., '45 (killed in action on Okinawa); Aug., '49 (buried at Frankfort, Ky.); Denison; Potter; see also Garfield.

BUDDINGTON, ARTHUR F.
Geology and Mineral Deposits of Southeastern Alaska, with Theodore Chapin. USGS Bulletin 800, 1929.
Some Eocene Volcanoes, with J.D. Fairchild. Reprinted from American Journal of Science, June, 1932.
See also Fuller in Bibliography.

BUEL, ARTHUR V. (v. 1878)
See Downs. Buel was a cartoonist in the Dawson district.

BUFFALO; see Bison.

BUFFUM, GEORGE TOWER (b. 1846)
Smith of Bear City. New York: Grafton Press, 1906. 248 pp. "Soapy" Smith and other sketches.

BUGBEE, WILLIS NEWTON
Echoes from the North. Syracuse: W.N. Bugbee Co., 1946. 168 pp. Eskimo legends.

BULDAKOV, MIKHAIL MATVYEVICH
Bancroft (director of Russian-American Co.); Chevigny (Chairman of Board); Dall (brig named for him built at Ross colony in 1819); Hulley (brother-in-law of Shelhikov).

BULIARD, ROGER P.
Inuk "Au dos de la Terre." English translation with some re-arrangement published at New York: Farrar, Straus and Young, 1951. 322 pp. Buliard's life as a priest among Eskimos of Victoria and the Coppermine region, Mackenzie District from 1934; sociological.
My Eskimos. New York: Farrar, Straus and Young, 1956. Juvenile.

BULKLEY, CHARLES S. (US Army officer; Engineer in chief, Western Union Overland Telegraph Expedition)
"Journal of the US-Russian Telegraph Expedition, 1865-67," mss. in Bancroft Library, also Portland Public Library. See also the following:
Alaska Life, March, '43 (R.L. Neuberger); *Alaska Sportsman*, Apr., '44; Bancroft (came to Sitka in 1865 for project); Brooks (appointed in 1864); Dall (Bulkley appointed Dall Director of the Scientific Corps which accompanied the expedition); Hulley (former military engineer, had built telegraph lines); Sherwood (*Explorations*); Wickersham (photo).

BULLARD, R. L.
Fighting Generals. Ann Arbor: University of Michigan Press, 1944.

BUNNELL, CHARLES ERNEST (1878-1956)
Alaska-Yukon Magazine, July, '12 (Smith-Bunnell-Weber, attorneys, Valdez); *Alaska Sportsman*, Feb., '49; Aug., '49; Feb., '50; Cashen; Chase (UA first president, 1921-49); Downs; Denison; Gruening; Hulley; Potter; Tewkesbury.

BURFORD, VIRGIL
North to Danger. New York: John Day Co., 1954. 254 pp. Autobiographical.

BURG, AMOS (b. 1903)
Numerous articles accompanied by Burg's own photographs in the following issue of *National Geographic Magazine:* July, 1930 ("Yukon Trail"); August, 1931 ("Mackenzie's Trail"); September, 1942 ("Alaska: Our Northwestern Outpost"); June, 1947 ("Inside Passage"); July, 1952 (*"North Star* Cruises Alaska's Wild West"; cruise of the Alaska Native Service vessel to 45 native villages); September, 1953 ("Along the Yukon Trail"); See also Frank Morris.

BURKE, CLARA MAY HEINTZ (b. ca. 1888)
Doctor Hap, with Adele Comandini. New York: Coward-McCann, 1961. 319 pp. Biography of Dr. Grafton Burke by his wife. She arrived in Alaska in 1906, he in 1908, both as Episcopal medical missionaries. Grafton Burke had been a member of Hudson Stuck's church at Dallas. The book contains much information on interior Alaskan life.

BURKE, GRAFTON ROSS (1884-1938)
Alaska Sportsman, Sept., '54; Burke; Franck (Ft. Yukon); Stuck (Stefansson at Ft. Yukon).

BURKETT, B. F.
"Mapping 13,000 square miles of Alaska," *Aviation*, 1929.

BURNETT, FREDERICK J.
"Gateway to the land of Gold," *Sunset*, June, 1929.

BURNETT, W. R.
The Goldseekers. New York: Doubleday, 1962. 283 pp.

BURNETT, O. LAWRENCE, Jr. and W. C. HAYGOOD
Soviet View of the American Past. Glenview, Ill.: Scott, Foresman & Co., 1964.

BURNEY, JAMES
See T-738 ff.

BURNS, WALTER NOBLE
A Year with a Whaler. New York: Outing Publishing Co., 1913. 250 pp. Narrative of whaling in the Bering and Chukchi Seas.

BURPEE, LAWRENCE JOHNSTONE (1873-1946)
Among the Canadian Alps. New York: John Lane Co., 1914. 239 pp.
Articles in the *Canadian Geographical Journal:*
"Campbell of the Yukon," April, 1945. (Campbell's discovery of the Pelly-Lewes-Yukon River intersystem.
"A Road to Alaska," November, 1940.
"Samuel Hearne Finds the Coppermine," March, 1946.
See also several chapters contributed to *Canada and Its Provinces*, edited by Shortt and Doughty, 1914-17.
On the Old Athabaska Trail. Toronto: Ryerson, 1926.
The Search for the Western Sea. Toronto: Musson Book Company, 1908. 2v.
See also T-3526.

BURR, AGNES RUSH
Alaska, Our Beautiful Northland of Opportunity. Boston: The Page Company, 1919. 428 pp.

BURREL, M.
"Alaska Thawing: Alaska Autumn (Poems),"
Antioch Review, XXI (Winter, 1961-62): 468-469.

BURROUGHS, JOHN (1837-1921)
Narrative of the Expedition (E.H. Harriman, 1899); see Harriman.
Far and Near. Boston: Houghton, Mifflin, 1924. 277 pp. Vol. XII of the Writings of John Borroughs.
Higginson (notes on Borroughs).

BURTON, MARY JUNE
Alaska. Columbus, Ohio: Merrill, 1948. 32 pp.

BUSCHMANN, JOHANN KARL EDUARD
See T-750.

BUSCHMANN, PETER
Alaska Sportsman, July, '54 (est. first cannery at Petersburg, 1897, town named for him); *Alaska-Yukon Magazine*, Feb., '12; *Alaska Weekly*, Sept., '51; Couch (son, Christian, first postmaster, 1900).

BUSH PILOTS
See Aviation.

BUSH, EDWARD F.
"Robert Service: Bard of the Klondike," *Alaska Journal*, IV (Spring, 1974): 105-112.

BUSH, RICHARD JAMES
Reindeer, Dogs, and Snow-shoes. New York: Harper and Brothers, 1871. 529 pp. Siberian exploration, 1865-66-67. Member of the US-Russian Overland Telegraph Expedition, Asiatic Division.

BUSIA, JOHNNY (3. 1957)
Alaska Sportsman, July, '48; Dec., '51; Nov., '53; Jan., '58.

BUSWELL, ARTHUR STEPHEN (b. 1922)
"Role of the Cooperative Extension Service in Alaska," unpublished master's thesis, University of Wisconsin, 1959.

BUTCHER, DEVEREUX
Exploring Our National Parks. Boston: Houghton, Miffin, 1954. 288 pp.
Exploring Our National Wildlife Refuges. Boston: Houghton, Mifflin, 1963. 340 pp.

BUTLER, EVELYN I. and GEORGE ALLEN DALE
Alaska: The Land and Its People. New York: Viking Press, 1957. 159 pp. Indian and Eskimo villages as viewed by itinerant ANS employees visiting 118 schools.

BUTLER, HUGH (US Senator, Nebraska)
Gruening (opponent of statehood).

BUTLER, RALPH E.
"The Blue Cow," *Alaska Sportsman*, Apr., May, '45. Whaling.

BUTLER, Sir WILLIAM FRANCIS (1838-1910)
The Great Lone Land. London: Low, 1872. 388 pp.

Wild Northland. London: Low, 1873. 358 pp. Both of these popular titles were reprinted several times, the latter as late as 1924.

BUTROVICH, JOHN, Jr. (b. 1910)
Alaska Life, June, '47 (Fairbanks insurance man; candidate for Governor, 1958, long legislative career); Tewkesbury (Territorial senator from 1945).

BUTSINSKII, P.
Zaselenie Sibiri. (Settlement in Siberia) Kharkov, 1889.

BUTTS, ROSE CURTICE
"Prisoners from Alaska," *Alaska Sportsman*, May, '48. This article by a teacher at the Eklutna native school is about the Attu children captured by Japanese in 1942.

BUYNITZKY, STEPHEN NESTOR
Land Rights of Natives in Alaska. Trans. of memo to Wm. Seward, 1867. In Alaska State Historical Museum.

BUZANSKI, P. M.
"Alaska, and Nineteenth Century American Diplomacy." *Journal of the West*, VI (July, 1967); 451-467.

BYERS, ARCHIE M.
The Timber Industry. Reprinted from Journal of Forestry, June, 1960.

BYRNES, MICHAEL
Brooks (reached Lake Atlin from Cassiar in 1867, via the Stikine or Taku Valley); Dall (employed by the Overland Telegraph Expedition to explore northern British Columbia routes); Higginson (reached Taku Arm of Tagish Lake); Raymond (explored Yukon River headwaters).

C

CAAMANO, JACINTO (often spelled Camano)
Account of a Voyage, 1790-91. Mss. in the Archivo General de la Nacion, Mexico City. See Wagner. Caamano apparently left San Blas in the company of Quimper. On a 1792 voyage Caamano explored the area just north of Dixon entrance, including Bucareli Bay and the entrance to Clarence Strait. Vancouver obtained a copy of Caamano's chart, and preserved his names.
"The Journal of Jacinto Caamano," trans. Harold Grenfell, ed. H.R. Wagner and W.A. Newcombe, *British Columbia Historical Quarterly*, July and October, 1938.
See also the following:
Bancroft (1792 voyage, and map); Dall; Wagner. The 1792 voyage of Caamano was the last of the Spanish voyages.

"CABIN FEVER"
Alaska Sportsman, June, '39 (radio helps); Dec., '56 (Dawson); Sharples (Skilak Lake).

CABRILLO, JUAN RODRIGUEZ (d. 1543)
Greenhow (first voyage north along Pacific coast, reached 38°N. Lat.); Dall; Wagner (full account).

CADE, TOM J.
"Ecology of the Peregrine and Gurfalcon Populations in Alaska," University of California, *Publications in Zoology*, 63 (1960): 151-289.

CADELL, HENRY MOUBRAY (1869-1934)
"The Klondike and Yukon Goldfields," *Scottish Geographical Magazine*, July, 1914. Reprinted in the Smithsonian Institution, Annual Report, 1914.

CADWALLADER, CHARLES LEE
See T-764.

CADZOW, DONALD A.
Native Copper Objects of the Copper Eskimos. New York: Museum of American Indians, 1920.

CAHLANE, VICTOR H.
A Biological Survey of Katmai National Monument. Wn.DC: GPO, 1959. 246 pp. Smithsonian Institution.

CAIRNES, DeLORME DONALDSON (1879-1917)
The Yukon-Alaska International Boundary. Ottawa: Gov't. Printing Bureau, 1914. 161 pp. Porcupine-Yukon system.

CAIRNES, RALPII
"Hazards of Climbing Mount McKinley," *Overland Monthly*, 1913.

CALASANZ, Sister MARIE JOSEPH (or CALA-SANCTIUN) (nee DERUYTER)
The Voice of Alaska. Lachine, Quebec: Sisters of St. Anne, 1935. 340 pp. Holy Cross mission from 1885 (founding) to 1905.

CALDWELL, ELSIE (b. 1882)
Alaska Trail Dogs. New York: R.R. Smith, 1945. 150 pp.

CALDWELL, J. B.
Introducing Alaska. New York: Putnam's Sons, 1947. 202 pp.
What to Expect in Alaska. Reprinted from *Alaska Sportsman*, February to July, 1945.
"Tackle Busters along the Highway," *Alaska Sportsman*, April, 1946.

CALE, THOMAS (b. ca. 1854)
Alaska-Yukon Magazine, March, '07 (photo); Apr., '08 (ten years of prospecting before going to Washington); Hulley (urged territorial government); Nichols; Shiels (served March 1907 to March 1909, 60th Congress); Underwood.

CALICO BLUFF
Chase (just above mouth of Seventy-mile River on the Yukon); Davis (strangely stratified rock bluff); Franck (between Yukon Crossing and Dawson); Stuck (ten miles below Eagle).

CALIFORNIA STATE DIVISION OF BEACHES AND PARKS
Fort Ross Historical Monument. Sacramento: State Publishing Office, 1956. 8 pp. Subsequent printings and revisions.

CALL, S. J.
Alaska-Yukon Magazine, July, '07 (on cutter *Bear*); Call accompanied Jarvis to Barrow with the reindeer drive in 1908; he was a surgeon.

CALLAHAN, JAMES MORTON (b. 1864)
The Alaska Purchase and Americo-Canadian Relations. Morgantown, W. Va.: W. Va. University Studies in American History, 1908. 44 pp.
American Relations in the Pacific, 1784-1900. Baltimore: Johns-Hopkins Press, 1901. 177 pp.
Russo-American Relations during the American Civil War. Morgantown, W. Va.: W. Va. University Studies in American History, 1908. 18 pp.

CALVIN, JACK
"Nakwasina Goes North," *National Geographic*, July, 1933. See also T-782 ff, and Ricketts, Edward.

CAMERON, AGNES DEAN (1863-1912)
The New North. New York: Appleton, 1910. 398 pp.

CAMERON, CHARLOTTE
A Cheechako in Alaska and Yukon. London: Unwin, 1920. 291 pp. Survey of Alaska in 1919.

CAMP, FRANK BERNARD (b. 1882)
Alaska Nuggets. Anchorage: Alaska Publishing Company, 1921. 45 pp. Poetry.

CAMP ROBBERS; see Canada Jay.

CAMPBELL, ARCHIBALD (b. 1787)
A Voyage Round the World, 1806-1812. New York: Broderick and Ritter, 1819. 219 pp. An account of an illiterate seaman shipwrecked on Sanak Island (between Unalaska and the Shumagins) while sailing with O'Cain on the *Eclipse*. O'Cain was the first American sea captain to induce Baranov to a trading arrangement. This work went through at least four editions.
The Restless Voyage. London: Harrap, 1949. 280 pp. A re-editing with additional documents.

CAMPBELL, C. S.
"The Anglo-American Crisis in the Bering Sea," *Mississippi Valley Historical Review*, XLVIII (1961): 393-414. 1890.

CAMPBELL, JOHN
"The Origin of the Haidaho of the Queen Charlotte Islands," *Transactions*, Royal Society of Canada, 1897.

CAMPBELL, JOHN N.
"The Tuktu Complex of Anaktuvuk Pass," *Anthropological Papers*, University of Alaska, 1961.

CAMPBELL, MARJORIE WILKINS
The Northwest Company. New York: St. Martin's Press, 1957. 295 pp.

CAMPBELL, ROBERT (1808-1894)
The Discovery and Exploration of the Youcon (Pelly) River. Winnipeg: Manitoba Free Press, 1885. 18 pp. Campbell was chief factor with the Hudson's Bay Company. He here briefly summarizes his exploratory work, 1838-1850, including discovery of the upper Yukon.
Two Journals of Robert Campbell, 1808-51 and 1850-53. Seattle: Shorey Book Store, 1958. Reprinted from typed copies.
See also the following:
Brooks (explored Pelly River, 1840 and 1842; Hudson's Bay Company's systematic explorations); Cameron (resume of Campbell's work); Dall; Higginson; Hulley (reached upper Stikine, 1838); Ogilvie (named Pelly and Lewes Rivers); Scidmore (est. post at Dease Lake); Stuck; Tompkins; Wickersham; Whymper.

CAMPBELL, THOMAS
The Pleasure of Hope. Reprint from Complete Poetical Works, Oxford University Press, 1907. In his speech to Congress on Alaska on April 9, 1867, Charles Sumner quoted from this poem of Campbell's which deals with exploration of the Arctic.

CAMPBELL, WILLIAM
Arctic Patrols. Milwaukee: Bruce Publications, 1936. 335 pp. Royal Canadian Mounted Police.

CAMSELL, CHARLES and M. W. MAXWELL
See T-800.

CANADA
See various Canadian subjects, e.g. Klondike, Yukon, Dawson, Mackenzie River, British Columbia, Alaska Highway, Robert Service, etc. See also the following:
Bureau of Statistics. *Trade of Canada with Asia.* Ottawa: King's Printer, 1933.
Department of Interior. *Report*, provisional boundary between Canada and Alaska, 1901.
Department of Interior. *Annual Report*, from 1897. Contains reports of Commissioner of the Yukon Territory and the Gold Commissioner.
Department of Interior. *The Yukon Territory.* Ottawa: GPB, 1907. 140 pp.
Department of Northern Affairs and National Resources. *Annual Report*, from 1954.
Department of Northern Affairs and National Resources, *Canadian Eskimo Art.* Ottawa: Queen's Printer, 1960. 42 pp.
Geological Survey. *Excursions in Northern B.C.,* Ottawa: GPB, 1913. 179 pp.
Northwest Mounted Police. *Reports*, from 1896. The reports from 1896 to 1899 contain much information on the Klondike.
Northwest Territories and Yukon Services. *Yukon Territory.* Ottawa, 1947.
Parliament, Senate. Special Committee on Sealing and Fisheries. *Proceedings.* Ottawa: King's Printer, 1934. 7v.
Royal Commission on Possibilities of Reindeer and Muskox Industries in the Arctic and Sub-arctic Regions. *Report.* Ottawa: King's Printer, 1922. 99 pp.
Travel Bureau. *Alaska Highway.* Ottawa, 1952.
The above listing is merely suggestive. For a survey of manuscript and bibliographical sources for

Canadian studies, particularly in relation to Alaska, see the Arctic Bibliography; see also Tourville under Canada.

CANADA
Encyclopaedia of Canada; see Encyclopaedia Candiana.

CANADA
See periodical indexes, including the *Alaska Sportsman*, and the historical journals, especially the *Canadian Historical Quarterly* and the *British Columbia Historical Quarterly.*

CANADA JAYS (Camp Robbers)
Alaska Sportsman, Jan., '52 (photo); June, '52; Sept., '52; Nov., '52 (magpie is similar); May, '54; Oct., '55; *Alaska-Yukon Magazine*, Dec., '07; Davis (unpalatable); James (Indian superstitions); Stuck (on Yanert).

CANADIAN ARCTIC EXPEDITION (1913-1916)
Anderson, Randolph (chief of the southern party); Canadian Arctic Expedition, *Report* (14v., King's Printer, 1919-46); Stefansson (*The Friendly Arctic*, expedition narrative); Stefansson (*Scientific American*, 1913).

CANADIAN BANK OF COMMERCE
Alaska Sportsman, June, 1954 (photo of staff at Dawson, 1899); Robert Service came to the Arctic working for this bank.

CANADIAN BOARD OF GEOGRAPHIC NAMES
Gazetteer of Canada-British Columbia. Ottawa: King's Printer, 1953. Prepared by the BC Department of Lands and Forests.
Gazetteer of Canada-Northwest Territories and the Yukon. (Provisional) Ottawa: Queen's Printer, 1959.

CANADIAN MINING LAWS
See material on the Klondike. See also Winslow (daily royalty replaced registration fee [$15], renewable at $100 per year; miners paid an average customs duty of 25% on supplies).

CANADIAN NATIONAL RAILWAYS
The Canadian Rockies and the Pacific Coast. Montreal, 1935.

CANADIAN NATIONAL STEAMSHIP COMPANY
The Midnight Sun. Montreal, 1930.

CANADIAN PACIFIC RAILWAY COMPANY
Roads to Adventure. n.p., 1932.

CANADIAN NORTHWEST MOUNTED POLICE
See Royal Canadian Mounted Police.

CANADIAN-US RELATIONS
See Alaska Boundary, and similar references; see also Alaska Diplomacy. See also the following:
Becker (Canadian government collected a 2-1/2% royalty on gold shipped from the Yukon); Davis (opposed White Pass railway construction, customs collection); Hawthorne (Gold Commissioner's

office); Ogilvie (free navigation of St. Lawrence ex-
changed for same of Stikine, Porcupine and Yukon);
Winslow (American complaints in the Klondike).

CANADA'S ALASKAN DISMEMBERMENT
Anonymous. Niagara-on-the-Lake: C. Thonger,
1904. 76 pp. Analytical examination of the fallacies
underlying the Tribunal award.

CANDLE (Seward Peninsula)
Alaska-Yukon Magazine, Apr., '07 (photo); Baker
(named for Candle Creek); Couch (post office from
1902); Colby (settled in 1901, named by miners for
scrubby local bush used by Eskimos for lighting);
Harrison; Hines (on the stampede); Pilgrim (204
miles from Nome by trail, turning point in All-
Alaska Sweepstakes).
This village should not be confused with another
of the same name, often shortened from Candle
Landing, south of McGrath in the Kuskokwim
valley. There is also a village of Candle Light, south
of Candle, on the Seward Peninsula.

CANDLEFISH
Arctander (on method of obtaining the oil); Bancroft (full descr., spelled eulachon [often spelled
ookakan]); Collis (food for whales); Davis (traded
by Chilkoots to interior Indians); Dufresne ("hooli-
gan"); Henderson; Jenkins; Petrof (found only
around Stikine).

CANE, CLAUDE RICHARD JOHN (b. 1859)
Summer and Fall in Western Alaska. London: H.
Cox, 1903. 191 pp. Account of Cook Inlet big game
hunt.

CANHAM, T. H.
Alaska-Yukon Magazine, Sept., '08 (26 years at
Nuklukayet, Rampart, Ft. McPherson, Ft. Selkirk);
Middleton (in *Sunday Magazine*, 1898); Stuck (at
Nuklukayet 1888-92); Canham was Archdeacon of
Selkirk.

CANNIBALISM
Arctander; Chase (natives at Kotlik ate child).

CANNING, GEORGE
See Alaska Diplomacy. See also Stapleton, A.G.
(life from 1822-27 [London: Longmans, 1831], 3v.,
includes treaty of 1825); Tompkins. See Bagot.

CANNING, STRATFORD
See Alaska Diplomacy, and the following:
Stuck (he and Nesselrode "ruled a line across a
map"); Tompkins.

CANOL OIL PROJECT
Alaska Sportsman, July, '44; March, '45 (com-
pleted); June, '45 (abandoned); March, '46; *Alaska
Life*, May, '44; Denison; Finnie; Griffin; Hixon
(*Canol* [Philadelphia: Dorrance, 1946]); Myers
(*Provincial News*, Edmonton, 1944); Sundborg. See
also *Canol: the Sub-arctic Pipeline and Refinery
Project*, San Francisco: privately printed (Bechtel-
Price-Callahan?), 1945. 220 pp. This project was
begun in 1942.

CANTWELL, GEORGE G.
The Klondike: A Souvenir. San Francisco: Rufus
Black, 1901.

CANTWELL, JOHN C. (US Revenue Cutter
Service officer)
*A Narrative Account of the Exploration of the
Kowak River*. Reprinted from the Report of the
cruise of the *Corwin*, 1884. Cantwell navigated the
Kobuk (here called Kowak) to Big Fish Lake in 1884
in a small boat. This report is the first description of
the area, and contains information on native life.
See the 1884 report of the *Corwin* for other re-
ports; see also Charles Townshend. See as well
report of the US Revenue Steamer *Nunivak* on the
Yukon River station, 1899-1901, Senate Document
No. 155, US Congress, 58th Congress, 2nd Session,
which contains social and economic information. See
also the following:
Baker (summary of work); Brooks (first up the
Kobuk); Harrison; Underwood.

CANYON CITY
Baker (named by prospectors); Becker (photo,
nine miles from Dyea); Couch (post office May to
November, 1898). Canyon City is mentioned in
many accounts of travel to the Klondike.

CAPPS, STEPHEN REID (1881-1949)
A Game Country without Rival. Reprinted from
National Geographic, January, 1917. On the pro-
posed Mount McKinley National Park. See the Arctic
Bibliography for Capps' numerous geologic studies.

CAPTAIN'S BAY
Baker (named in 1790 for Capt-Lieutenant
Mikhail Levashev by Sarichev; Levashev wintered
1768-69 at the head of the bay [southern arm of Unalaska Island] and named it St. Paul harbor after his
vessel); Bancroft (Zaikov explored bay in 1783,
Ledyard here in 1778, Billings' chief accomplishment
was through survey of this bay); Dall (thermal
spring [sulphur] here booms like cannon); Kitchener
(Unalaska [village] is on Iliuliuk Bay which leads
into Captain's Bay).

CARCROSS, Y. T.
Alaska Sportsman, Apr., '52; Nov., '53; Nov., '55
(photo); Becker (Carmacks married here); Cameron
(interview of Kate Carmack); Colby (named in
1904, contraction of Caribou Crossing, at north end
of Lake Bennett); Davis (between Lakes Bennett and
Tagish); Franck; Higginson (actual crossing is
between Lakes Bennett and Nares); Underwood;
Schwatka; Whiting (photo).

CARIBOO DISTRICT, B. C.
Tompkins (miners from Cariboo district worked
way up Fraser River and over the divide into the
Cassiar district; see also Hulley (Cariboo stampede
lasted 1859-65, many of the miners coming from
California via the Fraser rush).

CARIBOU
See the Arctic Bibliography. See also the follow-
ing:
Alaska Sportsman index; Allen, Joel ("New Cari-
bou from Kenai, in *Bulletin*, American Museum of
Natural History [1901]); Banfield ("Caribou Crisis,"
Beaver, Spring, 1956); Bee and Hall; Crisler;
Davis; Denison; Dufresne (last great migration
Circle-Eagle, 1926); Leopold and Darling; Ogilvie;
Savage; Seton, Ernest (*The Arctic Prairies*, Scrib-
ners, 1911 [415 pp.]); Underwood (graceful, stupid).

CARLISLE INDIAN SCHOOL (Pennsylvania)
Henderson (native girls from Unalaska Methodist Mission).

CARLSON, GERALD F.
Two on the Rocks. New York: David McKay, 1967. American school teacher on Little Diomede.

CARLSON, LELAND H.
"Nome: Mining Camp to Civilized Community," *Pacific Northwest Quarterly*, July, 1947.
An Alaskan Gold Mine. Evanston: Northwestern University Press, 1951. 178 pp. The Story of No. 9 above. Carlson was a professor of history at Northwestern and gathered information on this mine from Jafet Lindeberg, Carl Lomen and Antonio Polet.
"The Discovery of Gold at Nome," *Pacific Historical Review*, September, 1946.
"The First Mining Season at Nome, 1899," *Pacific Historical Review*, May, 1947.
"The Scandinavians and the Great Alaskan Gold Rush," *Yearbook*, Swedish American Historical Society, 1948.

CARLSON, PHYLLIS D.
"Alaska's First Census," *Alaska Journal*, I (Winter, 1971).

CARLSON, WILLIAM S. (US Air Force officer, President, University of Toledo)
Lifelines Through the Arctic. New York: Duell, Sloan and Pearce, 1962. 271 pp. Description of the opening of Arctic air routes during WW II. Laborator, Greenland, Edmonton-Fairbanks-Nome-Siberia, Aleutians, DEW, BMEWS, T-3.

CARMACK, GEORGE WASHINGTON (1860-1922)
My Experiences in the Yukon. Seattle: The Trade Printery, 1933. Privately printed by Marguerite Carmack.
"Talk Given at Inspiration Point," see Whiting.
"Thoughts, Tagish Lake, Christmas Eve, 1888," in Camp Hades, No. 23, Arctic Brotherhood, Fred Crewe.
See also the following:
Alaska Lfe, March, '43 ("Squaw Kate," who actually made the discovery of gold); *Alaska Sportsman*, Feb., '45; May, '51 (had planned coal mine before 1896); July, '51 (descr.); Atwood (*Gold Book*, entry shows Marguerite Carmack); Bankston; Becker (full photo); Brooks (life with Indians); Cameron; Clark; Cavis; Franck (fight for estate); Hulley; Ogilvie; Rickard; Tompkins; Whiting; Wickersham; Winslow. See also Klondike; Carmack, Kate.

CARMACK, KATE (ca. 1870-1920)
Alaska Life, March, '43; Becker (descr., lived near Carcross, where she is buried); Cameron (divorced by Carmack, she had one daughter).

CARMACKS
Alaska Sportsman, Nov. '53 (on Yukon 100 miles below Whitehorse); Sept., '54 (where the Whitehorse-Mayo Highway crosses the Yukon); George Carmack may have had a trading post near this location.

CARPE, ALLEN (d. 1932)
"The Ascent of Mount Bona," *American Alpine Journal*, 1931.
"The Mount Logan Adventure," *American Alpine Journal*, 1933.

CARPENTER, EDMUND SNOW
"Changes in the Sedna Myth among the Aivilik," *Anthropological Papers*, University of Alaska, May, 1955.

CARPENTER, FRANCES (b. 1890)
Canada and Her Northern Neighbors. New York: American Book Company, 1953. 438 pp.

CARPENTER, FRANK GEORGE (1855-1924)
Alaska: Our Northern Wonderland. Garden City: Doubleday, 1923. 319 pp.
Carpenter's Geographical Readers: North America. New York: American Book Company, 1910. 410 pp.

CARPENTER, HERMAN
Three Years in Alaska. Philadelphia: Howard, 1901. 105 pp.

CARRIGHAR, SALLY
Icebound Summer. New York: Alfred A. Knopf, 1953. 262 pp. Study of northern Alaska wildlife.
Moonlight at Midday. New York: Alfred A. Knopf, 1958. 392 pp. Sociological study of acculturation.
Wild Voice of the North. Garden City: Doubleday, 1959. 191 pp.
Five articles in *Sat. Eve. Post:*
"Nome: Cities of North America," January, 1951.
"Unalakleet," January, 1952.
"The Gold Rush Isn't Over Yet," January, 1954.
"The Party is Over for the Ekimos," February, 1954.
"I Tried to Outwit the Arctic," October, 1955.

CARRRINGTON, HUGH
Life of Captain Cook. London: Sedgwick and Jackson, 1939. 309 pp.

CARROLL, JAMES
Alaska Life, Jan., '46 (commanded the *Idaho* and *Ancon*, 1885, 1886); Collis (commanded the *Queen* in 1890 and took the *Idaho* to Muir Glacier in 1883); Gruening (selected "delegate to Congress"); Nichols; Scidmore; Young.

CARROLL, JAMES A. (1890-1963)
The First Ten Years in Alaska. New York: Exposition, 1957.

CARROTHERS, WILLIAM ALEXANDER
See T-854.

CARRUTHERS, JOSEPH
Captain James Cook, One Hundred and Fifty Years After. New York: Dutton, 1930.

CARSTENSEN, VERNON
The Public Lands. Madison: University of Wisconsin Press, 1968. 548 pp. Editor. Studies in the History of the Public Domain.

CARTER, CHARLES W. (1870-1961)
"Discovery of Juneau," *Alaska Life*, January, 1944. Carter was a Mayor of Juneau.

CARTER, CLARA M.
See Stuck; Clara Carter, a pioneer nurse, was at Allakaket, 1907-1912, and Skagway, 1902-1907. There is a photo in Stuck.

CARTER, JAMES C.
See T-857.

CARTER, NICHOLAS
See John Russell Coryell.

CARTER, THOMAS H.
The Laws of Alaska. Chicago: Callaghan & Co., 1900. 533 pp. A compilation of federal law for Alaska as of 1900, including the penal code, criminal procedure code, civil code, cession treaty, and the various acts, e.g., homestead, township, etc.

CASE, ROBERT ORMOND (b. 1895)
The Yukon Drive. Garden City: Doubleday, 1930. 359 pp.
West of Barter River. Garden City: Doubleday, 1941. 272 pp.

CASHEN, WILLIAM R.
Farthest North College President. Fairbanks: University of Alaska Press, 1972. Biography of Charles E. Bunnell, with information on the early history of the University of Alaska.

CASSIAR DISTRICT (B.C.)
Alaska Sportsman, May, '43; Sept., '47 (Fraser River strike in 1858, Cassiar in 1872, Moore's freight line, Wrangell to Glenora, 1873); Feb., '53 (Cassiar Asbestos Corporation); June, '53; May, '53 (photos); Andrews (gold discovered 1872 by McCullough and Thibert); Brooks; Chase (on freighting, and name [corruption of native "Casca"]); Dole (best yield 1874-1887); Clark (strike by Choquette on Stikine 1861); Morris (discovered by Thibert and companion in 1872, 8-1200 miners in 1870's); Scidmore (Choquette and Carpenter, 1861, Dease Lake accessible from sea); Tompkins (Cassiar claims centered on Dease Lake); Young (gold found at "Buck's Bar" on the Stikine, 1873-74 stampede).

CASSIAR BAR (in the Yukon River)
Alaska Sportsman, Sept., '54 (photo); Brooks (discovered in 1884 by Boswell, Franklin and Madison, first solid gold production on the Yukon); Cameron (near the Teslin River); Hulley; Chase (40 miles below Hootalinqua River); researchers should not confuse the Cassiar Bar, Yukon Territory, with the Cassiar District, northern British Columbia.

CASSIN, JOHN
See T-864.

CASTLE, N. H.
"A Short History of Council and Cheenik," *Alaska Pioneer*, June, 1912. Mr. Castle was an editor of the *Council City News*.
"Treatise on Searches and Seizures under Prohibition Laws in Force in Alaska," *Juneau Empire Printing*, January, 1922.

CASWELL, JOHN EDWARDS (b. 1913)
Arctic Frontiers. Norman: University of Oklahoma Press, 1956. 232 pp. Explorations in the Far North: DeHaven, Kane, Hayes, Hall, Schwatka, Howgate, Greely, Ray, Peary, Cook, and the *Jeannette*.
American Arctic Expeditions: Narratives, 1850-1909. Stanford: Stanford University Press, 1950. 173 pp.
See also the Arctic Bibliography, and *The Utilization of the Scientific Reports of US Arctic Expeditions, 1850-1909.* Stanford: Stanford University Press, 1951. 304 pp.

CATHERINE II, Empress of Russia, 1762-1796
See Pares' *A History of Russia*, and Riasanovsky's *History of Russia;* see also Alaskan Diplomacy, and material on the Russian period of Alaska. See also the following:
Bancroft; Chevigny; Hulley; Petrof; Tompkins.

CATHOLIC ENCYCLOPAEDIA
Alaska, a history of the Russian and later missions.

CATHOLIC MISSIONS IN ALASKA
Alaska Catholic, an intermittent periodical edited by A.B. Cain at Juneau; see *Alaska Life*, May, 1942. See also *Alaska Sportsman*, July, '43 (Hooper Bay); March, '57 (transfer of Holy Cross school to Copper Center); see also the Archives of the Prefecture Apostolic of Alaska at the Crosby Library, Gonzaga University, Spokane, Washington. See also the following:
Barnum (life of Seghers); Bosco; Calasanz; *Catholic Directory* (annual, New York: Alaska was created a Prefecture Apostolic in 1894, made a vicariate in 1916. The Diocese of Juneau was created in 1951, of Fairbanks in 1962, and of Anchorage in 1966.); Champagne; Crimont; Clut; DeBaets; Devine; Harrison; *Jesuit Missions* (monthly); Jette; Judge; Llorente; Morice; O'Connor; *Oregon Jesuit* (monthly, Portland); St. Anne's Academy; Santos; Savage; Seghers; Ursuline of Alaska; Wickersham.

CATHOLIC PRAYERS AND HYMNS
In the Tinneh Language. Koserefski, Indian Boys' Press, Holy Cross Mission, 1897. 22 pp. See also T-2352, 2259, 2260, 2790, 3830.

CATTO, WILLIAM
The Yukon Administration. Dawson: King Street Job Office, 1902.

CAUGHEY, JOHN WALTON
Hubert Howe Bancroft: Historian of the West. Los Angeles: University of California Press, 1946. 422 pp.
History of the Pacific Coast of North America. Lancaster: Lancaster Press, 1933. 406 pp. Also New York: Prentice-Hall, 1938.
"Hubert Howe Bancroft," *American Historical Review*, April, 1945.
"Problems of the Local Historian," *Pacific Historical Review*, March, 1943.

CAVAGNOL, JOSEPH J.
Postmarked Alaska. Holton, Kansas: The Gossip Printery, 1957. 107 pp. Saga of the Early Alaska Mails. Illus.

CAVANA, VIOLET VIRGINIA (b. 1874)
Alaska Bsketry. Portland: The Beaver Club, 1917. 50 pp.

CAWSTON, VEE
Matuk the Eskimo Boy. New York: Lantern Press, 1965.

CAXTON PRINTERS
"Idaho Firm Upholds Western Publishing," *Los Angeles Times*, October, 1951. Caxton has been publishing books on western themes, including history, since 1923.

CEASE, RONALD C. and JEROME R. SAROFF
The Metropolitan Experiment in Alaska. New York: Praeger, 1968. A Study of Borough Government.

CENOTAPH ISLAND (in Lituya Bay)
Alaska Sportsman, Feb., '38 (photo); Baker (named by LaPerouse, 1786); Bancroft (named L'Isle du Cenotaphe [a sepulcral monument erected in memory of a deceased person whose body is elsewhere]); Colby (cross on island); *National Geographic*, March, '35 (fox farm).

CENSUS OF ALASKA (Russian)
See the Wickersham Bibliography; see also Svetlana Fedorova, *The Population of Russian America*. For census data since 1867 see US, Bureau of the Census.

CENSUS OF ALASKA (United States)
See US, Department of Commerce, Bureau of the Census.
1880 . . . 33,426 (see Gruening)
1890 . . . 32,052 (see Carlson, P.D,)
1900 . . . 63,592
1910 . . . 64,356
1920 . . . 55,036
1930 . . . 59,278
1940 . . . 72,524
1950 . . .128,643
1960 . . .226,167
1970 . . .302,553

CHAFFEE, ALLEN
Sitka, the Snow Baby. Springfield, Mass.: McLaughlin, 1934. 115 pp. Juvenile.

CHAFFIN, YULE M.
Koniag to King Crab. Kodiak: Chaffin, Inc., 1967. 247 pp.

CHALMERS, J. W.
Fur Trade Governor. Edmonton: Institute of Applied Art, 1960. 190 pp. George Simpson, 1820-1860.

CHAMBERLIN, JO HUBBARD
"Klondike Stampede," *Reader's Digest,*" April, 1940.

CHAMBERLIN, JOSEPH C.
See US Department of Agriculture.

CHAMBERLIN, RALPH VARY and W. IVIE
See T-882.

CHAMBERS, ERNEST JOHN
The Royal North-west Mounted Police. Montreal: Mortimer Press, 1906.
The Unexplored West. Ottawa: Department of Interior, 1914. 361 pp.

CHAMISSO, ADELBERT von (1781-1838)
Descriptions of Kamchatka, etc. Vol. 3 of Kotzebue's *Puteshestvie v IUzhny Okean i v Beringov.* London: 1821.
A Sojourn at San Francisco Bay, 1816. San Francisco: Grabhorn Press, 1936.
See also the Arctic Bibliography (botanical works), and T-884 ff.

CHANCE, NORMAN A.
The Eskimo of North Alaska. New York: Holt, 1967. 107 pp.

CHANDALAR (River, village, Indians)
Alaska Sportsman, Apr., '57 (lake photo); *Alaska-Yukon Magazine*, March, '07 (new strike); Baker (two name derivations: "gens de Large" and John Chandlar, Hudson's Bay Co. factor); Castner (river mouth 25 miles below Fort Yukon); Colby; Couch (post office intermittent 1908-44); Dall (among the Indians here are Gens de Large, Gens de Rat, Gens de Foux, and Gens de Bois); Hulley (small stampede to river in 1906); Haywood (Gens de Rat, Gens des Foux, Gens de Bois are all locally called Loucheux); Stuck (voyageurs called the nomadic Indians "gens de large" because they moved about [over a large area of land], the river they frequented becoming river of the "gens de large," anglicized as Chandalar; Baker erred in accepting the notion that it was named for a "John Chandlar" of Hudson's Bay Company); Wickersham (no John Chandlar was ever employed by Hudson's Bay Company; name is anglicization of "Gens de Large.").

CHANDLER, EDNA WALKER and BARRETT WILLOUGHBY
Pioneer of Alaska. Boston: Ginn & Co., 1959. 179 pp. Story of Carl Ben Eielson.

CHAMPAGNE, JOSEPH ETIENNE
"First Attempts at the Evangelization of Alaska," *Etudes Oblate*, 1943. Brief history of the O.M.I. mission activity in Alaska, including expedition of Bishop Clut and Fr. Lecorre, 1872-73, from Fort McPherson to Fort Yukon and Saint Michael, but beginning with 1862.

CHAPIN, THEODORE SHEFFIELD (b. 1876)
The Nelchina-Susitna Region. Wn.DC: GPO, 1914. USGS. See Brooks' Mineral Resources for additional reports.

CHAPLIN, PETER
Journal and Log Book of Bering's First Expedition. Unpublished in its entirety. See Golder. Berkh edited the journal in his work on the Aleutian Islands.

CHAPMAN, CHARLES E.
"Catalogue of Materials in the Archivo General de las Indias," Berkeley, 1919.

CHAPMAN, JOHN WRIGHT (1858-1939)
A Camp on the Yukon. New York: Idlewild Press, 1948. 214 pp. Episcopal missionary who lived among the Eskimos at Anvik from 1887 to 1930. See also the Arctic Bibliography.

CHAPMAN, MAY SEELY
"The Animistic Beliefs of the Ten'a of the Lower Yukon," Hartford: Church Missions Publishing Co., 1939. 15 pp.
"Village Life at Anvik 50 Years Ago," *The Alaska Churchman*, May, 1946.

CHAPMAN, ROBERT MILLS (b. 1918)
"Interior Highlands of Eastern Alaska," in Howell Williams. See also the Arctic Bibliography.

CHAPPLE, JOE MITCHELL
"Discovering Alaska with President Harding," *McClure's Magazine*, October, 1923.

CHARD, CHESTER S.
"New World Migration Routes," *Anthropological Papers*, University of Alaska, December, 1958.
"Additions to Materials from Lake El'Gytkhyn, Chukchi Peninsula," *Anthropological Papers*, University of Alaska, December, 1960.
"Sternberg's Materials on the Sexual Life of the Gilyak," *Anthropological Papers*, University of Alaska, 1961. This is a translation of Lev Shternberg's "The Social Organization of the Gilyak" of 1933. The Gilyak inhabited the Amur River Region, including Sakhalin Island.

CHARLES, SIDNEY DEAN (1870-1959)
"Cordova," in *Alaska-Yukon Magazine*, December, 1910.
"The Conquering of the Copper River: How the 'Impossible' Railroad came to be Driven into the Alaskan Wilderness," *Alaska-Yukon Magazine*, December, 1910.
"History of Alaska's Third Legislature and Legislators," *Alaska Monthly*, May, 1917 to November, 1918.
See also the following:
Alaska Life, January, 1942 (biographical); *Alaska Sportsman*, May, 1959. At his death in 1959 Sidney Charles was editor of the *Ketchikan Daily News*.

CHARLEY'S VILLAGE (and CHIEF CHARLEY)
Ogilvie (photo); Schwatka (on western bank of the Yukon below Belle Isle, Tadoosh Indians here); Stuck (village, just above Charley Creek [Kandik Creek], was washed away in break-up of 1914; Charley Creek and Charley River are different streams); Wickersham (Indian hanged, Charley Riv. for murder of white man).

CHASE, WILLIAM HENRY (b. 1874)
Reminiscences of Captain Billie Moore. Kansas City: Burton Publishing Company, 1947. 236 pp. With his father and brothers, Billie Moore was one of the more widely known and respected early steam captains in Alaska. He was present shortly after the discovery of gold in the Cassiar in 1872. He was for many years a trader on the Yukon.
Alaska's Mammouth Brown Bears. Kansas City: B Burton Publishing Co., 1947. 129 pp.
The Sourdough Pot. Kansas City: Burton Publishing Co., 1943. 206 pp.
Pioneers of Alaska: Trail Blazers of By-gone Days. Kansas City: Burton Publishing Co., 1951. Chase was "Grand Historian" of the Pioneers. This volume includes a list of charter Pioneer members, and a list

of current members in 1950. Chase was two terms mayor of Cordova, retiring in 1962. See Tewkesbury, and the following:
Alaska Sportsman, July, '42; July, '57; *Alaska-Yukon Magazine*, December, 1910.

CHEECHAKO
Brooks (originally newcomer, now tenderfoot); Franck (pronounced "cheechalker"); Gruening (pronounced "cheechawker"); Hines (means migrant, as a bird); Harrison (derived from name of bird with short season in Alaska); James ("mangeurs de lard" is French for "green hands"); Rickard; Thomas (means "chee," lately new, and "chako," to become or come).

CHELYUSKIN EXPEDITION
The Voyage of the Chelyuskin, by members of the expedition; translated from the Russian by Alec Brown. New York: Macmillan, 1935. 325 pp. The *Chelyuskin*, attempting to reach Vladivostok from Leningrad by the Arctic route sank in the Chukchi Sea on February 13, 1934. The crew was rescued from a camp on drifting ice by aircraft.

CHENA (town)
Alaska Life, June, '49 (*Chena Times* of January 18, 1905 reviewed); *Alaska-Yukon Magazine*, Feb., '08; Jan., '09 (photo); Baker (west end of Chena Slough, incorporated 1903); Couch (post office 1903-18); Rickard (ten miles from Fairbanks in 1908); Stuck (history and demise); Wickersham.

CHENEGA (in Prince William Sound)
Baker (village on south end of island); Burford (descr.); Couch (post office from 1947).

CHENEY, WARREN (b. 1858)
The Way of the North. New York: Doubleday, 1905. 320 pp.
The Challenge. Indianapolis: Bobbs-Merrill, 1906. 386 pp.
His Wife. Indianapolis: Bobbs-Merrill, 1907. 395 pp.
"The Right to Revenge," *Sunset*, November, 1909.
"The Sentimental Lady," *Sunset*, April, 1911.

CHERNOFSKI (village, Unalaska Island)
Alaska Sportsman, Dec., '45 (sheep ranch); Baker (named by Sarichev, 1792); Denison (sheep); Dall; Miller (9000 sheep brought in 1914).

CHERNOV, IVAN (1790-1877)
Baker (summary, Creole pilot, contributed to Russian hydrographic charts); Bancroft (hostage in youth, commanded the *Polyfem*); Dall (examined Nuchek Harbor, 1830).

CHEVIGNY, HECTOR (b. 1904)
Lost Empire. New York: Macmillan, 1937. 356 pp. Nikolai Petrovich Rezanov.
Lord of Alaska. New York: Viking Press, 1942. 320 pp. Aleksandr Andreevich Baranov, and the Russian American Company.
Russian America: The Great Alaskan Venture, 1741-1867. New York: Viking Press, 1965. 247 pp.
See also *Alaskan Sportsman*, December, 1960, and *Alaska Life*, April, 1947. Since it is the only readily available work on Russian America for the general

reader and the casual student (Ballantine Books Comstock Editions published a paper edition in 1973), Chevigny's somewhat romanticized account is widely circulated. The researcher should consult Berkh on the Aleutian Islands, Khlebnikov's biography of Baranov, and R.A. Pierce's series on Alaska's Russian governors, among others.

CHICAGO RECORD
Klondike. Chicago: *Chicago Record*, 1897. 413 pp. Other editions, appearing nearly simultaneously, are listed in Tourville.

CHICHAGOF
Alaska Sportsman, June, '42 (mine closed due to labor strife); Dec., '55 (Hirst-Chicagoff mine described by employee W.E. Saunders); *Alaska-Yukon Magazine*, Oct., '07 (biog. Edward deGroff [b. 1860], President, Chichagoff Gold Mining Co.; mine discovered 1905); Couch (post office 1909-57); Morgan (story of mine, deGroff's death at Sitka); Tewkesbury (camp at northern end of Klag Bay, mine at Kimshan).

CHICHAGOF KING MINING COMPANY
"The Great Lesson of the Great Depression," Tacoma: Chichagof King Mining Company, 1934. 32 pp.

CHICHAGOV, VASILI I.
See the Wickersham Bibliography for accounts by Lomonosov, Sokolov, and others; see also T-2753, 3232, and 4236. In 1766 Levashev and Krenitzin were to sail from Okhotsk in a northeasterly direction and meet Chichagov, who was to come from Siberia through the Bering Strait. Due to shipwreck and scurvy the southern arm of the project did not sail. Chichagov led two expeditions along the north coast of Siberia in 1765 and 1766, but couldn't reach East Cape, also due to misfortune. Lomonosov read a paper on the project at a public meeting of the Imperial Academy of Sciences in St. Petersburg. It remained for Nordenskjold in the *Vega* to accomplish the northeast passage, but not until 1878-79.

CHICKAMIN (Glacier and River)
Alaska Sportsman, Aug., '37 (photo); Nov., '34 (ice worms); June, '51; March, '53 (photo at head of Portland Canal); Baker (river flows into Behm Canal); *Sunset*, July, '56.

CHICKEN (village southwest of Eagle)
Alaska Sportsman, May, '51; Baker; Couch (post office from 1903; Specht (*Tisha* [NY: St. Martin's Press, 1976]).

CHIGNIK
Alaska Sportsman, Dec., '37 (photo); Sept., '38; Baker (south shore, Alaska Peninsula); Colby; Couch (post office from 1901); Higginson (Castle Cape at entrance to bay); *National Geographic*, Sept., '31 (photo).

CHILBERG, JOHN EDWARD (d. 1956)
Alaska-Yukon Magazine, March, '07 (president, Alaska-Yukon-Pacific Exposition); July, '07 (photos); Feb., '09 (photos, article); *Daily Alaska Empire*, February, 1961 (Chilberg was banker in Seattle and Nome, probably son of Seattle banker Andrew C. Chilberg); Harrison (Eugene and B.A. apparently brothers of John E. Chilberg).

CHILBERG, JOSEPH
Alaska-Yukon Magazine, January, 1909 (opposed Wickersham for delegate in 1908); Nichols (backed by northern miners).

CHILDREN'S BOOKS
See Brinsmade in Bibliography; see also the index in the Tourville Bibliography for a listing of Juvenile literature.

CHILDS GLACIER
Alaska-Yukon Magazine, October and December, 1910 (photos); Abercrombie; Chase (photos); Denison (chiefly about railroad); Franck (trains stop for view); Rafferty (waves from breaking chunks are dangerous); Underwood; see also Miles Glacier.

CHILKAT (village)
Baker (Klukwan has been called "Chilkat Village"); Couch (post office 1890-99 [location given is erroneous]); Moser (on loose map Chilkat Post Office is shown on Chilkat Inlet, north of Pyramid Harbor, on the opposite side of the Inlet); Scidmore (one of the largest canneries in southeast Alaska on the opposite side of Chikat Inlet from Pyramid Harbor).

CHILKAT BLANKETS
Alaska Sportsman, Apr., '40; March, '42; March, '50; Dec., '51 (photo); Cameron (photo); Colby (process); Emmons; Scidmore (called narkheen [dance robes], also made by Haida and Tsimshian); Wickersham; Williams (rival Navajo).

CHILKAT TRAIL
Alaska Sportsman, Feb., '51 (Dalton or Chilkat Trail longer than Chilkoot, but can be used by packhorses); Rickard (bands of cattle driven over pass); Schwatka (route); Wells.

CHILKAT INDIANS; see Indians.

CHILKOOT BARRACKS; see Port Chilkoot.

CHILKOOT PASS (The Dyea Trail)
Alaska Sportsman, June, '48 (map, photos); Sept., '50 (Jack Marchbank went over pass on crutches); Dec., '51 (aerial tram completed in 1898); Jan., '52 (tramway); Nov., '52 (piano taken over pass); May, '54 (first women over pass in 1894); Oct., '54 (C.H. Barkdull says Mrs. Joe Ladue went over the pass several years before 1895); Andrews (Holt over pass in 1870[?], Edmund Bean and party in 1880, Schwatka in 1883); Davis (70 killed in avalanche); Mahoney; Scidmore (Scotchman over pass, Fort Selkirk to Chilkoot Inlet, in 1864; George Holt over to Yukon River in 1872, and again in 1874; Edmund Bean failed in 1877, but succeeded in 1880; Arizona prospectors over in 1882, Schwatka and Dugan and party in 1883; Schwatka (named it Perrier Pass); Wickersham (Soapy Smith's men on trail in 1898); Winslow (tram for freight only); Ogilvie called the pass Dyea, and it is today known by both names, and Chilkat and Chilkoot (Dyea) passes are often confused. Chilkat Pass is crossed by the present Haines-Haines Junction Highway; Chilkoot (Dyea) Pass and White Pass are reached from Skagway, the latter today crossed by the White Pass and Yukon Railway. Most widely circulated photographs of the passes during the Klondike rush are of Chilkoot (Dyea) Pass.

CHINA JOE (ca. 1834-1917)
Alaska Sportsman, Sept., '49 (photo; came to San Francisco at age 18, then to Wrangell, Cassiar, and Juneau; trading post at Juneau, then bakery; not expelled by miners when imported Chinese evicted; died at 83 in Juneau; charter member of '87 Alaska Pioneers); *Alaska Weekly*, Nov., '53 (name was Hi Chung); *Daily Alaska Empire*, October, 1960; Rickard (Wrangell, 1874, Juneau, 1881, owned home in Juneau); Yule, Emma S. ("China Joe," *Pacific Monthly*, August, 1910).

CHINA MARY (b. ca. 1880)
Alaska Sportsman, May, '50. China Mary voyaged from China at age 13, living two years in British Columbia. At age 15 she married a Chinese from Sitka to enter the United States. Her husband, who operated a restaurant in Sitka, died young, leaving her with two daughters. She then married a Scandinavian who started a dairy farm on Sawmill Creek. In 1950 she was a matron at the Sitka jail.

CHINESE IN ALASKA
Alaska Sportsman, May, '42 (Chinese buried at Lituya Bay); Oct., '54; Jan., '56; Oct., '56 (Chinese barred from Dawson); Brooks (difficulties at Juneau); Clark (Juneau troubles; cannery labor after 1906); Hawthorne (cannery workers die of scurvy or beri beri); Morris (flocked to Cassiar, resented by Indians at Sitka); Nichols (riots at Juneau and Douglas in 1886); Scidmore (all Chinese ordered out of the area at a Juneau meeting in May, 1882; Indians at Sitka objected to Chinese in 1879, and all but a few left the region); Sundborg (56 Chinese in Alaska in 1940).

CHINN, R. E.
"1968 Election in Alaska," *Western Historical Quarterly*, XXII (1969): 456-461.
"1970 Election in Alaska," *Western Historical Quarterly*, XXIV (1971): 234-242.

CHINOOK (lingua franca)
Boas (*Chinook Texts*); Thomas, Edward Harper (*Chinook: A History and Dictionary of Northwest Coast Trade Jargon*, Portland: Binfords and Mort, 1935); see also Smith (Americana). Chinook was a "universal" language used among traders and Indians on the Northwest coast, but it was not as common in Alaska as along the Canadian and lower coasts.

CHINOOK (warm wind)
Brown, Slater (*World of the West Wind* [Indianapolis: Bobbs-Merrill, 1961]); Davis (hot wind in December); O'Connor; Stuck; Underwood.

CHIRIKOF ISLAND
Alaska Sportsman, Jan., '35; Nov., '38; July, '39; March, '44; Feb., '48; *Alaska Weekly*, Oct., '50 (beef industry); Jan., '51; Aug., '51; Andrews (Bering discovered island, named it Tammanoi [Foggy]); Bancroft (Vancouver here 1794, Cook 1778); Bering-Golder; Dall; Denison (cattle here since 1886); Hilscher (Jack McCord failed in contract with army); Miller (Russians had convict settlement on island); Sundborg (Chirikof Cattle Co. has cattle and sheep on Sitkalidak Island); Tompkins; Vancouver (named it Tchirikov in his honor).

CHIRIKOV, ALEXEI ILICH (1703-1748)
Report of the Voyage of the St. Paul, see Golder, Bering's Voyages. See also the following:
Baker; Bancroft; Barbeau; Chevigny; Davidson; Divin (T-1301 ff); Golder; Laut, Agnes ("The Discoverer of Alaska," *Leslie's Magazine* [February, 1905]); Lebedev (T-2658); Solokov (T-4238); Staehlin (T-4276). The Alaska State Historical Library has in Russian on microfilm the Log of the St. Paul (135 pp.) and the Report to the Admiralty College (15 pp.)

CHISTIAKOV, PETER EGOROVICH (Governor, Russian America)
Andrews (Chief Manager, 1825-1830); Chevigny; Ivanshinstov (T-2308; Chistiakov voyaged with Muraviev in the *Elena* in 1824-26); Pierce (Russian Governors).

CHITTENDEN, NEWTON H.
Travels in British Columbia and Alaska. Victoria: 1882. 84 pp.

CHITTICK, VICTOR LOVITT OAKES (b. 1882)
Northwest Harvest. New York: Macmillan, 1948. 226 pp. Writers' Conference on the Northwest, Portland, Oregon, October-November, 1946.

CHITTY, ARTHUR BEN
Hudson Stuck of Alaska. New York: National Council of Churches, 1962.

CHKALOV, VALERII PAVLOVICH
See T-919.

CHOQUETTE, ALEXANDER ("Buck") (ca. 1828-1898)
Alaska Life, Jan., '46 (Stikine trader, moved to Prince of Wales Island in 1886); Brooks (a French-Canadian voyageur who worked for Hudson's Bay Company, found gold in the Stikine in 1861); Chase (managed a Hudson's Bay post 75 miles up the Stikine); Clark (died of hardships in the Klondike); Morris; Tompkins (est. post 1876); Young.

CHORIS, LOUIS (1795-1828)
Voyage Pittoresque autour du Monde. Paris: Firmin Didot, 1822. 149 pp. See VanStone on Choris in *Pacific Northwest Quarterly*, October, 1960.

CHRISTOE, ALICE HENSON
Treadwell: An Alaskan Fulfillment. Seattle, 1909. See also articles in the *Alaska-Yukon Magazine*.

CHRONOLOGIES
Baker (Introduction); Burney; Dall (list of historical events, 1542 to 1867 [detailed]); Greely (historical dates 1648 to 1925); Haycox (*Comparative Chronology of Alaska and America*, 1725-1973 [Alaska Department of Education, 1974]); Huber (selected events); Schafer (Pacific Coast history).

CHUGACH NATIONAL FOREST
See the Arctic Bibliography and the Wickersham Bibliography. The office of the Forest publishes numerous informational materials.

CHUGINADAK ISLAND (Aleutian)

Alaska Life, Sept., '44 (volcano tragedy, US Army); Colby (largest of the Islands of the Four Mountains); Garfield, *National Geographic*, October, 1948 (Mount Cleveland erupted in 1944).

CHUKCHI SEA

A portion of the Arctic Ocean lying north of Bering Strait, between Alaska and Siberia. See the Arctic Bibliography.

CHUKCHIS (Siberian Natives)

Alaska Sportsman, Aug., '56 (photo); Aldrich (called Masinkers by whalers, trading methods); Bancroft; Dall; James; Hulley; Pilgrim; Tompkins.

CHUKOVSKII, NIKOLAI KORNEEVICH

Voditeli Fregatov (Commanders of Warships). Moscow: 1947. 275 pp. Popular accounts of Kruzenstern's voyage on the *Nadezhda*, and Lisianskis trip around the world in 1803-06 on the *Neva*.

CHURCHILL, AWNSHAM, JOHN CHURCHILL and THOMAS OSBORNE

See Y-932 ff.

CIPOLLA, ARNALDO (b. 1879)

Norte America y los Norteamericanos. Santiago: Nascimiento, 1929. 264 pp. Translated from Italian to Spanish by Ramon Mondris.

CIRCLE CITY

Alaska Sportsman, Feb., '39 (houses warmed from hot springs); Nov., '48 (Bayne Beauchamp); Sept., '51 (Herminie Kitchen); Nov., '52; 1953; Dec., '54 and others; *Alaska-Yukon Magazine*, May, '09 (photo); Baker (named from supposed location on the Arctic Circle); Cameron; Carroll; Colby; Couch (post office from 1906); Davis; Denison; Hulley; Kitchener; Henderson (almost deserted in 1897, 1394 miles from St. Michael, forlorn location, 700 empty cabins); Martinsen (Ed Lung); Ogilvie (founded by McQuesten, 1894, 1894 photo); Ray (took possession of warehouses, 1897, issued supplies to destitute); Richardson (Circle business before 1897 transferred to Dawson after); Stuck (population in 1896, 3000); Sundborg; Tompkins (supply for Birch Creek; Capt. Ray on the Yukon); Walden; Wickersham (held court here).

CIRCLE HOT SPRINGS

Alaska Sportsman, numerous issues, Oct., '39 forward; consult Index; Colby; Couch (post office called Deadwood, 1905-1924, moved to new location and called Circle Hot Springs from 1924); Davis; Jacobin; Sundborg; Tewkesbury; see also the *Milepost* (Alaska Northwest Publishing).

CIVIL AERONAUTICS ADMINISTRATION (CAA)

Alaska Life, Oct., '46; *Alaska Sportsman*, Aug., '41 (149 aircraft and 184 pilots in Alaska); March, '49 (Yakutat); Denison; Gruening; Sundborg.

CIVILIAN CONSERVATION CORPS (CCC)

Franck (camps a failure?); Garfield and Forrest (totem restoration); Williams (age limits not imposed in alaska, Forest Service in charge in 1933); US Senate, Committee on Interior and Insular Affairs, 1935, Hearings (discrimination); Williams.

CLAH; see Philip McKay.

CLAMS

Numerous articles, see *Alaska Sportsman* Index; Denison (Cordova); Lipke (great size at Petersburg); Sundborg (razor clams at Cordova, butter clams in southeast Alaska); Tewkesbury (20 canneries); US Department of Interior (Mid-century Alaska).

CLARK, AUSTIN H.; see Henry B. Collins.

CLARK, DANIEL ELBERT (b. 1884)

"Manifest Destiny and the Pacific," *Pacific Historical Review*, March, 1932.

CLARK, DONALD W.

Kizhuyak Bay Excavation. Kodiak: Kodiak and Aleutian Historical Society, 1960, 28 pp.

CLARK, HAROLD BENJAMIN

A Doggerel Diary. New York: privately printed, 1937. 47 pp. Poetry.

"Up-stream for Mountain Goats," *Natural History*, December, 1937.

CLARK, HENRY WADSWORTH (b. 1899)

History of Alaska. New York: Macmillan, 1930. 208 pp. Henry Clark was manager of the Alaska Development Board in the 1940's.

Buck Coquette: Stampeder. Wn.DC: The Author, 1960. 152 pp.

CLARK, HORACE FLETCHER (d. 1928)

Miners' Manual. Chicago: Callaghan and Co., 1898. 404 pp.

CLARK, Mrs. IRVING M.

"A Tourist Sees Alaska," *Puget Soundings*, December, 1960.

CLARK, JOHN D. and L. SPRAGUE de CAMP

"Some Alaskan Place Names," *American Speech*, February, 1940.

CLARK, Lake

Baker (recorded as Lake Illiamna by Russians in 1802, rediscovered by John W. Clark, Nushagak trader, in 1891); Higginson (west of Redoubt Volcano, connected to Lake Illiamna by the Nogheling River); Underwood (50 miles long, narrow, 600' deep).

CLARK, M. (Florence Matilda)

Roadhouse Tales from Nome in 1900. Girard, Kansas: Appeal Publishing Co., 1902. 263 pp.

CLARK, SAMUEL F.

"Report on Hydroids collected on the coast of Alaska and the Aleutians," *Proceedings*. American Academy of Natural Sciences, 1876.

CLARK, SUSIE C.

Lorita: An Alaskan Maiden. Boston: Lee and Shepard, 1892. 171 pp.

CLARK, WALTER ELI (1869-1950) (Governor of Alaska, 1909-13)

"Alaska in 1959," *Collier's*, June, 1909.

Alaska. Boston: Marshall Jones Co., 1910. 192 pp.

Originally attributed to Governor Clark, the work was actually penned by Nathan Haskell Dole, Clark writing only the two page introduction. The same work with two additional chapters was published at Boston in 1910.

Clark wrote a number of popular periodical pieces; see the Wickersham bibliography. See also the following:

Alaska Sportsman, May, '50 (died at 81 in West Virginia); *Alaska-Yukon Magazine*, Sept., '09 (en route to Alaska); Feb., '12 (editorial criticizing Clark, who opposed home rule for Alaska; Clark's letter to Piggott); Dole; Gruening (Clark's ideas on home rule); Hulley ("not an Alaskan"); Nichols; Tompkins (suspected of representing "big" interests, Taft exercised poor judgment in the appointment); Wead (four stanzas praising the *Bear*).

CLARKE, TOM E.
Alaska Challenge: A Novel. New York: Lothrop, Lee and Shepard, 1959. 222 pp.
Back to Anchorage. New York: Lothrop, Lee and Shepard, 1961, 224 pp.
No Furs for the Czar. New York: Lothrop, Lee and Shepard, 1962. 191 pp.

CLARK'S POINT
Alaska Sportsman, Nov., '52 (photo); Feb., '53 (school photo); Baker (near mouth of Nushagak River, named in 1890 by Fish Commission, possibly in honor of Samuel Fessenden Clark of Williams College); Couch (post office from 1934); Clark's Point village has sometimes been called Stagarok.

CLAY, CASSIUS MARCELLUS (1810-1903)
See *Alaska Life*, January, 1946, and Tompkins. Clay was US Ambassador at St. Petersburg in 1858 when the Alaska purchase discussions were beginning. See Alaska purchase, and Robertson, James.
"Oration before Students and the Historical Class of Berea College, 1895," Richmond, Kentucky: Pantagraph, 1896. 10 pp.

CLAWSON, MARIAN and BURNELL HELD
The Federal Lands. Baltimore: Johns Hopkins Press, 1957. 501 pp.

CLEARY CITY and CLEARY CREEK
Alaska-Yukon Magazine, Apr., '07 (photo, over 1000 population); Jan., '09; July, '12; Baker (local name, from Gerdine, 1903); Cameron (mines produced over $5 million in 1906); Colby (1933 population 52, a few shacks); Couch (post office 1906-26); Kitchener (Frank Cleary was a watchman for E.T. Barnette at Fairbanks; Cleary strike 1902); Rickard; Stuck (Goldstream paid first, then Cleary); Wickersham (Frank Cleary elected first town recorder at Fairbanks).

CLEMENS, SAMUEL L. (Mark Twain) (1835-1910)
"The Esquimau Maiden's Romance," *Mark Twain's Library of Humor*, Vol. 12, New York, 1906.

CLEMENS, WILLIAM
"Report on the Aleutians," *Reader's Digest*, March, 1943.

CLEMENS, W. A. and G. V. WILBY
See T-952.

CLEMENTS, JAMES I.
See T-953.

CLERKE, CHARLES (d. 1779) (British Naval officer)
Bancroft; Cook (Vol. III of the Journal); Tompkins. Capt. Clerke succeeded to command of the Cook Expedition (3rd) upon the death of James Cook in February, 1779 in Hawaii.

CLEVELAND, BESS ANDERSON (d. 1894)
Frontier Formulas. Juneau: Totem Press, 1952. 212 pp.
Alaskan Cookbook. Berkeley: Howell-North, 1960. 164 pp.

CLEVELAND, RICHARD JEFFRY (b. ca. 1774)
A Narrative of Voyages and Commercial Enterprises. 2v. Cambridge: J. Owen, 1842.
Voyages and Commercial Enterprises on the Sons of New England. New York: Harper, 1886. 245 pp. Compiled from the journals and letters of Richard Cleveland. Cleveland commanded the Boston ship *Caroline*. He met Baranov while the latter was building the first Archangel post in the Alexander Archipelago. Cleveland warned Baranov about the natives whom he considered hostile.
In the Forecastle, or 25 Years a Sailor. New York: World Publishing Company, 1876. 407 pp.
See also the following:
Bancroft; Chevigny; Greenhow (first report of the existence of the Stikine); Tompkins.

CLIFTON, VIOLET MARY
The Book of Talbot. New York: Harcourt, Brace, 1933. 439 pp. Compiled from the diaries of John Talbot Clifton (1868-1928) who spent a few months in the Klondike in 1895, six months during the winter of 1897-98 with the Eskimos of Chesterfield Inlet, and ten months, 1901-02, in the Lena River area of Siberia.

CLIMATE; see Weather.

CLOVER PASS
Alaska Sportsman, July, '50 (church); May, '52 (photo); May, '53; Feb., '57; Baker (north end of Behm Canal, named by Coast Survey for Commander Richardson Clover); Dole (between Tongass Narrows and Loring); Lawrence (fishing); Scidmore (Clover, of the steamer *Patterson*).

CLOVER, RICHARDSON (US Naval officer)
Report, US Coast Survey, 1886. See comments in Baker.

CLOWES, WILLIAM LAIRD
The Royal Navy: A History. 7v. Boston: Little, Brown, 1899-1903.

CLUM, JOHN P. (b. 1851)
A Trip to the Klondike. St. Louis: Keystone View Co., 1899. 56 pp.
"Stirring Patriotic Address delivered at Fairbanks, Alaska, July 4, 1907," Fairbanks, 1907. 4 pp.
See also *Alaska-Yukon Magazine*, January, 1909

(photo; ran against Wickersham for delegate in 1908); Nichols (ran independently hoping for support from the Interior).

CLUNE, FRANK (1894)
Hands Across the Pacific. Sydney: Angus and Robertson, 1951. 304 pp.

CLUT, ISIDORE
"Journal du Voyage de Mgr. Clut au Territoire d'Alaska." Published in 1874 by the Missions of the Congregations of the Oblates of Mary Immaculate. Copy in the Library of the University of Ottawa, St. Joseph's Scholasticate. See also Champagne and Mousseau.

COACHMAN, LAWRENCE K. and C. A. BARNES
See T-962.

COAL
The following is a selective listing of potentially useful sources. The researcher should see the Arctic Bibliography, and the libraries and publications of the various government agencies, especially the Bureau of Land Management and other Interior bureaus. See also the following:
Alaska Life, Jan., '41 (map); June, '45 (origin of deposits); *Alaska Sportsman*, June, '40 (Healy mine largest in Alaska); June, '41 (output $680,000 in 1940); Sept., '41 (Perryville deposits, photo); Sept., '42 (Moose Creek); Feb., '47 (Homer); Oct., '47; Feb., '49 (Cape Lisburne); June, '49 (gov't. mines at Eska); July, '49 (Kachemak Bay); Aug., '49 (Capt. West of the *Corwin*); June, '50 (Homer); July, '52 (proposed development at Homer); Dec., '52 (Tyonek); June, '58 (1957 output over $7 million); *Alaska Weekly*, July, '51 (Kenai); *Alaska-Yukon Magazine*, Aug., '07 (Controller Bay); Feb., '08 (photo near Fairbanks); March, '08 (map); Jan., '09 (Tanana Valley); Dec., '09 (editorial on conservation); June, '10; Jan., '11 (Gov. Clark); Feb., '12 (critical of T. Roosevelt); Aldrich (Cape Lisburne); Bancroft (Coal Harbor, Cook Inlet mid-19th century); Clark; Carmack; Denison; Dole (Cook Inlet); Harrison; Hellenthal; Henderson; Higginson (Kachemak Bay); Glenn; Gruening (first considerable production in 1916; Navy; Lathrop at Nenana; Gov. Strong); Learnard (Susitna Valley); Lipke (Seldovia); Morris (Kuiu Island); Nichols (withdrawal); Petrof (American-Russian Co. at Graham Harbor); Scidmore (Admiralty Island); Stuck; Sundborg; Swineford (history); Underwood (history of mining); Williams (Herendeen Bay); Young (Guggenheims).

COAL BAY
Baker (three locations with this name are listed: [1] near Homer, [2] alaska Peninsula near the Shumagins, [3] Prince of Wales Island near Kasaan Bay; also Coal Harbor or Bay in Port Graham); Couch (near Homer, post office from 1892-1895).

COAL HARBOR
Baker (three locations with this name are listed: [1] head of Zachary Bay, Unga Island, [2] in Herendeen Bay, Alaska Peninsula, [3] Port Graham); Bancroft (in Graham Bay, Portlock in 1786, Fidalgo 1790; coal mined 1857); Couch (on Unga Island, post office 1902-12); Dall (coal on Unga Island valueless); Higginson; Hulley; Scidmore (errs in placing Russian mines in Kachemak Bay).

"COAL PARTY"; see Cordova Coal Party.

COAST AND GEODETIC SURVEY; see US Coast and Geodetic Survey.

COAST PILOT; see US Coast and Geodetic Survey.

COBB, JOHN NATHAN (1868-1930)
The Salmon Fisheries of the Pacific Coast. Wn.DC: GPO, 1911. 179 pp. Fisheries Commission. Contains history.

COBOL (Chicagof Island)
Boylan, Helen; see Martha Martin. Scene of "O Rugged Land of Gold".

COCHRAN, C. S. (US Revenue Cutter Service officer)
"The Bear: Most Famous of all Ships in the Arctic Service," *Proceedings*, US Naval Institute, 1929. See Wead, who reports that Cochran spent 20 years on the *Bear*, 8 as Captain.

CODY, HIRAM ALFRED (b. 1872)
An Apostle of the North. London: Seely, 1908. 385 pp. William Carpenter Bompas, D.D., first Bishop of Athabaska.
The Frontiersman. New York: Dutton, 1910. 342 pp.
On the Trail and Rapid. Philadelphia: Lippincott, 1911. Juvenile.

COCKE, ALBERT J.
"Dr. Samuel J. Call," *Alaska Journal*, IV (Summer, 1974): 181-189.

COE, CURTIS P.
The News-Letter. Kodiak. Edited by Coe (1899-1908) and George A. Learn (1908-1922). Coe was a Baptist missionary at Wood Island, Kodiak.

COE, DOUGLAS
Road to Alaska. New York: Julian Messner, 1943. 175 pp. Alaska Highway. Juvenile.

COCHRANE, JOHN D.
See T-965.

COHEN, FELIX S.
A Handbook of Indian Law. Wn.DC: GPO, 1941. Reprinted for the Department of Interior in 1958 under the title *Federal Indian Law*, edited by Frank B. Horne. The most significant compilation of American Indian law. Cohen was solicitor for the Department of Interior and involved in the early history of native claims. See references to his work in Gruening. See also *The Legal Conscience: Selected Papers of Felix S. Cohen*, edited by Lucy Kramer Cohen (New Haven: Yale University Press, 1960).

COLBERT, LEO OTIS (Director, US Coast and Geodetic Survey)
The US Coast and Geodetic Survey. Princeton: Princeton University Press, 1947. 28 pp. See also Wright and Roberts.

COLBY, MERLE ESTES (b. 1902)
A Guide to Alaska. New York: Macmillan, 1939. 427 pp. The work was produced under the Federal Writers Project, Works Progress Administration, and was highly regarded as a tourist manual. 53 persons collaborated in one capacity or another.
Alaska: A Profile with Pictures. New York: Duell, Sloane, and Pearce, 1940. 58 pp.
"Alaska Comes of Age," *Travel,* May, 1938.

COLDFOOT
Alaska-Yukon Magazine, Jan., '08; Apr., '08 (photo); March, '06 (Ida Williams); Baker (mining camp, middle fork, Koyukuk); Couch (post office 1902-08); Higginson (vegetables); Hulley; Kitchener (store, 1902); Stuck.

COLE, CASH (b. 1891) (Territorial Auditor, 1929-32)
Alaska Sportsman, Aug., '56 (lived in Juneau, 1894-1949; "elected" Governor in 1923); Jeffery; Tewkesbury.

COLE, CORNELIUS (1822-1924) (US Senator, California)
Memoirs. New York: McLaughlin Brothers, 1908. 354 pp. Cole was attorney for the principal stockholders of the Alaska Commercial Company. He attempted to negotiate a 25 year charter from the Russian government to succeed the Russian-American Company, a move unsuccessful because of the sale of Alaska. Cole's brother-in-law, Judge Burke, and General John F. Miller, Collector of the Port of San Francisco, were involved. It has been presumed that Cole, who was elected US Senator in 1867, used his influence to get the Pribilof Island seal contract for the Alaska Commercial Co. Gruening recalls that ACC's was the lowest of 13 bids. Clark also implies ethically questionable activity. It should be remembered that ACC had already purchased the bulk of the assets of the Russian-American Co., and were therefore possibly in a better position both to bid low and to fulfill the contract, which was, in any case, lucrative. See Hutchinson and Kohl; see also Sloss. See Farrar on Cole.

COLE, D.
"Allen Aylesworth on the Alaskan Boundary Award," *Canadian Historical Review,* LII (1971): 472-477.

COLEMAN, RUFUS ARTHUR
Northwest Books. Lincoln: University of Nebraska Press, 1949. 278 pp. Reviews of 600 titles.

COLLECTION OF DOCUMENTS ON ABORIGINAL RIGHTS
Documents and Copies pertaining to the transfer of Alaska, and to the formation of a Committee to report on aboriginal rights of Indians in Alaska. 1867-1892. Mss., Alaska State Historical Library.

COLLECTOR OF CUSTOMS, ALASKA
Letter and Reports, 1867-1882. Mss., Alaska State Historical Library.

COLLIER, ARTHUR JAMES
"A Survey of the Northwestern Portions of the Seward Peninsula," USGS Professional Paper, 1902. See Baker for a summary of Collier's work in Alaska.

COLLIER, WILLIAM ROSS and EDWIN VICTOR WESTRATE
The Reign of Soapy Smith. Garden City: Doubleday, 1935. 299 pp.

COLLINS, ERNEST BILBE (b. 1873)
Alaska Life, June, '47 (Speaker of the House, First Territorial Legislature, 1913); *Alaska Sportsman,* Apr., '55; *Alaska Weekly,* March, '51 (3 terms in the Senate, 4 times Mayor of Fairbanks); Tewkesbury.

COLLINS, HENRY BASCOM, Jr.
See the Arctic Bibliography for a complete listing of Collins' numerous publications on Arctic anthropology and archaeology. Most are short; they cover most of northern Alaska, including St. Lawrence Island. In *Alaska Sportsman,* January, 1956, Collins is quoted on the "land-bridge theory of the peopling of North America," suggesting that the Indians of North America migrated through the land-bridge, but that Eskimos and Aleuts came much later, over water. See David Hopkins.

COLLINS, PERRY McDONOUGH (1814-1900)
A Voyage down the Amour. New York: D. Appleton, 1860. 390 pp.
Overland Explorations in Siberia. New York: D. Appleton, 1864. 467 pp.
Statement. Origin, Organization, and Progress of the Russian-American Telegraph, Western Union Extension, Collins' overland line via Behring Strait, collated from documents in the "Russian Bureau" of the Western Union Telegraph Company. Rochester: *Evening Express,* 1866. 165 pp.
See also the following:
Alaska Life, Sept., '45 (Andrews, map); Bancroft (large privileges in Russia); Clark; Dall (US Consular agent at the mouth of the Amur); Brooks (project first advocated in 1857); Gruening (defended value of Alaska); Hulley; Henderson (US commercial agent in Siberia); James (he inspired the Western Union company); Petrof (secured charters from British and Russian governments); Shiels; Tompkins; Underwood; Wickersham (full story).

COLLINS, RAYMOND and SALLY JO COLLINS
See T-984 ff.

COLLINSON, Sir RICHARD (1811-1913)
Journal of the HMS Enterprise. London: S. Low, Marston, Searle and Rivington, 1889. In search of Franklin's ships, 1850-55. The *Enterprise* and *Investigator* under Collinson's command sailed from England early in 1850. Robert McClure captained *Investigator* (see McClure). *Enterprise* spent two winters in northern Canadian waters (1851-53) and a third in Camden Bay (1853-54), Alaska. While anchored in Port Clarence in 1851 Lieut. J.J. Bernard was sent up the Yukon to reconnoiter. He was killed in the massacre at Nulato of that year. This work is unusually thorough on Arctic knowledge to that time, and on the Franklin search to 1850. See also the following:
Alaska Life, May, '45 (Andrews); Back, George; Brooks (wintered on Walker Bay, north coast of Alaska); Dall; Greely; Mirsky; Stuck (Collinson Point named for him).

COLLIS, SEPTIMA MARIA (1842-1917)
A Woman's Trip to Alaska. New York: Cassell, 1890. 194 pp. Sitka in 1890.

COLLISON, WILLIAM HENRY (b. 1847)
In the Wake of the War Canoe. New York: Dutton, 1916. 351 pp. Collison was a sometime missionary among the ("head-hunting") Haida.

COLNETT, JAMES (1755-1806)
Journal Aboard the Argonaut. Toronto: Champlain Society, 1940. 328 pp. Colnett was the British captain who clashed with Estevan Jose Martinez at Nootka Sound (Vancouver Island) in 1789, the beginning of the Nootka Sound Controversy, a struggle over competing Spanish and British claims in the North Pacific. Colnett was sent to San Blas, the *Argonaut* a prize. English naval superiority assured the triumph of the British claim, and began the contraction of Spanish claims in the north.
A Voyage to the South Atlantic. London: W. Bennett, 1798. 179 pp. On extension of the southern whale fishery. Much of the work discusses the earlier voyage of the *Argonaut*, rather than this one in *Rattler*.

COLP, HARRY D. (d. 1950)
The Strangest Story ever Told. New York: Exposition Press, 1953. 46 pp. Prospectors at "devil's country" around Thomas Bay, north of Petersburg, early 20th century, which is represented as being "haunted."

COLUMBIA GLACIER
Alaska Sportsman, Dec., '37 (gold ore being mined on glacier); numerous other issues, see Index; Baker (named by the Harriman Expedition, 1899); Burroughs; Colby; Harriman; Higginson; Oliver; Vancouver (Vancouver's party was unimpressed with glaciers, even this one); Martin, Lawrence ("Columbia Glacier," *Review of Reviews* [July, 1911]).

COLUMBIA RIVER
Bancroft (Heceta sighted entrance; Gray entered and named); Dall (Broughton surveyed in *Jenny* [England]); Greenhow (Meares unable to find; Broughton claimed discovery); Meany (Gray tried nine days to enter, told Vancouver; Vancouver was convinced he could not enter); Vancouver (encounter with Gray).

COLUMBIAN EXPOSITION (Chicago, 1893)
Scidmore (the invitation to join the exposition on an equal footing with other territories was the first civil recognition of the district).

COLVILLE RIVER
Baker (named by Dease and Simpson, 1837, for Andrew Colville, whose name was spelled differently); Brooks (descr.); Dall (mouth seen only by whites; many mistook its mouth for the estuary of the Yukon, it being taken for a separate river [Kvikhpak]); Stuck (prehistoric trade route; Colville was Hudson's Bay Co. governor).

COLYER, VINCENT (1825-1888)
Bombardment of Wrangell. Wn.DC, 1870. 33 pp. In retaliation for the killing of the post trader, Leon Smith, by Indians in 1869. See Morris for notice of Colyer.

COMFORT, MILDRED HOUGHTON (b. 1886)
Peter and Nancy in the United States and Alaska. Chicago: Beckley-Cardy, 1940. 368 pp.

COMMANDER ISLANDS
"Contributions to the Natural History of the Commander Islands." Thirteen papers. *Proceedings,* US National Museum. Based largely on the work of Leonhard Stejneger. See Stejneger.

COMMERCE
See this topic in the Index of the Tourville Bibliography. See also the various federal agencies and territorial departments, e.g., US Department of Commerce, Bureau of the Census, Bureau of Customs, Steamboat Inspection Service, etc., and Commissioner of Mine Inspection, etc.

COMMERCE CLEARING HOUSE
Alaska Tax Reporter. Chicago, 1958.

CONE, CHARLES EDWARD (1862-1938)
Beyond the Skyline. New York: Boullion-Biggs, 1923. 90 pp. Poetry.

CONGREGATIONAL MISSIONS
Harrison (photo, Nome); Hulley (first mission 1890 at Cape Prince of Wales, then Valdez, Douglas, Nome; 1899 Dr. Wirth built hospital and library); Stewart (allotted Cape Prince of Wales as their territory); Stuck (H.R. Thornton was murdered by natives ["drunken"] at Cape Prince of Wales, W.T. Lopp carried on).

CONGRESS
See US Congress. Both Wickersham and Judson list numerous documents, speeches, reports, and committee materials (including hearings). The student should consult Frederick's Caches of Alaskana, and the listings of holdings of the National Archives, the Library of Congress and the various regional Federal Records Centers.

CONKEY COMPANY (Chicago); see Official Guide to the Klondike.

CONKLE, EARL JUDSON (b. 1906)
Alaska Gold. New York: Pageant Press, 1953. 77 pp. Poetry.

CONKLE, ELLSWORTH PROUTY (b. 1899)
200 Were Chosen: A Play in Three Acts. New York: French, 1937. 49 pp. Matanuska colony.

CONRAD, AUGUST W. (b. 1870)
See the Encyclopedia of American Biography. Conrad came to Alaska in 1898, mined at Rampart, Nome and Fairbanks where he became a popular figure.

CONRAD, EARL
The Governor and his Lady. New York: G.P. Putnam's, 1960. 433 pp. William Seward.

CONRAD, SHERMAN
"The Matanuska Valley Colonization Project," *Monthly Report,* April, 1936. FERA. (history and status).

CONSERVATION

Alaska Sportsman, Nov., '57; June, '58 (development more vital); *Alaska-Yukon Magazine*, Feb., '10 ("Conservation Gone Crazy"); Apr., '10; May, '10 ("conservation is preposterous"); Feb., '12 (danger of monopoly in the leasing system); Clark (Alaskan attitude); Denison; Gruening (Ballinger-Pinchot controversy); Hellenthal ("The Alaskan Melodrama"); Nichols; Whiting; Williams. See Ballinger-Pinchot controversy, Cordova Coal Party, etc.; see also Oil, Pipeline, etc.

CONSTANTINE, CHARLES P. (d. 1912) (Royal Northwest Mounted Police)

I Was a Mountie. New York: Exposition, 1958. Constantine established the post called Fort Constantine at Fortymile in 1895. See also the following: *Alaska-Yukon Magazine*, Sept., '08; Becker (his signature on Carmack's application for registering Discovery claim, Sept. 24, 1896); Kitchener (abolished bloomers for women, "froze" ACC store supplies at Dawson, gave destitute free steamer tickets down Yukon); Ogilvie (to Fortymile in 1894, became Agent-General for Yukon Territory, became Gold Commissioner); Ray (Constantine's fine cooperation); Tompkins; Winslow.

CONSTITUTIONS AND BY-LAWS OF INDIAN VILLAGES, ASSOCIATIONS, COMMUNITIES, ETC.

Wn.DC: GPO, 1950. Bureau of Indian Affairs. By village.

CONTROLLER BAY

Baker (named Comptroller's Bay by Cook); Brooks (coal and petroleum); Clark (unsatisfactory for large ocean vessels); Colby; Cook; Nichols (Taft restored certain lands to entry for Controller Railway and Navigation Co., "its windswept shores were unfit for the purposes of either transportation or politics"); Underwood (in reality a mud flat); for additional information on development see the Wickersham bibliography; see also Katalla, M.J. Heney, etc.

COOK, FREDERICK ALBERT (1865-1940)

To the Top of the Continent. New York: Doubleday, Page, 1908. 321 pp. Cook's claims to have been first to ascend Mount McKinley (1903, 1906), and to the North Pole, were refuted by many, in scholarly judgment, successfully. His account of his attainment of the Pole became first a major controversy, and then a scandal. See Robert Dunn, and Karl Decker; see also *Alaska Sportsman*, Jan., 1954.
My Attainment of the Pole. New York: Polar Publications, 1911. 604 pp.
Return from the Pole. New York: Pelligrini, 1951. 335 pp.
See also the following:
Dole (Cook's descr. from atop the McKinley summit); Washburn (in *American Alpine Journal*, 1946); see also *Alaska Sportsman*, September, 1956 and December, 1956 (letter from Andy Ferdinand who saw Cook immediately before, and after, his claimed ascent).

COOK INLET

Alaska Sportsman, Sept., '36; Apr., '38; March, '43; March, '56 (history: Cook, Dixon, Fidalgo, Vancouver); May, '49 (gold rush); Apr., '52 (Scotch captain poisoned Indians at Anchor Point to get furs); July, '52; Sept., '52; May, '53 (29 hour "swim" after explosion of gill-netter); Baker (Russians called it Kenai Bay; Sandwich named it in honor of Cook, who gave it no name); Brooks; Chevigny; Dall; Dole (tremendous tide); Higginson (Stepan Zaikov and Lebedev-Lastochkin erected forts); Kitchener (Russian forts were St. George on the Kasilof River, St. Nicholas on the Kenai; 11 ACC stations; NC Co. sold interests to Erskine in 1911); Petrof (Baranov sent disputants to Siberia for trial to end competition); Scidmore; Sherwood (*Cook Inlet Collection*); Shiels (gold rush); Thomas; Underwood (bore tide is sometimes 4 to 6 feet, roars); Vancouver (complete tour); Washburn.

COOK INLET HISTORICAL SOCIETY

Articles of Incorporation and By-laws. Anchorage, 1955.

COOK, JAMES (1728-1779) (officer, Royal Navy; explorer, navigator)

A Voyage to the Pacific Ocean. Vols. I and II by Cook, Vol. III by Capt. James King. London: G. Nicoll and T. Cadell, by order of the Admiralty, 1784. 3v. and atlas. This is the official edition; there have been many adaptations; see Smith's and Wickersham's bibliographies; see also the Tourville Bibliography. Following voyages for the British Admiralty it was a requirement that all officers and men turn in to the Admiralty all journals and diaries kept during the voyage. Pirated versions were not uncommon, however, and one such of Cook's third voyage was published in 1785, ostensibly written by Lieutenant John Rickman, but some say actually by John Ledyard. For materials on Cook see the Tourville Bibliography. Perhaps the best biography is that by John C. Beaglehole, published in 1974. Cook's contribution lay primarily in navigation and charting. As a navigator he was the equal of Columbus and Magellan. His extensive charting of the north Pacific coast of North America established for the first time an accurate notion of the geography of that coast in relation to Asia and the Arctic. His third voyage demonstrated Bering's first advanced contention of a strait between Asia and America, and laid to rest the possibility of finding a northwest passage. His journal is remarkably thorough, and shows him to have been systematic, determined and astute. For a sample of materials on Cook see the following:
Beaglehole (his edition of the Journals); Besand; Carruthers; Carrington; Denton (Far West Coast); Gould; Holmes; Kippis (perhaps still the best summary of the voyages); Kitson; Laut; Little; Lloyd; MacLean, A.; Munford (Ledyard's journal); Rienitis; Speck; Williamson.

COOK, JOHN ATKINS (1857-1937)

Pursuing the Whale. New York and Boston: Houghton, Mifflin, 1926. 344 pp. Quarter-century of whaling as told by a whaling captain. See also Faber and Kurt.

COOK, JOHN ATKINS and S. S. PEDERSON

Thar She Blows! Boston: Chapman and Grimes, 1937. 314 pp. In the Beaufort and Chukchi Seas.

COOK, JOSEPH J. and WILLIAM L. WISNER
Killer Whale! New York: Dodd, Mead, 1963.
Warrior Whale. New York: Dodd, Mead, 1966. A sperm whale off the Alaska Coast.

COOK, KATHERINE MARGARET
Public Education in Alaska. Wn.DC: GPO, 1937. 57 pp. Office of Education (Department of Interior) Sketch of country and its people, history of territorial schools, federal schools, and allied services (reindeer, cooperative stores, medical service. See also Reynolds, Florence, E., *Education of Natives.*

COOLEY, RICHARD A.
Alaska: A Challenge in Conservation. Madison: University of Wisconsin Press, 1966. 186 pp.
Politics and Conservation. New York: Harper and Row, 1963. 230 pp. The decline of the Alaska Salmon.
"North Country, A Geogaphical Study of Alaska," *Journal of the West*, VI (1967): 362-371.

COOLIDGE, LOUIS ARTHUR (1861-1925)
Klondike and the Yukon River. Philadelphia: H. Altemus, 1897. 213 pp.

COOMBS, CHARLES IRA (b. 1914)
Bush Flying in Alaska. New York: William Morrow, 1961. 93 pp.

COONTZ, ROBERT EDWARD (b. 1864) (US Naval officer)
From the Mississippi to the Sea. Philadelphia: Dorrance, 1930. 483 pp. Six years in Alaska.

COOPER, J. EARL
Alaska Sportsman, July, '57 (criticized for advocating capital punishment repeal); Sept., '57; Gruening (federal judge at Nome, 1952-53, former US Atty. at Anchorage).

COOPER, JOHN M.
Snares, Deadfalls and Other Traps. Washington: Catholic University, 1933. 144 pp. Algonquians and Athabaskans.

COOPER LANDING
Alaska Life, March, '44; *Alaska Sportsman*, May, '58 (Charles Lien); Baker; Couch (post office from 1947); Sharples.

COOPER, WILLIAM SKINNER
Several publications on glaciology in Alaska; see the Arctic Bibliography.

COOPER (metal)
Alaska Sportsman, Apr., '41 (none mined in 1940); Apr., '49 (photo of Gulkana nugget); Aug., '52 (Kennecott copper abandoned due to high cost); July, '53; Nov., '53; Sept., '54 (Hyder); Apr., '55 (B.C.); Nov., '55 (Wrangell); July, '56 (B.C.); *Alaska-Yukon Magazine*, Feb., '08 (map); Nov., '10 (Prince William Sound); Abercrombie; Allen; Bancroft; Davis (discovery of Kennecott district); Dole (discovery); Denison (Guggenheim, 1928-29 boom years); Gruening; Higginson (Guggenheims everywhere); Kinney; Nichols (Alaska Syndicate); Pilgrim (copper now only a gold ore byproduct);

Sundborg (Kennecott ceased in 1938, $227 million total production); Underwood (Ellamar, Latouche, Kennecott).

COPPER CENTER
Abercrombie (40 cabins in 1898); Baker (name first published in 1898, 300 miners wintered here in 1898); Colby (settled 1896); Couch (post office from 1901); Denison; *Jesuit Missions* (new boarding school, 1954); Powell (1899 "we found one man, and he was running a trading post"); Rice (1899 only a few prospectors remained); Sundborg (once site of agricultural experiment station); Tewkesbury (est. 1896, first white town in interior Alaska, native village ajoins settlement); Wickersham.

COPPER, BRYAN
Alaska, the Last Frontier. New York: William Morrow, 1973.

COPPER ISLAND (Commander Island group)
Bancroft; Colby (seal rookeries, copper deposits); Dall; Hulley (Basov in 1743).

COPPER RIVER
Abercrombie (expeditions); *Alaska Sportsman*, Aug., '39 ("Pioneers of the Copper River"); Feb., '49 (change in river course isolates Abercrombie Rapids); Oct., '52 (boat aground in Delta); Feb., '57 (photo of Chitina); Oct., '72 (freeze-up at Chitina); *Alaska-Yukon Magazine*, Feb., '10 (unusual photo near Tonsina); Oct., '10 (Andrews); Dec., '10 (near Tiekel); Allen (history: mouth discovered by Nagaiev in 1781, two Russian expeditions in 1796 fell short, partial explorations in 1798, 1803, 1819, 1843; in 1847 Serebrinnikov's party murdered by natives near the Tazlina, but leaders notes survived; C.G. Holt ascended to Taral in 1882, and John Bremner repeated this trip in 1884; Allen in 1885); Brooks (first successful ascent by Klimovskii in 1819); Baker (named by Nagaiev Miednaia [Copper], also called by native name, Atna); Bancroft (correctly located in 1779 by Bodega y Quadra); Dall; Dole (steamboats on upper reaches); Gruening (salmon depleted); Higginson (Miles and Childs Glaciers); Kochler; Petrof; Rafferty (military party descends river); Scidmore (Schwatka to the sea via the Copper in 1891); Tompkins (Russians called natives the Mednovskii [Copper]; Patochkin, 1798; Bazhenov, 1803; Klimovskii, 1819; Serebrinnikov in 1843 [to Trail]); Whiting; Wickersham (despairs Allen's attitude toward Atna natives). See also Kennecott, Atna natives, and Addison Powell.

COPPER RIVER AND NORTHWESTERN RAILROAD
Abercrombie (railway feasibility); *Alaska Life*, Jan., '41 (map); *Alaska Sportsman*, Nov., '38 (to be abandoned); March, '39 (Alaska Road Comm. will maintain line); June, '43 (Albert C. O'Neel); Feb., '49 (crosses Grinnel Glacier); Nov., '49 (construction photos); Jan., '51 (abandoned because of labor strikes and exhaustion of paying ore); Jan., '51 (first excursion train reached Chitina on Sept. 25, 1910); *Alaska-Yukon Magazine*, June '07 (planned to build to Yukon River); Aug., '09 (construction photos); Dec., '10 (photos); Beach (Iron Trail); Chase (first train from interior reached Cordova April 8, 1911); Colby; Franck (fare 10 cents per mile, photo of long

bridge); Goulet; Gruening (constr. cost $20 million); Davis; Hampton (Alaska a Morganheim barony); Higginson (construction battles); Hulley (construction obstacles); Nichols (Cordova Coal Party); Underwood (photo of $2 million bridge); Whiting (best on construction days).

COPPER RIVER HIGHWAY
Tewkesbury (to utilize 131 miles of abandoned railroad right-of-way to Chitina). See also *Alaska Weekly*, Dec., '50 (construction expected in next spring). There is a voluminous newspaper literature on the proposed highway, and several State Transportation Division studies. In 1970 the Sierra Club filed suit to prevent the construction, and in 1971 the federal government (Bureau of Land Management and National Park Service) announced intentions to consider a portion of the Copper River country for a possible national park and wilderness area. In 1975 a temporary settlement was reached postponing any highway development north of the Copper River delta for three years.

"COPPER RIVER JOE"
See Charles Henry Remington.

COPPER VALLEY SCHOOL
Newsletters, brochures and incidental materials in the Archive of the Catholic Diocese of Anchorage. Also *Corona Borealis*, the school yearbook, 1962-70. See also *Alaska Sportsman*, March, '57 (history, beginnings). The Copper Valley School was begun by Jesuit missionaries in 1956, replacing Holy Cross on the Yukon as Alaska's Catholic mission high school. The school closed in 1970. It was located at the junction of the Copper and Tazlina Rivers. See further references in the *Alaska Sportsman* Index.

CORBETT, JOHN
The Lake Country. Rochester: *Democrat and Chronicle* Printing, 1898. 161 pp. Visit to Sunrise on Cook Inlet.

CORDOVA
Alaska Development Board (Cordova District, 1951); *Alaska Life*, Nov., '38 (Wm. Chase); Nov., '40 (crab industry); Jan., '41 (crab and salmon); Feb., '42; Jan., '44 (photo); March, '46 (photo); Apr., '47 (crab); *Alaska Sportsman*, July, '36 (tourism); Aug., '39 (Johnny Walker); March, '42 (CR&WRR box cars used as dwellings); Apr., '44 (photo); Jan., '50 (cannery fire); Feb., '51 (Mt. Eccles photo); Jan., '52 (fire in downtown Cordova); March, '52 (photo Eyak lake); Feb., '53 (notes [erroneous derivation of name]); Jan., '55 (1923 photo); Nov., '56 (mailboat); Jan., '58 (salmon derby); and others, see Index; *Alaska-Yukon Magazine*, Aug., '09 (on first years of town by Grinnel with photos by Hegg); May, '10 (early photos); Dec., '10 (special issue on Cordova); July, '12 (notes); Baker (name of Cordova Bay changed in 1906 to Orca Bay to avoid confusion with bay of similar name near Dixon entrance; the bay was shown as Puerto Cordova on Vancouver's atlas, he either bestowing the name or copying Spanish usage; Orca was the name of the ships of the Pacific Steam Navigation Co. which operated a cannery on the bay from December, 1894); Beach (Iron Trail); Chase; Colby (errs in assuming Caamano named the

bay Cordova; Caamano did not voyage farther north than about 55°N. Lat.); *Cordova Daily Times*; Cordova Coal Party; Couch (post office from 1906); Elliott (Odiak cannery on Eyak lake); Franck (air photo, 1938); Borroughs (Orca had cannery and post office in 1898); Davis ([errs in thinking Caamano named bay for Cordoba in Spain]); Hulley; Nichols; Stuck; Sundborg; Tewkesbury; Tompkins (railroad problems); Vancouver (Mr. Johnstone's party visited Puerto Gravina ["named by Fidalgo"], and then surveyed Orca Bay without naming it; they did name Hawkins Island, and in a cove on the northwest of Hinchinbrook Island they found a cross on which was inscribed "Carolus IV, Hispan. Rex, An. 1790, Pr. Dn Salvador Fidalgo."); Wagner (Puerto Cordova named by Fidalgo, in honor of Luis de Cordova, captain-general of the navy; name adopted by Vancouver); Whiting (there was a cannery at Eyak; M.J. Heney changed the name Eyak to Cordova); Wilson; Young. See also Copper River, Kennecott.

"CORDOVA COAL PARTY"
Clark (citizens dumped inferior coal into bay); Gruening (May 5, 1911); Hellenthal (occurrence given much publicity); Hulley (after continued and futile protests against importation of foreign coal); Nichols (railroad imported Canadian coal; party occurred on May 3; no one arrested); Tompkins; Underwood (importation when there was already an abundance there).

CORDOVA DAILY TIMES
Cordova, Alaska. 1916. 32 pp. Also issued in 1914. *All-Alaska Review*, 1928, and again in 1930. The Cordova press also printed the *Chitina Weekly Leader*, at Cordova.

CORLEIS, W. H. R.
Hayes (independent Baptist missionary at Wrangell); Willard (from Philadelphia in 1879 with family); Wright (opened school in upper Taku village in 1881; in June 1882 established a mission station 12 miles below Juneau); Young (returned to states in 1882).

CORMACK, JOHN C.
"Building a Snow House," *Beaver*, 1940.

CORNEY, PETER (d. 1836)
Voyages in the North Pacific. Honolulu: Thrum, 1896. 138 pp. Trading voyages between the northwest islands and China, 1813-1818, with a description of the Russian settlements.

CORSER, HARRY PROSPER (1864-1936)
Totem Lore and the Land of the Totem. Juneau: Nugget Shop, 1934. 110 pp. Corser was a lecturer with the Pacific Steamship Company, having come to Alaska as a Presbyterian missionary. About 1904 he converted to the Episcopal faith.
Legends of Natives of Southeastern Alaska. Reprinted from *Alaska-Yukon Magazine*, October, 1908.
"Wrangell the Prosperous," *Alaska-Yukon Magazine*, October, 1911.
"Intellectual Life of the Thinklet Indians," *Alaska-Yukon Magazine*, July, 1912.
76 Page History of Alaska. n.p., 1927.

"History of Wrangell," *Alaska Year Book, Alaska Weekly*, 1927.
See also T-1086 ff.

CORSON, JOHN W.
See T-1091.

CORWIN (US Revenue Cutter)
Alaska Life, Nov., '41 (photo); *Alaska Sportsman*, Aug., '49 (her later history); Bancroft (Arctic cruise of 1885); Darling (winter photo at Nome); Hulley (C.H. Townsend in 1885, first suggested bringing reindeer to Alaska); Morris (vessel completed at San Francisco in 1877); Muir; Scidmore (Hootznahoo village shelled); Stuck (Corwin Coal Mine, 1890); Wead (sold into commercial service 1900).

CORY, TREVOR
The White Pass and Yukon Route. Seattle, 1901. 444 pp.

CORYELL, HUBERT VANSANT (b. 1889)
Klondike Gold. New York: Macmillan, 1938. 319 pp.

CORYELL, JOHN RUSSELL (1851-1924)
A Klondike Claim. New York: Street and Smith, 1897. 219 pp. Pseudonym for Coryell was Nicholas Carter.

COSGROVE, CHARLES H.
"Ketchikan: A Story of a Southeastern Mining Center," *Alaska's Magazine*, April, 1905.

COSTELLO, J. A.
The Siwash, Their Life, Legends and Tales. Seattle: Calvert Co., 1895. 169 pp.

COTTEN, BRUCE
An Adventure in Alaska. Baltimore: *Sun* Printing Office, 1922. 107 pp.

COTTER, FRANK; see O'Cotter.

COTTERILL, GEORGE FLETCHER (b. 1865)
The Climax of a World Quest. Seattle: Olympic Publishing Company, 1928. 226 pp. Puget Sound exploration; Juan de Fuca, George Vancouver.

COUCH, JAMES S.
Philately Below Zero: A Postal History of Alaska. State College, Pa.: American Philatelic Society, 1957. 81 pp. Many factual inaccuracies.
"Those Imported Musk Oxen," *Alaska Sportsman*, March, 1938. See criticism in *Alaska Sportsman*, June, 1958.
"Highway to History," *Alaska Sportsman*, January, 1957. Taylor Highway.
"Development of Hot Springs in Alaska," *American Philatelist*, August, 1953. Manley Hot Springs.

COUES, ELLIOTT
Fur-bearing Mammals. Wn.DC: GPO, 1877. 348 pp. US Geological and Geographical Survey of the Territories.

COUGHLAN, JOSEPH BULLOCK (US Naval officer)
Baker (Coast charts); Bancroft (succeeded Merriman in command of the *Adams*, which was replaced by the *Pinta* in 1884); Scidmore (buoys); Young.

COULTER, CHARLES C.
"The Native Alaskan and the Ethical Affinities of the Japanese," *Alaska Magazine and Canadian Yukoner*, May, 1900.

COUNCIL (Council City)
Alaska-Yukon Magazine, Apr., '07 (photo); Baker (on Niukluk River, Seward Peninsula); Castle; Colby (1938 descr.); Couch (post office 1950-53); Higginson (founded by Daniel P. Libby and party); Hulley (Libby party found gold here in March 1898; it was the Libby party who found gold at Anvil Creek); Rickard (population 200 in 1908); Stuck (Presbyterian church here); Tompkins; Underwood (max. pop. 3600; 1901 pop. 653; [Underwood est. the *Council City News* in 1902, selling his interest to his partner, Ella Fitz, in 1903]).

COUNCIL CITY AND SOLOMON RIVER RAILROAD
Harrison (16 miles in operation, 3 photos).

COUNCIL, MARY LEE
Alaska Life, Jan., '46 (secretary to Dimond and to Bartlett); Potter.

COURTNEY, WILLIAM B.
"Riding Alaska's Storms," *Colliers*, December, 1937.
"Christmas Zoo," *Colliers*, December, 1937.
"Pilgrim's Progress in Alaska: Matanuska Valley Project," *Colliers*, May, 1938.

COVARRUBIAS, MIGUEL (b. 1904)
The Eagle, the Jaguar, and the Serpent: Indian Art. New York: Alfred A. Knopf, 1954. 314 pp.

COVILLE, FREDERICK VERNON (1867-1937)
See the Arctic Bibliography. Coville described the work of Frederick Funston.

COWAN, ROBERT ERNEST (1862-1945)
A Bibliography of the History of California and the Pacific West, 1510-1906. San Francisco: Book Club of California, 1914. 342 pp. Cowan was one of the more important western Americana book collectors. This bibliography lists only 1000 of his 7000 titles. His collections were sold to the University of California (1897) and the University of California at Los Angeles (1936).

COWIE, DONALD
"To Japan via the Aleutians," *Queen's Quarterly* (Kingston, Ontario), May, 1942.

COX, BERNIECE
"Battle for Alaska," *Alaska Life*, December, 1942.

COX, EDWARD GODFREY
A Reference Guide to the Literature of Travel. n.p. 1938.

COXE, WILLIAM (1747-1828)
Account of the Russian Discoveries between Asia and America. London: T. Caddell, 1780. 367 pp. This work went through at least four editions, and includes numerous translations (usually partial). Coxe lived for some time in Russia, and was conversant in Russian and German. Although the work

is based much on second hand material, it was for many years the most comprehensive source of information on Russian early voyages. It is still the only source for some translations. It is said Catherine II gave Rev. Coxe permission to use the Russian archives and later had his work translated into Russian. See Tompkins, and Brooks.

A Comprehensive View of the Russian Discoveries. London: J. Nichols, 1787. 31 pp.

COYOTES
Alaska Sportsman, Jan., '40 (trapping near Matanuska); Sept., '40 (75 killed at Kachemak Bay); Apr., '41 (hides worth $5); Apr., '42 (turn over traps); Feb., '47 (hunt near Kasilof); Dec., '47 (first predatory coyote killed near Circle, 1923); July, '49 (bounty to $30); Apr., '50; July, '55 (photo); Apr., '57 (eat porcupines near Kenai); Oct., '60; May, '72; Dufresne; Franck; Stuck (followed white man into north country).

CRABS
Alaska Life, June, '49; *Alaska Sportsman*, Nov., '42 (Amok Island in Bering Sea); Dec., '42 (St. Lawrence Eskimos fish through ice); Aug., '43 (crab canning, Bering Sea); March, '45; March, '47 (photo); Apr., '47 (7 tons frozen flown to Calif.); Aug., '47 (Bering Sea floating cannery); Oct., '49; July, '50 (crab packers challenge foreign market); Apr., '51 (threatened by return of Japanese crabbers); June, '51 (Russian crabmeat barred); July, '51; June, '53 (Juneau tanner good quality, but not commercially feasible); Oct., '55 (ship live crabs to Seattle); Feb., '56; Apr., '56 (Cordova cannery); July, '56 (100,000 pounds brought into Kodiak, average male weighing 15 pounds); Sept., '56 (Kodiak); Feb., '57 (Homer); Apr., '67 (Dungeness); Feb., '71 (research); Sept., '72 (tanner); Denison (3 dungeness canneries at Cordova); Sundborg (king only recently fished commercially); Tewkesbury (experimental cannery ship in Bering Sea draws $1 million).

CRAIG
Alaska Sportsman, Aug., '38; Oct., '46; June, '48 (named for Craig Millar, uncle of Margaret E. Bell); Apr., '50; July, '50 (earthquake damage); Sept., '53; Oct., '53; Jan., '58 (Libby McNeil Libby cannery burned); *Alaska Weekly*, Dec., '50 (court ruling voids liquor prohibition); Hadman (7 year resident); Sundborg (half native population); Tewkesbury; Williams.

CRAIG, LULU ALICE
Glimpses of Sunshine and Shade. Cincinnati: Editor Publishing Company, 1900. 123 pp.

CRAIN, MEL
"When the Navy Ruled Alaska," US Naval Institute, *Proceedings*, LXXXI (1955): 199 ff.

CRANBERRIES
Alaska Life, June, '45 (varieties); *Alaska Sportsman*, Jan., '59; Oct., '68 (lowbush); Aug., '71 (wild berries of Alaska); Denison; Henderson (lowbush abundant); Parker (lowbush are lingon berries); Sundborg (bog lands of southeast well adapted to commercial cultivation); U of Alaska, Ext. Serv. (Bulletin, 1961).

CRANE, ALICE ROLLINS
Smiles and Tears from the Klondike. New York: Doxey's, 1901. 203 pp.
"Midnight Sun in the Klondike," *National Geographic*, February, 1901. In the same issue also "Northern Lights."

CRAWFORD, JOHN WALLACE (Captain Jack)
See T-1116; as well Judge (entertained at Dawson).

CREEKMORE, RAYMOND
Lokoski. New York: Macmillan, 1946. 48 pp. Juvenile.

CREIGHTON, DONALD
A History of Canada. Boston: Houghton, Mifflin, 1958. 619 pp.

CREWE, E. O.
Gold Fields of Alaska. Chicago: Cole, 1897. 61 pp. How to Get There.

CREWE, FRED
Poems of Klondyke's Early Days and Alaska's Long White Trail. Milwaukee: North American Press, 1921. 60 pp. Photographs of the Klondike stampede taken in 1897-98.
See T-1120 ff.

CRICHTON, CLARKE, Jr.
Frozen-in! London, 1930. Attempted rescue of the cargo of the *Nanuk* by Eielson and Borland.

CRILLON, MOUNT
Alaska Sportsman, Feb., '38 (photos); Baker (named by LaPerouse in 1786 for the French minister of Marine); Colby (Harvard-Dartmouth Expeditions, 1933-34); Washburn (in *National Geographic*, March, 1935).

CRIMONT, JOSEPH RAPHAEL (Catholic Archbishop of Alaska, 1917-45)
Sketch of the Martyrdom of Seghers. Victoria: Diggon-Hibben, 1944. 30 pp. Archbishop Crimont also wrote the entry on Alaska for the Catholic Encyclopedia. See also the following:
Alaska Sportsman, Apr., '44 (50 years in Alaska); Aug., '45 (died in Juneau, buried at the shrine of St. Terese); Denison; Calasanz (photo); Couch (first post master at Koserefsky, 1899); *Jesuit Missions*, July, '45; Jenkins (letter on the death of Bishop Rowe); Judge (arrived at Holy Cross, 1894); Robins; Santos (biography; became bishop in 1917); Savage (the work is virtually a biography of Bishop Crimont).

CRISLER, LOIS
Arctic Wild. New York: Harper and Row, 1958. 301 pp. Wolves.
"Break-up on the Yukon," *Alaska Sportsman*, August, 1958. See also *Alaska Sportsman*, October, 1957. Films made by Herb and Lois Crisler have been used by the Disney Studios.

CROFT, ANDREW
Polar Expedition. London: A. & C. Black, 1939. 268 pp.

CROMPTON, C. EDWARD
"The World's Greatest Seal Herd," *Travel*, January, 1932.

CROSBY, THOMAS (1840-1914)
Among the An-ko-me-nums. Toronto: Briggs, 1907. 243 pp. Flatheads of the Pacific Coast.
Up and Down the North Pacific Coast. Toronto: Methodist Mission Society, 1914. 243 pp. Mission ship. See Brooks, Morris, and Large. A Methodist missionary, Crosby served at Nanaimo, followed William Duncan at Fort Simpson, and was at Wrangell in 1876.

CROSNO, MAY FRANCES
Unpublished master's thesis on the Alaska purchase, University of California, 1926.

CROSKEY, ROBERT
"The Russian Orthodox Church in Alaska," *Pacific Northwest Quarterly*, LXVI (1975): 26-29.

CROSKEY, ROBERT and ROBERT NICHOLS
"The Conditions of the Orthodox Church in Russian America," *Pacific Northwest Quarterly*, LXIII (1972): 41-54. A translation of Bishop Innocent's (Veniaminov) 1839 report, published at St. Petersburg.

CROSS, VICTORIA
A Girl in the Klondike. New York: G. Munro's, 1898. 133 pp. Victoria Cross is a pseudonym for Vivian Cory.

CROSS, WILBUR
Ghost Ship of the Pole. New York: W. Sloane, 1960. 304 pp. Noble's *Italia*.

CROSSON, JOE (1903-1949)
Alaska Life, Aug., '40 (photo); Nov., '47; *Alaska Sportsman*, Sept., '49; Apr., '50 (Mt. Crosson and Crosson Glacier in Mt. McKinley National Park named in his honor); *Alaska Weekly*, Oct., '51 (widow); Franck (he and Harold Gillam found the Eielson wreckage); McGarvey; Potter.

CROUCH, T. W.
"Frederick Funston in Alaska, 1892-1894: Botany above the Forty-ninth Parallel," *Journal of the West*, X (1971): 273-306.

CROUSE, NELLIS MAYNARD (b. 1884)
The Search for the Northwest Passage. New York: Columbia University Press, 1934. 533 pp. Background theory and Ross, Parry, Franlin, Lyon, Back, Simpson, Dease, McClure, Kellett, Amundsen.
In Quest of the Western Ocean. New York: Morrow, 1928. 480 pp.
The Search for the North Pole. New York: R.R. Smith, 1947. 376 pp. Kane, Hayes, Jall, Nares, Greely, Nansen, Andree, Abruzzi, Peary.

CROWELL, N. H.
Sourdoughs All. Vancouver, Wn.: The Author, 1942. 250 pp.

CROYERE, LOUIS de l'ISLE de la (d. 1741)
Bancroft (brother [actually half-brother] of the map-maker, died at Petropavlovsk in 1741); Dall (with Chirikov, died of scurvy); Golder (spent some time on the Canadian frontier); Hulley (crossed Siberia); Tompkins (conducted expedition to Archangel and Kola Pass in 1727).

CRUMRINE, NINA (1889-1959) **and JOSEPHINE**
Alaska Life, July, '42 ("The Painters Crumrine"); June, '45 (paintings and poetry); Dec., '45 (photos mother and daughter); Aug., '48; June, '49; *Alaska Sportsman*, Aug., '41 (pastels of natives permanent in Juneau capitol bldg.); Oct., '42 (photo); Aug., '57 (photo); *Alaska Weekly*, July, '51 (Josephine a pupil of Ziegler); *Daily Alaska Empire*, Aug., '59 (mother dies at Juneau).

CULLEN, STEWART
The Wreck of the Wakamiya Maru. Reprinted from *Asia* (the American Magazine of the Orient), May, 1920. Drifting for months, it reached Unalaska in 1794. A castaway, its survivors were returned by the Russians to Japan in 1803.

CUMMING, JOHN ROSS (b. 1923)
"Metaphysical Implications of the Folklore of the Eskimos of Alaska," *Anthropological Papers*, 1954. University of Alaska.
"Survey of Teacher Status and Comparative Analysis of the Professional and Social Problems of Teacher Personnel in the Territory of Alaska," unpublished master's thesis, University of Washington, 1954.

CUMMINGS, CLARA E.
See "The Lichens of Alaska" in the Harriman report.

CUMMINS, HAROLD (b. 1893)
"Dermatoglyphics in Eskimos from Point Barrow," *Journal of Physical Anthropology*, Philadelphia, April, 1935.

CUNNINGHAM, CAROLINE
The Talking Stone. New York: Alfred A. Knopf, 1939. 118 pp. Early American stories told before the white man's day on this continent by the Indians and Eskimos. (Subtitle)

CUNNINGHAM, CLARENCE
Clark (coal claims finally denied); Hulley (Special Agent Jones reported that his 37 coal claims were fraudulent, but Ballinger ordered them cleared); Nichols; Tompkins (admitted he contemplated development of his claim into a company); see Ballinger-Pinchot controversy.

CUNNINGHAM, THOMAS PATRICK, S. J. (1906-1959)
Alaska Sportsman, Oct., '46 (photo; on King Island 11 years); May, '52 (Fr. Tom discusses Eskimos; intelligent, but will not work by schedule); March, '57 (at Barrow from 1954); *Daily Alaska Empire*, Sept., 59 (died of heart attack at Barrow); Franck (biog., son of New Zealand farmer); O'Connor (when ill and stranded at Wales, Sig Wien flew him to Nome); Potter (Wien); Santos (came to Alaska in 1936); Tewkesbury (biography).

CURRENT HISTORY
"Colonialism in Alaska," December, 1955.

CURRY

Alaska Life, March, '42 (Chef Maurikas); May, '42 (Maryl Brisky); June, '42 (photos of hotel clerk and matron); Colby (railroad passengers spend night here); Couch (post office from 1926); Denison (Curry was earlier known as Dead Horse); Franck (good food, high prices); Gruening (Congressman Charles F. Curry of Cliforia was Chairman of the House Committee on Territories after 1913); Poor (frame hotel with roaring mountain stream in back); Pilgrim (no Pullman cars on railroad; Curry hotel used instead); Tewkesbury (150 room hotel 248 miles from Seward, 130 from Anchorage).

CURTIN, WALTER RUSSELL

Yukon Voyage. Caldwell: Caxton Printers, 1938. 299 pp. Unofficial log of the *Yukoner.* Marooned in river ice the winter of 1897-98.

CURTIS, ASAHEL

Alaska Sportsman, June, '42 (photo); July, '42 (Log Cabin, B.C.); Aug., '42 (piloted boats in White Rapids); Dec., '64 ("Klondike Photographer"); Bankson.

CURTIS, CLAUDE H.

The Gospel in Alaska. San Francisco: Gospel Mission Press, 1946. 93 pp. War preaching in Alaska.

CURTIS, EDWARD S.

The North American Indian. 20v. Seattle: 1907-1930. There have been several editions of Curtis's full 20 volumes of photographic plates of the North American Indians, including Alaska, and several one volume abridgments. One complete reprint with supplement (4v. supplement) was published by Johnson Reprint Corp., New York, 1970. For Alaska photographers see Hegg, P.S. Hunt, and the Miles Brothers.

CURWOOD, JAMES OLIVER (1878-1927)

The Alaskan: A Novel of the North. New York: Cosmopolitan Book Corp., 1923. 326 pp. Reindeer and the Lomen Brothers are the setting.
Philip Steele of the Royal Northwest Mounted Police. Indianapolis: Bobbs-Merrill, 1911. 307 pp.
Steele of the Royal Mounted. New York: Burt, 1911. 306 pp.
The River's End. New York: Burt, 1919. 303 pp. About Conniston of the Royal Mounties.
The Valley of Silent Men. New York: Triangle Books, 1920. 298 pp. Three River country, Canada.
The Flaming Forest. New York: Toronto: C. Clark, 1921. 296 pp. Canadian Northwest. The last three titles as well in an anthology, *North Country Omnibus*, New York, Grosset and Dunlap.
"Hunting Walrus with the Eskimos," *Leslie's*, December, 1913.
"Gentlemen Unafraid," *Leslie's*, September, 1913. (Northwest Mounties).
See also "James Oliver Curwood and his Far North," in *The Bookman*, February, 1921. Curwood published 33 works, of which 31 were novels. His autobiography, *The Glory of Living*, was published in England.

CUSTOMS

Gruening (7 collectors in the first decade); Hulley (customs act of 1868); Morris (list of deputy collectors); Tewkesbury (Canadian regulations). Customs collectors were for a time the only civil representatives in Alaska, civil government not being created for the area until the organic act of 1884.

CZAP, IVAN M.

"The Bishop of Alaska's First Diocese," *Russian Orthodox Journal*, May, 1959.

D

DABOVICH, S.

The Holy Orthodox Church. Wilkes-Barre, Pa.: 1898. Liturgy.
The Lives of the Saints. San Francisco: Murdock Press, 1898. 127 pp.

DACHNOWSKY-STOKES, ALFRED P.

Peat Resources in Alaska. Wn.DC: GPO, 1941. 84 pp. Department of Agriculture.

DAFOE, JOHN W.

Clifford Sifton in Relation to His Times. New York: Macmillan, 1931. 552 pp.
"Alaska Boundary Dispute," in the boundary arbitration. Sifton was the British agent in the boundary negotiation.

DAHLAGER, JULES B. (ca. 1884-1952)

Alaska Sportsman, July, '37 (painting "Home of a Sourdough"); Nov., '43 (berry-picking with bears); Jan., '53 (died at Ketchikan, Sept., '52); *Alaska Weekly* (showing at Fairbanks); Chase (how he learned to paint at Cordova, 1921-29); Hulley (lifetime 2500 canvases).

DAIRYING

Alaska Sportsman, July, '56 (Matanuska); Calasanz (problems at Holy Cross); Denison; Hulley (Matanuska; Fairbanks); Sundborg; Tewkesbury (Juneau); see Agriculture.

DALBY, MILTON ARTHUR (b. 1904)

The Sea Saga of Dynamite Johnny O'Brien. Seattle: Lowman and Hanford, 1933. 249 pp. See also O'Brien, and Shiels.

DALE, GEORGE ALLAN (b. 1900)

Northwest Alaska and the Bering Sea Coast. Reprinted from *Societies Around the World*, ed. Irwin T. Sanders, Lexington, Ky.: University of Kentucky, 1952. Dale was an ANS officer from 1935 to 1949. In this article he notes his observations of changes in Eskimo life, including modes of travel, fishing techniques, cooking utensils, housing, and health and social customs. See also Evelyn Butler, and natives.

DALE, JOHN

See T-1154.

DALL, WILLIAM HEALEY (1845-1927)

Alaska and Its Resources. Boston: Lee and Shepard, 1870. 627 pp. The first major work published in English on Alaska. There were many errors in the work, and for the Upper Yukon Dall had only second-half accounts. Nonetheless, as an account of Alaska's potential and the attitude toward Alaska in the early years, the work was and is essential.

Among Dall manuscripts (see Frederick), there are the Dall Notebooks, in the Dall Papers in the Division of Mollusks (Dall was primarily an authority on mollusks) of the US National Museum in Washington, D.C. See also the Smithsonian Institution.

"Explorations in Russian America," *American Journal of Science*, January, 1868.

"A Critical View of Bering's First Expedition," 1725-30," *National Geographic*, May, 1890.

"Notes on an Original Manuscript Chart of Bering's Expedition of 1725-30," *Annual Report*, US Coast & Geodetic Survey, 1890.

"Remarks on the Natural History of Alaska," *Proceedings*, Boston Society of Natural History, 1868. This volume also includes the occasion when Dall suggested Alaska Range for the name of Alaska's central mountains.

Pacific Coast Pilot, Alaska, with Marcus Baker, 1883. (Wn.DC: GPO).

"Explorations in the Aleutian Islands," *Journal*, American Geographical Society, 1874.

Scientific Results of the Exploration of Alaska. Wn.DC: GPO, 1876. 276 pp. Smithsonian Institution Technical Paper, Dall's explorations of 1865-74.

"Alaska as it Is and Was," *Bulletin*, Philosophical Society of Washington, 1895. This contains an account of the work of the Scientific Corps of the Russian-American Western Union Overland Telegraph Expedition, 1865-68, and a description of the Coast Survey explorations in Alaska, 1871-80 under Dall's direction.

"Bancroft's Alaska: The Works of Hubert Howe Bancroft—*History of Alaska, 1730-1885*," in the *Nation*, February, 1886.

"A Yukon Pioneer, Mike Lebarge," *National Geographic*, April, 1898.

"A New Volcanic Island near Bogosloff Island," *Science*, January, 1884.

"Further Notes on Bogosloff Island," *Science*, January, 1885.

"The Metlakatla Mission in Danger," *National Geographic*, April, 1898.

"Marcus Baker," *National Geographic*, January, 1904.

Spencer Fullerton Baird: A Biography. Philadelphia: Lippincott, 1915. 462 pp. Contains correspondence relating to the organization of the Overland Telegraph Expedition. Baird was assistant secretary of the Smithsonian.

"On the Remains of the Later Pre-historical Man Obtained From Caves in Catherine Archipelago, and Especially From Caves of the Aleutian Islands," in *Contributions to Knowledge*, Wn.DC: GPO, 1878. Smithsonian Institution, Vol. 22.

"Tribes of the Extreme Northwest," *Contributions to North American Ethnology*, 1877. Wn.DC: GPO. Smithsonian Institution.

"On the Geological Aspects of Possible Human Immigration Between Asia and America," *American Anthropologist*, January, 1912.

"Reminiscences of Alaskan Volcanoes," *Scientific American*, July, 1918.

For a listing of Dall's technical papers, see the Tourville Bibliography and the Arctic Bibliography. Among secondary materials on Dall see the following:

Baker (biographical notes); Bancroft (Dall's story of the Nulato massacre); Brooks (life at St. Michael; influence on Congress re: the value of Alaska); Caswell (photo); Harriman; Herron (Juvenile); James (dall, at 20, was one of six men selected by Robert Kennicott to accompany him to Alaska to survey conditions along the proposed telegraph route to Siberia and St. Petersburg. After Kennicott's death on the Yukon in 1866, Dall succeeded him as head of the Scientific Corps); Scidmore (in his Alaska and Its Resources Dall gives a resume of the work of Veniaminov and Wrangell); see also these additional: Gabrielson; Morris (est. of native pop.); Nichols; Petrof; Stuck. See also Sherwood.

After plans for the Overland Telegraph collapsed in 1866, Dall remained in Alaska at his own expense. Later he worked for the US Coast Survey. Still later he served as paleontologist with the US Geological Survey, and as Curator of the Division of Mollusks and Tertiary Fossils at the National Museum in Washington. Numerous flora, fauna and geographical features in Alaska are named in his honor.

DALL, WILLIAM H., GEORGE M. DAWSON, and WILLIAM OGILVIE

The Yukon Territory. London: Downey and Co., 1898. 438 pp.

DALTON, JACK (1855-1944)

Alaska Sportsman, Jan., '42 (bagged largest bighorn sheep); Jan., '43 (resides Seaside, Oregon); March, '43 (biog.); Feb., '45 (died in San Francisco at age 89); July, '52 (drove cattle over Dalton trail to Ft. Selkirk); Aug., '52 (photo of Dalton and pack train with Indian packers); *Alaska Weekly*, Dec., '44 (obituary, was one of the 1880's pioneers); Brooks (1891 Dalton and Glave made second trip into Alsek basin and on to White River; first long pack trip in Alaska); Hawthorne (invented the Dalton sled [manufactured in Skagway] shot Jack McGinnis for slander); Hilscher (brought strawberry plants to Haines); Morgan (epic cattle drive of 1898; thrashed Tim Vogel for selling liquor to his men; told Birch to take his railroad off Dalton's property); Underwood; Walden; Williams (stories of his daring; a cousin of the Dalton Brothers of Kansas?).

DALTON TRAIL

Alaska Sportsman, Jan. '55 (Haines Highway follows old trail closely); Abercrombie (cattle were driven over trail to Rink Rapids); Brooks (from Pyramid Harbor to the top of the pass at the head of Klehini River); Denison (later life); Hawthorne (route ended at Ft. Selkirk on the Yukon); Rickard (over Chilkat Pass); Schwatka (Dr. Krause was the first to traverse this trail); Thompson (Juvenile); Wells; Winslow (descr.).

DANA, JOHN COTTON

The Far North-West. Newark: for the Travelers, 1906. 40 pp.

DANA, JULIAN
Sutter of California. New York: Harper's, 1917. 234 pp. John Sutter purchased most of the Russian properties in California when Fort Ross was liquidated in 1841. It was on other of Sutter's land later (1848) that the strike was made which initiated the California gold rush.

DANA, MARVIN
The Shooting of Dan McGrew. New York: Grosset & Dunlap, 1915. 317 pp. Based on the Robert Service poem.

DANENHOWER, JOHN WILSON (1849-1887)
Narrative of the Jeannette. Boston: Osgood, 1882. 102 pp. Synopsis of the cruise and detailed account of the retreat of the crew to Siberian shores.

DANIEL, HAWTHORNE (b. 1890)
Bare Hands. New York: Coward-McCann, 1929. 244 pp. Steamboat built on Devil's Island off the Alaska coast by four shipwrecked men.

DANKOLER, HARRY EDWARD (b. 1863)
James Griffin's Adventures in Alaska. Milwaukee: Yewdale, 1900. 276 pp.

DANNENBAUM, JED
"John Muir and Alaska," *Alaska Journal*, II (Autumn), 1972.

DARLING, ESTHER BIRDSALL
Baldy of Nome. San Francisco: Robertson, 1913. 75 pp. Well known dog story.
Boris, Son of Baldy. New York: Alfred A. Knopf, 1944.
Boris, Grandson of Baldy. Philadelphia: Penn Publishing Company, 1936. 317 pp.
Luck of the Trail. Garden City: Doubleday, 1933. 309 pp.
Navarre of the North. Garden City: Doubleday, 1930. 268 pp.
"Up in Alaska, A Poem," *Alaska-Yukon Magazine*, December, 1907.
"Forget-me-not," *Alaska Examiner*, Ketchikan, October 18, 1924. A portion of this poem is in the Session Laws of Alaska (Territory), the act designating the official Alaska flower.
The Break-up. New York: A.L. Burt, 1940. 320 pp.
No Boundary Line. New York: William Penn, 1942. 288 pp.
For secondary material on Esther Darling see the following:
Alaska Sportsman, Aug., '51; *Alaska Weekly*, Aug., '51 (Mrs. Darling at sourdough reunion in San Francisco); *Alaska-Yukon Magazine*, December, 1907; *Alaska-Yukon Gold Book* (at Nome, 1907-1917); Clark (Scotty Allan); Underwood (Scotty Allan); Wickersham (poems).

DARLING, FRANK FRAZER (b. 1903)
Pelican in the Wilderness. New York: Random House, 1956. 380 pp.

DARLING, ISOBEL
"Joaquin Miller's return from the Klondike," *Leslie's*, January, 1899.

DARNELL, RODNEY G.
"Brown Bears will Kill," *Field and Stream*, May, 1958.

DARSIE, RICHARD FLOYD
See T-1186.

DARTMOUTH COLLEGE LIBRARY
Dictionary Catalog of the Stefansson Collection on Polar Regions. Boston: G.K. Hall, 1967. 8v.

DASHKEVICH, ANTONY
Archangelo-Michaelovki (Cathedral of Michael the Archangel at Sitka). New York, 1899. 71 pp.

DAVENPORT, WALTER
"Great North Road: Highway from Vancouver to Alaska," *Collier's*, April, 1939.

DAVIDSON, DONALD C.
"The War Scare of 1854," *British Columbia Historical Quarterly*, October, 1941.
"Relations of the Hudson's Bay Company with the Russian-American Company on the Northwest Coast," *Brit. Col. Hist. Quarterly*, January, 1941.

DAVIDSON, DONALD THOMAS (b. 1919)
"The Geology and Engineering Characteristics of Some Alaskan Soils. *Bulletin*, Iowa Engineering Experimental Station, Ames, Iowa, 1959. 149 pp.

DAVIDSON, GEORGE (1825-1911)
The Alaska Boundary. San Francisco: Alaska Packers' Association, 1903. 235 pp. Covers the boundary from the 1825 Russo-British treaty to the decision of the Alaska Boundary Tribunal, 1903.
Francis Drake on the Northwest Coast. Transactions of the Geographical Society of the Pacific, 1908. 118 pp.
Tracks and Landfalls of Bering and Chirikov. San Francisco: Partridge, 1901. 44 pp.
"Report of George Davidson relative to the Resources and the Coast Features of Alaska Territory," *Annual Report*, US Coast & Geodetic Survey, 1867. Report of the US Coast Survey geographical reconnaissance on the cutter *Lincoln* of Sitka Harbor, St. Paul Harbor on Kodiak, and Iliukliuk and Captain's Harbors on Unalaska Island.
Coast Pilot of Alaska. Wn.DC: GPO, 1869. Southern boundary to Cook Inlet. See in this an interesting account of a Japanese junk wrecked in Alaskan waters.
"An Examination of Some of the Early Voyages of Discovery and Exploration on the Northwest Coast of America from 1539 to 1603. *Annual Report*, Coast and Geodetic Survey, 1886.
"The New Bogosloff Volcano in the Bering Sea," *Science*, March, 1884.
"Volcanic Eruption in the Bering Sea: The Recent Volcanic Eruption of St. John Bogoslov," Am. Geographical Soc., *Bulletin*, 1890.
"The Glaciers of Alaska that are shown on Russian charts or mentioned in Older Narratives," *Transactions*, Geographical Society of the Pacific, 1904.
See also the following:
Baker (made voluminous notes during 1867 summer in Alaska); Bancroft; Brooks (fixed Chirikov's landfall at Sitka Bay); Dall; Harrison (on

name of Nome); Lewis (biog.); Ogilvie (1869 at Chilkat); Scidmore (met Chilkat chief in 1867 and 1869, made Chilkat vocabulary); Sherwood (*Explorations*); Wagner; Wickersham (1869 eclipse); see also the Arctic Bibliography.

DAVIDSON GLACIER

Baker (named by Coast Survey in 1867, near head of Lynn Canal); Colby; Collis (visit 1890, excellent photo); Dall; Higginson; Scidmore; Young. All observers report Davidson as one of the most beautiful and inspiring in Alaska.

DAVIDSON, INNES N.

The Arctic Brotherhood. Seattle: Acme Publishing Co., 1909. 104 pp. History.

DAVIS, CAROL BERRY

Songs of the Totem. Juneau: Empire Printing Company, 1939. 48 pp. Thlingit songs in Thlingit and English.
Alaska Driftwood. Denver: Big Mountain Press, 1953. 80 pp. Poetry.

DAVIS, CHARLES HENRY (1807-1877) (Officer, US Navy)

Narrative of the North Polar Expedition. Wn.DC: GPO, 1876. 696 pp. Edition of the narrative of Captain Charles Francis Hall, commander of *Polaris*, on the 1871-73 search of the North Pole, with an account of Hall's death.

DAVIS, GEORGE THOMPSON BROWN (b. 1873)

Metlakahtla. Chicago: Ram's Horn Company, 1904. 128 pp.
An Indian Arcadia in Alaska. New York, 1904. Wm. Duncan.

DAVIS, HORACE

"Record of a Japanese Vessel Driven upon the Northwest Coast of North America and Its Outlying Islands," a paper read before the American Antiquarian Society annual meeting, April, 1872. Westover, Mass.: Hamilton, 1872. 22 pp.

DAVIS, JEFFERSON C. (1828-1879) (US Army officer)

Andrews (commander at Sitka, Indian troubles); Bancroft (Sitka Indian troubles); Scidmore (Seward was his "guest" at the "Castle" in 1869); Wickersham (Davis with Seward to view the 1869 eclipse at Klukwan).

DAVIS, JOHN WILLIAMS (b. 1873)

The Unguarded Boundary. Birmingham, England: Birmingham and Midland Institute, 1920. 36 pp. US-Canada border.

DAVIS, MARY LEE (b. 1890)

Uncle Sam's Attic. Boston: W. Wilde Co., 1930. 402 pp.
Alaska: The Great Bear's Cub. Boston: W.A. Wilde, 1930. 314 pp.
We Are Alaskans. Boston: W.A. Wilde, 1931. 335 pp.
Sourdough Gold. Boston: W.A. Wilde, 1933. 351 pp.

"Our Passage to Asia," *Virginia Quarterly Review*, July, 1928.
"Eskimo Butterfly," *Scribner's Magazine*, September, 1929.
"Climb Uncle Sam's Arctic Stair," *Independent Women*, April, 1935.
"Who Lives in Alaska?," *Scribner's Magazine*, May, 1923.

DAVIS, MAXINE

"I Saw Alaska at War," *Satevepost*, May, 1942.

DAVIS, NANCY YAW

"The Role of the Russian Orthodox Church in Five Pacific Eskimo Villages as Revealed by the Earthquake," *The Great Alaska Earthquake of 1964.* Human Ecology. Wn.DC: National Academy of Sciences, 1970. Committee on the Alaska Earthquake, Division of Earth Sciences, National Research Council. Old Harbor (Kodiak), Kaguyak, Ouzinkie, Afognak and Chenega.

DAVIS' PAINKILLER

See Sullivan.

DAVIS, ROBERT TYLER

Native Arts of the Pacific Northwest. Stanford: Stanford University Press, 1949. 165 pp.

DAVIS, WILLIAM MORRIS (ca. 1815-1890)

Nimrod of the Sea. New York: Harper's, 1874. 403 pp. Whaling.

DAVISON, LONNELLE

"Bizarre Battleground: the Lonely Aleutians," *National Geographic*, September, 1942.

DAVYDOV, GAVRIL IVANOVICH (1784-1809)

Dvukratnoe Puteshestvie v Ameriku (Two Voyages to America). St. Petersburg, 1810-1812. 2v. The voyages, by Davydov and Khvostov, were in 1802-04 and 1804-07, including crossings of Siberia. There is information in the volumes on Baranov and the Russian-American Company, with descriptions of life on Kodiak, Eskimos and also Tlingits, and some material on Kenai geography. See also Nikolai Aleksandrovich Khvostov, 1778-1809. See also the Arctic Bibliography, and T-1211 ff. See also the following:
Kotzebue; Sokolov, A.P. (as shown in Wickersham's bibliography); Baker; Bancroft (some American incidents; both officers were eventually killed while crossing the Neva River at night; both were supposedly heavy drinkers); Chevigny (on their meeting with Baranov at Kodiak); Petrof.

DAVYDOV, IURII VLADIMIROVICH

See T-1213.

DAWES, EFFIE LENORE (ca. 1871-1961)

I Reached for a Star. New York: Exposition Press, 1951.

DAWES GLACIER

Alaska Sportsman, Jan., '38 (photo); Baker (named by Coast Survey, 1891, for Henry Laurens Dawes, Massachusetts); Colby (12 miles from Sumdum, head of Endicott Arm, Stephens Passage); Muir (explored in 1880); Young (first, with Muir, to explore Endicott Arm).

DAWSON, CARL ADDINGTON
See T-1215.

DAWSON CREEK, B. C.
See Alaska Highway; see also Denison, Hulley, Sundborg.

DAWSON, GEORGE MERCER (1849-1901)
Report on an Exploration of the Yukon District. Montreal: Dawson Brothers, 1888. 277 pp. One object of this 1887 expedition was to determine where the Yukon or Pelly River crosses the 141st meridian (Alaska-Canada boundary).
"Notes on the Geology of Middleton Island," *Bulletin*, Geological Society of America, 1893.
"The Extinct Northern Sea-cow, and Early Russian Explorations in the North Pacific," *Canadian Field Naturalist*, January, 1894.
"Historical Notes on Events in the Yukon District," *Review of Historical Publications*, II: 173-189.
See also the following:
Alaska Sportsman, April, 1957; Colby (Director, Geological Survey, Canada; town named for him); Dall; Higginson; Henderson (son of McGill University Professor); Tolmie; Tompkins (Dawson and Ogilvie conduct surveys near boundary); Underwood (his travels).

DAWSON, LAFAYETTE (US Judge, 1885-1888)
Gruening (from Mo., more satisfactory than his predecessors); Shiels (at Sitka); Young (heavy drinker, but seemed moral; jury in his court refused to convict on the basis of Indian testimony).

DAWSON (City), Yukon Territory
Alaska Life, Dec., '41 (theater); July, '42 (on 1899 fire); *Alaska Sportsman*, Feb., '44 (dance hall girls); Aug., '44 (ice jam); Apr., '46; Jan., '48; July, '51; Dec., '51 (*Black Sand and Gold*, Edward Lung as told to Ella Lung Martinsen, installments to June, '54); Aug., '53 (fire of 1898); Sept., '54; Jan., '56 (origin of slide overlooking city); Sept., '56 (*I Married the Klondike*, installments to March, '57, by Laura Berton); Apr., '57, and others; see Index; *Alaska-Yukon Magazine*, March, '07; Sept., '08 (special issue on Dawson); Bankson; Beach; Beattie; Berton; Black; Bruce; Cameron; Chase; Couch; Curtin; Davis; Denison; Franck; Hellenthal; Henderson; Higginson; Jacobin; Judge; Kitchener; Lund; McKeown-Hawthorne; Morgan-Woods; Ogilvie; O'Connor; Rickard; Romig; Service; Tollemache; Underwood; Walden; Wiedemann; Winslow.

DAWSON NEWS
Golden Cleanup Edition, Dawson, 1902. Copy in Alaska State Historical Library.

DAWSON-WHITEHORSE STAGE
Cameron; Rickard (one trip weekly, 330 miles); Stuck (up the Nordenskjold River, cross the river at Yukon Crossing).

DAY, BETH
Glacier Pilot. New York: Henry Holt, 1957. 348 pp. Bob Reeve.

DAY, LUELLA
Tragedy of the Klondike. New York, 1906. "True facts of what happened in the gold fields under British rule."

DEAD HORSE GULCH
Alaska Sportsman, Apr., '45 (legend on tablet erected 1929); May, '57; Alaska-Yukon Gold Book (photo); Becker (unsanitary conditions); Cameron (exhaustion); Colby (between White Pass City and White Pass; another Dead Horse Gulch near Thompson Pass on the Richardson Highway); Franck (monument at Inspiration Point, 3 miles below White Pass); Hawthorne (horses not loaded correctly; last big pull to summit is through gulch); Tewkesbury; Whiting (formerly a crude Indian path); Willoughby (Mrs. Pullen stated there were 2500 bodies in the gulch at one time); Young (descr. plunges).

DEADMAN'S BAY (Kodiak Island)
Alaska Sportsman, Dec., '57 (photo); June, '58 (photo).

DeAHNA, HENRY C. (Customs Collector, Sitka, 1877-78)
Gruening (no pay for 358 days' service, as he failed to get Senate confirmation); Morris (critical).

DEANS, JAMES (b. 1827)
Tales of the Totems of the Hidery. Chicago: International Folk-Lore Association, 1899. 96 pp.

DEAN, D. M.
"Salmon and Sermons: Archdeacon Hudson Stuck and the Yukon River Cannery Controversy," *Journal of the West*, IX (1970): 552-566.

DeARMOND, DALE
Juneau: A Book of Woodcuts. Anchorage: Alaska Northwest Publishing, 1973.

DeARMOND, ROBERT NEIL (b. 1911)
The Founding of Juneau. Juneau: Gastineau Channel Centennial Association, 1967. 214 pp.
Some Names around Juneau. Sitka: Sitka Printing Company, 1957. 48 pp.
"Alaska's Panhandle," *Alaska Life*, January, 1948.
"The Army Takes the Sitka Census," *Alaska Life*, November, 1945.
"Names Make the Map," *Alaska Life*, August, 1949.
"The Wreck of the *James Allen*," *Alaska Life*, December, 1945.
"The Lady was a Trailblazer," *Alaska Sportsman*, July, 1958.
"The Ill-Favored Steamboat *Arctic*," *Alaska Journal*, I (Autumn, 1971).
See also the following:
Alaska Sportsman, August, 1953 (assistant to Governor); March, 1956 (photo, five years at Pelican); Couch (first postmaster at Pelican). See E. Atwood.

DEASE, PETER WARREN (1788-1868)
See Thomas Simpson.

DEASE LAKE
Alaska Sportsman, July, '54 (gold stampede in 1925); May, '55 (photo); Hulley (in the Cassiar boom of 1876).

De BAETS, MAURICE (1863-1931)
The Apostle of Alaska. Paterson, N.J.: St. Anthony Guild Press, 1943. 292 pp. Trans. Mary Mildred (Sister of St. Anne). Archdishop Charles Seghers. Seghers was martyred at Nuklukayet on the Yukon by a demented camp helper.

DEBORAH, MOUNT
Alaska Sportsman, Oct., '53; Nov., '54 (first ascent); *Alaska Weekly*, June, '51; Beckley, F. (*Appalachia*, Dec., '54; *Alpine Journal*, May, '55); Colby; Harrer; see also Allen and Wickersham on Allen.

DECISION, CAPE
Alaska Sportsman, Aug., '38 (photo); Hadman; Vancouver (named it in 1793, apparently in memorial to his determination to accurately delineate the extent of previous coastal discoveries in the North Pacific).

DECKER, KARL
"Dr. Frederick Cook—Fakir," *Metropolitan* (Magazine), January, 1910. See also Washburn.

DEE, HARRY
James Griffins' Adventures in Alaska. Milwaukee: J.H. Yewdale, 1903. 276 pp. Harry Dee is a pseudonym for Harry E. Dankoler.

DEER
See the Arctic Bibliography.

DEER MOUNTAIN
Alaska Sportsman, Nov., '43 (photo); Colby; Uyeda (Juvenile).

DEERING (village)
Alaska Sportsman, Dec., '57 (article by teacher); May, '58 (art. by Frank Engles, 1906-09; Eskimos feared horses); Baker (at mouth of Inmachuck River, south shore of Kotzebue Sound); Colby (mining camp); Couch (post office from 1901); Franck (photo); Harrison (photo; mines were on Inmachuk River, Kugruk River, and Candle Creek); Hilscher (Bess Cross); Stuck (native inhabitants removed at government expense to Noorvik in 1915); Tewkesbury.

DEFENSE OF ALASKA
The researcher should see the primary materials of the various military and civilian government agencies whose responsibility included the defense of Alaska in one capacity or another, e.g. the US Army, US Air Force, US Navy, US Coast Guard, Corps of Civil Engineers, etc. See also the various official histories of war and war theaters produced by the various branches, and also those monographs produced by military and civilian scholars. See as well biographical material and studies on important figures, e.g. Billy Mitchell, Simon Bolivar Buckner, Bob Reeve, etc. See also the following:
Alaska Life, Aug., '40; Feb., '41 (Stefansson); Nov., '41 (Woman's Bay); Jan., '42 (home defense); *Alaska Sportsman*, see the Index; *American Weekly*, June, '53 (Eskimo role); Andrews (early forts, WW I); Dimond (strategic value of Alaska); Driscoll; Ellsworth; Ford; Garfield (Thousand Mile War); Gruening; Gilman; Handleman; Hall; Hulley; Kitchener (WW I had little effect); Marston (Eskimo scouts); Morgan; Pilgrim (early military activity); Poor; Potter; Rutzebeck; Schwatka; Stein, Robert ("The Defense of Alaska," Wn.DC: Judd and Detweiler, 1910. 23 pp.); Sundborg; Tewkesbury (WW II bases); US Army (various publications by the command, USARAL); US Air Force (various publications by the command, Alaska Air Command); US Congress (see the documents produced by various times by the Committees on Military Affairs and later, the Armed Services Committees); Vidal.

deFILIPPI, FILIPPO
See Filippi, Filippo; see also T-1226 ff.

de FONTE, BARTOLOMEO
See Fonte, Bartolomeo de.

de FUCA, JUAN
See Fuca, Juan de.

DeGROFF, EDWARD (b. 1910)
Alaska-Yukon Magazine, Oct., '07 (photo); Hulley (NW Trading Co. sent him from Sitka to Juneau in 1881 to est. a store); Morgan (Sitka store, acquired Chichagof Mine died of appendicitis); Rickard (opened first Juneau store, was first Juneau postmaster, was secretary at meeting which changed name from Harrisburg to Juneau in 1881).

deLABILLIARDIERE, JACQUES JULIAN HOUTEN
See T-1234 ff.

De LAGUNA, FREDERICA (b. 1906)
The Archaeology of Cook Inlet. Philadelphia: University of Pennsylvania Press, 1934. 263 pp.
The Prehistory of Northern North America. Menasha, Wisc.: Society for American Archaeology, 1947. 360 pp. "Comparative and analytical discussion of the American and Asiatic origin and relationships of prehistoric Eskimo and Indian cultures."
Chugach Prehistory. Seattle: University of Washington Press, 1956. 289 pp.
Under Mt. St. Elias. Wn.DC: Smithsonian Institution, 1972. 3v.
"An Archaeological Reconnaissance of the Middle and Lower Yukon Valley, Alaska," *American Antiquity*, July, 1936.
"A Comparison of Eskimo and Paleolithic Art," *American Journal of Archaeology*, 1932-33.
"Eskimo Lamps and Pots," *Journal* of the Royal Anthropological Institute of Great Britain and Ireland, 1940.
"History of the Ever Useful Reindeer, Man's Sub-Arctic Ally," *Frontiers*, December, 1938.
"Indian Masks from the Lower Yukon," *American Anthropologist*, 1936.
"Mummified Heads from Alaska," *American Anthropologist*, 1933.
The Eyak Indians; see Kaj Birket-Smith.
"A Pottery Vessel from Kodiak Island, Alaska," *American Antiquity*, 1939.
"Preservation of Archaeological and Ethnological Material in Alaska," Alaska Science Conference, 1950.
"Some Dynamic Forces in Thlingit Society," *Southwestern Journal of Anthropology*, 1952.

"An Alaskan Stone Lamp," *Bulletin*, University Museum, University of Pennsylvania, Philadelphia, 1932.

"Ceremonial Paddles from the Eyak Indians," *Bulletin*, University Museum, March, 1934.

Eskimo and Tena Lamps and Cooking Pots. Copenhagen, 1938.

"Expedition to Alaska," University Museum, 1935. *Bulletin*.

"The Importance of the Eskimo in Northeastern Archaeology," in *Man in Northeastern North America*, ed F. Johnson, 1946.

"A Preliminary Sketch of the Eyak Indians," *Publications*, Philadelphia Anthropological Association, 1937.

"Peintures Rupestres Eskimo (Rock Paintings of the Eskimo)," *Journal*, Societe des Americanistes ee Paris, 1933.

"Some Problems in the Relationship between Tlingit Archaeology and Ethnology," *Memoirs*, suppl. to *American Antiquity*, 1953.

"Three Carvings from Cook Inlet, Alaska." *Bulletin*, University Museum, February, 1933.

Fog on the Mountains. New York: Doubleday, 1938. 275 pp.

"The Atna of Copper River, Alaska: The World of Men and Animals," *Folk*, II (1967/70).

DELANEY, ARTHUR K. (1841-1905)
Alaska Bar Association and Sketch of the Judiciary. San Francisco, 1901. 80 pp. Delaney was district judge at Sitka, 1895-97, and had previously served as commissioner of customs (1887-1889).

"An Account of a trip from Minnesota to Alaska in 1887," Ms. in Alaska State Historical Library.

See also *Alaska Monthly*, May, 1906.

DELAROV, EUSTRATE IVANOVICH
Bancroft (native of the Pelopponnesus, became a Moscow merchant, commanded the *St. Alexi* under Zaikov, Kamchatka to Prince William Sound, succeeded Samilov, preceded Baranov); Chevigny (returned to Russia in 1792); Dall (visited Three Saints Bay in 1788 by Lopez de Haro, became chief director of colonies [Golikov-Shelikhov] in 1790, succeeded by Baranov 1792); Hellenthal (fine character); Hulley; Tompkins.

DeLEEUW, ADELE
James Cook: World Explorer. Champaign: Garrard Publishers, 1963.

DELEGATE TO CONGRESS
Gruening (various bills, activities of delegates); Nichols; Naske; Shiels (list of terms of delegates to 1933).

DeLESSEPS, JEAN BAPTISTE BARTHELEMY
See T-1251 ff.

DELISLE, JOSEPH NICHOLAS
Nouvelles Cartes des Decouvertes. Paris, 1753. See Wagner. See also T-1257 ff. Delisle was a Frenchman who lived in St. Petersburg 21 years (1726-47). Frank Golder located the Delisle manuscripts in the Archives de la Marine in Paris. See also Waxel.

DeLONG, GEORGE WASHINGTON (1844-1881)
Voyage of the Jeannette. Boston: Houghton, 1883. 2v. The *Jeannette* sailed from San Francisco in 1879, calling at Bering Sea ports. She went adrift in ice near Herald Island in November, and after 19 months, was crushed and sank, northeast of the New Siberian Islands. Among the crew members who reached the Lena River delta in Siberia, DeLong and eleven others perished. See also the following:

Alaska Sportsman, Apr., '52 (photo); Caswell (photo); Danenhower; Ellsberg; Gilder; Melville; Mirsky; Muir; Newcomb; Perry; Prentiss; Samoilovich; Underwood; Williams.

DEMARCATION POINT
Baker (makes the boundary line on the Arctic coast, named by Sir John Franklin in 1826); Dall; Scidmore; Stuck.

DEMENTIEV, ABRAHAM MIKHAILOVICH
Bancroft (mate on *St. Paul* with Chirikov, commanded one of the lost boats on the American shore); Calasanz; Higginson; Hulley; Tompkins.

DENALI
Alaska Sportsman, Apr., '56 (citizens want old name restored); Stuck; Tewkesbury; Wickersham (legends).

DENALI HIGHWAY
Alaska Sportsman, Oct., '54 (construction); July, '56 (McKinley Park); Dec., '56; Dec., '57.

DENIS, FERDINAND JEAN (1798-1890)
Les California, l'Oregon, et l'Amerique Russe. Paris, 1849.

DENISON, BENJAMIN WEBSTER (b. ca. 1905)
Alaska Today. Caldwell, Idaho: Caxton Printers, 1949. 374 pp. 27 articles by Denison and four other contributors, describing Alaska at the close of World War II.

DENISON, MERRILL (b. 1893)
Klondike Mike, an Alaskan Odyssey. New York: William Morrow, 1943. 393 pp. Story of Mike Mahoney (1874-1951) who knew Jack London, Robert Service, "Soapy" Smith, "Tex" Rickard, and others. Successful with mining investments, Mahoney once carried a piano on his back over Chilkoot Pass, and on another occasion made a 400 mile dog sled trek with the frozen body of Judge Humes. See also *Alaska Sportsman*, September, 1955 for a story of Mahoney's fight with Tommy Burns.

DENISON, MURIEL
Susannah of the Yukon. New York: Dodd, 1937. 343 pp.

Susannah, A Little Girl with the Mounties. New York: Dodd Mead, 1941.

Susannah Rides Again. New York: Dodd Mead, 1941.

Susannah of the Mounties. New York: Random House, 1959.

DENNETT, TYLER
"Seward's Far Eastern Policy," *American Historical Review*, October, 1922.

DENNIS, ALFRED L. P.
Adventures in American Diplomacy, 1896-1906. New York: Dutton, 1928. 537 pp.

DENNIS, ARTHUR PIERCE
"Life on a Yukon Trail," *National Geographic*, Oct., 1899.

DENNIS, ISAAC C. (US Customs Collector)
Bancroft (report on rowdyism at Wrangell); Brooks (appoints Indian police to abate liquor traffic); Gruening (reported on military liquor manufacture and traffic); Morris (very efficient in dealing with liquor problem, but resigned because of lack of civil government and law enforcement).

DENNIS, JAMES TEACKLE (1865-1918)
On the Shores of an Island in the Sea. Philadelphia: Lippincott, 79 pp. Sitka via the Inland Passage.

DENNY, LUDWELL
"Danger at the Back Door: Alaska," *Washington News*, Aug. 26-31, 1940.

DENSMORE, FRANK
Alaska Life, Jan., '46 (prospected the Tanana in 1885); Brooks (arrived at Ft. Reliance from outside in Sept., '82); Chase (Mt. McKinley was known as Mt. Densmore from the early 1880's until 1896); Hulley (was first white man down the Yukon in 1882); Henderson (in 1897 had been in Alaska 12 years); Underwood (trader, explorer, ascended the Kuskokwim); Wickersham (at Andreavsky in 1887, explored the Nenana River); Winslow (Densmore and Spencer washed $24,480 from Eldorado Creek near Dawson in a single day, built a saloon).

DENTON, VERNON LLEWELLYN (1881-1944)
The Far West Coast. Toronto: Dent, 1924. 297 pp. Early exploration.

DENVER GLACIER
Alaska Sportsman, Nov., '55 (near Sawtooth Mt., White Pass Route); *Alaska-Yukon Magazine*, March, '10 (photo); Baker; Colby (on an arm of the Taku); Denison (tapped by trail).

De PONCINS, GONTRAN
Kabloona. New York: Reynal and Hitchcock, 1941. 339 pp. Title is northern Canada Eskimo name for white man. De Poncins spent time with Eskimos, describing his observations and conclusions in this volume. He judges that the primitive Eskimos he lived with had no capacity for generalization.

DEPPERMAN, W. H.
"Two Cents an Acre: Fiasco of the Collins Overland Telegraph through Alaska," *North American Review*, March, 1938.

DERIABIN, VASILI (also Derabin, Dershabin, Derzhavin)
Bancroft (accompanied Glazunov on expedition from St. Michael, murdered at Nulato); Brooks (to Nulato in 1841, massacre in 1851); Colby (cruel to Indians); Dall (rebuilt Nultao fort which had been destroyed in 1838 and 1839); Hulley; Petrof; Stuck; Whymper (Nulato fort was Fort Derabin); Zagoskin (with Malahov at Nulato in 1838 and 1839, traded at Nulato in 1842).

deROQUEFEUIL, CAMILLE
See T-1274 ff.

DERR, RONALD A.
Alaska Sportsman, Jan., '58 (Fairbanks, Alaska Visitor's Association).

DESJARDINS, JOSEPH-ALPHONSE
En Alaska. Montreal: Messager, 1930. 293 pp.

DESMOND, ALICE (b. 1897)
The Sea Cats. New York: Macmillan, 1946. 216 pp.
The Talking Tree. New York: Macmillan, 1947. 177 pp.

DeVIGNE, HARRY CARLOS (b. 1876)
The Time of My Life. Philadelphia: Lippincott, 1942. 336 pp. Long-time Alaska doctor; worked for the Bureau of Education, and was later Territorial Commissioner of Health. Autobiographical.
Pole Star, with Stewart Edward White. Garden City: Doubleday, 1935. 452 pp.
See also *Alaska Sportsman*, February, 1958.

DEVIL'S CLUB
Alaska Sportsman, July, '40 (photo); Nov., '41 (descr.); Oct., '47; Jan., '52 (also on rainier side of Cascades in Washington and Oregon); Feb., '53; Dec., '53; Dec., '55; and others, see Index; Anderson (descr.); Burroughs; Hayes (used to beat girls at Wrangell Institute, according to Mrs. McFarland); Schwatka ("devil sticks" a prophylactic against witchcraft); Scidmore; Sharples; Willoughby (very potent in weaving spells).

DEVIL'S THUMB
Alaska Sportsman, Jan., '47 (first ascent in 1946); Sept., '47 (1937 attempt); Sept., '49 (photo); May, '51 (photo); Baker (on mainland east of Frederick Sound, named in 1869 by Meade); Dole ("named with a generosity toward the powers of darkness"); Scidmore (viewed upon emerging from Wrangell); Sessions.

DEVINE, EDWARD JAMES (b. 1860)
Across Widest America. Montreal: *Canadian Messenger*, 1905. 307 pp. Miner's life at Nome and on Kotzebue Sound.

DEW LINE (Distant Early Warning system)
Alaska Sportsman, Nov., '56 (photo); Feb., '57 (18 radar stations on the Arctic coast); March, '57 (supply problems); May, '57 ("White Alice" radio network); Dec., '57 (complete); see also White Alice system.

DEWEY, MOUNT
Alaska-Yukon Magazine, Aug., '09 (poem); Baker; Colby; Stuck.

DeWINDT, HARRY (1856-1933)
Through the Gold Fields. New York: Harper, 1898. 314 pp.
My Restless Life. London: Grant Richards, 1909.
From Paris to New York. London: G. Newnes, 1904. 311 pp. The route taken led through Siberia and Alaska.
See also Kitchener, who remarks that DeWindt was a reporter at Dawson for the *London Times*.

D'WOLF, JOHN (1779-1872)

A Voyage to the North Pacific. Cambridge, Mass.: Welch, Bigelow, 1861. 147 pp. Known as "Northwest John," D'Wolf was the uncle of Herman Melville. In 1804, at age 24, he was master of the *Juno* of Bristol, R.I., for the Northwest Coast. Rezanov and Langsdorff purchased his vessel for $68,000. Remaining in Russian America, he sailed in 1806 with Rezanov and Langsdorff for Okhotsk, having become well acquainted with Baranov and Davydov. The party was marooned in Petropavlovsk for the winter, described by D'Wolf. In 1807 the party proceeded to Okhotsk, and overland to St. Petersburg, Rezanov dying at Krasnoyarsk. D'Wolf was probably the second American to make a trans-Siberian journey, after John Ledyard. His description is valuable of Russian America, Petropavlovsk, and St. Petersburg. Only 100 copies of this work were printed, and it is now rare. In 1968 Ye Galleon Press of Fairfield, Washington, printed 600 facsimile copies.

DEZHNEV, SEMEN IVANOVICH (ca. 1605-1673)

Otpiska Semen Dezhneva (Report of Semen Dezhnev to the Governor of Yakutsk, Ivan Pavlovich Akinfiev, concerning his sea voyage from the mouth of the Kolyma River to the mouth of the Anadyr River [1655]). Izvestia, 1948. If this report is accurate, Dezhnev passed the Bering Strait in 1648. Golder attacked the validity of the claim. See the following:

Alaska Sportsman, Feb., '35 (a visit to the small [five igloo] village of Dezhnev on East Cape [known to the Russians as Cape Dezhnev] by Mrs. Edith Plaut in 1934); Bancroft; Brooks; Dall; Clark; Fisher, Raymond (a reply to Golder, in *Pacific Historical Review*, August, 1956); Markov. See also the discussion of Russians in America previous to Bering in Svetlana Fedorova's *Population of Russian America*.

DICKEY, MIRIAM LOUISE

Alaska Life, Aug., '48 (secretary to Austin Lathrop, started radio station KFAR in Fairbanks); *Alaska Sportsman*, Nov., '54 (purchase of Taku Lodge near Juneau); Potter; Tewkesbury.

DICKEY, WILLIAM A. (d. 1939)

"Discoveries in Alaska," letter in the *New York Sun*, Jan. 24, 1897, in which the name McKinley is suggested for the mountain previously known as Denali and Mt. Densmore. Dickey describes his trip to the Susitna and Chulitna Rivers.

"The Sushitna River, Alaska," *National Geographic*, Nov., 1897. See also the following:

Brooks (on a prospecting trip in 1896 Dickey saw Mt.McKinley and estimated its height at over 20,000'); Couch (postmaster at Landlock on Prince William Sound, 1905, 1912); Colby (named mountain Denali in 1896, returned to Sunrise with story of its grandeur, returned to Susitna River in 1897, naming the mountain McKinley); Washburn.

DICKINS, EDMUND FINLAY

See Baker; Dickins compiled numerous US Coast and Geodetic Survey reports, and commanded the Coast Survey steamer *Gedney* in southeast Alaska waters in 1899-1905.

DICKINSON, GEORGE W.

The Alaska Central Railway. Seattle, 1903. 51 pp.

DICKINSON, GEORGE

Brooks (Indian wife opened mission at Haines the year before the Willards arrived); Morris (found quartz ledge on Tongass Narrows; in 1875 was trader at Howkan for Sherrick and Turk); Ogilvie (trader with J.J. Healey at Dyea in 1887); Willard (his son kept store at Haines, 1881); Young.

DICKINSON, JACOB McGAVOCK (1851-1928)
(US Secretary of War, 1909-1911)

"The Alaska Boundary Case," paper read before the American Bar Association, September, 1904. 32 pp. Reprinted in ABA *Transactions*, 1904. Dickinson represented the US at the boundary arbitration of 1903. His papers (40,000 items) are in the Tennessee State Archives. See also Alaska boundary.

DICKINSON, SARAH

Jackson (school at Haines in 1880); Morris (wife of George Dickinson the trader); Young (interpreter for missionaries at Wrangell; full Tongass Indian).

DIEBITSCH, E.

"Explorations in Alaska," *Goldthwaite's Geographical Magazine*, I (1890): 203 ff.

DIETZ, ARTHUR ARNOLD

Mad Rush for Gold. Los Angeles: *Times-Mirror Press*, 1914. 281 pp. Dietz headed a party from New York which tried to reach the Klondike over glaciers in the region of Disenchantment Bay, near Yakutat. All but four members of the party perished.

DIGBY, BASSETT

The Mammoth. New York: Appleton, 1926. 224 pp. Siberia.

DIKEMAN (Iditarod mining camp)

Couch (post office 1911-1915); Kitchener (photo NC Co. store in 1911, moved to Ruby 1912); Stuck (river navigation difficult).

DILL, W. S.

The Long Day. Ottawa: Graphic Publishers, 1926. 232 pp. Yukon Reminiscences, gold rush.

DILLER, JOSEPH S.

"Report on Atmospheric Sand Dust from Unalaska," *Nature*, 1884 (London).

"Volcanic Sand which fell at Unalaska," *Science*, 1884.

"Lava from the New Volcano on Bogosloff Island," *Science*, 1885.

DILLINGHAM

Alaska Sportsman, June, '48; Apr., '52; Dec., '56 (pop. 800); Jan., '58 (history, by R. DeArmond; town named for Senator Wm. P. Dillingham [1843-1923] of Vermont, who was part of the Nelson committee); *Alaska Weekly*, (7th Day Adventist school dormitory bldg. burned in 1950); Dec., '50 (Baker (at head of Nushagak Bay, post office from 1905); Colby (dominated by huge cannery, bunkhouse serving as hotel); Doward (says Snag Point was named Dillingham prior to 1935); Sundborg; Tewkesbury; Wickersham (Dillingham was at Rampart in 1903, admitted to Alaska bar in that year, village site selected and named in 1903, Wickersham establishing a commissioner's court at that time).

DILLON, PETER
See T-1296 ff.

DIMOND, ANTHONY JOSEPH (1881-1953)
"The Strategic Value of Alaska," *Military Engineer*, Jan., '41.

"The Aleutians," *New York Times Magazine*, Nov., 1942. Judge Dimond was born in New York state, came to Alaska in 1905, practiced law at Valdez in 1913, served as a Territorial Senator 1923-31, and was first elected delegate to Congress in 1933. He was appointed US District Judge at Anchorage in 1945. See the following:

Alaska Life, June, '40; Sept., '43 (by Neuberger); Feb., '45; *Alaska Sportsman*, March, '45 (editorial); Sept., '50; Sept., '53 (biographical); Denison; Shiels; Tewkesbury. See also Naske, and Herron.

DIPTHERIA
Clark (Nome epidemic, 1925, dog heroes); Stuck (Ft. Yukon and Circle, 1904, in upper Minchumina country, upper Kuskokwim, 1906); Walden (serum rushed to Nome over trail from Kaltag); Wead (sleds crossed Norton Sound on 1924-25 drive to save time).

DISCOVERY DAY (August 17)
Colby (celebrated in Yukon Territory, esp. Dawson, to commemorate the discovery of gold in the Klondike, 1896); Ogilvie (discovery described).

DISENCHANTMENT BAY
Baker (named Puerto del Desengano [Port of Undeception] by Malaspina in 1791, he not being deceived that the bay represented the entrance to a northwest passage; the English translation "disenchanted" is an error); Colby; Higginson (merges with Russell Fiord, which bends sharply to the south; "enchantment" would be more appropraite); Rickard (the earthquake of Sept. 1899 which damaged Muir Glacier, raised the beach of Disenchantment Bay 40 feet, and did serious damage in Yakutat Bay); Scidmore (Hooper, in 1890, pushed 60 miles back into this bay, and discovered Hubbard and Dalton Glaciers; in 1891 Prof. Russell explored the bay in a canoe and charted Russell Fiord); Underwood (earthquakes generated tremendous wave which toppled much ice); Vancouver (explored by Lt. Puget, named Digger's Sound).

DISTANT EARLY WARNING LINE; see DEW Line

DISTIN, WILLIAM L. (1843-1914) (Surveyor-General of Alaska, 1897-1913)
Alaska-Yukon Magazine, Sept., '07 (photo); DeArmond (Distin moved the Governor's Office from Sitka to Juneau in 1906).

DIVERS, DIVING
Alaska Sportsman, June, '51 (Jim Wadsworth); March, '54 (Wadsworth crippled by bends); Feb., '58 (60 Navy frogmen place charges on Arctic coast to clear ice for shipping); Burford (Alaska diving experiences).

DIVIN, VASILII AFANASEVICH
See T-1300 ff.

DIXON ENTRANCE
Alaska Sportsman, May, '56 (photo); Baker (discovered by Spaniards in 1774, and named Entrada de Perez; Dixon named it for himself in 1787; Meares named it Douglas Entrance for Capt. William Douglas of the *Iphigenia*; Tebenkov used the native name, Kaigani Strait); Bancroft (Perez here in 1774; Caamano in 1792 sought to establish the Spanish name; country north of Dixon entrance "universally acknowledged" as Russian in 1820); Clark (same latitude as Copenhagen); Dall (Bodega and Maurelle discovered Dixon Entrance in 1775 and named it Perez Entrance or Inlet); Greenhow (discovered by Juan Perez in 1774, named Perez Inlet by Bodega and Maurelle in 1775); Higginson (Dixon Entrance is in British Columbia); Hulley; Scidmore (also known as Granitza Sound); Vancouver (although Vancouver was in the vicinity of Dixon Entrance and named Cape Knox, he does not mention Dixon Entrance in his text); Wagner.

DIXON, FRANKLIN W.
Through the Air to Alaska. New York, 1930. 216 pp.

DIXON, GEORGE (d. ca. 1800)
A Voyage Round the World. London: G. Goulding, 1789. 360 pp. Portlock and Dixon were sent by the King George's Second Company to the Northwest coast in the *King George* and the *Queen Charlotte*. They arrived in Cook Inlet in 1786 and spent the winter in the Hawaiian Islands. In May of 1787 they found Meares and his crew aboard *Nootka* suffering from scurvy, in Prince William Sound. Dixon sailed south on the coast, exploring Yakutat Bay and Sitka Sound. Portlock remained at Nuchek to trade with the natives. Bancroft, Dall and Brooks point out that both Portlock and Dixon had been midshipmen with Cook on the third voyage. Dole reports on Dixon's comments about an Indian girl, who, he declared, "would have been considered handsome even in England," after he persuaded her to wash the paint from her face.

Remarks on the Voyages of John Meares, in a letter to that Gentleman. London: Stockdale, 1790. 37 pp.

Further Remarks on the Voyages of John Meares in which several important facts misrepresented in the said voyages relative to geography and commerce are fully substantiated, to which is added a letter from Captain Duncan containing a decisive refutation of several unfounded assertions of Mr. Meares and a final reply to his answer. London: Stockdale, 1791. 80 pp.

See also Meares, Howay, and Dixon-Meares Controversy.

Letter and Memorandum from Capt. George Dixon to Sir Joseph Banks regarding the fur trade on the Northwest coast, A.D. 1789. n.p.: White Knight Press, 1941. 6 pp. 125 copies.

See also T-1306 ff.

DIXON, JOSEPH SCATTERGOOD (b. 1884)
Birds and Mammals of Mount McKinley Park. Wn.DC: GPO, 1938. 238 pp. National Park Service. See also the Arctic Bibliography.

DIXON, ROLAND B.
"Tobacco Chewing on the Northwest Coast," *Amer. Anthropologist*, January, 1933.

DOBBS, ARTHUR (1689-1765)
An Account of the Countries Adjoining to Hudson's Bay. London: J.Robinson, 1744, 211 pp. Additions include a letter from Bartholomew de Fonte on his voyage to prevent ships attempting discovery of a northwest passage, and an abstract of all discoveries which have been published of the islands and countries in and adjoining to the great western ocean between America, India and China.
A Letter from a Russian Sea-officer. London: A. Linde and J. Robinson, 1754. 83 pp. Concerning del'Isle's chart and memoir relative to the new discoveries northward and eastward from Kamtschatka.

DOCKSTADER, FREDERICK J.
The American Indian in Graduate Studies. New York: Museum of the American Indian, 1957. 399 pp. Bibliography of theses and dissertations.
Indian Art in America. London: Studio Books, 1960. 224 pp.

DODGE, ERNEST S.
Northwest by Sea. New York: Oxford University Press, 1961. 348 pp. A compendium of Arctic cruises from the Cabots to *USS Skate.*

DODGE, HOWARD LEWIS (b. 1869)
Attraction of the Compass. Long Beach: Seaside Printing Co., 1916. 243 pp.

DODGE, WILLIAM SUMNER (US Customs Collector)
Oration delivered at Sitka, Alaska, July 4, 1868. San Francisco: Alta California Printing Co., 1868. 30 pp. See also the following:
Andrews (appt. customs collector at Sitka, October, 1867, his instructions to Vincent Colyer, Special Indian Commissoner, on demoralizing influence of soldiers at Sitka); Gruening (report on lighthouse needs, quoted on soldiers and native women); Hulley (published first issue of the *Alaska Times* at Sitka); Morris (appt. acting commissioner in August, 1867, report on the intelligence of the Indians); Nichols; Petrof (elected mayor of Sitka); Scidmore (entertained Sec. Seward at his home in Sitka, having accompanied him on the *Active* from San Francisco); Wickersham (edited *Murphy's Alaska Times*).

DODIMEAD, ALLAN J. et al; see T-1320 ff.

DOE, J.
"Reindeer have Brought Riches to Alaska," *Compressed Air Magazine*, New York, December, 1930.

DOGS AND DOG RACING
See the *Alaska Sportsman* Index; see also the following: Allan, A.A.; Bogoraz; Brooks; Cameron; Colby; Couch (listing of dog trail routes); Dall; Morgan, E.E.P.; Muir; Rickard; Seppala; Wickersham; Willoughby.

DOHERTY, BEKA and ARTHUR HEPNER
"Alaska: Last American Frontier," and "Baranov and Russian America," *Foreign Policy Reports*, December, 1942.

DOKLAD KOMITETA, etc.
Report of the Committee on Reorganization of Russian-American Colonies (in Russian). St. Petersburg: 1863-64. 2v.

DOLE, NATHAN HASKELL (1852-1935)
Our Northern Domain: Alaska. Boston: D. Estes, 1910. 237 pp. Written, apparently, completely from secondary sources, but exceptional.

DOLE, NATHAN HASKELL and G. WALDO BROWNE
Alaska, by Hon. Walter E. Clarke. Boston: Marshall Jones Co., 1910. This is Dole's work, with the chapters on seals and Bogosloff Island omitted, with an introduction by Clark and illustrations added.

DOLPHIN
Alaska-Yukon Magazine, Aug., '08 (photo); Aug., '10; Oct., '10; Nov., '10; Jan., '11 (photo of passengers); Hulley (four Senators arrive on *Dolphin* [incl. Dillingham]); Stuck (Baranov's second ship built at Resurrection Bay, after *Phoenix*, was called *Dolphin*).

DOME CITY (and Creek)
Alaska-Yukon Magazine, Feb., '08 (photo); Jan., '09 (photo); July, '12; Baker (local name, Fairbanks area tributary to Chatanika Creek); Couch (post office 1906-22); Cameron (produced $1,700,000 in 1906); Kitchener (strike by D.A. Shea; NC Co. had store here); Wickersham (Dome City cases involved big money).

DOMINION CREEK (near Dawson)
Bankson (scandal involving Gold Commissioner, July, 1898); Mahoney (1898 mining scandal brought new gold commissioner); Winslow (gold commissioner favored certain men with advance information).

DONAN, PATRICK
Alaska. San Francisco: Pacific Steamship Co., 1899. 37 pp. Land of Gold and Glacier.

DONNELLY, ELEANOR CECILIA (1838-1917)
A Klondike Picnic. New York: Benziger Brothers, 1898. 160 pp.

DONNELLEY AND ACHESON (Kodiak store)
Alaska Sportsman, Nov., '57 (took over merchandise business of W.J. Erskine in 1948).

DOOLITTLE, JAMES H.
Denison (grew up in Nome); Potter (Brigadier General).

DONSKOI, VLADIMIR; see T-1332 ff.

DORA
Alaska Life, March, '47; *Alaska Sportsman*, Jan., '40 (left mail service in 1917; succeeded by *Pulitzer*, *Dora* broke in two on the east coast of Vancouver Island in 1920); Oct., '53 (her sister ship, *Bertha*, wrecked in Uyka Bay in 1915); Brooks (40 years service begun in 1879); Burroughs; Henderson (Capt. Anderson aboard, 1897); Higginson (descr.); Hoke; Kitchener (launched for ACCo 1880, San

Francisco-St. Michael, touching at Kodiak and Unalaska, but not Turnagain Arm [Hope-Sunrise]; mail contract 1900, St. Michael, Golovin Bay, Nome, Port Clarence, York); Lipke (at Seward 1916); Oliver (many local children named for *Dora*); Ray (at Unalaska 1883 on annual voyage to Aleutian Island stations); Robins; Wead (picked up *James Allen* survivors 1894); Willoughby (story of cook on "lost" voyage in 1904); Winchell (photo; monthly mail to Unalaska.

DORBRANDT, FRANK
Alaska Life, June, '42 (tribute to Lester Busey); Franck (impulsive, encouraged Eielson to fly at time of fatal accident); Potter (story of 1929 fatal accident).

DORRANCE, JAMES FRENCH
The Golden Alaskan. New York: Macaulay, 1931. 311 pp.

DOROSHIN, PETER P.
Article (in Russian) on Prince William Sound and the Copper River in *Gornyi Zhurnal* (Russian Mining Journal), 1866. See also the Arctic Bibliography. See as well the following:
Baker (reconnaissance of gold resources in Alaska for the Russian-American Co. in 1847); Brooks (prospected on the Kenai Peninsula, took a few ounces of gold from the Russian River, first ever mined in Alaska); Dall (examined also Baranof Island and went to California); Dole (40 men worked with him); Golder; Petrof; Scidmore (Sitka); Underwood (effort abandoned after two years). Doroshin was a graduate of the Imperial Mining School at St. Petersburg. He was sent to the colonies in 1847 or 1848 where he prospected four years for gold and coal. Machinery for coal mining was shipped from Boston to Port Graham, but the operation was not economical.

DORSEY, GEORGE A.
"A Cruise among the Haida and Tlingit Indian Villages about Dixon's Entrance," *Appleton's Popular Science Monthly*, June, 1898.
"The Geography of the Tsimshian," *Amer. Antiquities*, Oct., 1897.

DOUGLAS (city, and Island)
Alaska Life, July, '45; *Alaska Monthly*, Sept.-Nov., '06; *Alaska-Yukon Magazine*, Sept., '07 (special issue); *Alaska Sportsman*, March, '40 (photo); Feb., '44; Feb., '54 (Mike Pusich); Baker (island named by Vancouver in 1794 for Bishop of Salisbury; town incorporated 1902; pop. in 1890 was 402); Bancroft; Clark (Treadwell Mines); Colby (Douglas bridge completed in 1935; Pierre Erusard found gold quartz in 1881); Couch (post office from 1887); Denison (Ski Bowl, Glory Hole); Hulley (mines flooded 1917); Nichols; Sundborg; Tewkesbury; Vancouver.

DOUGLAS, Sir JAMES (ca. 1803-1877) (Governor of British Columbia, 1858-1864)
Bancroft (ms. quoted on the raising of the British flag at Fort Stikine [formerly Ft. Dionysius], 1840); Hulley (before governorship worked for Hudson's Bay Company); Petrof (on Tlingit Indians and their god, Yealth); Sage.

DOUGLAS, MARY
See T-1335.

DOUGLAS, ROBERT DICK (b. 1912)
A Boy Scout in Grizzly Country. New York: Putnam's, 1929. 181 pp.
In the Land of Thunder Mountains. New York: Brewer, Warren and Putnam, 1932. 160 pp.

DOUGLAS, WILLIAM
Baker (sailed from China in 1788, reaches Meares at Nootka after visiting Cook Inlet); Bancroft (found "tickets of good usage" issued by the Russians in the hands of Cook Inlet natives); Dall; Greenhow (was supercargo on the *Iphiginia* with a Portugese captain; spent winter of 1788-89 at Hawaii; arrived at Nootka where he was arrested by Martinez on May 15 and released on May 26); Hulley; Tompkins; see also John Meares.

DOW, PETER
Alaska. Hot Springs, Arkansas, 1927. 128 pp. Dow spent 28 years in Alaska.

DOWARD, JAN S.
They Came to Wrong Way Home. Mountain View, Calif.: Pacific Press, 1961. 132 pp. Story of the founding of Aleknagik by Ray and Mabel Smith in 1930.

DOWNES, ANNE MILLER
Natalia. Philadelphia: Lippincott, 1960. 286 pp. Novel of Sitka at the time of the purchase.

DOWNIE, WILLIAM (1819-1894)
Hunting for Gold. San Francisco: California Publishing Co., 1893. 407 pp.

DOWNS, WINFIELD SCOTT (b. 1895)
Encyclopaedia of Northwest Biography. New York: American Historical Co., 1941. 515 pp.

DOWNING AND CLARKE, PUB.
Pocket Dictionary of the Chinook Jargon. San Francisco, 1898. 32 pp.

DOYLE, J. C.
"Alaska Likes Its Reapportionment," *National Civic Review*, LII (May, 1963): 271 ff.
"Alaska: On Its Way," *State Government*, XXXIII (Winter, 1960): 2-10.

DRAGE, THEODORE SWAINE
See T-1344.

DRAKE, Sir FRANCIS
Bancroft (concludes that Drake is the discoverer of the western coast from Cape Mendocino to the region of Cape Blanco); Brooks (first challenge to Spanish possession); Davidson (not in San Francisco Bay); Dall (Coronado and Cabrillo preceded Drake, having cruised the Pacific coast in 1542; Drake refitted in a California bay); Greenhow (named the western coast New Albion, anchored in a bay at about 38°N., the description of which fits either San Francisco Bay or Bodega Bay [although Drake's Bay has been advanced again recently]); Hulley; Laut; Speck; Wagner.

DRAKE, MARIE (b. 1878)
Alaskana: Our Last Frontier. Juneau: *Daily Empire*, 1938. 48 pp. Marie Drake served as secretary to the territorial commissioner of education, and wrote "Alaska's Flag," the Alaska official song, in 1927. See also the following:
Alaska Sportsman, Aug., '55; Brummit (says the song was written by a student at the Jesse Lee Home).

DRANE, FREDERICK B.
"From Chechako to Archdeacon," *Alaska Churchman*, April, 1930.

DRAPER, WILLIAM F.
"A Navy Artist Paints the Aleutians," *National Geographic*, Aug., '43.

DREANY, E. JOSEPH
A Maxton Book about Alaska. New York: Maxton Publishers, 1959. Unpaged.

DREBERT, FERDINAND (b. 1890)
Alaska Missionary. Bethlehem, Penn.: Moravian Book Shop, 1959. 165 pp. Experiences during 42 years on the Lower Kuskokwim and Bering Sea coast.
A Brief History of Bethel. Bethel, ca. 1942. Also Los Angeles: University of California, 1963, from the original.

DRIGGS, JOHN BEACH (1854-1914)
Short Sketches from Oldest America. Philadelphia: W. Jacobs, 1905. 163 pp. Arctic Alaska traditons and legends. Driggs was the first white missionary at Point Hope, where he was stationed by the Episcopal church for 18 years from 1890. See also the following:
Jenkins (excellent summary; Driggs was sent to Seattle in 1908 for rest, having become "eccentric." He returned living "beyond Cape Lisburne."); Stuck (full story of his later years).

DRISCOLL, JOSEPH (b. 1902)
War Discovers Alaska. Phildelphia: Lippincott, 1943. 351 pp. War construction, Matanuska colony, Gruening's Guerrilla's (Territorial Guard).

DRIVER, HAROLD E.
The Contribution of A.L. Kroeber. Baltimore: Waverly Press, 1962. 28 pp. Culture area theory and practice.
Indians of North America. Chicago: University of Chicago Press, 1961. 685 pp.

DRUCKER, PHILIP (b. 1911)
The Native Brotherhoods. Wn.DC: GPO, 1958. 194 pp. Modern intertribal organizations of the Northwest coast.
Indians of the Northwest Coast. New York: McGraw-Hill, 1955. 209 pp. Bureau of American Ethnology, Smithsonian.
Cultures of the North Pacific. San Francisco: Chandler Publishing Company, 1965. 243 pp.
"Archaeological Survey of the Northern Northwest Coast," *Bulletin 133*, Anthropological Papers No. 20, Bureau of American Ethnology. Exploration, trade, native-European contacts in the 18th and 19th centuries.

"Culture Element Distributions," *Northwest Coast*, Berkeley: University of California Press, 1950.

DRUM, MT.
Alaska Sportsman, Nov., '41 (photo); Allen (his names for the Wrangell peaks; Drum for the Adjutant-General of the Army); Colby (view from Edgerton Highway); Harrer, H. (in *Amer. Alpine Jrnl.*, 1955, on first ascent, 1954); Higginson (view from Tiekel Roadhouse, and the trail up the Chitina); Rohn (descr.); Wickersham (on Allen, on the view between the Gakona and Gulkana watersheds).

DRUMHELLER, EHRLICHMAN CO.
A Review of the Salmon Industry with particular reference to Pacific American Fisheries, Inc., Seattle. 1935. 27 pp.

DRURY, W. H. Jr.
See T-1359.

DRUZHININ, ALEXEI (d. 1763)
Bancroft (successful voyage 1752-57, of 1759 to Atka, Umnak and Sitkhin Islands; slain with most of his companions by natives at Unalaska in 1763); Berkh (of four vessels from Okhotsk in 1762 only two returned; all on Druzhinin's ship were slain save three, only one of which ever got back to Siberia); Coxe; Petrof (Druzhinin's crew first to suffer from changed attitude of the Aleuts).

DRYAD
Higginson (British brig repulsed by Russians upon attempting to enter the Stikine in 1833); Hulley; Petrof (following Wrangell's tenure as Governor, the Russians leased the main land to Hudson's Bay Co. [see C.I. Jackson, *Pacific Historical Review*, 1967]).

DUCHAINE, WILLIAM J.
"Integration in Alaska," *The Beaver*, Summer, 1961.

DUCHAUSSOIS, PIERRE JEAN BAPTISTE (b. 1878)
Mid Snow and Ice. London: Burns, Oates and Washbourne, 1923. 328 pp. Work of the Oblate Catholic missionaries in the Canadian Northwest.
The Grey Nuns in the Far North. Toronto: McClellan and Stewart, 1919. 287 pp. Catholic missions in the Northwest Territories.

DUCKERING, WILLIAM ELMHIRST (1882-1950)
Hulley (18 years Dean at U. of Alaska); Tewkesbury (biog., born in England, taught at U.B.C.).

DUCKS
See the Arctic Bibliography, and the *Alaska Sportsman* Index; see also the following:
Alaska-Yukon Magazine, July, '09 (Pacific eider); Bailey (dozen varieties descr); Brandt; Denison (surprising variety in Alaska); Gabrielson and Lincoln; Harriman; Henderson; Ray (eider migration; Ray's party killed 4-500 each year for food); Sundborg; Tewkesbury.

DUFFIELD, WILL WARD
See Baker for a listing of his US Coast & Geodetic Survey maps.

DUFRESNE, FRANK (b. 1895)
Alaska's Animals and Fishes. W. Hartford. Vt.: Countryman Press, 1946. 297 pp. Dufresne was a miner before serving as agent for the US Biological Survey in Alaska, and later worked for the Alaska Game Commission, from 1920.
My Way was North. New York: Holt, Rinehart and Winston, 1966. 274 pp. Autobiographical.
No Room for Bears. New York: Holt, Rinehart and Winston, 1965. 252 pp.
"An Alaska Angler Speaks Out," *Alaska Sportsman*, Jan., '35.
"Dog Mushing in Alaska," *Alaska Sportsman*, March, '36.
"The Game and Fur Belong to All the People," *Alaska Sportsman*, April, 1944.
"Grouse of Alaska," *Alaska Sportsman*, December, 1935.
Mammals and Birds of Alaska. Wn.DC: GPO, 1942. 37 pp. US Fish & Wildlife Service.
"Spotting Poachers: Alaska Game Protection Goes Modern," *Alaska Life*, March, 1941.
"What of Tomorrow?" *Alaska Sportsman*, April, 1937.
"Clarence Goes Stripfishing," *Alaska Sportsman*, June, 1935.
"Talking Totems," *Alaska Life*, July, 1945.
See also the following:
Alaska Sportsman, Jan., '48 (Chief, Div. of Information, US Fish & Wildlife Serv.); Aug., '50 (last five years before retirement in Wn.DC; retired 1950); *Alaska Weekly*, Sept., '55; Denison (a chapter by Dufresne); Potter.

DUFRESNE, KLONDY NELSON
See Nelson, Klondy.

DuHALDE, JEAN BAPTISTE (1674-1743)
The General History of China. London: J. Watts, 1763. 4v. This work contains a report and maps of Bering's first voyage from Kamchatka, making it apparently the first published report of the existence of the northwest coast of Pacific North America. Because the Russians did not themselves publish accounts of Bering's or others' voyages, and because there were no retracing of his routes by others before, it remained for James Cook to verify Bering's findings during his third voyage in 1778. On the first voyage Bering sighted St. Lawrence Island.

DULLES, FOSTER RHEA
Lowered Boats. New York: Harcourt, Brace, 1933. 292 pp. American whaling, including bowhead taking in the Chuchi Sea and the whaling disaster of 1871.

DUMOND, D.
An Archaeological Survey along Knik Arm. Fairbanks: University of Alaska Press, 1968.
A Summary of Archaeology in the Katmai Region. Eugene: University of Oregon Press, 1971.
"Toward a Prehistory of the Na-Dene, with a General Comment on Population Movements among Nomadic Hunters," *Amer. Anthropology*, CXXI (1969): 857-863.
"Toward a Prehistory of Alaska," *Alaska Review*, III (Fall 1967).

DUNAWAY, STELLA
"Hoonah," *Alaska Monthly*, December, 1906.

DUNBAR, M. J.
See T-1377 ff.

DUNCAN, RAY
"Juneau, Furlough Town," *Yank*, May, 1945. (Alaska edition).
"The Aleuts Go Home," *Yank*, May, 1945. (Alaska edition).

DUNCAN, SINCLAIR THOMSON (1828-1928)
From Shetland to British Columbia. Lerwick, Scotland: Charles J. Duncan, 1911. 282 pp.

DUNCAN, WILLIAM (1832-1918)
The Gospel in the Far West. London: Church Missionary House, 1869. 130 pp. Tsimshian Indian work.
Metlakahtla and the Church Missionary Society. Victoria: Munroe Miller, 1887. 44 pp. A defense of the position taken by the native Christians and their teachers, and an answer to the charges brought against them. Written mostly by William Duncan and Robert Tomlinson.
See the Tourville Bibliography, T-1380 ff; see also the following:
Alaska Sportsman, March, '43 (new monument); Aug., '45 (photo); Oct., '45 (editorial opposing reservation; 300 Metlakahtlans now living in Ketchikan); Dec., '45 (preferred to be called "Mister"); Dec., '49 (in the beginning some of the Indians wanted to kill him); Feb., '50; May, '55; Jan., '57; Beattie (on Marsden); Begg; Benyon (*Am. Anthro.*, 1941); Brooks; Chase; Clark; Colby; Collis (cannibalism was only acting, Duncan said); Davis; Denison; Higginson; Huber (*Ak. Sptsmn.*, Aug., '11); Hulley; Jackson; Jenkins (Episcopal view; Paul Mather, Metlakahtlan, became Episcopal priest); Matthews; Morris (has been smuggling goods into Alaska for a great many years); Scidmore (1884); Sessions (interviews with Duncan, Wellcome; letter of Duncan after his removal from Alaska); Smith (Biblio.); Stuck (critical of one-man rule; Bur. Educ. took over in 1914); Swineford (Duncan landed on Annette Island August 7, 1887); Tompkins (Duncan arrived June, 1857, Ridley came in 1879, move to Annette in 1887); Wellcome; Whymper (critical of notion that Duncan shouldn't have been a trader); Young.

DUNHAM, SAMUEL CLARKE (1855-1920)
The Goldsmith of Nome. Wn.DC: Neale Pub. Co., 1901. 80 pp. Verse.
The Men Who Blaze the Trail. New York: Barse and Hopkins, 1913. 126 pp. Poetry.
"Alaska to Uncle Sam," *Pacific Monthly*, 1900.
"The Chilkat or Dalton Trail," *Bulletin*, US Dept. of Labor, May, 1898.
"History of the City of Juneau," *Bulletin*, US Dept. of Labor, May, 1898.
See also the following:
Davis; Gruening; Harrison (Deputy Arctic Chief, Arctic Brotherhood); Wickersham (typed first issue of *Yukon Press*, Circle City, 1898; he was on the Yukon "writing up" labor conditions and data about the Dawson mining camp for the US Gov't.); see also Wickersham's Bibliography.

DUNN, ROBERT
The Shameless Diary of an Explorer. New York: Outing Publishing Co., 1907. 297 pp. Frederick Cook's claimed ascent of Mt. McKinley by a member of the party. See also six articles in *Outing Magazine*, 1904 on Cook. See also Wickersham's Bibliography.
The Youngest World. New York: Dodd, Mead, 1914. 492 pp.
"Conquering the Greatest Volcano," *Harper's*, March, 1909. On the first ascent of Mt. Wrangell.

DUNNING, WILLIAM ARCHIBALD
"Paying for Alaska." Some Unfamiliar Incidents in the Process," *Political Science Quarterly*, September, 1912.
Truth in History. New York: Columbia University Press, 1937. 228 pp.

DURANT, JOSEPH ("French Joe")
See Chase.

DURHAM, ROBERT C. and CLAYTON KNIGHT
Hitch Your Wagon. Drexel Hill, Penn.: Bell Pub. Co., 1950. 332 pp. The story of Bernt Balchen.

DURHAM, WILLIAM
Canoes and Kayaks. Seattle: Copper Canoe Press, 1960. 104 pp. Sources include E.W. Nelson, F. Boas, Jochelson, Birket-Smith, old Northwest coast voyages and others.

DURLACH, THERESA (b. 1891)
The Relationship System of the Tlingit, Haida and Tsimshian. New York: American Ethnological Society, 1928. 177 pp.

DUTCH HARBOR
Alaska Sportsman, May, '39 (photo); June, '46 (Japanese attack); Jan., '51 (Japanese attack); Nov., '53 (photo); Baker (so named for the tradition that a Dutch trader [ship] was the first to enter it; also called Udakta, Ougadakh and Ulakhta); Cahn (*Condor*, March, '47); Colby (pre-war descr.); Couch (post office, 1894-95, and 1936-41; from 1941 it was a naval post office); Dole (formerly called Lincoln Harbor); Grinnell (*Condor*, 1901); Gray; Higginson; Hulley; Jackson (reindeer report); Kitchener; Miller; Max; Oliver; Scidmore (Cook, 1778); Sundborg (weather); Tewkesbury; Walden.

DYEA
Alaska Life, July, '46 (unusual photo); *Alaska Sportsman*, June, '48 (map, photos, town and trail); Nov., '54 (1898 photo); *Alaska-Yukon Magazine*, (flogging a cache thief); Andrews (trading post and two saloons, in summer trail better than White Pass); Baker (also called Tyya, Dejah, Dayay, and Taiya); Colby (once had 10,000 [temporary] inhabitants, now one); Chase (1886 Healey's store was here, Bishop Seghers and party [11 people] had difficulty with Indians [108]); Couch (post office 1896-1902); Davis (first marshal killed by the barkeep); Hulley (Thomas Williams died at Healey's trading post after hardships en route from Fortymile in 1886-87; Klondike notes); Ogilvie (in 1887 there were at Dyea 138 Indians, Mr. and Mrs. J.J. Healey and George Dickinson); Pilgrim; Schwatka (Stick Indians served as "ferry" for the men; stone houses at head of Dayay River were simply loose boulders);

Scidmore (called Healey); Swineford (Dyea trail was used a dozen years before Skagway was ever thought of); Walden (trading post and a dozen Indian shacks); Winslow (gold rush conditions in Dyea).

DYER, E. JEROME
The Gold Fields of Canada. London: G. Philip, 1898. 268 pp. And how to get there.

DYKEMAN, KING
Whiting (joined the Klondike rush; later superior court judge in Seattle; heard suit against M.J. Heney).

DYKER, BOB
Get Your Man. London: Low, 1934. 244 pp. Royal Northwest Mounted Police; autobiographical.

DYNES, W. M.
Dynes' Tours of Alaska. Juneau: Dynes' Alaska Directory Co., 1922. 84 pp.

E

EAGLE
Alaska Life, Dec., '46; *Alaska Sportsman*, May, '41 (photo); June, '50 (H. Karsters helped lay out town); Sept., '54 (descr.); July, '55 (photo of fort); Jan., '57; Feb., '57; Aug., '59 (break-up); and others, see Index; Andrews (impatience at customs house); Baker (Belle Isle built 1881, Ft. Egbert 1899, Eagle incorp., 1901 [first in Alaska], military telegraph completed in 1903); Colby; Couch (post office from 1898); Davis (photo Ft. Egbert); Higginson (social life, sun returned Jan. 16); Kitchener (Belle Isle built by Mercier 1874, Harper and McQuesten here, named for the American eagle, only planned town of gold rush era, Wickersham arrived July, 1900, Amundsen in 1905); Purdy (Indian life); Rice (Major Ray succeeded Captain Richardson, 1899); Richardson (town building aided by prospect of government establishment); Rickard (in 1908 sign "mcQuesten and Co." still on store); Stuck (best town-site on Yukon, but subject to bitterly cold winds); Sundborg (river elev. 800' [1060' at Dawson]); Underwood (small amount of gold found on Mission Creek in 1896); Wickersham (Harper's post here 1875, called Fetutlin, court moved to Fairbanks in 1904).

EAGLES
See the Arctic Bibliography; see also *Alaska Life*, Jan., '46 (photo of young); *Alaska Sportsman*, see Index; *Alaska-Yukon Magazine*, July, '09 (photo, American bald eagle); Bailey; Brandt; Denison (prey on fox pups); Gabrielson (four varieties); Garland; Harriman; Miller (taken for bounty at Unalaska); Snyder (destruction of eagles in Alaska, in

Auk, April, 1926); Stuck (catches salmon in talons); Sundborg; Underwood; Willett (*Auk*, October, 1927); Williams (bald acquires white head in 4th year); Willoughby (Fr. Hubbard attacked by eagles in Aniakchak crater).

EAKIN, HENRY M.
"The Influence of the Earth's Rotation upon the Lateral Erosion of Streams," *Journal of Geology*, 1910. See also the Arctic Bibliography.

EARDLEY, A. J.
"Yukon Channel Shifting," *Bulletin*, Geological Society of America, March, 1938.

EARTHQUAKES
See Alaska Earthquakes; see also the Arctic Bibliography. See also the following:
Alaska Sportsman, March, '55 (heavy quake at Anchorage); Nov., '55 (moderate quake at Cordova); June, '46 (5 quakes in the Aleutians); Feb., '48 (in Tanana Valley); March, '50 (at Craig); Aug., '50 (at lake near Ketchikan); Adkins (quake of 1937, in *Bulletin*, Seism. Soc. of Am., 1940); Dall (near Russian Mission, 1867, severe at Sitka, 1847); Glenn (in Prince William Sound, 1899); Hines (at Unga, severe, 1788; boat sunk near Unimak Pass, 1871); Martin (*Bulletin*, Geol. Soc. of Am., 1910, 1899 quakes); Moye (*Bulletin*, Geol. Soc. of Am., 1915, quake of 1899); Powell (near Mt. Wrangell, 1899); Rice; Rickard (Sept. 1899, crushed Muir Glacier, affected Malaspina); Scidmore (at Sitka, 1880).

EAST, BEN
"Islands of Mist and Blood," series of articles in the *Grand Rapids Press*, August to December, 1942, numbering 19. Seal life on the Pribilofs.
"Sea Bird Cities in the Aleutians," *Natural History*, Feb., '43.
"Uncle Sam's Prize Fur Factory Closes Down," *Natural History*, April, 1943. Evacuation of the islands.
"The Sea Lions of Bogoslof," *Natural History*, Feb., 1946.

EAST CAPE
Alaska Sportsman, Aug., '49 (Siberian Eskimos visit Alaska-Yukon-Pacific Exposition in Seattle); Apr., '51 (Capt. Gottschalk walked from East Cape to Alaska in 1913); *Alaska-Yukon Magazine*, May, '08 (photo); Dall (13 miles from Diomedes, 54 miles from Cape Prince of Wales); Franck (200 inhabitants); Golder (Bering, and Dezhnev); Hulley; Ray, P. (*Golden Fleece* to Barrow); Wickersham.

EASTMAN, FRED; see T-1402.

EASTWOOD, ALICE (b. 1859)
"Description of Plants collected by Dr. Blaisdell at Nome," *Botanical Gazette*, 1902.

EATON (reindeer station)
Baker (on Unalaklik River, 10 miles above mouth, named for John Eaton, US Commissioner of Education); Couch (post office 1899-1901); Jackson (reindeer reports).

EATON, JOHN M. (US Commissioner of Education)
"Sheldon Jackson," *Alaska and Northwest Quarterly*, April, 1899.
"Sheldon Jackson: A Pioneer in the New West," New York: Women's Board of Home Missions of the Presbyterian Church, 1905. 15 pp. See also the following:
Alaska-Yukon Magazine, Aug., '08 (on Alaska's school needs); Gruening (recommended Sheldon Jackson for post of General Agent of Education); Nichols (placed Jackson in education post in Alaska).

EBERHART, BETH (b. ca. 1900)
A Crew of Two. Garden City: Doubleday, 1961. 286 pp. Salmon trolling near Ketchikan; autobiographical.

EBERSTADT, EDWARD and Sons; see Bibliography.

ECLIPSE EXPEDITIONS
Dall (1869; obtained local vocabulary at Plover Bay); Scidmore (Davidson and Seward at Klukwan in 1869); National Geographic Expedition, March, 1949, reported in *Asia and America*, 1948.

ECONOMIC TRENDS AND STUDIES
The following listing is selective; see the Arctic Bibliography, the various publications of the Alaska (Territorial) Development Board, the Alaska State Department of Commerce and allied departments and divisions, and the University of Alaska Institute of Social, Economic and Government Resarch. See also the following:
Alaska Life, Oct., '45 (detailed living costs); *Alaska Sportsman*, Sept., '50 (editorial); Oct., '50 (retail sales statistics); Nov., '50 (power rates); Jan., '51 (editorial); Sept., '51 (fisherman); July, '54 (groceries); *Alaska Weekly*, Feb., '51 (25% cost of living added to federal salaries); May, '51 and Aug., '51 (comparison statistics); *Alaska-Yukon Magazine*, July, '09 (C. Andrews on Alaska's resources); Browne; Caldwell; Davis; Eiteman; Fuller's Bibliography; Greely; Gruening; Harrison (table of gov't. income and expenditures, 1869-1904); Hellenthal (conservation); Henderson (Alaska resources compared with those of the province of Vologda, Russia); Kizer; Lewis; Martin; Nichols; Potter; Rickard; Rogers (*Transition*, and *Future*); Salin (in German); Sundborg; Tewkesbury; Underwood; see also Conservation, Oil, Fisheries, etc.; see also the resources on Alaska by the various federal agencies, e.g., US Congress, Committees on Interior, on Lands, etc., US Dept. of Commerce, US Dept. of Labor (Bureau of Labor Statistics), and the US National Resources Committee, US National Resources Planning Board, and the National Research Council. See also the Alaska Native Claims Settlement Act, and the various publications of the Federal-State Land Use Planning Commission established by the Act. See also the Alaska Planning Council and Alaska Task Force of the Bureau of Land Management, US Fish & Wildlife Service, and the National Park Service for proposals for the federal withdrawal of 80 million acres in Alaska for 28 federal recreation and protection areas.

EDDY, JOHN WHITTEMORE (b. 1872)
Hunting the Alaska Brown Bear. New York: Putnam's, 1930. 253 pp.
Hunting on Kenai Peninsula. Seattle: Lowman and Hanford, 1924. 90 pp.

EDELSTEIN, JULIUS C.
Alaska Comes of Age. New York: Putnam's, 1942. 62 pp. American Council, Institute of Pacific Relations, Far Eastern Pamphlets.
"Alaska: Pivot of Strategy," *New Republic*, May, 1942.

EDERER, BERNARD FRANCIS (b. 1900)
Through Alaska's Back Door. New York: Vantage Press, 1954. 162 pp. Canoe trip on the Athabaska River to the headwaters of the Mackenzie to Aklavik, then over the divide via the Ray, Bell and Porcupine Rivers to the Yukon.
"Aklavik to Fort Yukon," *The Beaver*, September, 1941.

EDGERTON HIGHWAY
Colby (named for Maj. Glen C. Edgerton, Chief Engineer, Alaska Road Commission); Sundborg; Tewkesbury.

EDINGTON, ARLO CHANNING (b. 1890) **and CARMEN BALLEN EDINGTON**
Tundra. New York: The Century Company, 1930. 334 pp. "Romance and Adventure on Alaskan Trails, as told by former Deputy Marshal Bert Hansen to the Edingtons," early 20th century.

EDITORIAL RESEARCH REPORTS; see Noyes, C.E.

EDMONTON ROUTE
Alaska Sportsman, March, April, May, 1955; Davis (All-Canadian route to the Klondike); Ogilvie; Romig (bitter experience).

EDNA BAY
Alaska Sportsman, Dec., '44 (logging); July, '56 (photo); Baker (shore of Kosciusko Island, named by Dickins, 1903-04); Couch (post office 1947-51).

EDUCATION
Three distinct organizations of education have existed in Alaska. From the earliest years towns taxed their inhabitants for school support, even though there was no civil provision for doing so until 1884 (first civil government act), or 1899 (town incorporation act), when incorporated towns were legitimized. In the 1880's the US Bureau of Education was authorized to establish schools for natives, often contracting this work to missionary groups (see Sheldon Jackson). This work was taken over in 1930 by the Bureau of Indian Affairs, when the Alaska Native Service was transferred from Education. Finally, the Territory of Alaska established schools for non-native children in areas outside incorporated towns (e.g., Chitina). After statehood such schools came to be administered by State-Operated Schools, under the Alaska Department of Education, and included schools in many native villages. In 1975 the state school system was decentralized, passing ad-ministrative control of schools into the hands of regional boards, still under the State Department of Education.
The researcher must examine material for the school system pertinent. For schools in incorporated towns, the town records and the territorial education commission. For territorial schools, the records in the office of the Commissioner of Education, including annual reports. For federal schools the records of first the US Bureau of Education and the General Agent for, and later Commissioner of Education in Alaska, and later, the records of the Bureau of Indian Affairs. See also the records of individual federal schools, e.g., Wrangell Institute, Mt. Edgecumbe, Eklutna, and White Mountain.
See also the following:
Alaska Life, July, '43 (general remarks on small schools); *Alaska Sportsman*, see Index; some significant articles are the following: Feb., '36 (source of school reports); Apr., '40 (the hiring of teachers without experience); Aug., '46 (territorial and city schools); June, '47 (Eklutna students transferred to Japonski Island); Oct., '50 (ANS has now 35 teachers who are native or part native); Nov., '50 (93 public schools, 667 teachers, 14,000 students); Aug., '51 (map of route of *North Star* school ship [supply]); Nov., '54 (all ANS schools to be transferred to territory); Dec., '56 (scarcity of teachers); *Alaska Weekly*, Feb., '51; March, '51 (teachers resign because of war scare); June, '51 (Protestant teachers in Catholic villages); *Alaska-Yukon Magazine*, Aug., '08 (survey of education, 1792-1908); Alaska Dept. of Educ. (*Alaska Dept. of Educ. and Education in Alaska, 1785-1966* [Juneau: Dept. of Educ., 1966]); Albee; Anderson and Eells (1935 survey of native education); Andrews (first school [Russian] at Kodiak; teachers killed); Arnold, C.B. (in *Alaska Life*, Sept., '38 on Douglas native school); Bancroft; Berto (Blue Ridge, Pilot Station); Brooks; Brooks and Kupper (Kenai teachers); Buchan and Allen (Pilot Point teachers); Calasanz (Holy Cross mission); Forrest (Wainwright teacher); Gruening; Harrison; Hilscher; Hulley; Jackson; Lavrisheff; Lopp; Meyers (Koyuk); Mayberry; Poole; Purdy (Eagle); Richards (Wainwright); Stewart (Jackson); Stuck; Underwood; Van Valin (Sinuk and Wainwright); Willard (Haines); Winchell (Unalaska); Wright (Haines).

EDMONDS, H. M. W.
The Eskimo of St. Michael. College: University of Alaska Press, 1966. 143 pp.

EDMONDS, DELTUS MALIN
The Toll of the Arctic Seas. New York: Holt, 1910. 449 pp.

EDWARDS, WILLIAM SEYMOUR (1856-1915)
Into the Yukon. Cincinnati: R. Clarke Co., 1904. 319 pp.

EELLS, WALTER CROSBY (b. 1886)
See three articles in the *Journal of Applied Psychology*, August, October, and December, 1933, on the educational achievement and general abilities of Alaska natives. See also Anderson, H.D.

EFIMOV, ALEKSEI VLADIMIROVICH
See T-1416.

EFIMOVA, ALEKSANDRA AFANAS'EVNA
See T-1422.

EIDE, ARTHUR HANSIN
Drums of Diomede. Hollywood: House-Warren, 1952. 242 pp. Transformation of the Alaskan Eskimo. Diomede, 1910. Norwegian teacher married to an Eskimo girl, teaching school.
New Stories From Eskimo Land. San Francisco: Harry Wagner, 1930. 214 pp. With Arthur S. and Ruth Palmer Gist.

EIELSON, CARL BEN (1897-1929)
See the following:
Chandler, E.W. (Pioneer of Alaska Skies, 1959); Coombs, C.J. (Alaska Bush Pilot, 1963); Herron (Wings Over Alaska, 1959); Potter, J. (Flying Frontiersman, 1956); Rolfsrud, E.N. (Brother to Eagle, 1952); Thomas, L. (Famous First Flights, 1968); Thomas, L. (Sir Hubert Wilkins, 1961); Wilkins, G.H. (Flying the Arctic, 1928); Willoughby, B. (Alaskans All, 1933).

EISENLOHR, LOUIS HENRY (b. 1859) **and RILEY WILSON**
Memories. Philadelphia: The Keystone Publishing Co., 1918. 96 pp.

EITEMAN, WILFORD JOHN (b. 1902) **and A. B. SMUTS**
"Alaska: Land of Opportunity—Limited," *Economic Geography*, January, 1951. Limitations on rapid economic expansion.
"Economic Basis of Prices in Alaska," *American Economic Review*, June, 1944.
"Population Pyramids," *Alaska Life*, June, 1944. Illustrating movement in and out of Alaska.

ELDER, WILLIAM
Biography of Elisha Kent Kane. Philadelphia: Lippincott, 1925. 416 pp. Exploration of the Canadian Arctic.

ELDRIDGE, GEORGE HOMANS
See geological reconnaissance reports listed in Baker.

ELAIDE, MIRCEA
Shamanism: Archaic Techniques of Ectasy. New York: Pantheon Books, 1964. 446 pp.

ELIOT, WILLARD AYRES
See T-1434 ff.

ELLEGOOD, DONALD R.
"The Quest for Alaskan History," *Alaska Review*, III (Fall, 1967).

ELLIOTT, HENRY WOOD (1846-1930)
Our Arctic Province. New York: Charles Scribner's Sons, 1886. 473 pp. Alaska and the Seal Islands. Superb description of Alaska: Russian occupation, Sitka, Mt. St. Elias, Resurrection Bay, Cook Inlet, Kodiak Island, sea otter, the Aleutians, sea lion, Eskimos at Nushagak, Yukon River, Arctic coast, walrus.
Report on the Seal Islands. Wn.DC: GPO, 1884. 10th Census, Vol. 8, 188 pp. Sealing industry on the Pribilofs 1872-74.

Report of the Condition of Affairs in the Territory of Alaska. Wn.DC: GPO, 1875. 277 pp. Mostly on the Pribilof Islands, primarily economic aspects of the sealing industry. Elliott Coues' "Ornithology of the Pribilof Islands" forms the ninth chapter of this work, as Coues' work forms significant chapters of other of Elliott's books.
"Ten Years' Acquaintance with Alaska," *Harper's*, Nov., 1877. Reviewed by W.H. Dall in the *Nation*, Nov., 1877; reply by Elliott in the *Nation*, Nov., 1877; answered by Dall in the *Nation*, December, 1877. This controversy centered on Elliott's opinion of the poor economic prospects for Alaska. Neither civil government nor military usefulness would come to Alaska, he thought. J. Nichols called Elliott "misguided." Elliott was accused of wielding influence in Washington on behalf of the Alaska Commercial Company which obtained the government contract for the seal harvest on the Pribilofs since he spent much of his time in Alaska studying the seal and the seal industry there. Elliott did not get on well with the government officials on the islands, a circumstance which strengthened the notion that he was in the company's employ. But William Gouverneur Morris believed Elliott's judgments were the result of sincere reflection and observation. Elliott's trouble, Morris suggested, was that while he knew the seal well, he knew literally nothing else about Alaska.
Elliott went to northern British Columbia with the southern half of the American section of the Overland Telegraph Expedition in 1867. Later he traveled to the Pribilofs as an assistant Treasury agent in 1872, by a special act of Congress in 1874, and at his own expense in 1876. He was an excellent naturalist, linguist and artist. He married a Creole woman who was spurned in Washington, DC. His pessimistic reports on Alaska were significant in the formation of early Congressional policy concerning Alaska.

ELLIOTT, LAWRENCE
"Anchorge Aweigh!" *The Rotarian*, December, 1960. Air age.
"Anchorage: The 'Mostest' Town in the USA," *Reader's Digest*, December, 1960.
"There's a Tidal Wave in Here," *Reader's Digest*, July, 1960. Lituya Bay.

ELLIS, CARLYLE
"The Winter's Crucial Battle on Copper River," *Alaska-Yukon Magazine*, June, 1910. Miles Glacier Bridge.

ELLIS, MULLETT
Tales of the Klondyke. London: Bliss Sands and Co., 1898. 164 pp.

ELLIS, WILLIAM
An Authentic Narrative. London: G. Robinson, 1782. 2v. Ellis was Cook's surgeon, on *Discovery* and *Resolution*.

ELLSBERG, EDWARD (b. 1891)
Hell on Ice. New York: Dodd, Mead, 1938. 421 pp. The *Jeannette*.
Cruise of the Jeannette. New York: Dodd, Mead, 1949. 275 pp. Juvenile.
"The Drift of the *Jeannette* in the Arctic Sea," paper read before the American Philosophical Society, 1940.

ELLSWORTH, CLARENCE EUGENE (b. 1882)
A Water-power Reconnaissance. Wn.DC: GPO, 1915. 173 pp. USGS.
Surface Water Supply. Wn.DC: GPO, 1915. 343 pp. USGS. Yukon-Tanana region.

ELLSWORTH, LINCOLN (1880-1951)
"At the North Pole," *Annual Report*, Smithsonian Institution, 1927. Ellsworth-Amundsen flight from Spitsbergen over the pole, and the unsuccessful 1925 flight, both in the lighter-than-air craft.
Beyond Horizons. Garden City: Doubleday, 1938. 403 pp.

ELLSWORTH, LYMAN R. (b. 1910)
Guys on Ice. New York: David McKay, 1952. 277 pp. 21 US Army personnel in the Pribilofs.
Halibut Schooner. New York: David McKay, 1953. 242 pp.

EMERSON, ALICE B.
Ruth Fielding in Alaska. New York: Cupples & Lean, 1926. 210 pp.

EMERSON, HARRINGTON (b. 1853)
"The Opening of Alaska," *National Geographic*, March, 1903.

EMERSON, WILLIAM CANFIELD (b. 1893)
The Land of the Midnight Sun. Philadelphia: Dorrance, 1956. 179 pp.

EMERY, GEORGE D.
The New Mining Law of Alaska. Seattle: Pioneer Printing, 1913. 25 pp.

EMMONS, GEORGE THORNTON (b. 1852)
The Basketry of the Tlingit. Memoir, Amer. Museum of Natural History, 1903.
Conditions and Needs of the Natives of Alaska. Wn.DC: GPO, 1905. 23 pp.
Jade in British Columbia and Alaska and Its Use by Natives. Museum of Natural History, New York. 1923. 53 pp.
"Copper Neckrings of Southern Alaska," *Amer. Anthro.*, 1908.
"Native Account of the Meeting between LaPerouse in Lituya Bay in 1786," *Amer. Anthro.*, 1911.
"Petroglyphs in Southeastern Alaska," *Amer. Anthro.*, 1908.
"The Whale House of the Chilkat," Amer. Mus. of Natural History, *Anthro. Papers*, 1916.
"The Chilkat Blanket," Amer. Mus. of Natural History, *Anthro. Papers*, 1907.
The Tahlton Indians. Philadelphia: University Museum of Pennsylvania, 1911. 120 pp.
"Tshimshian Stories in Carved Wood," *Amer. Mus. Jrnl.*, 1915.
"Slate Mirrors of the Tsimshian," Museum of Indian History, *Anthro. Papers*, 1921.
"Portraiture Among the North Pacific Coast Tribes," *Amer. Anthro.*, 1914.

ENCYCLOPEDIA ARCTICA
Unpublished typescript, 15v., in the Stefansson Collection at Dartmouth College. In 1946 the US Office of Naval Research contracted with Stefansson to publish the encyclopedia, but the project was abandoned in 1952. The work was completed as the Arctic Bibliography by the Arctic Institute of North America. See LeBaurdais.

ENCYCLOPEDIA OF NORTHWEST BIOGRAPHY
Ed. Winfield Scott Downs. New York: American Historical Company, 1941. 515 pp. Vol. 2 in 1942; Vol. 3 in 1943.

ENDICOTT, HENRY WENDELL (b. 1880)
Adventures in Alaska. New York: F.A. Stokes, 1928. 344 pp.

ENDRESEN, FRIDTJOF (b. 1894)
Alaska Kaller. Oslo: Bergendahl, 1956. 267 pp. Norwegians in Alaska, description and travel. The author visited the *Gjoa* at San Francisco in 1932.

ENEMARK D. C. and K. A. ANDERSON
See T-1468.

ENGEL, SAMUEL
See T-1469 ff.

ENGSTROM, EMIL
John Engstrom. New York: Vantage Press, 1956. 156 pp.

ENNIS, WILLIAM H.
"Journal," *Quarterly*, California Historical Society, March, 1954. Ennis was a member of the Overland Telegraph Expedition. He sailed from San Francisco for St. Michael in 1865 after five years of naval service. Parts I and III of his journal were found in a trunk sold at auction in San Mateo, California; Part II is still missing.

ENNOCK, CHARLES REGINALD
The Great Pacific Coast. London: G. Richards, 1910. 356 pp.

EPISCOPAL MISSIONS
Archer (Bompas Memoirs); Chapman; Cody (on Bompas); Driggs; Jeffery (Bishop Gordon); Jenkins (Bishop Rowe); Stuck; Tewkesbury (nurse Amelia Hill); see also the Wickersham bibliography. See Tourville, T-1478 ff, for service books in native dialects. See also William Duncan, and the periodical *Alaska Churchman*.

EPSTEIN, SAMUEL (b. 1909) **and BERYL WILLIAMS**
The Real Book About Alaska. Garden City: Doubleday, 1952. 191 pp. Juvenile, general.

ERDMANN, HUGO (1862-1910)
Alaska. (in German) Berlin: D. Reimer, 1909. 223 pp. Economic geography of the Yukon area immediately following the gold rush.

ERICKSON, EVERETT R. (Commissioner of Education, 1951-53)
See the reports of the territorial commissioner of education.

ERICKSON, GEORG ADOLF (1806-1877)
See the Arctic Bibliography.

ERNST, ALICE H.
Wolf Ritual of the Northwest Coast. Eugene: University of Oregon Press, 1952.

ERSKINE, WILSON FISKE
Katmai: A True Narrative. New York: Abeland-Schuman, 1962. 223 pp. Story of the 1912 Katmai eruption, witnessed by the author as a small boy, and reconstructed from interviews and letters. Wilson Erskine's father was the well known Kodiak merchant William J. Erskine.
White Water. New York: Abelard-Schuman, 1960. 256 pp. Seafaring around Kodiak Island 1923-54.

ERSPAMER, ALICE McGILL
Klondike Widow. New York: Pageant Press, 1953. 239 pp.

ESCHSCHOLTZ, JOHAN FRIEDRICH (1793-1831)
Zoologischer Atlas. Berling: G. Reimer, 1829-33. Eschscholtz accompanied Kotzebue on his second voyage around the world on *Predpriiatie* in 1823-26. Eschscholtz Bay, an arm of Kotzebue Sound, was named for him. See the Arctic Bibliography for more information on the five volume atlas.

ESKIMO LANGUAGE
The following is a selective secondary listing; see the various anthropological papers published by the University of Alaska, and the Arctic Bibliography; see also the following:
Barnum (grammar); Collins (comments on Swadesh); Gordon (Kuskokwim vocabulary); Hinz; Peck (grammar); Pilling; Smith, B. (for information on Netsvietov and the Kvipak mission); Swadish; Thalbitzer; Walton; Wells and Kelly.

ESKIMOS
See the Arctic Bibliography, and the *Alaska Sportsman* Index. See also the following:
Albee; Anderson (on Dr. Romig); Anderson and Eells; Andrews; Bandi (Eskimo Prehistory); Bancroft; Berto; Birket-Smith; Boas; Bogoraz; Brevig; Brower; Buchan; Buliard; Carrighar; Collins; Dale and Butler; Dall; De Laguna; Driggs; Eide; Forrest; Freuchen; Geist; Giddings; Gordon; Green; Helmericks; Holm; Holmberg; Hrdlicka; Ingstad; Jenness; Keithahn; Lantis; Lopp; Mason; Mathiassen; Meyers; Mikkelsen; Murdoch; Petitot; Pinart; Poncins; O'Connor; Oqiulluk; Oswalt; Rainey; Rasmussen; Richards; Rink; Rodahl; Schultz-Lorentzen; Spencer; Stefansson; Stuck; Swadesh; Thalbitzer; Thornton; Underwood; Van Stone; Van Valin.

The ESKIMO
Monthly periodical published at Nome, 1916-1918 by Walter C. Shields, District Superintendent of Schools.

The ESKIMO
Quarterly periodical published at Seattle by Clarence Andrews, 1936-1938.

The ESQUIMAUX
Newspaper issued in manuscript at Port Clarence, Russian America, and Plover Bay, Siberia, by John J. Harrington for employees of the Overland Telegraph Expedition, 1866, 1867, later issued in book form by Turnbull and Smith, San Francisco, 1867.

ESPINOSA y TELLO, JOSE de (1763-1815) **and M. F. de NAVARETE**
A Spanish Voyage and the Northwest Coast of America. London: Argonaut Press, 1930. 142 pp. A translation of *Relacion del Viaje Hecho por las Goletas Sutil y Mexicana en el ano de 1792* (Madrid: Imprenta Real, 1802; trans. Cecil Jane).
See also T-1496.

ESSIG, EDWARD OLIVER (b. 1884), **ADELE OGDEN, and CLARENCE J. DUFOUR**
"The Russians in California," *Quarterly*, California Historical Society, 1933.

ETCHES, JOHN CADMAN
An Authentic Statement of all the Facts relative to Nootka Sound, its discovery, trade, probable advantages to be derived from it, in an Address to the King. London, 1790. Published by Debrett, 26 pp. See Nootka Sound.
A continuation of an authentic statement of all the facts relative to Nootka Sound, its discovery, history, settlement, commerce, and the public advantages to be derived from it, with observations on a libel, which has been traced to a foreign ambassador; in a second letter by Argonaut. London: W.S. Fores, 1790. 34 pp. Etches was the supercargo with J. Meares.

ETOLIN, ADOLPH KARLOVICH
Etolin was a surveyor for the Russian-American Company before he became Russian Governor. On his governorship see Richard A. Pierce in *Alaska Journal*, 1972. For remarks on his hydrographic work see Baker.

EURYALUS; see T-1499 ff.

EVANGELICAL MISSION COVENANT CHURCH OF AMERICA
Covenant Frontiers. Chicago: E.M.C. Church of America, 1941. 244 pp. Edited by Peter Matson (China section), E.B. Larsson (Alaska section) and W.D. Thornbloom (Bd. of Missions). History of the mission at Yakutat, beginning in 1887, and Unalakleet, and Golovin, Elim and White Mountain, with notes on Mountain Village, Hooper Bay, Candle and Dime Creek. Includes photographs of most areas, and missionaries, up to 1940.

EVANS, ALLEN ROY
Meat: Tale of the Reindeer Trek, 1929-1935. London: Hurst, 1935. 288 pp. Journalist's story of an 1800 mile drive of 3000 reindeer from Buckland Bay, Kotzebue Sound, across Alaska and the Yukon to the reserve east of the Mackenzie River, a five year journey.

EVANS, ELWOOD (1828-1898)
History of the Pacific Northwest. Portland: North Pacific History Company, 1889. 2v.

EVANS, ROBLEY D.
A Sailor's Log. New York: Appleton, 1902. 466 pp. Sealing violations, Alaska coastal waters.

EVERETTE, OLIVER P.
God has been Northward Always. Seattle: Bradley Printing and Lithography Co., 1965. 96 pp. Poetry.

EVERMANN, BARTON WARREN

See the Wickersham Bibliography for miscellaneous early works on fisheries, salmon and fur seals especially, 1906-1921. Evermann was associated with David Starr Jordan and Henry Wood Elliott.

EWART, JOHN S.

The Kingdom of Canada. Toronto: Morang, 1908. 370 pp.

EXPLORATION

Baker; Bancroft; Barbeau; Brooks; Bush; Campbell; Dall; Denton; James; Kennicott; Laut; Ledyard; Mirsky; Muir; Sherwood; Speck; Stuck; Wickersham; Whymper; Young. Also US Congress, Senate, Committee on Military Affairs, Compilation of Narratives of Exploration of Alaska.

Listing of explorations:

American

Abercrombie	1884, 1898, 1899
Allen	1885
Baker	1873-80
Barnard	1898-1900
Beardslee	1879-80
Becker	1895
Blake	1863
Brooks	1898-1905
Cantwell	1884-85, 1899-1901
Clover	1885
Coghlan	1884
Collier	1900-04
Dall	1865-99
Davidson	1867-69
Dickins	1899-1905
Duffield	1897
Eldridge	1898
Elliott	1872-76
Faris	1898-1901
Flemer and Nelson	1898
Gerdine	1899
Gibson	1854-55
Gilbert	1900-01
Glass	1881
Glave	1890
Glenn	1898-99
Goodrich	1896
Grant	1905
Gray	1788-89, 1791-92
Hamilton	1904-05
Hanus	1879-81
Harber	1892
Harriman	1899
Hayes	1891
Helm	1886
Herron	1899
Hess	1903-05
Hooper, C.L.	1880-99
Hooper, S.L.	1881
Ingraham	1791-92
Jarvis	1897-98
Kendrick	1788-89, 1791
Leslie Exp.	1890-91
McGrath	1889-92
McLenegan	1885
Mansfield	1889-91
Marsh	1902-03
Martin	1903-05
Meade	1868-69

Mendenhall	1898-1902
Moffitt	1903-05
Moore, E.K.	1895-98
Moore, W.I.	1892-95
Moser	1897-1901
Muir	1879-81, 1890, 1899
Muldrow	1898
Murdoch	1881-83
Nelson	1877-81
Nichols	1881-83
N. Pac. Expl. Exp.	1854-55
Oliver	1903-05
Osgood	1902
Peters	1898-1904
Petrof	1880
Post	1898
Pratt	1898-1904
Prindle	1902-05
Putnam	1897-99
Ray	1881-83
Raymond	1869
Reaburn	1899-1902
Reid	1890-92
Ritter	1898-1904
Rohn	1899
Russell	1889-91
Schanz	1890-91
Schrader	1896-1902
Schwatka	1883-86
Snow	1886
Spencer	1900, 1903
Spurr	1896, 1898
Stanley-Brown	1891
Stockton	1889
Stone	1904-05
Stoney	1883-86
Symonds	1879-81
Tanner	1888-93
Thomas	1887-88
Topham	1888
Turner	1889-91
US Fish Commission	1888-1905
Wells	1890-91
Westdahl	1900-02
W.U. Telegraph Expedition	1865-67
Williams	1888
Witherspoon	1899-1905
Wright, C.W. and F.E.	1903-05

British

Barkley	1787
Beechey	1826-27
Colnett	1787
Cook	1778
Dease	1837
Dixon	1785-88
Douglas	1788-89
Franklin	1826
Hanna	1785-86
Meares	1786-89
Pender	1868
Portlock	1786-87
Simpson	1837
Strange	1786
Tipping	1786-87
Vancouver	1792-94

French

LaPerouse	1786

| Marchand | 1791 |
| Roquefeuil | 1818 |

German

Grewingk	1850
Krause	1882
Langsdorff	1804-05
Steller	1741

Russian

Archimandritov	1848-50
Bering and Chirikov	1741
Billings	1790-92
Chernov	1832-38
Coxe	1780
Davydov	1803
Doroshin	1848
Etolin	1818-45
Glotov	1763-66
Ilin	1818-42
Ingenstrem	1829-32
Khvostov	1803
Kotzebue	1816-17
Krenitsyn	1768-69
Krusenstern	1804-05
Kuritzien	1849
Levashev	1768-69
Lindenberg	1838
Lisianski	1804-05
Lutke	1827-28
Murashev	1839-40
Pribylov	1786
Sarychev	1790-92
Sauer	1790-92
Shishmarev	1816-21
Staniukovich	1827-28
Tebenkov	1831-50
Tikhmeniev	1861-63
Vasiliev	1819-22
Veniaminov	1824-34
Woronkovski	1836
Wesnesenski	1842-43
Zagoskin	1842-44
Zarembo	1834-38

Spanish

Arteaga	1779
Bodega y Quadra	1775-79
Caamano	1792
Eliza	1791, 1793
Fidalgo	1790
Galiano	1792
Heceta	1775
Malaspina	1791
Martinez y Zayas	1788-89, 1793
Maurelle	1775-79
Perez	1774
Quimper	1790
Valdes	1792

EXPLORATION COMPANY, LTD.; see T-1506.

EXPLORERS CLUB (New York)
Explorers Journal, a quarterly periodical published at New York from 1921.

EYERDAM, WALTER J.
"Lichens from Alaska: Thum Bay, Knight Island, Prince William Sound," *Biologist*, March, 1949.

F

FAIRBANKS
Alaska Life, Aug., '39 (named by E.J. Barnette for Senator Fairbanks, a friend of Wickersham); Sept., '39; May, '40 (University); Apr., '40 (Lathrop); Apr., '40 (dog derby); March, '40; March, '42 (creamery); Feb., '45 (Fairbanks issue); Nov., '46; June, '47 (photos); *Alaska Sportsman*, June, '36 (dog derby); July, '36 (ice carnival); March, '45; Aug., '47; Jan., '49; Feb., '54; March, '54, and other, see Index; *Alaska-Yukon Magazine*, March, '07; Feb., '08; Jan., '09 (history, with "first" photo); Jan., '09 (schools); July, '12; Cameron; Carrighar; Davis; Edington; Franck; Goulet; Griffin; Helmericks; Herron; Higginson (history); Hilscher; Jacobin; Kitchener; Potter; Rickard (history); Stuck; Underwood; Wickersham. See also the listings in the Tourville bibliography.

FAIRBANKS DAILY NEWS-MINER
The Low-down Truth on Alaska. Fairbanks: *News-Miner*, 1923. 48 pp.
There have been numerous special editions; see the Alaska Newspaper Index, prepared by the Alaska (State) Division of Libraries.

FAIRBANKS DAILY TIMES
See nine articles dealing with Mt. McKinley expeditions listed in Washburn.

FARB, PETER
Man's Rise to Civilization. New York: E.P. Dutton, 1968. 400 pp. As shown by the Indians of North America from Primeval Times to the Coming of the Industrial State. Also published in paper by Avon Books, 1969.

FARIS, JOHN THOMAS (b. 1871)
The Alaskan Pathfinder. New York: Fleming H. Revell, 1913. 221 pp. Sheldon Jackson.

FARIS, ROBERT LEE
"Survey of Kwikpak, Kawanak, and Aphoon Passes in the Yukon Delta," in *US Coast Survey Annual*, 1900.

FARQUHAR, FRANCIS PELOUBET
A Brief Chronology of Discovery in the Pacific Ocean from Balboa to Captain Cook's First Voyage, 1513-1770. San Francisco: Grabhorn Press, 1943. 14 pp.
A List of Publications Relating to the Mountains of Alaska (with Mildred P. Ashley). New York: American Alpine Club, 1934. 37 pp.
"The Exploration and First Ascents of Mt. McKinley," *Bulletin*, Sierra Club, June, 1949.
"Bradford Washburn's Photographs of Mt. McKinley," *Bulletin*, Sierra Club, June, 1950.

"Henry P. Karstens," *Amer. Alpine Jrnl.*, 1956. Karstens came to Alaska in 1897, climbed Mt. McKinley in 1913, and served as first superintendent of Mt. McKinley National Park, 1921-1928.

FARRAND, MAX
"District and Territory," *American Historical Review*, V (1899): 676-81.

FARRAR, VICTOR JOHN (b. 1886)
The Annexation of Russian America. Wn.DC: W.F. Roberts, 1937. 142 pp. An excellent work on the purchase of Alaska.
An Elementary Syllabus of Alaska History. Seattle, 1924. 19 pp.
The Purchase of Alaska. Wn.DC, 1934. 50 pp. 2nd edition, Wn.DC: W.F. Roberts Co., 1935.
"The Background of the Purchase of Alaska," *Washington Historical Quarterly*, April, 1922.
"Joseph Lane McDonald and the Purchase of Alaska," *Washington Historical Quarterly*, April, 1921.
"Senator Cole and the Purchase of Alaska," *Washington Historical Quarterly*, October, 1923.
"The Reopening of the Russian-American Convention of 1824," *Washington Historical Quarterly*, April, 1920.

FARRELLY, T. S.
"A Lost Colony of Novgorod in Alaska," *Slavonic and East European Review*, 1944. A letter written in 1794 by the monk Herman mentions Russians who supposedly came to Alaska from Novgorod about 1570 and settled near the town of Kasilov on the Kenai Peninsula. In this well known but highly criticized article, Farrelly suggests that the non-native construction of the houses in a site found near Kasilov in 1937 indicates the lost Novgorod colony existed there. See Brower. See also the discussion in Fedorova.

FAST, EDWARD GUSTAVUS
Catalogue of antiquities collected in the Territory of Alaska by Edward G. Fast, . . .consisting of more than 2000 most valuable and unique specimens. New York: Levitt, Strebeigh and Co., 1869. 32 pp.

FATHER HERMAN
See Herman of Valaam; see also Golder, Kashevarov, Shiels, and Valaam Monastery.

FEDERAL WRITERS' PROJECT
Whaling Masters. New Bedford: Old Dartmouth Historical Society, 1938.

FEJES, CLAIRE
People of the Noatak. New York: Alfred A. Knopf, 1966. 368 pp. See also T-1538.

FELDMAN, FRANCES LOMAS
Organization and Delivery of Human Services in Rural Alaska. Los Angeles: University of Southern California, 1971.

FELDMAN, T. C.
"The Federal Colonization Project in the Matanuska Valley," University of Washington, unpublished master's thesis, 1941.

FELL, SARAH
Threads of Alaska Gold. N.p., n.d., 35 pp. University of Washington Library.

FENWICK, GEORGE
An Athabaska Princess. New York: Alice Harriman Co., 1910. 156 pp.

FERBER, EDNA
Ice Palace. Garden City: Doubleday, 1958. 411 pp. This novel ran serially in the *Ladies Home Journal.*

FERGUSON (J. G.) PUBLISHING COMPANY
The Alaska Book. Chicago, 1960. 320 pp. 55 articles from *Alaska Sportsman*, and illustrations.

FERGUSON, ROBERT (1855-1935)
Arctic Harpooner. Philadelphia: University of Pennsylvania Press, 1938. 216 pp. Diary of a 16 month whaling voyage in the *Abbie Bradford*, 1878-79 in Hudson's Bay and at Marble Island.

FERNALD, KAY and KAY McDOWELL
Rubles to Statehood. Anchorage: K & K Enterprises, 1965. 132 pp. Numismatic items.

FERNANDEZ de NAVARRETE, MARTIN (1765-1844)
See Wagner. de Navarrete was chief hydrographer for the Spanish navy at the time of the first publication of the record of Spanish voyages to the Northwest coast.

FERRER de MALDONADO, LORENZO (d. 1625)
See Wagner. In 1609 Ferrer de Maldonado published an account (*Relacion del descubrimiento de estrecho de Anian*) of his discovery of a passage from the Atlantic to the Pacific, the famed northwest passage, above America, in 1588. A Portuguese geographer, he hoped to win reward and recognition. This claim was defended at Paris and Milan in 1790 and 1812, respectively. In 1791 Malaspina was sent to investigate the claim.

FERNOW, BERNHARD EDWARD (1851-1923)
"The Forests of Alaska," in Harriman.

FICTION
See this topic in the Tourville Bibliography, pp. 672-677.

FIDALGO, SALVADOR
See Wagner.

FIELD, HENRY MARTYN (1822-1907)
Our Western Archipelago. New York: Scribner's Sons, 1895. 250 pp.

FIELD, KATE
See eleven articles on Alaska in the early 1890's published primarily in *Kate Field's Washington* (periodical), but see also "Our Ignorance of Alaska," in the *North American Review*, 1889.

FIELD, WILLIAM OSGOOD, Jr.
"A Gazetteer of Alaskan Glaciers," *Transactions*, Amer. Geophysical Union, August, 1941.

FIELDHOUSE, FELICE
Yukon Holiday. New York: Longmans, Green, 1940.

FILIPPI, FILIPPO de (b. 1869)
The Ascent of Mt. St. Elias. New York: Stokes, 1900. 241 pp. Translated from the Italian original, describing a trip across the US to Seattle and then to Yakutat Bay and the ascent of Mt. St. Elias, with chapters on Malaspina, Seward, Agassiz, and Newton Glaciers.
"The Expedition of His Royal Highness Prince Louis of Savoy, Duke of Abruzzi, to Mt. St. Elias, Alaska," *American Alpine Journal*, 1898.

FINCK, HENRY THEOPHILUS (1854-1926)
The Pacific Coast Scenic Tour. New York: Scribner's, 1890. 309 pp.

FINDEISEN, HANS
See T-1555.

FINDLAY, ALEXANDER G.
A Directory for the Navigation of the Pacific Ocean. London: R.H. Laurie, 1851. 2v.

FINK, ALBERT
See T-1557 ff; pamphlets opposing Wickersham.

FINNEY, GERTRUDE E.
To Survive We Must Be Clever. New York: David McKay, 1966. 179 pp. Aleut language.

FINNIE, RICHARD (b. 1906)
Canada Moves North. New York: Macmillan, 1942. 277 pp. Northwest Territories in the 1940's.
Lure of the North. Philadelphia: David McKay, 1940. 227 pp. The western Arctic, between Herschel and King William Island.
Canol. San Francisco: Ryder and Ingram, 1945. 210 pp. The sub-Arctic pipeline and refinery project constructed by Bechtel-Price-Callahan for the Corps of Engineers, US Army, 1942-44, with documentary photographs.
Finnie has contributed numerous articles to Canadian journals on animals, oil, and Eskimos; see the Arctic Bibliography.

FINTON, WALTER L.
Alaska Bear Adventures. New York: Daniel Ryerson, 1937. 165 pp.

FISCHER, JOHANN EBERHARD (1697-1771)
See the Arctic Bibliography. Fischer succeeded Gerhard Friedrich Muller as historian on Bering's second expedition across Siberia. Local Siberian tribes are treated extensively. Fischer wrote in German, and Ivan Golubtsov translated the work into Russian in 1774. The work is titled *Siberian History from the Discovery of Siberia to the Conquest of that country by Russian Arms.*

FISH and FISHERIES
See the Arctic Bibliography; see also the following:
Alaska Packers Association (Annual Reports); *Alaska Sportsman*, see Index; Allen, E.W.; Annabel; Dufresne; Elliott; Ellsworth; Fishing Products

Laboratory; Jordan; Martin; Moser; *Pacific Fisherman* (monthly from 1904); Tanner; Tussing; US Bureau of Fisheries; US Fish & Wildlife Service; US Fish Commission (Bulletins from 1880); Wickersham; Wolfe. See *Alaska Fisheries Policy* by Arlon Tussing, et. al., published by the University of Alaska, Institute for Economic, Social and Government Research, 1972.

FISH, BYRON
Alaska. Seattle: Superior Publishing Co., 1965. 157 pp. Photography.

FISHER, EDNA MARIE (b. 1897)
"The Sea Otter," *Proceedings*, Pacific Science Congress, 1939. History of the sea otter fur trade, with statistics on skins, 1727-1938.
"Prices of Sea Otter Pelts," *California Fish and Game*, October, 1941.
"Early Life of a Sea Otter Pup," *Jrnl. of Mammalogy*, May, 1940.
"A Fractured Femur of the Alaskan River Otter," *Jrnl. of Mammalogy*, November, 1933.

FISHER, JAMES
The Fulmar. London: Collins, 1952. 496 pp.

FISHER, RAYMOND H.
The Russian Fur Trade, 1550-1700. Berkeley: University of California Press, 1943.
"Semen Dezhnev and Professor Golder," *Pacific Historical Review*, 1956.

FISHER, WALTER KENRICK (b. 1878)
See the Arctic Bibliography.

FISHER, WALTER L.
Address on the Alaska Problem, before the American Mining Congress at Chicago, October, 1911. Fisher was Secretary of Interior, and interested in railroad and coal lands in this address.

FISHER, WARREN SAMUEL
"A New Anobiid Beetle from Alaska," *Journal*, Academy of Sciences, 1938.

FITCH, EDWIN M.
The Alaska Railroad. New York: Frederick Praeger, 1967. 326 pp.

FITZ, FRANCES ELLA (b. ca. 1873)
Lady Sourdough. New York: Macmillan, 1941. 319 pp. At Nome in 1900 with Noyes and Anderson.

FITZGERALD, EMILY
An Army Doctor's Wife on the Frontier. Pittsburgh: University of Pittsburgh Press, 1962. 352 pp. Numerous letters on Sitka.

FITZGERALD, GERALD ARTHUR (b. 1898)
Surveying and Mapping in alaska. Wn.DC: GPO, 1951. USGS. Brief history, 1728-1950, resume of projects undertaken by the federal government from 1895, the techniques.
New Reconnaissance Maps of Alaska. In *Surveying and Mapping*, 1952. USGS.
"Mapping in the Arctic," *Photogrammetric Eng.*, 1954.

"Helicopter Revolutionizes Topographic Mapping of Remote Areas," *Civil Eng.*, 1954. Use of helicopters began in 1948; reduced field costs.

FITZGERALD, JOSEPH H.
"Alaska's Economy: Problems of Development," *Alaska Review*, III (Fall, 1968).

FLAGG, LOREN
"Kachemak Bay—Richest in the World?", *Alaska*, XLI (Feb., '75): 2-6.

FLAHERTY, ROBERT JOSEPH (1884-1951)
My Eskimo Friends. Garden City: Doubleday, 1924. 170 pp. Chiefly Hudson's Bay.

FLEMER, JOHN ADOLPH and JOHN NELSON
"Topographic Reconnaissance of the County about the Head of Lynn Canal in 1898," *Report*, US Coast & Geodetic Survey, 1899. Valleys of the Chilkat, Tairku, Klehini, Katzehin, Skagway and Taiya [Dyea] Rivers.

FLETCHER, ARCHIBALD LEE
Boy Scouts in Alaska. Chicago, 1913. Juvenile.

FLETCHER, INGLIS
Vilhjalmur Stefansson. New York: Nomad Pub. Co., 1925.

FLEURIEU, CHARLES PIERRE de CLARET, Comte de
Voyage Autour du Monde. London: Longman and Rees, 1801. 2v. This is an edition of Marchand's Journal of the voyage of 1790-92, with a significant introduction reviewing all northwest coast voyages to that time. The editing, however, takes speculative liberties with the date provided by the text.

FLINT, GEORGE M., Jr.
"Islands of the Bering Sea," in Howell Williams' *Landscapes of Alaska.*

FLINT, STAMFORD RAFFLES (b. 1847)
Mudge Memoirs. Truro: Netherton, 1883. 258 pp. Mudge was with Vancouver on *Discovery* at Nootka Sound.

FLODERUS, BJORN GUSTAV OSKAR
See T-1583 ff.

FLOOD, MILFORD
Arctic Journal. Los Angeles: Wetzel Pub. Co., 1950. 459 pp.

FLORA of ALASKA
See the Arctic Bibliography for the most complete collection of material on this subject; see also the following:
Alaska Sportsman, Apr., '36 (a department appearing intermittently through 1940); Aug., '48 (skunk cabbage); Sept., '56 (Iceland poppy); Feb., '57 (Ordway); Apr., '58 (wild rose); *Alaska-Yukon Magazine*, June, '07 (Gervais collection); Sept., '07 (Juneau gardens); Anderson; Black; Bongard; Burroughs; Chaney; Cooper; Coville; Davis; Eastwood; Griggs; Harriman; Heller; Henderson; Herder; Holm; Hooker; Hulten; Hutchison;

Jaques; Kellogg; Knowlton; Meeker; Mendenhall; Menzies; Merriam; Muir; Osgood; Pennell; Porsild; Raup; Roloff; Rothrock; Scammon; Schrader; Schwatka; Sharples; Simpson; Smith, P.; Steffen; Tatewaki and Kobayashi; Turner; Underwood; Vasey; White, H.; Wickersham; Williams; Wright.

FLORA, CHARLES and EUGENE FAIRBANKS
The Sound and the Sea. Bellingham: Pioneer Printing Co., 1968.

FLOWER, ROUSSEAU HAYNER
See T-1587.

FODOR, EUGENE, ROBERT C. FISHER and BARNETT D. LASCHEVER
The Pacific States. Litchfield, Conn.: Fodor's Modern Guides, 1963. 179 pp.

FOFONOFF, N. P. and F. W. DOBSON
Transport Computations for the North Pacific Ocean, 1955-58. Ottawa: Queen's Printer, 1960. 4v.

FOFONOFF, N. P. and C. K. ROSS
Transpost Computations for the North Pacific Ocean, 1959-61. Ottawa: Queen's Printer, 1961. 3v.

FOHN-HANSEN, LYDIA OLAVA (b. 1891)
Alaska Berries. Bulletin, University of Alaska Extension Service, 1955. 29 pp.
Sourdough Hotcakes. Bulletin, University of Alaska Extension Service, 1955. 3 pp.

FOLKLORE
Haywood, Charles. *A Bibliography.* Contains material for Tlingit, Tsimshian, Aleut, and Eskimo native traditions. (New York: Greenburg, 1951). Cites the following, among others: Bancroft, Barbeau, Beechey, Birket-Smith, Boas, Caamano, Collins, Dall, Driggs, Eells, Flaherty, Freuchen, Golder, Jette, Jewitt, Jochelson, Lang, Lantis, LaPerouse, Langsdorff, Lisianski, Lutke, Niblack, Portlock, Schwatka, Shelton, Strange, Wagner, Wellcome, Zagoskin.
See also the following:
Alaska Sportsman, Aug., '44 (octopus legend); Arctander (15 Tsimshian legends); Barbeau; Bogoraz; Boas (Tlingit, Haida and Tsimshian legends); Chapman (Tinnehs); Costello; Forrest; Garber; Garfield; Golder; Judson; Keithahn; Hallowell (bear ceremonies); Hatt (Asiatic influences); Jochelson (comparative); Koryak with American Indian; Lantis (Eskimo ceremonies); de Laguna (Ahtna); Rink (journal); Rasmussen; Schmitter; Swanton; Petitot; Wright, A. ("Athabaskan Tradition [Yukon animal tale]," *Jrnl. Amer. Folklore*, 1908); Wickersham (Denali); see also the *Alaska Sportsman* Index; see Totems.

FONDA, WILLIAM C. (d. 1938) ("Skagway Bill")
"Alaska as I Knew It," *Alaska Life*, August, 1940. Fonda's widow, author of this article, unveiled a statue of the well known miner, "The Prospector," in Sitka on Alaska Day, 1949.

FONTE, PEDRO BARTOLOME de (sometimes de la Fuente)
"A Letter from Admiral Bartholomew de Fonte,

Admiral of New Spain and Peru, and now Prince of Chile," *Monthly Miscellany*, London, April and June, 1708.

De Fonte was supposed to have made a voyage in 1640 from Peru to the Rio de los Reyes, represented in the account as entering the Pacific Ocean near Lat. 53°N. He continued up the river to the town of Conasset on Lake Belle where he found a large ship from Boston. In the conclusion of the account, however, he states clearly that there is no northwest passage. See a discussion of de Fonte in Greenhow, Burney, and Wagner. The account is often thought to be the work of James Petiver. Captain James Colnett believed he had discovered the Rio de los Reyes when he entered Douglas Passage. Caamano in 1792 found the end of the Channel, and Vancouver in 1793 further disproved the notion. Nonetheless, Delisle, Vaugondy, Jefferys and Navarrete all continued to advance the notion of the river in Europe. For references see the following:

Bancroft; Colby; Delisle; Greenhow; Hulley; Tompkins; Vancouver; Wagner.

FOOTE, DON CHARLES; see T-1594 ff.

FORBES, EDGAR A.
"How Canada Would Develop Asia," *Leslie's*, Nov., 1913.

FORBES, H. A.
Gazetteer of Northern Canada and Parts of Alaska and Greenland. Ottawa: Geographical Bureau, Department of Mines, 1948. 75 leaves. 2600 place names, derived primarily from Canadian government maps.

FORD, COREY (b. 1902)
Short Cut to Tokyo. New York: Scribner's Sons, 1943. 141 pp. War in the Aleutians.
Where the Sea Breaks its Back. Boston: Little, Brown, 1966. 206 pp. Wilhelm Steller in Alaska.

FORD, JAMES ALFRED (b. 1911)
Eskimo Prehistory in the Vicinity of Point Barrow, Alaska. New York: American Museum of Natural History, 1959. 272 pp.

FORDE, CYRIL DARYLL
Habit, Economy and Society. London: Methuen, 1943. 500 pp. Geographical introduction to ethnology.

FORREST, ELIZABETH CHABOT (b. ca. 1894)
Daylight Moon. New York: Stokes, 1937. 340 pp. Of husband and wife teachers who succeeded the Van Valins at Wainwright, about 1915-1918, and later taught at Akiak.

FORREST, GLADYS and B. FRANKLIN HEINTZLEMAN
Land Resources of Alaska. Portland: North Pacific Planning Project, 1944. 80 pp.

FORREST, LINN ARGYLE (b. 1905)
The Wolf and the Raven; see Viola Garfield.
Tale of an Alaska Whale; see A.M. Blackberry.
Mr. Forrest supervised restoration of totem poles in southeast Alaska, 1938-42.

FORSTER, GEORG (1754-94)
Cook, der Entdecker. Leipzig: P.G. Kummer, 1789. 222 pp. Forster was a contemporary student of north Pacific exploration; he published a number of commentaries on Meares and Douglas, Portlock, and the like, all in German.

FORSTER, HANS ALBERT; see T-1605.

FORSTER, JOHANN GEORG ADAM; see T-1606.

FORSTER, JOHANN REINHOLD (1729-1798)
History of the Voyages and Discoveries Made in the North. Dublin: White and Byrne, 1786. 489 pp. Translated from the German original. See also T-1609 ff.

FORT EGBERT; see Eagle.

FORT LISCUM (Valdez, 1900-1925)
Alaska-Yukon Magazine, June, '09 (photo); Andrews (est. by Abercrombie); Baker; Couch (post office 1900-22); Franck (abandoned 1924, had 600 men, converted to Dayville cannery 1929); Gruening; Hewitt (named for Spanish-American war hero); Niedieck (winter photo); US Army (*Building Alaska*, across the bay from Valdez, Co. G, 7th Inf.).

FORT YUKON
Alaska Sportsman, Jan., '56 (photo post office); Dec., '56 (caribou hunt); Aug., '57 (hospital opened 1917, closed 1957); Beaver; Carroll; Clut; Dall; Davis; Henderson; James; Kitchener; Melville, E. ("Discovery of the Site of Old Ft. Yukon," Anthro. Paper, Univ. of Alaska, 1958); Murray; Shore; Stuck; Wickersham.

FORTUINE, ROBERT
The Health of the Eskimos: A Bibliography, 1857-1967. Hanover: Dartmouth College Libraries, 1968. 87 pp.

FOSTER, JOHN WATSON (1836-1917)
The Alaskan Boundary Tribunal. Wn.DC: Judd and Detweiler, Printer, 1903. 14 pp.
"The Alaskan Boundary," *National Geographic*, Nov., 1899.
"Alaskan Boundary Tribunal," *National Geographic*, Jan., 1904.

FOSTER, WALTER BERTRAM (b. 1869)
In Alaskan Waters. Philadelphia: Penn. Pub. Co., 1903. 363 pp.

FOSTER, WILLIAM SOUTHMAYD (b. 1910)
Six articles in *American City*: Nov., '54, Anchorage; Dec., '54. Fairbanks; Oct., '54, Juneau; Sept., '54, Ketchikan; Aug., '54, statehood; Jan., '55, Seward, Valdez, Cordova.

FRAME, JOHN W.
Frame's Alaska Pocket Pilot. Ketchikan, 1929. 49 pp. 1000 Questions on the most wonderfully misunderstood country in the world asked and answered. Frame was a newspaper editor at various times in Juneau, Anchorage, Cordova, Valdez and Ketchikan, in the first quarter of the 20th century.

FRANCE, GEORGE W.
The Struggles for Life and Home. New York: Goldman, 1890. 607 pp. Pioneer home-building, 1865-89.

FRANCHERE, GABRIEL (1786-1863)
Narrative of a Voyage. New York: Redfield, 1874. 376 pp. Translated by J.V. Huntington. 1811-1814.

FRANCIS, FRANCES
War, Waves and Wanderings. London: Sampson Low, Marston, 1881. 2v. *Lancaster.*

FRANCIS, K. E.
"Outpost Agriculture: The Case of Alaska," *Geographic Review*, LVII (1967): 496-505.

FRANCK, HARRY ALVERSON (b. 1881)
The Lure of Alaska. New York: Stokes, 1939. 306 pp. Observations of a world traveler while on a summer tour of Alaska; perceptive observation, but much historical hearsay.

FRANKEL, HASKEL
Adventure in Alaska. Garden City: Doubleday, 1963. 142 pp.

FRANKLIN, F. K.
Cleft in the Rock. New York: Crowell, 1955. 250 pp.

FRANKLIN, Sir JOHN (1786-1847)
Narrative of a Second Expedition. London: J. Murray, 1828. 320 pp. 1825-27. Franklin descended the Mackenzie River and in the summer and fall of 1826 made his way westward along the Arctic coast to what is now Return Reef, Alaska. At Return Reef he was only 160 miles from Barrow, where a party from Beechey's ship awaited him. A smothering fog prevented the two groups' meeting, and the section of coast between remained unreported until 1837, by Dease and Simpson.
Franklin had commanded the *Trent* in an unsuccessful attempt to sail north of Spitzbergen in 1818. In 1819-22 he made his first explorations of the Canadian Arctic coast, east from the mouth of the Coppermine River. His third and final trip in the Canadian Arctic was made in 1845-47. He and 128 men aboard *Erebus* and *Terror* disappeared completely. In the succeeding years forty searching parties set out to find the missing men, Lady Jane Franklin herself outfitting four different ships. It was not until 1859 that the full story of Franklin's fate was determined by Leopold McClintock, who based his search on clues discovered by Dr. John Rae in 1854. Franklin's ships had met disaster on the shores of King William Island which lies between Victoria Island and Boothia Peninsula. Members of the crew had died of exhaustion and starvation after setting out to find aid. The search for Franklin resulted in extensive exploration of the Arctic regions. For further bibliography of Franklin see the Arctic Bibliography. See also the following:
Armstrong, A.; Sustin, H.T.; Collinson; Cyriax, R.J.; Davydov, I.V.; Great Britain (Franklin Search); Hooker, Wm. J.; Hooker, Wm. H.; Lamb, G.F.; Lambert, R.S.; Oxley, J.M.D.; Richardson, J.; Sargent; Seeman, B.C.; Simonds, P.L.; Skewes, J.H.; Smith, G.B.; Smucker, S.; Sutton, A.; Whymper, F.; Wright, N. See also Mirsky.

FRANKLIN, LUCIA J.
Stories and Facts about Alaska. Fairbanks: L.J. Franklin, 1921. 307 pp. Mining, farming, coal, oil.

FRASER, JAMES DUNCAN
The Gold Fever. Honolulu: The author, 1923. 100 pp.

FRASER, JAMES G.
Anthologia Anthropologica. London: P. Lund, Humphries & Co., 1939. 351 pp. Native races of America.
Totemism and Exogamy. London: Macmillan, 1910. 4v. Early forms of superstition and society.

FREDE, PIERRE
Aventures Lointaines. Paris: Firmin-Didot, 1890. 120 pp.

FREDERICK, ROBERT A.
Frontier Alaska. Special Issue, *Alaska Review*, Fall, 1967, Proceedings of the first Conference on Alaska History at Alaska Methodist University, 1967. Participants included Sherwood, Pierce, Nichols, Ellegood and others.
"Caches of Alaskana," *Alaska Review*, 1966. This is an important listing of manuscript and secondary sources on Alaska history in major public and private libraries in the United States collected by Professor Frederick of Alaska Methodist University. Frederick later became the first executive director of the Alaska Historical Commission.
Writing Alaska's History: A Guide to Research, Anchorage: Alaska Historical Commission, 1974. Articles on Alaska historical resources.
"On Imagination and New Paths: Our Multi-Frontier in the Far North," In *Frontier Alaska, Alaska Review*, 1967.

FREDERICK, SARADELL ARD
"Alaskan Eskimo Art Today," *Alaska Journal*, II (Autumn, 1972).

FREEMAN, ANDREW A.
A Case for Dr. Cook. New York: Coward-McCannd, 1961. 315 pp.

FREMONT, JOHN CHARLES (1813-1890)
Geographical Memoir. Philadelphia: McCarthy, 1849. 80 pp. On California, addressed to the US Senate, with extracts from Hakluyt's collection of voyages, LaPerouse's voyage, letter from Com. Jones to the Sec. of the Navy, etc.

FRENCH, LEIGH HILL (b. 1863)
Nome Nuggets. New York: Montross-Clarke-Emmons, 1901. 102 pp. Author was manager for the Nome Hydraulic Mining Company.
Seward's Land of Gold. New York: Montross-Clarke-Emmons, 1905. 101 pp.

FREUCHEN, PETER (1886-1957)
Arctic Adventure. New York: Farrar and Rinehart, 1935. 467 pp. Translated from the original

Danish which was published in Copenhagen in 1936. Freuchen went from Copenhagen to Greenland at 19 where he was later associated with Knud Rasmussen.

Eskimo. New York: Liveright, 1931. 504 pp. A novel of the Eskimos of Cape York in Northwest Greenland.

Ivalu, the Eskimo Wife. New York: Furman, 1935. 332 pp.

Ice Floes and Flaming Water. New York: Julian Messner, 1954. 242 pp.

Vagrant Viking. New York: Julian Messner, 1953. 422 pp.

The Law of Larion. New York: McGraw-Hill, 1952. 313 pp. Historical novel, Alaskan folklore, Nulato massacre.

Book of the Eskimos. New York: World Pub. Co., 1961. 441 pp.

Adventures in the Arctic. New York: Julian Messner, 1960. 383 pp.

Book of the Seven Seas. New York: Julian Messner, 1957. 512 pp.

It's All Adventure. New York: Julian Messner, 1938. 508 pp.

Men of the Frozen North. Cleveland: World Pub. Co., 1962. 315 pp.

Peter Freuchen Reader, ed. Dagmar Freuchen. New York: Julian Messner, 1965.

The Legend of Daniel Williams. New York: Julian Messner, 1956. 256 pp.

Freuchen married an Eskimo in Greenland where he lived most of his life. *Vagrant Viking* is autobiographical and describes his travels in Canada, Siberia, Scandinavia and Alaska, to which he made one trip. In an untranslated work called *White Man* he describes himself as a failure, primarily from the viewpoint of cultural integration. In one work he writes of himself, "Unfortunately, I froze my left leg off and that turned me into a writer." He knew many Arctic enthusiasts, and played in several films, including *Eskimo,* for which he came to Alaska in 1932. During World War II he was imprisoned by the Nazis, but escaped to Sweden. Later he came to America, married a fashion illustrator, and engaged for a lecture tour. He died in Anchorage in 1957 where he had come with Donald Macmillan, Bernt Balchen and Sir Hubert Wilkins to make a color television adventure series with Lowell Thomas, Sr. His systematic and scientific mind is displayed in all his works. For a complete bibliography see the Arctic Bibliography.

FREUCHEN, PETER and FINN SALOMONSEN
The Arctic Year. New York: Putnam's, 1958. 438 pp.

FREY, LUCILLE
Eyes Toward Icebergia. Anchorage: Alaska Methodist University Press, 1970.

FRYKMAN, GEORGE A.
"The Alaska-Yukon-Pacific Exposition, 1909," *Pacific Northwest Quarterly,* LIII (1962): 89-99.

FUCA, JUAN de (APOSTOLOS VALERIANOS) (d. 1602)
Bancroft; Binns; Colby; Cotterill; Denton; Greenhow; Hulley; Purchas; Speck; Wagner. Juan de Fuca served as a pilot on the Mexico-California coast. He claimed to have discovered a "broad inlet of the sea" in latitude 47°N. in 1592. Although some have defended the claim, most scholars have dismissed it. John Meares, the British trader, named the strait in 48°N. latitude the Strait of Juan de Fuca inthe late 18th century.

FUHRMANN, ERNST (b. 1886)
Tlinkit und Haida. Hagen: Foldwant, 1922. 46 pp.

FULLER, GEORGE WASHINGTON (b. 1876)
A History of the Pacific Northwest. New York: Alfred A. Knopf, 1931. 383 pp.

FULLER, GRACE HADLEY
Alaska: A Selected List of References. Wn.DC: GPO, 1943. Library of Congress. Designed to supplement the Wickersham bibliography.

Aleutian Islands: A List of References. Wn.DC: GPO, 1943. 41 pp. Library of Congress. Bibliographies, books, pamphlets and documents, periodicals.

FULLER, VERYL RICHARDS (1896-1935) **and ERVIN H. BRAMHALL**
Auroral Research at the University of Alaska. College: University of Alaska, 1937. 130 pp. On this subject see the Arctic Bibliography for the work of the Geophysical Institute at the University of Alaska.

FUNSTON, FREDERICK
"Over the Chilkoot Pass to the Yukon," *Scribner's Magazine,* November, 1896.

"Frederick Funston's Alaskan Trip," *Harper's,* 1895.

"Along Alaska's Eastern Boundary," *Harper's,* 1896.

"Across the Great Divide in Mid-winter," *Harper's,* 1900.

"Romance and Reality in a Single Life—General Frederick Funston," *Cosmopolitan,* 1899.

"Alaska Telegraph Lines," *Report,* Secretary of War, 1903. Brigadier General Funston commanded the Army of the Columbia (US Army forces in the Pacific United States). There is a similar survey in the Secretary of the Army's 1904 report.

"Botany of Yakutat Bay," Field Report, Division of Botany, *Contributions,* US National Herbarium, 1895.

See also "Frederick Funston in Alaska, 1892-1894: Botany Above the Forty-Ninth Parallel," Thomas W. Crouch, *Journal of the West,* X (1971): 273-306.

FUR FARMING
Alaska-Yukon Magazine, Feb., '12 (Thomas Vesey Smith on Middleton Island); *Alaska Sportsman,* July, '37; July, '39; March, '40; July, '43 (islands leased if not over 1000 acres); June, '45; July to Aug., '46 (on Nuka Bay); Dec., '47; Aug., '50; Apr., '51 (fox pelts down from 35,000 to 5000 in 10 years); Nov., '53 (farming obsolete); Caldwell; Carpenter; Colby; Denison; Greely; Gruening; Harriman; Hilscher; Judge; Pilgrim; Sundborg; Tewkesbury; US Dept. of Interior (Mid-century Alaska); Willoughby; Wolfanger (in *Economic Geography,* 1926).

FUR SEALS AND SEALING; see Pribilof Islands

FUR TRADE

Abercrombie; Alaska Commercial Company; *Alaska Sportsman*, June, '39 (fur auction, Anchorage); Sept., '41 (prices); Andrews; Anti-Monopoly Association; Bancroft; *Beaver;* Belden (*The Fur Trade of America* [New York: 1917]); Berkh; Brower; Campbell (*The Nor'westers* [New York: 1956]); Carter; Chevigny; Dall; Dawson; Elkins; Elliott; Fisher; Gardner; Garfield ("Fur for the Ladies," *Alaska Life*, Oct., '38); Golder; Golovin; Gruening; Howard; Huber (*Alaska Life*, Aug.-Dec., '39); Hudson's Bay Co.; Hulley; Khlebnikov; Kitchener; Klengenberg; Laut; Murray; Okun; Pallas; Pilder; Raymond; Tompkins; Underwood; Wrangell; Zagoskin.

G

GABRIEL, GILBERT WOLF (b. 1890)

I Got a Country. Garden City: Doubleday, 1944. 432 pp. Two lieutenants and a corporal in Alaska in 1942.

I, James Lewis. New York: Doubleday, 1932. 334 pp. Novel of the Astor Party.

GABRIELSON, IRA NOEL

Wildlife Refuges. New York: Macmillan, 1943. 257 pp.

"Some Alaskan Notes," *Auk*, Jan.- Apr., 1944. Log of a trip in the summer of 1940 along the south coast of Alaska, the Aleutians (eastern), Bering Sea islands and from Anchorage to Fairbanks, listing 191 species of birds.

GABRIELSON, IRA NOEL and FREDERICK C. LINCOLN

The Birds of Alaska. Harrisburg, Penn.; Stackpole Co., 1959. 922 pp. Compilation of the work of ornithologists in Alaska from 1741 with 50 page history of Alaska ornithology. "Alaska is relatively rich in water birds, poor in land birds."

GAGE, JOSEPH H.

Trail North to Danger. New York: Winston, 1952. 215 pp.

GAGNON, PAUL L.; see Beaver Report.

GAINES, RUBEN

Chilkoot Charlie. Sitka: Sitka Printing Company, 1951. 26 pp. Drawings by Dale De Armond. Poetry. See also the *Second Book of Chilkoot Charlie* and the *Third Book of Chilkoot Charlie* (1955 and 1957).

Mrs. Maloney. Sitka: Sitka Printing Co., 1955. 11 pp.

See also several volumes of anecdotes and vignettes drawn from Ruben Gaines' radio work in Anchorage entitled *Conservations Unlimited.*

GAIRDNER, GEORGE W. and A. G. HARRISON

See T-1674.

GALENA

Alaska Sportsman, October, 1954.

GALIANO, DIONISIO ALCALA and CAYETANO VALDES

Relacion del viage Hecho por las Goletas Sutil y Mexicana. Madrid: En La Imprinta Real, 1802. 186 pp. Voyage made in 1792. Translated in Wagner. See also Bancroft. Galinao came out from Spain with Malaspina in 1789. See also Espinosa y Tello and Cayetano Valdes.

GAMBELL, V. C.

Schoolhouse Farthest West. New York: Women's Board of Home Missions, 1910. 44 pp. St. Lawrence Island.

GANNET, HENRY (1846-1914)

"The General Geography of Alaska," *National Geographic*, May, 1901.

"The Harriman Alaska Expedition," *National Geographic*, December, 1899.

The Origin of Certain Names in the US. Wn.DC: GPO, 1902. 280 pp. USGS.

"Altitudes in Alaska," *Bulletin*, USGS, 1900.

"Geography of Alaska," in Harriman's *Alaska.*

GAPANOVICH, IVAN IVANOVICH (b. 1891)

"The Asiatic Origin of South American Man," Royal Asiatic Society, North China Branch, *Journal*, 1931.

GAPP, SAMUEL H.

Where Polar Ice Begins. Bethlehem: Moravian Church, 1928. 126 pp. Moravian missions.

Kolerat Pitsiulret. Bethlehem: Comenius Press, 1936. 108 pp. Early mission history.

GARBER, CLARK McKINLEY (b. 1891)

Stories and Legends of Bering Strait Eskimos. Boston: Christopher, 1940. 260 pp.

GARDNER, IRVINE M.

"Northern Sinecure," *The Beaver*, Winter, 1956. Daily life of a Hudson's Bay Co. manager.

GARDNER, LEE S.

The Optimist, American Plan. New York: Exposition Press, 1951. 105 pp.

GARFIELD, BRIAN

Thousand Mile War. New York: Macmillan, 1968. World War II in the Aleutians, from Dutch Harbor to Attu.

GARFIELD, VIOLA EDMUNDSON (b. 1899)

Meet the Totem. Sitka: Sitka Printing Co., 1951. 54 pp.

The Seattle Totem Pole. Seattle: University of Washington Press, 1940. 14 pp.

"Antecedents of Totem Pole Carving," *Proceedings*, Alaska Science Conference, 1956.

"Tsimshian Clan and Society," University of Washington, *Publications in Anthropology*, 1939.

"Contemporary Problems of Folklore Collecting and Study," University of Alaska, *Anthro. Papers*, 1953.

GARFIELD, VIOLA EDMUNDSON and LINN A. FORREST

The Wolf and the Raven. Seattle: University of Washington Press, 1948. 151 pp. Klawock and Ketchikan totem poles. In 1938 Mr. Forrest, regional architect with the US Forest Service, with CCC personnel, undertook restoration and relocation of the poles, a project long urged by the Department of Interior and the Governor of Alaska. The carving of new poles was done by Tlingit carvers. For notes on Mr. Forrest, anthropology professor at the University of Washington, see *Alaska Life*, May, 1941.

GARFIELD, VIOLA EDMUNDSON and PAUL S. WINGERT

The Tsimshian Indians and Their Arts. Seattle: University of Washington Press, 1966. 108 pp.

GARLAND, HAMLIN (1860-1940)

Long Trail. New York: Harper, 1907. 262 pp. Story of the Northwest Wilderness.

The Trail of the Goldseekers. New York: Macmillan, 1899. 264 pp. Garland traveled north with a companion from Ashcroft, B.C. to Quesnel (on the old Cariboo Trail), Hazelton (near the coast, but on the inside of the coast mountains), and Glenora, where he parted company with his companion, and went over the mountains to Wrangell, then to Skagway, White Pass, and Atlin Lake. He found the north foreboding, and returned to California, not without writing some Klondike poetry, however, nine of which were published in *McClure's Magazine*, April 1899. For further listings see Wickersham's bibliography.

GARRETT, W. E.

"Alaska's Marine Highway," *National Geographic*, June, 1965.

GARST, DORIS SHANNON (b. 1899)

Scotty Allan. New York: Messner, 1946. 238 pp. King of the Dog-team Drivers. See also Allan's autobiography.

Jack London: Magnet for Adventure. New York: Messner, 1944. 217 pp.

John Jewitt's Adventure. New York: Houghton-Mifflin, 1955. 211 pp.

GARTLEIN, CARL W.

"Unlocking Secrets of the Northern Lights," *National Geographic*, November, 1947.

GASSER, GEORGE WILLIAM (b. 1875)

"A Brief Account of Agriculture in Alaska," *Proceedings*, Alaska Science Conference, 1951. The work of seven agricultural experiment stations in Alaska, with notes on the Matanuska colony project.

Miscellaneous pamphlets and articles; see the following:

Cereal Growing in Alaska, 1926.
Farming Soils, 1943.
Livestock in Alaska, 1946.
The Matanuska Valley, 1946.
The Tanana Valley, 1946.
Growing Vegetables in Alaska, 1947.
Grass—Our Unsung Resource, 1948.
Agriculture in Alaska, 1948.
Grasslands in Alaska, 1948.
Growing Potatoes in Alaska, 1949.
The Grasses of Alaska, 1952.

Effect of Low Temperatures on the Growth of Tree Roots, 1953. All these were published by the Agricultural Experiment Stations in Alaska. See also Information for the Alaskan Farmer-Settler, published at Juneau in 1946 for the Alaska Development Board, 44 pp. For an analysis of Gasser and others as popularizers of Alaskan agricultural potential see Orlando Miller, *The Frontier in Alaska and the Matanuska Colony*.

GATES, WILLIAM CHARLES ("Swiftwater Bill") (1869-1937)

Alaska Life. July, '45, Aug., '45; Beebe; Beattie; Berton; Morgan; O'Connor; Wiedemann; Winslow. Gates, born William Charles Anloff, was a companion of Jack London at Dawson.

GEBHARD, ELIZABETH LOUISA (1859-1924)

The Life Adventures of the Original John Jacob Astor. New York: Bryan, 1915. 321 pp. See also K.W. Porter.

GEIST, OTTO WILLIAM and FROELICH G. RAINEY

Archaeological Excavations at Kukulik. Wn.DC: GPO, 1937. 391 pp. Bureau of American Ethnology. St. Lawrence Island. Largest mound found in the Bering Sea region, 1926-35. 50,000 artifacts were classified by Rainey, with appendicies in this work by Geist, and Roland, Snodgrass, Murie, Boekelman, and Paul Hopkins.

Aghvook, White Eskimo: Otto Geist and Alaskan Archaeology. Charles Keim. Fairbanks: University of Alaska Press, 1969.

Alaska Sportsman, Dec., '37 (by Geist on Eskimo grandmother on St. Lawrence Island); Aug., '55 and Feb., '58 (photo and biog. notes on Geist).

GEOGHEGAN, RICHARD HENRY (1866-1943)

The Aleut Language. Wn.DC: GPO, 1944. 169 pp. Dept. of Interior. This work was edited by Fredericka I. Martin (see below). Mr. Geoghegan based his grammar on the work of Veniaminov. See the Arctic Bibliography for a fuller listing of Geoghegan's work.

GEOGRAPHY

See exploration, and the Arctic Bibliography.

GEOLOGY

See the Arctic Bibliography, and full collection of USGS reconnaissance reports, special reports, bulletins, professional papers and Brooks' *Mineral Resources of Alaska*, at the USGS District Office in Anchorage, and at the Alaska State Historical Library. See also the following:

Alaska Life, June, '45; *Alaska Sportsman*, May, '44 (oil at Barrow); Feb., '48 (oil at Barrow); June, '48 (drilling at Barrow); Sept., '48 (oil on Iniskin Pen., Cook Inlet); Aug., '50 (photo, winterized rig); March, '52 (oil at Umiat); March, '53 (driller at Barrow); June, '53 (map, ice sheet); July, '53 (photo, conglomerate); Nov., '53 (closing, Barrow-Umiat field); May, '54 (Juneau area rising an inch a year); Sept., '54 (vegetation on nunataks); Apr., '55 (photo, Geophysical Institute); Jan., '57 (photo, mushroom rock); Baker (geologists as explorers); Beach (coal land, copper); Blake, T.; Blake, W.; Brooks; Cady; Dall; Denison; Grant; Grewingk; Gruening; Grye, G., et. al.; Leffingwell; Rickard; Russell, I.C.; Schrader; Spurr; Sundborg; Tewkesbury; Underwood; Williams, H.; Willoughby; Wickersham; see Oil. Consult the libraries and materials of government agencies, federal and state (and territorial) which have the responsibility of administering Alaska's resources and land.

GEORGE, JEAN CRAIGHEAD
The Moon of the Gray Wolves. New York: Crowell, 1969.

GEORGE, MARIAN M.
Little Journeys to Alaska and Canada. Chicago: A. Flanagan, 1901. 80 pp.

GEORGESON, CHARLES CHRISTIAN (1851-1931)
See the Arctic Bibliography for a complete listing of the numerous articles and pamphlets of C.C. Georgeson. By birth a Dane, Georgeson spent many years in Alaska with the various experiment stations. He pioneered Alaska agricultural observation and experimentation for the federal government. For commentary on his role see Miller, *The Frontier in Alaska and the Matanuska Colony.* See also two articles by Georgeson in *National Geographic*, "Possibilities of Alaska," 1902, and "Agricultural Capacity of Alaska," 1909. An example of Georgeson's work is "Agricultural Experiments in Alaska," in the *Yearbook* of the US Department of Agriculture, 1899. See also US Dept. of Agriculture.

GERDINE, THOMAS GOLDING
See Baker for a listing of Gerdine's USGS surveys of the Seward Peninsula, Chistochina River, Copper River Valley and the Tanana-Yukon region.

GERRISH, THEODORE
See T-1698.

GIANETTI, MICHELANGELO
Elogy of Captain Cook. Florence: G. Cambiagi, 1785. 87 pp.

GIBBONS, RUSSEL W.
See T-1704 ff. A vindication of Frederick Cook.

GIBBS, GEORGE (1815-1873)
Alphabetical Vocabulary of the Chinook Language. New York: Cramoisy, 1863. 23 pp.
Dictionary of the Chinook Jargon. New York: Cramoisy, 1863. 43 pp.
"Notes on the Tinneh or Chippewyan Indians of British and Russian America," *Annual Report.* Smithsonian Institution, 1866.

GIBBS, JAMES A., Jr. (b. 1921)
Sentinels of the North Pacific. Portland: Binfords and Mort, 1955. 232 pp. Pacific Coast lighthouses and light ships. Contains stories of the *Princess Kathleen*, Scotch Cap Light Station, and the *Baychime* (phantom ship).
Pacific Graveyard. Portland: Binfords and Mort, 1950. 192 pp. Story of ships lost at the Columbia River bar and vicinity.

GIDDINGS, JAMES LOUIS, Jr. (b. 1909)
Dendrochronology in Northern Alaska. Tucson: University of Arizona, 1942. 107 pp. Tree-ring research, 1937.
The Archaeology of Cape Denbigh. Providence: Brown University Press, 1964. 331 pp.
The Arctic Woodland Culture of the Kobuk River. Philadelphia: University Museum, University of Pennsylvania, 1952. 144 pp.
Ancient Men of the Arctic. New York: Alfred A. Knopf, 1967. 391 pp.
Giddings pioneered tree-ring research in northern Alaska, estimating from tree-ring counts from house timbers from excavations the age of the sites. See a listing of his articles on this methodology and his conclusions in the Arctic Bibliography. Giddings was an anthropologist with Brown University; he did considerable work in Cape Denbigh, and has published numerous articles on the problems of early man in the Arctic. See the following:
"Observations on the 'Eskimo type' of kinship and Social Structure," *Anthrop. Papers*, University of Alaska, 1952.
" 'Pillows' and Other Rare Flints," *Anthrop. Papers*, University of Alaska, 1956.
"Forest Eskimos: An Ethnographic Sketch of Kobuk River People in the 1880's," *Bulletin*, University Museum, University of Pennsylvania, 1956.
"Eskimos and Old Shorelines," *American Scholar*, XXXI (1962): 585-594.
"Round Houses in the Western Arctic," *Amer. Antiquity*, XXIII (1957): 121-135.

GIFFEN, NAOMI MUSMAKER
The Roles of Men and Women in Eskimo Culture. Chicago: University of Chicago Press, 1930. 113 pp.

GILBERG, AAGE (b. 1909)
Eskimo Doctor. New York: Norton, 1948. 229 pp. Gilberg was the first government doctor at Thule; the work presents a realistic picture of life in northern Greenland.

GILBERT, CHARLES HENRY (1859-1928)
"The Ichthyological Collections of the steamer *Albatross* During the Years 1890 and 1891," *Report*, Commissioner of Fish and Fisheries (US), 1893. Forty-five new species were found between Alaska and Oregon. For further publications see the Arctic Bibliography. See also Willis Horton Rich.

GILBERT, GEORGE
The Death of Captain James Cook. Honolulu: Paradise of the Pacific Press, 1926. 30 pp.

GILBERT, GROVE KARL (1843-1918)
Glaciers and Glaciation. New York: Doubleday, Page, 1904. 231 pp. This is volume three of the Harri-

man Expedition series. Glaciation is discussed generally, with observation of glaciers in Lynn Canal, Glacier Bay, Yakutat Bay, Prince William Sound, and the Kenai Peninsula.

GILBERT, JOHN JACOB
See Baker for a listing of Gilbert's Coast and Geodetic Survey reports, St. Michael to Golovin Sound, and on Unalaska and Unimak Islands, 1900-1901. Gilbert commanded the Coast Survey steamer *Pathfinder*.

GILBERT, KENNETH
Alaska Poker Stories. Seattle: Robert D. Seal, 1958. 147 pp.
Arctic Adventure. New York: Holt, 1947. 147 pp.
The Trap. New York: Holt, 1948. 138 pp.

GILBERT, WALTER EDWIN (1878-1950)
Arctic Pilot. London: Nelson and Sons, 1940. 256 pp. Flying north Canadian air routes in the 1920's.

GILDER, WILLIAM HENRY (1838-1900)
Schwatka's Search. New York: Scribner's, 1881. 316 pp. 1878-1880; Gilder accompanied Schwatka in search of Franklin's records, as a correspondent for the *New York Herald*.
"Among the Esquimaux with Schwatka," *Scribner's*, May, 1881.
Ice-pack and Tundra. New York: Scribner's, 1883. 344 pp. Search for the survivors of the *Jeannette*, 1881-82. USS *Rodgers* was the relief vessel; she voyaged through Bering Strait and the Chukchi Sea where she burned in St. Lawrence Bay. Account of finding the *Jeannette* survivors in Siberia, notes on the Chukchi, Yakuts and Petropavlovsk.

GILL, JOHN KAYE (1851-1929)
Gill's Dictionary of the Chinook Jargon. 17 editions from 1880-1910, 60 to 80 pages; 9th edition published in Portland.

GILLETT, J. M.; see T-1721.

GILLETTE, EDWARD; see T-1722.

GILLHAM, CHARLES EDWARD (b. 1898)
Raw North. New York: Barnes, 1947. 275 pp. 1935-40.
Sled Dog and Other Poems. Huntington, W.Va.: Standard Publications, 1950. 78 pp. Has biographical introduction.
Beyond the Clapping Mountains. New York: Macmillan, 1943. 134 pp.
Medicine Men of Hooper Bay. London: Batchworth, 1955. 142 pp. Eskimo folk tales.

GILLIS, CHARLES J.
Another Summer. New York: for private distribution, 1893. 76 pp. Yellowstone Park and Alaska.

GILMAN, ISABEL AMBLER
Alaska, the American Northland. Yonkers-on-Hudson: World Publishing Co., 1923. 343 pp. Geographical reader.
Alaskaland. New York: Harriman, 1914. 110 pp.
"In the Government Service," *Alaska-Yukon Magazine*, December, 1911. On Prof. W.T. Lopp.

GILMAN, WILLIAM
Our Hidden Front. New York: Reynal and Hitchcock, 1944. 266 pp. World War II Aleutian campaign.

GIST, ARTHUR STANLEY (b. 1883)
New Stories from Eskimoland. San Francisco: Harr, Wagner, 1930. 214 pp.

The GLACIER
Small monthly paper published at Wrangell from 1885 to 1888 by Samuel Hall Young, principal of the Tlingit Training Academy.

GLACIER BAY (and Glacier Bay National Monument)
Alaska Sportsman, July, '39 (nat. mon. enlarged from 1820 to 3850 sq. miles); Dec., '46; July, '53 (photo of glaciers); March, '58 (construction in Bartlett Cove); *Alaska-Yukon Magazine*, Aug., '08 (*Dolphin* first to land tourists at Muir Glacier since earthquake changed aspect); Allen, E.W. (*Mountaineer* [Seattle], 1925); Badlam ("Phantom City" glaciers); Ballou; Beach (Valley of Thunder); Brooks (bay discovered by Wood in 1877, explored by Muir and Young in 1879); Brown, D.M. (*Appalachia*, 1953, advance of glaciers); Burroughs (photos); Butcher, D. (*Exploring our Nat. Parks*); Clark; Colby; Collis (visit with Capt. Carroll, 1890); Cooper, W. (see the Arctic Bibliography for technical articles); Davidson (glaciers in Glacier Bay were known to the Russians); Dole; Gilbert; Grinnell (birds and mammals); Gruening (mon. est. 1925, farmers put out of business in 1927); Harriman (Burroughs, Muir); Higginson; Lawrence; Muir; Pilgrim ([*inaccurate*]); Reid; Romer (see the Arctic Bibliography); Scidmore; Sundborg; Tewkesbury; Underwood (Lt. Wood, 1877; Muir, 1879); Woollen; Wright; Young; see also the Arctic Bibliography for a more complete listing).

GLACIERS, GLACIOLOGY
Alaska Life, June, '45 (map on ice age); *Alaska Sportsman*, see Index; *Alaska-Yukon Magazine*, March, '08 (prospecting at Malaspina Glacier); July, '08 (Taku); Apr., '09 (Hubbard, Nunatak, Turner and Alexander Glaciers); March, '10 (by Andrews); Feb., '12; Bedlam; Blake; Brown, D. (*Appalachia*, 1952); Caldwell; Capps, S.R. (see the Arctic Bibliography); Burroughs; Carpenter; Clark; Colby; Davidson; Denison; Dole; Field, Wm. (see the Arctic Bibliography); Grant; Harriman; Hubbard (theory on glaciers); Juneau Ice Field Research Project (Arctic Bibliography); Lawrence, D.B. (dates and movement); MacDowell; Martin, L.; Mendenhall; Miller, M.; Muir; Pilgrim; Reid; Rickard; Russell; Schrader; Scidmore; Seton-Kerr; Sharp (Arctic Bibliography); Sundborg; Swineford; Tarr; Tewkesbury; Underwood; Washburn; Wickersham (*Alaska Magazine*, January, 1927 "glacial age soon to end"); Williams, H.; Wright, G.; Young.

GLADFELTER, KATHARINE ELEANOR
Under the Northern Star. New York: Friendship Press, 1928. 135 pp. A course of study on Alaska for junior boys and girls.

GLANZ, RUDOLF
The Jews in American Alaska, 1867-1880. New York, 1953. 46 pp. Includes bibliography.

GLASS, HENRY
See Baker for his work for the Coast and Geodetic Survey. Glass succeeded Beardslee on the Sitka station in 1881, commanding the *Jamestown* and *Wachusett*. He worked on several coast charts.

GLASSCOCK, C. B.
Lucky Baldwin. Indianapolis: Bobbs-Merrill, 1933. Elias Jackson ("Lucky") Baldwin was one of the Klondike miners who made and kept "big" money in the gold fields. He moved on to Nome, however, where he lost some money and sold his equipment. Upon his death in 1909 he left a $10 million estate, most of it accumulated from Nevada silver and California real estate.

GLAVE, E. J.
The Leslie Expedition to Alaska, 1890-91, with E.H. Wells and A.B. Schanz. Glave, with John Dalton, crossed Chilkat Pass (the Dalton Trail), and at Kusawa Lake crossed over to the headwaters of the Alsek River, descending that river to the Pacific. Glave wrote numerous articles on Alaska for *Leslie's* weekly magazine. See also Baker.

GLAVIS, LOUIS R.
Message transmitting, in response to Senate Resolution 112 of Dec. 21, 1909, original statement of charges made to the President by L.R. Glavis, together with other statements, letters, and records. Jan. 6, 1910. 805 pp. Senate Doc. No. 248, 61st Congress, 2nd session. Glavis was an assistant to Gifford Pinchot, Chief Forester, under Theodore Roosevelt. Glavis, with Pinchot, suspected the Cunningham coal claims as fraudulent, or intended by Cunningham to be turned over to the Guggenheim syndicate and consolidated in a corporate enterprise. This is the primary document in which Glavis and Pinchot outlined their suspicions, and accused Ballinger of aiding and abetting Cunningham. See Ballinger-Pinchot controversy.

GLAZUNOV, ANDREI
"Extract from the Journal of Andrei Glazunov, First Mate of the Imperial Russian Navy, during his voyage in the northwest of America," ed. James Van Stone. *Pacific Northwest Quarterly*, 1959. First appeared in Russian in Zhurnal Manufaktur i Torgovli, 1836. The complete original journal has never been published. Glazunov made an overland journey of 1400 miles in 140 days in 1833-34, traveling from St. Michael to the Anvik River, and down to the Yukon, over the portage to the Kuskokwim, and then northeast to the Stoney River, and back to St. Michael. He had originally planned to continue on to Cook Inlet, but did not.

GLAZEBROOK, G. P. de T.
The Hargrave Correspondence, 1821-43. Toronto: The Champlain Society, 1938. 472 pp. Concerns relationships between Hudson's Bay Company and the Russian-American Company in the early 19th century. See James Hargraves, and C. Ian Jackson.

GLEASON, H. A., Jr.
"A Note on Tanaina Sub-groups," *International Jrnl. of Anthrop. Linguistics*, 26 (1960): 248-51.

GLEASON, ROBERT J.
"Pioneer Mail Flight to Siberia," *Alaska Journal*, IV (1974): 122-124.

GLEAVES, ALBERT
The Life of an American Sailor. New York: George Doran, 1923. 359 pp. Rear Admiral William Hemsley Emory, USN.

GLENN, EDWIN FORBES (1857-1926)
Report on Explorations in Alaska (Cook Inlet, Susitna, Copper and Tanana Rivers). Wn.DC: GPO, 1899. US Army, Adjutant General's Office. See also Abercrombie.
"A Trip to the Tanana Region, 1898," in Compilation of Narratives, US Congress, Committee on Military Affairs.
"Explorations in and about Cook Inlet, 1899," in Compilation of Narratives.
Captain Glenn, for whom the Glenn Highway is named, with W.C. Mendenhall, explored a route northward from Port Wells, Prince William Sound, to the Tanana River, then to Rampart and Circle on the Yukon. He also explored in the Matanuska and Susitna River basins, one of the last areas of Alaska to come under the cognizance of military exploration. See also Marcus Baker.

GLENORA
Alaska Sportsman, June, 1960 (photo)

GLODY, ROBERT
A Shepherd of the Far North. San Francisco: Harr Wagner, 1934. 237 pp. Biography of Fr. William Francis Walsh, who was killed in the crash of the *Marquette*, a Catholic mission plane, at Kotzebue, the location of Fr. Walsh's mission. Ralph Wien was pilot of this flight. Also killed was Fr. Delon, another missionary. Wien Field at Kotzebue is named for Ralph Wien.

GLOSSARIES
Adams; Andrews (Eskimo and his Reindeer); Colby; Dall; Elliott; Henderson; Mason.

GLOTOV, STEPAN
Bancroft (first voyage to the Aleutians in 1758-62, to Umnak and Unalaska; second voyage in 1762-65 to Umnak; third voyage to Kodiak [discovery] 1763-64); Baker; Berkh; Coxe; Dall.

GLUBOK, SHIRLEY
The Art of the Eskimos. New York: Harper and Row, 1964. 48 pp.
The Art of the North American Indian. New York: Harper and Row, 1964. n.p.

GMELIN, JOHANN GEORG (1709-1755)
Flora Siberia. St. Petersburg: Academy of Science, 1747-1769. 4v. See also T-1741 ff.

GODDARD, PLINY EARLE (1869-1928)
Indians of the Northwest Coast. New York: American Museum of Natural History, 1924. 176 pp. Much on linguistics.

GODBEY, WILLIAM G.
"Up the Big, Big Road: Adventure on the Alaska Highway," *Alaska Review*, Spring, 1966.

GODSELL, PHILIP HENRY (b. 1889)

The Romance of the Alaska Highway. Toronto: Ryerson, 1944. 235 pp. A former field officer of the Hudson's Bay Co., Godsell here makes an economic commentary on the impact of the highway.

Arctic Trader. New York: Putnam's, 1934. 329 pp. As field officer for Hudson's Bay.

"The Passing of Herschel Island," *Royal Can. Mounted Police Quarterly*, 1942. The Mounted Police occupied this island from 1903 to 1940; other topics in the book include the Copper Eskimos, the lawlessness of whaling days, and Christian Klengenberg and his exploits.

"Old Trails to the Arctic," *Can. Geog. Journal*, 1934. Steamer passage from Ft. McMurray, Alberta, to Aklavik in the Mackenzie delta, with historical notes on river settlements.

Red Hunters of the Snows. Toronto: Ryerson, 1938. 324 pp. History of early contact between natives and white traders.

The Vanishing Frontier. Toronto: Ryerson, 1939. 287 pp. Saga of mounties and men of the last northwest.

See also T-2122.

GODWIN, GEORGE STANLEY (b. 1889)

Vancouver, a Life: 1757-1798. London: Philip Allan, 1930. 308 pp. This was the only biography until 1960, when Bern Anderson's work was published. The work includes a summary of the voyages, and an appendix provides correspondence and other documents. Godwin also published a novel of British Columbia, *Eternal Forest*, in 1929 (318 pp.).

GOETZ, DELIA

The Arctic Tundra. New York: William Morrow, 1958. 62 pp. Pictorial, juvenile.

GOETZE, O. D.

Souvenir of Northwestern Alaska. San Francisco: William Brown, n.d. 48 pp.

GOLD BOOK; see Fred Atwood.

GOLD RUSH; see Klondike.

GOLDBERG, ROBERT M.

Alaska Survey and Report. Anchorage: Alaska Research Institute, 1972, 1973. 2v. Statistical compilation of economic, governmental and social aspects of Alaska.

"Alaska," *Harper's Bazaar*, 1973.

GOLDER, FRANK ALFRED (1877-1929)

Bering's Voyages. An account of the efforts of the Russians to determine the relation of Asia and America. New York: American Geographical Society, 1922, 1925. 2v. Summary of contents: Bering's first voyage; Gvozdev's discovery of America, 1732; Bering's second expedition; Waxell's narrative; journal of the St. Paul (Chirikov); Bertholf's discussion of the routes; and in the second volume, biog. note on Steller; Steller's journal (this includes a Steller journal found first by Golder in Russia in 1917, a basic work on Alaska); Steller's notes on Bering Island and the sea cow; his letter to Gmelin; bibliography of Steller. The log book of St. Paul, not included in this work, was published in 1951 in Russian by Lebedev.

Russian Expansion on the Pacific, 1641-1850. Cleveland: A.H. Clark Co., 1914. 368 pp. Chapters on the administration of eastern Siberia in the 17th century, Russia and China on the Amur to 1689, critical examination of Deshnev's voyage, Kamchatka and the Kuriles, the Chukchi and the discovery of America. Golder here argues against the possibility of Deshnev's rounding East Cape in 1648. See also Raymond Fisher in the *Pac. Hist. Rev.*, 1956; see as well the discussion in Svetlana Fedorova, *Population of Russian America*. See reviews of this work by Golder in the *Wn. Hist. Q.*, 1915 (by C.L. Andrews), and *Geog. Journal*, 1916 (by J.F. Baddeley).

Guide to Materials for American History in Russian Archives. Wn.DC: Carnegie Institute, 1917. 177 pp. Vol. 2 in 1937. Golder worked in archives in St. Petersburg and Moscow from March to November, 1914. He also toured the Valaam monastery at Lake Ladoga (now in Finland). He made photostats of many documents, including diplomatic material to 1854, most of which is in the University of Washington Library, with copies in the Library of Congress.

Father Herman, Alaska's Saint. Originally published in 1915, apparently reprinted from the (Washington) State Agricultural College Journal, Pullman, this work was republished in 1968 in San Francisco by the Orthodox Christian Books and Icons Group, 66 pp. Fr. Herman was canonized by the American Orthodox Church in 1970.

"A Survey of Alaska," *Washington Historical Quarterly*, 1913.

"The Purchase of Alaska," *American Historical Review*, 1920.

"Mining in Alaska Before 1867," *Washington Hist. Q.*, 1916.

"The Russian Fleet and the American Civil War," *Amer. Hist. Rev.*, 1915.

"The Atitude of the Russian Government towards Alaska," a chapter in *The Pacific Ocean in History*, New York: Macmillan Co., 1917.

"Tales from Kodiak Island," *Jrnl. Amer. Folklore*, 1903.

"Aleutian Stories," *Jrnl. Amer. Folklore*, 1905.

"The Songs and Stories of the Aleuts," *Jrnl. Amer. Folklore*, 1907.

"Tlingit Myths," *Jrnl. Amer. Folklore*, 1907.

"A Kodiak Island Story," *Jrnl. Amer. Folklore*, 1907.

"Primitive Warfare among the Natives of Western Alaska," *Jrnl. Amer. Folklore*, 1909.

"Eskimo and Aleut Stories from Alaska," *Jrnl. Amer. Folklore*, 1910.

"Russian-American Relations in the Crimean War," *Amer. Hist. Rev.*, 1926.

"American Civil War through the Eyes of a Diplomat," *Amer. Hist. Rev.*, 1921.

"Russian Offer of Mediation in the War of 1812," *Pol. Sci. Q.*, 1916.

"Catherine II and the American Revolution," *Amer. Hist. Rev.*, 1915.

Professor Golder was born in Odessa, Russia, coming to the United States at age 3. Educated at Bucknell, he spent 3 years (1899-1902) as teacher and US Commissioner at Unga Island. There he gathered materials for his folklore articles. Earning his doctorate at Harvard (1909) he taught at

Missouri (Columbia), Boston University and the University of Chicago before going to Washington State College at Pullman (1910-1920). He taught at Stanford from 1921 until his death in 1929. Golder viewed Alaska as the final chapter in Russian expansion, although it was his interest in Alaska which led him to study the history of Russian expansion. In 1925 he edited Platanov's *History of Russia*, the *Documents of Russian HIstory, 1914-1917* in 1927, and with Lincoln Hutchinson, "On the Trail of the Russian Famine," and in 1928 "The March of the Mormon Battalion from Council Bluffs to California." His death in 1929 took a major scholar from the field of Russian and Alaskan history.

GOLDSCHMIDT, WALTER ROCH
Anthropology of Franz Boas. Menasha, Wisc.: American Anthropological Association, 1959. 165 pp. Essays on the centennial of his birth.

GOLDSON, WILLIAM
Observations on the Passage between the Atlantic and Pacific Oceans in two memoirs on the Straits of Anian and the discoveries of deFonte elucidated by a new and original map which is prefixed with an historical abridgment of discoveries in the North of America. Portsmouth: Mobray, 1793. 162 pp.

GOLDTHWAIT, R. P. et al
Soil Development and Ecological Succession. Columbus: Ohio State University Press, 1966. 167 pp. Muir Inlet.

GOLOVIN, PAULUS NIKOLAIEVICH (ca. 1823-1862)
Survey of the Russian Colonies in North America. Cong. Papers, 40th Congress, 2nd session, Ex. Document 177, a translation and abridgment of the original Russian. Golovin and Sergei Kostlivtsov were ordered to make an investigation of the affairs of the Russian-American Company in Alaska and California in 1860, as a part of the consideration for renewal of the company's charter. Among other of Golovin's recommendations was that Russians and natives be freed from company control. See the Arctic Bibliography, and Smith's Bibliography for a complete listing of Golovin's reports and the replies to them.

GOLOVNIN, VASILII NIKHAILOVICH (1776-1831)
See the Arctic Bibliography for a full review of Golovnin's circumnavigation in 1817-19, in *Kamchatka*. The account of the voyage, from Kronstadt via Cape Horn to Kamchatka and then Kodiak and Sitka, contains a full description of Sitka. Untranslated, Golovnin's accounts of the affairs of the Russian-American Company and living conditions of Aleuts in the settlements of the Company are highly critical, and are an important historical resource for study of the period. Golovnin had made an earlier journey, in 1810, which included a sledge journey in Kamchatka from Petropavlovsk to Nizhnekamchatsk, and a voyage from Petropavlovsk to Sitka and return. On Golovnin see also T-1763 ff.

GOODE, GEORGE BROWN (1851-1896)
The Fisheries and Fishery Industries of the US. Wn.DC: GPO, 1884-87. 7v. Goode wrote the sections on whaling and porpoises. Other sections are by J.A. Allen (seals and walruses), H.W. Elliott (fur seals, sea lions, sea otters), F.W. True (sea cows), T.H. Bean (fishery resources, cod fishery); N.P. Scudder (halibut, Davis Straits); Alonzo Clark (walruses and whales).

GOODENOUGH, WARD H.
Explorations in Cultural Anthropology. New York, 1964. Essays in Honor of George Peter Murdock; Eskimos of the Brooks Range.

GOODHUE, CORNELIA
Journey into the Fog. Garden City: Doubleday, 1944. 179 pp. Vitus Bering. See C.L. Andrews review in *Pac NW Q*, 1944.

GOODMAN, JOE R. et alii; see T-1775 ff.

GOODRICH, HAROLD BEACH (1870-1945)
History and Condition of the Yukon Gold District. See the annual report of the USGS for 1896-97. Goodrich, Spurr and Schrader made a geologic reconnaissance of the Chilkoot Pass route to the Klondike, and down the Yukon to St. Michael in 1896 (summer).

GORDON, GEORGE BYRON (1870-1927)
In the Alaskan Wilderness. Phildelphia: Winston, 1917. 247 pp. This is a report of a canoe voyage in 1907 on the Yukon from Whitehorse past Dawson to the Tanana and Kantishna, and then over to the Kuskokwim, for the University Museum of the University of Pennsylvania. The book describes the material culture of the Kuskokwim Eskimos. The University had sent out a previous expedition in 1905 which resulted in "Notes on the Western Eskimo," by Gordon, published in 1906 by the University Museum.

GORDON, Lord GRANVILLE ARMYNE
Nootka. London: Sands, 1899. 245 pp. Vancouver Island.

GORDON, MONA
The Mystery of LaPerouse. Christchurch, New Zealand: Bascanda, 1961. 187 pp.

GORDON, R. LESLIE
A Little Journey Through Alaska. Chicago: A. Flanagan, 1931. 144 pp.

GORDON, WILLIAM JOHN
Round About the North Pole. London: Murray, 1907. 294 pp. A history of exploration and research.

GORE, JOHN (ca. 1730-1790)
Capt. Gore commanded Cook's voyage after Clerke's death in 1779 including the excursion to Kamchatka. James King was his subordinate. Gore was content, however, to allow King's journal to be published as the official version of the expedition after Cook's death. Born in the colony of Virginia, Gore is honored by the naming of Gore Point on the southern tip of the Kenai Peninsula.

GORE, LOUISE C.
Soul of the Bearded Seal. Anchorage: Alaska Methodist University Press, 1967. 112 pp. Poetry.

GORHAM MANUFACTURING COMPANY

The Soul of Alaska. New York: Gorham Company, 1905. 96 pp. Photographic reproductions of bronzes by Louis Potter, of Tlingit life and habitat.

GORMAN, RICHARD F.

Fur Farming Opportunities in Alaska. Juneau: Alaska Development Board, 1947. 40 pp. On the fox and mink farming of Dr. C.K. Gunn.

GORRELL, JOSEPH R.

A Trip to Alaska. Newton, Iowa, 1905. 40 pp. Letters to the *Newton Herald* describing southeast Alaska.

GOSNELL, R. EDWARD (1860-1931)

A History: British Columbia. Victoria: Lewis Publishing Co., 1906. 783 pp. See also Scholefield.

GOSS, BARNEY

"Alaska's First Delegate Elect," *Alaska Journal,* II (Autumn, 1972).

GOULD, DOROTHY WHEATON

Beyond the Shining Mountains. Portland: Binfords and Mort, 1938. 206 pp. Capt. Vancouver, Astoria, gold rush, timber trade.

GOULD, MAURICE M. and KENNETH BRESSETT, KAYE and NANCY DETHRIDGE

Alaska's Coinage through the Years. Racine: Whitman Publishing Co., 1960. 46 pp. Illus. See also rev. ed. 1965, 176 pp. and bibliography.

GOULD, RUPERT THOMAS (b. 1890)

Captain Cook. London: Duckworth, 1935. 144 pp. See also the Arctic Bibliography.

GOULD, SYDNEY

Inasmuch: Church of England Missions in Canada. Toronto: Missionary Society of the Church of England, 1917. 285 pp. Northwest territories, Eskimos, Arctic Coast, Northwest passage.

GOULET, EMIL OLIVER (b. 1900)

Rugged Years on the Alaska Frontier. Philadelphia: Dorrance, 1949. 304 pp. Report of 16 years in Alaska, realistically presented. Goulet worked on the Copper River and Northwestern Railway at Chitina and Kennecott, and in the Paxson area and at Fairbanks. Prospecting at Miller Gulch, Alder Creek and other digs he made little more than wages. Goulet made his fortune in construction in Fairbanks during WW II, after which he left Alaska.

GOVERNMENT OF ALASKA

See the Arctic Bibliography, and the various publications of relevant government agencies, and the University of Alaska's Institute for Social, Economic and Government Research. See as well the following:

Russian Period: Fedorova; Khlebnikov; Okun; Pierce.

Cession to the US: Golder; Jensen; Shiels; etc., Purchase: Rousseau's report; Seward's speech; Shiels; Sumner's speech.

War Department: Gruening; Hulley.

Treasury Department (Customs officers, supported by the Navy and the Revenue Cutter Service): Beardslee; Gruening; Morris; see also Hulley.

Customs Act, 1868: Hulley.

Civil Government Act, 1884: Gruening; Hinckley; Pilgrim; Shiels. See also the list of judges, US Commissioners and US Marshal in Shiels.

Bering Sea Arbitration: Shiels.

Miners' Meetings: Hunt; see also Rodman Paul, *California Gold.*

Homestead Act, 1898: Gruening; Nichols.

Criminal Code, 1899: Gruening; Nichols.

Carter Act, 1900 (Civil Code, Capital removal, Incorporation of Towns, Increase in US Judges): Hulley; see also Gruening. See Spicer.

Boundary Dispute: see Boundary Issue, Boundary Tribunal.

Minook Decision, 1905 (declared US an integral part of the US as an incorporated territory, and at the same time established legal basis for Alaska native claims): Gruening; Hulley; Spicer; see also Cohen, and Washburn, W.

Alaska Delegate Bill: Hulley; Shiels (delegates listed).

Civil Government Act, 1912: Gruening; Hulley; Nichols; Spicer; Shiels (legislators listed).

Harding's speech at Seattle, 1923: Shiels.

Statehood: Fischer; Naske; see also Gruening. Constitutional Convention: Proceedings; Fischer (ISEGR). Tennessee Plan, Act of 1958: Gruening; Naske. See also Statehood.

See also the following:

Beardslee; Carter, T.H. (Laws of Alaska, 1900); Castle (on prohibition law enforcement, 1922); Castle (digest of cases, 1924); Charles and Southworth (mining law, 1906); Clarke, Horace (Miners' manual, 1898); Cohen (federal Indian [native] law); Delaney; Denison; Gruening; Gsovski (status of natives, Russian period); Harding; Haydon; Held and Garside (Harris mining district, 1887); Hills and Aushermann (mining laws, 1897); Hulley; Judson; Knapp; Morris; Naske; Nichols; Pilgrim; Reynolds (mining law); Roden (mining laws, 1913); Shiels; Spicer; Sumner; Thomas, Benj. P.; Tompkins; Wickersham.

GOVERNORS of ALASKA

See the Annual Reports of the Governors of Alaska to the Secretary of the Interior, and also messages, reports and miscellaneous materials. The official papers of the Office of the Governor of Alaska are housed in the Archive of the Alaska State Historical Library (Juneau), together with miscellaneous papers from the territorial period, such as those of the office of the Secretary, and some of the several commissions. Many of these papers are available on microfilm for research from the National Archives and Federal Records Service Center, Region 10, Seattle, Washington.

GRABER, ALMA HALL

East to Alaska. Sitka: Sitka Print Co., 1960. 30 pp. First Russian voyage to Sitka.

GRAHAM, ANGUS

The Golden Grindstone. Philadelphia: Lippincott, 1935. 304 pp. George M. Mitchell. Story of a prospecting party headed for the Klondike via the Slave and Mackenzie Rivers, and over the Peel and Wind Rivers. Injured along the way, Mitchell stayed several months with the Kutchin Indians.

GRAHAM, J. F.
Graham's Alaska Gold Fields Guide. Chicago:
Lomas Publishing Co., 1897. 30 pp.

GRAHAME, NIGEL B. M.
Bishop Bompas of the Frozen North. London:
Seeley, 1925. 60 pp. Juvenile.

GRANBERG, WILBUR J.
Voyage into Darkness. New York: Dutton, 1960.
190 pp. Juvenile.

GRAND TRUNK PACIFIC RAILWAY COMPANY
*Prince Rupert, the terminus of the Grand Trunk
Pacific Railway.* Montreal, 1911. 24 pp.

GRANT, DELBERT A. STEWART
Blazing a Gospel Trail to Alaska. Springfield, Mo.,
1944. 55 pp. Plane and jeep through Canada and
Alaska.

GRANT, ULYSSES SHERMAN (1867-1932)
USGS Bulletins 587(1915), 526(1913), and 443
(1910) on Prince William Sound and Kenai Peninsula
glaciers. Also American Geographical Society Bulletin, 1910-11 on the same subject.

GRAVES, S. H.
On the White Pass Payroll. Chicago: Lakeside
Press, 1908. 258 pp. By the president of the White
Pass and Yukon Railway.

GRAVES, WILLIAM P.
"Earthquake," *National Geographic*, July, 1964.

GRAVEL, MIKE (US Senator)
Jobs, and More Jobs. Anchorage: Mt. McKinley
Publishing, 1968.

GRAY, GRATTAN
"The Yukon's Coming Alive Again," *Maclean's
Magazine*, November, 1954. Mining and hydro-
electric development on the Upper (Taku) Yukon.

GRAY, ROBERT
Alaska-Yukon Magazine, Sept., '11; Dall; Denton; Bancroft; Godwin; Greenhow; Howell;
Hulley; Laut; Meany; Speck; Tompkins; Vancouver; Wagner.

GRAY, W. C.
Musings by Campfire and Wayside. New York:
Revell, 1936. 337 pp.

GREAT BRITAIN
See Alaska Diplomacy; Alaska Boundary. See also
Tourville.

GREEK CATHOLIC CHURCH
See Russian Orthodox Church.

GREELY, ADOLPHUS WASHINGTON (1844-
1935)
Handbook of Alaska. New York: Scribner's, 1909.
280 pp. Resources, products, attraction. Also
London edition and revised edition (1914).
Three Years of Arctic Service. New York: Scribner's, 1886. 2v. This is a report of Greely's expedition

of 1881-84 (the Lady Franklin Bay expedition) in
which Greely nearly lost his life. See Jeannette
Mirsky.
Report. The US Expedition to Lady Franklin's
Bay, Grinnell Land. Wn.DC: GPO, 1888. 2v. US
Army.
Handbook of Arctic Discoveries. Boston: Roberts
Brothers, 1896. 257 pp. Later editions as Handbook
of Polar Discoveries.
The Polar Regions in the 20th Century. Boston:
Little, Brown, 1928. 270 pp.
True Tales of Arctic Heroism. New York: Scrib-
ner's Sons, 1912. 385 pp. Staffe, Franklin, Ross,
Bedford Pim, Kane, Moon, Sonntag, Lady Jane
Franklin, Tyson, Parr, Schwatka, Bronlund, Nertuk,
and the Barrow whalers relief.
"Climatic Conditions of Alaska," *National Geo-
graphic*, 1898.
"The Economic Evolution of Alaska," *National
Geographic*, 1909.
"The Cartography and Observations of Bering's
First Voyage," *National Geographic*, 1892.
See also the Arctic Bibliography; see also Schley,
and Todd.

GREEN, FITZHUGH (b. 1888)
Bob Bartlett: Master Mariner. New York: Putnam's 1929. 211 pp. Juvenile.

GREEN, JOHN C.
See T-1845.

GREEN, JONATHAN S.
Journal of a Tour of the Northwest Coast. New
York: for C.F. Heartman, 1915. 104 pp. Reprinted
from the *Missionary Herald.* Voyage in 1829, descr.
with commentary on natives.

GREEN, PAUL (Aknik) (b. 1901)
I Am Eskimo—Aknik is My Name. Juneau: Alaska
Northwest Publishing, 1959. 86 pp. With Abbe Ab-
bott. Serially in *Alaska Sportsman*, Nov., '58-Aug.,
'59. Kivalina, Kotzebue Sound.

GREENAWAY, KEITH
See T-1848.

GREENHOW, ROBERT (1800-1854)
*The History of Oregon and California and Other
Territories on the Northwest Coast.* Boston: Little,
1844. 482 pp. The basic work before Bancroft.
Memoir, Historical and Political. New York: Putnam's, 1840. 228 pp. Previous to the above work,
this one was commissioned by the US State Department as a brief for Oregon claims, through the aegis
of Senator Linn.
Geography of Oregon and California. Boston:
Freeman, 1845. 120 pp. And the northwest coast.

GREENWOOD, AMY
Rolling North. New York: Crowell, 1955. 218 pp.

GREGORY, HOMER EWART (b. 1886)
North Pacific Fisheries. With Kathleen Barnes.
San Francisco: American Council, Institute of
Pacific Relations, 1939. 322 pp.

GREINER, JAMES
Wager with the Wind. Chicago: Rand McNally,
1974. 185 pp. Don Sheldon, McKinley pilot.

GREWINGK, CONSTANTIN CASPAR ANDREAS (1819-1887)
Beitrag zur Kenntniss der Orographischen und Geognostischen Beschaffenheit de Nord-West Kuste Amerikas. St. Petersburg: Gedruckt bey K. Kray, 1850. 351 pp. See Dall's summary of the significance of this work (p. 457). A description of coastal geography from San Francisco to Cape Lisburne and the Commander Islands, with special attention to Alaska surface features. Includes tables of volcanic disturbances, 1690-1844, and a summary of expeditions, 1542-1849.

GRIER, MARY CATHARINE
See T-1855.

GRIERSON, JOHN
Sir Hubert Wilkins. London: Robert Hale, 1960. 224 pp. Enigma of Exploration.

GRIFFIN, D. F.
First Steps to Tokyo. Toronto: Dent, 1944. 50 pp. Royal Canadian Air Force in the Aleutians.

GRIFFIN, DONALD REDFIELD (b. 1915)
"Alaska Bird Migrations," *Research Reviews*, July, 1951. See also the Arctic Bibliography.

GRIFFIN, HAROLD
Alaska and the Canadian Northwest. New York: W.W. Norton, 1944. 221 pp. Canol, Alaska Highway, Fairbanks, Whitehorse.

GRIFFITH, WILLIAM
See T-1859.

GRIGGS, ROBERT FISKE (1882-1962)
The Valley of the Ten Thousand Smokes. Wn.DC: National Geographic Society, 1922. 341 pp. Griggs led four expeditions into the Katmai region between 1915 and 1919. This volume contains a full story of the 1912 eruption.
Scientific Results of the Katmai Expedition. Columbus: Ohio State University, 1920. 492 pp.

GRIGOR'EV, A. A.; see T-1861 ff.

GRIGSBY, GEORGE B. (b. 1874)
"Biennial Report of the Attorney General, Territory of Alaska," *Daily Alaska Empire*, 1919. Grigsby was defeated three times for delegate of Alaska. See Gruening, and Nichols.

GRIMES, J. G.
Alaskan Gold. Boston: Badger, with Chapman and Grimes, 1936.

GRINNELL, GEORGE BIRD (1849-1938)
American Big Game. New York: Forest and Stream, 1904. 497 pp. Boone and Crockett Club. Mountain Sheep, Kodiak Bear, etc.
Hunting at High Altitudes. New York: Harper's, 1913. 511 pp.
"The Natives of Alaska," in Harriman's *Alaska* (expedition), 1902. Tlingits, Aleuts, Eskimos; Plover Bay, Chukotsk Peninsula, Port Clarence.
"The Salmon Runs, Cannery Techniques, etc.," in Harriman's *Alaska* (expedition), 1902.

Grinnell was a significant authority on American Indian life. See bibliography on his works in Smith-3880 ff.

GRINNELL, JOSEPH (1877-1939)
Gold Hunting in Alaska. Chicago: David Cook, 1901. 96 pp. Kotzebue Sound and Nome, from Grinnell's diary.
Birds of the Kotzebue Sound Region. Santa Clara, Calif.; Cooper Ornithological Club, 1900. 80 pp. Grinnell produced a large number of short works on Alaska bird life. See the Arctic Bibliography, and also the periodical *Condor*, January, 1940, which includes bibliography and biography.

GRINNELL, MICHAEL
Song of the Wild Land. New York: Pageant Press, 1952. 76 pp.

GROSVENOR, ELSIE MAY
"Alaska's Warmer Side,'" *National Geographic*, 1956.

GROSVENOR, GILBERT HOVEY (b. 1875)
"Harriman Alaska Expedition in cooperation with the Washington Academy of Sciences," *National Geographic*, 1899.

GRUBSTAKE PUBLISHING COMPANY
Klondike Grubstakes. Seattle, 1898. Issued monthly. Where to Get Them; What to Take.

GRUENING, ERNEST HENRY (1887-1974)
The State of Alaska. New York: Random House, 1954. 607 pp. Able statement of the thesis that neglect by the federal government to provide adequate government for Alaska had detrimental consequences.
An Alaskan Reader, 1867-1967. New York: Meredith Press, 1967. 443 pp. Selected and edited.
The Battle for Alaska Statehood. College: University of Alaska, 1967. 122 pp.
Let Us End American Colonialism. Alaska Constitutional Convention, Keynote Address, 1956.
Many Battles: The Autobiography of Ernest Gruening. New York: Liveright Press, 1973. 564 pp.
"The Political Ecology of Alaska," *Proceedings*, Alaska Science Conference, 1951; reprinted in *Scientific Monthly*, December, 1951.
"Alaska: Progress and Problems," *Scientific Monthly*, July, 1953.
"Strategic Alaska Looks Ahead," *National Geographic*, September, 1942.
"Alaska Proudly Joins the Union," *National Geographic*, July, 1959.
"Lonely Wonders of Katmai," *National Geographic*, June, 1963.
See also Sherwood Ross, *Gruening of Alaska*, and Alaska Statehood.

GRYC, GEORGE (b. 1919)
See the Arctic Bibliography.

GSOVSKI, VLADIMIR (b. 1891)
Russian Administration of Alaska and the Status of Alaskan Natives. Wn.DC: GPO, 1950. 99 pp. Senate Doc. 152, 81st Cong., 2nd Session. Excellent summary of legal basis for native status and native claims.

GUBSER, NICHOLAS J.
The Nunamiut Eskimos. New Haven: Yale University Press, 1965. 384 pp.

GUEMPLE, D. LEE
Inuit Spouse-Exchange. Chicago: University of Chicago Press, 1961. 133 pp.
"Alliance in Eskimo Society," *Proceedings,* American Ethnological Society, 1971.
"Eskimo Band Organization and the 'D.P. Camp' Hypothesis, *Arctic Anthropology,* IX (1972): 80 ff.

GUIDE BOOKS
See the following: Adams; Bedlam; Baedeker; Bright; Bruce; Burr; Caldwell; Cameron; Carpenter; Colby; Corser; Denison; Drake; Dynes; Franck; Greely; Harrington; Henderson; Herrin; Hart; Higginson; Hilscher; Itjen; Jacobin; Krug; Lanks; Rickard; Rossiter; Scidmore; Steward; Swineford; Tuttle; Underwood; Winslow; see also the US Dept. of Interior's *Mid-century Alaska.*

GUNTHER, ERNA
Northwest Coast Indian Art. Seattle: University of Washington Press, 1962. 101 pp.
Art in the Life of the Northwest Coast Indian. Seattle: Superior Publishing, 1966. 275 pp.
Indian Life on the Northwest Coast. Chicago: Univ. of Chicago Press, 1972. 271 pp. As seen by the early explorers and fur trappers of the late 18th century. Excellent study of attitudes as seen through artifact evaluation.

GVOZDEV, MIKHAIL SPIRIDONOVICH
Report on his voyage, July 23, to Sept. 28, 1732 in Golder, *Bering's Voyages.* Golder disputes this claimed first sighting of Alaska by Europeans. See also V.A. Divin.

H

HABERSHAM, ALEXANDER WYLLY
The North Pacific Surveying and Exploring Expedition. Phila.: Lippincott, 1857. See also Caswell.

HADLEIGH-WEST, FREDERICK
Exploratory Excavations at Sitka National Monument. Typescript. National Park Service. 1958.

HADMAN, VIRGINIA (b. 1908)
As the Sailor Loves the Sea. New York: Harper, 1951. 232 pp.
Alaska Fisherman's Almanac. Ketchikan: Daily Alaska Fishing News, 1947. 232 pp. Other editions other years.

HADWEN, ISAAC SEYMOUR (b. 1877) **and L. J. PALMER**
Reindeer in Alaska. Wn.DC: GPO, 1922. 74 pp. USDA.

HAGLUND, D. K.
"Alaskan Highway—Attendant Economic Development," *Assoc. of Amer. Geographers Annual,* 1960.

HAIG-BROWN, RODERICK LANGMERE (b. 1908)
Captain of the Discovery. Toronto: Macmillan, 1956. 181 pp. George Vancouver.
The Whale People. New York: William Morrow, 1963. 256 pp.

HAINES
Alaska Sportsman, Nov., '47; July, '42 (Col. Ripinski); March, '43 (Dalton Trail); May, '54 (BLM); Jan., '55; Apr., '55 (photo, cannery); Feb., '57; *Alaska-Yukon Magazine,* Sept., '09; March, '12; Colby; Cooley (history and resources); Higginson; Hulley; Kitchener; Ray; Rutzebeck; Scidmore; Sundborg; Tewkesbury; Vancouver; Willard; Wright; Young.

HAINES, JOHN
Winter News. Middletown, Conn.: Wesleyan University Press, 1966. 71 pp. Poetry.

HALE, CHARLES R.
Innocent of Moscow. Reprinted from *American Church Review,* July, 1877. See also Russian Orthodox Church.

HALE, HORATIO EMMONS
Ethnography and Philology. Philadelphia: C. Sherman, 1846. 666 pp. US Exploring Expedition, 1838-42, under Charles Wilkes. See also T-1899 ff.

HALL, ALICE
Songs of a Sourdough. New York: Pageant Press, 1953. 44 pp. Poetry.

HALL, CHARLES FRANCIS (1821-71)
Life with the Esquimaux. London: Low, 1864. 2v. Voyage of 1860-62 in search of John Franklin, to Davis Strait, Baffin Bay and Frobisher Bay. Hall claimed to have found relics of the voyage of Martin Frobisher three centuries earlier. Altogether Hall made three Arctic voyages. See the Arctic Bibliography.

HALL, EDWARD HAGMAN (1858-1936)
Alaska, Eldorado of the Midnight Sun. New York: Republic Press, 1897. 62 pp.

HALL, ERNEST FENWICK
Under the Northern Lights. Denver: Hall's Alaska Travelogs, 1932. 70 pp.

HALL, FREDERIC (b. 1825)
Laws of Alaska. Los Angeles: Prack and Blech, 1897. 32 pp. Pertaining to civil government, mines and land.

HALL, GEORGE LYMAN (b. 1913)
Sometime Again. Seattle: Superior Publishing Co., 1945. 217 pp. Personal experiences of a soldier stationed in Alaska from 1941.

HALL, OLOF
Youth North. Caldwell: Caxton Printers, 1936. 425 pp.

HALL, THOMAS; see T-1909.

HALLDORSON, M. A.
"The Matanuska Valley Colonization Project," unpublished master's thesis, University of Colorado, 1936.

HALLIDAY, WILLIAM MAY (b. 1866)
Potlatch and Totem. London: Dent, 1935. 240 pp. Recollections of an Indian agent.

HALLOCK, CHARLES (1834-1917)
Our New Alaska. New York: *Forest and Stream*, 1886. 209 pp.
Peerless Alaska. New York: Broadway Publishing Co., 1908. 224 pp.
"Two Hundred Miles up the Kuskokwim," *National Geographic*, February, 1898. Hallock founded *Forest and Stream*.

HALPERN, JOEL MARTIN
Eskimos of the Alaska Coast. New York: American Museum of Natural History, 1955. 6 pp. Deering and Wales.

HAMILTON, BASIL G.
Naming of Columbia River. Cranbrook, B.C.: *Cranbrook Courier*, n.d.

HAMILTON, ERNEST G.
See Moffit and George Martin for Hamilton topographic surveys of Kenai Lake and Controller Bay.

HAMILTON, JOHN TAYLOR
The Beginnings of the Moravian Mission in Alaska. Bethlehem, Pa.: Comenius Press, 1890. 23 pp.

HAMILTON, WILLIAM
"The Work of the Bureau of Education in Alaska," Lake Mohonk Conference, 29th Annual Meeting, Moravian Church, 1911 (W-2343). Hamilton was Asst. General Agent of Education in Alaska.

HAMILTON, WILLIAM
"Russian America," *American Scholar*, January, 1934.

HAMLIN, CHARLES SIMEON (b. 1868)
Old Times on the Yukon. Los Angeles: Wetzel Publishing Co., 1928. 172 pp. Dance halls and vaudeville.

HAMMERICH, LOUIS LEONOR (b. 1892)
"Russian Loan-words in Alaska," *Proceedings*, International Congress of Americanists, Cambridge, England, 1952. The process by which Russian words were adopted into the Eskimo language and analysis of their types (mostly pragmatic, some abstract).
"The Russian Stratum in Alaskan Eskimo," *Word*, 1954. Russian loan-words in Eskimo language.

HAMMES, LAUREL M.
"Characteristics of Housing for the Yukon-Kuskokwim Delta of Southwest Alaska," *Alaska Medicine*, March, 1965, 7 ff.

HAMMOND, JAY S. (Governor of Alaska)
Mr. Speaker! Naknek, Alaska: Fisherman's Publishing Co., 1962. 35 pp. Poetry, in the Alaska State Legislature where Hammond was a representative and senator.

HAMPTON, KATHLEEN
The Patch. New York: Random House, 1960. 312 pp.

HANDLEMAN, HOWARD
Bridge to Victory. New York: Random House, 1943. 275 pp. Retaking Attu. Handleman was an INS correspondent.
"Matanuska Valley," *Alaska Life*, March, 1944.

HANIGSMAN, ETHEL
Charming Alaska. Ketchikan, 1938. 28 pp. Verse over drawings.

HANSEN, A. H.
Tundra. New York: Century Company, 1930. 334 pp. Romance on Alaskan Trails, as told by former Deputy US Marshal Hansen to the Edingtons. See Edington and Edington.

HANSEN, H. P.
See T-1935.

HANSEN, HENRY P.
Arctic Biology. Papers presented at the 1957 and also the 1965 Biology Colloquia. Corvallis: Oregon State University, 1967. 294 pp.

HANSEN, MILDRED M.
Handbook for Freshman Legislators. Juneau, 1963.

HANSEN, SOPHUS E.
Tacoma to Anchorage and Kodiak. Seattle: Lowman and Hanford, 1919. 327 pp.
See also T-1938 ff.

HANSEN, WALLACE R.
The Alaska Earthquake. Wn.DC: GPO, 1966. 111 pp. USGS. Field investigations and reconstruction effort.

HANSON, EARL PARKER (b. 1899)
Stefansson: Prophet of the North. New York: Harper, 1941. 241 pp.
"The Far North Route to Europe," *Airway Age*, April, 1929.
"The Place of Aircraft in Polar Research," *Airway Age*, March, 1929.

HANSSEN, HELMER JULIUS (b. 1870)
Voyages of a Modern Viking. London: Routledge, 1936. 216 pp. Autobiographical. Hanssen was with Amundsen on the *Gjoa* and piloted the *Maud* in the northwest passage, 1918-22.

HARDCASTLE, ROMAINE
Alaska Day. Sitka: Alaska Day Festival, 1954 [?]. 80 pp.

HARDING, WARREN GAMALIEL (1865-1854)
Address on Alaska. Delivered at Seattle, July 27, 1923. 14 pp. See Willie F. Johnson and Thomas H.

Russell for Harding's views on Alaska; as well see Walter V. Woehlke. Harding brought with him to Alaska in 1923 Secretary Hoover and Secretary Wallace. Harold Ickes also was on the trip. See Gruening and Hulley.

HARGRAVE, JAMES (1798-1865)
The Hargrave Correspondence. Toronto; Champlain Society, 1938. 472 pp. 1821-1843. Concerns relations between Hudson's Bay Company and the Russian-American Company in the first half of the 19th century. See also Ian Nichols.

HARGRAVE, LETITIA (1813-1854)
The Letters of Letitia Hargrave. Toronto: Champlain Society, 1947. 310 pp. Hudson's Bay Co. and the Canadian Northwest.

HARGRAVES, DARROLL
"Eskimo Ivory Carvings of the Human Figure," *Alaska Journal*, IV (1974): 153-156.

HARJUNPAA, T.
"Lutherans in Russian Alaska," *Pac. Historical Review*, XXXVII (1968): 123-146.

HARP, ELMER, Jr.
"New World Affinities of Cape Dorset Eskimo Culture," *Anthrop. Papers*, May, 1953 (University of Alaska).

HARPER, W. A.
"Alaska Boundary Question: The Seattle Commercial Interst and the Joint HIgh Commission of 1898-99," *Journal of the West*, X (1971): 253-272.

HARRIMAN ALASKA EXPEDITION, 1899
Alaska. New York: Doubleday, Page, 1901 and later. 14v.
I Narrative of the Voyage; Glaciers, Natives: Burroughs, Muir, Grinnell
II History, Geography, Resources: Dall, Keeler, Gannett, Brewer, Merriam
III Glaciers, Glaciation: G.K. Gilbert
IV Geology, Paleontology: Emerson, Palache, Dall, Ulrich, Knowlton
V Cryptogamic Botany: Cardot, Cummings, Evans, Peck, Saccardo, Saunders, Theriot, Trelease
VI Not Printed (materials prepared)
VII Not Printed
VIII Insects Part I: Ashmead, Banks, Caudell, Cook, Currie, Dyar, Folsom, Heidemann, Kincaid, Pergande, Schwartz
IX Insects Part II: Ashmead, Coquillett, Kincaid, Pergande
X Crustaceans: Rathbun, Richardson, Holmes, Cole
XI Nemerteans, Bryozoans: Coe, Robertson
XII Enchytraeids, Tubioculous Annelids: Eisen, Bush
XIII Land and Fresh Water Mollusks, Hydroides: Dall, Nutting
XIV Shallow-water Starfishes: A.E. Verrill
The entire work was edited by Clinton H. Merriam. Following Harriman's death in 1910 the work was transferred to the Smithsonian, and all subsequent volumes were published under its authority. Volumes VI and VII were reserved for flowering plants, but the prepared manuscripts were not published. The expedition was arranged in cooperation with the Washington Academy of Sciences, and the

Proceedings of the Academy carried 30 additional papers, all but nine of which were printed in a re-publication of the original 14 volumes.

E.H. Harriman, railroad magnate, apparently conceived the Alaska expedition in conjunction with a proposed bear hunt on Kodiak Island. The steamer chartered for the voyage was large enough to accommodate numerous people in addition to the Harriman party, so scientists were invited along.

The expedition cruised the northwest coast from Seattle between May and July, 1899, reaching as far north as Port Clarence and Plover Bay, Siberia. Many photographs were made, and some poetry written (see, e.g., Sherwood, Cook Inlet Collection). John Burroughs wrote the narrative of the expedition, and William Dall contributed a brief history of Alaska.

See also the following:
"Harriman Alaska Expedition," *National Geographic*, 1899, by Henry Gannett.
"Harriman Alaska Expedition," *National Geographic*, 1899, by Gilbert Grosvenor.
Edward Henry Harriman, by John Muir. See further bibliography in Wickersham, and in Tourville.

HARRINGTON, REBIE
Cinderella Takes a Holiday in the Northland. New York: Revell, 1927. 269 pp.

HARRIS, A. C.
ALaska and the Klondyke Gold Fields. Chicago, Philadelphia: Monarch Books Co., 1897. 556 pp. See T-1958 for extended title.

HARRIS, A. S.
Alaska-cedar: a Bibliography. Wn.DC: GPO, 1969. USDA Forest Service, Pacific Northwest Forest and Range Experiment Station.

HARRIS, CHRISTIE
Once upon a Totem. New York: Antheneum, 1963. 160 pp.

HARRIS, JOHN
Navigantium atque Itinerantium Bibliotheca, or a complete collection of voyages and travels, consisting of above six hundred of the most auth•ntic writers. London: T. Osborne, H. Whitridge, ι.c., 1764. 3rd ed. 2v.

HARRIS, MAE EVANS
You can Alcan. Middleburg, Va.: Denlingers, 1959. 96 pp.

HARRIS, RICHARD T. (1833-1907)
An Account of the Discovery of Gold in the Harris Mining District. Handwritten manuscript in the state archive, Juneau, Alaska. Upon Harris' death at a home in Mt. Tabor, Oregon, in 1907, friends contributed to a fund to return his remains to Juneau (at one time called Harrisburg), where he was buried next to Joe Juneau. See *Alaska-Yukon Magazine*, December, 1908.

HARRISON, CHARLES
Ancient Warriors of the North Pacific. London: Witherby, 1925. 222 pp. Haida: laws, customs,

legends, history in the Queen Charlotte Islands.
The Hydah Mission. London: C.M. House, 1884
[?]. 23 pp.
"Haida Grammar," with A.F. Chamberlain,
Transactions, Royal Society of Canada, 1895.
See also T-1965 ff.

HARRISON, EDWARD SANFORD (1859-1910)
Nome and Seward Peninsula. Seattle: Metropolitan Press, 1905. 392 pp. History, descr., politics, 166 brief biographies.
Alaska Almanac. Seattle: Harrison Publishing Co., 1908-09. 2v. For the Arctic Club, Seattle. General profile. Harrison edited *Alaska-Yukon Magazine* from 1907 until his death in 1910. He had at one time lived in Nome.

HARRISON, GORDON SCOTT
Alaska Public Policy. College: University of Alaska Press, 1973. Institute for Social, Economic and Government Research. Current problems and issues.

HARSHBERGER, JOHN WILLIAM (1869-1929)
"Tundra Vegetation of Central Alaska directly under the Arctic Circle," in *Proceedings,* Amer. Philosopyhical Society, 1928.
The Forests of the Pacific Coasts. Helsinki, 1929. 5 pp.

HART, ALBERT BUSHNELL (1854-1943)
Extracts from Official Papers. New York: Lovell, 1892. 26 pp. Bering Sea controversy, 1790-1892. With Edward Channing.

HART, ROBERT G.
McKay's Guide to Alaska. New York: David McKay, 1959. 330 pp.

HARTE, FRANCIS BRET (1839-1902)
An Arctic Vision. Reprinted from *Yukon Press,* January 1, 1896. Quoted in Wickersham, and Stuck.

HARTESVELDT, RICHARD and JANE
Campsite Finder. San Martin, Calif.; Naturegraph Co., 1959. 80 pp. Alaska, British Columbia, Yukon Territory.

HARTING, JAMES; see T-1975.

HARTMANN, J. A. H.
"Exploration of Western Alaska by Moravians," in Sheldon Jackson's *Report* on Education in Alaska, 1886, with William H. Weinland. Hartman and Weinland made a reconnaissance of the lower Kuskokwim in 1884. See also Moravian Church, and William Weinland.

HARTT, A. C.
Movement of Salmon in the North Pacific. Vancouver: International Northern Pacific Fisheries Commission, 1956-58. (1962). 157 pp.

HARTWIG, GEORG LUDWIG (1813-1880)
The Polar World. New York: Harper, 1869. 486 pp. Kamchadals, Chukchis, Eskimos, Indians, also Wrangell; Steller, Kamchatka, Bering Sea, Alaska and Hudson's Bay Company. See also T-1977 ff.

HASELHURST, MAY A.
Days Forever Flown. New York: Gillis Brothers, 1892. 401 pp. Travel journal.

HASKELL, WILLIAM B.
Two Years in the Klondike and Alaska. Hartford: Hartford Publishing Co., 1898. 558 pp. Descr. Circle City and Rampart.

HASKIN, LESLIE LOREN (1882-1949)
Wild Flowers of the Pacific Coast. Portland: Metropolitan Press, 1934. 407 pp.

HASSEL, JOHANN GEORG H. (1770-1829)
See T-1985.

HASSELBORG, ALLEN E.
"Bird Notes from Admiralty Island," *Condor,* September, 1918.

HASWELL, ROBERT
Journal of Robert Gray's voyage in 1788-89, and 1790-92. Manuscript, published as an appendix to Bancroft's *History of the Northwest Coast,* Vol. I. See Wagner.

HATT, GUDMUND
"Early Intrusion of Agriculture in the North Atlantic Sub-arctic Region," *Anthrop. Papers,* University of Alaska, 1953. See also T-1987 ff.

HAUSER, WILLIAM E.
See T-1990.

HAVERLY, CHARLES E.
See T-1991.

HAWKES, CLARENCE
Silversheene, King of Sled Dogs. Springfield, Mass.: Milton, 1924. 234 pp.

HAWKES, ERNEST WILLIAM
Eskimo Land. Boston: Ginn and Co., 1914. 90 pp.
The Dance Festivals of the Alaskan Eskimo. Philadelphia: University of Pennsylvania, 1914. 41 pp. See also the Arctic Bibliography.

HAWKESWORTH, JOHN
See T-1997 (Captain Cook).

HAWKINS, JAMES E. and ELIZABETH A. DAUGHERTY
The Silver Fleece. Juneau: Alaska Rural Development Board, 1958. 55 pp. Economic study of the Bristol Bay region.

HAWTHORN, AUDREY
Art of the Kwakiutl Indians. Seattle: University of Washington Press, 1967. 472 pp.

HAWTHORN, HARRY BERTRAM, C. S. BELSHAW and S. M. JAMIESON
The Indians of British Columbia. Berkeley: University of California Press, 1958. 499 pp.

HAWTHORN, HARRY BERTRAM
A Survey of Contemporary Indians of Canada. Ottawa: Gov't. Printing Bureau, 1966. Indian Affairs Branch.

HAWTHORNE, MONT (1865-1952)
The Trail Led North. By Martha Ferguson McKeown. New York: Macmillan, 1948. 222 pp. Mont Hawthorne was a cannery manager in Alaska during the gold rush days. He also tried prospecting.
Alaska Silver. New York: Macmillan, 1951. 274 pp. Also by Martha Ferguson McKeown, niece of Mont Hawthorne.

HAYES, CHARLES WILLARD (1859-1916)
"Copper River as a Route to the Yukon Basin," *Journal,* Amer. Geographical Society, 1898. Hayes was a member of the Schwatka expedition of 1891.
"An Expedition through the Yukon District," *National Geographic,* May, 1892.

HAYES, FLORENCE SOOY (b. 1895)
Arctic Gateway. New York: Friendship Press, 1940. 132 pp.
A Land of Challenge. New York: Board of National Missions, Presbyterian Church of the USA, 1940. 32 pp.
The Eskimo Hunter. New York: Random House, 1945. 275 pp.
The Alaska Hunter. Boston: Houghton-Mifflin, 1959. 248 pp. Juvenile.

HAYES, JAMES GORDON (b. 1877)
Robert Edwin Peary. London: Richards, 1929. 299 pp.
Conquest of the North Pole. New York: Macmillan, 1934. 317 pp.

HAYNES, M. H. E. and H. WEST TAYLOR
Pioneers of the Klondyke. London: Sampson, Low, Marston and Co., 1897. 184 pp. Royal Northwest Mounted Police.

HAYNES, THOMAS S.
"The Nulato Massacre," *Alaska Life,* October, 1940. An account told to the author in 1904 by Chief Isaac of the Koyukuk Indians.

HAYS, LYDIA A.
See T-2007 ff.

HAYWOOD, CHARLES
A Bibliography of North American Folklore and Folksong. New York: Greenburg, 1951. 1292 pp. Broad scope of popular and technical literature.

HAZARD, JOSEPH TAYLOR (b. 1879)
Pacific Coast Trails. Seattle: Superior Publishing Co., 1946. 317 pp.

HAZELTON, ELIZABETH C., et. alii.
Alaskan Forget-me-nots. Seattle: Lowman and Hanford, 1923. 28 pp.

HEAD, HELEN SMITH
Death Below Zero. New York: Comet Press, 1953. 214 pp. Wiseman.

HEALTH
Parran, Thomas (b. 1892) and six others. *Alaska's Health.* Pittsburgh: University of Pittsburgh, 1954. A survey of the Alaska Health Survey Team to the Dept. of Interior.
See also *Alaska Natives and the Land,* Federal Field Committee Report, 1968.

HEALY, MICHAEL A.
Report of the Cruise of the Corwin. Wn.DC: GPO, 1889. 128 pp. Revenue Cutter Service. Bering and Chukchi Seas, Point Hope, Kobuk River, Pribilof Islands, Bogoslof Island, natives, fisheries; J.C. Cantwell, G.P. Merrill. Voyage of 1884.
Report of the Cruise of the Corwin. Wn.DC: GPO, 1887. 102 pp. Voyage of 1885. Includes Noatak River; S.B. McLenegan and C.H. Townshend. See the Arctic Bibliography also for the *Corwin* cruise of 1881 and the *Bear* cruises of 1897-98. On Healy see Wead. It was apparently Healy who suggested the importation of reindeer to Sheldon Jackson. Healy had two brothers, one of whom became bishop of Portland in Maine, and another, a Jesuit, who visited Alaska, including the Aleutians, in 1883.

HEARNE, SAMUEL (1745-1792)
A Journey from Prince of Wales' Fort. London: Strahan, 1795. 458 pp. From Hudson's Bay in 1769-72.
Journals of Samuel Hearne and Philip Turnor. Toronto: Champlain Society, 1934. 611 pp.
See Greenhow and Mirsky. Hearne's expedition was particularly important, for he demonstrated two significant concepts, that any northwest passage must lie north of the continental landmass, north of the mouth of the Coppermine River, and also that western man could live off the land in the manner of the Indian and survive (although on this latter point, see Stefansson, *Unsolved Mysteries of the Arctic,* in reference to the Franklin expedition).

HEAWOOD, EDWARD
A History of Geographical Discovery. Cambridge: Cambridge University Press, 1912. 475 pp. 17th and 18th centuries.

HECETA, BRUNA de
Diario de la Navegacion. . .Ano de 1775. Manuscript in the Archivo General at Mexico City. See Wagner. There is a copy in the Bancroft Library at the University of California, Berkeley. Heceta and Bodega y Quadra and Maurelle were instructed to reach 65°N. Lat., but only Bodega and Maurelle went beyond 49°N., reaching Bucareli Bay on the west coast of Prince of Wales Island. Wagner translated F. Sierra's account of the voyage (one of six) in the *Quarterly* of the Calif. Hist. Soc., in 1930. Heceta is often (and properly) spelled Hezeta.

HEFLIN, ALMA
Adventure was the Compass. Boston: Little, 1942. 285 pp. Airplane trip to Alaska.

HEGG, ERIC A.
Souvenir of Alaska. Seattle, 1900. 56 plates, no text. In 1888 Hegg opened a photographic studio in Bellingham, Washington. During the gold rush he operated in Dyea, Dawson and Nome. Later he served as photographer for the Guggenheim Alaska Syndicate at Cordova. He left Alaska after 20 years, eventually settling in California.

HEID, JOHN G. and G. W. GARSIDE
Local Mining Laws of Harris Mining District, Alaska. Juneau, 1887. 20 pp.

HEILPRIN, ANGELO (1853-1907)
Alaska and the Klondike. New York: D. Appleton, 1899. 315 pp. Summary of travel routes. Heilprin led a relief expedition to Peary at McCormick Bay, Greenland, in 1891. See the Arctic Bibliography, and *Bulletin*, Amer. Geographic Society, November, 1907.

HEINE, WILHELM
See the Arctic Bibliography.

HEINRICH, ALBERT
"Structural Features of Northwestern Alaska Eskimo Kinship," *Southwest Journal of Anthropology*, XVI (1960): 110-126.

HEINTZLEMAN, B. FRANK (b. 1888) (Gov. of Alaska, 1953-57)
Alaska Life, "For Future Farmers of Alaska," July, 1943.
Alaska Life, "Auto Ferry to Alaska," December, 1943.
Alaska Life, "They're Open, If You Can Cut It," October, 1945.
Alaska Magazine, "The Forests of Alaska as a Basis for Permanent Development," January, 1927.
American Forests, "Managing the Alaska Brown Bear," June, 1932.
Alaska Life, "Woodman, Where's that Ax?," October, 1938.
Journ. of Forestry, "Alaska Brown Bear Conservation," June, 1939.
Alaska Life, "Alaskan Peat Proffers Profits," October, 1939.
Alaska Life, "Sitka Spruce, An Alaska Industry that Needs Developing," October, 1940.
Journ. of Forestry, "Alaska—Modern Pioneering," June, 1960.
Puget Soundings, "Alaska Awakening," December, 1960.
Pulp-timber Resources of SE Alaska. Wn.DC: GPO, 1928. 34 pp. USDA, Forest Service.
A Plan for Management of the Brown Bear. Wn.DC: GPO, 1934. 20 pp. USDA.
"The Forests of Alaska," *Yearbook*, Department of Agriculture (US), 1949.

HEISTAND, HENRY OLCOT SHELDON (b. 1856)
The Territory of Alaska. Kansas City: Hudson-Kimberly, 1898. 195 pp.

HEIZER, ROBERT FLEMING (b. 1915)
Archaeology of the Uyak Site, Kodiak. Berkeley: University of California Press, 1956. 199 pp. Heizer assisted Ales Hrdlicka at this site in the summers of 1934 and 1935. The work is a study of the Hrdlicka collection housed in the US Naional Museum, Washington, DC.
"Notes on Koniag Material Culture," *Anthrop. Papers*, University of Alaska, 1952.
"Aconite Poison Whaling in Asia and America: An Aleutian Transfer to the New World," *Bulletin*, Amer. Bur. of Ethnology, 1943.

HELLENTHAL, JOHN ALBERTOS (1874-1944)
The Alaskan Melodrama. London: Allen and Unwin, 1936. 312 pp. Also New York: Liveright, 1936. Presents the thesis, supported by numerous factual inaccuracies, that Alaska has the worst government possible under the American system, and also that conservation policy is ruining Alaska's potential. On the whole, the work is a polemical plea for laissez-faire, opposing control of pelagic sealing and protection of the sea otter, and the fur seal generally. An extreme statement. See also an article on conservation in *Alaska Life*, January, 1944.

HELLER, CHRISTINE A.
Wild Edible and Poisonous Plants of Alaska. College: University of Alaska, 1953. 167 pp. Extension Serv.
Wild Flowers of Alaska. Portland: Graphic Arts Center, 1966. 104 pp.

HELLER, EDMUND (b. 1875)
"Mammals of the 1908 Alexander Alaska Expedition," *University of California Publications in Zoology, 1910.*

HELLER, HERBERT L.
Sourdough Sagas. Cleveland: World Publishing Co., 1967. 271 pp. Also Comstock Edition, Ballantine Books, 1971. Excerpts from gold rush diaries.

HELMERICKS, CONSTANCE (b. 1918)
We Live in Alaska. Boston: Little, Brown, 1944. 266 pp.
Hunting in North America. Harrisburg: Stackpole, 1956. 298 pp.

HELMERICKS, CONSTANCE and HARMON
We Live in the Arctic. Boston: Little, Brown, 1947. 329 pp. River boating on the Yukon and Koyukuk.
Our Summer with the Eskimos. Boston: Little, Brown, 1948. 239 pp. On the Colville, and at Beechey Point and Barrow.
Our Alaskan Winter. Boston: Little, Brown, 1949. 271 pp. Colville River and Aklavik.
The Flight of the Arctic Tern. Boston: Little, Brown, 1952. 321 pp. Flight to Barter Island, and supplying a scientific expedition.
"Back Home to the Arctic," *Life*, August, 1955.

HELMERICKS, HARMON (Bud) (b. 1917)
Arctic Hunter. Boston: Little, Brown, 1955. 142 pp.
Oolak's Brother. Boston: Little, Brown, 1953. 144 pp.
Arctic Bush Pilot. Boston: Little, Brown, 1956. 180 pp.
The Last of the Bush Pilots. New York: Alfred Knopf, 1969. 361 pp.

HELMERS, A. E.
"Alaska Forestry, A Research Frontier," *Journ. of Forestry*, June, 1960.

HENDERSON, ALICE PALMER
The Rainbow's End. Chicago: H.S. Stone, 1898. 296 pp. Steamer tour of Alaska, critical of the Russian Orthodox. Sheldon Jackson was a companion on the tour.

HENDERSON, DANIEL MacINTYRE (1880-1955)
From the Volga to the Yukon. New York: Hastings House, 1944. 256 pp. Wholly secondary account of Russian expansion in the north Pacific.

HENDERSON, LESTER DALE (1886-1945)
Alaska. Juneau: *Daily Alaska Empire,* 1928. 112 pp. Profile. Henderson was Commissioner of Education in Alaska from 1917 to 1930, and Superintendent of Schools at Burlingame from 1930 to 1945.
History of Education in Alaska, in *Report,* Commissioner of Education, 1918-1919. Also issued by the Alaska Territorial Department of Education.

HENDRYX, JAMES BEARDSLEY (b. 1880)
Connie Morgan in Alaska. New York: Putnam's, 1916. 341 pp.
Connie Morgan in the Fur Country. New York: Putnam's, 1921.
Snowdrift. New York: Putnam's, 1922. 381 pp.
North. New York: Putnam's, 1923. 334 pp.
Connie Morgan Hits the Trail. New York: Putnam's, 1929.
Blood on the Yukon Trail. New York: Putnam's, 1930. 305 pp.
Outlaws of Halfaday Creek. New York: Putnam's, 1935. 299 pp.
Connie Morgan in the Arctic. New York: Putnam's, 1936. 239 pp.
On the Rim of the Arctic. New York: Putnam's, 1948. 224 pp.
The Yukon Kid. Garden City: Doubleday Doran, 1934. 294 pp.
Badmen on Halfaday Creek. Garden City: Doubleday, 1950. 216 pp.
Black John of Halfaday Creek. Garden City: Doubleday Doran, 1939. 305 pp.
Blood of the North. Garden City: Doubleday Doran, 1938.
Courage of the North. Garden City: Doubleday, 1946. 251 pp.
Gold and Guns on Halfaday Creek. New York: Carleton House, 1942. 280 pp.
Gold is Where you Find It. Garden City: Doubleday, 1953. 191 pp.
It Happened on Halfaday Creek. Garden City: Doubleday Doran, 1944. 211 pp.
Justice on Halfaday Creek. Garden City: Doubleday, 1949. 220 pp.
Law and Order on Halfaday Creek. New York: Carleton House, 1941. 308 pp.
Murder on Halfaday Creek. New York: Doubleday, 1951. 191 pp.
Skullduggery on Halfaday Creek. Garden City: Doubleday Doran, 1946. 271 pp.
Strange Doings on Halfaday Creek. Garden City: Doubleday Doran, 1943. 269 pp.
The Czar of Halfaday Creek. Garden City: Doubleday Doran, 1940. 271 pp.
The Saga of Halfaday Creek. Garden City: Doubleday Doran, 1936. 189 pp.

HENEY, MICHAEL J.
See Herron, T-2079, and Whiting, T-4843.

HENLEY, G. F.
Guide to the Yukon-Klondyke Mines. Victoria: Province Publishing Co., 1897. 63 pp. Contains a report by William Ogilvie and diary of Archbishop Seghers.

HENRY, DAVID and KAY HENRY
Our Indian Language. Fairbanks: Summer Institute of Linguistics, 1966. 24 pp. Koyukon.
Dictionary of Indian Words. Fairbanks: Summer Institute of Linguistics, n.d., 11 pp. Koyukuk.
"Koyukon Classificatory Verbs," *Anthrop. Linguistics,* VII (1965): 80-88.
"Koyukon Locationals," *Anthrop. Linguistics,* XI (1969): 136-142.

HENRY, JOSEPH KAYE
Flora of Southern B.C. Toronto: W. Gage, 1915. 363 pp.

HENRY, MARGUERITE (b. 1902)
Alaska in Story and Pictures. Chicago: Whitman, 1941. 28 pp.

HENRY, WILL
The North Star. New York: Random House, 1956. 213 pp.

HERBERT, AGNES
Two Dianas in Alaska. With A. Shikara. London: J. Lane, 1909. 316 pp. Travel and hunting, Kodiak.
The Moose. London: Adam & Charles Black, 1913. 248 pp.

HERBERT, CHARLES F.
Alaska Mining Law Manual. Fairbanks, printed by *Jessens Weekly,* ca. 1966. 77 pp.

HERMAN, Fr. of Valaam Monastery
Zhizn Valaamskago Monakha German a. Life of the Valaam Monk, Herman. St. Petersburg: Synodic Press, 1894. 24 pp. See also the following:
Rochcau, V., "St. Herman of Alaska and the Defense of Alaska Native Peoples," *Orthodox Alaska,* II (1971); and Rochcau, V., "The Origins of the Orthodox Church in Alaska, 1820-1840," *Orthodox Alaska,* III (1971). See also Golder; Kashevaroff; Dall; Sarafian. See as well T-1534.

HERNDON, BOOTON
The Great Land. New York: Weybright and Tally, 1971.

HERRON, EDWARD ALBERT (b. 1912)
Alaska, Land of Tomorrow. New York: McGraw-Hill, 1947. 232 pp. Physical details of climate, geography and natural life. The best of Herron's works.
The Big Country. New York: Aladdin, 1953. 190 pp.
The Return of the Alaskan. New York: Dutton, 1955.
Dimond of Alaska. New York: Julian Messner, 1957. 190 pp.
First Scientist of Alaska. New York: Julian Messner, 1958. 192 pp. Juvenile.
Wings over Alaska. New York: Julian Messner, 1959. 192 pp. Carl Ben Eielson. Also Washington Square Press, 1967.

Alaska's Railroad Builder, Mike Heney. New York: Julian Messner, 1960. 192 pp. Juvenile.

The Conqueror of Mt. McKinley. New York: Julian Messner, 1964. Hudson Stuck.

HERRON, JOSEPH SUTHERLAND (b. 1869)
Explorations in Alaska, 1899. Wn.DC: GPO, 1900. 77 pp. War Department. Herron was a member of the Cook Inlet Military Exploring Expedition of 1899, under the command of Capt. Edwin Glenn. Dispatched at Orca, he crossed over Portage Glacier from Passage Canal to Turnagain Arm and on to Tyonek. From there he ascended the Yentna, crossed over to the Kuskokwim, and went out to the Yukon via Lake Minchumina. See also Baker.

HETZEL, THEODORE B.
Indian Rights and Wrongs in Alaska. Philadelphia: Indian Rights Association, 1961. 8 pp.

The Meek Do Not Inherit Alaska. Philadelphia: Indian Rights Association, 1962. 8 pp.

HEUSSER, CALVIN JOHN
Juneau Ice Field Research Project. n. pl., 1958. 7 pp.

Late Pleistocene Environments. New York: Amer. Geographical Society, 1960. 308 pp.

"Post-glacial Palynolgy and Archaeology in the Naknek River Drainage Area, Alaska," *American Antiquity,* XXIX (1963): 74-81.

HEWES, AGNES
A Hundred Bridges to Go. New York: Dodd, Mead, 1950. 275 pp.

HEWITT, JOHN MICHAEL (b. ca. 1870)
The Alaska Vagabond, Dr. Skookum. New York: Exposition Press, 1953. 284 pp. Ten years in Alaska, 1897-1908. Koyukuk, Army surgeon on telegraph construction, Nome to Circle City. Also Fort Liscum. Includes Gordon Bettles, Frs. Crimont and Ragaru, the Kokrines, "Swiftwater Bill," Major Strong, Billy Mitchell and W.P. Richardson.

HEYE, ARTUR (b. 1885)
In Letzten Westen. Zurich: A. Muller, 1939. 334 pp. Excellent photographs.

HEYERDAHL, THOR, SOREN RICHTER and HJALMAR RIISER-LARSEN
American Indians in the Pacific. Boston: Universitets Forlaget, 1952. Also Chicago: Rand McNally, 1953. 821 pp.

HIBBEN, FRANK CUMMINGS
Digging Up America. New York: Hill & Wang, 1960.

Treasure in the Dust. London: Cleaver-Hume Press, 1953.

HICK, GEORGE
Pioneer Prospector. Ed. Charles Bunnell. College: University of Alaska, 1954. 32 pp.

HICKEL, WALTER J. (Governor of Alaska) (US Sec. of Interior)
Who Owns America? Englewood Cliffs: Prentice-Hall, 1971. 328 pp.

"Wealth of the Land and the Growth of Alaska," *Journal of the West,* VI (1967): 357-361.

HIGGINSON, ELLA RHOADS (1862-1940)
Alaska, the Great Country. New York: Macmillan, 1908 and subsequent editions. 583 pp. Desc.; full treatment of SE, also Gulf to Tanana.

The Vanishing Race and Other Poems. Bellingham: C.M. Sherman, 1911. 28 pp.

HIGHWAYS and TRAILS
Alaska Life, Jan., '41 (Glenn Highway); Jan., '43 (Iliamna portage road, Cook Inlet to Bristol Bay); *Alaska Sportsman,* Sept., '41 (Cook Inlet-Lake Iliamna); Oct., '47 (bus., Haines-Fairbanks); Feb., '49 (Seward-Kenai); June, '49 (Slana-Tok); Nov., '50 (Thompson Pass open 2nd winter); Dec., '50 (Sterling Highway); May, '51 (Dawson, Eagle); Nov., '51 (Taylor Highway); Jan., '52 (Seward Highway); May, '53 (Hoover suggested Alaska-Siberia Highway in 1931); Apr., '54 (Nome-Bunker Hill); Oct., '54 (Denali Highway); Sept., '56 (possible SE highways); Nov., '56; Dec., '57 (mileage, Seattle, Great Falls); Feb., '58 (Nome-Fairbanks); and others, see Index. *Alaska Weekly,* Jan., '11 (road progress); see the Arctic Bibliography; Brooks; Caldwell; Chase; Colby; Denison (O'Hara); Gruening (Alaska Highway Patrol); Pilgrim; Tewkesbury; US Dept. of Interior (Mid-century Alaska); US NPS (recreational facilities); see also Alaska Highway, Richardson Highway.

HILDT, J. C.
Early Diplomatic Negotiations of the US with Russia. Baltimore: Johns Hopkins University Press, 1906.

HILL, EDGAR P.
See T-2105.

HILL, JAMES JEROME (1838-1916)
Address at the Opening of the Alaska-Yukon-Pacific Exposition, Seattle, June 1, 1909. 26 pp.

HILLS, W. JAMES, and B. M. AUSHERMAN
Klondike: Mining Laws, Rules and Regulations. Seattle: Lowman and Hanford, 1897. 143 pp.

HILLYER, WILLIAM H.
The Box of Daylight. New York: Alfred A. Knopf, 1931. 179 pp. Based on Boas' Tsimshian Mythology.

HILSCHER, HERBERT HENRY (b. 1902)
Alaska Now. Boston: Little, Brown, 1948. 299 pp. Based largely on interviews with faculty at the University of Alaska, the work presents a contemporary profile. Hilscher was editor of *Alaska Life,* public relations director with the University, a member of the Alaska Development Board, has worked in public relations in Anchorage.

"How We May Speed the Social Progress of Alaska," *Proceedings,* Alaska Science Conference, 1952.

HILSCHER, HERBERT HENRY and MIRIAM HILSCHER
Alaska, USA. Boston: Little, Brown, 1959. 243 pp. Development of Alaska.

HIMMELHEBER, HANS
See T-2113.

HINCKLEY, THEODORE C.
The Americanization of Alaska, 1867-1897. Palo Alto: Pacific Books, Inc., 1972. 234 pp.
"The Americanization of Alaska," *Alaska Journal,* I (1971).
"Alaska as an American Botany Bay," *Pacific Hist. Review,* XLII (1973): 1-19.
"Journal of a Trip to Alaska in 1878," *Journal of the West,* V (1966): 25-70.
"A Proposed Icelandic Colony," *Alaska Journal,* IV (1974): 2-9.
"Publicist of the Forgotten Frontier," *Journal of the West,* IV (1965): 27-40.
"Reflections and Refractions: Alaska and Gilded Age America," *Alaska Review,* III (1967).
"Sheldon Jackson and Benjamin Harrison: Presbyterians and the Administration of Alaska," *Pacific Northwest Quarterly,* LIV (1963): 66-74.
"Sheldon Jackson as Preserver of Alaska's Native Heritage," *Pacific Historical Review,* XXXIII (1964): 411-424.

HINDS, RICHARD BRINSLEY
See T-2116 ff.

HINE, CHARLES COLE (1825-1897)
A Trip to Alaska. Milwaukee: King, Fowle, 1889. 64 pp.

HINES, JOHN CHESTERFIELD (b. 1877)
Minstrel of the Yukon. New York: Greenberg, 1948. 231 pp. Hines lived at Nome from 1900 to 1906.

HINTON, ARTHUR CHERRY
The Yukon. Philadelphia: Macrae Smith, 1955. 184 pp. with Philip H. Godsell. Popular history.

HINZ, JOHN (ca. 1874)
Grammar and Vocabulary of the Eskimo Language. Bethlehem, Pa.: Moravian Church, 1944, and 1955. 199 pp. Kuskokwim.

HIPPLER, ARTHUR E.
Eskimo Acculturation. College: University of Alaska, 1970. A Selected, Annotated Bibliography.

HIRSCH, DAVID I.
"Glottochronology and Eskimo-Aleut Prehistory," *Amer. Anthropologist,* LVI (1954): 825-38.

HISTORY of ALASKA
See Bibliography. See also the following:
Andrews; Bancroft; Brooks; Brown; Chase; Clark; Gruening; Huber; Hulley; Nichols; Ogilvie; Pilgrim; Shiels; Tompkins; Wickersham. See also Early Explorations; Purchase of Alaska, and other topics.

HISTORY — JEANNETTE
History of the Adventurous Voyage and Terrible Shipwreck. New York: DeWitt, 1882. 95 pp.

HISTORY of the WRONGS of ALASKA
See Anti-Monopoly Association.

HITCHCOCK, MARY E.
Two Women of the Klondike. New York: Putnam's, 1899. 495 pp.

HIXON, ARTHUR T. (b. 1916)
Canol. Philadelphia: Dorrance, 1946. 284 pp.

HOARE, JOSEPH McCORMICK (b. 1918)
"Interior Highlands of Western Alaska," in Howell Williams. See Geology.

HODGE, FREDERICK WEBB
Handbook of American Indians North of Mexico. Wn.DC: GPO, 1907, and 1912. 2v. Bur. of Ethnology. Hodge also assisted Edward S. Curtis with a multivolume work.

HODGINS, THOMAS (1828-1910)
"The Alaska-Canada Boundary Dispute under the Anglo-Russian Treaty of 1825; the Russian-American-Alaska Treaty of 1867; and the Anglo-American Conventions of 1892, 1894, and 1897; An Historical and Legal Review," *Contemporary Review,* 1902 (Toronto). Reprinted, Toronto: W. Tyrell, 1903. 26 pp.
The Alaska Boundary Tribunal and International Law. Toronto: Carswell, 1904. 24pp.

HOEMAN, V. N.
"Pyramid Peak, Unalaska," *Alaska Review,* Spring, 1966.

HOFF, SYD; see T-2135.

HOFFMAN, WALTER JAMES (1846-1899)
"Graphic Art of the Eskimo," based on the collections in the National Museum, *Annual Report,* US National Museum, 1895.
Comparison of Eskimo Pictographs. Wn.DC: Judd & Detweiler, 1883. 19 pp.
"Our Native Indian Pictography," *Bulletin,* Catholic University, April, 1897.

HOFMANN, CHARLES
Frances Densmore: A Biography. New York: Museum of American Indians, 1967.

HOFSINDE, ROBERT
The Indian Medicine Man. New York: William Morrow, 1966.

HOGGATT, WILFORD BACON (b. 1865)
(Governor of Alaska)
See Hoggatt's annual reports to the Sec. of Interior, 1906-1909. See also Wickersham's bibliography for a listing of Hoggatt's Congressional testimony. Hoggatt was the first Alaska governor to reside at Juneau. See the *Alaska-Yukon Magazine,* Sept., '07, July, '07, and Dec., '07. See also Whiting.

HOIJER, H., et. alii.
Studies in Athabaskan Languages. Berkeley: University of California Press, 1963. 154 pp. Seminar papers, Summer Institute of Linguistics, University of Oklahoma, 1958.

HOKE, HELEN
Alaska, Alaska, Alaska. New York: Franklin Watts, 1960. 244 pp. Excerpts from the following: Colby;

Muir; Young; Joaquin Miller; Burroughs; Willough-by (on Fr. Hubbard); Service (Sam McGee); Epstein and Williams (gold rush); Dunham; London; Hines; Brower; Eva Best; Morenus; Banks; Beach; Gilman (SS *Dora*); Potter; Stewart; Gilman (Alaska).

HOKKAIDO UNIVERSITY
See T-2145 ff.

HOLBROOK, SILAS
Sketches by a Traveler. Boston: 1830. 315 pp. See also T-2147.

HOLLAND, EDWARD
To the Yukon and the Klondike Gold Fields. San Francisco, 1897. 56 pp.

HOLLAND, RICHARD ROWE (b. 1891)
150th Anniversary of the Arrival of Capt. George Vancouver, at Burrard Inlet, 1792. N.p., 1942, 8 pp.

HOLM, GUSTAV FREDERIK (1849-1940)
See the Arctic Bibliography.

HOLM, WILLIAM
Northwest Coast Indian Art. Seattle: University of Washington Press, 1965. 144 pp.

HOLMES, J. J.
Silent Songs of the North. Eureka, Calif.: 1926. 52 pp. Poetry.

HOLMES, LEWIS
The Arctic Whaleman. Boston: Wentworth, 1857. 296 pp. Whaling in the Bering and Chukchi Seas, wreck of the *Citizen* in 1852, 9 months with the Chukotsk Peninsula natives.

HOLMES, MAURICE
An Introduction to the Bibliography of Capt. Cook. London: Edwards, 1936. 59 pp.
Captain James Cook, R.N., F.R.S.: A Bibliographical Excursion. London: Edwards, 1952.

HOLY CROSS
Alaska Sportsman, Jan., '41; March, '55 (Brother Hess here from 1914); Calasanz; Cameron; Colby; Couch; Greely (photo); Helmericks; Henderson; Hewitt; Higginson; Hrdlicka; Hubbard; Hulley; Judge; Llorente; Robins; Santos; Savage; Stuck; Walden; Wickersham.

HOLZWORTH, JOHN MICHAEL (b. 1888)
The Wild Grizzlies of Alaska. New York: Putnam's, 1930. 417 pp. For the American Biological Society. Careful study of brown bears and grizzly bears in Southeast Alaska and on the Kenai Peninsula; a plea for protection.
The Twin Grizzlies of Admiralty Island. Philadelphia: Lippincott, 1932. 250 pp.

HOMER
Alaska Life, June, '44 (fur farms); *Alaska Sportsman,* Oct., '38; Jan., '41; Oct., '45 (named for Homer Pennock, manager, Alaska Gold Mining Co.); Nov., '45; Dec., '45; June, '47; June, '50 (hydroelectric plant); Dec., '50 (wild berry products); Apr.,

'52; July, '52; Nov., '53; May, '54; Dec., '54; Jan., '60, and others, see Index; Burroughs; Colby; Denison; Higginson; Sundborg; Winslow.

HONCHARENKO, AGAPIUS
Russian and English Phrase Book. San Francisco: Roman and Co., 1868. 100 pp.
The School and Family Russian-American Primer. San Francisco, 1871. 48 pp.
See also *Alaska Herald.* Honcharenko published the *Alaska Herald* at San Francisco from 1868 to 1872, semi-monthly. Supposedly a Greek or Russian monk, authorities assert he was never in Alaska. Petrof called the paper "chiefly a blackmailer of corporations." The paper was dual language, and is said to be the first to use the word "Alaska" in its title. Kitchener asserts Honcharenko was hired by the Alaska Commercial Company to write a Russian primer for use on the Pribilof Islands. The *Herald,* on the other hand, was vitriolic in its denunciation of that company as monopolistic, nativist and exploitive. The *Katalla Herald* "charged" Honcharenko with encouraging strife among the Russians in Alaska by claiming they were owed certain monies by the US government. After Honcharenko sold the paper in 1872 its anit-monopoly agitation ceased.

HONEYMAN, A. VANDOREN
Reindeer Land. Plainfield, N.J.: 1905. 100 pp. Juvenile.

HONIGMANN, JOHN J.
The World of Man. New York: Harper, 1959. 971 pp.
"Child Rearing Patterns among the Great Whale River Eskimos," *Anthro. Papers,* University of Alaska, 1953.
"The Attawapiskat Swampy Cree," *Anthro. Papers,* University of Alaska, 1956.
"The Great Whale River Eskimo," *Anthro. Papers,* University of Alaska, 1960.

HOOKER, Sir WILLIAM JACKSON (1785-1865)
The Botany of Capt. Beechey's Voyage. London: H.G. Bohn, 1841. 485 pp.
Flora Boreali Americana. London: H.G. Bohn, 1840. 2v.
A Brief Memoir of the Life of Mr. David Douglas. London: H.G. Bohn, 1838. 104 pp.

HOOPER, CALVIN LEIGHTON (1842-1900)
Report, Cruise of the Corwin. Wn.DC: GPO, 1881. Revenue Cutter Service, cruise of 1880.
Report, Cruise of the Corwin. Wn.DC: GPO, 1883. Revenue Cutter Service, cruise of 1881. On this cruise, in addition to his regular duties, Hooper sought information on the missing *Jeannette,* and missing American whalers. See also Muir.
Report on the Sea Otters of Alaska. Wn.DC: GPO, 1897. 35 pp. Bureau of the Census. Report on the otter grounds along the Aleutian Islands and Kodiak Island. See also Baker.

HOOPER, SAMUEL LEIGHTON
The Discovery of Wrangel Island. San Francisco: California Academy of Sciences, 1956. 27 pp. The landing was made by *Corwin* in 1881. This work contains also a biographical sketch of Calvin Hooper (father of Samuel Hooper), including his service in the Bering Sea Patrol.

HOOPER, WILLIAM HULME (1827-1854)
Ten Months Among the Tents of the Tuski. London: J. Murray, 1853. 417 pp. Relates voyage of the *Plover*, 1848-51, with a winter in Plover Bay. Hooper also made two trips up the Mackenzie River to Fort Simpson, and returned overland (east) to England. The work describes native life.

HOOPES, DAVID
Alaska in Haiku. Rutland, Vt.: C.E. Tuttle, 1972.

HOPKINS, DAVID MOODY
The Bering Land Bridge. Stanford: Stanford University Press, 1967. 495 pp.
"Thaw Lakes and Thaw Sinks in the Imuruk Lake Area, Seward Peninsula, Alaska," *Journ. of Geology*, March, 1949.
"Seward Peninsula," with J.P. Hopkins, in Howell Williams.
"Geological Background of the Iyatayet Archaeological Site, Cape Denbigh, Alaska," *Bulletin*, Geological Soc. of America, 1952.

HORNADAY, WILLIAM TEMPLE (1854-1937)
Our Vanishing Wild Life. New York: Scribner's, 1913. 411 pp.
Camp Fires in the Canadian Rockies. London: Laurie, 1906. 374 pp.

HOSLEY, EDWARD H.
"The McGrath Ingalik," *Anthro. Papers*, University of Alaska, 1961.

HOTOVITSKY, DMITRI (d. ca. 1952)
Alaska Life, July, '44 and Jan., '45, "Hotovitsky's Log." See also T-5017.

HOUGH, EMERSON (1857-1923)
See T-2189 ff.

HOUGH, WALTER (1859-1935)
"The Lamp of the Eskimo," *Annual Report*, US National Museum, 1896. See also the Arctic Bibliography.

HOUSE, BOYCE
Friendly Feudin': Alaska vs Texas. San Antonio: Naylor Co., 1959. 64 pp.

HOUSTON, CHARLES S.
"Denali's Wife," (Mt. Foraker), *Appalachia*, 1934. See also *Amer. Alpine Journ.*, 1935.

HOWARD, OLIVER OTIS (1830-1909)
"A Visit to Alaska in 1875," in *Compilation of Narratives* (US Congress). See also Wickersham's Bibliography. Howard urged that Honcharenko's charges against the Alaska Commercial Co. be investigated, and so argued in an appendix to one edition of this report. He urged some form of civil government be appointed for Alaska, and wrote a brief article on the native chiefs Fernandeste, Sitka Jack, and Annahootz, in *St. Nicholas*, May, 1908. He employed Alexander Choquette as an interpreter.

HOWAY, FREDERICK WILLIAM (1867-1943)
(Provincial Judge)
Captain George Vancouver. Toronto: Ryerson, 1932. 32 pp.

Presidential Address: *The Early Literature of the North West Coast.* Ottawa: Royal Society of Canada, 1924. 31 pp.
The Dixon-Meares Controversy. Toronto: Ryerson, 1929. 156 pp. Also New York: Da Capo Press, 1969 (reprint). Presents John Meares as a selfish, unprincipled fur trader.
Voyages of the Columbia to the Northwest Coast. Boston, 1941. Also New York: Da Capo Press, 1969 (reprint). 518 pp.
Zimmerman's Captain Cook. Toronto: Ryerson, 1930. 120 pp. Limited edition of 250.
"The Fur Trader in Northwestern Development," in *The Pacific Coast in History*, Howay, et. alii. New York: Macmillan, 1917. 535 pp.
"A List of Trading Vessels in the Maritime Fur Trade," *Proceedings*, Royal Society of Canada, 1930 to 1934 (five installments).
"Letters Relating to the Second Voyage of the Columbia," *Oregon Historical Quarterly*, June, 1923.
"A Yankee Trader on the Northwest Coast, 1791-95," *Washington Historical Quarterly*, April, 1930.
Builders of the West. Toronto: Ryerson, 1929. 251 pp.
"On the New Vancouver Journal," *Washington Hist. Q.*, 1915.
"Notes on Cook's and Vancouver's Ships," *Wn. Hist. Q.*, 1930.
"Early Navigation on the Strait of Juan de Fuca," *Oregon Hist. Q.*, 1911.
"Four Letters from Richard Cadman Etches to Sir Joseph Banks," *Br. Col. Hist. Q.*, April, 1942.
British Columbia, the Making of a Province. Toronto: Ryerson, 1928. 289 pp.
British Columbia and the United States; see Henry Forbes Angus.
See also Scholefield, *British Columbia from Earliest Times.*

HOWE, R. S.; see T-2205.

HOWGATE, HENRY W.
See T-2206.

HRDLICKA, ALES
Alaska Diary, 1926-31. Lancaster, Pa.: Jaques Cattell, 1943. 414 pp.
The Aleutian and Commander Islands. Philadelphia: Wistar Institute of Anatomy and Biology, 1945. 630 pp.
An Eskimo Brain. New York: Knickerbocker Press, 1901. 49 pp.
The Anthropology of Kodiak Island. Philadelphia: Wistar Institute of Anatomy and Biology, 1944. 486 pp.
"The Coming of Man from Asia in the Light of Recent Discoveries," *Annual Report*, Smithsonian Institution, 1935.
"Anthropological Survey in Alaska," *Annual Report*, Bureau of American Ethnology, 1929. Yukon, Tanana, coastal Eskimo, Prince William Sound to Point Barrow.
"The Eskimo of the Kuskokwim," *Amer. Journ. of Physical Anthrop.*, 1933.
"The Genesis of the American Indian," *Proceedings*, Internat'l. Congress of Americanists, 1915.
"Remains in Eastern Asia of the Race of People that Peopled America," Smithsonian Miscellaneous Collections, 1912.

See the Arctic Bibliography for a complete bibliography of Hrdlicka's Alaska work. Curator of the Physical Anthropology section of the Smithsonian Institution, Hrdlicka carried on field research in many parts of the world. See also *Alaska Sportsman*, February, 1937.

HUBBACK, THEODORE RATHBONE
To Far Western Alaska. London: Ward, 1929. 332 pp. Big game hunting. *Short shrift by this industry book*

HUBBARD, BERNARD ROSECRANS (1888-1962)
Mush, You Malemutes! New York: America Press, 1932. 179 pp. Stories of Fr. Hubbard's travels in Alaska.
Cradle of Storms. New York: Dodd, 1935. 285 pp. More travelogue in Alaska.
Alaskan Odyssey. London: Hale, 1952. Reprint of the last 100 pages of *Mush, You Malemutes!*
One Hundred Pictures of Little Known Alaska. New York: America Press, 1935. 72 pp.
"Geologic Features of Aniakchak and Veniaminov Craters," *Journal*, Washington Academy of Sciences, 1931.
See also Robert Dick Douglas.

HUBER, LOUIS R.
100 Events that Built Alaska. Ketchikan: Alaska Magazine Publishing Co., 1944. 50 pp. See also *Alaska Life*, July, 1941.
"The Road to the Top of the Continent," *Travel*, July, 1947.
"Flight over Katmai," *Alaska Sportsman*, April, 1951.
"Incredible Conquest of Mt. McKinley," *Natural History*, December, 1949.

HUCULAK, MYKHAYLO
When Russia was in America. New York: Heinman Press, 1971.

HUDSON, WILL E.
Icy Hell. London: Constable, 1937. 307 pp. Newsreel cameraman in the Aleutians and Siberia.

HUDSON'S BAY COMPANY
Alaska Sportsman, Sept., '54 (Trader's Cove, Stephens passage); *Alaska-Yukon Magazine*, Feb., '08; Bancroft; Barbeau; *Beaver;* Brooks (Ft. Stikine); Bryce, George (*History*); Campbell; Chevigny; Clark; Colby; Dall; Davidson; Donald; Davidson, Gordon C. (*History of the Northwest Co.*, U. Calif. Press, 1918); Denison; Gardner; Godsell; Greenhow; Gruening; Hulley; James, James A.; Kitchener; MacKay; Morris; Murray; Simpson; Alexander; Simpson, Sir George; Stuck; Tompkins; Willson; Wright, Julia.

HUGHES, CHARLES CAMPBELL
An Eskimo Village in the Modern World. Ithaca: Cornell University Press, 1960. 419 pp.
"Eskimo Ceremonies," trans. from I.K. Voblov, *Anthrop. Papers*, University of Alaska, 1959.
"Under Four Flags: Recent Cultural Change among the Eskimos, Alaska," *Current Anthrop.*, VI (1965): 27-41.
"An Eskimo Deviant from the 'Eskimo' Type of Social Organization," *Amer. Anthrop.*, LX (1958): 1140 ff.

"Observations on Community Change in the North: An Attempt at Summary," *Anthropologica*, V (1963): 69-81.

HUISH, ROBERT (1777-1850)
A Narrative of the Voyages of Capt. Beechey. London: W. Wright, 1836 [?]. 508 pp. Voyage of 1825-28.
The North-West Passage. London: McGowan, 1851. 418 pp.

HULBERT, HOMER B.
In Search of a Siberian Klondike. New York, 1903. Biography of Washington B. Vanderlip.

HULBERT, WINIFRID
The Bishop of All Beyond. New York: Friendship Press, 1948. 24 pp. Sheldon Jackson.

HULLEY, CLARENCE CHARLES (b. 1907)
Alaska, 1741-1953. Portland: Binfords and Mort, 1953. 406 pp. New edition entitled *Alaska: Past and Present* in 1958.
"A Historical Survey of the Matanuska Valley Settlement in Alaska," *Pacific Northwest Quarterly*, October, 1949. Hulley was professor of history at the University of Alaska, 1945-55. His *Alaska: Past and Present* is perhaps the most adequate and useful general history of Alaska readily available for wide use. Andrews, Gruening, Bancroft and Dall are all available in libraries, but are out of print.

HULTEN, ERIC (b. 1894)
Flora of the Aleutian Islands. Stockholm: Thule, 1937. 397 pp.
Flora of Alaska and the Yukon. Lund: Gleerup, 1941-50. 3v. The first major comprehensive work of its kind.
Outline of the History of Arctic and Boreal Biota during the Quaternary Period. Stockholm: Thule, 1937. 168 pp.
"History of the Botanical Exploration of Alaska and Yukon Territories from the Time of Their Discovery to 1940," *Botaniska Notiser*, 1940.

HULTKRANTZ, AKE
Conceptions of the Soul among North America Indians. Stockholm, 1953. 545 pp.
The North American Indian Orpheus Tradition. Stockholm, 1957. 340 pp.

HUNT, CORNELIUS E.
The Shenandoah. New York: G.W. Carlton, 1867. 273 pp. This was the last Confederate cruiser. Operating in North Pacific waters, she was unaware of the end of the American Civil War until well after the armistice at Appomattox. Her success against northern shipping was remarkable. This work is by one of her officers.

HUNT, HARRIET E.
Ketchikan: First City of Alaska. Ketchikan: Journal Printing, 1909. 64 pp. Descr.

HUNT, LAWRENCE
The Curse of the Killer Whale. New York: Funk and Wagnalls, 1963. 186 pp.

HUNT, ROCKWELL D.
"Hubert H. Bancroft: His Work and His Method," *Publications*, Calif. Historical Society, 1911. See also Caughey.

HUNT, WILLIAM R.
North of 53º. New York: Macmillan Press, 1974. 328 pp. Thorough, popular detail of the successive gold rushes from the Klondike to Nome and back to the interior. One of the better descriptions of all the rushes.
Arctic Passage. New York: Charles Scribner's Sons, 1975. Settlement in the Bering Sea region, and Alaska-Siberian contact.
Alaska: A Bicentennial History. New York: W.W. Norton, 1976. xvi & 200 pp. Amer. Assoc. for State and Local History. Perhaps the best summary of the American period in Alaska in print, treating ably post-WW II development, conservation, oil, and less well, the native claims act. Supersedes Hulley and Gruening as the most useful summary of Alaska since 1867.
"Harry de Windt: He Blew it at Chilkoot Pass," *Alaska Journal*, I (1971).
"Soldier on the Yukon," *Journal of the West*, X (1971). Capt. Charles Farnsworth at Fts. Gibbon (Tanana) and Egbert (Eagle), circa. 1900.
William Hunt is Professor of History at the University of Alaska, College. He was the winner of the 1976 Historian of the Year award given annually by the Alaska (State) Historical Society.

HUNTING and TRAPPING
A vast subject for Alaska studies; virtually every summary, survey, travel account and reminiscence of Alaska mentions hunting and trapping. Trapping land mammals for fur pelts first became a major enterprise in Alaska after the 1880's, particularly as the interior river basins were explored (for record) and became known to prospectors and adventurers. In this early period the Alaska Commercial Company posts were the major purchaser. See the Index for *Alaska Sportsman* and *Alaska Magazine;* see as well the index in the Tourville bibliography. In addition, see the following:
Annabel; Auer; Beach, William; Bond; Borden; Cane; Crisler; Chase; Endicott; Finton; Grinnell; Hayes; Helmericks; Holzworth; Hubback; McCracken; McGuire; Radclyffe; Schwatka; Scull; Seton-Karr; Sheldon; Shore; Thomas, W.; Williams, J.; Young, G.

HUNTINGTON, JAMES and LAWRENCE ELLIOTT
On the Edge of Nowhere. New York: Crown Publishers, 1956. 183 pp. Koyukuk region.

HUSSEY, KEITH M.
See T-2241 ff.

HUTCHINSON, JOSEPH H.
The Wandering Gentile. San Francisco: Commercial News Publishing Co., 1914. 12 pp. Sketch of Alaska.

HUTCHINSON, KOHL & Co.
See Alaska Purchase; see also Sloss. Perhaps the most useful summary of the role of Hutchinson and Kohl in the purchase of Alaska and later the Alaska Commercial Company appears in Jensen's *The Alaskan Purchase and Russian-American Relations*. See Alaska Commercial Company. See the articles by Gilbert and by Sharrow in addition.

HUTTON, J. E.
A History of the Moravian Missions. London: Moravian Publications Office, 1923. 550 pp.

HWUI SHAN
See Speck, and Vining.

HYDE, JOHN (1848-1929)
Wonderland. Chicago: Rand McNally, 1888. 94 pp.
Northern Pacific Tour. St. Paul: W.C. Riley, 1888. 94 pp. For the Northern Pacific Railroad; tour guide.

HYDROGRAPHY
See the Arctic Bibliography.

HYLANDER, CLARENCE J.
Wildlife Community. Boston: Houghton, Mifflin & Co., 1965.

I

ICELANDIC IMMIGRATION (proposed)
See Morris; Petrof; Olafsson.

ICKES, HAROLD L. (Sec. of Interior)
Not Guilty. Wn.DC: GPO, 1940. 50 pp. Dept. of Interior. Official inquiry into the charges made by Glavis and Pinchot against Richard A. Ballinger, Sec. of Interior, 1909-1911. See articles on Ickes in *Alaska Life*.

IDITAROD
Alaska-Yukon Magazine, Dec., '09; June, '10; Nov., '10 (photo); Dec., '10; Feb., '12 (trail completed to Seward); Colby; Couch (post office 1910-29); Hulley; Kitchener; Mahoney; Parker (novel); Stuck; Young (miners).

ILIN, PETER IVANOVICH (1818-1842)
"Survey of the Eastern Coast of Kamchatka," *Journal*, Russ. Hydrographic Dept., 1852. See Baker.
"Survey of Ilina Bay on the Western Shore of Chichagof Island," in Sarychev's *Atlas*.

ILLARION, Fr. (b. 1818)
See translated excerpts in Alaska Church Collection, University of Alaska (Robe and Lavriskev). See also *Preliminary Survey* by Barbara Sweetland

Smith. Illarion's Journals are in the Russian Orthodox Alaska Archive, and the National Archives in
Washington.

ILLINGWORTH, FRANK (b. 1908)
Highway to the North. London: Ernest Benn,
1955. 297 pp. Alaska Highway.
North of the Circle. New York: Philosophical
Library, 1952. 254 pp. A collection of articles.
Pete of Icy Bay. New York: Coward-McCann,
1951. 245 pp. Juvenile.

INDIANS
See also Aleuts; Basketry; Eskimos; Folklore; In-
dian Languages; Indian Reservations; Indians,
Origin; Metlakatla; Totem Poles; see also Alaska
Natives; Alaska Native Claims Settlement Act. See
also the following:
Alaska Sportsman, Nov., '37 (communal houses);
July, '38 (ed.; Indians not businessmen or farmers);
March, '39 (petroglyphs); May, '40 (animals were
people); May, '42 (Indians but defense bonds);
Dec., '42 (shamans); March, '43 (Indian girl
with sourdough); July, '43 (same); Oct., '44 (land
rights); Dec., '44 (ed. land rights); Jan., '47
(Haines); May, '47 (Hazelton); Aug., '47 (Mud
Bight); Sept., '47 (copper shield); Dec., '47 (Eklutna); Jan., '48 (Pennock Is.); Feb., '48 (Kwakiutl
photo); Aug., '48 (Chilkat mythology); May, '49
(Kenaitzie photo); July, '49 (Kenaitzes); Dec., '49
(potlatch outlawed by missionaries and government); Oct., '50 (fear of responsibility); Jan., '51
(Leask Cove); Feb., '51 (masks); June, '51 (original
culture vanishing); June, '51 (Chief Skowl's men fire
first guns in warfare); July, '51 (115 yr. old Tlingit
woman); Apr., '52 (white pirate poisons Indians at
Anchor Pt.); Oct., '52 (why Indian culture remained
stone age); March, '53 (Tongass forest receipts im-
pounded to settle Indian claims); June, '53 (Yukon
Indians claim Tananas bad people); Apr., '54 (101
yr. old Tlingit); June, '54 (Hoonah dance customs);
Aug., '54 ("squaw candy" is hard smoked salmon);
Dec., '55 (govt. aid, fish shortage); Jan., '56 (1852
Indian still living); Apr., '56 (torches); Sept., '56
(tilt of head to left indicates laziness, Tlingit theory);
Feb., '58 (Zimovia Strait site); Jan., '59 (Ft. Yukon);
March, '59 (Brooklyn carved totem); Dec., '59 (land
rights); Jan., '60; and other, see Index; *Alaska Life*,
Dec., '44 (land rights); June, '45 (land rights); Aug.,
'45 (Army adult school); *Alaska-Yukon Magazine*,
Nov., '08 (tribes distinguished); see as well these:
Abercrombie (Ahtna); Adam, L. (see Arctic Bib-
lio.); Adams, Ben; Alaska Native Foundation;
Allen, H. (Ahtna); Allen, R. (Anthrop. Pap., UA);
Andrews; Arctander; Arnold, C. (*Alaska Life*, Sept.,
'38); Aronson, J. (see Arctic Bibliography); Badlam;
Baily, G. (observations in 1879, see Arctic Biblio.);
Ballou; Bancroft; Barbeau; Beardslee; Beaver;
Benyon, Wm. (see the Arctic Biblio.); Berlin Royal
Museums; Berry, M.; Bigjim; Binning; Birket-
Smith; Boas; BC Dept. Educ.; Bronson (on mis-
treatment of Indians, see Arctic Biblio.); Brooks;
Bruce; Bruet; Burroughs; Butler and Dale; Cad-
wald (*Alaska Life*, Dec., '40); Calasanz; Carpenter;
Chamberlain, A. (Arctic Biblio.); Chapman, J.;
Chase (Arctic Biblio.); Chevigny; Cohen; Colby;
Collis; Collison; Cook; Crosby; Culin (Arctic Bib-
lio.); Curtis (Arctic Biblio.); Dall; Davis; Davis,

N.; Davy, G. (Arctic Biblio.); Davydov; Dawson;
de Laguna; Daugherty; Denison; Dixon; Dixon, R.
(Arctic Biblio.); Dole; Dorsey, G. (Arctic Biblio.);
Drucker; Durlach; Eells; Elliott; Ely; Emmons;
Emerson; Fellows, F. (Arctic Biblio.); Fleurieu;
Fuhrmann; Fed. Field Comm.; Garfield, V.; Gar-
land; Galligher; Gibbs; Goddard; Golovnin; Gor-
ham; Graham; Green, J.; Green, P.; Grinnell;
Gsovski; Hadleigh-West; Halliday; Hallowell
(Arctic Biblio.); Harriman; Harrison, C.; Haekel
(Arctic Biblio.); Harrington (Arctic Biblio.); Hayes;
Helmericks; Herron; Higginson; Holmberg; Honig-
man; Howard, O.; Hrdlicka; Hulley; Ingraham;
Inverarity; Jackson; Jacobsen; Jenkins; Jenness;
Jette; Jones, L.; Jones, S. (Arctic Biblio.); Judge;
Juvenal; Keithahn; Kelly, E. (Arctic Biblio.);
Knapp and Dorr; Kotzebue; Krause, A.; Krieger,
H.; Langsdorff; Lathan; Learnard; Leechman
(Arctic Biblio.); LeFebre, C. (Arctic Biblio.);
Lemert (alcohol, Arctic Biblio.); Lenoir (Arctic Bib-
lio.); Lindquist; Lisianski; McClellan, C. (Arctic
Biblio.); McCullagh; McDonald, N.; McKennan;
MacLeod (Arctic Biblio.); Marchand, J. (Arctic
Biblio.); Marchand, E.; Marshall; Mason; May-
berry; Mendenhall; Menzel; Morice, A. (Arctic
Biblio.); Muir; Morgan, L.; Murdoch; Murray;
Newcombe; Niblack; Nathan; Nichols; Niedieck;
Oberg; Olson, R. (Arctic Biblio.); Osgood; Park;
Parsons, E.; Petrof; Pierce, W.; Pilgrim; Pinart;
Powell; Purdy; Rainey; Raymond, C.; Replogle;
Richardson, J.; Sapir, E. (Arctic Biblio.); Schmitter
(Arctic Biblio.); Schwatka; Scidmore; Scouler (Arc-
tic Biblio.); Seaton-Karr; Shepard; Shotridge (Arc-
tic Biblio.); Smith, H. (Arctic Biblio.); Sniffen and
Carrington (Arctic Biblio.); Spurr; Stuck; Sullivan,
R.; Swanton; Swineford; Underwood; US Adj.
Gen.; US Army; US Cong.; US Dept. Int.; US Rev.
Cut. Serv.; US Treas. Dept.; Vahl; Vancouver;
Van Stone; Veniaminov; Washburne; Wellcome;
Whymper; Wickersham; Wike; Willard; Wrangel;
Wright, J.; Young, S.; Zagoskin. See also Arnold, R.

INDIAN LANGUAGES
Boas; Chapman (Anvik); Dall; Davidson, G.;
Davydov; Goddard; Harrison; Jette; Kruzenstern;
Legoff; Miller, R.; Morice; Murray; Mason; Os-
good; Petitot; Pilling; Pinart; Powell; Sapir;
Schott; Scouler; Shafer; Strange; Swanton; Wick-
ersham; Wolff; Zagoskin; see also the Arctic Bib-
liography, and the publications of the Department of
Anthropology of the University of Alaska.

INDIAN RESERVATIONS
Alaska Sportsman, Oct., '45 (Ickes policy); Apr.,
'48 (Karluk); Bancroft; Cohen; Price; US Congress,
Senate Comm. on Interior and Insular Affairs; see
also Gruening.

INDIAN ORIGINS, MIGRATIONS
Alaska Sportsman, May, '58 (E.K. Allen); Ban-
croft (Native Races); Barbeau (*Geog. Rev.*, July, '45,
"Aleutian Route"); Barbeau (*Proc.*, Pac. Sci. Conf.,
1933, Siberian origins); Barbeau (*Sci. Monthly*,
Apr., '33, Asian survivals in Indian songs); Birdsell
(Viking Fund Summer Sem. in *Phys. Anthrop.*);
Birket-Smith (Scand. Naturalist Conf. 1929); Boas
(*Proc.*, Int. Congl of Americanists, 1902, Jesup
Exped.); Boas (in *Amer. Aborigines*, ed. D. Jenness

[1933 Pac. Sci. Conf.]); Boas (Int. Cong. of Americanists, 1908, Jesup Exped.); Boas (*Sci. Monthly*, 1929); Boas (Int. Cong. of Amer., 1924); Brooks, C. (SF, Acad. Sci, 1876, *Japanese Wrecks*); Buschmann, J.K.E. (Arctic Biblio.); Campbell, J. (*Transact.*, Roy Can. Inst., 1898, Denes [NA] and Tungus [Asia], concl. challenged by Morice); Davis, Horace (*Record of Japanese Vessels driven upon the Northwest Coast*); Fewkes, J. et. alii. (Amer. Anthrop., 1912); Goddard, F. (*Int. Journ. of Am. Ling.*, 1920); Hatt (*Proc.*, Pac. Sci. Conf., 1933); Hatt (Arctic Biblio.); Hopkins (*Bering Land Bridge Theory*); Hrdlicka (*Ann. Rpt.*, Smithsonian, 1935); Hrdlicka (Remains in E. Asia); Ives, R. (*Am. Antiquity*, 1956); Jenness (anthology of papers, Pac. Sci. Conf., 1933, titled *The American Aborigines*); Jenness (Rpt. to Int. Cong. of Anthrop. and Ethnol. Sci., Copenhagen, 1938); Jochelson (Int. Cong. of Amer., 1904); Jones, L.; Keithahn; Leechman (*Can. Hist. Rev.*, 1935); MacLeod, Wm. (Anthrop. Ephemeris, 1929); Mason; Morice (*Trans.*, Roy. Can. Inst., 1915); Petitot (Int. Cong. of Amer., 1875); Shafer, R. (*Int. Jour. of Amer. Ling.*, 1952).

INGERSOLL, W. T.
"Lands of Change: Four Parks in Alaska," *Journal of the West*, VII (1968): 173-192.

INGRAHAM, JOSEPH
Journal of the Voyage of the Brigantine *Hope* from Boston to the Northwest Coast of America, 1790-92. In the Provincial Archives, Victoria, BC. Unpublished.

INGSTAD, HELGE MARCUS (b. 1899)
Nunamiut: Among Alaska's Eskimos. New York: W.W. Norton, 1954. 303 pp. Ingstad spent the winter of 1949-50 with Eskimos of Anaktuvuk Pass who had lived on the Arctic coast near the Yukon border as late as 1938 (from 1918). The village then numbered 65.
The Land of Feast and Famine. New York: Alfred A. Knopf, 1933. 332 pp. Narrative of 1930-31 sojourn near Great Slave Lake.

INNIS, HAROLD ADAMS (b. 1894)
Settlement and the Mining Frontier. Toronto: Macmillan, 1936.

INNOKENTII; see Veniaminov.

INNOKO
"Innoko Mining District," *Mining and Scientific Press*, 1909. See also the following:
Alaska-Yukon Magazine, Nov., '07; Nov., '08; Sept., '09; Chase (gold disc. winter of 1906-07); Hulley; Stuck.

INSECTS; see the Arctic Bibliography.

INSIDE PASSAGE
Alaska Life, July, '38; Jan. ff, '40; Jan., '56; *Alaska Sportsman*, May, '36; May, '43 (Ripple Rock blasted); July, '47; Oct., '48 (shipwreck); Oct., '52 (labor strike); Nov., '55; Dec., '55 (SS *Yukon*); Apr., '57; Oct., '58 (*Maggine Murphy*); July, '58; May, '59; Nov., '59; Dec., '59; others, see Index; *Alaska-Yukon Magazine*, Jan., '11; Badlam; Ballou; Bright; Bruce; Burroughs; Cameron; Clark, S.;

Colby; Davis; Denison; Godwin; Hart; Hansen; Greely; Higginson; Lukens; Miller; Morgan; Pierrepont; Pilgrim; Pinkerton; Schwatka; Scidmore; Stuck; Vancouver; Wardman; Winslow; Wolfe; Woollen. See also Shipwrecks.

INTERNATIONAL ASSOCIATION for QUATERNARY RESEARCH
See T-2273.

INTERNATIONAL BOUNDARY COMMISSION
President Grant's 4th Annual Message to Congress (42nd), recommending Congressional provision of a Joint Commission on the Alaska-British Columbia boundary, Dec. 2, 1872.
Joint Report of the US and Br. Commissioners on the Alaskan-Canadian Boundary. Wn.DC: GPO, 1898. 15 pp.
Joint Maps of the International Boundary between the US and Canada along the 141st Meridian, surveyed and monumented 1907-13, under a convention of April 21, 1906. Wn.DC: USGS, 1918. 41 maps.
Joint Report, Survey and Demarcation of the International Boundary between the United States and Canada along the 141st meridian, etc. Wn.DC: GPO, 1918. 305 pp. 41 maps. Department of State.
Joint Report, Survey and Demarcation of the Boundary between Canada and the United States, Tongass Passage to Mt. St. Elias. Ottawa: Gov't. Printing Bureau, 1918. 356 pp. See also Alaskan Boundary Dispute.

INTERNATIONAL BUREAU of the AMERICAN REPUBLICS
See Pan-American Union.

INTERNATIONAL FISHERIES COMMISSION
See T-2276 ff.

INTERNATIONAL NORTH PACIFIC FISHERIES COMMISSION
See T-2279 ff.

INTERNATIONAL PACIFIC HALIBUT COMMISSION
See T-2284 ff.

INTERNATIONAL POLAR EXPEDITION, 1882-83
Report, Internat'l. Polar Exped. Wn.DC: GPO, 1885. 695 pp. US Congress. House Ex. Doc., 44, 48th Cong., 2nd Sess. Narrative of the expedition, with ethnographic sketch of natives by Lt. Patrick Henry Ray; specimens, natural history, John Murdoch; census of natives, and vocabulary; flora and fauna. Additional contributors included Dall, Asa Gray, Charles Riley, and Charles Schott.

INTERNATIONAL SOCIETY for the EXPLORATION of the ARCTIC REGIONS
See T-2287.

INVERARITY, ROBERT BRUCE (b. 1909)
Art of the Northwest Coast Indians. Berkeley: University of California Press, 1950. 243 pp.
Movable Masks and Figures. Bloomfield Hills, Mich.: Cranbrook Institute of Science, 1941.

Northwest Coast Indian Art. Seattle: State Museum, University of Washington, 1946. 36 pp.

Visual Files Coding Index. Bloomington: Indiana University Press, 1960. 185 pp.

IRELAND, WILLARD E.

"James Douglas and the Russian-American Company, 1840," *Br. Col. Hist. Quarterly*, January, 1941.

IRTEL, IGUMEN

"Alaska, the Battleground of Orthodoxy," *Russian Orthodox Journal*, February, 1954.

IRVING, LAURENCE

Birds of Anaktuvuk Pass, Kobuk and Old Crow. Wn.DC: GPO, 1960. 409 pp. Smithsonian Institution. Based on studies from 1947 to 1957.

"On Naming Birds of the Arctic," *Anthrop. Papers*, University of Alaska, 1958.

"Stability in Eskimo Naming of Birds on Cumberland Sound," *Anthrop. Papers*, University of Alaska, December, 1961.

IRVING, WASHINGTON (1783-1859)

Astoria. Numerous editions, the first about 1836. John Jacob Astor encouraged Irving to do a story of the fur trade and trappers (see Porter, *John Jacob Astor*), providing him with numerous letters and reports from men in the west. Chapter 57 of *Astoria* (sub-titled Anecdotes of an Enterprise beyond the Rocky Mountains) concerns a voyage by a fur agent named Hunt on the old *Beaver* to "Sheetka" in 1812. At Sitka Hunt met "Count" Baranov. See Bancroft, who quotes Irving on Baranov.

IRVING, WILLIAM N.

"Evidence of Early Tundra Cultures in Northern Alaska," *Anthrop. Papers*, University of Alaska, May, 1953.

"An Archaeological Survey of the Susitna Valley," *Anthrop. Papers*, University of Alaska, December, 1957.

"Ruins from Central Alaska," *Amer. Antiquity*, XX (1955): 380-383.

IRWIN, DAVID (b. 1911)

One Man Against the North. With Franklin M. Reck. New York: Crowell, 1940. 244 pp. Irwin lived among the Eskimos of the Arctic from 1933 to 1935. See another edition, with John Sherman O'Brien.

IRWIN, DON LOUIS (b. 1888)

"Status and Accomplishments of Agricultural Research in Alaska," Alaska Science Conference, 1950.

The Position of Agriculture in Alaska's Current Economy. With Hugh A. Johnson. Published jointly by the University of Alaska and the USDA, 1953. 15 pp.

See the Arctic Bibliography for a complete bibliography of Irwin's works on Alaska agriculture. Irwin was general manager of the ARRC in the Matanuska Valley, and director of the agricultural experiment station at Palmer. See O. Miller.

ITJEN, MARTIN (d. 1942)

The Story of the Tour on the Skagway. Skagway, n.p., 1934. 82 pp. Itjen was a promoter and tour booster at Skagway. See the *National Geographic*, September, 1942. See also the *Alaska Sportsman*, Index.

IVANSHINSTOV, N.

Obozrienii Russkikh Krugosvietnykh Puteshetvii. Summary of Russian Round-the-World Voyages. Published serially in *Zap. Gidr. Dep.* (Journ. of the Hydrographic Dept.) in 1849. Thirty-eight voyages, as follows:

Krusenstern (*Nadezhda* [Hope])	1803-06
Lisianski (*Neva*)	1803-06
Hagemeister (*Neva*)	1806-07
Golovnin (*Diana*)	1807-09
Lazarev, M.P. (*Suvarov*)	1813-16
Kotzebue (*Rurik*)	1815-18
Hagemeister (*Kutuzov*)	1816-18
Ponafidin (*Suvarov*)	1816-18
Golovnin (*Kamchatka*)	1817-19
Bellinghausen (*Vostok* [*Orient*])	1819-21
Lazarev, M.P. (*Mirnyi* [*Peace*])	
Vasiliev, M.N. (*Otkrytie* [*Discovery*])	1819-22
Shishmarev (*Blagonamierennyi* [*Good Intent*])	1819-22
Ponafidin (*Borodino*)	1819-21
Dokhturov (*Kutuzov*)	1820-22
Klochkov (*Rurik*)	1821-22
Kiseakovski (*Elizaveta*)	1821-22
Tulubiev and Krushchev (*Apollon*)	1821-24
Filatov (*Ajax*)	1821-22
Lazarev, M.P. (*Kreiser*)	1822-25
Lazarev, A.P. (*Ladoga*)	1822-25
Kotzebue (*Predpriiatie* [Enterprise]	1823-26
Chistiakov and Muraviev (*Elena*)	1824-26
Dokhturov (*Smirni*)	1824-25
Wrangel (*Krotki*)	1826-27
Staniukovich (*Moller*)	1826-29
Lutke (*Seniavin*)	1826-29
Khromchenko (*Elena*)	1828-31
Hagemeister (*Krotki*)	1828-30
Khromchenko (*Amerika*)	1831-33
Von Shants (*Amerika*)	1834-36
Tebenkov (*Elena*)	1835-36
Berens (*Nikolai*)	1837-39
Khadnikov and Woewodski (*Nikolai*)	1839-41
Zarembo (*Nasliednik Alexander*)	1840-41
Yunker (*Abo*)	1840-42
Vonliarliarski (*Irtysh*)	1843-45
Nevelskoi (*Baikal*)	1848-49

J

JACKSON, HARTLEY HARRAD THOMPSON
(b. 1881)
*Literature on the Natural History of the Arctic
Region.* Wn.DC: GPO, 1949. 48 pp. US Fish &
Wildlife Service. Bibliography.

JACKSON, SHELDON (1834-1909)
Alaska, and Missions on the North Pacific Coast.
New York: Dodd, Mead, 1880. 327 pp. About 1883
a separate chapter on natives was added, though the
entire work deals primarily with the missionary
effort among the natives.
Facts about Alaska. New York: Women's Home
Missions, Presbyterian Church, 1894. 22 pp.
Report on Education in Alaska. Wn.DC: GPO,
1886. 93 pp. Sen. Ex. Doc. No. 85, 49th Cong., 1st
Sess. Jackson first assumed the post of General Agent
for Education in Alaska in 1885.
Report on Introduction of Domestic Reindeer into
Alaska. Sixteen such reports were compiled between
1890 and 1906, with no reports in 1891 and 1892
and two in 1894. Normally they are about 150 pages
in length. From 1907 the reindeer report was included in the annual report of the US Commissioner
of Education (see US Office of Education). Sheldon
Jackson arranged for the importation of reindeer
from Siberia in hopes of providing an economic and
stabilizing force for Alaskan Eskimos. The experiment was largely unsuccessful.
The Native Tribes of Alaska. Ocean Grove, N.J.:
National Assembly, 1883. Reprinted from *Sixty Addresses, Christian Educators in Council*, ed. J.C.
Hartzell.
On Sheldon Jackson see the following:
Stewart, Robert L.; Faris, J.T.; Brady; see also
Brooks; Henderson; Hulley; see as well Hinckley;
and Andrews (*Alaska Life*, Sept., '43). Jackson was
born in Minaville, NY, and from 1858 to 1885 was a
successful missionary in the American west. From
1879 with the publication of his study of Alaskan
missions he was regarded as an authority, and was
appointed General Agent for Education in Alaska.
For a full bibliography see the Arctic Bibliography
and Wickersham's bibliography. See also T-2310 ff.

JACOBIN, LOUIS (b. 1889)
Guide to Alaska and the Yukon. Los Angeles:
Wetzel Pub. Co., annually from 1946. See *Alaska
Life*, March and May, 1945.

JACOBSEN, JOHAN ADRIAN (b. 1853)
*Captain Jacobsen's Reise an der Nordwestkuste
Amerikas.* Leipzig: M. Spohr, 1884. 431 pp. 1881-
83 expedition in British Columbia and Alaska gathering artifacts for the Royal Museum of Berlin,
mainly among the Tlingits, the Eskimos, and the Ingalik. See also the Arctic Bibliography.

JACQUOT, LOUIS
"Alaska Natives and Higher Education, 1960-72,"
unpublished doctoral dissertation, University of
Oregon, School of Education, 1974.

JAGGAR, THOMAS A.
Journal, Technology Expedition to the Aleutian
Islands, 1907. Boston: Ellis, 1908. 37 pp. Volcanoes.
Volcanoes Declare War. Honolulu: Paradise of
Pacific, Ltd., 1945. 166 pp.
"Mapping the Home of the Great Brown Bear,"
National Geographic, 1929. Pavlof Volcano.

JAMES, BUSHROD WASHINGTON (1836-1903)
Alaskana. Philadelphia: Porter and Coates, 1892.
368 pp. Poetry and legend.
Alaska: Its Neglected Past, Its Brilliant Future.
Philadelphia: Sunshine Publishing Co., 1897. 444
pp.

JAMES, JAMES ALTON (b. 1864)
*The First Scientific Exploration of Russian Amer-
ica and the Purchase of Alaska.* Chicago: North-
western University, 1942. 276 pp. Includes Henry
Bannister's journal of his months at St. Michael for
weather observation (and contemplation), and
Robert Kennicott's diary while with the Scientific
Corps, with considerable analysis of Alaska's role.

JAMES, SAM
Taming the Arctic Shrew. Anchorage: Color Art
Printing, 1963. 22 pp. Poetry.

JAMESON, EARLE C.
*A Glimpse of the 2nd Alaska Territorial Legis-
lature.* Juneau: Empire Printing Co., 1915. 36 pp.
The Golden Northland. Juneau: Empire Printing,
1923. 54 pp. Legislative souvenir manual with biographical sketches.

JAMISON, PAUL L. and STEPHEN L. ZEGURA
"An Anthropometric Study of the Eskimos of
Wainwright," *Arctic Anthrop.*, VII (1970): 125-143.

JANE, CECIL
A Spanish Voyage to Vancouver. London: Argonaut Press, 1930. 142 pp. 1792 voyage of the
schooners *Sutil* and *Mexicana* to the Strait of Juan de
Fuca.

JANE, FRED T.
The Imperial Russian Navy. London: W. Thacker
& Co., 1899.

JAPANESE (in Alaska)
"Japanese Seal Poachers," *Outlook*, August, 1896.
"Japanese Discovery of Alaska: Kwankai-ibun,"
Asia Magazine, May, 1920. 1794 landing of outcasts
at Unalaska.
"Japanese in Alaska," *Outlook*, August, 1906.
"Record of Japanese Vessels Driven Upon the
Northwest Coast," paper read before the American
Antiquarian Society, 1872, by Horace Davis.
"Japanese Wrecks, Stranded and Picked up Adrift
in the North Pacific Ocean, Ethnologically Con-
sidered," paper read before the California Academy
of Sciences, 1875.

JAQUES, FLORENCE PAGE (b. 1890)
As Far as the Yukon. New York: Harper, 1951. 243 pp. Travel.

JARVIS, DAVID H.
Report, Cruise of the US Revenue Cutter *Bear.* Wn.DC: GPO, 1900. Lt. Jarvis with three companions was landed on Nunivak Island. They collected reindeer and drove them to Barrow for the relief of American whalers marooned there, and reported to be starving. Jarvis later became a customs collector, and later still worked for the Northwest Fisheries Co., an affiliate of the Alaska Syndicate. He became a political figure of note and influence. He was credited with suppressing a smallpox epidemic at Nome in 1899. Gruening reports (p. 337) that Jarvis committed suicide when he was named in an action by the federal government to recover for fraud in the sale of coal to Army posts in Alaska. Two other company officials were convicted and received prison sentences. See *Alaska-Yukon Magazine,* December, 1908.

JARVIS, J. R.
"Cape Nome Gold Rush," *Journ. of the West,* IX (April, 1970): 153-195.

JARVIS, WILLIAM HENRY POPE
The Great Gold Rush, Toronto: Macmillan, 1913. 355 pp.

JEANCON, JEAN A., and FREDERIC H. DOUGLAS
Northwest Coast Indians. Denver: Denver Art Museum, 1930.

JEANNETTE
Caswell; DeLong; Ellsberg; Gilder; *History of the Jeannette;* Melville; Muir (*Corwin*); Newcombe; Perry, R.; Stuck; see also the following:
Alaska Sportsman, June, '43; April, '52; Hulley; US Congress, House Misc. Doc. No. 66, 48th Cong., 1st Sess. (Committee on Naval Affairs).

JEBB, RICHARD
Studies in Colonial Nationalism. London: Edward Arnold, 1905. Chapter on the Alaska boundary.

JEFFERY, EDMOND C.
Alaska. Anchorage: Jeffery Publishing Co., 1955. 212 pp. Who's Who.

JEFFERYS, THOMAS
The Great Probability of a Northwest Passage. London: 1768. 155 pp. Jefferys also translated into English C.F. Muller's *Voyages from Asia to America.* See also T-2336 ff.

JENKINS, JAMES TRAVIS
Whales and Modern Whaling. London: H.F. & G. Witherby, 1932.

JENKINS, THOMAS (b. 1871)
The Man of Alaska; Peter Trimble Rowe. New York: Morehouse-Gorham, 1943. 340 pp. Bishop Rowe was the first Episcopal Bishop of Alaska, serving from 1895 to 1942. Jenkins was Bishop in Alaska as well, building St. John's Church, Ketchikan. Bishop Rowe is buried at St. Peters-by-the-Sea, Sitka, which he built.

JENNESS, DIAMOND (b. 1886)
Dawn in Arctic Alaska. Minneapolis: Univ. of Minnesota Press, 1957. 222 pp. This is primarily a history of the Stefansson expedition from 1913 to 1919. It includes the story of the loss of the *Karluk,* Stefansson's principal ship.
"Archaeological Investigations in Bering Strait, 1926," in *Bulletin,* National Museum, Canada, 1928.
"The Eskimo of Northern Alaska: A Study in the Effect of Civilization," *Geographical Review,* February, 1918.
"Little Diomede Island, Bering Strait," *Geog. Rev.,* Jan., 1929.
"Prehistoric Culture Waves from Asia to America," *Journal,* Washington Academy of Sciences, Jan., 1940. Concl.: No extensive migration across the Bering Strait, except perhaps Eskimo, since early centuries of the Christian era; Kamchatka-Aleutian route also ruled out. Resemblances between Paleo-Asiatics and modern New Mexico Indians do not demand a post-Christian migration.
The People of the Twilight. New York: Macmillan, 1928. Chicago: University of Chicago Press, 1959. 251 pp. Two years among primitive Eskimos at Coronation Gulf, Arctic Ocean.
"Stray Notes on the Eskimo of Arctic Alaska," *Anthrop. Papers,* University of Alaska, 1953.
See also the Arctic Bibliography.

JENSEN, B. B.
"Alaska's Pre-Klondike Mining: The Men, the Methods, and the Minerals," *Journ. of the West,* VI (1967): 417-432.

JENSEN, RONALD J.
The Alaska Purchase and Russian-American Relations. Seattle: University of Washington Press, 1975. 185 pp. Excellent summary.

JESSON, EDWARD R.
"From Dawson to Nome on a Bicycle," *Pac. Northwet Quart.,* July, 1956. Trip made in 1900.

JESUIT MISSIONS
A monthly periodical published in New York. The magazine carried numerous articles on the Alaska missions. See also *Oregon Jesuit.* Catholic mission activity in Alaska seems to have begun with four Oblates of Mary Immaculate who preached along the Yukon River in 1862, to 1873, the Canadians Seguin, Petitot, Lecorre, and Monsignor Clut. Archbishop Charles Seghers of Victoria came in 1877. Jesuits from Italy, France, Spain, Ireland, Canada and the US came later, with US Jesuits exercising jurisdiction from 1912. Secular priests were introduced in all but the most remote areas in the 1960's.

JETTE, JULES (ca. 1864-1927)
Catholic Church, Liturgy and Ritual in the Tinne Language. Winnipeg: Free Press, 1904. 124 pp.
"The Jottings of an Alaskan Missionary," unpub. ms. in Jesuit Archives, Oregon Province, Crosby Library, Gonzaga University, Spokane, Washington.
"On the Language of the Ten'a," *Man* (anthrop.), 1907-09.
"L'Alaska," *Revue Canadienne,* Spring, 1893.
See also the Arctic Bibliography. On Jette see the following: Cameron; Savage; *Jesuit Missions,* 1958.

JEWITT, JOHN RODGERS (1783-1821)
A Journal Kept at Nootka Sound. Boston, 1807. Reprint, Boston: Goodspeed, 1931. 91 pp.
Narrative of the Adventures and Sufferings of John R. Jewitt. New York, 1815. 166 pp. Written by Richard Alsop.
See also Aumack (*Rivers of Rain*) and Garst (*John Jewitt's Adventure*). Jewitt was an armorer on the *Boston* which was attacked by Chief Maquinna while lying in Nootka Sound in March, 1803. Only two men survived, kept in captivity for four years. The books relate Jewitt's observations.
The Captive of Nootka. New York: Peaslee, 1835. 259 pp. See also T-2353 ff.

J. L. S.; see Staehlin von Storcksburg, Jakob. Also see Neue Nachrichten.

JOCHELSON, WALDEMAR (Vladimir Il'ich) (1855-1937)
Aleut Folk Lore. New York: Columbia University Press, n.d.
Archaeological Investigations in the Aleutian Islands. Wn.DC: Carnegie Institute, 1925. 145 pp.
History, Ethnology and Anthropology of the Aleut. Wn.DC: Carnegie Institute, 1933. 91 pp.
"Scientific Results of the Ethnological Section of the Riabushinskii Expedition," *Proceedings*, Internat'l. Cong. of Americanists, 1912.
"The Aleut Language and Its Relation to the Eskimo Dialects," *Proceedings*, Internat'l. Cong. of Americanists, 1912.
"The Aleutian Language in the Light of Veniaminov's Grammar (in Russian), *Bulletin*, Akademiia Nauk SSSR, Spring, 1919.
"The Ancient and Present Kamchadal and the Similarity of Their Culture to that of the Northwestern American Indians," *Proceedings*, Internat'l. Cong. of Americanists, 1928.
"Archaeological Investigations in Kamchatka," reprinted as *Carnegie Institute Publication No. 388*, 1928. Includes data on Japanese shipwrecks, early Russian fur tribute, history of early explorations, etc.
The Koryak. New York: Stechert, 1905-08. 842 pp.
"The Mythology of the Koryak," *Amer. Anthrop.*, 1904. Comparative.
Peoples of Asiatic Russia. New York: Amer. Museum of Natural History, 1928. 259 pp.
"Past and Present Subterranean Dwellings of the Tribes of Northeastern Asia and Northwestern America," *Proceedings*, Internat'l. Cong. of Amer., 1906.
Jochelson spent a lifetime studying the cultures of peoples on both sides of the Bering Sea. See the Arctic Bibliography for a full listing of his many works.

JOERG, WOLFGANG LOUIS GOTTFRIED
Brief History of Polar Exploration. New York: American Geographical Society, 1930. 50 pp. From the advent of aviation. See also T-2360 ff.

JOHANSEN, DOROTHY O. and CHARLES M. GATES
Empire of the Columbia. New York: Random House, 1957.

JOHN, BETTY
Seloe, the Story of a Fur Seal. Cleveland: World Publishing Co., 1955. 185 pp.

JOHNSHOY, WALTER
Apaurak in Alaska: Social Pioneering Among the Eskimos. Philadelphia: Dorrance, 1944. 325 pp. T.L. Brevig.

JOHNSON, ALBERT (b. 1869)
The Defense of Alaska: The Union of the White Race and the Problem of Universal Peace. Speech in the US House of Representatives, August, 1913. Wn.DC: GPO, 1913. 14 pp.

JOHNSON, ALBIN
See Covenant Frontiers.

JOHNSON, EBENEZER
A Short Account of a Voyage. Boston, 1798. In the years 1796-98. See Smith's Bibliography, S-5235 ff.

JOHNSON, FREDERICK
"An Archaeological Survey of the Alaska Highway, 1944," *Amer. Antiquity*, XI (1946): 183-86.

JOHNSON, HUGH ALBERT (b. 1913)
Present and Potential Agricultural Areas in Alaska. Palmer, Alaska: Agricultural Experiment Station, 1953. 28 pp.
Urban Use of Alaskan Farm Products. Palmer: Agr. Exp. Sta., 1953. 20 pp.
Family Farm Agreements for Alaska. College: Univ. Ext. Serv., 1953. 20 pp.
Using Alaska's Native Grasslands. College: Univ. Ext. Serv., 1954. 12 pp.
Land Occupancy, Ownership and Use. Palmer: Agr. Exp. Sta., 1956. 31 pp. Kenai Peninsula.
See the Arctic Bibliography for a full listing of Johnson's works, and O. Miller for his role in Matanuska Valley agriculture.

JOHNSON, HUGH A. and KEITH L. STANTON
Matanuska Valley Memoir. Palmer: Univ. of Alaska and US Agri. Exp. Sta., 1955.

JOHNSON, HUGH A. and HAROLD T. JORGENSON
The Land Resources of Alaska: A Conservation Foundation Study. New York: University Publishers, 1963. 551 pp. For the University of Alaska.

JOHNSON, MADINE
Journey of Enchantment. New York: Exposition Press, 1956.

JOHNSON, MARGARET S. and HELEN LOSSING JOHNSON
The Smallest Puppy. New York: Harcourt Brace, 1940. 88 pp.

JOHNSON, WILLIAM E.
Alaska, Through the Rhymes of a Construction Stiff. Seattle: Craftsman Press, 1956. 72 pp.

JOHNSON, WILLIS F.
Life of Warren G. Harding. Philadelphia: John C. Winston, 1923. 288 pp.

JOHNSTON, ALVA
The Legendary Mizners. New York: Farrar, Straus and Young, 1953. See also Addison Mizner, and E.D. Sullivan.

JOHNSTON, SAMUEL PERRY (b. 1865)
The Alaska Commercial Company, 1868-1940. San Francisco: E.E. Wachter, Printer, 1940. 65 pp.

JONAS, CARL
Beachhead on the Wind. Boston: Little, Brown, 1945. 212 pp. Aleutians in WW II.

JONES, CHARLES D.
Vagrant Verse by Charley. Nome: Nome Publishing Co., 1962.

JONES, CHARLES J.
Buffalo Jones' 40 Years of Adventure. Topeka: Crane & Co., 1899. 469 pp. Preservation.

JONES, DOROTHY M.
"Child Welfare Problems in An Alaska Native Village," *Social Service Review,* XLIII (1969): 296-309.

JONES, DOUGLAS N.
"Alaska's Economy: The State of the State," *Alaska Review,* Fall, 1966.

JONES, ERNEST LESTER (1876-1929)
Report of Alaska Investigations in 1914. Wn.DC: GPO, 1915. 155 pp. Report by the Deputy Commissioner of Fisheries of the Bureau of Fisheries steamer *Albatross'* Alaska fish investigation; also fur seals and fur farming.

JONES, H. WENDY
Man and the Mountain. Anchorage: Alaskan Printing Co., and Graphic Arts Press, 1962. 76 pp. Paintings of Sydney Laurence.

JONES, HERSCHEL V.
Adventures in Americana, 1492-1897. New York: W.E. Rudge, 1928. 2v.

JONES, JOHN WILLIAMS
The Salmon. New York: Harper, 1959. 19 pp.

JONES, LAURA BUCHAN
See Laura Buchan.

JONES, LIVINGSTON FRENCH (1865-1928)
A Study of the Thlingets of Alaska. New York: F.H. Revell, 1914. 261 pp.
Indian Vengeance. Boston: Stratford Company, 1920. 68 pp. Livingston Jones was pastor of Memorial Presbyterian Church, Juneau, 1905-1913.

JONES, N. W.
Indian Bulletin for 1868. N.pl.: C.A. Alvord, 1869. 26 pp. Brief account of Chinese voyages to the northern coast of America, name interpretation.

JONES, ROBERT D.
"A Municipal Farmer," *Alaska-Yukon Magazine,* August, 1907. Dyea; Klatt ranch.
"Sitka Today," *Alaska-Yukon Magazine,* October, 1907.

"Correspondence of a Crook: Soapy Smith," *Alaska-Yukon Magazine,* January, 1908.
"The Washington-Alaska Military Cable and Telegraph System," *Alaska-Yukon Magazine,* July, 1907.

JONES, STUART E.
"Charting our Sea and Air Lanes," *National Geographic,* February, 1957. US Coast and Geodetic Survey.

JONES, WILLIAM BENJAMIN (b. 1866)
The Argonauts of Siberia. Philadelphia: Dorrance, 1927. 165 pp. Prospecting and Trading.

JORDAN, DAVID STARR (1851-1931)
The Days of Man. Yonkers-on-Hudson, New York: World Book Company, 1922 2v. Autobiographical.
The Fur Seals and the Fur Seal Islands. Wn.DC: GPO, 1898-99. 4v. US Treasury Department. With Leonhard Stejneger, Frederick Lucas, J.F. Moser, Charles H. Townsend, George A. Clark, Joseph Murray, and others.
Matka and Katik: A Tale of the Mist Islands. San Francisco: Whitaker and Ray, 1897. 68 pp.
"Bogoslofs," *Pop. Sci. Monthly,* December, 1906.
"The Silent City of Muir Glacier," *Pop. Sci. Monthly,* June, 1897.
"Colonial Lessons of Alaska," *Atlantic Monthly,* November, 1898.

JORDAN, G. F.
"Redistribution of Sediments in Alaskan Bays and Inlets," *Geographic Review,* LII (1962): 548-558.

JORDAN, JED
Fool's Gold. New York: John Day, 1960. 255 pp. An unrefined account of Alaska in 1899.

JORDAN, MARILYN
"Trolling Poles," six installments in *Alaska Sportsman,* September, 1947 to February, 1948.

JOSEPHSON, KARLA
Use of the Sea by Alaska Natives: A Historical Perspective. University of Alaska, Arctic Environment Information and Data Center (Anchorage), 1974.

JOSLIN, FALCON
"Agriculture in the Tanana Valley," *Alaska-Yukon Magazine,* November, 1909.
Alaska: Proposed Legislation for Government Construction of Railroads and Leasing of Coal Lands. An Address, 15th Session, American Mining Congress, Spokane, 1912. 20 pp.
The Needs of Alaska. Address, annual meeting, American Mining Congress, 1921.
See Wickersham's Bibliography.

JOY, EDMUND STEELE
The Right of Territories to Become States of the Union. Newark, N.J.: Advertizer Printing House, 1892.

JUDGE, CHARLES JOSEPH (d. ca. 1907)
An American Missionary. Baltimore: J. Murphy, 1904. 293 pp. William H. Judge, S.J. Born in Baltimore in 1850, Judge came to Alaska in 1890, to Holy Cross Mission. He went to Nulato (1892-94) and

Fortymile (1895-97), and followed the gold rush to Dawson, where he built a hospital. He was regarded as particularly selfless, dying of pneumonia at Dawson in January, 1899.

JUDGE, JAMES
"The Blue Foxes of the Pribilof Islands," Amer. Breeder's Assn. *Annual Report*, 1908.
See also the Arctic Bibliography.

JUDSON, KATHARINE BERRY (b. ca. 1880)
Subject Index to the History of the Pacific Northwest and of Alaska, as found in the United States Government Documents, Congressional Series, in the American State Papers, and in other Documents, 1789-1881. Prepared for the Seattle Public Library. Olympia: Lamborn, Public Printer, 1913. 341 pp. Published by the Washington State Library.
Pacific Northwest. Seattle Public Library, 1910. 12 pp.
Myths and Legends of Alaska. Chicago: A.C. McClurg, 1911. 148 pp.

JUNEAU
Adams; *Alaska Life*, Aug., '39; Aug., '40; Sept., '41; Nov., '41; Feb., '42 (night photo); Jan., '44; July, '45 (Juneau issue); Dec., '46; Feb., '47; Aug., '48, and others; *Alaska Sportsman*, see Index; *Alaska Searchlight* (see the Alaska State Historical Library); *Alaska Weekly*; *Alaska-Yukon Magazine*, Sept., '07 (special Gastineau issue); March, '07 (photo); March, '10; Apr., '10; Dec., '11; Andrews; Badlam; Beach; Beckley, F. (*Amer. Alpine Journ.*, 1950); Boyle (*Alaska Mag.*, '27); Bright; Brooks; Bruce; Butler and Dale; Cameron; Carpenter; Carter; Chase; Colby; Collis; Corser; Couch; Davis; DeBaets; DeArmond; DeVighne; Denison; Dole; Foster; Franck; Greely; Gruening; Harris, R.; Hart; Hellenthal; Henderson; Herron; Higginson; Hilscher; Hulley; Jacobin; Jenkins; Kitchener; Krug; Kuehnelt-Leddihn; Miller, M.M.; Morgan and Keithahn; Muir; Munoz; Nichols; Petrof; Pierce (newspaper clippings from 1889); Pilgrim; Potter; Rickard (summary, capital move); Rossiter; Rutzebeck; Savage (Crimont); Scidmore; Shiels; Small; Stuck; Sundborg; Swineford; Taylor, C.; Tewkesbury; Tompkins; Underwood; Vancouver; Ward; Willoughby; Winslow; Young.

JUNEAU ICECAP or ICEFIELD
Alaska Sportsman, Oct., '54 (photo); Nov., '54 (snow fleas); March, '55 (photo); July, '55 (research project); Aug., '55 (photo Grumman SA 16); Aug. '56; July, '59; *Geogr. Review*, Oct., '49 (research proj.); Griscom (*Harvard Mountaineering*, June, 1951); Magoun (*Apalachia*, June, 1949); Miller, M.M.; Putnam (*Apalachia*, Dec., 1949).

JUNEAU, JOE (1836-1899)
Bancroft; Clark; Colby; Denison; Hulley; Morgan (had restaurant in Dawson); Tompkins; Wickersham; Winslow; *Alaska Sportsman*, June, '41 (photo, memorial); *Alaska-Yukon Mag.*, Sept., '07 (photos, Juneau, Harris); Dec., '08 (graves); n. 1887 was chosen as the year before which Alaska residence was required for membership in the Alaska Pioneers because $87.00 was the cost of returning Harris' body to Juneau for burial in 1907; see Harris.

JUVENAL, IEROMONAKH (d. 1796)
Journal, partial, trans. Ivan Petrof, in *Papers*, Kroeber Anthropological Society, 1952. This journal is reported to have been in the possession of Fr. Shashnikon at Unalaska at one time. See also Smith, B.

K

KACHADOORIAN, REUBEN
Effects of the Earthquake (1964) on the Communities of Kodiak and Nearby Islands. Wn.DC: GPO, 1967. USGS.

KALLINIKOV, N. F.
See T-2404.

KANE, ELISHA KENT (1820-1857)
Arctic Explorations; The Second Grinnell Expedition. Philadelphia: Childs and Peterson, 1856. 2v. In search of Franklin, 1853-55.
The US Grinnell (First) Expedition in Search of Sir John Franklin. New York: Harper, 1853. 552 pp. 1850-51.
See the Arctic Bibliography for further works; see also biographical material by William Elder, and M. Jones.

KANE, PAUL
Wanderings of an Artist among the Indians of North America. London: Longmans, 1859. 455 pp.

KANE, THOMAS L.
Alaska and the Polar Regions. New York, 1868. 32 pp.

KANGUK and WILLIAM ALBEE
Kanguk, a Boy of Bering Strait. Boston: Little, Brown, 1939. 116 pp.

KANTISHNA (District)
Alaska Sportsman, Dec., '50; Dec., '42; Aug., '47; June, '48; March, '50, and others, see Index; Colby; Couch (post office 1905-06, and 1929-36); Hall (Fannie Quigley and Johnny Busia); Stuck (strike in 1905); Wickersham (changed Dugan River to Kantishna).

KARELIN, DMITRII BORISOVICH (1913-1953)
Moria Nashei Rodiny (Seas of Our Country). Leningrad: 1954. 342 pp.

KARO, H. A.
Emergency Charting of the Alaska Earthquake Disaster Area. Manila, 1964. 20 pp. United Nations.

KARR, H. W.
Shores and Alps of Alaska. London, 1887. 262 pp.

KARLUK (vessel)
Bartlett; Chafe, E. (*Geog. Journ.*, May, 1918); McConnell (*Harper's*, Feb., 1915); Stefansson; Wead. Serving as Stefansson's flagship in 1913, the *Karluk* (Capt. Bartlett) was caught in ice near Flaxman Island and drifted to the vicinity of Wrangel Island where she sank in January, 1914. The crew managed to sail to safety.

KARLUK (village)
Alaska Sportsman, June, '58 (river mouth nearly closed, great runs over); Bancroft; Couch (post office 1892-1906, and from 1930); Hawthorne; Higginson; Scidmore.

KARSTENS, HENRY P. (1878-1955)
Alaska Sportsman, June, '50; Brooks; Chase; Farquhar; Washburn (Karsten's diary of Mt. McKinley ascent). Karstens was first superintendent of Mt. McKinley National Park.

KASAAN NATIONAL MONUMENT
Alaska Sportsman, July, '40 (cannery photo); Oct., '41 (photo); Colby; Corser; Krieger; Young (knew village before desertion).

KASHEVAROFF, ANDREW P. (1863-1940)
Alaska Historical Museum. Juneau: Alaska Hist. Assn., 1922. 61 pp.
Annual Report to the Governor, Librarian and Curator, Alaska Historical Library and Museum. Odd years, 1923-39.
"Father Herman," reprinted from *Valaam Monastery Ascetics*, St. Petersburg, 1872.
"Ivan Veniaminov, Innocent, Metropolitan of Moscow," *Alaska Magazine*, January, 1927.
"Uncle Sam Takes Possession," *Alaska Magazine*, Jan., 1927.
On Kashevaroff, see the following:
Dynes' Tours; Franck; *Sunset*, April, 1923; Willoughby.

KASHEVAROV,   ALEKSANDR   FILIPPOVICH (1809-1870)
See T-2416.

KATALLA
Alaska-Yukon Magazine, Aug., '07 (J.F.A. Strong); March, '08 (coal); Colby; Couch (post office here 1904-43; former post office, Controller Bay); Higginson (poor harbor, railroad problems); Nichols (coal troubles); Whiting ("birth" and "death"); Willoughby; see also the *Katalla Herald*, published 1907-09.

KATMAI NATIONAL MONUMENT
Alaska Sportsman, see Index; Bancroft (small Russian station here, oil on lake); Chase (1912 eruption described); Colby; Franck; Hubbard; Griggs (authority); Hart (tourism); Stuck; Sundborg; Underwood (effects of the eruption on Kodiak Island, and the *Dora*); Wead (*Bear* and *Manning* at Kodiak, 1912); Willoughby; Winslow.

KAVANAUGH, ETHEL (b. 1901)
Wilderness Homesteaders. Caldwell, Idaho: Caxton Printers, 1950. 303 pp. Autobiographical.

KAWAGLEY, DOLORES
Yupik Stories. Anchorage: Alaska Methodist University Press, 1975.

KEELER, CHARLES
Days Among Alaska Birds. In Harriman's *Alaska*, Vol. 2.

KEELER, NICHOLAS EDWIN (b. 1851)
A Trip to Alaska in 1905. Cincinnati: Ebbert and Richardson, 1906. 115 pp.

KEEN, DORA
"Studying Alaskan Glaciers," *Bulletin*, Geog. Soc., Philadelphia, 1915.
"Exploring Harvard Glacier," *Harper's*, 1915.
"Arctic Mountaineering by a Woman: Mt. Blackburn," *Scribner's*, 1912.
"The First Expedition to Mt. Blackburn," *Bulletin*, Geog. Soc., 1912.
"First up Mt. Blackburn," *World's Work*, 1913.
"Woman in the Wilderness," *Harper's*, 1914.

KEEN, J. H.
Trans. *Portions of the Book of Common Prayer in Haida.* London: Society for Promoting Christian Knowledge, 1899. 39 pp.

KEEP, JOSIAH
West Coast Shells. San Francisco: Whitaker and Ray, 1904. 300 pp. Also Stanford University Press, 1935.

KEESING, ELDEE
Gorham's Gold. Boston: R.G. Badger, 1915. 357 pp.

KEIM, CHARLES
Aghvook: White Eskimo. College: University of Alaska Press, 1969. 313 pp. Otto Geist and Alaska Archaeology.

KEIM, DeBENNEVILLE RANDOLPH
Our Alaskan Wonderland and Klondike Neighbor. Wn.DC: Harrisburg Publishing Co., 1898. 352 pp.

KEITHAHN, EDWARD LINNAEUS (b. 1900)
"Adventure: Stranger than Fiction," *Alaska Sportsman*, December, 1938.
"Willi Waw: Kodiak Man," *Al. Sports.*, June, 1948.
"There's Magic in the Arctic," *Al. Sports.*, July, 1942.
"The Husky is Much the Larger Breed," *Al. Sports.*, Nov., 1943.
"Eskimo Christmas," *Al. Sports.*, Dec., 1939.
Igloo Tales. Lawrence, Kansas: US Indian Service, 1950. 142 pp.
Alaska and Hawaii. New York: Macmillan, 1956. 312 pp.
"Let's Lease an Island," *Al. Sports.*, June, 1941.
"An Outpost of Civlization in the Arctic," *Travel*, Aug., 1927. Shishmaref.
"Chirikov First Saw Land," *Al. Sports.*, Feb., 1941.
"Alaska Ice, Inc.: History of Operations of the Ice Industry in Alaska in 1850," *Pacific Northwest Quarterly*, Apr., 1945.

"The Cremation of Chief Kowee," *Al. Sports.*, March, 1955.

"Legend and Fact about Glass Floats," *Sunset*, Sept., 1949.

"When Animals were People," *Al. Sports.*, May, 1940.

"Alaska's Copper Currency," *Al. Sports.*, May, 1942.

"Human Hair as a Decorative Feature in Tlingit Ceremonial," *Anthrop. Papers*, University of Alaska, 1954.

"Curators Aren't Born That Way," *Alaska Life*, Dec., 1943.

"Hunting Without a Gun," *Al. Sports.*, Jan., 1937.

"Fishing Without a Hook," *Al. Sports.*, Oct., 1937.

"A Tribute to Old Man Raven," *Al. Sports.*, June, 1937.

"It's All Very Confusing," *Al. Sports.*, July, 1944. Plant naming.

"The Secret of Petroglyphs," *Al. Sports.*, March, 1939.

"The Petroglyphs of Southeastern Alaska," *Amer. Antiquity*, Oct., 1940.

"The Tools of the Petroglyph Mason," *Proceedings*, Alaska Science Conf., 1940.

"God's Demons and Ancestral Spirits," *Al. Sports.*, Dec., '42.

Monuments in Cedar. Ketchikan: Ray Anderson, 1945. 160 pp.

"Notes on the Origin of the Totem Pole," *Proceedings*, Alaska Science Conf., 1951.

"Return of the Raven," *Al. Sports.*, April, 1940.

"Story of the Lincoln Totem," *Al. Sports.*, May, 1943.

Alaska for the Curious. Seattle: Superior Publishing Co., 1966. 160 pp.

Eskimo Adventure: Another Journey into the Primitive. Seattle: Superior Publishing Co., 1963. 170 pp.

See also T-2428, ff.

KELLETT, HENRY
Narrative of the Voyage of HMS Herald. London: Reeve, 1853. 171 pp. In search of Franklin, Kellett, commanding *Herald*, discovered and named Herald Island, northwest of Bering Strait, and was the first to sight Wrangel Island, which he mistook for the continent. See Mirsky. Kellett was in Kotzebue Sound in 1849.

KELLOGG, ALBERT (1813-1887)
"Botany," *Annual Report*, US Coast and Geodetic Survey, 1867.

KELLOGG, C. E. and I. J. NYGARD
The Principal Soil Groups of Alaska. Wn.DC: GPO, 1951. USDA.

KENAI PENINSULA
Bancroft; Berkh; Chevigny; Cook; Coxe; Dall; Davydov; Grewingk; Holmberg; Hrdlicka; Khlebnikov; Langsdorff; Lisianski; Lutke; Pallas; Petrof; Sarychev; Sauer; Shelekhov; Tarenetski; Tikhmenev; Tompkins; Vancouver; Veniaminov; Whymper; see also Sherwood (Cook Inlet Collection).

KENAI (village)
Bancroft (Konovalov built Ft. St. Nicholas, 1791; Zaikov succeeded Konovalov, 1793; Fr. Juvenal here 1796, Baranov, 1800); Brooks (teacher's life, 1911-14); Baker; Chevigny; Swineford; Vancouver; see also Sherwood (Cook Inlet Collection). See also Fedorova.

KENDRICK, JOHN; see Wagner.

KENDRICK, SYLVESTER J.
Chilkoot Pass, and Songs of Alaska. Los Angeles: Coast Printing Co., 1926. 61 pp. Poetry.

KENEDY, P. J. and Sons
Official Catholic Directory. Lists Catholic churches and mission stations in Alaska, with priests assigned. Lists also schools and hospitals. Annual.

KENNAN, GEORGE (1845-1924)
Tent Life in Siberia and Adventures among the Koriaks. New York: Putnam's, 1870. 425 pp. While with the Overland Telegraph Expedition.
E.H. Harriman: A Biography. Boston: Houghton, 1922. 2v.
"A Dog-sledge Journey in Kamchatka and Northeastern Siberia," *Amer. Geog. Soc. Journal*, 1876.
"Siberia: Exile's Abode," *Amer. Geog. Soc. Journal*, 1882. Tompkins remarks that Kennan provided the first account of the Siberia exile system with this work.

KENNAN, GEORGE F.
"Russia and the Alaska Purchase," *Amer. Foreign Serv. Journal*, February, 1938.

KENNECOTT COPPER CORPORATION
Annual Report, from 1915. See also the following:
"The Great Bonanza Copper Mine," *Alaska-Yukon Magazine*, December, 1910. See also notes in *Alaska Sportsman*, August, 1952 and May, 1957. See as well N.H. Dole. The Kennicott Glacier in the upper Chitina River valley was named by explorers in the late 19th century. The Guggenheim-Morgan people named the Kennecott Copper Corporation from a USGS map of the area on which Robert Kennicott's name on the glacier had been misspelled. For further information on the Kennecott Copper Corp. see the annual reports of the governors of the territory of Alaska, and the *Cordova Times*.

KENNEDY, HOWARD ANGUS
The Book of the West. Toronto: Ryerson Press, 1925. 205 pp. Canada.

KENNEDY, KAY J.
The Wien Brothers' Story. Fairbanks, 1967. 38 pp.

KENNICOTT, ROBERT (1835-1866)
Journal, printed in James Alton James, in which there is a bibliography of Kennicott's writings on natural history.
Journal, in *Transactions*, Chicago Academy of Sciences, 1867-69, which also includes a biography.
See also Stearns, and as well, Taylor.
"Russian America," by J. Kershner, in *Alaska Life*, June, '46. See also Sherwood.

KENT, ROCKWELL
A Northern Christmas. New York: American Artists Group, 1941. 26 pp.
Rockwellkentiana. New York: Lakeside Press, 1933. 100 pp.
Wilderness. New York: Putnam's, 1920. 217 pp. See also T-2443.

KERN, EDITH (b. ca. 1866-1941)
A Little Journey to Alaska. Chicago: Flanagan, 1901. 95 pp. Juvenile.
Little Journeys to Alaska and Canada. Chicago: Flanagan, 1923. 94 pp.

KERNER, ROBERT JOSEPH (b. 1887)
Russian Expansion to America. Chicago: Bibliographical Society of America Papers, 1931. 129 pp. Chevigny calls this the most complete bibliography on the subject.
Northeastern Asia: A Selected Bibliography. Berkeley: University of California, 1939. 2v.

KESSEL, BRINA, ROBERT B. WEEDEN and GEORGE C. WEST
Bird-finding in Interior and Southcentral Alaska. N.pl.: Alaska Ornithological Society, 1967. 42 pp.

KETCHIKAN
Alaska Life, Jan., '42 (Sid Charles); Jan., '44; Sept., '45 (Ketchikan issue); Aug., '48; *Alaska Sportsman*, see Index; *Alaska-Yukon Magazine*, March, '07 (photo); Aug., '09; Atwood; Bashford (*Al. Sports.*, March, '48); Bell; Bright; Browne; Caldwell; Cameron; Carpenter; Colby; Corser; Denison; Dole; Forster; Franck; Greely; Gruening; Hadman; Higginson; Herron; Hulley; Jacobin; Jenkins; Kitchener; Kuehnelt-Leddihn (*Geog. Review*, July, '46); Lawrence; McCarthy (*Amer. Forests*, Apr., '53, on Heintzleman); Meals (*Alaska Mag.*, 1927); Nichols; Oliver; Poor; Potter; Rossiter; Ryan; Scidmore; Stuck; Sundborg; Tewkesbury; Underwood; Uyeda; Vancouver; Ward; Willoughby; Wolfe.

KHLEBNIKOV, KIRIL TIMOFEEVICH (1780-1838)
Aleksandr Andreevich Baranov. St. Petersburg: Naval Press, 1835. Trans. Richard Pierce and published by Limestone Press, Kingston, Ontario, 1973. 209 pp.
Materials on the History of Russian Settlements along the Shores of the Eastern Ocean. In Russian. In four parts. The first two parts are by V.M. Golovnin. Part III contains notes by Khlebnikov on Russian colonies in America from 1800 to 1818, including Ft. Ross. Part IV contains exploration accounts, and Khlebnikov's notes on the Tlingit uprising of 1802.
Memoirs of California. Trans. A.G. Mazour in *Pacific Historical Review*, September, 1940. See the Arctic Bibliography for a full listing of Khlebnikov's works.

KHROMCHENKO, VASILII STEPANOVICH (d. 1849)
See the Arctic Bibliography, and James Van Stone.

KHVOSTOV, NIKOLAI ALEKSANDROVICH
See Gavril Ivanovich Davydov; see also Baker.

KING, JAMES
See T-2458 ff.

KING, A. RICHARD
The School at Mopass: A Problem of Identity. New York: Holt, Rinehart and Winston, 1967. Case Studies in Education and Culture.

KINGSTON, WILLIAM HENRY GILES (1814-1880)
Captain Cook: His Life, Voyages, and Discoveries. London: Religious Tract Society, 1871. 352 pp.

KIP, WILLIAM INGRAHAM
The Early Jesuit Missions in North America. Albany: Pease and Prentice, 1866. 325 pp.

KIPLING, RUDYARD (1865-1936)
"The Rhyme of the Three Sealers," in *The Seven Seas*, New York: Appleton, 1896. 209 pp.
"The White Seal," in *Jungle Book*, London: Macmillan, 1894.
"Lukannon," *Metropolitan Magazine*, March, 1907.

KIPPIS, ANDREW (1725-95)
The Life of Captain James Cook. London: G. Nichols & G.G.J. & J. Robinson, 1788. 527 pp.
Voyages Round the World from the Death of Captain Cook. New York: Harper, 1844. 410 pp.
Voyages Round the World Performed by Captain Cook. London: Cowie, Low & Co., 1826. 2v.

KIRBY, W. W.
A Journey to the Youcon, Russian America. Smithsonian Institution, Annual Report, 1864.

KIRK, ROBERT C.
Twelve Months in Klondike. London: Heinemann, 1899. 273 pp.

KIRKLAND, LOLA
Grandma Goes to the Arctic. Philadelphia: Dorrance, 1957. 279 pp.

KIRKWOOD, DEAN
The Salmon Industry in Alaska. Portland: C.C. Chapman Co., 1909. 59 pp.

KIRWAN, ARCHIBALD LAURENCE PATRICK
The White Road. London: Hollis and Carter, 1959. 374 pp. Polar exploration.

KITCHENER, LOIS DELANO (b. 1914)
Flag Over the North: The Story of the Northern Commercial Company. Seattle: Superior Publishing Co., 1954. 349 pp.
"The Fighting Earth Movers," *Alaska Life*, July, 1946.

KITSON, ARTHUR
Captain James Cook. New York: Dutton, 1907. 525 pp.
The Life of Captain James Cook. London: Murray, 1911. 334 pp.

KITTLITZ, FRIEDRICH HEINRICH
See T-2479.

KITTO, FRANKLIN HUGO (b. 1880)

Yukon: Land of the Klondike. Ottawa, 1929. 45 pp.

"The Survival of the American Bison in Canada," *Geog. Journ.*, May, 1924.

KIZER, BENJAMIN HAMILTON (b. 1878)

The US-Canadian Northwest. Princeton: Princeton University Press, 1943. 71 pp.

The North Pacific International Planning Project. New York: Institute of Pacific Relations, American Council, 1942.

KLABEN, HELEN and BETH DAY

Hey, I'm Alive! New York: McGraw-Hill, 1964.

KLAPPHOLZ, LOWELL

Gold! Gold! New York: McBride, 1959. 207 pp.

KLEBER, L. C.

"Alaska, Russia's Folly," *History Today*, XVII (1967): 229-235.

KLEIN, D. R., R. A. RAUSCH, and W. TROYER

The Status of the Brown Bear in Alaska. Wn.DC: GPO, 1958. Bur. Sport Fisheries, US Fish & Wildlife Serv.

KLEINFIELD, JUDITH

"Cognitive Strengths of Eskimos, and Implications for Education," Institute for Social, Economic and Government Research (ISEGR), *Occasional Paper No. 3, 1970.*

"Achievement Profiles of Native Ninth Graders, Fairbanks, Alaska," ISEGR, University of Alaska, 1970.

"Effective Teachers of Indian and Eskimo High School Students," ISEGR, University of Alaska, 1972.

"Using Nonverbal Warmth to Increase Learning: A Cross-cultural Experiment," ISEGR, University of Alaska, 1973.

"A Long Way from Home," ISEGR, University of Alaska, 1973.

"Land Claims and Native Manpower," ISEGR, University of Alaska, 1973.

Judy Kleinfield has been associated also with the Alaska Federation of Natives, and the Alaska Native Foundation.

KLEINSCHMIDT, F. E.

"A Hunter's Paradise," *Field and Stream*, August, 1910.

KLENGENBERG, CHRISTIAN (1869-1931)

Klengenberg of the Arctic: An Autobiography. London: J. Cape, 1932. 300 pp. Point Hope, Barrow, Herschel Island, and Rymer Point on Victoria Island.

KLONDIKE

Significant amounts of gold were found in the Klondike district of the Yukon Territory in 1896, on Rabbit, later Bonanza Creek, a tributary of the Klondike River, about 15 miles above its confluence with the Yukon. The discovery was made by George Carmacks or his Indian wife, on the advice of a Canadian, Robert Henderson. Carmacks was accompanied by two Indians, "Skookum Jim" and "Tagish Charley." The find was sufficiently significant to

spark a major rush to the territory by prospectors who had been panning for gold in the northwest since at least the 1850's when gold was discovered on the Frazer River, and the 1870's when it was found in the Cassiar district.

By the time news of the Klondike discovery reached the outside, all the important gold bearing creeks and lands had already been staked. But the hordes who came to Alaska went on to further strikes in the Chena basin, and at Nome, as well as minor rushes in such places as Ruby, Rampart, Iditarod and the like. Gold mining became an economic and political mainstay of Alaskan development.

Perhaps the best general work on the Klondike rush is that by Pierre Berton, which includes an excellent bibliography, with annotations. There are many very misleading and erroneous materials printed on the Klondike, making it mandatory for the researcher to seek authoritative judgment in evaluating any such book.

Along with Berton, see the following:

Adney; Allan; Anzer; Archer; Atwood; Armstrong; Auzias de Turenne; Averill; Bankson; Banon; Beach; Beattie; Becker; Beebe; Bell; Berton; Black; Bruce; Burns; Camsell; Canton; Carmacks; Cody; Collier; Coolidge; Cory; Coryell; Craig; Crane; Crewe; Cunynghame; Curtin; Dafoe; Dalby; Davis; Day; Denison; DeWindt; Dietz; Dill; Donnelly; Droonberg; Dow; Dunn; Edwards; Ellis; Fetherstonhaugh; Fraser; Garland; Garst; Graham; Graves; Grinnell; Hamlin; Harris; Haskell; Haverly; Hawthorne; Hayne; Hegg; Heilprin; Henderson; Hitchcock; Holland; Hunt; Ingersoll; Jarvis; Judge; Keeler; Keim; Kirk; Kitchener; LaRoche; Laytha; Leisher; Leonard; Lloyd-Owen; London; Longstreth; Lung; Lynch; MacDonald; McKeown; McLain; Mahoney; Margeson; Medill; Miers; Mizner; Morgan; Morrell; O'Connor; Ogilvie; Page; Palmer; Pike; Pocock; Prather; Price; Pringle; Quiett; Quinan; Rickard; Robertson; Romig; Roper; Sabin; Samuels; Scearce; Schwatka; Secretan; Service; Sharp; Sola; Spurr; Stanley; Steele; Stone; Sullivan; Thompson; Tollemach; Treadgold; Trelawney; Tuttle; Walden; Whiting; Wickersham; Wiedemann; Williamson; Winchester; Winslow; Young; Zaccarelli.

The following are Klondike guide books:

Alaska Commercial Co.; Aubert; Bramble; Caldwell; Cantwell; Chicago Record; Clark; Clements; Colliery Engr. Co.; Conkey; Coolidge; Crewe; Goodman; Grubstakes Pub. Co.; Hall; Heistand; Henley; Hills; Hinton; Ingersoll; Klondyke Mining Laws; Kootenay Guide; Ladue; Leehey; Leonard; Lindsey; Lord and Co.; Lowman and Hanford; Lugrin; Marvin; Miners' News; Montague; North Amer. T. & T. Co.; Ogilvie; Paramore; Rinfret; Stansbury; Washington and Alaska SS Co.; Wells; Wilson.

See as well T-2487 ff, the Arctic Bibliography, and the following:

Alaska Sportsman, Index; *Alaska-Yukon Magazine*, Sept., '08 (on the discovery); Nov., '08; May, '09; March, '10 (Lone Star first quartz mill); Brooks; Cameron; Chase; Clark; Colby; Caldwell; Higginson; Hulley; Hunt; Meeker; Nichols; Stuck; Sullivan; Wickersham; Wharton; Willoughby.

KLONDIKE "KATE"

See Kathleen Rockwell.

KNAPP, EDWARD EVERETT
Ah-re-gay: King of the Northland. Springfield, Mass.: Milton Bradley Co., 1931. 384 pp.

KNAPP, FRANCES
The Thlinkets of Southeastern Alaska. Chicago: Stone and Kimball, 1896. 197 pp.

KNAPP, LYMAN E.
"A Study upon the Legal and Political Status of the Natives of Alaska," *American Law Register,* XXX: 325-339.

KNIGHT, CLAYTON and ROBERT C. DURHAM
Hitch Your Wagon: The Story of Brent Balchen. Drexel Hill, Pa.: Bell Publishing Co., 1950. 332 pp. See also Balchen's autobiography.

KNIGHT, FRANK
Young Captain Cook. New York: Roy Publishing Co., 1966.

KNOPF, ADOLPH (b. 1882)
"The Probable Tertiary Land Connection between Asia and North America," *Bulletin,* University of California Department of Geology, 1910.

KNOWLTON, FRANK HALL
"Notes on Collection of Inter-glacial Wood from Muir Glacier," *Journ. of Geology,* 1895.

KNOX, THOMAS K.
The Voyage of the Vivian to the North Pole and Beyond. New York, 1885.

KODIAK and KODIAK ISLAND
Alaska Life, Apr., '40 (church bells); Nov., '41; Oct., '43; Sept., '48; *Alaska Sportsman,* see Index: Ameigh; Andreev; Baker; Bancroft; Barnaby; Bean; Blake; Burroughs (with a famous eulogy of Kodiak); Brooks; Caldwell; Campbell; Capps; Chevigny; Clark; Colby; Couch; Dall; Davidson; Davis; Davydov; Denison; Dole; Douglas; Erskine; Elliott; Golder; Golovnin; Greely; Griggs; Gruening; Hall; Hart; Heizer; Herbert; Higginson; Hilscher; Howard; Hrdlicka; Hulley; Jacobin; Jeffery; Kashevaroff; Kellogg; Kitchener; Kruzenstern; Langsdorff; Lantis; Lisianski; Lutke; Miller; Morris; Petrof; Potter; Sarychev; Sauer; Schuessler; Scidmore; Shepard; Sundborg; Swineford; Tanner; Tewkesbury; Thomas; Tompkins; Vancouver; Vrooman; Wead; Whymper; Willoughby; Winslow; Wolfe; Woollen.

KOENIG, DUANE
"Ghost Railway in Alaska: The Story of the Tanana Valley Railroad," *Pacific Northwest Quarterly,* January, 1954.

KOHAUT, KAREN
Alaska Natives in Higher Education. ISEGR, University of Alaska, 1974.

KOHLSTEDT, EDWARD DELOR
William Duncan. Palo Alto: National Press, 1957. 82 pp.

KOLARZ, WALTER
Peoples of the Soviet Far East. London: Philip, 1954. 193 pp.

KOO, TED SWEI-YEN
See T-2506 ff.

KOSMOS, GEORGE
Alaska Sourdough Stories. Seattle: Seal and West, 1956. 30 pp.

KOTZEBUE
Alaska Sportsman, Index; Aldrich (dozen igloos, 1887); Baker; Bancroft; Beechey; Colby; Franck (Quakers discourage Eskimo dancing); Giddings; Hart; Hulley; Illingworth; Kotzebue; McElwaine; O'Connor; Poor; Seemann; Stoney; Stuck; Swineford; Van Stone; Winslow. Although the site shows evidence of long use, the contemporary village of Kotzebue is of relatively recent origin. Former villages here were known as Kikiktak, Kikitaruk, and Point Blossom. Hudson Stuck commented on the disappearance of native names for the site. Tourism began here in 1947.

KOTZEBUE, AUGUSTUS von
See Dall. A. Kotzebue was the father of Otto Kotzebue.

KOTZEBUE, OTTO EVSTAFEVICH (1878-1846)
See the Arctic Bibliography. Kotzebue made numerous Arctic voyages. In 1816 he discovered Kotzebue Sound, and sighted the Krusenstern Promontory, and the Diomede Islands. In 1821 an English version of his 3 volume *Voyage to the Southern Ocean and Bering Strait* was issued. It should not be confused with an abridged version published in England the same year. See also *A New Voyage around the World in 1823-25,* 2v. (London: Henry Colburn and Richard Bentley, 1830). See also T-2516 ff.

KOVACH, MICHAEL GEORGE
"The Russian Orthodox Church in Russian America," unpublished doctoral dissertation, University of Pittsburgh, 1957.

KOWELUK, BOB and RICHARD APPLETON
The Outlook: Alaska Natives and their Careers. Anchorage: Alaska Methodist University Press, 1975.

KOYUK
Inman, Dorothy; articles in *Alaska Sportsman,* Sept., Nov., '42; Apr., Oct., Dec., '43; also Robert Inman, May, '43; see also Meyers (critical of Eskimos). The Inmans were school teachers.

KOYUKUK RIVER
Alaska Sportsman, Dec., '35 (prospectors); Jan., '40; Sept., '41 ($35,000 from Nolan Creek); Apr., '53 (photo); Oct., '54 (only 150 Koyukuk Indians remaining, in Huslia and Koyukuk); *Alaska-Yukon Magazine,* Oct., '08 (first marriage); Allen; Bancroft; Brooks (river discovered by Malakov, miners abandon steamers); Dall; Davis; Helmericks; Hulley; Higginson; Marshall; Stoney; Stuck; Wickersham; Zagoskin.

KOZELY, LADO A.
Community Facts Survey: Eklutna. Anchorage: Bureau of Indian Affairs, 1963.

KRADER, LAWRENCE
"Recent Trends in Soviet Anthropology," *Biennial Review of Anthropology*, 1959 (ed., B. Siegel).

KRAFT, WALTER C.
"Heceta: A Name with a Split Personality," *Names*, Dec., 1959.

KRASHENINNIKOV, STEPAN PETROVICH
See T-2531 ff.

KRASILOVSKY, PHYLLIS
Benny's Flag. Cleveland: World Publishing Co., 1960. unp.

KRATT, IVAN FEDOROVICH
Velikii Ocean (The Great Ocean). Leningrad, 1950. 552 pp.

KRAUSE, AUREL (1848-1908)
The Tlingit Indians. Seattle: University of Washington Press, 1956. 310 pp. Trans. of 1885 edition.

KRENITSIN, PETER KUZMICH and MIKHAIL LEVASHEV
See the Arctic Bibliography. Russian naval officers, Krenitsin and Levashev sailed from Kamchatka to the Aleutians on a significant voyage of exploration and charting in 1768-69.

KRESGE, DAVID, SUSAN R. FISON and ANTHONY R. GASBARRO
Bristol Bay: A Socio-economic Study. ISEGR, University of Alaska, 1974.

KRIEGER, HERBERT WILLIAM (b. 1889)
"Archaeological and Ethnological Studies in Southeast Alaska," Smithsonian Institution, *Miscellaneous Collections*, 1927.
"Indian Villages of Southeast Alaska," Smithsonian Institution, *Annual Report*, 1927.

KRUG, WERNER G.
Sprungbrett Alaska. Hamburg: Hoffmann and Campe, 1953. 368 pp.

KRUZENSHTERN, IVAN FEDOROVICH (1770-1846)
See the Arctic Bibliography for a complete bibliography. See also T-2549 ff. Kruzenshtern made numerous voyages from Kronstadt to Arctic waters, the first in 1804-05 with the Rezanov diplomatic mission to Japan. In 1827 he published an atlas of the Pacific. In 1856 Longmans, Green of London published an English translation of some of his Memoirs, edited by his daughter. And in 1813 Richard B. Hoppner translated his *Voyage Around the World in 1803-1806* (London: J. Murray, 1813, 2v.).

KUEHNELT-LEDDIHN, ERIK R. von
"Cities and Towns of Alaska," *Geog. Review*, July, 1946. Observations on development.

KUGELMASS, J. ALVIN
Roald Amundsen: A Saga of the Polar Seas. New York: Julian Messner, 1955. 191 pp.

KUMMER, FREDERIC ARNOLD (b. 1873)
The Perilous Island: A Story of Mystery in the Aleutians. Philadelphia: Winston, 1942. 212 pp.

KUNST, JAAP
Ethnomusicology. The Hague: Martinus Jijhoff, 1959. 303 pp.

KURSH, HARRY
This is Alaska. Englewood Cliffs: Prentice-Hall, 1961. 286 pp.

KUSHNER, HOWARD I.
Conflict on the Northwest Coast. London: Greenwood Press, 1975. xii & 225 pp. American-Russian Rivalry in the Pacific Northwest, 1790-1867. Essays the thesis that conflict and rivalry, particularly over economic resources, instead of amity, led to the Russian decision to sell its American possession to the U.S.
"The Russian Fleet and the American Civil War: Another View," *The Historian*, August, 1972.

KUSKOKWIM RIVER
Alaska Sportsman, see Index; Anderson; Bancroft; Clark; Dall; Gapp; Gordon; Helmericks; Hrdlicka; Hubback; Kitchener; Kutchin; Lipke; Pike; Petrof; Raymond; Schwalbe; Smith, B.; Spurr; VanStone; Wells; Zagoskin.

KUZNETSOV, I. V.; see T-2576.

L

LABILLARDIERE, JACQUES JULIEN HOUTON de (1755-1834)
An Account of a Voyage in Search of LaPerouse. London: Debrett, 1800. 2v. Labillardiere was a naturalist.

LABOR
See James Foster ("The Western Federation Comes to Alaska [*Pac NW Q*, Oct., 1975]). See also Gruening. See also Alaska (Ter.) Dept. of Labor, and US Dept. of Labor.

LADA-MOCARSKI, VALERIAN
Bibliography of Books on Alaska Published before 1868. New Haven: Yale University Press, 1969. 567 pp. This excellent volume includes facsimiles of title pages, and a full English translation of all titles listed.

LADUE, JOSEPH
Klondyke Nuggets. New York: American Technical Book Co., 1897. 92 pp.
Klondyke Facts. Montreal: J. Lovell, 1897. 205 pp. Ladue founded and named the town Dawson. From Plattsburg, New York, Ladue joined Harper and McQuesten on the Yukon in 1882. He built the first cabin and saloon on the Dawson site.

LA FAY, HOWARD
"DEW Line: Sentry of the Far North," *National Geographic*, '58.

LAFORTUNE, BELLARMINE (1869-1947)
A Collection of Prayers. Nome, 1916. 49 pp. See also Helen Savage.

LAGUNA, FREDERICA; see de Laguna.

LALOR, WILLIAM G.
"Submarine through the North Pole," *National Geographic*, 1959.

LAMBERT, CLARA (b. 1898)
The Story of Alaska. New York: Harper, 1940. 40 pp.

L'AMOUR, LOUIS
Sitka. New York: Appleton-Century-Croft, 1957. 245 pp.

LANDRU, JACK
Sled Dog of Alaska. New York: Dodd, Mead, 1953. 184 pp.

LANE, CHARLES D.
See Wild Goose Mining and Trading Company.

LANE, FRANKLIN KNIGHT (1864-1921)
"Progress of the Alaska Railroad," *Railway Age*, 1919 (2).
"Red Tape in Alaska," *Outlook*, 1915.
"Freeing Alaska from Red Tape," *North American*, 1915.
See Anne W. Lane and Louise H. Wall, *The Letters of Franklin K. Lane, Personal and Political* (Boston: Houghton, 1922; 473 pp.); see also Gruening. See also Scott Bone (*Sat. Eve. Post*, 1925).

LANE, FREDERICK A.
The Geatest Adventure: The Story of Jack London. New York: Aladdin Books, 1954. 192 pp.

LANE, ROSE WILDER
He Was a Man. New York: Harper, 1925. 380 pp. Jack London.

LANE-POOLE, STANLEY
Life of the Rt. Hon. Stratford Channing. New York, 1888. 2v.
See diplomacy; see Tompkins.

LANG, JOHN
The Story of Captain Cook. London: T.C. & E.C. Jack, 1906. 119 pp.

LANGSDORFF, GEORG HEINRICH (1774-1852)
Voyages and Travels in Various Parts of the World. London: Colburn, 1817. 617 pp. Kamchatka expedition, 1815. Vol. 2, Unalaska, Kodiak, Sitka, etc.
See Chevigny for an interpretation of the relationship between Rezanov and Langsdorff.
Langsdorff's Narrative of the Rezanov Voyage to Neuva California. San Francisco: T. Russell, 1927. 158 pp.
See also the Arctic Bibliography.

LANKS, HERBERT CHARLES (b. 1899)
Highway to Alaska. New York: Appleton-Century, 1944. 200 pp.

LANSING, ROBERT
"The Questions Settled by the Award of the Alaskan Boundary Tribunal," *Bulletin*, Amer. Geog. Soc., 1904.

LANTIS, DAVID W.
Alaska. Garden City: Doubleday, 1957. 64 pp.
"A Habitat of Early Man," *Geog. Review*, 1955. Cape Denbigh.

LANTIS, MARGARET (b. 1906)
"Mythology," *Journ. Amer. Folklore*, 1938. Kodiak Island.
"Alaskan Whale Cult," *Amer. Anthrop.*, 1940.
"Social Culture of the Nunivak Eskimo," *Transactions*, Amer. Philosophical Society, 1946.
Alaska Eskimo Ceremonialism. New York: J.J. Augustin, 1947. 127 pp.
"Security for the Alaskan Eskimo," *Papers*, Inter-American Conf. on Indian Life, Peru, 1948.
"Mme. Eskimo, an Artist," *Natural History*, February, 1950.
"Reindeer Industry," *Arctic*, April, 1950.
"Religion of Eskimos," in *Fern's Forgotten Religions*, New York, Philosophical Library, 1950.
"Present Status of Alaskan Eskimos," Paper, Alaskan Science Conference, 1950.
"The Social Sciences," *Reports*, US Public Health Service, May, 1953.
"The Trend of Science in Alaska," US Public Health Service, *Reports*, May, 1953.
"Where are the Social Sciences in Alaska?" *Sci. Monthly*, 1953.
"Social Anthropological Research in Alaska," *Proceedings*, Alaska Science Conference, 1952.
"Nunivak Eskimo Personality Revealed in Mythology," *Anthrop. Papers*, University of Alaska, 1953.
"Opportunities for Sociological Research in Alaska," *Amer. Soc. Review*, 1953.
"Edward William Nelson," *Anthrop. Papers*, University of Alaska, 1953.
"Problems of Human Ecology," *Arctic*, 1955.
Eskimo Childhood and Interpersonal Relationships. Seattle: University of Washington Press, 1960. 215 pp. This is a kind of sequel to *Alaskan Eskimo Ceremonialism*.
"Folk Medicine and Hygiene: Lower Kuskokwim and Nelson Island-Nunivak," *Anthrop. Papers*, University of Alaska, 1959.
"The Mythology of Kodiak Island, Alaska," *Journ. of Amer. Folklore*, 1938.
"The Nunivak Eskimo Personality as Reflected in Mythology," *Anthrop. Papers*, University of Alaska, 1953.
"Factionalism and Leadership: A Case Study of Nunivak Island," *Arctic Anthrop.*, 1972.
Ethnohistory in Southwestern Alaska and the Southern Yukon. Lexington: University of Kentucky Press, 1970.
See also Edward Spicer. See the Arctic Bibliography.

LANTZEFF, GEORGE V.
Siberia in the 17th Century. Berkeley: University of California, 1943.

LAPEROUSE, JEAN FRANCOIS de GALAUP, Comte de (1741-1788)
A Voyage Round the World. London: J. Johnson, 1798. 3v. 1785-88.
The First French Expedition to California: Laperouse in 1786. Los Angeles: G. Dawson, 1959. 145 pp.
Louis XVI commissioned the Laperouse expedition in 1785. While exploring the northwest coast south of Yakutat in 1786 two small boats were lost, with their crews, in a tidal bore at the entrance to Lituya Bay. Later, both ships of the expedition, the *La Boussole* and *L'Astrolabe*, were wrecked at the South Pacific island of Vanikoro. The disappearance of the ships remained a mystery, however, until 1826, when Peter Dillon of the *St. Patrick* brought back relics of the ships from natives at Vanikoro. Apparently, all survivors from one vessel perished by massacre. Certain survivors of the other had lived on the islands until a few months before Dillon's arrival.
See the following:
Allen, E.W.; Barbeau; Bayly; Labillardiere; Marshall; Rossel; Speck; Wagner.

LARGE, RICHARD GEDDES
The Skeena: River of Destiny. Vancouver: Mitchell Press, 1957. 180 pp.
Prince Rupert: Gateway to Alaska. Vancouver: Mitchell Press, 1960. 210 pp.

LaROCHE, FRANK
En Route to the Klondike. Chicago: W.B. Conkey, 1896. Photographic.

LARSEN, ESTHER LOUISE
"The Eskimos, An American People," *Anthrop. Papers,* University of Alaska, 1957. Partial translation of a 1756 paper.

LARSEN, HELGE EYVIN (b. 1905)
Ipiutak and the Arctic Whale Hunting Culture. New York: Amer. Museum of Natural History, 1948. 276 pp. With Froelich G. Rainey. Based on expeditions by the authors and J.L. Giddings.
The Circumpolar Conference in Copenhagen. Copenhagen: Ejnar Munksgaard, 1960. 92 pp.
For a full bibliography of articles see the Arctic Bibliography, and Karen Workman's bibliography of Alaskan Archaeology.

LARSON, FREDA
Glad Lee, the Cross-eyed Bear. New York: Exposition Press, 1951. Juvenile.

LATHAM, EDWARDS MATHEWS (b. 1910)
Statehood for Hawaii and Alaska. New York: Wilson, 1953. 197 pp.

LATHAM, ROBERT CORDON
The Native Races of the Russian Empire. London: H. Bailliere, 1854. 340 pp.

LATHROP, WEST
Dogsled Danger. New York: Random House, 1956. 247 pp.
Jet: Sled Dog of the North. London: 1958. 254 pp.
Juneau, the Sleigh Dog. New York: Random House, 1942. 279 pp.
Northern Trail Adventure. New York: Random House, 1944. 217 pp.

LAUFE, ABE; see E.M. Fitzgerald.

LAUGHLIN, WILLIAM SCEVA (b. 1909)
"Contemporary Problems in the Anthropology of Southern Alaska," *Proceedings,* Alaskan Science Conference, 1950.
"Aleut Health Problems," *Proc.,* Alaska Science Conf., 1950.
"The Aleut-Eskimo Community," *Anthrop. Papers,* Univ. of Alaska, 1952.
"The Alaska Gateway Viewed from the Aleutian Islands," *Papers,* Physical Anthropology of the American Indian, Viking Fund Publication, 1951.
"Blood Groups, Morphology, and Population Size of the Eskimos," Cold Spring Harbor Symposia on Quantitative Biology, 1950.
"A New View of the History of the Aleutians," *Arctic,* 1951. With G. H. Marsh.
"Archaeological Investigations on Umak Island, Aleutians," *Arctic Anthrop.,* I (1962): 108-110.
"Bering Strait to Puget Sound: Dichotomy and Affinity between Eskimo-Aleuts and American Indians," in *Arctic Inst. of NA, Technical Paper No. 11,* 1962.
"The Earliest Aleuts," *Anthrop. Papers,* Univ. of Alaska, 1963.
"Eskimos and Aleuts: Their Origins and Evolution," *Science,* CXLII (1963): 633-645.
"Human Migrations and Permanent Occupation in the Bering Sea Area," in Hopkins, *Bering Sea Land Bridge.*
Laughlin, an authority in migration interpretation, concludes that Aleuts appear to have come to the Alaska mainland in two waves, one beginning 4000 years ago, the other within the last 1000 years.

LAURIDSEN, PETER (1846-1923)
Vitus J. Bering: Discoverer of Bering Strait. Trans., Julius E. Olsen. Chicago: S.C. Griggs & Co., 1889. 223 pp.

LAUT, AGNES CHRISTIAN (1871-1936)
Vikings of the Pacific. New York: Macmillan, 1905. 349 pp.
The Conquest of Our Western Empire. New York: McBride, 1927. 363 pp.
The Fur Trade of America. New York: Macmillan, 1921. 341 pp.
See also Wickersham's bibliography; these works tend toward romanticization.

LAVRISCHEV, TIKHON I. (d. 1937)
"History of Education in Alaska," unpub. doctoral dissertation (D.Ed), University of California, 1935.
See Alaska Church History, Documents relative to the History of the Orthodox Church in Alaska, University of Alaska History Research Project, 1935-37.

LAWING, NELLIE NEAL (1874-1956)
Alaska Nellie. Seattle: Seattle Printing and Publishing Company, 1940. 201 pp. Nellie Lawing operated a roadhouse on Kenai Lake on the Alaska Railroad. Many famous visitors traveling the railroad were feted to her hospitality. See Jeffery, and Tewkesbury. See also *Alaska Sportsman,* July, 1939 and January, 1957. Paul I. Irwin, a Methodist missionary at Seward made tape recordings with Nellie Lawing between 1948 and 1951.

LAWRENCE, DONALD BUERMANN (b. 1911)
"Estimating Dates of Recent Glacier Advances and Recessions," *Transactions*, Amer. Geophysical Union, 1950.
"Glacial Fluctuation for Six Centuries in Southeastern Alaska," *Geog. Review*, 1950.
"Recent Glacier History of Glacier Bay, Alaska," Amer. Philosophical Soc., *Yearbook*, 1950.

LAWRENCE, EDWARD A. (b. 1907)
Clover Passage. Caldwell: Caxton Printers, 1954. 260 pp.

LAWRENCE, GUY
"Yukon Telegraph Service," published serially in the *Alaska Sportsman*, October, 1958 to May, 1959. The Klondike rush prompted construction of a telegraph line from Circle City to Lake Bennett, where connection could be made by trail to Skagway and southbound steamers. Later, a line was put through to Atlin, and to Telegraph Creek, Hazelton and Quesnel, following the old Overland Telegraph route of 1865. Lawrence worked on this line for 40 years. This work is constructed from his diary.

LAWS and GOVERNMENT of ALASKA;
See Government.

LAYCOCK, GEORGE
Alaska: The Embattled Frontier. Boston: Houghton Mifflin, 1971.

LAYTHA, EDGAR (b. 1910)
North Again for Gold. New York: Stokes, 1939. 360 pp. Canada.

LAZAREV, ALEKSEI PETROVICH
See the Arctic Bibliography.

LAZAREV, M. P.
See the Arctic Bibliography.

LAZELL, J. ARTHUR
Alaskan Apostle: The Life Story of Sheldon Jackson. New York: Harper, 1960. 218 pp.

LEACOCK, STEPHEN BUTLER (1869-1944)
Adventures of the Far North. Toronto: Glasgow, Brook, 1914. 152 pp. Arctic exploration.

LEARNARD, H. G.
Report, in Reports of Explorations of the Territory of Alaska, 1898. Wn.DC: GPO, 1899. Adjutant-General's Office, US Army. Portage Bay, Turnagain Arm, Resurrection Bay, Kenai Peninsula, Sushitna and Talkeetna Rivers. Includes information on natives.

LEBEDEV, D. M.
See the Arctic Bibliography.

LE BOURDAIS, DONAT MARC (b. 1887)
Northward on the New Frontier. Ottawa: Graphic Publishers, 1931. 311 pp. With Lomen on the schooner *Herman* to Wrangel Island, Siberia, in 1924.
Stefansson, Ambassador of the North. Montreal: Harvest House, 1963. 204 pp. Relations with the Canadian govt.

LEDYARD, JOHN (1751-1789)
A Journal of Capt. Cook's Last Voyage. Hartford, Conn.: N. Patten, 1783. 208 pp. Ledyard was an American adventurer who sailed with Cook in 1776. With the aid of Benjamin Franklin, Thomas Jefferson, and the Marquis de Lafayette, Ledyard undertook a journey west to east across Europe and Asia, intending too to cross North America from Oregon to New England (1786-87). However, he was returned to St. Petersburg from Siberia by order of the Russian government. Jared Sparks wrote a biography of Ledyard. See also Munford, and Augur. A ms. copy of Ledyard's journal is available in the Dartmouth College Library. See Jared Sparks.

LEE, CHARLES A.
Aleutian Indian and English Dictionary. Seattle: Lowman and Hanford, 1896. 23 pp.

LEE, FRANK C.
Alaska Highway Poems. Mason City, Iowa: Kiipto Co., 1944.

LEE, NORMAN
Klondike Cattle Drive. Vancouver: Mitchell Press, 1960.

LEEHEY, MAURICE DANIEL
Mining Code for Use of Miners and Prospectors in Washington and Alaska. Seattle, 1900. 103 pp.

LEFFINGWELL, ERNEST de KOVEN (b. 1876)
The Canning River Region. Wn.DC: GPO, 1919. 251 pp. USGS.
"Flaxman Island: A Glacial Remnant," *Journ. of Geol.*, 1908.
"Ground-ice Wedges," *Journ. of Geol.*, 1908.

LEIBERMAN, ELIAS
The American Short Story: A Study on the Influence of Locality on its Development. Ridgewood, N.J.: The Editor, 1912.

LEIGHTON, ALEXANDER and CHARLES C. HUGHES
"Notes on Eskimo Patterns of Suicide," *Southwestern Journal of Anthropology*, VII (1955): 327-338.

LeJEUNE, JOHN MARY (b. 1855)
Chinook and Shorthand Rudiments. Kamloops, B.C.: 1898. 15 pp.

LENSEN, GEORGE ALEXANDER
Russia's Eastward Expansion. Englewood Cliffs: Prentice-Hall, 1964.

LEONARD, JOHN WILLIAM (b. 1849)
The Gold Field of the Klondike. Chicago: Marquis, 1897. 216 pp.

LEONTY, Rt. Rev.
"The History of the Russian Orthodox Church in America," *Russian Orthodox Journal*, 1943-45.

LEOPOLD, ALDO STARKER (b. 1913)
Wildlife in Alaska. New York: Ronald Press, 1953. 129 pp. Conservation.

"Effects of Land Use on Moose and Caribou in Alaska," *Transactions*, North American Wildlife Conference, Wn.DC: 1953.

LEPOTIER, ADOLPHE AUGUSTE MARIE (b. 1898)
See the Arctic Bibliography.

LEROI-GOURMAN, ANDREE (b. 1911)
See the Arctic Bibliography.

LESLIE, FRANK (Expedition of 1890-91)
Narratives, by E.J. Glave, Alfred B. Schanz, and E.H. Wells. In vols. 70-73 of *Leslie's Illustrated Newspaper*, 1890-91. From Pyramid Harbor, Lynn Canal, to St. Michael, via the Yukon, Tok, Tanana and Chilkat Rivers. Also the Kuskokwim, Nushagak and Lower Yukon in winter. Sponsored by Frank Leslie. See E. Wells.

LESSNER, ERWIN CHRISTIAN
Cradle of Conquerors: Siberia. Garcen City: Doubleday, 1955.

LES TINA, DOROTHY (b. ca. 1920)
Icicles on the Roof. New York: Abelard-Schuman, 1961. 181 pp. Well written about Bethel after WW II by ex-Army woman.
Alaska: A Book to Begin On. New York: Holt, Rinehart and Winston, 1962. Juvenile.

LEVANESVSKII, SIGISMUND
See T-2693 ff.

LEVCHENKO, G. I.
See the Arctic Bibliography.

LEWIS and DRYDEN
Marine History of the Pacific Northwest. Portland: Lewis and Dryden Printing Co., 1895. 494 pp.

LEWIS, GEORGE EDWARD (b. 1870)
Yukon Lyrics. Portland: 1925. 69 pp.
Nick of the Woods. Portland: Jensen, 1916. 222 pp.
See also T-2696 ff.

LEWIS, F. MARTIN
Alaska: Its Economy and Market Potential. Wn.DC: GPO, 1959. 61 pp. Dept. of Commerce.

LEWIS, JAMES CONRAD
Black Beaver; The Trapper. Chicago: Robert O. Law Co., 1911. 58 pp.

LEWIS, OSCAR
George Davidson: Pioneer West Coast Scientist. Berkeley: University of California Press, 1954. 146 pp. See also Morgan Sherwood.

LIEK, HARRY J.
"The Second Ascent of Mt. McKinley," *Sierra Club Bulletin*, 1933.

LIGHTHOUSES of ALASKA
Alaska Life, Aug., '48 (Cape Spencer); *Alaska Sportsman*, Aug., '38 (Cape Decision, Eldred Rock, Cape Hinchinbrook); July, '39 (Scotch Cap); Sept., '39 (Five Finger); Apr., '54 (operation, bibliog-raphy); May, '54 (Cape Spencer); Sept., '54 (Ninilchik); Feb., '55 (Scotch destroyed); other, see Index; Gibbs (Scotch Cap destroyed); Gruening; Jeffery (Pt. Retreat, Cape Spencer, Sentinel Is., Mary Is.); Snow; Willoughby; see also Alaska Dept. of Parks, *Aids to Navigation in Alaska History*, 1974.

LIN, PETER C.
"Alaska's Population and School Enrollments," *Review of Business and Economic Conditions*, VIII (1971).

LINDBERGH, ANNE S. (b. 1906)
North to the Orient. New York: Harcourt, Brace, 1935. 255 pp. Flight in 1931 over Canada and Alaska from Wn.DC, with chapters on Aklavik, Barrow, King Island and Kamchatka.

LINDLEY, ALFRED D.
See the Arctic Bibliography for articles on the Lindley-Liek expedition on Mount McKinley.

LINDQUIST, WILLIS
Alaska, the Forty-ninth State. New York: McGraw-Hill, 1959. 111 pp.

LINDSAY, DAVID MOORE (b. 1862)
A Voyage to the Arctic. Boston: D. Estes, 1911. 233 pp. In the whaler *Aurora*.

LINDSEY, DOUGLAS
Alaska. Stockton, Calif.: T.W. Hummel, 1897. 24 pp.

LINDSLEY, AARON LADNER (1817-1891)
Sketches of an Excursion to Southern Alaska. N.p.: 1879.

LIPKE, ALICE CUSHING
Under the Aurora. Los Angeles: Suttonhouse, 1938. 286 pp. Autobiographical novel.

LIPSHITS, B. A.
See the Arctic Bibliography.

LISIANSKII, IURII FEDOROVICH (1773-1837)
Voyage Round the World in the Years 1803-06. London: J. Booth, 1814. 388 pp. Trans. Lisianski commanded the *Neva*, Kruzenstern the expedition. Kruzenstern carried Rezanov to Japan, while Lisianski hurried to Sitka, where the guns of the *Neva* made the difference in Baranov's successful offensive against the Sitka Indians in 1804.
On Lisianski see also the Arctic Bibliography, and T-2723 ff.

LITTLE, ARTHUR, Co.
Report to the State of Alaska. Cambridge: Harvard University Press, 1961.

LITTLE, C. H.
"Captain Cook in Alaska," *Canadian Geographic Journal*, LXXIX (1964): 134-141.

LITUYA BAY
Alaska Sportsman, Feb., '38 (photos); Feb., '49; Oct., '58 (earthquake); others, see Index; Bancroft; Brooks (beach gold); Colby; Dall; Higginson;

Hulley; Miller; LaPerouse; Scidmore (native legend); Williams, J. (native legend; miner hanged here 1899). See also deLaguna and Gunther.

LLORENTE, SEGUNDO (b. 1906)
See the Arctic Bibliography for a series of works published at Mexico City in Spanish about Jesuit missionary activity in Alaska. Fr. Llorente served in the Alaska Territorial Legislature.

LLOYD, CHARLES CHRISTOPHER
The Voyages of Captain James Cook. London: Cresset, 1949. 384 pp.

LLOYD, FREEMAN
"Working Dogs of the World," *National Geographic*, 1941.

LLOYD-OWEN, FRANCES
Gold Nugget Charlie. London: Harrap, 1939. 259 pp. Charles E. Masson.

LOCKLEY, FRED (b. 1871)
History of the First Free Delivery Service of Mail in Alaska. Portland: the Author, 1955. 12 pp.

LOMEN, CARL JOYS (b. 1880)
Fifty Years in Alaska. New York: David McKay, 1954. 302 pp. Autobiographical. See also Clarence Andrews' opposition to the Lomen Brothers' reindeer operations.
"Camel of the Frozen Desert," *National Geographic*, 1919.

LOMEN, HELEN
Taktuk: An Arctic Boy. Garden City: Doubleday, 1928. 139 pp.

LOMONOSOV, MIKHAIL VASIL'EVICH
See T-2752 ff.

LONDON, JACK (1876-1916)
Call of the Wild. New York: Macmillan, 1903. 327 pp. Publication of this story of "Buck," a Husky sled dog brought immediate and enduring fame to London as a writer of naturalist fiction.
White Fang. New York: Macmillan, 1905. 327 pp. Heroic story of part wolf-part dog who responds to kind treatment.
Sea-Wolf. New York: Macmillan, 1904. 366 pp. This story of marine lawlessness was said to be modeled on "Dynamite" Johnny O'Brien, and Abe McLean, sometimes suggested as leader of a Japanese raid on the Pribilof Islands in 1906 (after publication of *Sea-Wolf*). The cutter *Bear* was used for *Ghost* in a film made of *Sea-Wolf*. See Robert De Armond in *Alaska Life*, May, 1946, and Gordon James in *Alaska Life*, January and March, 1947.
Burning Daylight. New York: Macmillan, 1910. 361 pp. Story of a Klondike millionaire. London spent the winter of 1897-98 at Stewart in the Yukon with Elam Harnish (1871-1941) upon whom this novel is based. Klondike Mike Mahoney figures as well.
A Daughter of the Snows. Philadelphia: Lippincott, 1902. 334 pp.
Children of the Frost. New York: Macmillan, 1902. 261 pp.
Lost Face. New York: Macmillan, 1910. 240 pp.

Scorn of Women. New York: Macmillan, 1906. 256 pp.
The Son of the Wolf: Tales of the Far North. Boston: Houghton, Mifflin, 1900. 251 pp.
The God of His Fathers and Other Stories. New York: McClure Phillips, 1901. 299 pp.
The Faith of Men, and Other Stories. New York: Macmillan, 1904. 286 pp.
Love of Life, and Other Stories. New York: Macmillan, 1907. 265 pp.
Revolution, and Other Essays. New York: Macmillan, 1910. 309 pp.
Smoke Bellew Tales. New York: Century, 1912. 385 pp.
The Sun-Dog Trail, and Other Stories. Cleveland: World Publishing Co., 1951. 251 pp.
Best Short Stories of Jack London. New York: Permabooks, 1949. 243 pp. and other editions.
For a complete listing of Jack London anthologies, of which there are many, see T-2754 ff. For material on London see the following:
Bland, Henry M. *Jack London*, reprint of "Jack London, Traveler, Novelist and Social Reformer," *Craftsman*, 1906.
Garst, Shannon. *Jack London: Magnet for Adventure*.
Lieberman, Elias. *The American Short Story*.
London, Charmain. *The Book of Jack London*. New York: Century, 1921.
London, Joan. *Jack London and His Times*. New York: Doubleday, Doran, 1939.
Morgan, E.R. *Jack London*.
Stone, Irving. *Jack London: Sailor on Horseback*. Boston: Houghton, Mifflin, 1938. New York: Doubleday, 1947.
Jack London came to Skagway in 1897, and crossed Chilkoot Pass to Whitehorse Rapids where he earned $3000 piloting boats. He was then 21. He went on to Dawson, and during the winter became snowbound at Stewart, Yukon, Terr. He is said to have lost all his teeth to scurvy. During the winter of 1898-99 he, Rex Beach, and others formed something of a literary colony at Rampart on the Yukon in Alaska. He went to Nome in 1899, and then back to California from where he started north. Unlike Beach, London did not use factual settings for his stories, instead concentrating on form and style. Although his stories are much more widely known than Beach's, they tend to misrepresent many aspects of life in Alaska. On London's stories in relation to Alaskan realities, see Franck, Clark, and Stuck. For literary criticism of London see the scholarly journals. See also the secondary sources listed in Tourville following T-2785.

LONGSTRETH, THOMAS MORRIS (b. 1886)
In Scarlet and Plain Clothes. New York: Macmillan, 1933. 365 pp.
The Silent Force. New York: Century, 1927. 383 pp.
The Force Carries On. Toronto: Macmillan, 1954. 182 pp.

LONNEUX, MARTIN J.
Graded Catechism in Innuit. Chaneliak, Alaska.

LOPEZ, de HARO, GONZALO
See Wagner. Landing on Montague Island in 1788, Lopez de Haro claimed all surrounding land

for Spain. He next visited Delarov (Shelikhov's agent) at Three Saints Bay on Kodiak, and later still, Unalaska. In 1790 he became involved in the Nootka Sound controversy on Vancouver Island.

LOPP, WILLIAM THOMAS (1864-1939)
See Richards for "Pioneer Education in Northwest Alaska."
White Sox: The Story of the Reindeer in Alaska. Yonkers: World Book Co., 1924. 76 pp. Lopp was chief of the Alaska division of the Bureau of Education (Dept. of Interior), 1908-1925. See Gilman, and also Andrews in *Alaska Life*, August, 1944. See also Thornton, H.R.

LORAIN, S. H.
Lode-tin Mining at Lost River, Seward Peninsula. Wn.DC: GPO, 1958. 76 pp. Dept. of Interior, Dept. of Mines.
"Government Assistance to Mining in Alaska," *Proceedings*, Alaska Science Conference, 1951.

LORING, CHARLES G.
See T-2797.

LOUBAT, JOSEPH FLORIMOND
Narrative of the Mission to Russia in 1866. New York, 1873. Gustavus Vasa Fox, Assistant Secretary of the Navy.

LOUISIANA PURCHASE EXPOSITION (St. Louis, 1904)
The Exhibition of the District of Alaska. St. Louis: Woodward and Tiernan, 1904. 56 pp.

LOWTHER, BARBARA J.
Bibliography of British Columbia: Laying the Foundations, 1848-1899. With the assistance of Muriel Land. Prepared under the auspices of the Social Sciences Research Centre, University of Victoria. Victoria, BC: University of Victoria Press, 1968.

LOYENS, WILLIAM J.
"The Koyukon Feast for the Dead," *Arctic Anthropology*, II (1964): 133-148.
"The Changing Culture: Nulato Koyukon Indians," unpublished doctoral dissertation, University of Wisconsin, 1966.

LUBBOCK, ALFRED BASIL (1876-1944)
The Arctic Whalers. Glasgow: Brown, Ferguson, 1937. 483 pp.

LUCAS, FREDERICK AUGUSTUS (1852-1929)
"Animals Recently Extinct or Threatened with Extermination," *Annual Report*, U.S. National Museum, 1889.

LUCIA, ELLIS
Klondike Kate: The Life and Legend of Kitty Rockwell. New York: Hastings House, 1962. 305 pp.

LUCIER, CHARLES
"Buckland Eskimo Myths," *Anthrop. Papers*, University of Alaska, 1954.
"Noatagmiut Eskimo Myths," *Anthrop. Papers*, University of Alaska, 1958.

LUCIER, CHARLES, JAMES VAN STONE and DELLA KEATS
"Medical Practices and Human Anatomical Knowledge among the Noatak Eskimos," *Ethnology*, VII (1960): 251-264.

LUCIW, WASYL and THEODORE LUCIW
Ahapius Honcharenko and the Alaska Herald. Toronto: Slavia Library, 1963. 120 pp. The editor's life, and an analysis of his newspaper.

LUDECKE, EDWARD
"Our First Troops in Alaska," *Alaska-Yukon Magazine*, 1907. Ludecke was a colonel with the Ninth Infantry at Sitka in 1867.

LUGRIN, CHARLES HENRY (b. 1846)
Yukon Gold Fields: Map Showing Routes. Victoria: *British Colonist*, 1897. 32 pp.

LUIGI, Duke of ABRUZZI (1873-1933)
La Stella Polare nel mar Artico. Milano: Hoepli, 1903. 2v. English translation, London: Hutchinson, 1903.
Farther North than Nansen. London: Bell, 1901. 702 pp. See also Filippi, Filippo de.

LUKENS, MATILDA BARNES
The Inland Passage. N. pub., 1889. 84 pp.

LULL, RODERICK
Call to Battle: A Novel. Garden City: Doubleday, 1943. 304 pp. Japanese attack on the Pacific Coast.

LUND, ROBERT
The Alaskan. New York: John Day, 1953. 366 pp. A novel of Seward, faithless love and alcohol.

LUNDBORG, EINAR (b. 1896)
The Arctic Rescue: How Nobile was Saved. New York: Viking Press, 1929. 221 pp. From Spitzbergen by plane.

LUNG, EDWARD BURCHELL (1867-1956)
Black Sand and Gold. New York: Vantage Press, 1956. 419 pp. Klondike.

LUTGEN, KARL
Two Against the Arctic. New York: Pantheon Press, 1957. Trek to Barrow.

LUTHIN, REINHARD H.
"The Sale of Alaska," *Slavonic and East European Review*, XVI (1938): 168-182.

LUTKE, FEDOR PETROVICH (1792-1882) Also Litke.
See the Arctic Bibliography. This rare work chronicles a circumnavigation of 1826-29. See also Baker.

LUTZ, HAROLD J.
Aboriginal Man and White Man as Causes of Fires. New Haven: Yale University Press, 1959. 49 pp.
"Fires as an Ecological Factor in the Boreal Forest of Alaska," *Journal of Forestry*, June, 1960.

LYNCH, JEREMIAH (1849-1917)
Three Years in the Arctic. London: Arnold, 1904. 280 pp.

LYNN CANAL
Alaska Sportsman, Aug., '40 (photo); July, '42; Dec., '56; Burroughs; Colby; Denison; Higginson; Rutzebeck; Scidmore; Vancouver; Willard; Wright. See also Haines, Skagway, Port Chilkat; see also US Coast and Geodetic Survey.

M

MABEE, JACK
Sourdough Jack's Alaskan Cookery. Nevada City, Calif.: Mathis, Osborn, Woods, 1959. 37 pp.

MANVILLE, R. H. and S. P. YOUNG
Distribution of Alaska Mammals. Wn.DC: GPO, 1965. Bur. of Sport Fisheries.

MARSH, GORDON H.
A Stone Lamp from Yukon Island, Alaska," *Anthrop. Papers,* University of Alaska, 1956.

MATHIASSEN, THERKEL
"Notes on Knud Rasmussen's Archaeological Collections from the Western Eskimo," *Proceedings,* International Congress of Americanists, 1928.
"Some Specimens from the Bering Sea Culture," *Indian Notes,* VI (1930): 33-56.
"The Present State of Eskimo Archaeology," *Acta Archaeologica,* II (1931).

McBRIDE, JAMES L.
The Smoky Valley Claim. Caldwell: Caxton Printers, 1948. 260 pp. Juvenile.

McBRIDE, WILLIAM D.
Saga of the Riverboats. Reprinted from *Cariboo and Northwest Digest,* 1948-49.

M'CLINTOCK, Sir FRANCIS LEOPOLD (1819-1907)
The Voyage of the Fox: A Narrative of the Discovery of the Fate of Sir John Franklin. London: J. Murray, 1859. 403 pp. In 1854 Dr. John Rae of Hudson's Bay Company met an Eskimo on the western shore of Boothia Peninsula who supplied positive clues to the fate of Franklin. M'Clintock completed the riddle by finding the actual remains. M'Clintock found the only feasible passage by Montreal Island, through Rae Strait, the route later followed by Amundsen's first northwest passage.

M'CLURE, Sir ROBERT JOHN Le MESURIER (1807-1873)
The Discovery of the North-West Passage. London: Longman, 1856. 405 pp. M'Clure, in *Investigator,* wintered in Prince of Wales Strait between Banks and Victoria Islands, sailing from the west (Bering Strait). Though later forced to give up his ship, he and his men sailed in boats on through, eventually getting back to England.

McCOLLOM, PAT
"The Art of Alex Combs," *Alaska Journal,* IV (1974): 156-162.
"Artist Machetanz," *Alaska Journal,* IV (1974): 32-40.

McCONNELL, RICHARD GEORGE (1857-1942)
Report on Exploration of the Yukon and Mackenzie Basins. Montreal: W.F. Brown, 1891. 163 pp. Canadian Geological Survey.
Report on the Klondike Gold Fields. Ottawa: King's Printer, 1901. 71 pp. Can. Geol. Survey.

McCORKLE, RUTH
The Alaskan Ten-footed Bear. Seattle: R.D. Seal, 1958. 39 pp.

McCORMICK, ALMA
Adventure was the Compass. Boston: Little, Brown, 1942. 285 pp.

McCRACKEN, HAROLD (b. 1894)
God's Frozen Children. New York: Doubleday, 1930. 291 pp. Amer. Museum of Nat. History Siberian Arctic Expedition.
Alaska Bear Trails. New York: Doubleday, 1931. 260 pp.
The Last of the Sea Otters. Philadelphia: Stokes, 1942. 98 pp.
The Biggest Bear on Earth. Philadelphia: Lippincott, 1944. 113 pp.
Son of the Walrus King. Philadelphia: Lippincott, 1944. 128 pp.
Sentinel of the Snow Peaks. Philadelphia: Lippincott, 1945. 151 pp.
The Beast that Walks Like Man. New York: Hanover House, 1955. 319 pp.
Iglaome. New York: Century, 1930.
Hunters of the Stormy Sea. Garden City: Doubleday, 1957. 312 pp.
The Flaming Bear. Philadelphia: Lippincott, 1951. 222 pp.
Beyond the Frozen Frontier. New York: Robert Speller, 1936. 233 pp.
Pirate of the North. Philadelphia: Lippincott, 1953. 213 pp.
Roughnecks and Gentlemen. Garden City: Doubleday, 1968. 441 pp.
The Caribou Traveler. Philadelphia: Lippincott, 1949. 204 pp.
The Story of Alaska. Garden City: Doubleday, 1956. 57 pp.
Toughy: Bulldog of the Arctic. Philadelphia: Lippincott, 1948. 202 pp.

McCRACKEN, HAROLD and HARRY Van CLEVE
Trapping. New York: A.S. Barnes, 1947. 196 pp.

McCURDY, HORACE WINSLOW
The H.W. McCurdy Marine History of the Pacific Northwest. Seattle: Superior Publishing Co., 1966. 706 pp.

MacDONALD, ALEXANDER
In Search of El Dorado. London: Unwin, 1905. 291 pp.
The White Trail. London: Blackie, 1908. 392 pp.

McDONALD, ARCHIBALD
Peace River. Ottawa: J. Durie, 1872. 119 pp. Journal.

McDONALD, LUCILE SAUNDERS
Bering's Potlatch. London: Oxford University Press, 1944. 232 pp.
Search for the Northwest Passage. Portland: Binfords and Mort, 1958. 142 pp.
Down North. London: Oxford University Press, 1943. 274 pp.

McDONALD, MALCOLM (b. 1901)
The Favorites of Fate. New York: Exposition Press, 1954.

McDONALD, NORMAN C.
Fish the Strong Waters. New York: Ballantine Books, 1956. 184 pp.
Witch Doctor. New York: Ballantine Books, 1959. 143 pp.

McDONALD, ROBERT
See T-2872 ff.

M'DOUGALL, GEORGE FREDERICK
The Eventful Voyage of HM discovery ship Resolute. London: Longman, 1857. 530 pp. See Sir Edward Belcher.

McELWAINE, EUGENE
The Truth about Alaska. Chicago: The Author, 1901. 445 pp.

McFARLAND, JEANNETTE
One Mad Scramble. Cambridge, Ohio: Southeastern Publishing Co., 1940. 116 pp. Southeast travel.

McFEAT, TOM
Indians of the North Pacific Coast. Seattle: University of Washington Press, 1967. 270 pp.

MacFIE, HARRY (b. 1879)
Wasa-Wasa: A Tale of Trails and Treasure in the Far North. New York: W.W. Norton, 1951. 288 pp. From 1897.

McGARVEY, LOIS (1885-1959)
Along Alaska Trails. New York: Vantage Press, 1960. 200 pp.

MacGOWAN, KENNETH
Early Man in the New World. New York: Macmillan, 1950. 260 pp.

MacGOWAN, M.
The Hard Road to Klondike. London: Routledge & Kegan Paul, 1962. 150 pp.

McGRATH, J. E.
"The Alaskan Boundary Survey," *National Geographic,* 1893.

McGUIRE, JOHN A.
In the Alaska-Yukon Game Land. Cincinnati: S. Kidd, 1921. 215 pp.

MACHETANZ, FREDERICK (b. 1908)
Panuck: Eskimo Sled Dog. New York: Scribner's, 1939. 94 pp. Unalakleet.
On the Arctic Ice. New York: Scribner's, 1940. 105 pp. Reindeer.
On Fred Machetanz as artist see McCollom, and T-2901 ff.

MACHETANZ, SARA
Rick of High Ridge. New York: Scribner's, 1952. 177 pp.
Where Else but Alaska. New York: Scribner's, 1954. 214 pp. Travel and autobiography.
A Puppy Named Gih. New York: Scribner's, 1957. 28 pp.
Barney Hits the Trail. New York: Scribner's, 1950. 195 pp.
Robie and the Sled Dog Race. New York: Scribner's, 1964. 176 pp.
Seegoo: Dog of Alaska. New York: Scribner's, 1960. 204 pp.
The Howl of the Malemute. New York: Scribner's, 1954. 214 pp.
"A Cabin in Matanuska," *Alaska Sportsman,* March-April, 1951.
"Disappearing Lake," *Alaska Sportsman,* October, 1952.

MACK, GERSTLE
Lewis and Hannah Gerstle. New York: The Author, 1953. Early story of Hutchinson and Kohl.

MacKAY, DOUGLAS (1900-1938)
The Honourable Company: A History of Hudson's Bay Co. Indianapolis: Bobbs-Merrill, 1936. 396 pp.

MacKAY, D.
"The Collins Overland Telegraph," *Br. Columbia Hist. Quarterly,* V (1946).

McKAY, PHILIP
See Arctander (taught Duncan the Tsimshian language); Brooks (began mission work in Alaska); Hayes; Morris; Scidmore; Young.

McKEE, LANIER
The Land of Nome. New York: Grafton, 1902. 260 pp. Noyes, Mackenzie and the Alaska Gold Mining Co.

McKELVIE, BRUCE ALASTAIR (b. 1889)
Maquinna the Magnificent. Vancouver: Daily Province, 1946. 65 pp. John Jewitt and the *Boston;* see also Jewitt, and Bancroft.

McKENNAN, ROBERT A.
The Upper Tanana Indians. New Haven: Yale University Press, 1959. 226 pp.
The Chandalar Kutchin. Montreal: Arctic Institute, 1965. 156 pp.

MACKENZIE, ALEXANDER (1763-1820)
Voyages from Montreal on the River St. Lawrence. London T. Cadell, 1801. 412 pp. Mackenzie was the first to explore to the Arctic Ocean, in 1789. Later he explored the Fraser to the Pacific, in 1793. His influence on western exploration was considerable.

McKEOWN, MARTHA FERGUSON (b. 1903)
Alaska Silver. New York: Macmillan, 1951. 274 pp.
The Trail Led North. New York: Macmillan, 1948. 222 pp.

McKINLEY, Mount
Alaska Life, Nov., '38; Feb., '44 (hotel in war years); March, '44; Apr., '45; *Alaska Sportsman,* see Index; *Alaska-Yukon Magazine,* Apr., '08; Jan., '09; Nov., '09 (editorial on Cook); Aug., '10 (mountain misnamed); *Alpine Journal* (London), Feb., '03; Aug., '04; Aug., '11; Nov., '13; Nov., '42; May, '43; *American Alpine Journal,* '29; '46; '49; *American Geographic Society Bulletin,* '12. See also the following:
Adams, Ansel; Beach; Beckey (in *Appalachia,* Dec., '54); Brooks; Browne; Butcher; Cameron; Capps (incl. USGS bulletins); Colby; Cook, F.A.; Corser; Couch; Denison; Dickey (namer); Dixon; Dunn; Elliott; Farquhar; Francis (in *Appalachia,* Dec., '52); Franck; Gardey (in *Am. Alpine J.,* '55); Gruening (on park administration); Hackett (in *Mazama,* Dec., '51); Hart; Henderson; Higginson; Holden (see Arctic Biblio.); Huber; Humphreys (in *Appalachia,* Dec., '52); Korner (in *Appalachia,* Dec., '53); Laurence (see Hulley); Lipke; McLean (in *Am. Alpine J.,* '55); Mailan; Murie; *National Geographic,* see Index; Pearson (*Satevepost,* Dec., '53); Roloff (in *Trail and Timberline,* Feb., '47); Scudder (in *Am. Alpine J.,* '53); Sheldon; Snow (*Alaska-Yukon Mag.,* '10 [misnaming]); Stephenson; Stuck; Underwood; Washburn (see a full bibliography of Washburn's articles in the Arctic Bibliography); Wickersham; Winslow; Wood (in *Amer. Alpine J.,* '55).

McLAIN, CARRIE M.
Gold Rush Nome. Portland: Graphic Arts Center, 1969. 23 pp.
Pioneer Teacher. Portland: Graphic Arts Center, 1970. 70 pp.

McLAIN, JOHN SCUDDER (b. 1853)
Alaska and the Klondike. New York: McClure, Phillips, 1905. 330 pp. Senate Committee on Territories trip.

McLENEGAN, SAMUEL B.
"Exploration on the Kowak River," *Report,* Corwin, 1884.
"Exploration of the Noatak River," *Report,* Corwin, 1885.

MacMASTER, Sir DONALD (1846-1922)
The Seal Arbitration. Montreal: Brown, 1894. 65 pp.

MacMILLAN, MIRIAM
Etuk, the Eskimo Hunter. New York: Dodd, Mead, 1950. 177 pp. Juvenile.
Kudla and His Polar Bear. New York: Dodd, Mead, 1953. 96 pp. Juvenile.

McMILLION, OVID MILLER
New Alaska. Ann Arbor: Edwards Brothers, 1939. 216 pp.

MacMULLEN, JERRY
Star of India: the Log of an Iron Ship. Berkeley: Howell-North, 1961. 133 pp. Alaska Packer's Assn.

McMURRAY, DeVON
All Aboard for Alaska. Boston: Heath, 1941. 159 pp.

McMURRAY, FLOYD IVAN (b. 1891)
Westbound. New York: Scribner's 1943. 394 pp.

MacNAIR, H. F.
"The Log of the *Caroline,*" *Pacific Northwest Quarterly,* January, 1938.

McNEER, MAY
The Alaska Gold Rush. New York: Random House, 1960. 186 pp.

McNEILLY, MILDRED MASTERSON
Heaven is too High. New York: Hampton, 1944. 432 pp.
Praise at Morning. New York: Morrow, 1947. 409 pp.

MacNEISH, RICHARD S.
"The Engigstciak Site of the Yukon Arctic Coast," *Anthrop. Papers,* May, 1956. University of Alaska.
"Man out of Asia as seen from the Northwest Yukon," *Anthrop. Papers,* May, 1959. University of Alaska.
Investigations in Southwest Yukon. Andover, Mass.: Peabody Foundation for Archaeology, 1964.

MACOUN, JAMES MELVILLE
See T-2945 ff.

McPHERSON, HALLIE M.
"The Projected Purchase of Alaska," *Pac. Hist. Review,* 1934.
"The Interest of William McKendree Gwin in the Purchase of Alaska," *Pac. Hist. Review,* 1934.

McQUESTEN, LEROY NAPOLEON (1836-1909)
See letter to Albert McKay in the Bunnell collection in the University of Alaska archive. According to Ogilvie, McQuesten loaned his diary to a would-be historian, was never able to recover it. Arriving on the Yukon in 1873, McQuesten was active in the founding of Ft. Reliance, Fortymile, Circle and Eagle. He is often associated with Harper. See Heller, and Berton. See also B.B. Jensen, "Alaska's Pre-Klondike Mining," *Jour. West* (July, 1967).

MADDREN, ALFRED GEDDES
Smithsonian Exploration in Alaska in 1904. Wn.DC: GPO, 1905. 117 pp. Smithsonian Misc. Publication. Mammoth fossils.

MADSEN, CHARLES (1884-1953)
Arctic Trader. New York: Dodd, Mead, 1957. 273 pp. G. Madsen served as interpreter on *Bear* and

Thetis. C. Madsen was a trader who owned several vessels in the whale trade. Later he operated a store on Kodiak.

MAHONEY, MIKE
See Merrill Denison.

MAHR, AUGUST C.
The Visit of the Rurik to San Francisco in 1816. Stanford: Stanford University Press, 1932.

MAKAROVA, R. V.
"Expeditions of Russian Traders in the Pacific Ocean in the 18th Century" (in Russian), *Voprosy Geografii*, 1950. Basov, Stepan Glotov, Pushkarev, and Andreian Tolstykh. See the Arctic Bibliography.

MALASPINA di MULAZZO, ALESSANDRO (1754-1810)
Viaje Politico-Cientifico Alrededor del Mundo por las Corbetas Descubierta y Artievida. Madrid: Imp. de la Viuda Ehijos de Abienze, 1885. 681 pp. On this circumnavigation Malaspina was ordered to search the northwest coast for a passage. At Yakutat Bay in 1791 he became convinced of the unlikelihood of the passage's existence (see Disenchantment Bay). It was Malaspina's misfortune to be in jail when the journals of the voyage of *Sutil* and *Mexicana* to Puget Sound were published with an account of the earlier voyage of the *Descubierta*. Dall named the glacier in 1874. See Wagner. See also T-2956 ff.

MALDONADA; see Ferrer de Maldonado.

MALLETTE, GERTRUDE ETHEL (1887)
Chee-cha-ko. New York: Doubleday, 1938. 299 pp.

MALLINSON, FLORENCE LEE
My Travels and Adventures in Alaska. Seattle: Seattle-Alaska Co., 1914. 200 pp.

MANFIELD, NORMA B.
Keeper of the Wolves. New York: Rinehart, 1934. 305 pp.

MANNING, CLARENCE A.
Russian Influence on Early America. New York: Library Publishers, 1953. 216 pp.

MANNING, WILLIAM RAY
"The Nootka Sound Controversy," *Annual Report,* American Historical Association, 1904.

MANSFIELD, HARRY BUCKINGHAM
"Surveys in Southeastern Alaska," in *USGS Reports,* 1890.

MANWARING, G. E.
My Friend the Admiral: The Life, Letters and Journals of Rear-Admiral James Burney, F.R.S., the Companion of Captain James Cook and Friend of Charles Lamb. London: Geo. Routledge, 1931. 314 pp.

MARCHAND, ETIENNE (1755-1793)
Voyage Autour de Monde pendant les annees 1770-92. Paris: Imprimerie de la Republique, 1798.

Although Baker ignores Marchand, Bancroft, Barbeau, Greenhow, Hulley, and of course, Wagner all comment on this voyage.

MARGESON, CHARLES ANSON
Experience of Gold Hunters in Alaska. Hornellsville, New York: the Author, 1899. 297 pp. Valdez glacier, Copper River, Tonsina prospecting.

MARINE RESEARCH SOCIETY
The Sea, the Ship, and the Sailor: Tales of Adventure from the Log Books and from Original Narratives. Salem, Mass.: Marine Research Society, 1925.

MARKHAM, Sir ALBERT HASTINGS (1841-1918)
Life of Sir John Franklin and the Northwest Passage. London: G. Philip, 1891. 324 pp.
A Whaling Cruise in Baffin's Bay and the Gulf of Boothia. London: Lowe, Marston, etc., 1874. 319 pp. *Polaris* rescue.

MARKHAM, Sir CLEMENTS ROBERT (1830-1916)
The Lands of Silence. Cambridge: University Press, 1921. 539 pp.
Life of Admiral Sir Leopold McClintock. London: Murray, 1909. 370 pp.
"Expedition of Lt. F. Schwatka to King William Land," *Proceedings,* Royal Geographic Society, 1880.
"Measures for the Search and Relief of the *U.S. Jeannette* Arctic Expedition," *Proceedings,* Royal Geographic Society, 1882.
"On the Next Great Discovery: The Beaufort Sea," *Geographic Journal,* 1906.

MARKOV, ALEKSANDR
See T-2972.

MARKOV, SERGEI I.
See the Arctic Bibliography.

MARSH, GORDON
"A Comparative Study of Eskimo-Aleut Religion," *Anthrop. Papers,* University of Alaska, 1954.
"A Stone Lamp from Yukon Island, Alaska," *Anthrop. Papers,* University of Alaska, 1956.

MARSH, ROY SIMPSON
Wings and Runners: Tom's Alaska Adventures. New York: Stokes, 1932. 258 pp.
Kang. Philadelphia: Macrae Smith Co., 1962.
Moog. Phildelphia: Macrae Smith Co., 1958.

MARSH, S. J.
"Notes on a Remarkable Journey made in the Winter of 1902-03 from Camden Bay on the Arctic Coast to Fort Yukon, via Kuselik Creek, Barter River, Canning River, East Fork, Chandalar River," in Brooks' *Report on the Geography and Geology of Alaska,* Wn.DC: GPO, 1906. USGS Professional Paper No. 45.

MARSHALL, EDISON (b. 1894)
Seward's Folly. Boston: Little, Brown, 1924. 312 pp. Fiction. Sitka.

The Sleeper of the Moonlit Ranges. New York: Cosmopolitan, 1925. 311 pp. Aleutian Islands. Fiction.

Ocean Gold. New York: Harper, 1925. 383 pp.

Child of the Wild. New York: Cosmopolitan, 1926. 297 pp.

Princess Sophia. Garden City: Doubleday, 1958. 381 pp.

The Deadfall. New York: Cosmopolitan, 1927. 290 pp.

The Deputy at Snow Mountain. New York: H.C. Kinsey, 1932. 284 pp.

The Doctor of Lonesome River. New York: Cosmopolitan, 1931. 294 pp.

The Far Call. New York: Cosmopolitan, 1928. 284 pp.

The Fish Hawk. New York: A.L. Burt, 1929. 290 pp.

The Land of Forgotten Man. Boston: Little, Brown, 1923. 306 pp.

The Missionary. New York: Cosmopolitan, 1930. 288 pp.

The Snowshoe Trail. Boston: Little, Brown, 1921. 324 pp.

MARSHALL, JAMES STIRRAT and CARRIE MARSHALL

Adventures in Two Hemispheres. Vancouver: Talex Printing Service, 1955. 208 pp. George Vancouver.

Pacific Voyages. Portland: Binfords and Mort, 1960. 100 pp.

Vancouver's Voyage. Vancouver: Mitchell Press, 1967. 228 pp.

MARSHALL, JAMES VANCE

A River Ran Out of Eden. London: Hodder and Stoughton, 1962. 128 pp.

MARSHALL, ROBERT (1901-1939)

Arctic Village. New York: Smith and Haas, 1933. 399 pp. Wiseman, on the Koyukuk. This book was a Literary Guild selection. Marshall lived at Wiseman 15 months and records numerous tales and legends, and includes in the work many photographs. Most important, he includes much on daily living.

Arctic Wilderness. Berkeley: University of California Press, 1956. 171 pp. Letters among Arctic friends, mostly on mountain climbing.

Doonerak or Bust. N. pl.: the Author, 1938.

North Doonerak, Amawk and Apoon. N. pl.: the Author, n.d.

MARSTON, MARVIN

Men of the Tundra: Eskimos at War. New York: October House, 1969. 227 pp. This is Col. Muktuk Marston's story of the organization and work of the Eskimo scouts during WW II.

MARTIN, ANNA

Around and About Alaska. New York: Vantage Press, 1959. 95 pp.

MARTIN, FRANCES F.

Nine Tales of Raven. New York: Harper and Row, 1951. 60 pp.

MARTIN, FREDERICKA I.

Sea Bears: The Story of the Fur Seal. Philadelphia: Chilton Co., 1960. 201 pp.

The Hunting of the Silver Fleece: Epic of the Fur Seal. New York: Greenberg, 1946. 328 pp. Authoritative.

The Aleut Language. For a full citation see the Arctic Bibliography; this is a translation of Veniaminov.

"Pribilofs' Sealers-Serfs of the North," *Newsletter*, Inst. of Ethnic Affairs, 1948.

MARTIN, GEORGE CURTIS (1875-1943)

"The Recent Eruption of Katmai Volcano in Alaska," *National Geographic*, 1913.

"The Petroleum Fields of the Pacific Coast of Alaska," USGS *Bulletin*, No. 250, 1905.

"A Reconnaissance of the Matanuska Coal Fields, Alaska," USGS *Bulletin*, No. 289, 1906.

MARTIN, LOUISE ANITA

North to Nome. Chicago: A. Whitman, 1939. 316 pp.

MARTIN, LAWRENCE (b. 1908)

"The National Geographic Researches in Alaska," *National Geographic*, June, 1911.

"The Hubbard Glacier," *Popular Science Monthly*, 1910.

MARTIN, MARTHA (ca. 1896-1959)

O Rugged Land of Gold. New York: Macmillan, 1953. 223 pp.

Home on the Bear's Domain. New York: Macmillan, 1954. 246 pp. Partially autobiographical.

MARTIN, PAUL SIDNEY, GEORGE I. QUIMBY and DONALD COLLIER

Indians Before Columbus. Chicago: University of Chicago Press, 1947. 582 pp.

MARTINDALE, THOMAS

Hunting in the Upper Yukon. Philadelphia: G.W. Jacobs, 1913. 320 pp.

MARTINEZ, ESTEBAN JOSE

Diary of a Voyage North with Perez in 1774. Mss. in Archivo General de la Nacion, Mexico City. See Wagner. See other diaries listed in the Arctic Bibliography.

Martinez was the central figure in the Nootka Sound controversy, in which the Spanish seized two English ships, only to be forced to release them later, acknowledging the superiority of Britain on the seas and on the northwest coast.

MARTINSEN, ELLA LUNG and EDWARD BURCHALL LUNG

Black Sand and Gold. New York: Vantage Press, 1956. 419 pp.

Trail to North Star Gold. Portland: Metropolitan Press, 1969. 359 pp.

MARVIN, FREDERICK ROWLAND (1847-1918)

Yukon Overland: The Gold Digger's Handbook. Cincinnati: Editor Publishing Co., 1898. 170 pp.

MASIK, AUGUST (b. 1888)

Arctic Nights' Entertainment. London: Blackie, 1935. 234 pp.

MASON, GEORGE F.
Animal Tracks. New York: William Morrow, 1943. 95 pp.

MASON, MICHAEL HENRY (b. 1900)
The Arctic Forests. London: Hodder and Stoughton, 1924. 320 pp. Takudh-Kutchin people and language.

MASON, OTIS TUFTON (1838-1908)
"Basket-work of the North American Aborigines," *Report*, US National Museum, 1884.
Indian Basketry. New York: Doubleday, 1904. 2v. See also the Arctic Bibliography.

MASTERSON, JAMES RAYMOND
See Pallas, Peter Simon.

MATANUSKA VALLEY
Alaska Life, March, '41; March, '44; Dec., '45; May, '46; *Alaska Sportsman*, see Index; Adams; Andrews; Andrews, R. (Agricultural Experiment Station, College); Bright; Castner (in reports of explorations); Chase; Conkle; Conrad; Colby; Couch; Dale, R. (*Climate*, [GPO]); Denison; Franck; Gasser; Glenn; Hanson, H. (Dept. of Interior, '44); Hart; Hayes; Hellenthal; Herron; Hilscher; Hulley; Krug; Leonard; Machetanz; Martin, G.; Moore, C.; Morgan and Keithahn; Pilgrim; Potter; Rockie, W.; Rossiter; Smitter; Stone, K.; Sundborg; Underwood; US Dept. of Interior (Mid-century Alaska); Willoughby; Winslow. See also Orlando Miller, *The Frontier in Alaska and the Matanuska Colony* (New Haven: Yale University Press, 1975); see as well Alaska Rural Rehabilitation Corporation.

MATHER, JOHN RUSSELL (b. 1923)
"Microclimatic Investigations at Point Barrow, 1957-58," Laboratory of Climatology, *Publications*, 1956.

MATHEWS, RICHARD
The Yukon. Holt, Rinehart and Winston, 1968. 313 pp.

MATHIASSEN, THERKEL
Archaeological Collections from the Western Eskimos. Copenhagen: Gyldendalske, 1930. 100 pp. Trans. W.E. Calvert.
Report on the Expedition. Copenhagen: Gyldendalske, 1945. 121 pp.

MATLOCK, ALMA HARWELL
Teaching Above the Arctic Circle. N. pl.: 1967. 24 pp.

MATTESON, H. H.
The Trap. New York: W.J. Watt, 1921. 293 pp.

MATTHEWS, COURTLAND W.
Aleutian Interval. Seattle: Frank McCaffrey, 1949. 61 pp. Poetry.

MATTHEWS, MARK A.
Survey Conditions of Indians in the United States. Wn.DC: GPO, 1939. Senate Committee on Indian Affairs.

MATTHIESSEN, PETER
Oomingmak: The Expedition to the Musk Ox Island. New York: Hastings House, 1967. 85 pp.

MAULE, FRANCIS I.
El Dorado "29" along with Three Other Weird Alaskan Tales. Philadelphia: Winston, 1910. 124 pp.

MAURELLE, FRANCISCO ANTONIO
Journal of a Voyage in 1775. London: J. Nicols, 1781. Maurelle sailed on the *Sonora* commanded by Bodega y Quadra. They were accompanied by Bruno de Heceta, who became separated and discovered the mouth of the Columbia River. Bodega and Maurelle discovered Sitka and named its prominent mount San Jacinto, later named Edgecumbe by Cook. See Wagner, and the Arctic Bibliography.

MAURY, JEAN WEST
Old Raven's World. Boston: Little, Brown, 1931. 284 pp.

MAY, CHARLES P.
Animals of the Far North. New York: Abelard-Schuman, 1963.

MAYBERRY, FLORENCE
Dachshunds of Mama Island. New York: Doubleday, 1963.

MAYBERRY, GENEVIEVE
Eskimo of Little Diomede. Chicago: Follett Publishing Co., 1961.
Sheldon Jackson Junior College: An Intimate History. New York: Board of National Missions of the Presbyterian Church of the United States of America, 1953. 40 pp.
"Ships that Pass in the Night," *Alaska Life*, 1944. *Bear*, *Boxer*, and *North Star*. See also other articles in *Alaska Life*, March, '44 (Aleut evacuees on Burnett Inlet), Jan., '45, March, '46, and March, '47.

MAYOKOK, ROBERT
Eskimo Customs. Nome: Nome Nugget Press, 1951. 36 pp.
Eskimo Life. Nome: Nome Nugget Press, 1951. 21 pp.
Eskimo Stories. Nome: Nome Nugget Press, 42 pp. 1960.
The Alaskan Eskimo. N. pl.: n. pub., n. d. 11 pp.

MAYOL, LURLINE
The Big Canoe. New York: Appleton-Century, 1933. 257 pp. Haida stories.
The Talking Totem Pole. Akron: Saalfield, 1930. 142 pp.

MAZOUR, ANATOLE G.
"Dimitri Zavalashin: Dreamer of a Russian-American Empire," *Pacific Historical Review*, March, 1936.
"Doctor Yegor Scheffer; Dreamer of a Russian Empire in the Pacific," *Pac. Hist. Rev.*, March, 1937.
"Prelude to Russia's Departure from America," *Pac. Hist. Rev.*, September, 1941.
"The Russian-American Company: Private or

Government Enterprise?" June, 1944.

"The Russian-American and Anglo-Russian Conventions of 1824-25," *Pac. Hist. Rev.*, 1945.

MEAD, FRANK S.
On Our Own Doorstep. New York: Friendship Press, 1948. 167 pp.

MEADE, RICHARD WORSAM
Account of a Cruise through the Alexander Archipelago in the Winter of 1868-69. Wn.DC: GPO, 1869. 29 pp. *USS Saginaw.* US Navy.

MEALS, JOHN EDWARD
"Alaska—Empire or Wasteland?" *Alaska Magazine*, Jan., 1927.

"Ketchikan, the 'First City,' " *Alaska Magazine*, Jan., 1927.

"A Trip to Skagway, What to See in the Garden City," *Alaska Magazine*, Jan., 1927.

Meals was one of the editors of the *Pathfinder of Alaska*, official organ of the Pioneers of Alaska, and invaluable source of information and perspective on the history of early American Alaska.

MEANY, EDMOND STEPHEN (1862-1935)
Vancouver's Discovery of Puget Sound. New York: Macmillan, 1907. 344 pp. Portraits and biographies of the men honored in the naming of geographic features.

A New Vancouver Journal of the Discovery of Puget Sound. Seattle, 1915. 43 pp.

"The Naming of Seward in Alaska," *Washington Historical Quarterly*, April, 1907.

"Alaska's Provisional Delegate to Congress," *Alaskan Mag. and Canadian Yukoner*, 1900.

Meany was for many years professor at the University of Washington. See the Arctic Bibliography for further references.

MEARES, JOHN (ca. 1756-1809)
Voyages made in the years 1788 and 1789 from China to the Northwest Coast of America. London: Logographic Press, 1790. 372 pp.

Meares set up as a trader in Calcutta after retirement from the Royal Navy. He took the *Nootka* to Unalaska in 1786 where he was entertained by Delarov. He was caught by winter in Prince William Sound where half his crew died of scurvy, the remainder being saved only by the timely arrival of Dixon in the *Queen Charlotte*. Later Meares would accuse Dixon of indifference, however, claiming that Portlock, also in the Sound on the *King George* (traveling with Dixon) was more helpful. Portlock extracted a promise from Meares not to trade on the northwest coast. In 1788 Meares lived with the Indians at Nootka Sound, and discovered and named the Strait of Juan de Fuca. When he sailed for China in 1789 he left the northwest coast for good. He had left two ships in the Nootka area, however, the *Iphigenia* and the *Northwest America*, which were seized by the Spanish in the famous Nootka Sound controversy. Meares presented a memorial to Parliament for damages. Dixon contested his right to damages; see Dixon. Many historians have characterized Meares as mendacious. For full bibliography on Meares see the Arctic Bibliography; see also Speck; Bancroft; Barbeau; Denton; Greenhow; Hulley; Tompkins, and Wagner. See as well Nootka Controversy. See also T-3052 ff.

MEARS, ELIOT GRINNELL
Maritime Trade of Western United States. Stanford: Stanford University Press, 1935. 583 pp.

Pacific Ocean Handbook. Stanford: Stanford University Press, 1967; also Stanford: James Ladd Delkin, 1944.

MECHAM, KATHRYN WINSLOW
See Kathryn Winslow.

MEDICINE, ARCTIC
Rodahl; Romig.

MEDILL, ROBERT BELL
Klondike Diary: True Account of the Klondike Rush of 1897-98. Portland: Beattie & Co., 1949. 188 pp.

MEEKER, EZRA (1830-1928)
Ventures and Adventures of Ezra Meeker. Seattle: Rainier Printing Co., 1908. 384 pp.

The Busy Life of 85 Years of Ezra Meeker. Seattle: the Author, 1916. 399 pp.

MELDGAARD, JORGEN
Eskimo Sculpture. New York: Clarkson N. Potter, 1960. 48 pp.

MELIN, MARGARET
Modern Pioneering in Alaska. New York: Pageant Press, 1954. 78 pp.

MELVILLE, GEORGE WALLACE (1841-1912)
In the Lena Delta: A Narrative of the Search for Lieut-Commander De Long. Boston: Houghton Mifflin, 1885. 497 pp. Melville was chief engineer of the *Jeannette*. This account includes the story of the Greely Relief Expedition.

MELVILLE, HERMAN
Moby Dick, or the White Whale. First published in 1851.

MELZACK, RONALD
The Day Tuk became a Hunter. New York: Dodd, Mead, 1967. 92 pp.

MENAGER, FRANCIS M.
The Kingdom of the Seal. Chicago: Loyola University Press, 1962. 203 pp. Catholic mission at Hooper Bay.

MENDELSOHN, S.
"Native Problem," *Economist*, August, 1967.

"Plane Country," *Economist*, August, 1967.

"Alaska after the Flood," *Economist*, August, 1967.

MENDENHALL, T. C.
"The Alaska Boundary Line," *Atlantic*, 1896.

MENDENHALL, T. C., J. E. McGRATH and J. W. TURNER
"Alaska Boundary Survey," *National Geographic*, 1893.

MENDENHALL, WALTER CURRAN (b. 1871)
"A Reconnaissance from Resurrection Bay to the Tanana River in 1898," *Annual Report*, USGS, 1898.

"A Reconnaissance in the North Bay Region, 1900," in *Reconnaissances of the Cape Nome and Norton Bay Regions*, USGS, 1900.

"Reconnaissance from Fort Hamlin to Kotzebue Sound," *Annual Report*, USGS, 1902.

Mineral Resources of the Mount Wrangel District. With F. Schrader. USGS Professional Paper, 15, 1903.

"The Wrangel Mountains, Alaska," *National Geographic*, 1903.

MENZEL, DOROTHY
"Papers Relating to the Trial of Feodor Bashmakof for Sorcery at Sitka in 1829." In *Papers*, Kroeber Anthropological Society, 1951. Bashmakov was a converted Tlingit Indian who had become a priest. He supposedly employed shamanism in an attempt to cure a fellow Indian. The translation of the trial transcript (in the Bancroft Library) was done by Ivan Petrof.

MENZIES, ARCHIBALD
Journal of Vancouver's Voyage, April to October, 1792. Victoria: W.H. Cullin, 1923.

"Menzies' Journal Relating to Visits to California," *California Historical Society Quarterly*, 1924.

"Menzies' Journal Relating to Hawaii," *Hawaii Historical Society*, n.d.

Menzies did not get on well with Vancouver, and was recommended for court martial at the end of the voyage. He refused to surrender his journal, according to the custom.

MENZIES, DONALD
The Alaska Highway: Saga of the North. Edmonton: Stuart Douglas, 1943. 48 pp.

MERK, FREDERICK
Fur Trade and Empire: George Simpson's Journal. Cambridge: Harvard University Press, 1931. 370 pp.

MERRETT, JOHN
Captain James Cook. New York: Criterion Press, 1957.

MERRIAM, CLINTON HART (1855-1942)
"Bogoslof, Our Newest Volcano," *Harriman's Alaska*, Vol. II. See also the Arctic Bibliography.

MERRILL, ELDRIDGE W. (d. 1932)
Alaska-Yukon Magazine, '07 (photos); *American Magazine* (by Barrett Willoughby); Willoughby.

MERRILL, ELMER DREW
The Botany of Cook's Voyages and Its Unexpected Significance. Waltham, Mass.: Chronica Botanica, 1954. 224 pp.

MERRILL, RUSSELL HYDE (1894-1929)
Alaska Sportsman, April, '58; Potter (Merrill disappeared on September 16, 1929, on a flight to a gold mine). Merrill Field and Merrill Pass are named for Russell Merrill, as is Merrill Wien.

MERRILL, SAMUEL
"Personal Recollections of John Muir," *Sierra Club Bulletin*, February, 1928.

MERTIE, JOHN BEAVER (b. 1888)
"Geologic Features of Alaska," *Transactions*, New York Academy of Sciences, 1939.

"Mountain Building in Alaska," *American Journal of Science*, 1930.

See the Arctic Bibliography for Mertie's USGS reconnaissance reports for Alaska.

METHODIST MISSIONS
Brummitt; Crosby; Fisk; Guernsey; Hamilton; Hayes; Henderson; Hulley; Large; Moore, D.; Morris; Oliver; Underwood; Winchell; Wise (in *Methodist Quarterly*, 1881); Young.

METLAKATLA (also Metlakahtla)
Alaska Sportsman, see Index; Arctander; Barbeau; Begg; Brooks; Brown; Colby; Collis; Couch; Davis; Dole; Franck; Grinnell; Harriman; Hayes; Higginson; History of Metlakatla (report to Sec. of Interior, ca. 1953 [typewritten copy advertised by Arthur H. Clark Co.], incl. Indian petitions, claims to industry ownership, etc.); Hulley; Kohlstedt; Matthews; Marsden; Morris; Ridley; Scidmore; Sessions; Stock; Stromstadt; Stuck; Swineford; Underwood; Wellcome; Wickersham; Wiedemann; Winslow; see also the Arctic Bibliography. See also William Duncan, and Annette Island.

MEYER, JACOB GIBBLE (b. 1884)
Our American Neighbors. Chicago: Follett, 1953. 462 pp.

MEYERS, WALTER E.
Eskimo Village. New York: Vantage Press, 1957. 125 pp. Koyuk, near the head of Norton Sound.

MEZHOV, VLADIMIR IZMAILOVICH (1831-1894)
See the Arctic Bibliography.

MICKEY, BARBARA HARRIS
"The Family among the Western Eskimo," *Anthrop. Papers*, University of Alaska, 1955.

MIDDLETON, CHRISTOPHER (d. 1770)
A Vindication of the Conduct of Captain Christopher Middleton. London: J. Robinson, 1743. 206 pp.

A Reply. London: G. Brett, 1744. 192 pp.

A Rejoinder. London: Cooper, Brett and Amey, 1745. 156 pp.

MIDDLETON ISLAND
Alaska Sportsman, Apr., '50 (Thomas V. Smith); *Alaska-Yukon Magazine*, Feb., '12 (Thomas V. Smith); Colby; Gruening (Air Force, 1950); Underwood (fox farming); Willoughby.

MIKKELSEN, EJNAR (b. 1880)
Conquering the Arctic Ice. London: W. Heinemann, 1909. 470 pp. Beaufort Sea to Valdez.

Frozen Justice. New York: Alfred A. Knopf, 1922. 230 pp.

Mirage in the Arctic. London: Rupert Hart-Davis, 1955. 216 pp.

"Report of the Mikkelsen-Leffingwell Expedition," *Bulletin*, Am. Geog. Soc., 1907.

MILEPOST, The
Published annually by Alaska Northwest Publishing Company, a full guide to Alaska travel.

MILES, CHARLES
Indian and Eskimo Artifacts of North America. New York: Henry Regnery, 1963. 244 pp.

MILLER, BASIL WILLIAM
Ken in Alaska. Grand Rapids: Zondervan Publishing House, 1944. 71 pp.
Koko and the Eskimo Doctor. Grand Rapids: Zondervan Publishing House, 1949. 88 pp.
Koko—King of the Arctic Trail. Grand Rapids: Zondervan Publishing House, 1947. 74 pp.
Koko on the Yukon. Grand Rapids: Zondervan Publishing House, 1954. 88 pp.

MILLER, DON JOHN (b. 1919)
Geology of Possible Petroleum Provinces of Alaska. Wn.DC: GPO, 1959. 132 pp. USGS. Annotated bibliography.
"Gulf of Alaska Area," in Howell Williams' *Landscapes of Alaska.*
Giant Waves in Lituya Bay, Alaska. Wn.DC: GPO, 1960. 86 pp. USGS.
See also the Arctic Bibliography.

MILLER, GERRIT SMITH and R. KELLOGG
North American Recent Mammals. Wn.DC: GPO, 1955. 954 pp. Smithsonian Institution.

MILLER, H.
"Russian Opinion on the Cession of Alaska," *American Historical Review*, April, 1943.

MILLER, JAMES MARTIN
Discovery of the North Pole. Philadelphia: George A. Parker, 1909. 428 pp. Frederick Cook's own story.

MILLER, JOAQUIN
"Stampedes on the Klondike" *Overland Monthly*, 1897.
"In a Klondike Cabin," *Leslie's*, 1899.
Complete Poetical Works. Philadelphia: Porter and Coates, 1892. See the poem, "Alaska."
See *Alaska Review*, 1966 for "To Chilkoot Pass, 1897: An Uncollected Eyewitness Report."
See also Miller, Juanita, *My Father: C.H. Joaquin Miller, Poet* (Oakland: Tooley-Towne, 1941; 218 pp.).
Miller wrote exaggerated poetical materials from the Klondike, in many cases distorting reality. His works were very popular.

MILLER, MAX CARLTON (b. 1901)
The Great Trek: The Story of the Five-year Drive of a Reindeer Herd. Garden City: Doubleday, 1935. 224 pp. 3000 head sent by the Lomen brothers on contract to the Canadian government.
Fog and Men on Bering Sea. New York: Dutton, 1936. 271 pp. On *Northland*, which replaced *Bear*.

MILLER, MAYNARD MALCOLM
"Aerial Survey of Alaskan Glaciers, 1947," *Appalachia*, 1948.
"First American Ascent of Mt. St. Elias," *National Geographic*, 1948.

"Yahtsetesha," *American Alpine Journal*, 1947.
"Alaska's Mighty Rivers of Ice," *National Geographic*, 1967.
Miller writes with the Juneau Ice Field Research Project.

MILLER, MIKE
Off the Beaten Path in Alaska. Juneau: Alaskabooks, 1970. 116 pp.
Soapy. Juneau: Alaskabooks, 1970. 122 pp.

MILLER, POLLY and LEON MILLER
Lost Heritage of Alaska. Cleveland: World Publishing Co., 1967. 320 pp.

MILLER, RAY E.
"A Strobo-photographic Analysis of a Tlingit Indian's Speech," *Internat'l. Journ. of Amer. Linguistics*, 1930.

MILLS, DAVID
The Canadian View of the Alaskan Boundary Dispute. Ottawa: Government Printing Bureau, 1899. 23 pp.

MILLS, STEPHEN E. and JAMES W. PHILLIPS
Sourdough Sky. Seattle: Superior Publishing Co., 1969. 176 pp. Photographic.

MILTON, JOHN P.
Nameless Valleys, Shining Mountains: The Record of an Expedition into the Vanishing Wilderness of Alaska's Brooks Range. New York: Walker & Co., 1970.

MILTON, Viscount and W. B. CHEADLE
The Northwest Passage by Land. London: Cassell, 1865. 394 pp.

MINER'S GUIDE to ALASKAN and YUKON RIVER GOLD FIELDS
San Francisco: Alaskan and Yukon River Gold Fields Bureau of Information, 1898.

MINING
History: *Alaska Life*, Feb., '41; *Alaska Monthly*, Oct., '07; *Alaska-Yukon Magazine*, May, '09; Golder; Shiels; USGS *Mineral Resources of Alaska*, annual from 1901, Alfred Brooks (extremely useful).
General: *Alaska Life*, Jan., '42 (death of Alaska mining); June, '45; *Alaska Sportsman*, Dec., '38 (editorial); Dec., '42 (gold mines closed to release workers for work producing strategic metals); Dec., '48 (editorial); Oct., '53 (editorial); *Alaska-Yukon Magazine*, Sept., '07 (discovery at Juneau); Brooks; Denison; Gruening; Harrison; Hilscher; Hurja (13 articles in Mining and Scientific Press [SF, 1914-15]); Kinzie; Rickard; Sundborg; Underwood; US Dept. of Interior (*Mid-century Alaska*); Wickersham. See also Mary Berry, and the Alaska Territorial Bureau of Mines and the Alaska State Commissioner of Natural Resources; see also T-85-88, T-2075, T-3861 ff, T-3940. See also the Arctic Bibliography.

MIRSKY, JEANNETTE (b. 1903)
To the North! New York: Viking Press, 1934. 386 pp. The story of Arctic exploration from earliest times to the present.

To the Arctic! New York: Alfred A. Knopf, 1948. 334 pp. Same.

The Westward Crossings: Balboa, Mackenzie, Lewis and Clark. New York: Knopf, 1946. 365 pp.

Elisha Kent Kane and the Sea-faring Frontier. Boston: Little, Brown, 1954. 201 pp.

MISSIONS and MISSIONARIES

Anderson; Andrews; Arctander; Badlam; Bancroft; Barbeau; Beattie; Brevig; Brooks; Brower; Bruce; Brummitt; Calasanz; Champagne; Chapman; Chevigny; Clark; Clut; Cody; Colby; Crosby; Curtis; Dall; De Baets; Denison; Drebert; Driggs; Faris; Gapp; Golder; Greely; Griesemer (in *Alaska Life* [Aug., '46] on S. Hall Young); Hayes; Helmericks; Henderson; Fr. Herman (German); Higginson; Hubbard; Hulley; Hutton; Jackson; Jenkins (on Bishop Rowe); Jette; Johnshoy; Judge; Juvenal; Larsson; Large; Lazell (on Jackson); Llorente; Moore (in *Alaska Sportsman*, Jan., '41 [on Holy Cross Mission], July, '43 [on Hooper Bay]); Morgan; Morris; Mousseau; Muir; O'Connor; Oliver; Owens; Romig; Santos; Savage; Schwalbe; Seghers; Smith, B.; Smith, M.; Stewart; Stuck; Svenska; Tompkins; Tucker; Underwood; Vahl; Veniaminov; Wellcome; Willard; Winchell; Winn; Wright; Young.

MITCHELL, JOHN MURRAY

See the Arctic Bibliography.

MITCHELL, MAIRIN

The Maritime History of Russia, 1848-1948. London: Sedgwick and Jackson, 1949. 544 pp.

MITCHELL, WILLIAM (1879-1936)

General Greely: The Story of a Great American. New York: Putnam's, 1936. 242 pp. See also Mirsky.

MIZNER, ADDISON

The Many Mizners. New York: Vere Publishing Co., 1932. The Mizners were prominent entrepreneurs, gamblers and entertainers in the Klondike era, operating in Dawson and Nome. See Sullivan, and Johnson; see also O'Connor. See T-3149 ff.

MJELDE, MICHAEL JAY

Glory of the Seas. Middletown, Conn.: Wesleyan University Press, 1969. 303 pp. Whaling.

MOBERG, D. R.

"1958 Election in Alaska," *Western Political Quarterly*, March, 1959.

MOFFIT, FRED HOWARD (b. 1874)

The Fair Haven Gold Placers, Seward Peninsula. Wn.DC: GPO, 1905. 85 pp. USGS. For a full bibliography on Moffit see the Arctic Bibliography.

MOLENAAR, DEE

"Mt. St. Elias: The First Ascent," in *Sierra Club Bulletin*, May, 1947.

MOLLUSKS

See Dall; see also the Arctic Bibliography.

MONROE, FRANCIS (1855-1940)

See Savage.

MONROE, ROBERT D.

"An Excursion to Wrangell, 1896," *Pac. Northwest Q.*, 1959. Philip C. Van Buskirk.

MONTAGUE, PHIL S.

Ready Reference and Hand Book of the Klondyke and Alaskan Gold Fields. San Francisco: Hicks-Judd Co., 1897. 58 pp.

MONTGOMERY, IVIL J. (b. ca. 1895)

"This Library Gets Around," *Pacific Coaster*, 1962.

MONTGOMERY, RICHARD GILL (b. 1897)

Pechuck: Lorne Knight's Adventures in the Arctic. New York: Dodd, Mead, 1932. 291 pp. Knight sailed on the *Polar Bear* in 1915, and later joined Stefansson's Canadian Arctic expedition in 1917-18.

Adventures in the Arctic. New York: Dodd, Mead, 1932. 281 pp. Same.

Husky: Co-pilot of the Pilgrim. New York: Holt, 1942. 271 pp.

MONTGOMERY, RUTHERFORD GEORGE (b. 1896)

Iceblink. New York: Holt, 1941. 288 pp. Juvenile.

Seecatch: Story of a Fur Seal. Boston: Ginn, 1955. 124 pp.

Amikuk. Cleveland: World Publishing Co., 1955. 204 pp.

MONTHLY MISCELLANY

See the Arctic Bibliography. See also de Fonte.

MOORE, JOHN BASSETT

"The Alaskan Boundary," *North Amer. Review*, Oct., '99.

History and Digest of the International Arbitrations. Wn.DC: GPO, 1898. 6v.

MOORE, J. BERNARD

Skagway in Days Primeval. New York: Vantage Press, 1968. 202 pp.

MOORE, TERRIS (b. 1908)

"Mt. Fairweather is Conquered at Last," *Sportsman*, Oct., '31.

"Mt. Sanford: An Alaskan Ski Climb," *Amer. Alpine J.*, 1939.

Mt. McKinley: The Pioneer Climb. Fairbanks: University of Alaska Press, 1967. 202 pp.

MOORE, WILLIAM I.

"Surveys made by the Coast and Geodetic Survey Steamer *Patterson* in Southeastern Alaska waters in 1892, 1893 and 1894," in *USC&GS Reports*.

MOOSE

See the Arctic Bibliography; see also *Alaska Sportsman* Index.

MORENUS, RICHARD

Alaska Sourdough: The Story of Slim Williams. Chicago: Rand McNally, 1956. 278 pp.

MOREY, WALTER

Gentle Ben. New York: Dutton, 1965. 191 pp.

Gloomy Gus. New York: Dutton, 1970. 256 pp.

Home is the North. New York: Dutton, 1967. 223 pp.

Kavik the Wolf Dog. New York: Dutton, 1968. 192 pp.

MORGAN, AUDREY and FRANK MORGAN
"Alaska's Russian Frontier: Little Diomede," *National Geographic*, 1951.

MORGAN, BERNICE BANGS
The Very Thought of Thee. Grand Rapids: Zondervan, 1952. 136 pp. Autobiographical, descriptive.
"Chilkoot Veterans," *Alaska Life*, April, 1948.

MORGAN, EDWARD E. P. (ca. 1871-1939)
God's Loaded Dice: Alice, 1897-1930. Caldwell: Caxton Printers, 1948. 298 pp. Alaska Steamship Co. and numerous famous Alaskans.

MORGAN, JULIET and EDWARD KEITHAHN
Alaska and Hawaii. New York: Macmillan, 1950. 312 pp. Juvenile.

MORGAN, LAEL
And the Land Provides: Alaskan Natives in a Year of Transition. New York: Doubleday, 1974. 316 pp. Alaska Native Claims Settlement Act.
The Woman's Guide to Boating and Cooking. Freeport, Me.: Wheelwright Co., 1968. 246 pp.

MORGAN, LEN
Klondike Adventure. New York: Nelson, 1940. 199 pp. Juvenile.

MORGAN, MURRAY CROMWELL (b. 1916)
Bridge to Russia: Those Amazing Aleutians. New York: Dutton, 1947. 222 pp. Historic and contemporary survey.
Dixie Raider: The Saga of the CSS Shenandoah. New York: Dutton, 1948. 336 pp. Operations in the Bering Sea.
Skid Road. New York: Viking, 1951. 280 pp. Seattle.
One Man's Gold Rush. Seattle: University of Washington Press, 1967. 215 pp.

MORGAN, WILLIAM GERRY (b. 1868)
The Trail of the Cheechako in Alaska. Wn.DC: McQueen, 1928. 46 pp.

MORICE, ADRIAN GABRIEL (1859-1938)
"The Dene Languages," *Transactions*, Royal Canadian Institute, 1889.
"Dene Roots," *Transactions*, Royal Can. Inst., 1892.
"The Unity of Speech among the Northern and Southern Dene," *Amer. Anthrop.*, 1907.
"The Use and Abuse of Philology," *Trans.*, Royal Can. Inst., 1899.
"Northwestern Denes and Northeastern Asiatics," *Trans.*, Royal Can. Inst., 1915.
"The Western Denes: Their Manners and Customs," *Proceedings*, Royal Can. Inst., 1888.
"Notes Archeological, Industrial, and Sociological on the Western Denes," *Trans.*, Royal Can. Inst., 1892.
The History of Northern Interior British Columbia. Toronto: Briggs, 1904. 349 pp.
History of the Catholic Church in Western Canada. Toronto: Musson, 1910. 2v.

The Catholic Church in Western Canada. Winnipeg: Canadian Publishers, 1931. 26 pp.
The Catholic Church in the Canadian Northwest. Winnipeg: Canadian Publishers, 1936. 83 pp.
Fifty Years in Western Canada. Toronto: Musson, 1930. 267 pp. Memoirs.
Thawing out the Eskimos. Boston: Society for the Propagation of the Faith, 1943. 188 pp.

MORISON, SAMUEL ELIOT
History of US Naval Operations in WW II: The Aleutians, Gilberts, and Marshalls. Boston: Little, Brown, 1951.
The Maritime History of Massachusetts. Boston: Houghton, 1931.
"American Strategies in the Pacific Ocean," *Oregon Hist. Q* (March, 1961).

MORRELL, WILLIAM PARKER (b. 1899)
The Gold Rushes. London: Black, 1940. 426 pp.

MORRIS, FRANK, W. R. HEATH, and AMOS BURG
Marine Atlas. Seattle: P.B.I. Publishing Co., 1959.

MORRIS, IDA DORMAN
A Pacific Coast Vacation. New York: Abbey Press, 1901. 255 pp.

MORRIS, WILLIAM ALFRED
"Origin and Authorship of the Bancroft Pacific States Publications," *Oregon Historical Quarterly*, 1903. See also Pierce. Morris was a friend of F. Fuller Victor, one of Bancroft's many authors who most resented his taking full credit for the Pacific works. She gave Morris many clues to identification of the various authors. See also Caughey.

MORRIS, WILLIAM GOUVERNEUR
Report on the Customs District, Public Service, and Resources of Alaska Territory. Wn.DC: GPO, 1879. 163 pp. This is one of the more important sources for Alaska history for the period immediately after cession. See Gruening.

MORROW, HONORE
Argonaut. William Morrow: 1933. 316 pp.

MORROW, WILLIAM W.
The Spoilers. Reprinted from the *Calif. Law Review*, 1916. Nome case with Noyes and Anderson.

MORSKOI SBORNIK
See the Arctic Bibliography, and V.M. Golovnin.

MORTIMER, GEORGE
See T-3203 ff.

MORTON, ARTHUR SILVER (1870-1945)
A History of the Canadian West to 1870-71. London: Nelson, 1939. 987 pp.
Sir George Simpson: Overseas Governor of the Hudson's Bay Company. Portland: Binfords and Mort, 1944. 310 pp.
The Northwest Company. Toronto: Ryerson, 1930. 32 pp.

MOSER, JEFFERSON FRANKLIN

"The Salmon and Salmon Fisheries of Alaska," Report of the US Fish Commission steamer *Albatross*, *Bulletin*, US Fish Commission. Wn.DC: GPO, 1899. A full survey taken from Cape Prince of Wales to Cook Inlet in 1898.

"Alaska Salmon Investigations in 1900 and 1901," *Bulletin*, US Fish Commission. Wn.DC: GPO, 1902.

"Alaska: Hydrographic Notes and Sailing Directions," *Bulletin*, US Coast and Geodetic Survey, 1903.

See also the Arctic Bibliography.

MOUNT McKINLEY NATURAL HISTORY ASSOCIATION

Mt. McKinley National Park: Alaska Colorbook. Amsterdam, New York: Noteworthy Co., 1968. 32 pp.

MOUNT WRANGELL COMPANY

Short Story of Alaska and the Yukon. Boston, 1898.

MOUNTAINS and MOUNTAINEERING

Alaska Magazine, Jan., '27 (49 peaks listed); Alpine journals (*Alpine Journal* [London]; *Amer. Alpine J.*; *Appalachia*; *Canadian Alpine J.*; *Sierra Club Bulletin*); Arctic Bibliography; Beardslee (in *Field and Stream*, Nov., 1879); Bent (in *Geog. Rv.*, June, '19); Brooks; Dunn (see Wickersham Bibliography); Hazard; Keen (see Wickersham); Macbeth (in *Alaska-Yukon Magazine*, Oct., '11); *National Geographic*, see Index; Pilgrim; Russell; Seton-Karr (in *Proc.*, Royal Geog. Soc., May, 1887); Washburn (indispensable for the McKinley student); Wickersham.

See also the following:

Alaska Range	Brooks
Mt. Alverston	Bates; Clifford
Akutan Crater	Hubbard
Aniakchak Crater	Douglas; Morgan; Hubbard
Mt. Augusta	Reynolds
Mt. Bona	Baxter; Hart
Mt. Brooks	Ames; Humphreys; Scudder
Mt. Cleveland	Morgan
Mt. Cook	Miller, T.; Mohling
Mt. Crillon	Washburn
Mt. Deborah	Beckey; Harrer
Mt. Deception	Washburn
Mt. Drum	Harrer; Hart; Henderson
Mt. Eielson	*Alaska Sportsman*, '46, 47
Mt. Fafnir	West
Mt. Fairweather	Dall; Washburn
Mt. Foraker	Brown, T.; Washburn
Mt. Hayes	Korff; Washburn; Whitney
Hayes Range	Ferris
Mt. Hess	Paige
Mt. Hubbard	Bates; Clifford
Mt. Hunter	Beckey; Harrer; Henderson; Washburn
Mt. Jordan	Baxter
Katmai	Griggs; Hubbard; Morgan
King Peak	Hart; Reynolds; Schoening; Thayer
Mt. LaPerouse	Seitz
Mt. Logan	Foster; Miller, T.; Mohling
Mt. McArthur	Mohling
McCall Peak	*Explorer's Journal*

Mt. McKinley	see Mt. McKinley
Mt. Mather	Humphreys; Scudder
Mt. Natazhat	Lambart
Prince Wm. Sound	Field
Russell Fiord	Putnam
Mt. St. Agnes	Dyhrenfurth; Washburn
Mt. St. Elias	Broke; Dall; DeLay; Miller, M.; Putnam; Russell; Seton-Karr; Williams
Mt. Sanford	Moore
Scott Peak	Ames
Mt. Sharkstooth	West
Mt. Shishaldin	Higginson
Tulik Crater	Morgan
Unimak Island	Higginson; Westdahl
University Peak	Blumer; Hart; Houston; Reynolds; Sanders
Mt. Vancouver	Bruce-Robertson; Hainsworth; Odell
Mt. Veniaminov	*Alaska Sportsman*, Aug., '39; March, '54; Sept., '55; Hubbard
Mt. Witherspoon	Nielsen; West
Mt. Wrangell	Allen; *Alaska Sportsman*, Nov., '41; Beiser; Colby; Dunn; Korff; Mendenhall; Rice; Powell; Rohn

In all cases see the Arctic Bibliography.

MOUNTEVANS, EDWARD RATCLIFFE GARTH RUSSELL EVANS

See T-3213 ff.

MOURELLE, FRANCISCO ANTONIO

See Maurelle.

MOUROT, N. O.

"Flying in Alaska," *Popular Aviation*, July, 1928. Photos of Crosson, Wilkes and Eielson.

MOZEE, YVONNE

"An Interview with Rei Munoz," *Alaska Journal*, Spring, 1974.

MOZINO SUAREZ de FIGUEROA, JOSE MARIANA (1757-1819)

See the Arctic Bibliography.

MUDGE, ZACHARIAH ATWELL (1813-1888)

Fur-clad Adventurers. New York: Phillips and Hunt, 1880. 342 pp. Alaska and Kamchatka. Telegraph, 1865.

Arctic Heroes. New York: Nelson and Phillips, 1875. 304 pp.

MUELLER, R. J.

A Short Illustrated Topical Dictionary of Western Kutchin. Fairbanks: Summer Institute of Linguistics, 1964.

MUIR, JOHN (1838-1914)

Travels in Alaska. Boston: Houghton Mifflin, 1915. 326 pp. This is Muir's major work on Alaska, as revealing of his own view of nature as it is of the glaciers of southeast Alaska which captivated him. He tells of his stay at Wrangell, and his travels in Glacier Bay with S. Hall Young.

The Cruise of the Corwin. Boston: Houghton, 1917. 278 pp. 1881 search for DeLong and the *Jean-*

nette. This includes Muir's observations of Unalaska, the Aleuts, Chukchis, Bering Sea islands, Plover Bay, St. Michael, first landing on Wrangel Island, whaling wrecks, and the Eskimos.

Stickeen: The Story of a Dog. Boston: Houghton, 1909. 73 pp.

Our National Parks. Boston: Houghton Mifflin, 1901. 382 pp.

"Notes on the Pacific Coast Glaciers," in *Harrimans Alaska.*

"Alaska," *American Geologist*, May, 1893.

On John Muir, see the following:

John Muir: A Pictorial Biography. Seattle: Lowman and Hanford, 1938. 105 pp.

The John Muir Book. Seattle: Cooperative Printing Co., 1925. 71 pp.

The Wilderness World of John Muir. Henry B. Kane. Boston: Houghton Mifflin, 1954. 332 pp.

The Writings of John Muir. Ed., William Frederic Bade. 10v. Boston: Houghton Mifflin, 1915-24.

The Life and Letters of John Muir. Ed., William Frederic Bade. Boston: Houghton Mifflin, 1924. 2v.

John of the Mountains: The Unpublished Journals of John Muir. Boston: Houghton Mifflin, 1938. 459 pp. Few of these relate to Alaska.

A Synthesis of Muir Criticism. William B. Rice. Reprinted from *Sierra Club Bulletin*, June, 1943.

John Muir Memorial Number. Sierra Club Bulletin, 1916.

For a full bibliography on John Muir see the Arctic Bibliography, and T-3221 ff. See also *Alaska-Yukon Magazine*, April, 1907. See as well Washburn, and Norman. See also Swift.

MUIR, JOHN REID
The Life and Achievements of Captain James Cook. London: Blackie, 1939. 310 pp.

MULDROW, ROBERT
"Mount McKinley Notes," *National Geographic*, Aug., 1901. See also the 20th *Annual Report* of the USGS (1899) for the narrative of Muldrow's survey of the Susitna Valley with George H. Eldridge. See also Baker.

MULLER, GERHARD FRIEDRICH (1705-1783)
Voyages from Asia to America. London, 1761. 120 pp. Muller traveled with Bering in 1741, and published a map of the voyage in 1754. His work was corrected by Cook. See the Arctic Bibliography.

MULLER, MARTIN (b. 1902)
See the Arctic Bibliography.

MULLER, SIEMON WILLIAM (b. 1900)
Permafrost. Wn.DC: GPO, 1945. 231 pp. US Army, Military Intelligence. See the Arctic Bibliography.

MUNFORD, JAMES KENNETH (b. 1912)
John Ledyard: An American Marco Polo. Portland: Binfords and Mort, 1939. 308 pp.

John Ledyard's Journal of Captain Cook's Last Voyage. Corvallis: Oregon State University Press, 1963. 264 pp.

"Did John Ledyard Witness Captain Cook's Death?" *Pac. Northwest Quarterly*, April, 1963.

MUNGER, JAMES F.
Two Years in the Pacific and Actic Oceans. New York: J.R. Howlett, Printer, 1852. 80 pp. Natives, whaling. Reprint: Fairfield, Wn.: Galleon Press, 1967.

MUNOZ, JUAN
Juneau: A Study of the Gastineau Channel Area. Juneau: Totem Press, 1956. 120 pp.

"Cliff Dwellers of the Bering Sea," *National Geographic*, 1954. King Island.

MUNRO, JOHN A.
The Alaska Boundary Dispute. Toronto: Copp Clark, 1967. 169 pp. See also Penlington.

MUNRO, WILFRED HAROLD
Tales of an Old Seaport. Princeton: Princeton University Press, 1917. 292 pp. Bristol, Rhode Island.

MUNROE, KIRK (1850-1930)
The Fur-seal's Tooth. New York: Harper, 1894. 267 pp.

Snow-shoes and Sledges. New York: Harper, 1895. 271 pp.

MURASHEV, MIKHAIL
See the Arctic Bibliography, and Baker.

MURDOCH, JOHN (1852-1925)
"Contributions to the International Polar Expedition, 1882-83," in *Report*, International Polar Expedition to Point Barrow. See the Arctic Bibliography.

"Animals Known to Eskimos," *American Naturalist*, Oct., 1898.

"The East Greenlanders," *Am. Nat.*, 1887.

"Legendary Fragments from Point Barrow," *Am. Nat.*, 1886.

"Popular Errors Regarding the Eskimo," *Am. Nat.*, 1887.

"Seven New Species of Crustacea," *Proceedings*, US National Museum, 1884.

"Remarkable Eskimo Harpoon from East Greenland," *Proc.*, US Nat. Museum, 1888.

"Pt. Barrow and NW Greenland Eskimo Boot Strings Compared," *American Anthropologist*, 1898.

"History of the 'Throwing Stick' which Drifted from Alaska to Greenland," *Amer. Anthrop.*, 1890.

"Siberian Origins of Customs of Western Eskimos," *Amer. Anthrop.*, 1888.

"Ethnological Results of the Point Barrow Expedition," *Annual Report*, Bureau of American Ethnology, 1892.

See a fuller listing in the Arctic Bibliography.

MURDOCK, GEORGE PETER (b. 1897)
Ethnographic Bibliography of North America. New Haven: Yale University Press, 1941. 168 pp.

Our Primitive Contemporaries. New York: Macmillan, 1934. 614 pp.

Rank and Potlatch among the Haida Indians. New Haven: Yale University Press, 1936. 20 pp.

MURIE, ADOLPH (b. 1899)
A Naturalist in Alaska. New York: Devin-Adair Co., 1961. 302 pp.

Birds of Mt. McKinley, Alaska. San Francisco: Pisani Printing Co., 1963. 86 pp.

Mammals of Mt. McKinley National Park, Alaska. San Francisco: Pisani Printing Co., 1962. 56 pp.

"Wildlife of Mt. McKinley National Park," *National Geographic*, 1953.

"Wilderness North," *Pacific Discovery*, 1953.

"Nesting Records, Arctic Willow Warbler," *Condor*, 1956.

"The Wandering Tattler: Notes on Nesting," *Wilson Bulletin*, 1956.

MURIE, MARGARET (b. 1902)
Two in the Far North. New York: Alfred A. Knopf, 1962. 438 pp. Autobiographical.

"We Explore the Sheenjeck," *Alaska Sportsman*, 1960.

MURIE, OLAUS JOHAN (b. 1889)
"Planning for Alaska's Big Game," Alaska Science Conf., *Papers*, 1952.

"Return to Denali," *Sierra Club Bulletin*, 1953.

"Wildlife Introductions in Alaska," *Transactions*, North American Wildlife Conf., 1940.

"Aleutian Cruise," *Travel*, 1942.

A Field Guide to Animal Tracks. Boston: Houghton Mifflin, 1954.

Fauna of the Aleutian Islands and Alaska Peninsula. Wn.DC: GPO, 1959. 406 pp. US Fish and Wildlife Service.

See also the Arctic Bibliography.

MURPHY, EMILY FERGUSON (1868-1933)
Bishop Bompas. Toronto: Ryerson, n.d. 30 pp.

MURPHY, ROBERT
The Haunted Voyage. New York: Doubleday, 1961. Bering.

The Warmhearted Polar Bear. Boston: Little, Brown, 1957. 48 pp.

MURRAY, ALEXANDER HUNTER (1818-1874)
Journal of the Yukon, 1847-48. Ottawa: Government Printing Bureau, 1910. 125 pp. From Ft. McPherson to the Porcupine and Yukon, and the building of Ft. Yukon. General information. Robert Kennicott visited Ft. Yukon in 1860, guest of James Lockhart, then chief factor for Hudson's Bay Co.

MURRAY, GLADYS HALL
Mystery of the Talking Totem Pole. New York: Dodd Mead, 1965. 208 pp.

MURRAY, HUGH (1779-1846)
Historical Account of Discoveries and Travels in North America. London: Rees, 1829. 2v.

MURRAY, ROBERT K.
The Harding Era: Warren G. Harding and His Administration. Minneapolis: University of Minnesota Press, 1969.

MURTAUGH, WILLIAM J.
"The Homes of Nome," *Alaska Journal*, Winter, 1974.

MYERS, BEN L.
A Short Story of the Metlakatla Christian Mission. Palo Alto: the Author, 1954. 32 pp.

MYERS, C. V.
Through Hell to Alaska: A Novel. New York: Exposition Press, 1955. 264 pp. Canol.

MYERS, HARRY M. and WILLIAM A. MYERS
Adventures in McKinley Park. N. pl.: Provincial News, 1933. 40 pp.

Back Trails. Lapeer, Mich.: the Author, 1933.

MYERS, HORTENSE and RUTH BURNETT
Carl Ben Eielson: Young Alaska Pilot. Indianapolis: Bobbs-Merrill, 1960. 190 pp.

Vilhjalmur Stefansson: Young Arctic Explorer. Indianapolis: Bobbs-Merrill, 1966.

MYERS, JOHN L.
The Great Land. New York: Board of Home Missions, n.d. 6 pp.

MYERS, LEONARD (b. 1827)
"Purchase of Alaska," Speech in the House of Representatives, July 1, 1868.

MYRON, ROBERT
Mounds, Towns and Totems. Cleveland: World Publishing Co., 1966. 127 pp.

N

NAHANNI VALLEY
See Patterson.

NAISH, CONSTANCE and GILLIAN STORY
English-Tlingit Dictionary. Fairbanks: Summer Institute of Linguistics, 1963. 81 pp.

NAMES, Geographic
Arctic Bibliography; Baker ("Alaskan Geographic Names," *Annual Report*, USGS, 1899); Callarman, B. (*Alaska Life*, March, '45); Couch; Davidson ("Copper River of Alaska," *Transactions*, Geog. Soc. of Pacific, 1902); Davidson ("Report on Resources, Coast Features of Alaska," *Annual Report*, USC&GS, 1867); DeArmond (*Alaska Life*, Aug., '49); Gr. Britain, Hydrographic Dept., "Bering Sea and Strait Pilot," (1920); Lilian, S. (*Alaska Sportsman*, Aug., '40); Marshall ("Reconnaissance, Koyukuk Valley," *Mineral Res. of Alaska, 1931,* [USGS]); *Names*, Journal of the Amer. Name Soc.; Orth, Donald J. (*Dictionary of Alaska Place Names*); Ransom, J.E.; Sealock, R.B. and P.A. Seely (*Biblio. of Place Name Literature* [Chicago, 1948]); Steward (*Names*, Dec., '56 [on the name "Alaska"]); US Bd. on Geog. Names (6th Rpt., 1933); US Bd. on Geog. Names (see the Arctic Bibliography); US Dept. of Commerce, C&GS ("Geographic Names in the Coastal Areas of Alaska," [1939-40]); Walbran; Winn (*Alaska Life*, May, 1944).

NANSEN, FRIDTJOF (1861-1930)
Farthest North. New York: Harper, 1897. 2v. Norwegian vessel *Fram* in 1893-96.
Eskimo Life. London: Longmans, Green, 1893. 350 pp. Greenland.
The First Crossing of Greenland. London: Longmans, Green, 1890. 2v. Nansen and Sverdrup in 1888.
"To the North Pole by Airship," *Forum*, April, 1926. Plans for the future.
See also the Arctic Bibliography.

NASKE, CLAUS M.
An Interpretive History of Alaskan Statehood. Anchorage: Alaska Northwest Publishing Co., 1973.
"103,350,000 Acres," *Alaska Journal*, 1972.
"Little Men Demand Statehood for Alaska," *J. of the West*, 1974.

NATIONAL ACADEMY OF SCIENCES
The Great Alaska Earthquake of 1964. Wn.DC: Nat. Acad. of Sciences, 1968. 446 pp.

NATIONAL GEOGRAPHIC SOCIETY
See Index.
America's Wonderlands. Wn.DC: Nat. Geog. Soc., 1923.
Great Adventures with the National Geographic. Wn.DC: Nat. Geog. Soc., 1963. 504 pp.
See also T-3274 ff.

NATIONAL RESOURCES PLANNING BOARD
"Postwar Economic Development of Alaska," *Regional Development Plan, Report for 1942.* Wn.DC: GPO, 1947.

NATIVES; see Alaska Natives; Indians; Eskimos; Aleuts.

NAVAL GOVERNMENT at Sitka
Bancroft; Andrews; Gruening; Hulley; Nichols; Scidmore; see also Beardslee, and Tompkins. The naval vessels at Sitka during this period were the following:

HMS *Osprey*, A'Court	1879
USS *Jamestown*, Beardslee	1879-80
USS *Jamestown*, Glass	1880-81
USS *Wachusett*, Lull	1881
USS *Wachusett*, Glass	1881-82
USS *Adams*, Merriman	1882-84
USS *Adams*, Coghlan	1884
USS *Pinta*, Nichols	1884

See also Beardslee.

NAVARRETE, MARTIN FERNANDEZ de
See Fernandez de Navarrete, Martin.

NEATBY, LESLIE H.
The Quest of the Northwest Passage. New York: Crowell, 1958. 194 pp.

NELSON, EDWARD WILLIAM (1855-1934)
Report on Natural History Collections Made in Alaska Between 1877 and 1881. Wn.DC: GPO, 1887. 337 pp. US Army. Nelson's stay at St. Michael with sledge trips to adjoining regions.
"The Eskimo about Behring Strait," *18th Annual Report*, Bur. of Amer. Ethnology, 1896-97. Life and custom.

Wild Animals of North America. Wn.DC: Nat. Geogr. Soc., 1918.
"Birds of Bering Sea and the Arctic Ocean," *Cruise of the Revenue Steamer Corwin*, 1881.
"On the Source of the Jadite Implements of the Alaskan Innuit," *Proceedings*, US National Museum, 1884.
See also the Arctic Bibliography. On Nelson see the following:
Baker; Goldman (*Auk*, 1935); Hooper (Cruise of the *Corwin*); Lantis ("Edward William Nelson," *Anthrop. Papers*, Univ. of Alaska, 1954); Oehser (*The Land*, Spr., 1950).

NELSON, KLONDY ESMERALDA (b. 1897)
Daughter of the Gold Rush. With Corey Ford. New York: Random House, 1958. 173 pp.
"I was a Bride of the Arctic," *Sat. Eve. Post*, 1956.

NELSON, RICHARD K.
Hunters of the Northern Forest. Chicago: University of Chicago Press, 1973. 429 pp.

NELSON, URBAN C.
"The Forest-Wildlife Resources of Alaska," *J. of Forestry*, 1960.

NENANA
Alaska Sportsman, Feb., '43; March, '54; Sept., '55 (closing of Episcopal mission school); Dec., '57 (steamboat *Nenana*); July, '55 (ice pool started in 1906); Cameron, Colby; Couch; Chase; Franck; Kitchener; Stuck; Tewkesbury; Winslow.

NEUE NACHRICHTEN
See T-3933. A 1776 publication (Hamburg and Leipzig) on the relationship between Asia and NorthAmerica, variously ascribed to Johann Schultz, Jean-Benoit Schérer and August Schlözer. See L. Stejneger.

NEUMAN, DANIEL SAHEYAUSE
Practical Medical Manual for Alaska Missionaries and Teachers. Nome: Press of the Nome Daily Nugget, 1911, 100 pp.

NEVSKII, V. V.
Pervoe Puteshestvie Rossiian Vokrug Sveta. (First Russian Voyage around the World) Moscow, 1951. 272 pp. Krusenstern and Lisianski in 1803-06. Bibliography.

NEW YORK TIMES
See Index.

NEWCOMBE, CHARLES FREDERIC (b. 1851)
The First Circumnavigation of Vancouver Island. Victoria: King's Printer, 1914.
"The Haida Indians," *Proceedings*, Internat'l. Congress of Americanists, Quebec, 1906.
"The McGill Totem Pole," *Ottawa Naturalist*, 1918.

NEWELL, EDYTHE W.
The Rescue of the Sun, and Other Tales. Chicago: A. Whitman, 1970. 142 pp.

NEWELL, GORDON R. and JOE WILLIAMSON
Pacific Steamboats: From Sidewheeler to Motor Ferry. Seattle: Superior Publishing Co., 1958. 196 pp.

NEWELL, GORDON R.
SOS North Pacific: Tales of Shipwrecks. Portland: Binfords and Mort, 1955. 216 pp.

NEWELL, IRWIN MAYER
See T-3299 ff.

NEWSPAPERS
See Wickersham, W-4984-5211. See also Nichols, pp. 425-27. See as well the microfilm index of Alaska newspapers being prepared by the Alaska State Library. See also the following:
Alaska Life, March, '43; July, '41; July, '45; Jan., '46. See also De Armond, Underwood.

NIBLACK, ALBERT PARKER (1859-1929)
"The Coast Indians of Southern Alaska and Northern British Columbia," *Annual Report*, US National Museum, 1888. Life and habits, Skeena River to Prince William Sound.

NICHOLS, HENRY EZRA
Alaska Coast Pilot. rev. ed. Wn.DC: GPO, 1891. See also Baker.

NICHOLS, IRBY C.
"Russian Ukase and the Monroe Doctrine," *Pacific Historical Review*, Feb., 1967.

NICHOLS, JEANNETTE (b. 1890)
Alaska. Cleveland: Arthur H. Clark, 1924. 456 pp. A History of its Administration, Exploitation, and Industrial Developments during its First Half Century under the Rule of the United States. Nichols served as secretary to Wickersham when he was Alaska delegate.

NIEDLIECK, PAUL
Cruises in the Bering Sea. Trans. London: Ward, 1909. 252 pp. Natives, and game. In 1906 from the Gulf of Anadyr to Nome, and the Aleutians.

NIKOLAI, Bishop of the Aleutians and Alaska
See T-3308 ff.

NILSSON, EINAR
"Mt. McKinley Diary," *Sierra Club Bulletin*, June, 1943.

NISHIMOTO, SETSUO
Report on Whale Marking in the North Pacific, 1950. Tokyo: Fisheries Agency of the Japanese Government, 1951. 245 pp.

NIXON-ROULET, MARY F.
Our Little Alaskan Cousin. Boston: Houghton, 1909. 138 pp. Juvenile.

NOBILE, UMBERTO (b. 1885)
With the Italia to the North Pole. London: Allen and Unwin, 1930. 358 pp. By air.
"Navigating the *Norge* from Rome to the North Pole and Beyond," *National Geographic*, Aug., 1927.

NOICE, HAROLD H.
With Stefansson in the Arctic. New York: Dodd Mead, 1924. 269 pp.

NOME
Alaska Life, Feb., '43 (Noyes); Jan., '44; March, '44; May, '45; and others; *Alaska Sportsman*, see Index; *Alaska-Yukon Magazine*, March, '07 (history); July, '07 (mining); Aug., '07; Nov., '07; Dec., '07; Aug., '08 (shipping); March, '09 (prominent men); Apr., '09 (mushing to Valdez); Albee ('34 fire); Allen, A. (dog races); Andrews; Arnell (*Alaska Life*, Feb., '48); Bankson; Baker; Beach; Blake; Brevig; Bright; Brooks; Cameron; Carlson, L.; Carpenter; Carrighar; Chase; Clark, H.; Clark, M.; Colby; Couch; Critchfield (in *Econ. Geog.*, Oct., '49); Darling; Davis; Devine; Dole (on name); Dunham; Eastwood; Eisenlohr; Ellis (*Eng. Mining J.*, 1915); Enders-Schichanowsky; Fitz; Forrester (*Alaska Sportsman*, Nov., '45); Franck; French; Garst; Goetze; Greely; Grinnell; Griffiths (in *Compilation of Narratives*); Gruening; Harrison; Hart; Hawthrone; Hellenthal; Hewitt; Higginson; Hilscher; Hines; Hulley; Hunt; Hutchison; Jacobin; Jarvis; Jenkins; Johnston; Kirillov (see the Arctic Bibliography); Kitchener; Kuehnelt-Leddhin; Lindbergh; Lockley; Lomen; McElwaine; McKee; McLain; Madsen; Mahoney; Martin, L.; Mikkelsen; Miller, Max; Mizner; Morrow; Nelson, Klondy; Osborne; Pilgrim; Poor; Potter; Rickard; Robinette; Robins; Rossiter; Samson; Samuels; Savage; Schrader; Stevens; Stuck; Sullivan, E.; Sullivan, M.; Sundborg; Tewkesbury; Thompson, D.; Tompkins; Trelawney-Ansell; Trezona; Tulchinskii (see the Arctic Bibliography); Underwood; US Army (*Compilation of Narratives*); US Dept. of Interior (Mid-century Alaska); Walden; Wead; Wickersham; Willoughby; Winslow; Wirt; Young.

NOONAN, DOMINIC A. (b. 1883)
Alaska: The Land of Now. Seattle: Sherman Printing Co., 1921. 134 pp. Poetry.
Alaska: The Land of Plenty. New York: Pageant Press, 1960. 163 pp. Poetry.

NOOTKA, and NOOTKA SOUND CONTROVERSY
Anderson, B.; Bancroft; Barbeau; Brooks; Colby; Colnett; Cook; Denton; Etches; Greenhow; Godwin; Howat; Hulley; Kippis; McDonald; Marshall; Martinez; Meares; Mozins; Perez; Speck; Tompkins; Vancouver; Wagner. See also T-730, T-997. Nootka Sound was discovered by Martinez and Perez in 1774, and again by Cook in 1778. It was a popular anchorage for trading vessels. In 1789 the Spanish captured British vessels here on a charge of trespass (see Colnett, and Meares), but returned the ships when war threatened. In 1792 Vancouver was sent out to accept the Spanish surrender.

NORDENSKIOLD, NILS ADOLF ERIK (1832-1901)
See T-3323 ff.

NORDENSKIOLD, NILS OTTO GUSTAF
See T-3336 ff.

NORMAN, CHARLES
John Muir, Father of our National Parks. New York: Julian Messner, 1957. 191 pp.

NORMAN, ROSTEN
Big Road. New York: Rinehart, 1946. 233 pp.

NORRIS, LUTHER
See Wiedemann.

NORTH AMERICAN COMMERCIAL COMPANY
See the Arctic Bibliography.

NORTH AMERICAN TRANSPORTATION and TRADING COMPANY
Alaska and the Gold Fields of Nome. Chicago, 1900. 136 pp.

NORTH PACIFIC EXPLORING EXPEDITION
Manuscript journals, see Baker. See also Caswell, and Habersham, and Heine. The expedition was sent by J.P. Kennedy in 1853 to make hydrographic surveys for the navy, and to conduct scientific research. Captain Cadwalader Ringgold was the initial commander, succeeded by Captain John Rodgers. The *Vincennes* and *Fenimore Cooper* conducted coast surveys, the latter the first US vessel (government) to negotiate the Bering Strait. The *John Hancock* charted whaling grounds in the Sea of Okhotsk and the Gulf of Amur, while the *Fenimore Cooper* charted the Aleutian Islands.

NORTH PACIFIC PLANNING PROJECT
Report of Progress, 1943. Wn.DC: National Resources Planning Board, 1943. 39 pp.

NORTH PACIFIC PUBLISHING COMPANY
North Pacific Almanac. Seattle, 1890.
North to Alaska. A Guide to Travelers in the "Land of the Future." Victoria: 20th Century Advertising Ltd., 1968. 86 pp.

NORTHERN PACIFIC RAILROAD COMPANY
Alaska. St. Paul, n.d. 31 pp.
The Alaska-Yukon-Pacific Exposition. St. Paul, 1909. 45 pp.
Puget Sound and Alaska. St. Paul, 1916. 32 pp. See also T-3353 ff.

NORTHRUP, TRUMAN
Arctic Raider. Boston: W.A. Wilde, 1936. 320 pp. Fiction based on reality.

NORTHWEST BOOKS
Report of the Committee on Books. Inland Empire Council of Teachers of English, Aug., 1933. Missoula: Montana State University, 1933. 69 pp.
Northwest Books: First Supplement. Lincoln: University of Nebraska Press, 1949. 278 pp.

NORTHWEST MAPPING SERVICE
New Alaska Highway Packet. Seattle: 1948. 8 pp.

NORTHWEST PASSAGE
Alaska Life, Aug., '39 (Kellems, from Alaska to Baffin Bay in *Pandora*); *Alaska Sportsman,* Jan., '55 (MP patrol boats); Feb., '58 (US Coast Guard); Alexander, P. (*North-West and North-East Passages* [Cambridge: Cambridge University Press, 1915]); Amundsen (first transit, 1903-07); Armstrong, Sir A.; Barrow, J.; Beaufoy (in Daines Billington); Bodilly (on Capt. James); Brown, J.; Christy (Luke Foxe and

James of Bristol); Crouse; Colby; Caswell; Cook, James; DeFonte; Delisle; Ferrer de Maldonado; Fernandez de Navarrete; Godwin; Golder; Goldson; Greenhow; Huish (on Capt. John Ross and on Beechey); Hulley; Johnson; Larsen (*Voyage of the RCM Police Schooner St. Roch* [Ottawa: 1945]); Leveson-Cower (*Beaver*, 1936); M'Clure (discoverer, 1850-54); McDonald, Maldonado (see Ferrer de Maldonada); Middleton; Mirsky; Neatby; Neuberger; Osborn; Parry; Pickersgill; Randall; Robinson; Ross; Salva; Speck; Stone (in *Bulletin*, Am. Geog. Soc., 1903); Swaine (on Capt. Francis Smith); Tranter; Tompkins; Vancouver; Wyld; Wagner.

NOURSE, JOSEPH EVERETT
Narrative of the Second Expedition of Capt. Chas. F. Hall. Wn.DC: GPO, 1879. Sen. Ex. Doc. No. 27, 45th Cong., 3rd Sess. For Hall's life see Caswell, and notes in Mirsky.

NOVO y COLSON, PEDRO de (1846-1931)
See T-3361 ff.

NOYES, CHARLES E.
"Present and Future Development of Alaska," *Editorial Research Papers* (Wn.DC: Ed. Res. Reports, 1939).

NOYES, SHERMAN A.
Faith Creek. New York: Vantage Press, 1956. 150 pp.

NOZIKOV, NIKOLAI NIKOLAEVICH
Russian Voyages around the World. London: Hutchinson, 1941. 165 pp. Trans. E. and M. Lesser. Contains an introduction on Russian circumnavigations and company exploitation of the native population.

NUKLUKAYET
Alaska Sportsman, June, '55 (NC Co. post, history [Ft. Adams, Ft. Weare, Ft. Gibbons, etc.]); Allen (in *Compilation of Narratives*); Baker (at Tanana and Yukon Rivers); Dall; DeBaets; Chase; Kitchener; Raymond; Santos; Schwatka; Stuck; Whymper.

NULATO
Alaska Sportsman, Oct., '40; March, '46; Allen; Bancroft; Colby; Dall; Helmericks; Haynes (massacre, in *Alaska Life,* Oct., '40); Higginson; Hrdlicka; Hulley; James; Judge; Llorente; O'Connor; Petrof; Raymond; Rickard; Santos; Savage; Schwatka; Stuck; Sundborg; Tompkins; Whymper; Wickersham; Zagoskin.

NUNN, GEORGE EMRA (b. 1882)
Origin of the Strait of Anian Concept. Philadelphia: 1929. 36 pp.

NUTCHUK
See Simeon Oliver.

O

OAK, HENRY LEBBEUS (1844-1905)
"Literary Industries: A Statement on the Authorship of Bancroft's Native Races and History of the Pacific States. San Francisco: Bacon Printing Co., 1893. 89 pp. Criticism of Bancroft's authorship claims; cp Pierce on Petrof, and see Bancroft.

OAKES, PATRICIA
A State is Born. New York: Harcourt Brace, 1958.
The Alaska Voters' Guidebook. Central, Alaska: 1962.

OBERG, KALERVO (b. 1901)
"The Social Economy of the Tlingit Indians," unpublished doctoral dissertation, University of Chicago, 1937.
"Crime and Punishment in Tlingit Society," *Amer. Anthrop.*, 1934.

O'BRIEN, JOHN A. (1851-1931)
See letter to Archie Shiels' *Seward's Icebox.* See also Dalby, M.A., Andrews, R.W., and Herron.

O'BRIEN, JOHN SHERMAN (1898-1938)
Alone Across the Top of the World. Chicago: Winston, 1935. 254 pp. David Irwin.

O'BRIEN, P. J.
Will Rogers. Philadelphia: Winston, 1935. 288 pp.

O'CONNELL, C.
"Alaska: District to Territory," unpublished master's thesis, University of Washington, 1935.

O'CONNOR, HARVEY
The Guggenheims: The Making of an American Dynasty. New York: Covici Friede, 1937.

O'CONNOR, PAUL, S. J. (b. 1897)
Eskimo Parish. Milwaukee: Bruce, 1947. 134 pp.

O'CONNOR, RICHARD
High Jinks on the Klondike. Indianapolis: Bobbs-Merrill, 1954. 284 pp.
Jack London: A Biography. Boston: Little, Brown, 1964. 430 pp.

O'COTTER, PAT
Rhymes of a Roughneck. Seward: the Author, 1918. 92 pp. Pseudonym for Frank J. Cotter (d. 1942).

ODALE, TOM
"Some Alaska Adventures," *Alaska Journal,* Winter, 1974.

OFFICIAL GUIDE TO THE KLONDIKE
Chicago; Conkey Company, 1897. 296 pp.

OFFICIAL PAPERS, Great Britain and Spain
London: Debrett, 1790. 100 pp. See Nootka Sound Controversy.

OGDEN, ADELE
The California Sea-otter Trade, 1784-1848. Berkeley: University of California Press, 1941. 251 pp.
"Russian Sea-otter and Seal Hunting on the California Coast, 1803-1841," in *The Russians in California,* California Historical Society, 1933.

OGILVIE, DAVID SHEPHERD (b. 1923)
A Kandid View of Kiska. New York: William-Frederick Press, 1945. 31 pp. War poems.

OGILVIE, WILLIAM (1846-1912)
Early Days on the Yukon. New York: John Lane, 1913. 306 pp. One of the most valuable works on the gold rush. Ogilvie, an official Canadian surveyor, went to Dyea in 1887 where he found the JJ Healy's and George Dickinson and 138 Indians, his object an accurate recording of the border, particularly on the Yukon River. With Capt. William Moore and the Indian Skookum Jim he explored White Pass, which he named for Thomas White, Canadian Interior Minister. He met McQuesten and Harper on the Yukon, who were then using the Indian name for the Klondike, "Tron Deg." His story of the discovery of gold comes from participation. He surveyed claims, and arbitrated disputes. See also Pierre Berton, and William Hunt.
The Klondike Official Guide. Toronto: Hunter, Rose, 1898. 153 pp. Published by authority of the Department of Interior, Dominion of Canada.
Lecture on the Klondike Mining District. Victoria: Wolfenden, 1897. 14 pp.
Lecture on the Yukon Gold Fields. Victoria: Wolfenden, 1897. 32 pp.
Information Respecting the Yukon District. Ottawa: GPB, 1897. 64 pp.
"Down the Yukon and Up the Mackenzie," *Canadian Magazine,* 1893.
See also Henderson, and Higginson.

OHMER, EARL NICHOLAS (1882-1955)
"The Future of Fur Ranching," *Alaska Sportsman,* July, 1937. See *Alaska Weekly,* Nov., '55 and *Alaska Sportsman,* March, 1956.

OIL
Alaska Department of Law (*Comments on the Proposed Trans-Alaska Pipeline* [Juneau, 1971. 192 pp.]); Alaska Legislature, (Joint) Pipeline Impact Committee (Files: 4 reels microfilm, 1972 [Alaska State Library]); Alaska Legislature, Senate, Commerce Committee (Transcripts, Hearings on Pipeline Legislation [Juneau, 1972. 2v.]); *Alaska Oil and Gas Yearbook* (Anchorage, from 1960); *Alaska Petroleum Directory* (title varies: e.g., Alaska Petroleum and Industrial Directory) (Anchorage: Petroleum Publications, Inc., from 1959); Alderman, Morris A. (*The World Petroleum Market* [Baltimore: Johns Hopkins University Press, 1972. 438 pp.]); Alyeska Pipeline Service Company (*Oil from the Arctic* [Bellevue, Wn.: n.d. unpaged]); Alyeska Pipe-

line Service Company (*Summary Project Description of the Trans-Alaska Pipeline* [Anchorage, 1971. 64 pp.]); Ball, Max Waite (*The Fascinating Oil Business* [Indianapolis: Bobbs-Merrill, 1940. 444 pp.]); Ball, Max Waite (*Petroleum Withdrawals and Restorations affecting the Public Domain* [Wn.DC: GPO, 1916. 427 pp. USGS]); Bates, James Leonard (*The Origin of Teapot Dome: Progressives, Parties and Petroleum, 1909-1921* [Urbana: University of Illinois Press, 1963. 278 pp.]); Berry, Mary (*Alaska Natives and the Trans-Alaska Pipeline: The Politics of Oil*); Brown, Tom (*Oil on Ice: Alaska Wilderness at the Crossroads* [San Francisco: Sierra Club, 1971. 189 pp.]); Chasan, Daniel Jack (*Klondike '70: The Alaskan Oil Boom* [New York: Praeger, 1971. 184 pp.]); Cicchetti, Charles J. (*Alaskan Oil: Alternate Routes and Markets* [Baltimore: Johns Hopkins University Press, 1972. 142 pp.]); Clark, James A., et alii (*The Chronological History of the Petroleum and Natural Gas Industries* (Houston: Clark Book Co., 1963. 317 pp.); Cooper, Bryan (*Alaska: The Last Frontier* [New York: William Morrow, 1972. 248 pp.]); Dalton, James W. (*Survey of the Future Growth of the Petroleum Industry and its Impact on Anchorage* [Anchorage: Chamber of Commerce, 1958. 109 pp.]); Frankel, Paul H. (*Essentials of Petroleum: Key to Oil Economics* [New York: A.M. Kelley, 1969. 188 pp.]); Giddens, Paul (*Early Days of Oil* [Gloucester, Mass.: P. Smith, 1964. 149 pp.] Pictorial); Hendricks, Thomas A. (*Resources of Oil, Gas and Natural Gas Liquids in the US and the World* [Wn.DC: GPO, 1965. 20 pp.] USGS); Herbert, Charles F. (*Alaska and Northwest Canada Economic Activities* [Wn.DC: GPO, 1968. 2v.] Prepared for the Federal Field Commission for the Development of Planning in Alaska); Herndon, Booton (*The Great Land* [New York: Weybright and Talley, 1971. 241 pp.); Hoult, David P. (*Oil on the Sea* [New York: Plenum Press, 1969. 114 pp.]); Johnson, Arthur Menzies (*Petroleum Pipeline and Public Policy, 1906-1959* [Cambridge: Harvard University Press, 1967. 555 pp.]); Joint (US-Canada) Economic Committee (*North Pacific Study* [Portland: US Section, Joint Economic Committee, 1944. 1v. various pagings]); Lachenbruch, Arthur H. (*Some Estimates of the Thermal Effects of a Heated Pipeline in Permafrost* [Wn.DC: GPO, 1970. 23 pp.] USGS); W.J. Levy Consult. Corp. (*Economic Considerations Bearing on the Valuation of Alaskan Crude Oil and State Policy on Pipelines* [Juneau: Alaska Legislative Affairs Agency, 1970. 1v. various pagings]); Arthur D. Little, Inc. (*Potential Use for Alaska's Energy Resources: Report to the State of Alaska* [n.pl., 1961. 117 pp.]); Lovejoy, Wallace F. and Paul T. Homan (*Economic Aspects of Oil Conservation Regulations* [Baltimore: Johns Hopkins University Press, 1967. 295 pp.]); Martin, George C. (*The Petroleum Fields of the Pacific Coast of Alaska and the Bering Coal Field* [Wn.DC: GPO, 1905. 64 pp.] USGS); Martin, George C. (*Preliminary Report on Petroleum in Alaska* [Wn.DC: GPO, 1921. 83 pp.] USGS); McKinney, Carl M. (*Analysis of Some Crude Oils from Alaska* [Wn.DC: GPO, 1959. 29 pp.]); Miller, Don John (*Geology of Possible Petroleum Provinces in Alaska* [Wn.DC: GPO, 1959. 132 pp.] with Tom G. Paine and George Gryc); Noxness, Ron (*The Long Pipe* [St. Louis: Committee for Environmental Information, 1970. 13 pp.]); Netschert, Bruce C. (*The Future Supply of Oil and Gas* [Baltimore: Johns

Hopkins University Press, 1958. 134 pp.); Noggle, B. (*Teapot Dome: Oil and Politics in the 1920's* [Baton Rouge: Louisiana State University Press, 1962]); O'Connor, Richard (*The Oil Barons: Men of Greed and Grandeur* [Boston: Little, Brown, 1971. 502 pp.]); Odell, Peter R. (*Oil and World Politics* [Harmondsworth: Penguin Books, 1970. 188 pp.]); Pierce N. (*Pacific States*); Pratt, Wallace, E. (*World Geography of Petroleum* [Princeton: Princeton University Press, 1950. 464 pp.]); Schaefer, Joseph E. (*Alaska's Economy in Case of a National Economic Pause* [Wn.DC: GPO, 1968. 59 pp.] Prepared for the Federal Field Commission for the Development of Planning in Alaska); Sell, George (*The Petroleum Industry* [New York: Oxford University Press, 1963. 276 pp.]); Tanzer, Michael (*The Political Economy of International Oil and Undeveloped Countries* [Boston: Beacon Press, 1969. 435 pp.]); Tussing, Arlon (*Alaska Pipeline Report* [University of Alaska, Institute for Social, Economic and Government Research, 1971. 138 pp.]); US Congress, Senate, Committee on Interior and Insular Affairs (Hearings, Trans-Alaska Pipeline [91st Cong., 1st Sess., 1969]); US Dept. of Interior (*Final Environmental Impact Statement on the Proposed Trans-Alaska Pipeline* [Wn.DC: GPO, 1972. 6v.]); US Dept. of Interior, Office of Economic Analysis (*Economic Analysis of the Economic and Security Aspects of the Trans-Alaska Pipeline* [Wn.DC: GPO, 1972. 2v.]); US Geological Survey (*Exploration of Naval Petroleum Reserve No. 4* [Wn.DC: GPO, 1956]); University of Alaska, Institute of Marine Science and Institute of Water Resources (*Baseline Data Survey for the Valdez Pipeline Terminal Environmental Study to TAPS* [College, 1969. 240 pp.]); Werner, Morris R. and John Starr (*Teapot Dome* [New York: Viking Press, 1969. 306 pp.]); See also the Arctic Bibliography; see as well Alaska Natives.

OKAKOK, GUY (b. 1903)
Okakok's Alaska: Selections from Point Barrow News. Fairbanks: P.E.O. Sisterhood, 1959. 31 pp.

OKLADNIKOV, A. P.
Ancient Population of Siberia and Its Culture. Cambridge: Harvard University Press, 1959. Peabody Museum of Archaeology and Ethnology Russian Translation Series. Cp. Svetlana Fedorova.

OKUN, SEMEN BENTSIONOVICH
The Russian-American Company. Trans. Carl Ginsburg. Cambridge: Harvard University Press, 1951. 311 pp. Cp. B. Smith. For a complete bibliography on Okun's works in Russian consult the Arctic Bibliography.

OLD HARBOR
Alaska Sportsman, April, 1949; Couch. On the southeast shore of Kodiak Island.

OLIVER, EDMUND H.
The Canadian Northwest. Ottawa: Publications of the Canadian Archives, 1914. 2v. Contents include documents relating to relations between the Hudson's Bay Co. and the Russian-American Co.

OLIVER, ETHEL ROSS
Aleutian Boy. Portland: Binfords and Mort, 1959. 196 pp. Juvenile.

OLIVER, NOLA NANCE (b. 1880)
Alaskan Indian Legends. New York: Field-Doubleday, 1947. 69 pp. Juvenile.

OLIVER, PASFIELD
The Memoirs and Travels of Mauritius Augustus Count de Benyowsky. New York: Macmillan, 1893. 399 pp. See also Nicholson.

OLIVER, SIMEON (b. 1903)
Son of the Smoky Sea. New York: Julian Messner, 1941. 245 pp.
Back to the Smoky Sea. New York: Julian Messner, 1946. 225 pp. See also T-3368 ff.

OLIVER, VINCENT J.
"Ice Fog in Interior Alaska," *Proceedings*, Alaskan Science Conference, 1950.

OLSEN, MICHAEL L.
A Preliminary List of References for the History of Agriculture in the Pacific Northwest and Alaska. Davis, Calif.: University of California, 1968. 58 pp. A cooperative project by the Agricultural History Branch, Economic Research Service, US Dept. of Agriculture, and the Agriculture History Center.

OLSON, B. G. and MIKE MILLER
Blood on the Arctic Snow and Other True Tales of Far North Adventure from Alaska Sportsman. Seattle: Superior Publishing Co., 1956. 279 pp.

OLSON, RONALD LeROY
Adze, Canoe and House Types on the Northwest Coast. Seattle: University of Washington, 1927. 38 pp. Reprint, Seattle: University of Washington Press, 1967. 234 pp.

OLSON, SIGURD F.
Runes of the North. New York: Alfred A. Knopf, 1963. 254 pp.

OMAN, LEILA
Eskimo Legends. Nome: Nome Publishing Co., 1965.

O'MALLEY, HENRY
Fur Seal Industry of the Pribilof Islands. Wn.DC: GPO, 1930. 15 pp. US Bur. of Fisheries.
Sport Fishing in Alaska. Wn.DC: GPO, 1933. 18 pp. US Bur. of Fisheries.

O'MEARA, WALTER ANDREW
The Savage Country: A History of the Men of the Northwest Company. Boston: Houghton Mifflin, 1960.

O'NEILL, HAROLD E.
The Auroral Drama. Aurora, Missouri: Burney Brothers Publishing Co., 1937. 327 pp.

O'NEILL, HESTER
The Picture Story of Alaska. New York: David McKay, 1951. 49 pp. Juvenile.

O'NEILL, WIGGS J.
Steamboat Days on the Skeena River. Kitimat, BC: Northern Sentinel Press, 1960. 35 pp.

OQUILLUK, WILLIAM A.
People of Kauwerak: Legends of the Northern Eskimo. Anchorage: Alaska Methodist University Press, 1973.

OREGON HISTORICAL QUARTERLY
Published at Portland by the Oregon Historical Society.

OREGON JESUIT
Published at Portland by the Oregon Province of the Jesuit (Society of Jesus) Fathers.

ORLOV, B. P.
See T-3418.

ORMOND, CLYDE
Bear! Black, Grizzly, Brown, Polar. Harrisburg: Stackpole, 1961.

ORTH, DONALD J.
Dictionary of Alaska Place Names. Wn.DC: GPO, 1967. 1084 pp. USGS.

ORVIG, SVENN
McCall Glacier, Alaska. Montreal: Arctic Institute of North America, 1961. 30 pp. Meteorological observations, 1957-58.

OSBORNE, ALICE
"Nome's Early Years," *Alaska Journal*, Winter, 1974.

OSBORN, HENRY FAIRFIELD
The Age of Mammals in Europe, Asia and North America. New York, 1919.
"John Muir," *Sierra Club Bulletin*, 1916.

OSCHINSKY, LAWRENCE
The Most Ancient Eskimos. Ottawa: University of Ottawa, 1964. 112 pp.

OSGOOD, CORNELIUS B.
The Ethnology of the Tanaina. New Haven: Yale University Press, 1937. 229 pp.
Ingalik Material Culture. New Haven: Yale University Press, 1940. 500 pp.
Contributions to the Ethnology of the Kutchin. New Haven: Yale University Press, 1936. 188 pp.
Ingalik Mental Culture. New Haven: Yale University Press, 1959. 195 pp.
Ingalik Social Culture. New Haven: Yale University Press, 1958. 289 pp.
The Distribution of the Northern Athabaskan Indian. New Haven: Yale University Press, 1936. 23 pp.
Winter: The Strange and Haunting Story of a Lone Man's Experiences in the Far North. London, 1955. 255 pp.

OSGOOD, HARRIETT (b. 1905)
Yukon River Children. New York: Oxford University Press, 1944. 80 pp.

OSGOOD, JUDY
"Christmas in Kotzebue," *Puget Soundings*, 1960.

OSGOOD, WILFRED HUDSON (1875-1947)
A Peculiar Bear from Alaska. Chicago, 1909. 3 pp.
"Big Game of Alaska," *National Geographic*, 1909.

Biological Investigations in Alaska and Yukon Territory. Wn.DC: GPO, 1909. 96 pp. US Biol. Survey on the Yukon.

A Biological Reconnaissance of the Base of the Alaska Peninsula. Wn.DC: GPO, 1904. 86 pp. US Biol. Survey.

The Fur Seals and Other Life of the Pribilof Islands. Wn.DC: GPO, 1916. 172 pp. US Bur. of Fisheries.

Natural History of the Queen Charlotte Islands. Wn.DC: GPO, 1901. 87 pp.

"Mastodon Remains in the Yukon Valley," *Proceedings,* Biological Society of Washington, 1905.

See the Arctic Bibliography for a full listing of Osgood's lesser works.

OSTERVALD, JEAN FREDERIC
See T-3434 ff.

OSWALT, WENDELL H.
Alaskan Eskimos. San Francisco: Chandler Publishing Co., 1967. 297 pp.

Mission of Change in Alaska: Eskimos and Moravians on the Kuskokwim. San Marino: Huntington Library, 1963. 170 pp.

Napaskiak: An Alaskan Eskimo Community. Tucson: University of Arizona Press, 1963. 178 pp.

This Land Was Theirs: A Study of the North American Indian. New York: Wiley & Sons, 1966. 560 pp.

"The Archeology of Hooper Bay Village," *Anthrop. Papers,* Univ. of Alaska, 1952.

"The Saucer-shaped Lamp of the Eskimo," *Anthrop. Papers,* Univ. of Alaska, 1953.

"Recent Pottery from the Bering Strait Region," *Anthrop. Papers,* Univ. of Alaska, 1953.

"Regional Chronologies in Spruce of the Kuskokwim River," *Anthrop. Papers,* Univ. of Alaska, 1954.

"Prehistoric Sea Mammal Hunters at Kailia, Alaska," *Anthrop. Papers,* Univ. of Alaska, 1955.

"A New Collection of Old Bering Sea Artifacts," *Anthrop. Papers,* Univ. of Alaska, 1957.

"A Western Eskimo Ethnobotany," *Anthrop. Papers,* Univ. of Alaska, 1957.

"Eskimos and Indians of Western Alaska, 1861-1868: Extracts from the Diary of Fr. Illarion," *Anthrop. Papers,* Univ. of Alaska, 1960. See also B. Smith.

"Three Eskimo Communities (Napaskiak, Pt. Hope, and Eskimo Pt., NWT)," *Anthrop. Papers,* Univ. of Alaska, 1960.

"Historical Populations in Western Alaska and Migration Theory," *Anthrop. Papers,* Univ. of Alaska, 1962.

"The Kuskokwim River Drainage, Alaska," *Anthrop. Papers,* Univ. of Alaska, 1965.

"Dated Houses at Squirrel River, Alaska," *Tree Ring Bulletin,* 1949.

"Northeast Asian and Alaskan Pottery Relationships," *Southwestern Journal of Anthropology,* 1953.

OSWALT, WENDELL H. and JAMES VAN STONE
"The Ethnoarcheology of Crow Village, Alaska," *Bulletin,* Bur. of Amer. Ethnology, 1967.

"Partially Acculturated Communities: Canadian Athabaskans and West Alaska Eskimos," *Anthropologia,* 1963.

OWENS, FERN ROYER
The Sky Pilot of Alaska. Mountain View, Calif.: Pacific Press, 1949. 176 pp. Biography of Harold L. Wood (1890-1944); Seventh Day Adventist missionary.

P

PACIFIC CLIPPER LINE, Seattle
Seattle to the Nome Gold Coast. Seattle: Richardson, 1900. 44 pp.

PACIFIC COAST STEAMSHIP COMPANY, San Francisco
Alaska Excursion. Chicago: Poole Brothers, 1915. 18 pp. and other years.

Alaska: The Marvelous Land of Gold and Glacier. San Francisco, 1899. 37 pp.

All About Alaska. San Francisco, 1887. 32 pp.

Four Thousand Miles North and South From San Francisco. San Francisco, 1896. 75 pp.

The Alaska Indian Mythology. San Francisco, 1915. 12 pp.

Yukon Territory, Alaska and Puget Sound. San Francisco, 1902. 75 pp.

PACIFIC HISTORICAL REVIEW
Quarterly, published by the Pacific Branch of the American Historical Association from 1932.

PACIFIC NORTHWEST QUARTERLY
Quarterly, published at the University of Washington; formerly the *Washington Historical Quarterly,* 1906-32. See also Erik Bromberg.

PACIFIC STATES NEWSPAPER DIRECTORY
San Francisco: Palmer and Ray, 1888. 348 pp. Directory of all newspapers in California, Oregon, Washington, Idaho, Utah, Nevada, Arizona, New Mexico, Montana, Alaska, Wyoming, British Columbia, Texas, Colorado, Sandwich Islands, and Mexico. Includes periodicals.

PACIFIC STEAMSHIP COMPANY, San Francisco
Alaska: Top o' the World Tours. Seattle, 1924. 31 pp.

Cruising the World's Smoothest Waterway. Seattle, 1929. 27 pp.

PACKARD, WINTHROP
The Young Ice Whalers. Boston: Houghton Mifflin, 1903. 397 pp.

PAGE, ELIZABETH MERWIN (b. 1889)
Wild Horses and Gold. New York: Farrar and Rinehart, 1932. 362 pp. A herd of horses driven from Wyoming to the Klondike in 1897.

PAGE, ROGER
This is Kodiak. Kodiak: Roger Page, 1969. 64 pp. Photographic.

PAIGE, SIDNEY (b. 1880)
"A Growing Camp in the Tanana Gold Fields," *National Geographic,* 1905. See also the Arctic Bibliography.

PALEONTOLOGY
See the Arctic Bibliography.

PALLAS, PETER SIMON (1741-1811)
See the Arctic Bibliography.

PALMEDO, ROLAND
Ski New Horizons. New York: Doubleday, 1961. 319 pp.

PALMER
Alaska Sportsman, see Index; *Alaska Weekly,* numerous issues, 1950-51; Couch (George Palmer est. trading post, 1899; post office from 1917); Colby; Franck; Hayes; Hulley; Sundborg; Winslow. See also Matanuska Valley.

PALMER, FREDERICK (b. 1873)
In the Klondyke. New York: Scribner, 1899. 218 pp. Notes on Canadian policy. See also T-3479 ff.

PALMER, LAWRENCE JOHN (1893-1945)
See the Arctic Bibliography for authoritative papers on reindeer.

PAN PACIFIC PROGRESS
Alaska. Los Angeles, 1930. Includes articles by G.A. Parks, S.C. Bone, O.F. Ohlson, and others.

PANETH, PHILIP
Alaskan Backdoor to Japan. London: Alliance Press, 1943. 108 pp. Numerous inaccuracies.

PAPANIN, IVAN DMITRIEVICH (b. 1894)
Life on the Ice Floe. New York: Hutchinson, 1940. 240 pp. Journal, 1937-38.

PARAMORE, EDWARD E., Jr.
The Ballad of Yukon Jake. New York: Coward-McCann, 1928. 42 pp.

PARAMORE, H. H.
The Practical Guide to America's New Eldorado. St. Louis: Myerson, 1897. 64 pp.

PARISH, PEGGY
Ootah's Lucky Day. New York: Harper and Row, 1970. 63 pp. Juvenile.

PARK, WILLIAM ZERBE
Shamanism in Western North America. Evanston: Northwestern University Press, 1938. 166 pp.

PARKER, HERSCHEL CLIFFORD
See the Arctic Bibliography for numerous articles on the climbing of Mt. McKinley.

PARKER, MARY M.
This Was Alaska. Seattle: Tewkesbury Publishing Co., 1950. 237 pp.

PARKER, ROBERT R. and WALTER KIRKNESS
King Salmon and the Ocean Troll Fishery. Juneau: Dept. of Fisheries, 1956. 64 pp. Research paper.

PARKER, SEYMOUR
"Eskimo Psychopathology in the Context of Eskimo Personality and Culture," *Amer. Anthrop.,* 1962.

PARKER, WALTER
International Fisheries Regimes of the North Pacific. Anchorage: University of Alaska, 1974. Arctic Environment Information and Data Center.

PARKINSON, EDWARD S.
Wonderland. Trenton: MacCrellish and Quigley, 1894. 259 pp.

PARRAN, THOMAS, et alii
Alaska's Health. Pittsburgh: University of Pittsburgh Press, 1954. var. pag.

PARRY, EDWARD (1830-1890)
Memoirs of Rear Admiral Sir Edward Parry. London: Longmans and Roberts, 1857. 403 pp.

PARRY, Sir WILLIAM EDWARD (1790-1855)
Journal of a Voyage for the Discovery of a North-West Passage. London: Murray, 1821-24. 2v.
Journal of a Second Voyage. London: Murray, 1824-25.
Journal of a Third Voyage. London: Murray, 1828. 229 pp.
Three Voyages. New York: Harper, 1842. 2v.

PARTON, JAMES (1822-1891)
Life of John Jacob Astor. New York: American News Co., 1865. 121 pp. See also Kenneth Porter.

PARTRIDGE, BELLAMY
Amundsen, the Splendid Norseman. New York: Stokes, 1929. 276 pp.

PARTRIDGE, WELLES MORTIMER
Some Facts About Alaska and Its Missions. Peabody, Mass.: C.H. Shepard, 1900. 46 pp.

PATCHELL, SARAH ELIZABETH
My Extraordinary Years of Adventure and Romance in the Klondike and Alaska. London: Stockwell, 1939. 397 pp.

PATHFINDER OF ALASKA
Published by the Pioneers of Alaska, monthly, at Valdez, 1919-1925. Editors include John W. Frame, Harry G. McCain, and John E. Meals. Also published at Cordova and Anchorage.

PATTERSON
See *Alaska Sportsman,* Feb., '55 (built 1882; wrecked, Cape Fairweather, 1938); see also *Pacific Coastal Liners,* Gordon Newell and Joe Williamson. See also Newell.

PATTERSON, R. M.
"The Nahany Lands," *Beaver,* Summer, 1961, and *Alaska Sportsman,* May, 1947. The Nahanni River

region of the Northwest Territories is an area of unexplained disappearance.

PATTERSON, RUSSEL H.
"Effect of Prolonged Wet and Cold on the Extremities," *Army Medical Bulletin*, April, 1944. Attu exposures.
"War Casualties from Prolonged Exposure to Wet, and Cold," *Surgery, Gynecology, and Obstetrics*, Jan., '45.

PATTY, ERNEST NEWTON
"The Known Tin Deposits of Alaska," *Eng. and Mining J.*, April, 1929.
"Placer Mining in the Sub-Arctic," *Western Miner*, Apr., '45.
"Solar Thawing Increases Profit from Sub-Arctic Placer Gravels," *Transactions*, Amer. Inst. of Mining and Metallurgical Engrs., 1951.
North Country Challenge. New York: D. McKay, 1969. 272 pp. Ernest Patty was president of the University of Alaska, 1953-60. See Cashen.

PATTY, STANTON H.
"[Vitus] Bering's Grave," *Alaska Journal*, Winter, 1971.
"A Conference with the Tanana Chiefs," *Alaska Journal*, Spring, 1971.
"Felix Pedro—A Mystery [of his Burial Place]," *Alaska Journal*, Autumn, 1971.

PAUL, FRANCES LACKEY (b. 1889)
Spruce Root Basketry of the Alaska Tlingit. Wn.DC: GPO, 1954. 80 pp. BIA.
Home Care of the Tuberculous in Alaska. Lawrence, Kansas: US Indian Service, 1947. 117 pp.

PAUL, RODMAN W.
"Patterns of Culture in the American West," *Alaska Review*, Fall, 1967.

PAUL, WILLIAM L., Sr.
"The Real Story of the Lincoln Totem," *Alaska Journal*, Summer, 1971.

PAVLOV VOLCANO
Alaska Sportsman, Nov., '37 (layer of ashes); Baker (Alaska Peninsula); Colby; Dall (active 1762 and 1786); Kennedy (USGS *Bull.* 1028 [1955]); Wickersham.

PEARSON, GRANT HAROLD
My Life of High Adventure. Englewood Cliffs: Prentice-Hall, 1962. 234 pp. With Philip Newill.
The Seventy Mile Kid. Los Altos: Calif.: the Author, 1957. 13 pp.
The Taming of the Denali. Los Altos, Calif.: the Author, 1957. 21 pp. See also *Alaska Sportsman* Index.

PEARY, JOSEPHINE
My Arctic Journal. Philadelphia: Contemporary Pub. Co., 1893. 240 pp.
The Snow Baby: A True Story. New York, 1901. 84 pp.

PEARY, ROBERT EDWIN (1856-1920)
Northward over the Great Ice. New York: Stokes, 1898. 2v. Greenland in 1886, and 1891-97. Smith Sound Eskimos.

Nearest the Pole. London: Hutchinson, 1907. SS *Roosevelt* to Cape Sheridan, Ellesmere Island.
The North Pole. New York: Stokes, 1910. 373 pp. Peary Arctic Club expedition.
Secrets of Polar Travel. New York: Century, 1917. 313 pp.
Vilhjalmur Stefansson. New York: Nomad Pub. Co., 1925. 53 pp.

PEATTIE, ELLA W.
A Journey Through Wonderland. Chicago: Rand McNally, 1890. 94 pp. For the Northern Pacific Railroad.

PECK, EDMUND JAMES (1850-1924)
Eskimo Grammar. Ottawa: Surveyor General's Office, 1919. 92 pp. Peck was a missionary at Little Whale River.

PEDERSEN, ELSA
Alaska. New York: Howard-McCann, 1969.
Alaska Harvest. New York: Abingdon Press, 1961. 192 pp.
Cook Inlet Decision. New York: Atheneum Press, 1963.
Dangerous Flight. New York: Abingdon Press, 1960. 224 pp.
Fisherman's Choice. New York: Atheneum Press, 1964.
House Upon a Rock. New York: Atheneum Press, 1968. 218 pp.
Mystery on Malina Straits. New York: Ives Washburn, 1963. 116 pp.
Petticoat Fisherman. New York: Atheneum Press, 1969. 231 pp.
The Mountain of Gold Mystery. New York: Ives Washburn, 1964. 122 pp.
The Mountain of the Sun. New York: Abingdon Press, 1962. 224 pp.
The Mystery of the Alaska Queen. New York: Ives Washburn, 1969. 145 pp.
Victory at Bear Cove. New York: Abingdon Press, 1959. 207 pp.
"The Red Plane," *Alaska Sportsman*, Aug., '47.

PEDERSEN, THEODORE (b. 1905)
"Call All Hands," *Alaska Sportsman*, April, '44. Whaling.

PEKARSKII, PETR PETROVICH (1828-1872)
See the Arctic Bibliography, on Steller.

PELICAN CITY
Alaska Sportsman, May, '54; June, '54; July, '54; Sept., '54; Oct., '54; March, '55 (photo, Helvig Christenson with Kalle Raatikainen, founder; biographical notes); Aug., '57 (photo); Couch (post office from 1939; R. DeArmond, first postmaster); Gruening (Norton Clapp, Tacoma, cold storage owner); Tewkesbury; *Alaska Life*, Dec., '47 (K. Raatikainen, "Pelican Charlie").

PENDER, JANE
Kotzebue: Two Worlds. Fairbanks: The Lettershop, 1970. 20 pp.

PENICK, JAMES, Jr.
Progressive Politics and Conservation: The Ballinger-Pinchot Affair. Chicago: University of Chicago Press, 1968.

PENLINGTON, NORMAN
The Alaska Boundary Dispute: A Critical Reappraisal. Toronto: McGraw-Hill, Ryerson, 1972. See also Munro.

PENNANT, THOMAS (1726-1798)
Arctic Zoology. London: H. Hughs, 1784-87. 2v. The polar world as then known.

PENROSE, CHARLES VINICOMBE
A Memoir of James Trevenen. London: Navy Records Society, 1959. James Cook.

PEREZ, JUAN
See the Arctic Bibliography.

PERKINS, ANGIE (1854-1921)
San Diego to Sitka. Knoxville: S.B. Newman, 1902. 88 pp.

PERKINS, BRADFORD
Prologue to War. New York: Random House, 1959. 244 pp. See also Kenneth Porter.

PERKINS, DEXTER
The Monroe Doctrine, 1823-26. Cambridge: Harvard University Press, 1927. See also Monroe Doctrine.

PERMAFROST
See the Arctic Bibliography.

PERRON, JOSEPH (b. 1864)
See Savage.

PERRY, RICHARD
The Jeannette. Chicago: Coburn and Cook, 1882. 840 pp. Summary of all voyages.

PERRY, RICHARD
The World of the Polar Bear. Seattle: University of Washington Press, 1966. 195 pp.
The World of the Walrus. New York: Taplinger, 1968. 162 pp.

PETER, RICHARD
The Ballad of Joe Juneau. Juneau: the Author, 1962. 36 pp.

PETERS, WILLIAM JOHN
Juneau Special Map. Wn.DC: GPO, 1904. USGS. See also Baker.

PETERSBURG
Alaska Life, Jan., '44; Jan., '46 (special ed.); *Alaska Sportsman,* see Index; *Alaska-Yukon Magazine,* Feb., '12 (photos); Andrews, R. (photo Peter Buschmann, Norwegian founder [1897]); Caldwell; Cameron; Colby; Couch (post office from 1900); Corser; Davis; Denison; Franck; Griffin (*Alaska Life,* Sept., '46); Jacobin; Lipke; Sundborg; Underwood; Winslow.

PETERSON, LEAH JANE
This is Alaska. Seattle: Pacific Books, 1958. 107 pp.

PETERSON, MARTIN SEVERIN (b. 1897)
Joaquin Miller: Literary Frontiersman. Stanford: Stanford University Press, 1937. 198 pp.

PETERSON, ROGER TORY
See T-3552 ff.

PETITOT, EMILE FORTUNE STANISLAS JOSEPH (1838-1917)
See the Arctic Bibliography for a full bibliography. Unfortunately, none of Fr. Petitot's numerous works seem to have been translated from the French.

PETROF, IVAN (b. 1842)
Report on the Population, Industries, and Resources of Alaska. Reprinted from US Census, *Reports,* 1880. Wn.DC: US Census Office, 10th Census, 1884. 189 pp. Petrof was an excellent choice to do the census report on Alaska. He could get from place to place easily under primitive conditions, he was fluent in Russian, he had apparently studied Russian-American Co. records from Sitka (in Washington, DC), and he had been in Alaska in 1878 on the Cutter *Rush.* However, he tended to exaggerate and even fabricate where he could not get adequate information, and he apparently did not visit any number of places he easily could have. Petrof's population figures were later disputed, and the 1890 census (after the 1884 civil government act) are at some considerable disparity with Petrof's for 1880 plus what is known about growth.
See Richard Pierce, (*Pac. NW Q.,* 1968) for a discussion of Petro's career and character. See also Sherwood.
"Alaska," in US Bureau of Statistics (Treasury Department), *Report on the Internal Commerce of the US, 1890* (Wn.DC: GPO, 1891). Contains a historical sketch as well as description.
"Geographical and Ethnological Notes on Alaska," *Transactions and Proceedings,* Geog. Soc. of the Pac., July, 1891.
Alaska Appeal, semi-monthly periodical, published at San Francisco, March, 1879 to April, 1880.
"The Limits of the Innuit Tribes on the Alaska Coast," *American Naturalist,* 1882.
See also Bancroft, *History of Alaska.* Petrof contributed to Bancroft's *History,* perhaps writing most of the sections. See William Morris, who assigns authorship to Petrof, Bancroft, Bates and Nemos. See also Bancroft's own account in his *Literary Industries.*
Petrof was born in St. Petersburg in 1842. Initially a military interpreter, a speech impediment acquired as a young man forced him to other pursuits. He served with the Union in the American Civil War, attaining the rank of lieutenant. He was apparently hired by the Russian-American Co. for work at Sitka but was placed in charge of a post on Cook Inlet. Later, as customs officer he took a seized vessel (*Constitution*) from Kodiak to San Francisco in 1870. There he became a literary assistant for H.H. Bancroft. He toured Alaska in 1878 looking for "all available" archives (Bancroft), and then worked with documents in Washington, DC. His work with the 1880 census is well known. From 1892 his career is clouded. He slanted some translations of Russian materials in favor of the US in the Bering Sea controversy, and was discovered by the British (Andrews, Pierce). He was apparently trying to ingratiate himself with the US government (Tompkins). Brooks praised his knowledge of geography, but Nichols felt all of his material suspect. Young testified to his capacity for whiskey. Marcus Baker

found his work very useful for his catalogue of place names, and the maps he published in 1880 and 1882 are very accurate.

PETROLEUM
See Oil.

PETTINGILL, OLIN SEWALL, Jr.
The Bird Watcher's America. Berkeley: University of California Press, 1966. 441 pp.

PETTITT, GEORGE ALBERT
Primitive Education in North America. Berkeley: University of California Press, 1946. 182 pp.

PEWE, TROY LEWIS (b. 1918)
Permafrost and Its Effects on Life in the North. Corvallis: Oregon State University, 1966. 40 pp.
The Periglacial Environment: Past and Present. Montreal: McGill-Queen's University Press, 1969. 487 pp. See also the Arctic Bibliography.

PHILATELY
Andrews, C.L. (*Alaska Life*, Feb., '46); Arnold, C. (*Alaska Life*, July, '38); Cavagnol; Couch; Gambell, F. (*Alaska Life*, Apr., '47); Gould and Bressett; Koestler; Roberts, R. (*Alaska Life*, June, '41); *Rossica* (periodical on Russian postal history, Philadelphia, ed. Gregory B. Salisbury); Salisbury (see *Rossica*); Startin (in *Stamp Collecting*, 1959); Tchilinghirian and Stephen. See also the Wickersham bibliography.

PHILLIPS, ALAN
The Living Legend. Boston: Little, Brown, 1957. 328 pp. RCMP.

PHILLIPS, ELLIS L., Jr. (b. 1921)
Alaska Summer. Glen Head, NY: the Author, 1938. 32 pp.

PHILLIPS, JAMES W.
"Name Origins: Prudhoe Bay and Duke Island," *Alaska Journal*, Summer, 1974.

PHILLIPS, PHILLIP LEE
Alaska and the Northwest Part of North America, 1588-1898. Wn.DC: GPO, 1898. Maps. Reprint: NY: Burt Franklin, 1970. 119 pp. Maps in the Library of Congress.

PHILLIPS, R. A. J.
Canada's North. Toronto: Macmillan, 1967. 306 pp.

PHILLIPS, RICHARD
See T-3574 ff.

PHILLIPS, WALTER SHELLEY
Totem Tales. Chicago: Star Publishing Co., 1896. 326 pp.
Indian Fairy Tales. Chicago: Star Pub. Co., 1902. 326 pp.
The Chinook Book. Seattle: Davis, 1913. 118 pp.

PICKERSGILL, RICHARD
A Concise Account of Voyages. London: Bew, 1782. 69 pp.

PIERCE, FRANK RICHARDSON
Rugged Alaska Stories. Seattle: Frank McCaffrey, 1950.

PIERCE, NEAL R.
The Pacific States of America. New York: W.W. Norton, 1972. 387 pp.

PIERCE, RICHARD A.
"Alaska in 1867 as Viewed from Victoria," *Queen's Quarterly*, Winter, 1967.
"Prince D.P. Maksutov: Last Governor of Russian America," *Journ. of the West*, 1967.
"Alaska's Russian Governors: Chistiakov and Wrangel," *Alaska Journal*, Autumn, 1971.
"Alaska's Russian Governor's: Murav'ev, 1820-25," *Alaska Journal*, Summer, 1971.
"Alaska Treasure: Our Search for the Russian Plates," *Alaska Journal*, Winter, 1971.
"New Light on Ivan Petrof, Historian of Alaska," *Pacific Northwest Quarterly*, January, 1968.
"The Russian Period of Alaskan History," *Alaska Review*, Fall, 1967.
"Two Russian Governors: Hagemeister and Yanovskii," *Alaska Journal*, Spring, 1971.
Richard Pierce, Professor of History at Queen's University, Kingston, Ontario, has edited a number of works on the Russian period of Alaska history at Limestone Press, Kingston. Among these are the following:
Fedorova, Svetlana, *Population of Russian America.*
Khlebnikov, Kiril, *A.A. Baranov.*
Howay, F.W., *List of Trading Vessels in the Maritime Fur Trade, 1785-1825.*
Pierce, R.A., *Arrivals and Departures from the Port of Sitka.*

PIERCE, W. H.
Thirteen Years of Travel and Exploration in Alaska. Lawrence, Kansas: Journal Publishing Co., 1890. 224 pp. Cassiar, Juneau, Klondike, an Indian battle on the Tanana.

PIERREPONT, EDWARD WILLOUGHBY
Fifth Avenue in Alaska. New York: Putnam's, 1884. 329 pp.

PIET, JOSEPHUS M.
The Land of the Midnight Sun. n.pl.: Schinner, 1925. 20 pp.

PIKE, WARBURTON MAYER
Through the Subarctic Forest. London: Arnold, 1896. 295 pp.

PILDER, HANS (b. 1885)
See the Arctic Bibliography.

PILGRIM, MARIETTE SHAW (b. 1898)
Alaska: Its History, Resources, Geography and Government. Caldwell: Caxton Printers, 1939. 296 pp. Weak on the Russian era, otherwise general coverage, if somewhat romanticized.
Oogaruk, the Aleut. Caldwell: Caxton Printers, 1947. 223 pp. Juvenile. See Brinsmade.

PILLING, JAMES CONSTANTINE (1846-1895)
Bibliography of the Eskimo Language. Wn.DC: GPO, 1887. 116 pp.

Bibliography of the Athapascan Languages. Wn.DC: GPO, 1892. 125 pp.

Bibliography of the Algonquin Languages. Wn.DC: GPO, 1891. 614 pp.

Bibliography of the Chinookan Languages. Wn.DC: GPO, 1893. 81 pp.

PILOT POINT
Buchan and Allen. Ugashik Bay, north coast, Alaska Penin.

PILOT STATION
Berto (teacher, 1925-28). Lower Yukon.

PILZ, GEORGE E. (1844-1926)
"Reminiscences of Pioneer Days in Alaska," Ms., Bunnell Collection, University of Alaska Archive, and Alaska State Library. Pilz was a German mining engineer who emigrated to America in 1867. Working his way west to San Francisco, he went to Sitka, where he was moderately successful. Staking others to prospect for him, a common practice, he sent Richard Harris and Joe Juneau to work on the Gastineau Channel. The two made the find which later developed into the Treadwell stamping operation. After forays in South America, Pilz went to the Fortymile district, dying at Eagle in 1926. See Andrews in *Alaska Life*, Feb., '44.

PINART, ALPHONSE LOUIS (1852-1911)
See the Arctic Bibliography and T-3591 ff.

PINCHOT, GIFFORD (1865-1946)
Who Shall Own Alaska? Reprinted from *Saturday Evening Post*, Dec., '11.

Breaking New Ground. New York: Harcourt, Brace and Co., 1947. See also Ballinger-Pinchot Affair, Penick, etc.

PINKERTON, JOHN
A General Collection of the Best and Most Interesting Voyages and Travels in All Parts of the World. London: Longman, Hurst, Rees and Orme, 1808-14. 17v.

PINKERTON, KATHRENE SUTHERLAND (b. 1887)
Three's a Crew. New York: Carrick and Evans, 1940. 316 pp. Autobiographical, 1923-30.

Wilderness Wife. London: Harrap, 1939. 302 pp. Autobiographical, 1910-20.

Two Ends to Our Shoestring. New York: Harcourt, Brace, 1941. 362 pp. Autobiographical.

Hidden Harbor. New York: Harcourt, Brace, 1951. 278 pp.

Second Meeting. New York: Harcourt, Brace, 1956. 204 pp.

Steer North! New York: Harcourt, Brace, 1962. 219 pp.

Tomorrow Island. New York: Harcourt, Brace, 1960. 217 pp.

Year of Enchantment. New York: Harcourt, Brace, 1957. 224 pp.

PIONEER'S HOME, Sitka
Alaska Life, Feb., '41; *Alaska Sportsman*, see Index; *Alaska Weekly*, Oct., '50 (Laura G. Gamble, first woman) (biog. Skagway Bill Fonda and wife); Jan., '51 (168 persons listed); Apr., '51 (history;

opened 1913, new buildings from 1932); Andrews (photo); Chase (descr., photos); Colby; Denison; Franck; Gruening; Hulley (by first legislature); Potter; Tewkesbury.

PIONEERS of ALASKA
Alaska Sportsman, June, '41 (photo, Juneau memorial); July, '55; Jan., '56; Aug., '39 (residency prior to 1910); *Alaska Weekly*, March, '51 (E.B. Collins); Chase (organized 1907 at Nome; presidents, 1907-51); *Pathfinder*. See also *Alaska-Yukon Magazine*, Dec., '08 ('87 Pioneers Association; origin of idea, 87 people each contributing $1 to return remains of Richard Harris to Juneau; persons living 1887 eligible).

PIPES, NELLIE
See John Meares.

PLACE, MARIAN TEMPLETON
The Yukon. New York: Ives Washburn, 1967. 211 pp.

POETRY in Alaska
Partial listing: Albertson, C.; Allen, E. (*Al. Life*, Sept., '46); Allen, J. (Dynes); Allen, L. (W-1335); Andrews, C.; Atwood, F. (*Gold Book*); Auldridge (*Al. Life*, May, '47); Baranov, A.A. (Shiels); Bates, R. (Reed); Best, E. (W-5263); B., J.S. (Reed); Black, E. (Reed); Blackman, H. (*Al. Life*, Dec., '45); Blanchard, E. (*Al. Life*, Jan., '47); Bonner, C.A. (*Al. Life*, May, '49); Buckner, M. (*Al. Life*, July, '42); Bugbee, Haydon and Porter (*Poems on Alaska* [Sitka, 1891]); Burroughs; Camp, F. (*Al. Life*, June, '46); Carmack (Whiting); Cole, L. (*Ak. Sp.*, Sept., '42); Cone, C. (W-5284, *Pathfinder*, Wickersham); Conkle; Connell, L.; Cotter, F. (Wickersham); Craig (W-5288); Crawford (W-5289); Crewe (W-5290); Dall; Darling (Wickersham); Davis, C.; Dawes, L.; Dawson, E. (*Ak. Sp.*, June, '43); Dell, C. (*Al. Life*, Nov., '48); "Denali" (Wickersham); DeVere (Wickersham); Dog-Puncher's Song (Walden); Drake (Chase); Dunham (Davis, Bankson, Wickersham); Durant, J. (Chase); Reed, Wickersham; Edgecomb, G. (*Al. Life*, May, '47); Farrar; Firkins (W-5312); Flynn (*Al. Life*, Apr., '48); Fordham (*Al. Life*, July, '45); Gaines; Garland; Gaylord (Wickersham); Gaynel, L. (*Al. Life*, Feb., '46); Gilman, I. (W-5320); Gilmore, M. (A-Y, '11); Gilmour (W-5322); Gross (W-1335); Hamlin (Wickersham); Hanigsman; Harper (W-5325); Harriman; Harrison (Wickersham); Harte (Wickersham); Haydon (Reed); Haynes (*Al. Life*, Feb., '48); Higginson; Higgs (W-5331); Hines (Wickersham); Holic (*Al. Life*, July, '46); Hood (Judge); Ironsides (*Ak. W.*, Sept., '51); Isaacson (*Al. Life*, Jan., '42); James; James, S.; Keeler; Kelly (Reed); Kendrick; Kipling; Knibbs (Wickersham); Krill (*Al. Life*, March, '46); Lamborn (Reed); Lanier; Laverne (S-5769); Lawing (*Al. Life*, March, '42); Lee; Lewis (W-5347); Little (*Ak. W.*, Oct., '51); McAllister (*Al. Life*, July, '46); Mackay (W-5356); MacLennan (W-5357); Massey (W-5368); Maule (W-5369); Metcalfe (Wickersham); Miles (W-5371); Miller, J.; Moore (*Al. Life*, Dec., '46); Noonan; O'Connor, J. (*Al. Life*, March, '42); O'Cotter; Ogilvie; Olafson (W-5381); Otterson (W-5384); Paramore; *Pathfinder*; Phillips, F. (Reed); Powell (W-5388); Ray-

nor (*Ak. W.*, June, '50); Reed, Elmer; Reese (Reed); Richardson, R. (*Ak. Sp.*, Apr., '43); Rider-Smith (*Ak. Life*, Jan., '47); Royal (Reed); Sabine (Wickersham); Salisbury; Samarkand (*Al. Life*, July, '46); Sauerdo; Service; Shaw (Reed); Sheldon, C. (W-5403); Shepherd (Wickersham); Shields, M.; Shields, W. (W-5404); Slater (Wickersham); Smith, H. (*Al. Life*, May, '44); Smith, J. (W-5406); Smith, W. (S-9620); Snow, M. (Pilgrim); Sutherland, H. (W-5413); Taber (W-5415); Terry (*Al. Life*, Nov., '48); Thayer (W-5416); Thompson, U. (Chase); Tompson, C. (W-1335); Tranter (*Al. Life*, Aug., '48); Truesdell (W-5421); Van Note (Reed); Walden, A.; Wahl (*Al. Life*, Dec., '43); Walker (*Al. Life*, Jan., '42); Weston (*Ak. Sp.*, March, '43); Whiting; Whytton; Wickersham; Wiedemann; Worman (Bankson); Yanert (*Jessen's*, Oct., '58); Young, A. (*Al. Life*, Jan., '42); Young, S.; Z., Q. (W-5429).

POETRY SOCIETY OF ALASKA
One Hundred Years of Alaska Poetry, 1867-1967. Denver: Alan Swan, 1966.

POINT BARROW; see Barrow.

POINT HOPE
Alaska Sportsman, March, '42 (ancient Ipiutak village had 4000 pop.); Apr., '42 (entire site now a cemetery); Nov., '42 (Pt. Hope light maintained in winter for sled drivers); Feb., '55; Aug., '56; Apr., '57; July, '51, and see Index; Aldrich (famine of 1885-86); Baker (history of name "Tigara," named by Beechey for Sir William J. Hope); Brower (story of Attungowrak); Colby; Couch (post office from 1905); Driggs; Edson, in Stuck; Giddings; Henderson; Hoare (see the Wickersham bibliography); Jenkins; Knapp (see the Wickersham bibliography); Miller (ghost town); Poor; Rainey; Smith, G.; Stuck; Van Valin (photo); Wead.

POKROVSKII, ALEKSEI ALEKSEEVICH (b. 1875)
See the Arctic Bibliography.

POLAND, EDWIN C.
Alaska: A Colored Map. Otherwise known as Kroll's Map of Alaska. Seattle: Kroll Map Co., 1951 and subsequent editions. Still one of the better Alaska maps.

POLARIS EXPEDITION
Hall, Charles Francis (persuaded the US Navy to give him a tug for the Franklin search in 1871); Mirsky; Tyson, George (*Arctic Experiences* [New York: Harper, 1874]).

POLEVOI, N. A.
See the Arctic Bibliography; see also Khlebnikov.

POLEVOI, I. I.
See the Arctic Bibliography; Anadyr region, 1912.

POLITOVSKII, V. G. (1807-1867)
See the Arctic Bibliography; Russian-American Co.

POLK, R. L. and Co.
Alaska-Yukon Gazetteer and Business Directory. Seattle: R.L. Polk and Co., 1903 and subsequent editions.

POLLAK, GUSTAV
See T-2020; Michael Heilprin and his sons.

POLLOCK, ELLEN
Helene of the Yukon. N.pl.: the Author, 1940. 257 pp.

POLLOCK, HOWARD W.
The State of the 70's. New York: Boyer Organization, Inc., 1970. 162 pp.

POLNOE, SOBRANIE ZAKONOV ROSSIISKOI IMPERII
See the Arctic Bibliography; laws of the Russian Empire.

POLONSKII, A. S.
See the Arctic Bibliography; material on Chirikov and Bering.

POMEROY, EARL SPENCER
The Territories and the United States, 1861-1890. Philadelphia: University of Pennsylvania Press, 1947. 163 pp.
The Pacific Slope. New York: Alfred A. Knopf, 1965. 403 pp. History of California, Oregon, Washington, Idaho, Utah and Nevada.

PONCINS, GONTRAN de MONTAIGNE, Vicomte de (b. 1900)
Kabloona. With Lewis Galentiere. New York: Reynal and Hitchcock, 1941. 339 pp. Kabloona is Eskimo for white man. Experiences at King William Island, 1938-39.
Eskimos. New York: Hastings, 1949. 104 pp.
The Ghost Village. New York: Doubleday, 1954. 222 pp. In the *Audrey*, from the Coppermine, through the Beaufort Sea to Bering Strait and the Aleutians, 1939.
See also the Arctic Bibliography and T-3638.

PONIATOWSKI, MICHEL (b. 1922)
See the Arctic Bibliography.

POOLE, C. P.
"Two Centuries of Education in Alaska," unpublished doctoral dissertation, University of Washington, 1948.

POOLE, FRANCIS
Queen Charlotte Islands. London: Hurst and Blackett, 1872. 347 pp.

POOLE, LYNN and GRAY POOLE
Danger! Iceberg Ahead! New York: Random House, 1961. 81 pp. Juvenile.

POOR, HENRY VARNUM (b. 1888)
An Artist sees Alaska. New York: Viking Press, 1945. 279 pp. US Army Project, 1943, military installations in Alaska.

PORSILD, ALF ERLING (b. 1901)
Reindeer Grazing in Northwest Canada. Ottawa: F.A. Acland Printers, 1929. 46 pp.
"Contributions to the Flora of Alaska," *Rhodora*, 1939.
"Flora of Little Diomede Island," *Transactions*, Royal Society of Canada, 1938. See also the Arctic

Bibliography for published and manuscript materials.

"A [Alaskan] Seal for the Government," *Alaska Journal*, Spring, 1971.

PORT CHILKOOT (also Ft. William Seward and Chilkoot Barracks)

Alaska Life, Apr., '48; *Alaska-Yukon Magazine*, March, '12 (photo); Chase (1920 photo); Franck (1938); Gruening (est. during gold rush, declared surplus in 1947); Potter (1940).

PORT CLARENCE (Libbysville, Teller)

Baker (named by Beechey in 1827 for the Duke of Clarence, called Kaviaiak Bay by the Russians); Brooks (telegraph lines, 1867; whalers waited here for ice to open); Dall; Burroughs; Hulley; Swineford (descr.); Wead (*Bear* trading with natives); Wickersham.

POTTER, KENNETH WIGGINS (b. 1905)

John Jacob Astor: Businessman. Cambridge: Harvard University Press, 1931. 2v. Kenneth Porter was for many years Professor of History at the University of Oregon.

PORTER, ROBERT PERCIVAL (1852-1917)

Report on Population and Resources of Alaska. Wn.DC: GPO, 1893. Bur. of Census, 11th Census.

PORTER, STEPHEN C.

Pleistocene Geology of Anaktuvuk Pass. Montreal: Arctic Institute of North America, 1966. 100 pp.

PORTER, ZOE

The Alaska Primer. San Francisco: Harr Wagner Pub. Co., 1926. 174 pp.

PORTLAND ART MUSEUM

Native Arts of the Pacific Northwest. Stanford: Stanford University Press, 1949. 165 pp. Rasmussen Collection.

PORTLOCK, NATHANIEL (1748-1817)

A Voyage Round the World. London: Stockdale and Goulding, 1789. 384 pp. For notes see George Dixon. Voyage in 1785-1788. Numerous editions. Both Dixon and Portlock were in the employ of the King George's Sound Company. See also the following:

Baker (both officers served under Cook in 1778); Bancroft; Brooks; Denton; Hulley; Speck; Tompkins; Wagner; see also T-1606, T-3304, T-3780.

POST, WILLIAM SCHUYLER

"Report of the Kuskokwim Expedition," with Josiah E. Spurr, in *Maps and Descriptions*, USGS, 1899. See Baker for notes. The party left the head of Cook Inlet, descended the Kuskokwim, proceeded to the Nushagak, and then crossed the Alaska Peninsula to Katmai to meet the *Dora*. See also *Alaska Magazine*, 1975.

POTIEKHIN, V.

See the Arctic Bibliography.

POTILOVSKII, V. G.

See the Arctic Bibliography.

POTTER, CLINT

Sitka Sketches. Anchorage: Alaska Northwest Pub. Co., 1970. 52 pp.

POTTER, JEAN CLARK (b. 1914)

Alaska Under Arms. New York: Macmillan, 1942. 200 pp. Profile of Alaska, 1941. Cp. Neal Pierce, 1972.

The Flying North. New York: Macmillan, 1947. 261 pp. Bush flying in Alaska.

Flying Frontiersmen. New York: Macmillan, 1956. 212 pp. Juvenile.

"World's Craziest Pilot, Archie Ferguson," *Satevepost*, 1945.

POTTER, LOUISE

A Study of a Frontier Town in Alaska: Wasilla to 1959. Hanover, N.H.: R.E. Burt, 1963. 104 pp.

Alaska Highway Flowers. N.pl.: the Author, 1966. 40 pp.

Old Times on Upper Cook Inlet. Anchorage: The Book Cache, 1967. 43 pp.

Roadside Flowers of Alaska. Thetford Center, Vt.: Burt, 1962. 610 pp.

Wild Flowers along Mt. McKinley Park Road. Hanover, N.H.: Roger Burt, 1969. 145 pp.

POWELL, ADDISON MONROE (b. 1856)

Trail and Camping in Alaska. New York: Wessels, 1909. 379 pp. Powell spent ten years, 1898-1908, in Alaska as a government scout and prospector. This volume is well illustrated, with many Copper River photographs.

"The Gakona and Chistochina Rivers," in *Compilations of Narratives* (US Congress).

"James Germansen, Pioneer," *American Magazine*, 1931.

Echoes from the Frontier. New York, 1909. Poetry.

POWELL, EDWARD ALEXANDER (b. 1879)

The End of the Trail. New York: Scribner, 1914. 462 pp.

Marches of the North. New York: Century, 1931. 311 pp.

"Where to Find a Fortune," *American Magazine*, 1931.

POWELL, JOHN WESLEY (1834-1902)

"Indian Linguistic Families of America, North of Mexico," *Annual Report*, US Bureau of American Ethnology, 1885-87. Powell was the explorer of the Colorado River, and an early supporter of the Smithsonian Institution and the Bureau of Ethnology. See Wallace Stegner, *Beyond the 100th Meridian.*

POWERS, ALFRED

Alaska: America's Last Frontier. Cleveland: Travel League, 1921. 14 pp.

Animals of the Arctic in Action and Adventure. New York: David McKay, 1965. 272 pp.

POWERS, HOWARD ADORNO (b. 1904)

"Alaska Peninsula, Aleutian Islands," in Howell Williams. See also the Arctic Bibliography.

PRATHER, J. B.

The Land of the Midnight Sun. Douglas, Alaska, 1899. Photography.

PRATT, JOHN FRANCIS

"Reports on Surveys in Alaskan Waters by the Coast Survey steamer *Patterson*, 1899-1904," in USC&GS Reports. See also Baker. Pratt conducted surveys in the vicinities of St. Michael, Cape Dyer, Scammon Bay, Port Safety and Golfnin Bay, among others. See Patterson.

PREBLE, EDWARD ALEXANDER (b. 1871)

A Biological Survey of the Pribilof Islands. Wn.DC: GPO, 1923. 255 pp. US Biol. Survey.

PRENTICE, HARRY

The Boy Explorers, or The Adventures of Two Boys in Alaska. New York: A.L. Burt, 1895. 314 pp.

PRENTISS, HENRY MELLEN

The Great Polar Current: Polar Papers Old and New. Cambridge: Riverside Press, 1897. 153 pp. Delong-Nansen-Peary.

PRESBYTERIAN CHURCH in the USA

The Presbyterian Church in Alaska, 1877-1885. Wn.DC: McGill, 1886. 13 pp.

The Relation of the Presbytery to Alaska. Portland: Ellis Printing Co., 1900. 12 pp.

PRESBYTERIAN MISSIONS

Andrews; Badlam; Beattie; Brooks; Bruce; Clark; Faris; Greely; Griesemer (in *Alaska Life*, Aug., '46); Hayes; Howard; Hulley; Jackson; Lazell; Lindsley; Mayberry; Morris; Muir; Stewart; Willard; Winn (in *Alaska Life*, Jan., '43); Wright; see also John Brady, James Condit; J.F. Cross, Sheldon Jackson, David Waggoner, and S. Hall Young. See also Stewart's life of Jackson.

In 1880 Henry Kendall, Secretary-President of the Presbyterian Board of Home Missions, invited representatives of the Methodists, Baptists and Episcopalians to meet with Sheldon Jackson to discuss missionary activity in Alaska. The group agreed on a division of territory, as follows:

Presbyterians, southeast Alaska, and Pt. Barrow
Episcopalians, the Yukon valley
Baptists, Kodiak Island and Cook Inlet
Methodists, Aleutian and Shumagin Islands
Moravians, Kuskokwim and Nushagak valleys
Congregationalists, Cape Prince of Wales

PREVOST, JULES L.

See the Arctic Bibliography for translations of scripture and hymns into Indian dialects on the Yukon; see also the Wickersham bibliography. One of these, *Book of Songs to Christ*, 16 pages, is reputed to be the first book printed in the interior of Alaska, at Ft. Adams (St. James Mission) in 1894.

"The Tanana Mission," in *Spirit of Missions*, May, 1906. See also *Spirit of Missions*, June, 1897 and May, 1903.

For material on Prevost see the following: Henderson, Stuck and Wickersham.

PRIBILOF ISLANDS (SEALS AND SEALING)

Alaska Commercial Co.; *Alaska Life*, May, '43 (on Fr. Baranoff); March, '44 (migration); Aug., '44 (Aleuts in southeast Alaska); Sept., '44; Oct., '45; Dec., '46; July, '48 (migration); May, '49; *Alaska Sportsman*, see Index; Andrews, C.; Andrews, R.; Austin, O. and F. Wilke (US F&WS Rpt., 1950 on Japanese sealing); Baker, R. (US F&WS Rpt., 1950, 1957); Bancroft; Barth (USGS *Bulletin*, 1956); Bartholomew (*Trans.*, N. Am. Wildlife Cong., 1953); Bee and Hall; Berlioz and Jouanin; Bertram (*Arctic*, 1950); Blond; Bower; Brass (*J. of Royal Asiatic Soc.*, 1897); Brown (see Stanley-Brown); Burroughs (Harriman); Carpenter; Carter (*Fur Seal Arbitration* [Paris: Chamerot and Renouard, 1893]); Carver (*Murrelet*, 1928); Chevigny; Colby; Dall; Davis; Denison; Desmond; Dole; Drake, F. (*USS Albatross*, 1894-95); Driscoll; Dufresne; Eklund and Larson (*Am. J. of Hygiene*, March, '56, polio epidemic); Elliott; Ellsworth; Enders (*Trans.*, N. Am. Wildlife Conf., 1945); Evermann; Fouke Fur Co. (*Romance of Alaska Sealskin* [St. Louis, 1954, 7th ed.]); Franck; Freuchen (*Saga of the Fur Seals*, 1955); Gibbons (*Trans.*, N. Am. Wildlife Conf., 1947); Goode, G., J. Allen and H.W. Elliott (see the Arctic Bibliography for papers of fisheries); Greely; Gruening; Hanna (see the Arctic Bibliography); Harrington (*J. of Wn. Acad. of Sci.*, 1947); Hart; Heath (Rpt., Cmdr. of Fisheries, 1910); Hellenthal; Higginson; Hough; Hulley; James; Jochelson; Jones, E.; Jordan; Judge; Kaplin; Kenyon K. (see the Arctic Bibliography); Kitchener; Kittlitz; Kotzebue; Langsdorff; Laut; Lembkey (US F&WS, 1910); London, J.; Lugrin; Lutke; McLain; Macmaster; MacMillan (*Forest and Outdoors*, July, '35, Aug., '48); Mailliard (*Condor*, May, '21, Jan., '23, May, '26); Martin, F.; Merriam (*Proc.*, Biol. Soc. of Wn., 1892); Miller, Max; Morris; Munroe; Olyroyd (see the Arctic Bibliography); O'Malley (US F&WS, 1930); Osgood, W.; Parker, G. (*Proc.*, Pac. Sci. Cong., 1926); Petrof; Pilgrim; Preble; Roberts, B. (*Polar Record*, July, '45); Sanford (*Comm. Fisheries Rev.*, Apr., '49); Sarychev; Sauer (see the Arctic Bibliography); Scheffer (*P. NW. Q.*, Apr., '48; also the Arctic Bibliography); Scidmore; Seeman (*Econ. Geog.*, 1937); Shepard; Shiels; Stanley-Brown, J. (*Bulletin*, US F&WS, 1893) (*J. Am. Geog. Soc.*, 1894); Stanton (*Behring Sea Controversy* [New York: King, 1892]); Stejneger; Steller; Sundborg; Swineford; Taylor, F.H.C., M. Fujinaga, and F. Wilke (*Rpt. of Biologists* [Wn.DC: GPO, 1955]); Tewkesbury; Thompson (Ak. Sci. Conf., 1950); Tomasevich, J. Stanford: Food Res. Inst., 1943); Tompkins; Townsend; Tyler (SF, 1887); Underwood; USAF (automatic weather stations); US Bur. Fisheries (*Alaska Fishery and Fur Seal Industries* [Wn.DC: GPO, 1911-45], rpts. of admin., natives, fur-seal patrol, etc.); US Coast Guard (*Rpt.*, Oceanographic Cruise, *Chelan*, 1936 [2v.]); US Cong., Hse. Comm. on Merchant Mar. and Fisheries (*Fur Seal and Other Fisheries of Alaska* [50th, 2nd Sess., 1889]); US Cong., Hse. Comm. on Claims (*Fur Seal Investigations in Ak* [64th, 1st Sess., 1916]); US cong., Hse. Comm. on Ways and Means (*Alaska Commercial Co.* [44th, 1st Sess., 1876]); US Cong., Sen. Comm. on Commerce (*Alaska Fur Seals* [69th, 1st Sess., 1926] Elliott, govt. contracts); US Cong., Sen. Comm. on Commerce (*Fur Seals* [67th, 2nd & 4th Sess., 1923] Elliott); US Dept. of Agr. (*Fur Supply of the US*, 1930); US Dept. of Commerce, C&GS (Coast Pilot); US Dept. of Interior (*Fishery Res. of the US* [79th, 1st Sess. Sen. Doc. 51, 1945]); US Dept. of Interior (*Pribilof Islands Survey Group* [1949; ms.], native conditions [found equal to elsewhere, criticism of US F&WS unwarranted]);

US Dept. of State (Memorandum, etc., dealing with Russian seizures of US ships [*Cape Horn Pigeon*, Sea of Okhotsk, 1892; *James Hamilton Lewis*, Copper Island, 1892; *C.H. White*, Commander Islands, 1892; *Kate and Anna*, Commander Islands, 1892] [57th, 1st Sess., 1900; also privately printed]); US Dept. of State (*Bulletin*, 1957 [US, Canada, Japan, USSR fur seal convention]); US F&WS (*Alaska Fishery and Fur Seal Industries* [1948-50], a continuation of Bur. Fisheries annual reports); US Rev.-Cutter Serv. (Rpts. of the *Corwin* cruises); Veniaminov (Notes on the Unalaska Islands district [in Russian], 1840, 3v.); Wardman; Wead; Wickersham (Bibliography); Wilbur (*J. of Mammalogy*, 1952); Wilke (*Trans.*, N. Am. Wildlife Conf., 1954); Willoughby; Wooding (*Can. Geog. J.*, 1955); Wormwith (in *Canada and its Provinces* [1914-17]).

PRIBYLOV, GERASSIM GAVRILOVICH (d. 1796)
Bancroft (disc. St. George Is., 1786, St. Paul, 1787; navigator of Billings exped.); Chevigny; Baker; Colby; Hulley; Kitchener (islands sighted by Synd 1767?); Martin (legends and artifacts); Miller (on Pribylov's ordering an officer hanged); Petrof.

PRICE, ARCHIBALD GRENFELL
The Explorations of Captain Cook in the Pacific as told by Selections of His Own Journals, 1768-79. New York: Limited Editions Club, 1957.

PRICE, E. V.
See the Arctic Bibliography.

PRICE, JULIUS MENDES (d. 1924)
From Euston to Klondike. London: Low, 1898. 301 pp.

PRIESTLEY, HERBERT INGRAM
"The Log of the *Princesa*," *Oregon Hist. Q.*, 1920. Estevan Jose Martinez.

PRIESTLEY, W. E.
"The Susitna: Alaska's Land of Promise," *Alaska-Yukon Magazine*, September, 1909.
"Down the Tanana River on a Raft," *Alaska-Yukon Magazine*, April, 1910.
"The Voyage of the *Dora*," *World Wide Magazine*, June, 1911.
"The Kuskokwim River: Alaska's Neglected Highway," *Alaska-Yukon Magazine*, July, 1909.
See also Wickersham's Bibliography.

PRINCE, BERNADINE LeMAY
The Alaska Railroad in Pictures, 1914-1964. Anchorage: Ken Wray Print Shop, 1964. 2v. Edition limited to 1000.

PRINCE OF WALES, CAPE
Alaska Sportsman, Dec., '38 (photo; 60 miles from Asia); Baker (named by Cook); Miller (photo); see also Wales.

PRINCE OF WALES ISLAND
Alaska Sportsman, March, '38 (wildlife); Oct., '55 (largest US island); Dec., '57 (uranium); Baker (earliest use of name in Anglo-Russian Treaty of 1825); Vancouver (named islands he assumed to lie to the west of Clarence Strait, Prince of Wales Archipelago).

PRINCE RUPERT, BC
Alaska Life, Oct., '45 (American soldiers); March, '46 (Neuberger); *Alaska Sportsman*, July, '54 (Cariboo and Skeena Highways); Sept., '56 (building of town); March, '58 (photo); Apr., '58 (photo); others, see Index; *Alaska-Yukon Magazine*, Feb., '08 (photo of Prince Rupert, for whom town named); Colby; Grand Trunk Pacific; Gruening; Large (history); Wolfe.

PRINCE WILLIAM SOUND
Alaska Sportsman, Nov., '56 (mail route); March, '58 (photo); others, see Index; Baker (named by Cook, called by Russians Chugach Gulf); Burford; Burroughs (in Harriman); Cook; Higginson; Petrof; Scidmore; Tompkins (entered by Russian Zaikov, 1783). See Jacobsen (*Exploring Prince William Sound*).

PRINDLE, LOUIS MARCUS
See various USGS publications on gold rush districts.

PRINGLE, GEORGE CHARLES FRASER (1873-1949)
Adventures in Service. Toronto: McClelland and Stewart, 1929. Presbyterian mission.
Tillicums of the Trail. Toronto: McClelland and Stewart, 1922. 253 pp.

PROSSER, WILLIAM THORNTON
"Oil First in Solving Alaska's Fuel Problem," *Alaska-Yukon Magazine*, April, 1911. Katalla.
History of Alaska and the Klondike. Seattle, and New York: Northern Historical Assn., 1912. 12 pp. Prospectus. See the Wickersham bibliography.

PROTESTANT EPISCOPAL CHURCH in the USA
Alaska. New York: Domestic Committee, 1883. 20 pp.
That Great Land Alaska. New York: National Council, 1949. 63 pp.
Morning and Evening Prayer, in Eskimo. New York: Fisher and Thul, 1923. 91 pp.
Book of Common Prayer: Portions in Haida. London: 1899. 29 pp.
Service Book. New York: Bible and Common Prayer Book Soc., 1908. 109 pp.

PROVINCIAL PUBLISHING CO., Vancouver, BC
A Gazetteer of British Columbia. Vancouver, 1909. 114 pp.

PRUITT, WILLIAM O., Jr.
Animals of the North. New York: Harper and Row, 1967. 173 pp.

PUBLIC ADMINISTRATION SERVICE, Inc.
Proposed Organization of the Executive Branch, State of Alaska. Chicago: PAS, Inc., 1958. 268 pp.
Constitutional Studies. Juneau: Alaska Statehood Committee, 1955. 3v. For Alaska statehood.
Proposed Plan for Personnel Administration, State of Alaska. Chicago: PAS, Inc., 1959. 112 pp.

PUHR, CONRAD
Modern Alaska and the Alcan. Anchorage: Puhr Publishing, 1955. 108 pp.

PULLEN, HARRIET SMITH (1859-1947)

Alaska Sportsman, Aug., '40 (husband died 1895 leaving four children); March, '43 (notes on career); June, '43 (Pullen house severely damaged by fire); *Alaska Weekly*, Oct., '51 (home owned by granddaughter); Cameron; Colby; Denison; Franck; Willoughby. In 1974 the Pullen collection, owned by a granddaughter in Lynnwood, Washington, was sold at auction. The State of Alaska (legislature) failed to appropriate money to obtain the collection. See T-4894.

PURCHAS, SAMUEL

Purchas, His Pilgrimes. London: 1625-26. 5v. Juan de Fuca's alleged discovery.

PURCHASE OF ALASKA

Alaska Life, Nov., '38 (F.K. Lane says 1.4 million paid for Alaska, and 5.8 million for Russian naval visits to US ports during the Civil War); Jan., '46 (did Cassius Clay buy Alaska); Asquith (*Coast*, Aug., 1907); Bailey; Bancroft; Bicknell (*Territorial Acquisitions* [Boston, 1899]); Bishop (*Nat'l. Republican*, 1923); Brown, Wm. (*Atlantic*, June, 1905); Bruce (*Romance of Am. Expansion* [New York, 1909]); Callahan; Clay; Cole; Dall (*Nation*, 1877); Dennett (*Am. Hist. R.*, 1922); Dole; Dunning; Elliott (*Nation*, 1877); Farrar; Golder; Higginson; Heistand; Hulley; James; Jackson, I.; Jackson, S.; Kennan; Koch (*A-Y Mag.*, '11); Lansdale (*Ak. Monthly*, '06); Luthin; McCoy (*Acq. of Alaska* [U. Cal., 1912]); McElroy (*Winning the Far West* [NY, 1914]); McPherson; Miller, H.; Nichols; Price (*Americana*, Apr., '10); Reid; Sato (Johns Hopkins studies, 1886); Schafer; Shiels; Seward; Spaight (*Roy. AF Q.*, Jan., '53); Sumner (Memoirs, Speech); Swineford; Tompkins; US Cong. (see citations in Wickersham's bibliography); Walker, R.J. (W-4138); Williams, S. (*NY's Part in History* [NY, 1915]). See also Seward. See especially R. Jensen, *Alaskan Purchase.*

PURDY, ANNE (b. 1905)

Dark Boundary. New York: Vantage Press, 1954. 79 pp. Eagle, natives, school teacher, 1905-1910.

PUTNAM, GEORGE ROCKWELL

Mariner of the North: Life of Captain Bob Bartlett. New York: Duell, Sloan and Pearce, 1947. 246 pp.

Lighthouses and Lightships of the US. Boston: Houghton Mifflin, 1917. 308 pp.

PUYALLUP PRESS

The Story of Ezra Meeker. Puyallup, 1939. 48 pp.

PYLE, ERNEST TAYLOR

Home Country. New York: Wm. Sloane Assoc., 1947. 472 pp.

Q

QUADRA; see Bodega y Quadra.

QUAKER MISSIONS

Alaska Weekly, Aug., '51 (Noatak, Deering, Kivalina, Shungnak, Selawik, Noorvik, Kotzebue); Couch; Franck; Greely (began at Douglas); Hayes (1887 missions at Douglas and Kake); Hulley; O'Connor; Stuck (tobacco and alcohol banned; under the direction of California Quakers).

QUEENY, EDGAR MONSANTO (b. 1897)

Cheechako: Story of an Alaska Bear Hunt. New York: Scribner's, 1941. 133 pp.

QUIETT, GLENN CHESNEY (1895-1936)

Pay Dirt: Panorama of American Gold Rushes. New York: Appleton-Century, 1936. 506 pp.

QUIMBY, GEORGE IRVING

Aleutian Islanders: Eskimos of the North Pacific. Chicago: Chicago Museum of Natural History, 1944. 48 pp.

Periods of Prehistoric Art of the Aleutians. Chicago: Field Museum of Natural History, 1945. 16 pp.

The Sadiron Lamp of Kamchatka as a Clue to the Chronology of the Aleut. N.pl.: 1946. Reprinted from *Amer. Antiquity*, 1948.

See also T-3010.

QUIMPER, MANUEL

Journal of a Voyage to the Strait of Juan de Fuca, Ms. in the Archivo General, Mexico City. See translation in Wagner's *Spanish Explorations in the Strait of Juan de Fuca.* Failing to find Colnett at Nootka in 1790, Quimper explored the strait, and then returned to San Blas.

QUINAN, W. R.

"Discoverer of the Yukon Gold Fields: A Note on Klondike History," *Overland Mag.*, October, 1897.

QUINN, VERNON (b. 1881)

Picture Map Geography of Canada and Alaska. Philadelphia: Lippincott, 1944. 114 pp.

R

RAASCH, GILBERT OSCAR
Geology of the Arctic. Toronto: University of
Toronto Press, 1961. 3v. First Internat'l. Symposium
on Arctic Geology.

RABLING, HAROLD
The Story of the Pacific. New York: Norton, 1965.

RABOT, CHARLES
See the Arctic Bibliography.

RADAU, HANNS; see T-3718 ff.

RADCLYFFE, CHARLES ROBERT EUSTACE
Big Game Shooting in Alaska. London: Ward,
1904. 292 pp. Hunting on the Kenai Peninsula in
1903; current hunting laws.

RADFORD, ARTHUR W.
"Three Months at Elevation Eleven Thousand,
Alaska," *Aeronautic Review*, December, 1929. Aerial
survey in Alaska.

RAE, JOHN (1813-1893)
Narrative of an Expedition. London: Boone,
1850. 247 pp. Hudson's Bay to Committee Bay,
1846-47. See T-1820, T-1823, T-2836.

RAGATZ, LOWELL J.
A Bibliography of Articles. London: Thomas,
1935. 2v. Sub-title: Descriptive, Historical and Sci-
entific Articles on Colonies and other Dependent
Territories appearing in American Geographic and
Kindred Journals through 1934.

RAILROADS
Alaska Central Railroad; Alaska Home Railroad
(Gruening; Hulley; Nichols; see also Alaska Rey-
nolds Development Co.); *Alaska Life*, Aug., '42
(through Canada to Alaska); Oct., '42 (C.L. An-
drews); June, '49 (Tanana Mines RR); Alaska
Northern Railway Co. (new name for re-organized
Alaska Central Railway Co.; see Fitch; Gruening;
Nichols; also *Alaska Life*, Oct., '42); Alaska Railroad (see this heading); Alaska Reynolds Development Co. (*Alaska Life*, Oct., '42; Colby; Hulley;
Nichols; Sherman [*Pacific Monthly*, Nov., '06];
Whiting; also Beach [*Iron Trail*]); *Alaska Sportsman*, Apr., '55 (Chickamin River, Behm Canal);
Aug., '59; *Alaska Weekly* (numbers in 1950 and
1951 contain several articles on plans for a Canadian
rail connection between Alaska and continental US);

Am. Geog. Soc., *Bulletin*, 1913, and 1915 (Alaska
and Prince William Sound rail routes); Andrews;
Brooks; Brown, A. (*A-Y Mag.*, June, '07); Colby (all
roads); Copper River & Northwestern Railway (see
this heading); Council City and Solomon River Rail-
road (Gruening; Harrison); Denison (Copper
River); DeWindt (*Metro. Mag.*, '02); Franck; Gil-
pin; Gruening; Harrison; Hilscher; Hulley;
Jennings (Ottawa, 1898 [Stikine River-Teslin Lake]);
Koenig (*P. NW. Q.*, Jan., '54); McFarlin (*Sci.
Amer.*, May, '16); Miller, O.; Nichols; Pilgrim;
Potter; Prince; *Rev. of Revs.*, March, '04; Ryan
(*A-Y Mag.*, Sept., '08); Seward Penin. Railroad
(Harrison; Hulley; see also Nome); Stuck; Sund-
borg; Tanana Valley Railroad (Andrews; Hulley;
Joslin [*A-Y Mag.*, Jan., '09]); Koenig; TVRR Annual
Rpts.; Tewkesbury; Tuttle; US Cong., Hse. Comm.
on Interest. and For. Commerce (*Transportation in
Alaska* [80th Cong., 2nd Sess., 1948]); US Alaska RR
Commission; White Pass and Yukon Railroad (see
this heading); Whiting; Winslow.

RAINE, WILLIAM MacLEOD (b. 1871)
The Yukon Trail. Boston: Houghton, 1917. 323
pp.

RAINEY, FROELICH GLADSTONE (b. 1907)
"Archaeology in Central Alaska," *Anthrop.
Papers*, Amer. Mus. of Nat. Hist., 1939 (Copper and
Tanana Valleys).
"Eskimo Chronology," *Proceedings*, Nat. Acad.
Sci., 1936. (Otto Geist, Kukulik, 1931-35).
"Eskimo Prehistory," *Anthrop. Papers*, Amer.
Mus. of Nat. Hist., 1941. (Panuk Islets).
"Culture Changes on the Arctic Coast," *Trans.*,
NY Acad. of Sci., Apr., '41 (Point Hope, 1940).
"A New Form of Culture on the Arctic Coast,"
Proc., Nat. Acad. of Sci., March, 1941. (Ipiutak,
Point Hope, 1939).
"The Ipiutak Culture at Point Hope, Alaska,"
Amer. Anthrop., 1941.
"Native Economy and Survival in Arctic Alaska,"
Applied Anthrop., 1941. Reindeer industry.
"Whale Hunters of Tigara," *Anthrop. Papers*, Am.
Mus. of Nat. Hist., 1947.
"Alaskan Highway: An Engineering Epic," *Na-
tional Geographic*, 1943.
"Discovering Alaska's Oldest Arctic Town," *Na-
tional Geographic*, 1942. Point Hope.
"Eskimo Archeology in 1950," *Proc.*, Alaskan
Science Conf., 1950.
"Old Eskimo Art," *Natural History*, 1937.
"Mystery People of the Arctic," *Natural History*,
1941.
"The Significance of Recent Archaeological Dis-
coveries in Inland Alaska," *Society for American
Archaeology*, 1953.
"Louis Giddings: 1909-1964," *Amer. Anthrop.*,
1965.
"Radiocarbon Dating in the Arctic," *Amer.
Antiquity*, 1959.

RAISZ, ERWIN JOSEPHUS (b. 1893)
Landform Map of Alaska. Wn.DC: Army Map
Service, 1948.

RAMBEAU, MARJORIE (b. 1889)
Notes on her Dawson experience by Fred Atwood
in *Alaska Life*, December, 1941; Davis.

RAMME, RICHARD A.
"Commercial Flying in Alaska," *Aviation*, March, 1942.

RAMPART
Alaska Sportsman, March, '42 (gold discovered by John Minook; pop, 1500); *Alaska-Yukon Magazine*, Dec., '08 (ms. book, circa 1893-96); Beach (Barrier); Cameron; Couch (post office from 1898); Colby; Davis (Duncan, Rickard, Beach; 8th infantry); Denison (agr. exp. sta.); Franck; Henderson (village called Minook originally); Hulley (Gasser); Kitchener (deserted 1910; $20,000 gold dust stolen from AC Co. warehouse, 1900); Stuck; Young.

RAMPART FORUM
Published in mimeograph by Sam Hubbard, Jr., in 1898, at Rampart. It carried advertisements, news (often rumors), and information, selling at $1 per copy. Beach, Brainard and Roy Norton were contributors.

RAMPART HOUSE
Alaska Sportsman, May, '42 (New Rampart House photo); *Alaska-Yukon Magazine*, Sept., '08 (Anglican mission founded 1882); Chase (Showman's House); Colby; Stuck. The original Hudson's Bay post was at the confluence of the Porcupine and Yukon Rivers, in what was later determined to be Russian, then American territory.

RAMPARTS OF THE YUKON RIVER
Alaska Sportsman, Apr., '57 (dam site); Cameron; Gruening; Higginson (Upper Ramparts, Ft. Selkirk to Dawson); Judge; Stuck.

RAND, AUSTIN LOOMER (b. 1905)
Mammals of the Yukon. Ottawa: King's Printer, 1945. 93 pp.
Mammals of the Lower Half of the Alaska Highway. Ottawa: King's Printer, 1944. 50 pp.

RAND McNALLY and Co.
Rand McNally Guide to Alaska and the Yukon. Chicago, 1922. 175 pp. See earlier edition, 1903.

RANGASWAMI, M. R.
"On the Very Large Pacific Earthquake of Nov. 10, 1938," *Bulletin*, Seismological Soc. of America, 1941.

RANSOM, JAY ELLIS (b. 1914)
"Stories, Myths and Superstitions of Fox Island Aleut Children," *J. of Amer. Folklore*, 1947.
"Derivation of the word *Alaska*," *Amer. Anthrop.*, July, 1940. Meaning is "mainland," as in Stewart.
"If You Want to Be Correct, Say Alaxsxaq," *Alaska Life*, Sept., 1941.
"Aleut Semaphore Signals," *Amer. Anthrop.*, July, 1941.
"The Bogoslof Islands," *Alaska Life*, August, 1948.
"Caribou on the Yukon," *Alaska Life*, December, 1940.
"Mister Muskrat," *Alaska Life*, August, 1940.
"No More Songs Along the Yukon?" *Alaska Life*, June, 1949.
"The People of the Aleutians," *Alaska Life*, June, 1943.

"Bread, Butter and Muskrats," *Ak. Sportsman*, Aug., 1942.
"Down There is the Yukon River," *Ak. Sports.*, July, 1941.
"I Took My Bride to the Aleutians," *Ak. Sports.*, July, 1939.
"Sheep Raising on Umnak," *Alaska Sportsman*, April, 1939.
"The Wreck of the *Umnak Native*," *Alaska Sportsman*, Feb., 1941. See also the Arctic Bibliography.
"Writing as a Medium of Acculturation among the Aleut," *Southwestern J. of Anthrop.*, 1945.
"Aleut Linguistic Perspective," *SW J. of Anthrop.*, 1946.

RANSOM, M. A.
"Alaska: Top of the Axis," *Proc.*, US Naval Inst., 1939.

RAPAPORT, STELLA F.
Reindeer Rescue. New York: Putnam's, 1955. 120 pp. Juvenile.

RASMUSSEN, KNUD JOHAN VICTOR (1879-1933)
Alaskan Eskimo Words. Copenhagen: Gyldendalske Boghandel, 1941. 83 pp. Greenland and Labrador.
The Alaskan Eskimos. Copenhagen: Glydendalske Boghandel, 1952. 291 pp.
Across Arctic America. New York: Putnam's, 1927. 388 pp.
Adjustment of the Eskimos to European Civilization. Repr. from *Proc.*, Pac. Science Congress, 1934. Reponse to admin. and govt. in Greenland and Alaska.
The Eagle's Gift. Garden City: Doubleday, 1932. 235 pp. See also the Arctic Bibliography, and T-233, T-431, and T-2530. Rasmussen was a prolific writer on Arctic subjects. See also Freuchen's *Arctic Adventure*.

RATHBONE, A. D.
"New Key to the North," *Scientific Amer.*, June, 1943.

RAUP, HUGH MILLER (b. 1901)
"Botanical Problems in Boreal America," *Bot. Rv.*, 1941. With bibliography.
"Expeditions to the Alaska Military Highway, 1943-44," *Arnoldia*, 1944. Expeditions of the Arnold Arboretum of Harvard University.
"Forests and Gardens along the Alaska Highway," *Geog. Review*, January, 1945.
"Vegetation along the Alaska Highway," *J. of the NY Bot. Garden*, August, 1945.

RAUSCH, ROBERT LLOYD (b. 1921)
"Notes on the Nunamiut Eskimo, and Mammals of the Anaktuvuk Region," *Arctic*, December, 1951.
"Observations on a Cyclic Decline of the Lemmings," *Arctic*, December, 1950.
See a full bibliography in the Arctic Bibliography. See also T-2574 and T-4001.

RAVENHILL, ALICE
A Corner Stone of Canadian Culture. Victoria: King's Printer, 1944. 103 pp. Indians of BC.

RAVENSTEIN, ERNEST GEORGE
"Sitka and the Russian Territories in America,"
Bentley's Miscellanies (London, 1855), v. 38.
   The Russians on the Amur. London, 1861. Dis-
covery and colonization.

RAVENSTOCK, RUTH E.
"Dairy of the Arctic," *Alaska Life*, March, 1942.
C.T. Hinckley and Charles Cresmer.

RAY, CARLETON
"Three Whales that Flew," *National Geographic*,
1962.

RAY, CHARLES
See University of Alaska.

RAY, DOROTHY JEAN
   Artists of the Tundra and the Sea. Seattle: Uni-
versity of Washington Press, 1961. 170 pp.
   Eskimo Masks: Art and Ceremony. Seattle: Uni-
versity of Washington Press, 1967.
   The Eskimos of Bering Strait, 1650-1898. Seattle:
University of Washington, 1975. 305 pp.
   "19th Century Settlement and Subsistence Patterns
in Bering Strait," *Arctic Anthrop.*, 1964.
   "Pictographs near Bering Strait, Alaska," *Polar
Notes*, 1966.

RAY, LOUIS LAMY (b. 1909)
   "Some Minor Features of Valley Glaciers," *J. of
Geol.*, 1935.
   "Alaskan Glacier Positions in 1931," *Proc.*, Geol.
Soc. of Amer., 1933.
   "Studies of Certain American Glaciers in 1931,"
Bulletin, Geol. Soc. of America, 1936.

RAY, PATRICK HENRY (1842-1911)
   "Narrative," in *Rpt. of the Internat'l. Polar
Exped. of 1882-83.* See version also in Compilation
of Narratives. Includes an account of the destruction
of the whaler *North Star* by ice floes in 1882.
   "Ethnographic Sketch of the Natives of Pt.
Barrow," in the same *Report*, Wn.DC: GPO, 1884.
See also John Murdoch.
   "Meteorology," in the same report.
   "Arctic Experiences at Pt. Barrow," *Proc.*, Royal
Geog. Society, November, 1884.
   *Report of Action in Relief of People in the Yukon
River Country.* Wn.DC: GPO, 1899. US Cong.,
House Doc. 244, 55th Cong., 3rd Sess., 1899. 123
pp. P.H. Ray, W.P. Richardson, Sheldon Jackson
and others.
   "Alaska Gold Fields," *Compilation of Narratives.*
Contains Ray's letters on the critical food shortage at
Dawson, 1897, a shortage later disputed.
   "Relief of the Destitute in the Gold Fields, 1897,"
in *Compilation of Narratives.* Arriving from Nor-
way, reindeer destined for the Yukon died due to
unsuitable grazing conditions.
   "Relief of the Destitute of the Yukon Region,
1898," in *Compilation of Narratives.* With W.P.
Richardson. See a fuller treatment of the reindeer
relief expedition in Caswell; see also Baker.

RAYMOND and WHITCOMB CO.
See T-3756 ff; Alaska tours.

RAYMOND, CHARLES (1842-1913)
   *Report of a Reconnaissance on the Yukon River,
1869.* Wn.DC: GPO, 1871. 113 pp. US Cong.,
Senate Exec. Doc. 12, 42nd Cong., 1st sess. Raymond was sent to determine if the Hudson's Bay Co.
post of Ft. Yukon was on American territory, as it
was. This report contains valuable ethnographic information, and an analysis of the economic impact
of the Hudson's Bay Yukon trade. See Baker for an
analysis of Raymond's work.

REA, ELLA M.
   Castaways of the Yukon. Boston: Meador Publishing Co., 1936. 298 pp.

READ, FRANCIS
   G.I. Parson. New York: Morehouse-Gorham Co.,
1945. 117 pp.

READ, JOHN E.
   Nansen in the Frozen World. Philadelphia: A.J.
Holman Co., 1897. 560 pp.

REAT, LORAINE
   Alaskan Days. Seattle: Farwest, 1944. 46 pp.

REDDAWAY, W. F.
   The Monroe Doctrine. New York: Harper's, 1902.
345 pp. See Dexter Perkins, and Alaska Diplomacy.

REDDING, ROBERT H.
   Aluk, An Alaskan Caribou. Garden City, Doubleday, 1967. 107 pp.
   Mara, the Weasel. Garden City: Doubleday,
1968. 138 pp.
   North to the Wilderness. Garden City: Doubleday, 1970. 187 pp.

REED, A. H. and A. W. REED
   Captain Cook in New Zealand. Wellington: Reed,
1951. 262 pp.

REED, BYRON L.
   "The Contribution of the Coast Guard to the
Development of Alaska," *US Naval Institute*, May,
1929.

REED, ELMER
   *The Kobuk Maiden and other Alaska Sourdough
Verses.* Juneau: Elmer Reed, 1933. 34 pp. From
newspapers published in the territory, 1866-1933,
incl. Edwin Black, Haydon, Marie Drake, French
Joe, Charles Royal, Emma Lamborn, Emma Shaw,
and others.

REED, JOHN CALVIN (b. 1905)
   "Recent Investigations by the USGS of Petroleum
Possibilities in Alaska," *Bulletin*, Am. Assoc. of
Petroleum Geol., 1946.
   Alaska and the Geological Survey, repr. from *Sci-
entific Monthly*, Oct., 1949.
   "The Geological Survey in Alaska: Field Season of
1949," *Arctic*, 1949.
   "The Physical Sciences in Alaska: Past, Present
and Future," *Proc.*, Alaskan Science Conference,
1951.
   "Record of the First Approach to Mt. McKinley,"
Amer. Alpine Journal, 1955. Location of the cairn
placed by Brooks in 1902, found by Reed and others
in 1954.

"Exploration of Naval Petroleum Reserve Number 4, 1944-53," *USGS Prof. Paper*, 1958.

"The United States turns North," *Geog. Review*, 1958. Contemporary profile of Arctic scientific projects.

"Geological Evolution of Southeastern Alaska," in Howell Williams.

See also the Arctic Bibliography.

REED, WILLIAM
The Phantom of the Poles. New York: Rockey, 1906. 283 pp. Hollow earth theory.

REEVE, ROBERT
See T-1218 and T-3658; see Day, Potter.

REID, CHARLES F.
"Federal Support and Control of Education in the Territories and Outlying Possessions," *J. of Negro Education*, July, 1938.

Education in the Territories and Outlying Possessions. New York: Columbia University Press, 1940. 593 pp.

REID, HARRY FIELDING (1859-1944)
"Report on an Expedition to Muir Glacier," *Annual Report*, USC&GS, 1891.

"Studies of Muir Glacier," *National Geographic*, 1892.

"Glacier Bay and Its Glaciers," *Annual Report*, USC&GS, 1894. See Baker. Reid taught at Case Institute and Johns Hopkins. Reid Glacier and Reid Inlet in Glacier Bay are named for him.

REID, VIRGINIA HANCOCK
The Purchase of Alaska: Contemporary Opinion. Long Beach: Press-Telegram, 1939. 134 pp.

REINDEER In Alaska
Alaska Sportsman, see Index; *Alaska-Yukon Magazine*, July, '07 (deer from Lapland to Circle); Aug., '08; Dec., '08 (relief for whalers); July, '12 (Underwood); Bankson (Lapp reindeer in Dawson); Bauer, H.A. (*Arctica*, 1935; history); Bertholf, E. (*Harper's*, 1899; whalers); Bogdanovich, K. (Arctic Bibliography); Brovig, T.; Brower, C. (Arctic Bibliography); Brooks; Bush; Calasanz (Holy Cross herds failed); Callan (*Alaska Life*, March, '46 [Lomens]); Cameron; Chase; Colby; Darling; (*Oryx*, Aug., '54 [Caribou, reindeer, moose]; *Listener*, Nov., '53 ["Man, Caribou, and Lichen"]); Davis, M.; De Laguna; Denison; Dole; Eicher (*Alaska Life*, July, '43); Evans; Faris; Franck; Franklin, L.; Glenn; Grosvenor (*Ann. Rpt.*, Smithsonian, 1902); Gruening; Hadwen and Palmer; Harrison (Kjelsberg, foreman at Haines); Hawkes (*Anthropos. Ephemeris*, 1913); Henderson; Higginson; Hulley; Hurja (*Overland*, 1914); Jackson; James; Kelley (*Nat'l. Rv.* [London], 1932), Lantis (basic); LeBourdais; Leopold and Darling; Lomen, C. (*National Geographic*, 1919; *Forest and Outdoors*, 1946); Lomen, G. (*Amer. Wildlife*, 1920); Lopp; McLain; Miller, M.; Muir; Northrup; O'Connor; Olson; Osgood; Palmer; Pilgrim; Poor; Porsild (Arctic Bibliography); Presnall (*Trans.*, N. Am. Wildlife Conf., 1943); Rainey; Ray; Roberts; Rood (*Ak. Life*, 1938); Savage; Scheffer (*Sci. Amer.*, 1951); Sonenfeld; Stefansson; Stewart; Stuck; Swineford; Tewkesbury; Tompkins; Underwood; US Adj.-Gen.

Off. (see Herron); US Bureau of Educ. (Jackson); US Bur. Fisheries (Alaska Fishery and Fur Seal Industries, 1945); US Cong., House, Military Affairs (Yukon relief [1899]); US Congress, Senate, Indian Affairs (Alaska reindeer [1939]); US Dept. Interior (Arctic Bibliography); US Rev. Cutter Serv. (*Bear*); Van Valin; Wead; Weiss (Arctic Bibliography); White, T. (*New Outlook*, Aug., '33); Wickersham.

REMINGTON, CHARLES HENRY (b. 1859)
A Golden Cross on Trails from the Valdez. Los Angeles: White-Thompson, 1939. 200 pp. By Copper River Joe (pseud.). Over the Valdez Glacier in 1898.

REMLEY, DAVID A.
"Crooked Road: Oral History of the Alaska Highway," *Alaska Journal*, Spring, 1974.

The Crooked Road: The Story of the Alaska Highway. New York: McGraw-Hill, 1976. 305 pp.

RENGSTROM, ARTHUR G.
Bibliography on Aviation in Alaska. Wn.DC: Library of Congress, 1944. 39 pp. Mimeo.

REPLOGLE, CHARLES
Among the Indians of Alaska. London: Headley Brothers, 1904. 182 pp. Douglas Island.

RETTIE, JAMES CARDNO
Papers on Base-line data for Alaska, 1944, for the North Pacific Planning Council; see the Arctic Bibliography.

REVENUE-CUTTER SERVICE
Burns, W. (Wickersham Bibliography); Butler, R. (Wickersham Bibliography); Brown, J. (W-5652); Henderson (W-5654); Jackson (*National Geographic*, Jan., '96); Pedros (W-5656); Price; Sheppard (W-5658); Stockton (*National Geographic*, 1890); Suplee (W-5660); Wead.

REVILLAGIGEDO, JUAN VINCENTE, Count (1740-1799)
Instructions to his Successor. (In Spanish.) Mexico City: Imprenta C.A. Guiol, 1831. 353 pp. Caamano named the island bearing Revillagigedo's name.

REX, ROBERT W.
See T-3792 ff.

REYNOLDS-ALASKA DEVELOPMENT CO.
See T-3794 ff.

REYNOLDS, FLORENCE E.
The Education of Native and Minority Groups: A Bibliography. With Katherine M.O. Cook. Wn.DC: GPO, 1933, 1935. 2v. US Office of Education (Dept. of Interior), Bulletins No. 12 and 63.

REYNOLDS, JOSEPH W.
Reynold's Handbook of the Mining Laws of the US and Canada. Chicago: W.B. Conkey Co., 1898. 359 pp.

REYNOLDS, ROBERT
Alaska. New York: Liveright, 1972. Photography.

REYNOLDS, ROBERT R.
"Pacific and Alaska Defenses: Remarks in the Senate," *Congressional Record*, 77th Cong., 2nd sess. pp. 1674 ff.

REZANOV, NIKOLAI PETROVICH (1764-1807)
The Rezanov Voyage to Nueva California in 1806. Thomas Russell. San Francisco: T. Russell, 1926. 104 pp. English translation, Langsdorff narrative.
For material on Rezanov see the following:
Alaska Life, Feb., '43 (Andrews); May, '48 (Conception de Arguello); Atherton; Brooks; Chevigny; Colby; Fedorova; Gruening; Harte; Henderson; Hulley; Khlebnikov; Petrof; Rickard; Tompkins; Yarmolinsky.

RHODE, CECIL E.
"When Giant Bears Go Fishing," *National Geographic*, Aug., 1954.

RHODE, CLARENCE J. and WILL BARKER
Alaska's Fish and Wildlife. Wn.DC: GPO, 1953. 60 pp. US F&WS. Supersedes the 1942 publication *Birds and Mammals of Alaska.*

RHODES, CHARLES C.
See August Sonntag.

RICE, HERBERT H.
Report of the Commission (Highway), 1933. Wn.DC: GPO, 1933. 116 pp. US Dept. of State.

RICE, JOHN F.
"From Valdez to Eagle City," in *Compilation of Narratives*, US Congress. Rice was a Quartermaster's Clerk in Abercrombie's 1899 expedition to the Valdez Glacier and the Klutina River.

RICH, EDWIN ERNEST
John Rae's Correspondence with the Hudson's Bay Company. London: Russell, 1953. Arctic expedition of 1844-45.
Hudson's Bay Company, 1670-1870. Toronto: Macmillan, 1960. 3v.

RICH, WILLIS NORTON (b. 1885)
Salmon Tagging Experiments in Alaska. Wn.DC: GPO, 1924. Subsequent reports were issued (US F&WS) in 1926, 1927, and 1930, some authored by Charles Gilbert and Seton Thompson.

RICHARDS, EVA LOUISE ALVEY (d. 1956)
Arctic Mood: A Narrative of Arctic Adventures. Caldwell: Caxton Printers, 1949. 282 pp. Superbly written; Wainwright, 1924-27. See also Forrest. Ms. Richards married C.L. Andrews.

RICHARDS, H. G. and R. W. FAIRBRIDGE
Annotated Bibliography of Quaternary Shorelines, 1945-1964. Philadelphia: Academy of Natural Science of Philadelphia, 1965. 280 pp.

RICHARDSON, HAROLD W.
Alcan: America's Glory Road. Repr. from *Engineering News-Record*, 1942.

RICHARDSON, Sir JOHN (1787-1865)
Arctic Searching Expedition. London: Longmans, 1851. 516 pp. Franklin search, incl. journal of

Richardson and Rae on the Mackenzie, the Arctic and the Coppermine in 1849. See also the Arctic Bibliography.
The Zoology of Captain Beechey's Voyage. London: Russel, 1839. 156 pp.
The Zoology of the Voyage of HMS Herald, 1845-51. London: L. Reeve, 1854. 171 pp.

RICHARDSON, WILDS PRESTON
"Relief of the Destitute in the Gold Fields," in *Compilation of Narratives*, US Congress. 1897 at Dawson and Fort Yukon.
"Relief of the Destitute in the Yukon Region," in *Compilation of Narratives.* 1898. With P.H. Ray.
"The Mighty Yukon as Seen and Explored," in *Compilation of Narratives*, 1899. Winter conditions.
"Report of Action in Relief of People in the Yukon River Country," US Congress, House, Doc. No. 244, 55th Cong., 3rd sess. Includes reports of Jackson, Wells and others.
"Road Building in Alaska," *Alaska-Yukon Magazine*, 1907.
See also the following:
Alaska Sportsman, July, '56; Brooks; Chase (commanded WW I expedition in Russia); Colby; Davis (commander at Eagle; also Archangel in Russia); Gruening (Pres., Ak. Bd. of Rd. Comm., US Army, 1905-1917); Underwood; Wickersham (opposed Alaska RR; opposed Wickersham).

RICHARDSON HIGHWAY
Alaska Life, July, '40 (photo of R.E. Sheldon and first auto in Alaska, 1905); Nov., '40 (war on tolls); *Alaska Sportsman*, Jan., '56 (Sheldon started stage service over highway to Fairbanks until 1926); other, see Index; *Alaska Weekly*, Aug., '50 (highway kept open first winter, 1949-50, cost $600,000); Apr., '51 (competition hurts ARR); Brooks (sled road est. by Richardson 1906; horse trail to Thompson Pass est. by Abercrombie in 1899, extended to Eagle by 1904); Colby; Couch (mail route to CR&NW RR when road washed out); Denison; Franck; Gruening ($9 per ton freight toll to help ARR; little more than wagon road in 1940); Hayes; Hulley; Kitchener (details on stage line); Mahoney; Potter (drivers lock toll collector in toll house); Stuck (horse stage three times weekly); Wickersham (1905 Valdez to Fairbanks in 14 days).

RICHMOND, VOLNEY (1871-1957)
Alaska Sportsman, Oct., '57 (president Northern Commercial Co., 1921-1957); Kitchener (*Flag over the North* virtually a biography of Richmond).

RICHWOOD, A. M.
"Joseph Billings," *Geographic Journal*, June, 1966. Russian Expedition, Northeast, 18th century.

RICKARD, GEORGE LEWIS ("Tex") (1871-1929)
Alaska Sportsman, Oct., '57; *Alaska Weekly*, June, '50 (Sam Mingus of California on his experiences with Rickard, Beach, et al); Berton; Bankston (owned the Northern Saloon at Dawson); Davis (worked in saloon at Rampart); Harrison (member first city council at Nome, 1901); Hines (his saloon was long wooden bldg. with two story false front); Mahoney (kept his riches); O'Connor (promoted fights; owned Great Northern Saloon at Nome); Rickard, M.; Samuels (biography); *Sat. Eve. Post*,

Dec., '55; Sullivan (close friends with Mizner; left for Nevada in 1904); Wickersham (photo Nome city council).

RICKARD, MAXINE ELLIOTT
Everything Happened to Him. New York: Stokes, 1936. 368 pp.

RICKARD, THOMAS (d. 1952)
Through the Yukon and Alaska. San Francisco: Mining and Scientific Press, 1909. 392 pp. Excellent survey of mining activity in 1908.
Retrospect: An Autobiography. New York: McGraw-Hill, 1937. 402 pp. Rickard published a mining journal in San Francisco in the 1920's.
The Romance of Mining. Toronto: Macmillan, 1945. 450 pp.
See also Wickersham's bibliography for early articles on mining. See also the following:
"The Klondike Rush," *Br. Col. Hist. Q.,* July, 1942.
Historic Backgrounds of BC. Vancouver: Wrigley, 1948. 358 pp.

RICKER, ELIZABETH MILLER
Seppala: Alaskan Dog Driver. Boston: Little, 1930. 295 pp. Much of this is written by Leonard Seppala.

RICKMAN, JOHN
Journal of Captain Cook's Last Voyage. London: 1781. A surreptitious account, one of 50.

RICKS, MELVIN (1896-1964)
Earliest History of Alaska. Anchorage: Cook Inlet Historical Society, 1970. This is a collection of three early sources: Berkh's *Chronological Sketch of the Aleutian Islands,* Shelikhov's *Account of a Journey in 1785,* and Khlebnikov's biography of A.A. Baranov. See the note on Mel Ricks at the beginning of this volume.
Directory of Alaska Postmasters and Postoffices, 1867-1963. Ketchikan: Tongass Publishing Co., 1965. 72 pp.

RIDGEWAY, ROBERT (1850-1929)
Catalogue of a Collection of Birds. Repr. from *Proc.,* US National Museum, 1893. C.H. Townsend's collection taken on the US Fish Comm. steamer *Albatross,* 1888.
The Birds of North and Middle America. Continued by Herbert Friedmann. *Bulletin,* US National Museum, Parts I-IX, 1901-1946. Wn.DC: GPO. The most comprehensive work on the birds of North America.
See also the Arctic Bibliography.

RIDLEY, WILLIAM (b. 1836)
Senator MacDonald's Misleading Account of his Visit to Metlakatla exposed by the Bishop of Caledonia, 1882. London, 1882. 12 pp.
Snapshots from the North Pacific: Letters of Bishop Ridley. London: Church Missionary Society, 1903. 192 pp. Ridley was to have taken over the Tsimshean mission in BC in 1879, but because of strong differences of opinion, William Duncan went to Metlakatla in Alaska with most of the Indians.

RIEDER, KEITH K.
Cheechako First Class. Manchester, Maine: Falmouth Pub. House, 1953. 200 pp.

RIEGEL, ROBERT E. and ROBERT G. ATHEARN
America Moves West. New York: Holt, Rinehart and Winston, 1964. 651 pp.

RIENTIS, REX and THEA RIENTIS
The Voyages of Captain Cook. London: Paul Hamlyn, 1968. 157 pp.

RIESENFELD, STEFAN A.
Protection of Coastal Fisheries under International Law. Washington: Carnegie Endowment for International Peace, 1942. 296 pp.

RIGGS, RENEE COUDERT (d. 1962)
Animal Stories from Eskimo Land. New York: Stokes, 1923. 113 pp.
Igloo Tales from Eskimo Land. New York: Stokes, 1928. 132 pp.

RIGGS, THOMAS, Jr. (1873-1945) (Governor of Alaska, 1918-1921)
"Marking the Alaska Boundary," *National Geographic,* 1909.
"Surveying the 141st Meridian," *National Geographic,* 1912.
"A Close Call," *Alaska Sportsman,* Feb., 1935.
"The Alaska Boundary," *Alaska Sportsman,* Feb., 1939.
"Geodetic Work of the International Boundary Commission," in *Geodetic Operations in the US, 1936-38.* Wn.DC: GPO, 1939. US C&GS.
"The Alaska Highway," *World Affairs,* 1942.
See also the following:
Brooks (with J.D. Craig set the boundary post on the Arctic coast in 1912); Cameron; Colby; Gruening; Hulley (joined the stampede in 1897, in Yukon three years); Jenkins; Wolfe.

RINGGOLD-RODGERS EXPEDITION
See North Pacific Exploring Expedition.

RINK, HINRICH JOHANNES (1819-1893)
Tales and Traditions of the Eskimo. London: Blackwood, 1875. 472 pp.
The Eskimo Tribes. London: Longmans, Green, 1891. 2v. Distribution and characteristics.
"The 'Throwing Stick' of Alaska," *Amer. Anthrop.,* 1891.
"On a Safe Conclusion which can be Drawn concerning the Origin of the Eskimo," *Journal,* Anthrop. Inst. of Gr. Br. and Ireland, 1896.
See also the Arctic Bibliography.

RINK RAPIDS
Alaska Sportsman, Nov., '38 (near Five Finger Rapids, which was given the name Rink by Schwatka); Davis; Franck; Hawthorne (worse than expected); Higginson; Rickard; Schwatka (named the rapids after Dr. Henry Rink, of Christiania, a well known authority on Greenland); Stuck.

RIOBO, JUAN
"Alaska in 1779: Narrative of a Voyage in *La Princesa,* in company of Bodega y Quadra," in *Historical Records and Studies.* New York: US

Catholic Historical Society, 1918. Fr. Riobo was chaplain on the voyage. This manuscript was discovered in the library of the University of Santa Clara where it had lain unnoticed for over a century.

RIPINSKY, SOLOMON (b. 1859)
"The Natives of Chilkat, Alaska," *Alaska-Yukon Magazine*, March, 1908. Ripinsky operated a trading post at Chilkat. See *Alaska Sportsman*, July, 1942, for biography. He was also a teacher, and worked in the cannery. Seton-Kerr apparently named Geissen Hill near Haines in Rapinsky's honor in 1890.

RITTER, HOMER PETER
Surveys of the Copper River Delta. Annual Report, US C & GS, 1908. See also notes on Ritter in Baker.

ROADS
See Highways and Trails.

ROBARTS, VICTORIA P.
Let's Go to Alaska. Los Angeles: Wetzel, 1951. 108 pp.

ROBERTS, BRIAN BIRLEY
"Notes on the Barrow Collection of Arctic Equipment," *Geog. Journal*, May, 1940.
"The Reindeer Industry in Alaska," *Polar Record*, July, 1942.
"The Study of Man's Reaction to a Polar Climate," *Polar Record*, July, 1943.
"Notes on Physiological Work on Heat Loss from the Human Body," *Polar Record*, July, 1943.
"Sound Effects in Polar Conditions," *Polar Record*, Jan., '44.
"The Protection of Fur Seals in the North Pacific Ocean," *Polar Record*, July, 1945.

ROBERTS, DAVID
Deborah: A Wilderness Narrative. New York: Vanguard Press, 1970. 188 pp.
The Mountain of My Fear. New York: Vanguard Press, 1968.

ROBERTS, KENNETH
Northwest Passage. Garden City: Doubleday, 1937. 709 pp.

ROBERTS, LESLIE (b. 1896)
The Mackenzie. New York: Rinehart, 1949. 276 pp.

ROBERTS, LLOYD
Samuel Hearne. Toronto: Ryerson, 1930. 27 pp.

ROBERTS, MARJORIE
See T-3835 ff.

ROBERTSON, DOUGLAS S.
To the Arctic with the Mounties. Toronto: Macmillan, 1934. 309 pp.

ROBERTSON, ELSIE
Where the Sea Flag Floats. Elgin, Ill.: 64 pp.

ROBERTSON, FRANK G. and BETH KAY HARRIS
Soapy Smith: King of the Frontier Con Men. New York: Hastings House, 1961. 244 pp.

ROBERTSON, J. A.
List of Documents in Spanish Archives. Wn.DC: GPO, 1910.

ROBERTSON, JAMES ROOD
A Kentuckian at the Court of the Tsars: the Ministry of Cassius Marcellus Clay to Russia, 1861-1862, and 1863-1869. Berea, Ky.: Berea College, 1935.

ROBERTSON, WILLIAM NORRIE
Yukon Memories. Toronto: Hunter-Rose, 1930. 359 pp. Klondike, 1898-99.

ROBERTSON, WYNDHAM
Oregon: Our Rights and Title. Wn.DC: Gideon, 1846. 203 pp.

ROBINETTE, ALLAN M.
Facts about Cape Nome. Seattle: Cape Nome Information and Supply Bureau, 1900. 64 pp. See T-3841.

ROBINETTE, GRADY
Rebel of the Yukon. Anchorage: June Robinette, 1967. 49 pp.

ROBINS, ELIZABETH (1862-1952)
The Magnetic North. New York: Stokes, 1904. 417 pp.
Come and Find Me. New York: Century Co., 1908. 531 pp.
Raymond and I. New York: Macmillan, 1956. 344 pp. Superb description of Nome in 1900.
"Alaskan Boundary," *Fortnightly Review* (London), 1903. Some opinions on those who cross it.

ROBINSON, G. D.
Exploring Aleutian Volcanoes. Repr. from *National Geographic*, 1948.

ROBINSON, JOHN
"Alaska's Russian Heritage," *Puget Soundings*, Seattle, December, 1960.

ROBINSON, JOHN LEWIS (b. 1918)
Conquest of the Northwest Passage by the RCMP. Repr. from *Can. Geog. Journal*, Feb., 1945.

ROBINSON, R. R.
"Forest and Range Fire Control in Alaska," *Journal of Forestry*, June, 1960.

ROCHE, ALFRED R.
"A View of Russian America in Connection with the Present War," *Trans.*, Literary and Historical Society of Quebec, 1856. Plan for British conquest.

ROCKIE, WILLIAM ALLAN (b. 1890)
"Matanuska from Lazy Mountain," *Soil Conservation*, May, 1941.
"Pitting on Alaska Farm Lands," *Geog. Review*, Jan., 1942.
"A Picture of Matanuska," *Geog. Review*, July, 1942.
"What of Alaska?" *Soil Conservation*, January, 1946.
See Orlando Miller, *The Frontier in Alaska and the Matanuska Colony*.

ROCKWELL, KATHLEEN ELOISA (1876-1957)
"Klondike Kate"
Alaska Life, Dec., '39 (helped Alexander Pantages get started in vaudeville); *Alaska Sportsman*, Apr., '38; Feb., '44; Aug., '44; Jan., '47; July, '48 (Bend, Oregon); Jan., '50 (near Jefferson, Oregon); May, '54 (early photo); March, '57; May, '57 (long obituary); May, '58 (husband [Wm. Van Buren] died at Everett, Wn.); Alaska-Yukon Gold Book; Davis, Lucia (full biography); Morgan; Willoughby (first husband, Floyd Warner, divorced her; second, John Matson [married her in 1933], died in 1946 in the Yukon at 83; third, Van Buren, survived her by one year).

ROCKWELL, ROBERT H.
"Too Close to Bears," *Natural History*, March, 1941.

ROCKWOOD, ELEANOR RUTH
Books on the Pacific Northwest for Small Libraries. New York: Wilson, 1923. 55 pp.

RODAHL, KARE (b. 1917)
The Ice-capped Island: Greenland. London: Blackie, 1946. 142 pp. 1939-40 Swedish-Norse expedition to determine the relationships between vitamins in Arctic foodstuffs and the diseases of scurvy and beri-beri.
"Notes on the Prevention and Treatment of 'Spekk-finger,' " *Polar Record*, January, 1943. An occupational problem.
The Toxic Effect of Polar Bear Liver. Oslo: Dybwad, 1949. 90 pp. See also the Arctic Bibliography.
"Vitamin B-1 Content of Arctic Plants and Animal Tissue," *Trans. & Proc.*, Botanical Soc. of Edinburgh, 1944-45.
Vitamin Sources in the Arctic. Oslo: Dybwad, 1949. 64 pp.
"The Vitamin A Content and Toxicity of Bear and Seal Liver," *Biochemical Journal*, July, 1943.
North: The Nature and Drama of the Polar World. New York: Harper, 1953. 237 pp. Story of the establishing of the US Air Force station T-3 on an ice island at approx. 88° 17'N., 166°W, in 1951-52.
"Ice Islands in the Arctic," *Scientific American*, 1954. Islands T-1, T-2 and T-3.
"Arctic Survival Problems," in *Collected Papers on Aviation Medicine*, London: NATO Advisory Group for Aeronautical Research, 1955.
Comparative Sweat Rates of Eskimos and Caucasians. Fairbanks: Ladd Air Force Base, 1957. 20 pp.
Human Acclimatization to Cold. Fairbanks: Ladd Air Force Base, 1957. 50 pp.
Smilets Folk. Oslo: Gyldendahl, 1957. 188 pp.
Eskimo Metabolism. Oslo: Brogger, 1954. 83 pp.
Nutritional Requirements under Arctic Conditions. Oslo: Norsk Polarinstitutt, 1960. 58 pp.
Studies in the Blood and Pressure of the Eskimo. Oslo: Norsk Polarinstitutt, 1954. 79 pp.
The Last of the Few. New York: Harper and Row, 1963. 208 pp. Eskimos of Barter Island, Anaktuvuk Pass, Kotzebue, Gambell and the Pribilovs.
"US Air Force Survival Ration Studies in Alaska," *Arctic*, August, 1950.

RODEN, HENRY (b. 1874)
The Alaska Mining Law. N.pl.: n.p., 1913. 20 pp.
Alaska Mining Law: Federal and Territorial. Juneau: the Author, 1950. rev. ed. 121 pp.
Compiled Laws of Alaska, 1933. Juneau: Alaska Territory, 1934. 1224 pp.
See also the following:
Alaska Life, March, '40; *Alaska-Yukon Magazine*, Jan., '09 (Fairbanks attorney, biog.); Tewkesbury. Roden was a member of the first territorial legislature in 1913. He was attorney-general of Alaska 1941-45. He emigrated from Switzerland in 1898.

RODERICK, JOHN R.
"Early History of Oil in Alaska," *Alaska Petroleum Directory*, 1962-63 edition. Excellent summary of all material with all the photographs which could be located. Includes also a reprint of Prosser's article in *Alaska-Yukon Magazine*, 1911.
"Random Thoughts on Politics in Alaska," *Puget Soundings*, December, 1960.

RODLI, AGNEW SYLVIA
North of Heaven: A Teaching Ministry Among the Alaskan Indians. Chicago: Moody Press, 1963. 180 pp. Nikolai.

ROGERS, GEORGE WILLIAM (b. 1917)
Alaska in Transition: The Southeast Region. Baltimore: Johns Hopkins Press, 1960. 384 pp.
The Future of Alaska: Economic Consequences of Statehood. Baltimore: Johns Hopkins Press, 1962. 311 pp.
Change in Alaska: People, Petroleum and Politics. Seattle: University of Wash. Press, 1970. 279 pp.
"Alaska's Economic History," *Alaska Review*, Fall, 1967.
"Alaska: From Frontier to 49th State," *Business Horizons*, Winter, 1958.

ROGERS, GEORGE and RICHARD COOLEY
Alaska's Population and Economy. College: Institute for Business, Economic and Government Research, 1963.

ROHN, OSCAR
"Geology of the Wrangell Mountains," in *Compilation of Narratives*, US Congress.
"Reconnaissance of the Chitina River and Skolai Mountains," in Abercrombie, *Copper River Military Exploring Expedition.* See also the note in Baker.

ROLFSRUD, ERLING NICOLAI
Lanterns over the Prairies. Deerwood, Minnesota: the Author, 1950.
Brother to the Eagle. Alexandria, Minn.: Lantern Books, 1952. 181 pp. Carl Ben Eielson.

ROLLINS, ALICE (1847-1897)
From Palm to Glacier. New York: Putnam's, 1892. 145 pp.

ROLOFF, LOUISE L.
"Attu Flowers," *Trail and Timberline*, July, 1947.
"Skiing Possibilities near McKinley," *Trail and Timberline*, February, 1947.

ROLT-WHEELER, FRANCIS W.
The Boy with the US Life-Savers. Boston: Lothrop and Shepard, 1915. 346 pp.
The Boy with the US Survey. Boston: Lothrop and Shepard, 1909. 381 pp.

ROMIG, EMILY CRAIG (1871-1957)
The Life and Travels of a Pioneer Woman in Alaska. Colorado Springs: the Author, 1945. 136 pp. A valuable work for its relation of conditions on trails to the Klondike. Emily Craig left Chicago with her husband, A.C. Craig, in August, 1897 in a party of 14 persons led by one Warmolts. The trip had been advertised as a six-week trip to Dawson with food for one year at a cost of $500. The party reached Ft. Resolution on Great Slave Lake on October 12 where Warmolts absconded with all the cash, but leaving considerable supplies. The party continued on, with Emily Craig as cook and general helper, reaching Dawson on Aug. 30, 1899, via Ft. McPherson (July, 1898). Mrs. Romig reports the census at Dawson in 1900: 5404 Americans, 3364 British subjects, 83 Germans. The Craigs went on to Nome, leaving there in 1909, Craig becoming chief carpenter on the Alaska Railroad, and dying in 1928. Emily Craig worked as a nurse in the government hospital at Anchorage, there meeting Dr. Joseph Romig, whom she married. The Romigs lived in Colorado Springs from his retirement in 1938.

ROMIG, JOSEPH HERMAN (1872-1951)
A Medical Handbook for Missionaries. Philadelphia: Boericke and Tafel, 1904. 259 pp.
Annual Report of the Moravian Mission at Bethel. Bethlehem, Pa.: Moravian Mission Society, 1899.
The Raven of the Eskimos. Colorado Springs: the Author, 1943. 34 pp. Dr. Romig's medical training was paid for by the Moravian Missionary Society with the understanding that he would serve as a missionary a number of years after medical school. Remaining in Alaska after his term, he served variously as US Commissioner, superintendent of schools, and railroad surgeon at Anchorage. Often referred to as the "dog team doctor" from his work in the Kuskokwim region from 1896, his biography is told by Eva Greenslit Anderson.

ROOD, J. SIDNEY (b. 1901)
"This Reindeer Business," *Alaska Life*, September, 1938.

ROPER, EDWARD
A Claim on Klondyke. Edinburgh: Blackwood, 1899. 312 pp.

ROPPEL, PATRICIA
"Sumdum," *Alaska Journ.*, Summer, 1971.
"Sealevel: A Ghost Mining Town," *Alaska Journ.*, Winter, 1971.
"Alaskan Lumber for Australia," *Alaska Journ.*, Winter, 1974.

ROQUEFEUIL, CAMILLE de
A Voyage round the World between the Years 1816-1819. London: Phillips, 1923. 112 pp. See also the Arctic Bibliography. Roquefeuil's voyage took him to Nootka in 1817 and Sitka in 1818 where he contracted with Hagemeister in the manner of the old contracts between Baranov and the Americans.

At Prince William Sound, however, he was attacked by Tlingits, and 30 of his Aleut hunters killed. After paying for these ($90 each) he brought a load of produce from California for Sitka, and then left for the Pacific and Europe.
See also the following:
Andrews, Bancroft, and Wickersham's bibliography.

ROSCOE, W. F.
Ice-bound. New York: Vantage Press, 1954. 132 pp. Salmon industry; fiction.

ROSE, MARC A.
"Japanese Poaching in Alaskan Waters," *Reader's Digest*, 1937.

ROSENBERG, FRANTZ
Big Game Hunting in British Columbia and Norwy. London: Hopkinson, 1928. 261 pp.

ROSS, ALEXANDER (1783-1856)
Adventures of the First White Settlers on the Oregon or Columbia River. London: Smith, Elder, 1849. 352 pp. Much on John Jacob Astor. See also Porter, and Speck.

ROSS COLONY (ZASELENIE ROSSA, KALIFORNIA)
Alaska Life, Sept., '41 (Bodega Bay, 1812; Farallones Islands, 1812-40); Andrews; Bancroft; Belcher (settlement descr.); Chevigny; Dall; Ermann; Essig-Ogden-Dufour; Fedorova; Khlebníkov; Manning; Petrof; Tarasaidze; Thompson, R.; Tikhmenev; Tompkins; Torrubia; Wagner. See also Sutter, Bodega Bay.

ROSS, EDWARD A.
Proposed Cession of Alaska Panhandle to Canada. N.pl.: n.p., 1912. 10 pp.

ROSS, EMILY LINDSLEY (1861-1939)
Aaron Ladner Lindsley, founder of Alaska Missions. Portland: Board of National Missions of the Presbyterian Church, 1927. 12 pp. See also Hill, Lindsley.

ROSS, FRANK E.
"American Adventures in the Early Marine Fur Trade with China," *Chinese Social and Political Science Review*, 1937.

ROSS, Sir JOHN (1777-1856)
A Voyage of Discovery made under the orders of the Admiralty. London: Murray, 1819. 435 pp. This was part of a several pronged investigation of the Arctic in the year 1818, including Ross, Parry, Buchan, and Franklin. Ross's ships discovered Melville Bay, Cape York, Prince Regents Bay, Whale Sound and Carey's Islands. See Mirsky.
Narrative of a Second Voyage in Search of a Northwest Passage. London: Webster, 1835. 2v. Voyage of 1829-33.
See also the Arctic Bibliography.

ROSS, PONTUS HENRY (1879-1937)
Haymaking at Kenai Experiment Station. Wn.DC: GPO, 1907. 13 pp. Agr. Exp. Sta.

ROSS, SHERWOOD
Gruening of Alaska. New York: Best Books, 1968. 224 pp.

ROSSE, IRVING C.
"The First Landing on Wrangell Island," *Journal,* Amer. Geog. Soc., 1883. The *Corwin* in 1881.
"Medical and Anthropological Notes on Alaska," US Rev. Cutter Serv., *Report of the Corwin,* 1881.

ROSSIISKO-AMERIKANSKAYA KOLONIIA
See the Arctic Bibliography; and T-3888 ff.

ROSSIISKO-AMERIKANSKAYA KOMPANIYA
See the Arctic Bibliography, and T-3890 ff.

ROSSITER, HARRIET ISABEL
Alaska Calling: A Laugh on Every Page. New York: Vantage Press, 1954. 200 pp.
Indian Legends from the Land of Al-ay-es-ka. Ketchikan: Ketchikan Chronicle, 1925. 30 pp.

ROSSMAN, DARWIN LUCIAN (b. 1915)
"Layered Basic Intrusive, Fairweather Range," *Bulletin,* Geol. Soc. of Amer., Dec., 1954.
"Geology and Ore Deposits in the Reid Inlet Area, Glacier Bay, Alaska," *Reports,* USGS, 1935.
"Ore Deposits on Northwestern Chichagof Island," in *Reports,* USGS, 1955.
See also the Arctic Bibliography.

ROSSMAN, EARL
Black Sunlight: A Log of the Arctic. New York: Oxford University Press, 1926. 231 pp.

ROST, ERNEST CHRISTIAN
Mount McKinley. Wn.DC: J.D. Milane & Sons, 1914. 33 pp.

ROSTEN, NORMAN
The Big Road. New York: Rinehart, 1946. 233 pp.

ROTHERY, AGNES EDWARDS (b. 1888)
The Ports of British Columbia. Garden City: Doubleday, 1943. 279 pp.

ROTHROCK, JOSEPH TRIMBLE (1839-1922)
"List of, and Notes upon, the Lichens collected by Dr. T.H. Bean in Alaska, in 1880," *Proc.,* US National Museum, 1884.
"Sketch of the Flora of Alaska," *Annual Report,* Smithsonian Institution, 1867. From the WU Telegraph Expedition, 1866.

ROUNSEFELL, GEORGE
See the Arctic Bibliography.

ROUQUETTE, LOUIS-FREDERIC (1884-1926)
The Great White Silence. Trans. New York: Macmillan, 1930. 233 pp.

ROUSSEAU, LOVELL H.
"Report from Portland, Oregon, Dec. 1867, to the Secretary of State, on the Transfer of Alaska," in Shiels.

ROWE, L. L.
"The *USS Gannett* visits Alaska," *Proc.,* US Naval Institute, June, 1938.

ROWE, PETER TRIMBLE (1856-1942)
See Jenkins; see also Cairns, Carter, Weems and Ziegler. Bishop Rowe, a Canadian, served the Episcopal church in Alaska from 1895 to 1942, living at Sitka from 1895 to 1912, and at Vancouver and Seattle. See also T-1104, T-2338, and T-4781.

ROWLEY, DIANA
Arctic Research. Montreal: Arctic Inst. of North Amer., 1955. 261 pp. Current status, and problems.

ROYAL, CHARLES ELLIOTT
The Trail of a Sourdough: Rhymes and Ballads. Toronto: McClelland and Stewart, 1919. 168 pp.

RUBEL, ARTHUR J.
"Partnership and Wife-exchange among the Eskimo and the Aleut," *Anthrop. Papers,* University of Alaska, 1961.

RUBINSTEIN, MARION
"The Ice-man Cometh—with a Lasso," *Seattle Times,* Sept. 16, 1962. Marketing glacier ice at Juneau.

RUDENKO, SERGEI IVANOVICH
The Ancient Culture of the Bering Sea and the Eskimo Problem. Toronto: University of Toronto Press, 1961. 186 pp. Archaeological excavations on the northeast Siberian coast.

RUGGIERI, VINCENZO
See T-3913.

RUNGIUS, CARL
See T-452, T-3879, T-4099.

RUNNALS, FRANK E.
A History of Prince George. Vancouver: Wrigley, 1946. 197 pp.

USS RUSH
See Kitchener (Capt. George Bailey washed overboard, 1880); Hulley (seized American and Canadian sealers, 1887); Morris (crew and armament descr., 1887); Shepard; Wead (inaugurated floating court, 1910); Wickersham. See also *Alaska Sportsman,* Sept., '47 (photo of Indian who served on *Rush*).

RUSK, CLAUDE E.
"On the Trail of Dr. Cook," *Pacific Monthly* (Portland), Oct.-Nov., 1910. Refutes the claims.

RUSSELL, ANDREW
Grizzly Country. New York: Alfred A. Knopf, 1967. 302 pp.

RUSSELL, FRANCIS
The Shadow of Blooming Grove: Warren G. Harding and His Times. New York: McGraw Hill, 1968. 447 pp.

RUSSELL, FRANK (1868-1903)
Explorations in the Far North. Iowa City: University of Iowa Press, 1898. 290 pp. In 1892-94. From a base at Ft. Rae Russell lived with Indians near Great Slave Lake, then negotiated the Mackenzie River to Herschel Island, Pt. Barrow, and Cape Chaplina.

RUSSELL,   FREDERICK   STRATTEN   and CHARLES MAURICE YONGE
The Seas: Our Knowledge of Life in the Sea. London: Warne, 1963. 376 pp.

RUSSELL, ISRAEL COOK (1852-1906)
Glaciers of North America. Boston: Ginn & Co., 1897. 210 pp.
Volcanoes of North America. Boston: Ginn & Co., 1897. 346 pp.
"Existing Glaciers of the US," *Ann. Report,* USGS, 1884.
"Mt. St. Elias Expedition," *Bulletin,* Amer. Geog. Soc., 1890.
"The Expedition of the Nat. Geog. Soc. and the USGS," *Century Mag.,* 1891.
"An Expedition to Mt. St. Elias," *Nat. Geog.,* 1891.
"Height and Position of Mt. St. Elias," *Nat. Geog.,* 1892.
"Mt. St. Elias and its Glaciers," *Amer. J. of Science,* 1892.
"Second Expedition to Mt. St. Elias," *Ann. Report,* USGS, 1891-1892.
"Origin of the Gravel Deposits Beneath Muir Glacier," *Amer. Geologist,* 1892.
"Malaspina Glacier," *J. of Geology,* 1893.
"A Journey up the Yukon River," *Bulletin,* Amer. Geog. Soc., 1895. St. Michael to Ft. Selkirk.
"Mountaineering in Alaska," *Bulletin,* Amer. Geog. Soc., 1896.

RUSSELL, THOMAS C.
Mourelle's Voyage of the Sonora in the Second Bucareli Expedition. Trans., D. Barrington. San Francisco: T.C. Russell Press, 1920. 120 pp.
The Rezanov Voyage to Nueva California in 1806. Trans. T.C. Russell, San Francisco: T.C. Russell Press, 1926. 104 pp.
Langsdorff's Narrative of the Rezanov Voyage to Nueve California in 1806. Trans. T.C. Russell. San Francisco: T.C. Russell Press, 1930.
Narrative of a Voyage to California Ports in 1841-42. Ed. T.C. Russell. S.F.: Russell Press, 1930. 232 pp.
Russell operated his own press in San Francisco putting out quite limited editions to sell to reference libraries.

RUSSIAN-AMERICAN COMPANY
The company was formed in 1799 by acknowledging what had become a virtual monopoly of the Shelikhov-Golikov Company, which had been granted a limited monopoly in 1795, due to the success of the company and the efforts of Nikolai Rezanov, who married Shelikhov's daughter, Shelikhov himself dying in 1796. The early history of the company, and particularly Shelikhov's establishment of a permanent colony is told in the following: Andrews, Bancroft, and also in Berkh, Chevigny, Fedorova, Gruening, Hulley, Klebnikov, and in others. Granted a 20 year charter in 1799, renewal came in 1821, after a reorganization which saw the retirement (see Chevigny, Fedorova, and Khlebnikov) of manager Baranov, and the determination to use naval officers as managers, and incidentally, to keep out the American traders. The most progressive manager was probably von Wrangel. For the middle period see Fedorova, and Pierce and Okun.

The charter was renewed again in 1844, but by then a lease had been granted the Hudson's Bay Co. to trap the mainland adjacent to the Alexander Archipelago (see I. Jackson), and Ft. Ross had proved uneconomical (see Chevigny). Discussions about an American purchase began as early as 1856, and, though interrupted by the Civil War, were virtually complete by 1862. For the purchase see Jensen and Pierce. See the following:
Records of the Russian-American Co. (microfilm, Library of Congress, 77 rolls; available, University of Alaska, untranslated); *Documents Relating to the History of Alaska* (Alaska Church History; Rockefeller project, 1935-38, Cecil Robe and Tikhon Lavrischev, available at the University of Alaska). See also the following: Adamov, A.G.; Andreev; Andrews; Baker; Bancroft; Berkh; Brooks; Bush; Cheney; Chevigny; Clark; Colby; Dall; Davydov; Dole; Doroshin; Ermann; Fedorova; Glazunov; Golder; Golovin; Golovnin; Greenhow; Grewingk; Gruening; Gsovski; Haynes; Herman (German); Higginson; Holmberg; Hough; Hulley; Ireland; Irving; James; Kennan; Khlebnikov; Kittlitz; Khromchenko; Kotzebue; Krusenstern; Langsdorff; Laut; Lepotier; Lipshits; Lisianski; Lutke; McCracken; McNeilly; Makarova; Manning; Markov; Mazour; Mehnert; Menzel; Mitchell; Ogden; Okun; Oliver; Petrof; Ostrovskii; Pilder; Pilgrim; Pinart; Politovskii; Roche; Sarafian; Scidmore; Shashkov; Shemelin; Shiels; Simpson; Sliunin; Sokolov and Kushnarev; Speck; Sturdza; Swineford; Tebenkov; Tikhmenev; Tompkins; Underwood; Van Stone; Veniaminov; Vishnevskii; Whymper; Wrangell; Zagoskin; Zavalishin.
See also Baranov; Sitka; Purchase of Alaska; Russian Orthodox Church. See as well James Gibson (*Imperial Russia in Frontier America* [Cambridge: Harvard Univ. Press, 1975]).

RUSSIAN-AMERICAN RELATIONS
Adamov; Adams, E.; Adams, J.Q.; *Alaska Life,* July, '40; Oct., '44; June, '47; *Alaska Sportsman,* Nov., '40 (Alaska sale claimed illegal); Feb., '43; Sept., '43 (Soviets send prints of Peter the Great and Catherine II); Aug., '47; Nov., '54 (ice island occupied); Oct., '57 (battleships visited St. Michael in 1913); *Alaska Weekly,* June, '51 (Moscow Rose beamed to Nome); *Amer. Hist. Review,* Apr., '13 (correspondence of Russian Ministers in Washington, 1818-1825); Bailey; Brooks; Callahan; Collins; Denison; Franck; Golder; Greenhow; Gruening; Keber; Lipke; McNeilly; Manning; Mazour; Miller; Morris; Norwood; Ogilvie; Parry; Potter; Scidmore; Slavin; Stefansson; Tarsaidze; Thomas; Tompkins; Underwood; Vsemirnyi.
See also Alaska Diplomacy; Purchase of Alaska.

RUSSIAN-AMERICAN   TELEGRAPH   EXPEDITION
See Western Union Overland Telegraph Expedition.

RUSSIAN MISSION
Alaska-Yukon Magazine, Nov., '10 (photo); Cameron (church locked and dusty in 1919); Chase; Colby (portage to Kuskokwim now deteriorating); Couch (post office here 1922-52); Davis; DeBaets (founded 1847); Helmericks (Betsch); Henderson (descr.); Hulley (founded 1844); Rickard (Russian mission at Holy Cross); Savage (descr.); Stuck.

RUSSIAN ORTHODOX CHURCH

Alaska Life, July, '49 (Vladimir Donskoi, priest at Sitka, 1889); *Alaska Sportsman*, July, '39 (Kochergin in church at Umnak, photo); June, '55 (notes on the three bar cross); *Alaska Weekly*, Nov., '51 (Bishop John Zlobin tours Alaska parish); Allen, Robert (*Quar. J. of the Lib. Cong.*, "Alaska before 1867 in Soviet Literature," [July, 1966]); Andrews; Bancroft; Basanoff, V. (*Orthodox Alaska*, "Archives of the Russian Church in Alaska in the Library of Congress," [May, 1970]), (also *Pacific Historical Review*, 1933); Bensin, Basil (*History of the Russian Orthodox Greek Catholic Church of North America* [New York, 1941]), (*Orthodox Alaska*, "Blessed Herman of Alaska," [September, 1969]); Blomkvist, E.E. (*Oregon Historical Quarterly*, "A Russian Scientific Expedition to California and Alaska, 1839-49: The Drawings of I.G. Voznesenskii," Trans., Dmytryshyn and Crownhart-Vaughan [June, 1972]); Bolkovitinov, N.N. (*Oregon Historical Q.*, "Russia and the Declaration of the Non-colonization Principle: New Archival Evidence," Trans. Dmytryshyn [June, 1971]); Bolshakoff, Serge (*The Foreign Missions of the Russian Orthodox Church* [New York: Macmillan, 1943]); Brooks; Buzanski, Peter M. (*J. of the West*, "Alaska and Nineteenth Century American Diplomacy," [July, 1967]); Chevigny; Collins; Dall; Dorosh, John (*Quar. J. of the Lib. Cong.*, "The Alaskan Russian Church Archives," [August, 1961]); Fedorova; Gibson, James P. (*Pacific Northwest Quarterly*, "Russian America in 1833," [Jan., 1972]); Gilder, William (*Alaska Journal*, "St. Michael, 1881," [Spring, 1973]); Gilbert, Benjamin F. (*J. of the West*, "Arts and Sciences in Alaska, 1784-1910," [October, 1962]); "The Alaska Purchase," [April, 1964]); Golder, F. (*Guide*) (*Alaska Journal*, "The Attitude of the Russian Government toward Alaska," [Spring, 1971; repr.]) (*Orthodox Alaska*, "Father Herman, Alaska's Saint," [Fall, 1972]); Gsovski; Hanable, William (*Alaska Journal*, "New Russia. . .Yakutat Bay in 1796," [Spring, 1973]); Hieromonk Antonius (*Orthodox Alaska*, "Reminiscences and Impressions on the Formal Transfer of the Territory of Alaska to the United States," [Fall, 1972]); Henderson (unfavorable comment); Hines (beloved priest at Nome); Howard (service in Sitka, 1875); Hulley; Jackson; James (native baptisms); John, Fred and Katie John (*Alaska Journal*, "The Killing of the Russians at Batzulnetas Village. . .Oral History from the Copper River Region, recorded by B. Stephen Strong," [Summer, 1973]); Kovach, Michael (unpub. doc. dissert., U. Pittsburgh, 1957, "The Russian Orthodox Church in Russian America"); Kroeber Anthropological Society Papers (Journal of Hieromonk Juvenal up to his murder in 1795, reputedly [Spring, 1952]); Lada-Mocarski; Lantis; Leonty; Lipke (blessing on the waters); McCollom, P. (*Alaska Journal*, "The Story of Icons," [Winter, 1972]); Michael, Henry N. (*Lieutenant Zagoskin's Travels in Russian America, 1842-1844* [Toronto: U. of Toronto Press and the Arctic Inst. of N. Amer., 1967]); Morris (Nicholas Metropolsky priest at Sitka were Aleut); Nichols, R. and R. Crosskey (*Pac. NW Q.*, "The Condition of the Orthodox Church in Russian America: Innokentii Veniaminov's History of the Russian Church in Alaska," [April, 1972]); Nikolai (see W-5750 ff); Okun; Oliver (photo, Unalaska; Hotovitzki's singing; Pontelief's blessing);

Orthodox Alaska ("Letters of Bishop Innocent," Trans. from Barsukov's *Pisma Innokentiia* [Nov., '69 and Jan., '70]), ("Missionary Oath," [Fall, 1972]), ("Notes and Impressions during Travel in Alaska and the Aleutian Islands by Right Rev. Nicholas, Bishop of the Aleutians and Alaska," [Fall, 1972]), ("Saint Herman: Two Documents Concerning his Life," [March, 1971]), ("Seventy-five Years Ago in Alaska," [Dec., 1972; repr. from *Russian Orthodox American Messenger*, 1897]), ("Three Journals of Abbot Nicholas, 1858-1860, 1862-1863, 1864," [June, 1972]), ("Travel Journal of Hieromonk Illarion, 1861-1868," [March, 1971]), ("Travel Journal of Priest Jacob Netsvetov, 1828-1842," [March, 1972]); Oswalt, W. (*Mission of Change in Alaska: Eskimos and Morvaians on the Kuskokwim* [San Marino: Huntington Library, 1963]), ("Eskimos and Indians of Western Alaska, 1861-68: Extracts from the Diary of Fr. Illarion," [*Anthrop. Papers*, U. of Alaska, 1960]), ("Historical Populations in Western Alaska and Migration Theory," [*Anthrop. Papers*, U. of Alaska, 1961]), ("The Kuskokwim River Drainage," [U. of Alaska, *Anthrop. Papers*, 1965]); Patty, S. ("Bering's Grave," *Alaska Journal* [Winter, 1971]), ("Mission to Zagorsk: A Visit to the Tomb of the Great Russian Alaskan, Fr. Ivan Veniaminov," *Alaska Journal* [Spring, 1972]); Pierce, R.; Petrof; Putinsky (W-5752); Ray, D. ("Nineteenth Century Settlement and Subsistence Patterns in Bering Strait," *Arctic Anthrop.* [1965]); Rochcau, Vsevolod ("The Origins of the Orthodox Church in Alaska, 1820-1840," *Orthodox Alaska* [Nov., 1971, Jan., 1972]), ("St. Herman of Alaska and the Defense of Alaskan Native People," *Orthodox Alaska* [Jan., 1970, March, 1970]); Sarafian, Winston (unpub. doc. dissert., UCLA, 1970, "Russian American Company Employee Policies and Practices, 1799-1867"); Scidmore (see transferred to San Francisco, 1868); Shalamov (W-5753); Sherwood (*Alaska and Its History, Cook Inlet Collection*); Smith, B. (*Preliminary Survey*); Stuck; Sturdza (W-5758); Tompkins; Valaam Monastery (*Centenary of the Russian Church in America* [St. Petersburg, 1894] [unpublished typescript trans. by N. Gray, Kodiak, 1925 available at St. Herman's Pastoral School of the Russian Orthodox Church in Alaska]); Van Stone, James (*Eskimos of the Nushagak*), ("Nushagak: A Russian Trading Post in Southwest Alaska," *Alaska Journal* [Summer, 1972]), ("An Annotated Ethnohistorical Bibliography of the Nushagak River, Alaska," *Fieldiana* [1964], ("Akulivikchuk: A Nineteenth Century Eskimo Village on the Nushagak River," *Fieldiana* [1970]), ("Tikchik Village: A Nineteenth Century Village Community in Southwestern Alaska," *Fieldiana* [1966]), ("Kihik: An Historic Tanaina Indian Settlement," *Fieldiana* [1969]), ("Exploring the Copper River Country," *Pac. NW Q.* [1967]), ("Russian Exploration in Interior Alaska: An Extract from the Journal of Andrei Glazunov," *Pac. NW Q.* [1959]); Veniaminov; Watkins, Albert (unpub. master's thesis, University of Alaska, 1961, "A Historical Study of the Russian Orthodox Church in Alaska"); Wickersham (see this heading in the bibliography).

RUSSIAN RIVER

Alaska Sportsman (see Index); Baker; Colby; Franck; Hulley (Doroshin; on Doroshin see also Sherwood, *Cook Inlet Collection*).

RUSSIANS in AMERICA
Adamkiewicz (*Dalhousie Review*, 1948); Adam-
ov; *Alaska Sportsman*, June, '40 (search for Levan-
evsky plane); June, '58 (Kenai); *Alaska Weekly*,
Sept., '51 (deaths at Ouzinkie from steam bath);
Anderson; Andreev; Andrews; Aronson; Asmous;
Bains; Bancroft; Bannister; Barbeau; Bartz; Bell;
Berg; Berkh; Blomkvist; Bonch-Osmolovskii;
Brooks; Chevigny; Clark; Cook; Corser; Coxe;
Dall; Dawson; Denison; Denton; Divin; Efimov;
Farrelly; Fedorova; Fitzgerald; Gapanovich;
Golder; Granberg; Golovin; Greenhow; Gruening;
Hammerich; Hartwig; Henderson; Higginson;
Huber; Hulley; James; Karelin; Kennan; Kolarz;
Ledyard; Lepotier; McDonald; McCracken; Maka-
rova; Manning; Markov; Martin; Meals; Meany;
Morgan; Morris; Muller; Munford; Pallas; Potter;
Rechnoi Transport; Sarychev; Sauer; Shenitz;
Sparks; Speck; Staehlin; Stejneger; Steller;
Tarsaidze; Tompkins; Usov; Vahl; Veniaminov;
Vancouver; Wagner; Waxell; Whymper; Wicker-
sham; Woolen; Wrangel; Wright; Zagoskin. See
also Baranov, Purchase of Alaska; Alaska Diplo-
macy; Russian-American Company; Russian Ortho-
dox Church; Veniaminov.

RUSSO-FINNISH WHALING COMPANY
Bancroft (1849-54, half owned by Russian-
American Co.); Hulley; Petrof; Wickersham (bib-
liography).

RUSTGARD, JOHN (b. 1863)
Home Rule for Alaska. Juneau: 1927. 39 pp.

RUTZEBECK, HJALMAR (b. 1888)
Alaska Man's Luck. New York: Boni and
Liveright, 1920. 260 pp. Autobiographical, Lynn
Canal.
My Alaska Idyll. New York: Bone and Liveright,
1922. 296 pp.
Sailor with a Gun. New York: Pageant Press,
1957. 182 pp. Autobiographical, Fort Seward.

RYAN, JAMES C,
Report of the Commissioner of Education, 1950.

RYAN, JOHN JOSEPH (b. 1922)
The Maggie Murphy. New York: Norton, 1951.
224 pp. Autobiographical. Ryan worked for the
Anchorage Times and the *Fairbanks News-Miner*,
where he published a column, "Sourdough Jack
Sez."

RYAN, RICHARD S.
Testimony before legislative committees in Washington, DC. See the Wickersham bibliography. Ryan
was involved with legislation relating to coal, telegraph, and railroads.

S

S., J. B.; see T-4332, Steller, Geo.

S., J. L.; see Neue Nachrichten.

SABIN, EDWIN LEGRAND
Klondike Pardners. Philadelphia: J. Lippincott,
1929. 286 pp.

SABIN, JOSEPH
*Dictionary of Books Relating to America from
Discovery*. New York, 1868-1936. See Wagner.

SABINE, BERTHA W.
A Summer Trip among Alaskan Missions. Hartford: Church Missions Pub. Co., 1910. Episcopal.

SAGE, WALTER N.
Sir James Douglas and British Columbia.
Toronto: Univ. of Toronto Press, 1930. 398 pp.

St. ANNE'S ACADEMY, Victoria, BC
*St. Anne's in British Columbia and Alaska, 1858-
1924*. Victoria: Sisters of St. Anne, 1924. 106 pp.

St. ELIAS, Mt.
Alaska Sportsman, see Index; *Alaska-Yukon Mag-
azine*, Apr., '07; Apr., '09; *Appalachia*, June, '54
(first ascent); Baxter (*Sierra Club Bulletin*, 1951);
Broke; Brooks; Bruce; Clifford (*Can. Alpine J.*,
1952); Colby; Dall; Davis (*Can. Alpine J.*, 1958);
Dole; Filippi; Golder; Hainsworth (*Amer. Alpine
J.*, 1950); Hanna (*Pac. Discovery*, 1952); Houston
(*Amer. Alpine J.*, 1956); Hulley; Josendal (*Appa-
lachia*, 1952); Kauffman (*Can. Alpine J.*, 1947);
Lilley (*Amer. Alpine J.*, 1957); Luigi; McGowan
(*Amer. Alpine J.*, 1954); Miller, M. (*Amer. Alpine
J.*, 1947); Miller, T. (*Can. Alpine J.*, 1954); Mohling
(*Mountaineering*, 1953); Molenaar (*Sierra Club
Bul.*, 1947); Odell; Ortenburger (*Amer. Alpine J.*,
1957); Putnam (*Appalachia*, 1947); Reynolds (*Can.
Alpine J.*, 1953; *Amer. Alpine J.*, 1955); Russell, I.
(*Bulletin*, Amer. Geog. Soc., 1896); Sanders (*Appa-
lachia*, 1955); Schoening (*Am. Alpine J.*, 1953);
Schwatka; Scidmore; Seton-Karr (*Proc.*, Royal
Geog. Soc., 1887) (*Shores and Alps of Alaska* [Lon-
don: Low, Marston, 1887]); Steller; Stuck; Thayer
(*Amer. Alpine J.*, 1953); Topham (*Proc.*, Royal
Geog. Soc., 1889); Underwood; Vancouver;
Wallerstein and Clarke (*Pacific Discovery*, 1958);
Waxell; Wead; Wickersham; Williams, Wm.
(*Scribner's*, Apr., '89).

St. LAWRENCE ISLAND
Alaska Life, March, 46; *Alaska Sportsman*, Dec.,
'37 (photo, Oktokoyuk, medicine man); Nov., '42

(heating fuels expensive); Sept., '45; July, '49 (Dick Dundas); Nov., '51 (photo, Cape St. Elias light); June, '52 (dead walruses from Siberia); Nov., '53 (ice pool); Jan., '60 (John Angalook), and Index; Aldrich (Clerk Island); Baker; Burroughs (deaths due to whiskey reported to the Harriman expedition); Colby (native name of island is Chibukak); Collins; Dole (suggests starvation in winter of 1879-80 due to extreme cold); Elliott; Friedmann (*Proc.*, US Nat. Museum, 1932); Geist; Golder; Gruening; Henderson (suggests entire population of 400 starved in 1878, remains found in 1880 by revenue cutter); Higginson (discovered by Bering in 1728); Hrdlicka; Hughes (*Amer. Anthrop.*, 1958); Hulley; Jackson (suggests 1878 starvation due to rum purchased the previous season rendering population unable to prepare food for winter); Lutke; Midlo and Cummins (*Am. J. of Phys. Anthrop.*, 1931); Mikami (*Ak. Sportsman*, 1935 [Geist]); Miller, M. (descr. of bodies found by *Corwin*, 1880); Moore (*Am. Anthrop.*, 1923, 1928); Muir; Nelson; Nordenskiold; Oetteking (see the Arctic Bibliography); Pa. U. (*Bulletin*, 1958 [Univ.-Ackerman exped. to St. Lawrence Island]); Petrof (in *Comp. of Narratives*); Rainey; Sarychev; Smith (*Ak. Sports.*, Oct., '37 [whale hunting]); Stuck; Van Valin.

St. MARY'S HOSPITAL (Dawson)
1897-98 to 1947-48: Golden Jubilee. Dawson, 1948. 16 pp.

St. MATTHEW ISLAND
Alaska Sportsman, Dec., '40; Aug., '55 (reindeer pop. to be reduced, now 500 from 20 left by CG during the war); Oct., '57; Baker; Burroughs; Dall (nearly all Russians here starved winter of 1810 as sea mammals disappeared); Dawson (*Bulletin*, Geol. Soc. of Amer., 1894); Hanna (see the Arctic Bibliography); Kittlitz; Raymond (in *Comp. of Narratives*); Stresemann (*Ibis*, Apr., '49 [birds from Cook's voyage]); US Coast Pilot.

St. MICHAEL
Alaska Sportsman, Aug., '39 (Whymper drawing); Aug., '49 (notes by West of *Corwin*); Feb., '50 (photo, church); March, '53 (photo, floating saloon); Aug., '53 (descr. by *Bear* crewman); May, '56 (blockhouse photo); May, '57 (descr.); Oct., '57 (by Corlett, lieut. at St. Michael in '13); Andrews (photos, trading stas.); Baker (named for Capt. Michael Dmitrievich Tebenkov, initially called Mikhailovskii); Bannister (journal of 1865-67); Blount; Cameron; Chase; Colby; Couch (post office from 1897); Davis (1899); Dole (founded 1833, unsuccessfully attacked by Unaligmiuts, 1836); Franck; Henderson; Hersey (*Auk*, 1917); Hewitt (Army doctor, 1897-1908); Higginson; Hulley; James (Kennicott, Bannister and Dall, 1865-67); Judge (letter, 1890-91); Kitchener (AC Co.); Miller (1935); Muir; Nelson; Ogilvie; Petrof (in *Comp. of Narratives*); Ray (letter, 1897); Raymond (in *Comp. of Narratives*); Rickard (photo); Schwatka; Scidmore; Swineford; Tompkins; Underwood; Wead; Whymper; Zagoskin.

St. TERESE SHRINE, Juneau
Alaska Life, May, '42 (built by LeVasseur, 1936); July, '42; July, '45 (photo); *Alaska Sportsman*, June, '41; June, '42; Couch (post office, 1938-46); Munoz (northernmost American Catholic shrine); Savage.

SALAMANCA, LUCY
"Photographing the Unknown," *National Republic*, 1930.
"Uncle Sam's Last Frontier," *National Republic*, 1931.

SALISBURY, HAROLD
Poems of Alaska. Nome: Nugget Press, 1954. 64 pp.
Alaskan Songs and Ballads. Portland: Metropolitan Press, 1967. 111 pp.
The Great Land: Poems of Alaska. Anchorage: Ken Wray Press, 1969. 79 pp.

SALISBURY, OLIVER MAXSON (b. 1888)
Quoth the Raven. Seattle: Superior Pub. Co., 1962. 275 pp. Journal, Klawock, 1926-27.

SALMON
Alaska Life, June, '43; March, '47; *Alaska Sportsman*, see Index; *Alaska Weekly*, March, '51 (Ak. Salmon Inst. est.); June, '51 (pricing); Sept., '51 (Skeena River rock slide); Beach; Brooks; Cameron (Ketchikan cannery); Carpenter; Clark; Colby; Cobb; Denison; Dole (Karluk); Dufresne; Franck; Greely; Gruening; Harriman; Hawthorne; Hellenthal; Henderson; Hilscher; Hubbard; Hulley; James; Jacobin; Morris; Moser; Petrof; Potter; Pilgrim; Rich; Rogers; Savage; Schaefers and Fukuhara; Schwatka; Scidmore; Stuck; Sundborg; Tewkesbury; Tussing; Underwood; US F&WS; Vancouver; Walden; Willoughby; Wilson; Willimovsky; Winslow; Wolfe; Young.

See also Fish and Fisheries.

SALMONBERRIES
Alaska Sportsman, Feb., '53 (descr.); Davis; Harriman (descr., Burroughs); Henderson; Morris (Russians called it Morosky; anti-scorbutic; ripens when salmon run); O'Connor; Willard.

SALT, HARRIET
The Alaska Railroad, repr. from *Mighty Engineering Feats* (Phila.: Penn. Pub. Co., 1937).

SALVATION ARMY in Alaska
Alaska Magazine, Winter, '50 (Dawson to Skagway in 1899; successful with natives; McGill, Bloss, St. Clair [Hoonah], Willard [Angoon], and Newton [Kake]); *Alaska-Yukon Magazine*, Sept., '08 (Evangeline Booth); Bankson (Dowell to Dawson in 1898); Hawthorne (Dawson); Tewkesbury (1950 missions at Angoon, Anchorage, Hoonah, Juneau, Kake, Ketchikan, Klawock, Metlakatla, Petersburg, Saxman, Sitka, Tenakee and Wrangell).

SAMSON, SAM (b. 1869)
The Eskimo Princess. Stevenson, Wn.: Columbia Gorge Pubs., 1941. 48 pp. Autobiographical, Nome, 1900.

SAMUELS, CHARLES
The Magnificent Rube: Life and Gaudy Times of Tex Rickard. New York: McGraw Hill, 1957. 301 pp.

SAMWELL, DAVID
A Narrative of the Death of Captain James Cook. Honolulu: Hawaiian Historical Society, 1916. 26 pp.

SANTOS, ANGEL
See the Arctic Bibliography.

SARGENT, EPES
See T-3960 ff.

SARGENT, R. H. and FRED MOFFITT
"Aerial Photographic Surveys in Southeastern Alaska," *Bulletin*, USGS, 1929.

SARAFIAN, WINSTON LEE
Unpublished doctoral dissertation, UCLA, 1970, "Russian American Company Employee Policies and Practices, 1799-1867." See Russian Orthodox Church.

SARNOFF, PAUL
Ice Pilot: Bob Bartlett. New York: Julian Messner, 1966. 161 pp.

SARYCHEV, GAVRIIL ANDREEVICH (1763-1830)
See the Arctic Bibliography, and T-3964 ff.

SATTERFIELD, ARCHIE
Alaska Bush Pilots in the Float Country. Seattle: Superior Pub. Co., 1968. 176 pp.

SAUER, MARTIN
An Account of a Geographical and Astronomical Expedition. London: Cadell, 1802. 414 pp. Billings, 1787, St. Petersburg, to Yakutsk and Okhotsk, thence to Kolyma to the Arctic, and attempts to sail eastward; also voyages to Alaska in 1789-92; see Wagner.

SAUNDERS, L. F.
"Warden of the Aleutians," *Sunset*, 1926.

SAVAGE, ALMA HELEN (b. 1900)
Dogsled Apostles. New York: Sheed and Ward, 1942. 231 pp. Catholic missions.
The Forty-ninth Star, Alaska. New York: Benziger Brothers, 1959. 180 pp. Catholic notables.
Smoozie: The Story of an Alaska Reindeer Fawn. New York: Sheed and Ward, 1941. 68 pp. Juvenile.
Eben the Crane. New York: Sheed and Ward, 1944. 74 pp. Juvenile.
Holiday in Alaska. Boston: Heath, 1944. 80 pp. Juvenile.
Kulik's First Seal Hunt. Paterson, NJ: St. Anthony Guild Press, 1948. 114 pp.
"Oldest Bishop Knows Dutch Harbor," *Catholic World*, 1942.

SAVAGE, RICHARD HENRY (1846-1903)
The Princess of Alaska. New York: Neely, 1894. 420 pp.

SAWIN, H. A.
"Bucket Dredge Installed at Goodnews Bay," *Eng. and Mining J.*, 1938.

SAYLER, HARRY L.
The King Bear of Kodiak Island. Chicago: Reilly & Britton, 1912. 268 pp. Sayler's pseudonym was Elliott Whitney.
The Airship Boys Due North. Chicago: Reilly & Britton, 1910. 335 pp.

SCAMMAN, EDITH
"A List of Plants from Interior Alaska," *Rhodora*, 1940.
"Ferns and Fern Allies of the Central Yukon Valley," *Amer. Fern J.*, 1949.

SCAMMON, CHARLES MELVILLE (1825-1911)
The Marine Mammals of the North-western Coast of North America. New York: Putnam's, 1874. 319 pp. Includes an account of the Pacific whale fishery.
See also the Arctic Bibliography.

SCARBOROUGH, C. W.
"The Journey that Failed," *Alaska Journal*, Winter, 1974.

SCARTH, W. H.
Report on Trip to the Yukon. Ottawa: GPB, 1897. 13 pp. Scarth was an inspector with the RCMP.

SCEARCE, STANLEY (b. 1879)
Northern Lights to the Fields of Gold. Caldwell: Caxton Printers, 1939. 390 pp. Autobiographical, Klondike. See also *Alaska-Yukon Magazine*, Sept., '08.

SCHAEFERS and FUKUHARA
"Offshore Salmon Explorations Adjacent to the Aleutian Islands, June-July, 1953," *Commercial Fisheries Review*, US F&WS, 1954.

SCHAFER, JOSEPH (1867-1941)
The Pacific Slope and Alaska. Philadelphia: G. Barrie's Sons, 1904. 436 pp. Very brief on Alaska.
A History of the Pacific Northwest. New York: Macmillan, 1905. 321 pp.

SCHANZ, ALFRED B.
Chapter on the Nushagak District, in the Eleventh Census. Schanz was a member of the expedition sent to Alaska in the spring of 1890 by Frank Leslie's Illustrated Newspaper. See E.J. Glave; see also Baker.

SCHEFFER, VICTOR B. and KARL W. KENYON
"The Fur Seal Comes of Age," *National Geographic*, Apr., '52.
Seals, Sea Lions and Walruses. Stanford: Stanford University Press, 1958. 179 pp.
The Year of the Seal. New York: Scribner's Sons, 1970. 213 pp.
The Year of the Whale. New York: Scribner's Sons, 1969. 205 pp.

SCHERER, J. B.
See the Arctic Bibliography.

SCHERMAN, KATHARINE
See the Arctic Bibliography. The Schermans conducted an ornithology expedition to the region of Baffin Bay in 1954 sponsored by the New York Zoological Society and the Arctic Institute of North America.
Spring on an Arctic Island. Boston: Little, Brown, 1956. 331 pp.

SCHLEDERMANN, PETER and W. OLSON
"Archaeological Survey of the C.O.D. Lake Area, Minto Flats," *Anthrop. Papers*, University of Alaska, 1969.

SCHLEIN, MIRIAM
Oomi, the New Hunter. New York: Abelard-Schuman, 1955. 109 pp.

SCHLEY, WINFIELD SCOTT (1839-1911) **and J. R. SOLEY**
The Rescue of Greely. New York: Scribner's, 1885. 227 pp. See also Greely.
Greely Relief Expedition of 1884. Wn.DC: GPO, 1887. 75 pp. US Navy.

SCHLOZER, AUGUST LUDWIG von
See the Arctic Bibliography.

SCHMITT, WALDO LASALLE (b. 1887)
"Alaska King Crab Investigations, 1940," *Explorations and Field Work of the Smithsonian Institution in 1940.* Wn.DC: GPO, 1941.

SCHMITTER, FERDINAND (b. 1876)
Upper Yukon Native Customs and Folk-lore. Wn.DC: GPO, 1910. Smithsonian.

SCHMUCKER, SAMUEL MOSHEIM (1823-1863)
Arctic Explorations and Discoveries during the 19th Century. New York: Miller, Orten, 1857. 517 pp. Ross, Parry, Back, Franklin, McClure, etc., incl. Kane's search for Franklin.
See also the Arctic Bibliography.

SCHOENBERG, WILFRED, P., S. J.
Jesuits in Oregon. Portland: Oregon Jesuit, 1959. 64 pp. Alaska is in the Oregon Jesuit Province. Includes a photo of Archbishop Seghers.

SCHOETTLER, ARTHUR E.
"Industrial Education in Alaska," *Industrial Education*, May, 1938.
"Vocational Education in Alaska," *Industrial Arts and Vocational Education*, March, 1938.

SCHOLEFIELD, ETHELBERT OLAF STUART (1875-1919) **and FREDERICK W. HOWAY**
British Columbia from the Earliest Times. Vancouver: Clarke, 1914. 4v. Vol. 2 is by Howay; Vols. 3 and 4 are biographical.
A History of British Columbia. Vancouver: B.C. Historical Association, 1913. 2v.

SCHOOLING, WILLIAM
The Hudson's Bay Company. London: Hudson's Bay Co., 1920. 129 pp.

SCHORR, ALAN EDWARD
Supplement to Orth's Alaska Placenames. College: University of Alaska, 1974.

SCHOTT, CHARLES ANTHONY (1826-1901)
"Terrestrial Magnetism," *Report*, Internat'l. Polar Expedition, 1884. US Congress, 48th Congress, House Exec. Doc. 44 (2nd Sess., 1885).
See also the Arctic Bibliography.

SCHRADER, FRANK CHARLES (1860-1944)
A Reconnaissance in Northern Alaska. Wn.DC: GPO, 1904. 139 pp. USGS Koyukuk, John, Anaktuvuk and Colville Rivers, Arctic Coast.
"Reconnaissance of a Part of Prince William Sound and the Copper River District, 1898," *Annual Report*, USGS, 1899. Schrader was geologist with US Army Expedition No. 2 in 1898.
The Geology and Mineral Resources of a Portion of the Copper River District. Wn.DC: GPO, 1901. 94 pp. USGS. Valdez, Kotsina, Strelna, Tana Glacier, and return.
Preliminary Report on the Cape Nome Gold Region. Wn.DC: GPO, 1900. 56 pp. USGS. Based on 1899 survey.
"Recent Work of the US Geological Survey in Alaska," *Bulletin*, Amer. Geog. Soc., 1902.
"The Cape Nome Gold District," *National Geographic*, 1900.
See also the Arctic Bibliography.

SCHUCHERT, CHARLES
Atlas of Paleogeographic Maps of North America. New York: John Wiley, 1955. 177 pp.

SCHULTZ, GWEN
Glaciers and the Ice Age: Earth and Its Inhabitants during the Pleistocene. New York: Holt, Rinehart and Winston, 1963. 128 pp.

SCHULTZ, J. L.
See the Arctic Bibliography, and Neue Nachrichten.

SCHULTZ, LEONARD
"A New Genus and Two New Species of Cottoid Fishes from the Aleutian Islands," *Proc.*, US National Museum, 1938.

SCHULTZ-LORENTZEN CHRISTIAN WILHELM (b. 1873)
See the Arctic Bibliography.

SCHULTZE, AUGUSTUS
See the Arctic Bibliography, and T-4013 ff.

SCHWAB, HENRY B. deV.
"Early Chapters in the History of Mt. McKinley," *Amer. Alpine J.*, 1933.
See also *Alpine J.* (London), 1932, and *Amer. Alpine J.*, 1932 for articles on the Cape-Koven tragedy of 1932.

SCHWALBE, ANNA BUXBAUM
Dayspring on the Kuskokwim: The Story of Moravian Missions in Alaska. Bethlehem, Pa.: Moravian Press, 1951. 264 pp. Bethel and the Nushagak area, from 1884 to 1951.

SCHWARTZKOPF, KARL-AAGE
The Alaska Pilot. New York: Franklin Watts, 1961. 118 pp. Juvenile.
The Actic Pilot. New York: Franklin Watts, 1962. 136 pp. Juvenile.

SCHWATKA, FREDERICK (1849-1892)
Along Alaska's Great River. New York: Cassell, 1885. 360 pp. Popular account of the Yukon.
A Summer in Alaska. St. Louis: J.W. Henry, 1891. 418 pp. An enlarged edition of *Along Alaska's Great River*.
Report of a Military Reconnaissance in Alaska, 1883. Wn.DC: GPO, 1885. 121 pp. Official narrative, condensed. Much material on natives, and 20 maps.

"Exploration of the Yukon River in 1883,"
Journal, Amer. Geog. Soc., 1884.
  Nimrod of the North. New York: Cassell, 1885. 198
pp. Animals and hunting.
  Wonderland: or Alaska and the Inland Passage.
Chicago: Rand McNally, 1886. 96 pp.
  Address, Annual Meeting. Amer. Geog. Soc.,
1880. See Caswell for a discussion of Schwatka's
1878-80 expedition in search of Franklin.
  "Letter of Lieut. F. Schwatka, US Army, Com-
manding the Franklin Search Party," *Journal*, Amer.
Geog. Soc., 1880.
  The Search for Franklin. London: Nelson, 1886.
127 pp. See also Gilder.
  "The Igloo of the Innuit," *Science*, 1883.
  "The Alaska Military Reconnaissance of 1883,"
Science, 1883.
  "The Middle Yukon," *Science*, 1884.
  "The Implements of the Igloo," *Science*, 1884.
  The Children of the Cold. Boston: Educational
Publications Co., 1899. 212 pp.
  "Two Expeditions to Mt. St. Elias," *Century*,
Apr., 1891.
  See also the Arctic Bibliography. Schwatka con-
ducted a Franklin search expedition in 1878-80, his
exploration of the Yukon in 1883, and an expedition
to the Mt. St. Elias region for the *New York Times* in
1886. Baker records a Schwatka expedition in 1891,
from Lynn Canal and Taku Inlet, via the Lewes and
Teslin Rivers, the White River and Skolai Pass, and
the Chitina and Copper Rivers to Prince William
Sound. Results were published in *National Geographic* (1892) by Charles Willard. See also *Alaska
Life*, Nov., '44 by Charles Erskine Scott Wood.

SCHWIEBERT, ERNEST
  Salmon of the World. New York: Winchester
Press, 1970. 63 pp.

SCHWEINIT, P. de
  "The Moravian Mission on the Kuskokwim," *Missionary Review of the World*, 1890.

SCIDMORE, ELIZA RUHAMAH (1856-1928)
  *Alaska: Its Southern Coast and the Sitkan Archi-
pelago*. Boston: Lothrop, 1885. 333 pp. Based on
summer cruises of 1883 and 1884, coincident with
navy rule in Alaska.
  *Appleton's Guide-book to Alaska and the North-
west Coast*. New York: Appleton, 1893. 167 pp.
  "The Discovery of Glacier Bay," *Nat'l. Geog.*,
1896.
  "The Mt. St. Elias Expedition of Prince Luigi
Amadeo of Savoy, 1897," *Nat'l. Geog.*, 1898.
  "The Stikine River in 1898," *Nat'l. Geog.*, 1899.
  "The First District of Alaska from Prince Frederick
Sound to Yakutat Bay," *Eleventh Census*, 1890.
  "Alaska," *Reports*, Director of the Mint, 1883, and
1884.
  "The Disputed Boundary between Alaska and
British Columbia," *Century Magazine*, 1891.
  "The Alaska Boundary Question," *Century Mag-
azine*, 1896.
  "Recent Explorations in Alaska," *Nat'l. Geog.*,
1893, 1894.
  "The Northwest Passes to the Yukon," *Nat'l.
Geog.*, 1898.

SCORESBY, WILLIAM (1760-1829)
  *Seven Log-books Concerning the Arctic Voyages
of Captain William Scoresby, Senior*. New York:
Explorers Club, 1917.

SCORESBY, WILLIAM (1789-1857)
  Memorials of the Sea: My Father. London: Long-
man, Brown, 1851. 232 pp. Greenland whaling.
  An Account of the Arctic Regions. Edinburgh:
Constable, 1820. 2v. Whaling, natural history.

SCOTT, ERASTUS HOWARD (b. 1855)
  Alaska Days. Chicago: Scott, Foresman, 1923.
106 pp. Personal narrative, Inland Passage, Alaska
Railroad.

SCOTT, F. P. and L. R. WYLIE
  "Alaskan Earthquake Observed at Washington,"
Popular Astronomy, 1937.

SCOULER, JOHN
  "On the Indian Tribes Inhabiting the Northwest Coast of America," *Journal*, Royal Geog. Soc.,
1841.

SCRIPPS INSTITUTION of OCEANOGRAPHY
  Oceanic Observation of the Pacific, 1956. Berkeley: University of California Press, 1963. 485 pp.

SCRUTATOR
  *The Impracticability of a North-west Passage for
Ships*. London: Valpy, 1824. 182 pp.

SCULL, EDWARD MARSHALL (b. 1880)
  Hunting in the Arctic and Alaska. Philadelphia:
Winston, 1914. 304 pp.

SEA COWS (Rhytina)
  Baer (see the Arctic Bibliography); Buchner (see
the Arctic Bibliography); Elliott; Golder (Waxell);
Gruening; Huish (reports last taken in 1768);
Pallas; Stejneger (see the Arctic Bibliography);
Steller; Waxell.

SEA LIONS
  Alaska Sportsman, see Index; *Alaska-Yukon Magazine*, Apr., '07; Burroughs (in Harriman); Dole
(quotes Elliott); Dufresne; Elliott; Harriman;
Henderson; Kenyon and Scheffer; Newcombe;
Petrof; Wolfe (Canadian cutter bombed sea lions to
protect salmon).

SEALOCK, RICHARD BURL and P. A. SEELY
  *Bibliography of Place Name Literature, US,
Canada, Alaska, and Newfoundland*. Chicago:
American Library Association, 1948. 331 pp.

SEALS, Bearded
  Dufresne (Nunivak to the Polar ice); Kitchener
(oogruk, Eskimo name).

SEALS, Fur
  See Pribilof Islands.

SEA OTTERS
  Alaska Life, Sept., '45; *Alaska Sportsman*, see
Index; *Alaska Weekly*, July, '50 (Amchitka); An-
drews; Barabash-Nikiforov ("Sea Otters of the Com-

mander Islands," *J. of Mammalogy* [1935]); Barbeau; Brandt (see Arctic Bibliography); Brooks; Chevigny; Colby; Dufresne; Dall; Dole (Belkofski); Erman (descr.); Elliott; Fischer, E.; Golder; Gruening (protection; Belkovski); Hanna (*J. of Mammalogy*, 1923); Henderson (still good catches in 1897, pelts bringing $150); Higginson (Belkovski); Hooper; Hulley; Jochelson; Jones, R. (*Proc.*, Alaskan Science Conf., 1951); Jones, R. ("Present Status of the Sea Otter in Alaska," *Trans.*, N. Amer. Wildlife Conf., 1951); Kenyon and Scheffer (*Seals, Sea-lions and Sea Otter of the Pac. Coast* [Wn.DC: GPO, 1953], US F&WS); Kenyon (*Oryx*, 1957); Kirkpatrick, C. (*Arctic*, 1955); Kitchener (statistics after Russians; 5000 annual average 1870-1890); Loganov (Arctic Bibliography); McCracken; McDonald, L.; MacMillan (*Forest and Outdoors*, 1949); Malkovich (Arctic Bibliography); Marakov (Arctic Bibliography); May (*Nat. History*, 1943); Mertens (Arctic Bibliography); Miller; Murie (*J. of Mamalogy*, 1940); Ogden (Arctic Bibliography); Paramonov (Arctic Bibliography); Petrof; Pilgrim; Pocock (*Proc.*, Zoological Soc. of London, 1928); Preble (*Biol. Survey of the Pribilof Islands*, USBS, 1923); Rausch (*Ecology*, 1951); Scammon (*Amer. Naturalist*, Apr., 1870); Scheffer (*J. of Mammalogy*, 1951) (*Nature*, 1950; Scheffer and Wilke (*J.*, Wn. Acad. of Sci., 1950); Schiller (*Biol. Bull.*, 1954); Schwatka; Scidmore; Snow; Steller; Strassen (Arctic Bibliography); Swineford (Belkovski, Sannahk Island); Tanner (*Albatross*); Tillenius (*Beaver*, 1955); US Bur. Fish (annual report from 1911); US Dept. Interior (*Mid-century Alaska*); US Rev. Cutter Serv. (Hooper); Vancouver; Wilke (*J. Wildlife Management*, 1957); Williams (*J. of Mammalogy*, 1938); Wrangel; Wright. See also the Arctic Bibliography.

SEALS, Hair
Alaska Sportsman, see Index; *Alaska Weekly*, Apr., '51 (bounty in salmon areas); Aldrich; Allen (*Bulletin*, Amer. Museum of Natural History, 1902); Burroughs; Dufresne; Harriman; Miller; Pilgrim; Swineford; Williams, J.

SEALS, Ribbon
Alaska Sportsman, Feb., '58; Dufresne (distributed sparingly; stripes).

SEALS, Ringed
Dufresne (most abundant, Kuskokwim north).

SEATTLE, Washington
Binns, *Gateway: Story of the Port of Seattle*; Morgan, M.; see also Herron; Underwood. See also Alaska-Yukon-Pacific Exposition.

SEATTLE CHAMBER OF COMMERCE, ALASKA BUREAU
Alaska: Our Frontier Wonderland. Seattle, 1916. 112 pp.

SEATTLE ELECTRIC COMPANY
Souvenir Guide of the Alaska-Yukon-Pacific Exposition. Seattle, 1909. 64 pp.

SEATTLE FUR EXCHANGE
A Story in Pictures: Seattle Fur Exchange. Seattle, 1928. 22 pp.

SEATTLE, JOHN MUIR SCHOOL
John Muir: A Pictorial Biography. Seattle: Lowman and Hanford, 1938. 105 pp.
The John Muir Book. Seattle: Cooperative Printing, 1925. 71 pp.

SEATTLE POST-INTELLIGENCER
Facts on Alaska. Seattle, 1904. 16 pp.

SEATTLE REPUBLICAN
Northwestern Negro Progress Number: Alaska-Yukon-Pacific Exposition, 1909. Seattle: H.R. Cayton, 1909. 78 pp.

SEATTLE WRITERS' CLUB
Tillicum Tales. Seattle: Lowman and Hanford, 1907. 308 pp.

SECRETAN, JAMES HENRY EDWARD (1852-1926)
To Klondyke and Back. London: Hurst and Blackett, 1898. 260 pp.

SEE ALASKA
Periodical published by George Huff. Alaska Statehood Number, July, 1959. 50 pp.

SEED, H. G. and S. D. WILSON
The Turnagain Heights Landslide in Anchorage, Alaska. Berkeley: University of California Press, 1966. 37 pp.

SEEMANN, BERTHOLD CARL (1825-1871)
Narrative of the Voyage of HMS Herald, 1845-51. London: Reeve, 1853. 2v.
The Botany of the Voyage of HMS Herald. London: Reeve, 1854.

SEGAL, LOUIS
The Conquest of the Arctic. London: G.G. Harrap and Co., 1939. 248 pp. Contains a chronology of Arctic voyages, 1870-1918.

SEGHERS, CHARLES JOHN (1839-1886) **Catholic Archbishop**
DeBaets (*Apostle of Alaska*); Henley (diary, in *Guide to Yukon-Klondike Mines*); *Catholic Sentinel* (Portland: letters, 1877-78; see W-1058); Crimont; Calasanz; Judge; Wickersham; Young. See also Bosco. Seghers was martyred at Yissetlatch, near Nulato, by Francis Fuller, mentally deranged, in 1886. Seghers had been on the Yukon in the season of 1877-78, and at Unalaska and Kodiak in 1873. Seghers established a mission at Wrangel in 1879. See also G. Steckler.

SELDOVIA
Alaska Sportsman, see Index; Baker (called Seldevoi, meaning herring, by Tebenkov; native name is Chesloknu); Colby; Couch (post office from 1898); Higginson; Johnson (USGS, typescript, open file series no. 246, 1954); Kitchener (NC Co. store here and elsewhere in Cook Inlet, but in 1911 moved to Erskine in Kodiak District sale); Lipke (autobiographical, after 1916); Sherwood (in Cook Inlet Collection); US Dept. of Interior (*Mid-century Alaska*).

SELL, GEORGE
The Petroleum Industry. New York: Oxford University Press, 1963. 276 pp.

SELLE, RALPH ABRAHAM
The Daughter of the Midnight Sun. Houston: Carroll Printing Co., 1933. 32 pp.
Luck and Alaska. Houston: Carroll Printing, 1932. 186 pp.
The Lure of Gold. Houston: Carroll Printing, 1932. 32 pp.

SELSAM, MILLICENT ELLIS
The Quest of Captain Cook. New York: Doubleday, 1962. 128 pp. Juvenile.

SELTZER, CARL C.
"The Anthropometry of the Western and Copper Eskimos," *Human Biology*, Sept., 1933.

SEMYONOV, Y.
The Conquest of Siberia. London: George Routledge, 1944. Trans. E. Dickes.

SENTER, GANO E.
Kawoo of Alaska. Denver: Sage Books, 1964. 113 pp. Shipwrecked seamen among the Tlingit.

SEPPALA, LEONHARD (b. 1877)
Alaska Sportsman, March, '36; Dec., '36; June, '37; Dec., '37; Feb., '55 (Norseman's League medal); Feb., '60 (retirement to Seattle), and Index; *Alaska Weekly*, Dec., '50 (7 months visit to Norway); June, '51; Cameron; Colby (on Balto and Togo); *Encycl. of NW Biog.*; Potter (photo with Will Rogers); Ricker (autobiography, as told to Mrs. Ricker).

SEREBRENNIKOV, RUF (d. 1848)
See the condensation, translated, of Serebrennikov's account of his trip up the Copper River in 1847-48 in Allen's narrative in the *Compilation of Narratives*. Sent by Tebenkov to explore the Copper, Serebrennikov and his men were presumably massacred by the Ahtna. His notes were turned over to Russians by Eyak Indians, who supposedly got them from Ahtna traders. See also Brooks, and Hulley. See also B.S. Strong.

SERVICE, ROBERT (1874-1958)
The Spell of the Yukon and Other Verses. New York: Barse, 1907. 99 pp. Numerous other editions.
"Law of the Yukon," *Canadian Magazine*, 1907.
Songs of a Sourdough. Toronto: Ryerson, 1907. 108 pp.
Ballads of a Cheechako. New York: Barse, 1909. 137 pp.
The Trail of '98: A Northland Romance. New York: Grosset, Ryerson, 1910. 514 pp. Other editions.
Rhymes of a Rolling Stone. New York: Dodd, Mead, 1912. 172 pp.
The Pretender: A Story of the Latin Quarter. New York: Dodd, 1915. 349 pp.
Rhymes of a Red Cross Man. New York: Barnes, 1916. 192 pp.
Ballads of a Bohemian. New York: Barse, 1921. 220 pp.

The Poisoned Paradise. New York: Dodd, 1922. 412 pp.
The Roughneck. New York: Barse, 1924. 448 pp.
The Master of the Microbe. Toronto: McClelland, 1926. 424 pp.
The House of Fear. New York: Dodd, 1927. 408 pp.
Why Not Grow Young. New York: Barse, 1928. 226 pp.
Bar-room Ballads: A Book of Verse. London: Ernest Benn, 1940. 206 pp.
The Complete Poems of Robert Service. New York: Dodd, Mead, 1942. 1027 pp.
Ploughman of the Moon: An Adventure into Memory. New York: Dodd, Mead, 1945. 472 pp. Autobiographical.
Service was a Scot. He left home while in high school. Though some of his verses were accepted by boys magazines, he worked a time as a bank clerk, and then migrated to British Columbia as a farmhand. Drifting around the west coast for a few years, he finally returned to British Columbia and worked for the Canada Bank of Commerce. Transferred to Whitehorse, he began to write verses of the north. Some of these, sent east to be bound as Christmas gifts, proved so popular that Service's fame and fortune were made. He later traveled, served as an ambulance driver in France during the First War and later still retired to the Riviera. Never a resident of Alaska, Service embodied in his poetry the spontaneous, transparent, pragmatic approach to life often identified with the north.
Harper of Heaven, a Record of Radiant Living. New York: Dodd, Mead, 1948. 452 pp.
See *Alaska Life*, Nov., '45; see also *Alaska Journal*, Summer, 1974. See also Illingworth for a critical interpretation of Service's influence on the north. See also Bush, Cameron, Davis and Franck.

SESSIONS, FRANCIS CHARLES (1820-1892)
From Yellowstone Park to Alaska. New York: Welch, Fracker, 1890. 186 pp.
"Alaska," in *Magazine of Western History*, 1886.

SETCHELL, WILLIAM ALBERT (1864-1943)
See the Arctic Bibliography.

SETON-KARR, HEYWOOD WALTER (b. 1859)
Shores and Alps of Alaska. London: Low, Marston, 1887. 248 pp. This includes the diary of John Bremner.
Bear-hunting in the White Mountains. London: Chapman and Hall, 1891. 156 pp.
"The Alpine Regions of Alaska," *Proc.*, Royal Geog. Soc., 1887.
"Explorations in Alaska and Northwest British Columbia," *Proc.*, Royal Geog. Soc., 1891.
Ten Years' Travel and Sport in Foreign Lands. London: Chapman and Hall, 1890. 179 pp.

SEWARD
Alaska Life, Apr., '40; June, '40 (photo); March, '41 (on moving railway terminal); Jan., '42; Jan., '44; Oct., '44 (marathon); Jan., '45; Feb., '46 (phantom signals on Mt. Marathon); Oct., '46; *Alaska Sportsman*, see Index; *Alaska Weekly*, Jan., '51; Feb., '51; Sept., '52 (early history); *Alaska-Yukon Gold Book*; *Alaska-Yukon Magazine*, July,

'11 (Ballaine on Seward beginnings); *Alaska's Health*, Feb., '55; *Amer. Geog. Soc.*, Dec., '15; Baker; Chase; Colby; Couch (post office from 1895); Davis; Denison; Dole; Forbes (*Leslie's Weekly*, 1913); Franck; Gruening (Ballaine promoted Alaska Central RR); Helmericks; Higginson; Hilscher; Hulley; Jacobin; Lipke; Lund; McDonald (*Alaska Health*, 1958); Meany ("The Naming of Seward in Alaska," *Wn. Hist. Q.* [Apr., '07]); Pedersen (*Ak. Sports.*, Aug., '59) (*Alaska-Yukon Mag.*, July, '11); Phillips (*Alaska Health*, Dec., '52); Pilgrim; Poor (descr); Seward C. of C. ("The City of Seward, Alaska"); Shiels; Stuck; Underwood; Vancouver. See also the Arctic Bibliography.

SEWARD, Fort William H.
See Port Chilkoot.

SEWARD, FREDERICK W.
Reminiscences of a Wartime Statesman and Diplomat, 1830-1915. New York: Putnam, 1916. 489 pp.
The Autobiography of William Henry Seward from 1801 to 1834. New York: Derby and Miller, 1891. 822 pp.

SEWARD GLACIER
Baird and Salt; Baker; Odell; Russell; Sharp; Wood, Walter (*Arctic*, 1948).

SEWARD-ANCHORAGE HIGHWAY
Alaska Sportsman, Oct., '56; Tewkesbury.

SEWARD PENINSULA
Bertholf; Brooks; Collier (USGS, 1902); Critchfield (*Econ. Geog.*, Oct., '49); French; Harrison; Higginson; Hopkins (USGS); Hulley; Jacobsen; Knopf, A. (USGS); Lucier (*Anthrop. Papers*, Univ. of Alaska, 1958); Lupo (*Trans.*, Ill. State Acad. of Science, 1923); Mendenhall (USGS); Nordenskiold; Schrader; Seeman; Shapiro; Smith (USGS, 1908); Stuck; Taylor (*Ak. Sports.*, 1947); US Coast Pilot; US Rev. Cutter Serv. (Annual Reports). See also D. Ray.

SEWARD PENINSULA RAILROAD
Alaska Sportsman, Dec., '47 (photo); Oct., '53; Feb., '58 (history); *Alaska-Yukon Magazine*, March, '07 (photo of wharf terminal); March, '09; Colby; Franck (old locomotive); Wickersham.

SEWARD, WILLIAM HENRY (1801-1872)
The Works of William H. Seward. Boston: Houghton Mifflin, 1884. 5v.
Address on Alaska at Sitka, August 12, 1869. Boston: Old South Works, 1902. 16 pp.
Alaska. (Speech at Sitka). Wn.DC: Philip and Solomons, 1869. 31 pp.
Autobiography of William H. Seward from 1801 to 1835. New York, 1877. 822 pp. Compiled by F. Seward.
William H. Seward's Travels around the World. New York, 1873. 788 pp. Edited by Olive R. Seward.
Report of the Hon. William H. Seward, Secretary of State, on Alaska. US Congress, 40th Cong., 2nd Sess., House Exec. Doc. No. 177 (1868). Contained in President Johnson's message in answer to a resolu-

tion of the House, transmitting correspondence of Seward, Kennicott, Collins and Kirtland.
See also the following:
Baker, G. (*Life of Seward* [New York, 1855]); Bancroft (*Life of Seward* [New York, 1900; 2v.]); Bemis (*American Secretaries of State* [New York, 1958]); Bradford (*Union Portraits* [New York, 1916]); Conrad (*Governor and His Lady* [New York, 1959]); Conrad (*Seward for the Defense* [New York, 1956]); Farrar (*Purchase of Alaska*); Seward, F. (*Reminiscences of a War-time Diplomat, 1830-1915* [New York, 1916]).
See also the following:
Alaska Life, June, '40 (woman who knew Seward); Aug., '44; *Alaska Sportsman*, Jan., '54 (Seward totem); Oct., '56; *Alaska Weekly*, March, '51; April, '51; Andrews; Bancroft; Brooks; Bruce (*Outlook*, July, '08); Colby; Franck; Harvey (*Putnam's*, June, '07); Higginson; Hulley; Mahan, A.T. (*Harper's*, Sept., '97); Manning; Morris; Nichols; Petrof; Pilgrim; Ray (on Tanana being called Seward); Scidmore (Alaska trip); Tarsaidze; Pennington; Tekesky; Underwood; Van Deusen, G.G. See also Paolino, E. (*The Foundations of the American Empire* [Ithaca: Cornell Univ. Press, 1973]). See Purchase of Alaska.

SEYMOUR NARROWS
Alaska Sportsman, Oct., '37 (photo); Nov., '55 (photo); Dec., '55 (blasting plan); Colby; Hawthorne; Higginson (Vancouver Island; wrecks: *Saranac*, 1875; *Wachusett*, 1875; *Grappler*, 1883 with many lives); Schwatka (highway); Scidmore (descr. ship losses, grounding of USS *Suwanee*; 70 Chinese lost on *Grappler*); Underwood.

SGIBNEV, A. S.
See the Arctic Bibliography; history of Kamchatka.

SGROI, PETER P.
Why the US Purchased Alaska. College: University of Alaska Press, 1970. 64 pp.

SHABELSKII, AKHILL
See the Arctic Bibliography.

SHAFER, JOSEPH
Alaska's Economy in Case of a National Economic Pause. Wn.DC: GPO, 1968. 59 pp. Fed. Field Comm. for the Development of Planning in Alaska.

SHAFER, ROBERT
"Athapaskan and Sino-Tibetan," *Internat'l. J. of Amer. Ling.*, January, 1952.

SHAIASHNIKOV, I.
See the Arctic Bibliography, and T-4083.

SHAKES, Chief (several)
Alaska Sportsman, Sept., '47 (Stikine chief); June, '48 (history of Stikines); March, '54 (photo); Apr., '55; March, '56; *Alaska-Yukon Magazine*, Oct., '08 (photos, notes); Andrews; Barbeau; Corser; Dole; Higginson; Morris ("bad Indian"); Muir; Scidmore; Wright; Young.

SHALAUROV (d. ca. 1767)
Coxe (Russian navigator, attempted to double East

Cape from mouth of the Lena, in 1761-63 and 1764-67; possibly killed by Chukchis on second attempt).

SHANNON, G.C.
"Alaskan Cities Preparing for Home Rule," *Public Management*, October, 1958.

SHANNON, TERRY
A Dog Team for Ongluk. Chicago: Children's Press, 1962. 32 pp.
Kidlik's Kayak. Chicago: Albert Whitman, 1959. 40 pp.
Ride the Ice Down. San Carlos, Calif.: Golden Gate Junior Books, 1970. 78 pp.
Tyee's Totem Pole. Chicago: Albert Whitman, 1955. 48 pp.

SHAPIRO, HARRY LIONEL (b. 1902)
The Alaskan Eskimo. New York: Amer. Museum of Natural History, 1931. 37 pp.

SHARP, ROBERT PHILLIP (b. 1911)
"Accumulation and Ablation on the Seward-Malaspina Glacier System," *Bulletin*, Geol. Soc. of Amer., July, 1951.
Glaciers. Eugene: University of Oregon Press, 1960. 78 pp.

SHARPLES, ADA WHITE (b. 1891)
Alaska Wild Flowers. Stanford: Stanford University Press, 1938. 156 pp.
Two Against the North. New York: Dial Press, 1961. 252 pp. Autobiographical; homesteading, Skilak Lake, Kenai Peninsula.

SHASKOV, S. S. (1841-1882)
See the Arctic Bibliography, and T-4095.

SHAW, CHARLES L.
"Warpath to Alaska," *Canadian Business*, April, 1942.

SHAW, CHARLES
The Wilderness of Denali. New York: Charles Scribner's Sons, 1930. 412 pp.

SHAW, GEORGE COOMBS (b. 1877)
Vancouver's Discovery of Puget Sound. Seattle: Rainier Printing Co., 1933. 23 pp.
The Chinook Jargon and How to Use It. Seattle: Rainier Printing Co., 1909. 65 pp. See also the Arctic Bibliography.

SHEARER, M. H.
"A Geographical Survey of the Region," *J. of Geography*, May, 1936. Matanuska Valley.

SHELDON, CHARLES (1867-1928)
The Wilderness of the Upper Yukon. New York: Scribner's, 1911. 354 pp. Exploration for Wild Sheep.
The Wilderness of the North Pacific Coast Islands. New York: Scribner's, 1912. 246 pp. Hinchinbrook Island, Nuchek history (Charles Swanson, trader there in 1907, left with sea-otter).
The Wilderness of Denali. New York: Scribner's, 1930. 412 pp.

"Hunting the Big Bear on Montague Island," *Scribner's*, June, 1912.
"Mount McKinley," *Proc.*, National Parks Conference, Dept. of Interior, 1917. On creation of the nat'l. park.
See also the Arctic Bibliography; also T-610, T-1012 and T-4809.

SHELDON, DON
See James Greiner.

SHELEKHOV, GRIGORII IVANOVICH (1747-1795)
For a full bibliography of accounts by Shelekhov see the Arctic Bibliography. Some few works have been translated:
Journal of the Voyages of Gregory Shelekhof, a Russian Merchant from Okhotsk on the Eastern Ocean to the Coast of America in 1783-87. London: W. Tooke, 1795. 42 pp. Trans. unknown. This is Vol. II of *Varieties of Literature*, compiled by Tooke. Margaret Lantis shows a ms. translation by Petrof in the Bancroft Library at the University of California. Other editions. See T-4656.
See also the following:
Adamov (in Russian); *Alaska Life*, Aug., '48 (on Natalii Shelikhova); *Alaska Sportsman*, June, '52 (letter on model town); Andreev (see English translation); Andrews (see also in *Alaska Life*, Dec., '42); Brooks; Bancroft; Chevigny; Colby; Dall; Dole; Fedorova; Gruening; Higginson; Hulley; Kitchener; Okun; Petrof; Rodionov (in *D. of Am. Biog.*); Sarafian; Scidmore; *Syn Otechestva;* Swineford; Tikhmenev; Tompkins; Underwood; Wickersham; Willoughby; Yarmolinski (*Bulletin*, NY Public Lib., '32).
See also T-4101, T-4 ff, T-3475, T-3814, T-4656.

SHELFORD, VICTOR E.
The Ecology of North America. Urbana: University of Illinois Press, 1963. 610 pp.

SHELTON, WILLIAM
Indian Totem Legends of the Northwest Coast Country. Chilocco, Okla.: Indian Agricultural School, n.d. 17 pp.
The Story of the Totem. Everett, Wn.: Kane & Harcus, 1923. 80 pp. Also 1935.

SHEMELIN, FEDOR
See the Arctic Bibliography.

SHENANDOAH, CSS
Alaska-Yukon Magazine, March, '07 (Capt. Waddell)); Aldrich (burned 30 vessels); Brooks (only vessel to carry the Confederate flag around the world); Colby; DeArmond (*Alaska Sportsman*, July, '37; repr. Anchorage *Daily News*, 1974); Eberhardt (*Alaska Life*, Sept., '46); Holloway (*Conn. Q.*, 1898); Hulley; Hunt, C. (*The Shenandoah* [NY, 1910]); Miller; Scidmore; Underwood; Whittle (Norfolk, 1910); Whymper. See B.F. Gilbert.

SHENITZ, HELEN A. (b. 1895)
"Vestiges of Old Russia in Alaska Today," *Proc.*, Alaskan Science Conf., 1953. Cultural traditions.
Our Good Father. Repr., *Russian-Orthodox Journal*, 1957.
"Fr. Veniaminov: The Enlightener of Alaska," *Amer. Slavic and East European Review*, 1959.

SHEPARD, F. P. and R. F. DILL
See T-4110.

SHEPARD, ISABEL SHARPE (b. 1861)
The Cruise of the US Steamer Rush in the Behring Sea. San Francisco: Bancroft, 1889. 257 pp. Descr., 1889.

SHEPARD, THOMAS ROCHESTER
Placer Mining Law in Alaska. New Haven: S. Field, 1909. 16 pp.

SHEPARD'S CITATIONS
Shepard's Alaska Citations: Cases and Statutes. Colorado Springs: Shepard's Citations, 1959.

SHEPHERD, W. R.
Guide to the Material for the History of the US in Spanish Archives. Wn.DC: GPO, 1907.

SHEPPARD, MORRIS
Reserve Officer's Training Corps Unit at the University of Alaska. Wn.DC: GPO, 1940. US Cong., Senate, 76th Cong. 3rd Sess., Committee on Military Affairs.

SHERMAN, DEAN F.
Alaska Cavalcade. Seattle: Alaska Life Publishing Co., 1943. 304 pp.
"Get Your Tin in Alaska," *Alaska Life*, April, 1943.

SHERMAN, K. L.
See the Arctic Bibliography.

SHERMAN, R. O.
"From Klukwan to the Yukon," *Alaska Journal*, Summer, 1974.
"The Village of Klukwan," *Alaska Journal*, Spring, 1974.

SHERMAN, STEVE
"Ruby's Gold Rush Newspapers," *Alaska Journal*, Autumn, 1971.

SHERWOOD, MORGAN B.
Exploration of Alaska, 1865-1900. New Haven: Yale University Press, 1965. 207 pp. US Army exploration of Alaska; classic. 2nd Printing, 1969.
Alaska and Its History, ed. Seattle: University of Washington Press, 1967.
The Cook Inlet Collection, ed. Anchorage: Alaska Northwest Publishing, 1974.
The Politics of American Science, 1939-Present, co-ed. Chicago: Rand McNally, 1965. Also Cambridge: MIT Press, 1972.
"George Davidson and the Acquisition of Alaska," *Pacific Historical Review*, May, 1959.
"A Pioneer Scientist in the Far North," *Pacific Northwest Quarterly*, April, 1962.
"An Historical Note on 'A Reconsideration of the Lancashire Cotton Famine,' " *Agricultural History*, July, 1963.
"Ivan Petroff and the Far Northwest," *Journal of the West*, July, 1965.
"Ardent Spirits: Hooch and the *Osprey* Affair at Sitka," *Journal of the West*, July, 1965.
"Science in Russian America," *Pacific Northwest Quarterly*, January, 1967.

"Federal Policy for Basic Research: Presidential Staff and the National Science Foundation, 1950-1956," *Journal of American History*, December, 1968.
"Mining and Public Policy in Alaska: An Essay Review," *Pacific Northwest Quarterly*, January, 1970. Repr. *Alaska Journal*, Spring, 1971.
"Urban Renewal on the Last Frontier," *International J. of Environmental Studies*, March, 1971.
"Staying Afloat in the Patent Office," *American West*, May, 1971.
"Technology and Public Policy," in Kranzberg and Pursell, eds., *Technology and Western Civilization* (Ne York, 1967).
"The Significance of Alaska's Past," in R. Frederick, ed., *Frontier Alaska* (Anchorage, 1968).
"L.R. Jones, Plant Pathologist," in E. James, ed., *Dictionary of Amer. Biog.*
"Alaska," and sketches (Sitka, Baranov, Veniaminov, Jackson, Allen, Lathrop) in H. Lamar, ed. *Reader's Encyclopedia of the American West* (New York, 1975).

SHIELDS, WALTER C. (d. 1918)
The Ancient Ground. Nome: Keenok Club, 1918. 47 pp. Poetry.

SHIELS, ARCHIBALD WILLIAMSON (b. 1878)
Early Voyages of the Pacific. Bellingham: Union Printing Co., 1931. 61 pp.
Seward's Icebox. Bellingham: Union Printing Co., 1933. 419 pp. Very useful.
"Veniaminov in Alaska," *British Columbia Historical Q.*, 1947.
The Purchase of Alaska. College: University of Alaska Press, 1967. 207 pp.
See also the Arctic Bibliography, and T-4116 ff.

SHILLINGLAW, JOHN JOSEPH (b. 1830)
A Narrative of Arctic Discovery. London: W. Shoberl, 1850. 348 pp. Franklin search.

SHIMKIN, DEMITRI BORIS
The Economy of a Trapping Center: The Case of Fort Yukon. New York: Johnson Reprint Co., 1966. 21 pp. From *Econ. Dev. and Social Change* (Chicago, 1955. V. 3).

SHINEN, MARILENE
"Marriage Customs of the St. Lawrence Island Eskimos," *Anthropologica*, 1963.

SHINKWIN, ANNE D.
"Early Man in the Brooks Range: The Tuktu-Naiyak Sequence," unpublished master's thesis, George Washington University, 1964.

SHIPPEN, FRANCES
"Alaska's Bishop," *Cathedral Age*, June, 1942.

SHIPWRECKS
Alaska Life, Aug.-Nov., '41 (History of Alaska Transportation: *Beaver, Labouchere, Growler, Thomas Woodward*); Dec., '41 (chart by L. Huber with locations of 177 strandings and wrecks in Alaska, 1900-17, incl. *Dora, City of Topeka, Princess*

May, Islander, California); March, '44 (*Crown City*, Nome); Nov., '44 (*Northwestern*, Dutch Harbor); Dec., '45 (*James Allen*, Amlia Island, 1894; 25 men); Feb., '46 (Baranov); May, '46 (*State of California*, Gambia Bay, 1913; *Princess May*, 1910; *Princess Sophia*, 1918; *Islander*, Pt. Hilda, Douglas Island, 1901, 42 persons; *Tahoma*, Buldir Island), May, '46 (*Yukon*, Seward); Oct., '46 (*Webster*, Atka Island, 1890); Feb., '48 (*Alaska*, 1900, Nome); July, '49 *Ancon*, 1889, Naha Bay); *Alaska Sportsman*, Aug., '38 (*Koshun Maru*, Scotch Cap); March, '39 (*Patterson*, Cape Fairweather); May, '39 (*Patterson* cargo); Jan., '40 (*Pulitzer*, Chignik; was Aleutian mail boat succeeding *Dora*, which broke in two off Vancouver Island); Sept., '41 ("Ghosts of Alaskan Commerce": *Karluk*, 1830, Kodiak; *Sivutch*, 1831, Atka; *Chilkat*, 1837, Cape Edgecumbe; *Clara Nevada*, 1898, Lynn Canal; *Discovery*, 1902, Nome [disappeared]; *Islander*, 1901, Juneau; *Princess May*, 1910, Lynn Canal; *State of California*, 1913, Gambier Gay; *Ancon*, 1890, Loring; *Aleutian* [see Newell and Williamson]; *Patterson*, 1938, Cape Fairweather; *Mackay*, 1938, Kanak Island, Controller Bay; *Alaska*, 1940, Prince Rupert; *Oaxaca* [see Newell and Williamson]; *Depere* [see Newell and Williamson]; *Admiral Evans* [see Newell and Williamson]; *Cucarao*, 1913; *Alki*, 1917, Pt. Augusta; *Jabez Howes* [see Newell and Williamson]; *Armeria*, c. 1913; *Bertha*, 1915, Uyak [burned]; *Mariechen*, c. 1907, False Bay; *Mariposa*, 1917, Straits Island; old SS *Denali*; *Kennecott*, 1923, Graham Island; *Yucatan*, 1910, Icy Strait; *Tuckahoe*, 1941, Katalla; *Kvichak*, c. 1941, Canadian coast); Dec., '42 ("Caught in the Arctic": *Java*, 1870, East Cape; *Oriole*, 1871, Plover Bay; *Monticello*, 1871, Pt. Belcher; also story of 32 whalers lost near Pt. Belcher, 1219 persons aboard being rescued by 7 other vessels; Eskimos looted and burned all ships save *Minerva*, which was beached and returned to SF the following year); Apr., '46 (*Yukon*, 1946, Johnstone Bay, near Seward, 11 lost); May, 46 (*Donbass* [Russian] broke in two near Adak, 1946; *Sackett's Harbor* broke in two near Attu, 1946); June, '46 (*Venus*, 1946, Zarembo Island); Aug., '46 ("Wreck of the *Yukon*": *State of California*, 1913, Gambier Bay; *Mariposa*, 1917, Sumner Strait; *John Straub* and *Arcata* [torpedoed, WW II]; *Delwood*, WW II, Massacre Bay; *North Wind*, WW II, Shumagins; Mt. McKinley, WW II, Unimak Pass; *Clevedon*, WW II, Yakutat [explosion]); Oct., '46 (stern half of *Sackett's Harbor* leased by Anchorge for power); Nov., '46 (*Cougar*, 1946, Shelikov Strait, 8 lost); Apr., '47 (*Alaska*, 1947, Cordova, "jinx" ship); Apr., '47 (*North Sea*, 1947, Bella Bella); Aug., '47 (old *Alaska*, 1921, off California, 42 lost); Nov., '47 (*Diamond Knot*, 1947, Port Angeles); March, '48 (*Prince George*, 1945, Gravina Island); May, '48 (US Navy lost 21 vessels [all types] in Alaskan waters in the period 1941-45); March, '49 (photo, *Princess May*, 1910, on reef); Apr., '49 (photo, *Mariposa*, 1915, aground, Bella Bella); Aug., '49 (*Sunset*, 1949, False Pass, 5 lost); Sept., '49 (photo, *Ancon*, 1889, Naha Bay); Aug., '49 (*Hazel B III*, 1949, Stikine River); Oct., '49 (*Clarksdale Victory*, 1947, Hippa Island, Ketchikan, 49 lost); Jan., '51 ("Sinking of the *Vermay*", 1950); March, '51 (photo, *Pomare*, 1949, Snow Pass, aground); June, '51 (*Islander* raised after 33 years); Feb., '53 (photos, *Princess Kathleen*, 1952); July, '53

(photo, *North Sea*, Bella Bella, aground); Oct., '53 (photo, *Bertha*, 1915 Uyak Bay, aground); Oct., '54 (photo, *Alki*, 1917, aground); Oct., '54 (photo, *Dode*, 1910); Feb., '55 (*Patterson*, 1938, Cape Fairweather); Nov., '55 (photo, *North Sea*, Bella Bella, aground); Dec., '55 (blast Ripple Rock, Seymour Narrows, where 32 vessels have snagged and five sunk); Jan., '56 (tug *Harold J.*, 1955, Shishmaref, 3 men [vanished]); Feb., '58 (*Cottage Queen*, 1899, Seymour Narrows); Oct., '37 (*Windsor*, 1936, Strait of Georgia); Dec., '37 (*Limit*, 1937, Chatham Strait [vanished]); *Alaska-Yukon Gold Book* (23 victims of *Islander*, 1901; notes, *Clara Nevada*, down in 6 hours from explosion, south of Skagway; *State of California*, 1913, Gambier Bay; list of victims, *Princess Sophia*, 1918); *Alaska-Yukon Magazine*, March, '10 (*Ohio*, *Farallon*, *Yucatan*, and others); Sept., '09 (*Ohio*, 1909, Heikish Narrows); Aldrich (*Napoleon*, 1885, Cape Navarin; whalers of 1871, map; whalers, 1876, great loss of life; Japan, 1870, East Cape; *Mt. Wollaston* and *Vigilant*, 1879, Herald Island [disappeared]); Andrews (*St. Peter* [Bering], 1741, Commander Islands; *Three Saints*, 1790, Unalaska [Baranov]; *Orel*, 1799, Prince William Sound; *Phoenix*, *St. Michael* and *St. Alexander*, 1799, between Alaska and Siberia; *Avoss*, 1799, Sitka; *St. Nicholas*, Destruction Island [Washington]; *Neva*, 1813, Cape Edgecumbe; *Alexander*, 1813, Kurile Islands; *Karluk*, 1830, Kodiak; *Sivutch*, 1831, Atka; *Chilkat*, 1837, Cape Edgecumbe; *Jeannette*, 1881, Siberian coast; *Rodgers*, 1882, East Cape [burned]; *Navarch*, 1897, Icy Cape; *Laurada*, 1898, Bering Sea; *Jane Grey*, 1898 [foundered at sea]); Andrews ("Marine Disasters of the Alaska Route," *Wn. Hist. Q.*, 1916; lists 400); Andrews, R. (*Zapora*, 1937, Admiralty Island; *Grant*, 1911, Banks Island; *Onward Ho*, 1915 [disappeared]; *Columbia*, *Ella G.*, *Melalo*, *Alameda*, *G.R. Hughes*, 1911-21, B.C. waters [all halibuters]; *Alice*, 1914, Cape Decision [halibut schooner]; *Constance*, 1919, Cape Suckling; *Washington*, 1922, Cape Suckling; photo, *Princess Sophia*, 1918; photo, *Farallon*, 1910, Cook Inlet, aground); Bankson (*Clara Nevada* sank with all on board; *Corona*, 1898); Baychimo (Hudson's Bay Co. derelict drifting from 1931; see *Alaska Sportsman*, June, '35 and Dec., '35 for notes on abandonment; also Oct., '37 and July, '57; see also Miller); Beach (*Ohio* fictionalized in *Iron Trail*); Becker (photo, *Alki*; photo, *Colorado*, Wrangell Narrows); Berkh (*Neva* [in Russian] St. Petersburg, 1817); Brooks, Brooks, C. ("Japanese Wrecks, Stranded and Picked up Adrift in the North Pacific Ocean, *Proc.*, Cal. Acad. of Sci. [1876]); Brower (*Lady Kindersly*, 1924, off Barrow; *Navarch*, 1897); Chase (*Pacific*, 1873, Cape Flattery, 500 lost; *Islander*, *Del Norte*, *Princess Louise*, *Yucatan*, all in Lynn Canal); Chevigny; Curtin (river boats); Davis, H. (*Record of Japanese Vessels Driven on the Northwest Coast of America* [Worcester, 1872]); DeLong (*Jeannette*); Dole (*Royal Charlie* seized and scuttled by Admiralty Island natives, 1857, crew murdered); Gibbs (*Princess Kathleen*, 1952; Scotch Cap Light disaster of 1946; *Koshun Maru*, 1930, Scotch Cap; *Baychimo*, 1931, Arctic); Gruening (Knapp recorded 10 shipwrecks for 1889, and 10 more by 1891; partial list of wrecks in Rept. of the Sec. Commerce for 1914 [incl. *Armeria* and Rev. Cut. *Tahoma*]; 1915 Congressman Humphrey of Seattle read into the *Cong. Record* a list of 260 Alaskan wrecks with a loss of 449 lives; Alaska Bureau, Seattle C. of C. listed in 1918 426 ships lost in Alaskan waters, with a loss of 862 lives; 1912 Senator Wilson of Washington testified that 77 ships lost in preceding 15 years; US C&GS in 1916 listed rocks bearing names of wrecked ships [Potter Rock; Ohio Rock; Idaho Rock; California Rock; City of Topeka Rock; Colorado Rock; Fortuna Str.; Mariposa Rock; Orizaba Reef; Sennett Point; Tahoma Reef; Wayanda Ledge, Yukon Reef]); *Jeannette* (see DeLong); *Karluk* (sank Jan. 11, '14 85 miles south of Wrangel Island [Wead]; Stefansson; Bartlett); Khramtsov (*Disaster of the Heir of Alexander* [in Russian] *Morskoi Sbornik*, 1848); Markov (*Eyewitness Account of the Wreck of the Neva* [in Russian; St. Petersburg, 1850]); Morgan (*Ohio*, 1910, Milbank Sound; M.J. Heney was aboard; *Mariposa*, 1918, picked up pirates from wrecked *Alki*, was later wrecked in Sumner Strait; *Alaska* [ex-*Colon*], 1918, Bald Bluff in Hiekish Narrows, saved; *Princess Sophia*, Vanderbilt Reef; *Alaska* [ex-*Colon*], 1922, Cape Mendocino; *Aleutian*, 1928, Uyak Bay); Morris (*Suwanee* and *Saranac*; *Growler*, Prince of Wales Island, all hands; *George S. Wright*, Devil's Reef, Sea-otter group; *Langley*, Chatham Strait); Newell and Williamson (photos, *Alki* and *Zapora*; *Clara Nevada*, 1898, Lynn Canal; *Elsie*, *Sitka*, *Alexandria*, *Louise*, *J. Kennedy*, *St. Lawrence*, all 1898; *Whitelaw*, *Alfred J. Beach*, *Mono*, *Marquis of Dufferin*, *Stikine Chief*, *Eliza Anderson*, *Anita*, *Brixham*, *Stirling*, *Guardian*; *Alpha*, Yellow Island Light; *Islander*, 1901, Juneau [raised 1934, scrapped, 1952]; photo, *Princess May*; *George S. Wright*, 1873, disappeared after leaving Tongass Island for Portland; photo, *Olympia*, 1910, Prince William Sound; *Valencia*, 1906, Vancouver Island; *Star of Bengal*, 1908, Coronation Island, 110 lost; photo, *C.S. Holmes*, 1950, Vancouver Island; photos, *Princess Sophia*, 1918, Vanderbile Reef; *Yukon*, 1946, Seward; *State of California*, 1913, Gambier Bay; bibliography); Poor (*Crown City*, Nome); Potter (*Mt. McKinley*, mysterious; other transports, WW II); Scidmore (*Saranac*, 1875, Seymour Narrows; *Grappler*, 1883, Seymour Narrows; *Suwanee*, Queen Charlotte Sound; *Eureka*, 1883, Peril Strait, *George S. Wright*, 1873); (*Ancon*, 1889, Loring; *George S. Wright*, 1873; *Royal Charlie*, 1866, Kuiv village; *Wayanda*, *Eureka*, Peril Strait); Sievernyi (*St. Nikolai*, 1808 [in Russian]); Stefansson (*Karluk*); Tompkins (index of losses); US Treas. (W-7434, W-7505); US Rev. Cutter Serv. (W-7608); US Senate (W-9490, W-9491); US House (W-9933); Wead (*Star of Bengal*, 1908, 110 men in boiling surf; *Karluk*; *Tahoma*, 100 miles off Agattu; Cutter *Perry*, 1910, St. Paul Island; Cutter *McCulloch*, 1917, San Francisco, collision); Whiting (*Portland*; *Ohio*, 1909); Wiedemann (*Eliza Anderson*); Wolfe (*Princess Sophia*; photo, *Princess May*; *Alaska*, Swanson Bay, BC, Capt. Nord; *Venus*, off Kodiak, near-wreck). See also *Baychimo*, *Islander*, *Jeannette*, *Karluk*, *Princess Sophia*, *Shenandoah*.

SHIRAS, GEORGE III
"White Sheep, Giant Moose, and Smaller Game of the Kenai Peninsula," *National Geographic*, 1912.
Hunting Wildlife with Camera and Flashlight. Wn.DC: Nat. Geog. Soc., 1935. 2v.

SHISHALDIN, Mt.
Alaska Sportsman, Feb., '39 (cp. Fujiyama); March, '45 (photo); Apr., '47 (eruptions); Dec., '46; Jan., '51 ("Smokin' Moses"); Aug., '56 (last eruption Jan., '47); June, '57 (descr.); Oct., '57 (photo); Bancroft (attempted ascent in 1872); Baker (Sarychev named, 1790); Dall (flames, 1824, 1827-29, 1838); Dole; Fuller (*Everybody's*, 1907); Henderson; Higginson; Hubbard (climbed); Harriman (Burroughs' descr.); Petrof; Potter; Sarychev; Sauer; Scidmore; Washburn; Whymper; Wickersham; Williams, H. See also Unimak Island and Unimak Pass.

SHISHMAREF
Alaska Sportsman, March, '47; Feb., '57 (Eskimo Cook Book prepared by children); Oct., '57 (George Ahgupuk); Baker (name from cape and inlet, named by Kotzebue, 1816 for member of party); Colby (pop. 200); Couch (post office, 1901-02 and from 1924); Poor (descr.).

SHISHMAREV, GLIEB SEMENOVICH
See the Arctic Bibliography; see also Baker; Grewingk; see also Krusenstern.

SHOEMAKER, WILLIAM RAWLE
"A Summer among the Seals," *United Service*, 1894. Unalaska.

SHORE, EVELYN BERGLUND (b. ca. 1917)
Born on Snowshoes. Boston: Houghton Mifflin, 1954. 209 pp. Fort Yukon and the Salmon River. See also *Alaska Sportsman*, Nov. '42.

SHORT, WAYNE
The Cheechakoes. New York: Random House, 1964. 244 pp.
This Raw Land. New York: Random House, 1968. Autobiog.

SHORTALL, LEONARD
Eric in Alaska. New York: William Morrow, 1967. 48 pp.

SHORTT, TERENCE M. (b. 1910)
The Summer Birds of Yakutat Bay, Alaska. Toronto: Royal Ontario Museum of Zoology, 1939. 30 pp.

SHOTRIDGE, FLORENCE (d. 1917)
"The Life of a Chilkat Indian Girl," *Museum Journal*, University of Pennsylvania, September, 1913. Autobiog.

SHOTRIDGE, LOUIS (b. 1883)
"Indians of the Northwest," *Museum J.*, 1913.
"House Posts and Screens and the Heraldry," *Museum J.*, 1913.
"My Northland Revisited," *Museum J.*, 1917.
"A Visit to the Tsimshean Indians," *Museum J.*, 1919.
"Keyt-gooshe, 'Killer Whale's Dorsal Fin,'" *Museum J.*, 1919.
"War Helmets and Clan Hats of the Tlingit Indians," *Museum J.*, 1919.
"Ghost of Courageous Adventurer," *Museum J.*, 1920.

"Tlingit Woman's Root Basket," *Museum J.*, 1921.
"Land Otter-man," *Museum J.*, 1922.
"The Emblems of the Tlingit Culture," *Museum J.*, 1928.
"How Ats-ha Followed the Hide of his Comrade to Yek Land," *Museum J.*, 1930.
See the notes in the Arctic Bibliography on the above articles. Shotridge assisted Boas on his grammar.

SHRIEVER, LUCILLE W.
Alaskan Verses from Native Folklore. Montreal: Marlin Publ. Co., 1969. 57 pp.

SHTEINBERG, EVGENII L'VOVICH
See the Arctic Bibliography, and T-4137.

SHUMAKER, CECIL LEE
Do You Know? New York: Exposition Press, 1967.

SHURTLEFF, BERTRAND LESLIE
Two Against the North. Indianapolis: Bobbs-Merrill, 1949. 274 pp. Juvenile.
Colt of the Alcan Road. Indianapolis: Bobbs-Merrill, 1951.
Escape from the Icecap. Indianapolis: Bobbs-Merrill, 1952.
Long Lash. Indianapolis: Bobbs-Merrill, 1952.

SIBERIA
See the following: Bancroft; Berkh; Bush; Butsinskii; Cook; Fisher, R.; Golder; Henderson; Herron; Kennan; Kittlitz; Krasheninnikov; Lantzeff; Lessner; Muller; Nordenskiold; Pallas; Pekarskii; Pierce; Polevoi; Ravenstein; Sachot; Sliunin; Slovtsov; Struve; Tompkins. The name is derived from Siber, Russian for Isker, the capital of the Tartar kingdom of Kuchum Khan.

SICKELS, DOROTHY J.
Eskimos: Hunters of the Arctic. Garden City: Doubleday, 1941. 20 pp.

SIDDALL, W. R.
"The Yukon Waterway in the Development of the Interior of Alaska," *Pacific Historical Review*, 1959.

SIEBERT, ERNA and WERNER FORMAN
North American Indian Art. New York: Tudor Publ. Co., 1967. Incl. Tlingit.

SIERRA CLUB
Publishers of the *Sierra Club Bulletin* on mountaineering, conservation and ecology, and occasional books on Alaska themes. See Tom Brown, *Oil on Ice.* See also *Wilderness in a Changing World* (San Francisco, 1966 [255 pp.]).

SILENT CITY
Badlam (photos); Bruce (illustrations); Jordan; Rickard; Scidmore. In the 1880's one Dick Willoughby, claiming to be a professor, circulated a faded photograph, later demonstrated to be of Bristol, England, which he said was a mirage photographed near Muir Glacier.

SILLARS, ROBERTSON
The North Pacific and Alaska. New York: Columbia University, 1942. 19 pp.

SILOOK, ROGER
In the Beginning. Anchorage: Anchorage Printing Co., 1970. 31 pp.

SILVERBERG, ROBERT
Scientists and Scoundrels. New York: Crowell, 1965. Frederick Cook.

SILVERS, CONNIE
Alaska Highway Souvenir and Travel Guide. Anchorage: the Author, 1963. 200 pp.

SIMMONDS, PETER LUND
Sir John Franklin and the Arctic Regions. Buffalo: G.H. Derby & Co., 1852. 396 pp.

SIMMONS, GEORGE
Target Arctic. Philadelphia: Chilton Books, 1965. 420 pp.

SIMONSEN, SIGURD J.
Among the Sourdoughs. New York: Fortuny's, 1940. 153 pp.

SIMPSON, ALEXANDER (b. 1811)
The Life and Times of Thomas Simpson. London: R. Bentley, 1845. 424 pp. T. Simpson, nephew of Sir George Simpson, was the first explorer to reach Barrow from the east. Franklin reached it from the west in 1826. Simpson, with Dease, set out in 1837 to chart the unmapped coast.
The Oregon Territory. London: R. Bentley, 1846. 60 pp.

SIMPSON, Sir GEORGE (1792-1860)
Narrative of a Journey Round the World. London: Colburn, 1847. 2v. 1841-42.
An Overland Journey Around the World. Same as above.
Narrative of a Voyage to California Ports. San Francisco: Thomas Russell, 1930. 232 pp.
Fur Trade and Empire: G. Simpson's Journal. Cambridge: Harvard University Press, 1831. 370 pp.
Journal of Occurrences in the Athabaska Department. Toronto: Champlain Society, 1938. 498 pp.
See also the following:
Bancroft (Ft. Stikine, Sitka, 1841; overland to Ft. Vancouver and Sitka, then California, then Sitka again in 1842, thence to Okhotsk and Siberia to London); Brooks; Higginson; Hulley (leased the coastal strip for Hudson's Bay Co. in 1839; Gov. McLoughlin of Ft. Stikine murdered; agreement with Etolin to ban liquor sales to Indians); McDonald (1828); Morton; Ogilvie; Petrof (Stikine lease); Tompkins (descr. of Veniaminov). See also T-4161 ff.

SIMPSON, JOHN
See the Arctic Bibliography, and T-1826, T-1832, and T-3907.

SIMPSON, THOMAS (1808-1840)
Narrative of the Discoveries on the North Coast of America. London: R. Bentley, 1843. 419 pp. 1836-39.
"An Account of the Recent Arctic Discoveries by Messers. Dease and T. Simpson," *Journal*, Royal Geog. Soc., 1838.

"An Account of Arctic Discovery on the Northern Shore of America in the summer of 1838," *Journal*, Royal Geog. Soc., 1839.
See also T-4160, and T-4326.

SINCLAIR, BERTRAND WILLIAM (b. 1878)
North of Fifty-three. New York: Grosset, 1914. 345 pp.

SIND, Lt.; see Synd.

SINROCK, MARY
Alaska-Yukon Gold Book (Seward Peninsula reindeer herder, one of whose party discovered gold near where Nome now is situated; information was communicated to Council City, bringing Price, Gordon, Lindeberg, Lindbloom and Brynteson); Davis (photo); Dole (Mary Andrewuk, had 300 reindeer in 1905); Machetanz; Van Valin (Sinuk, 8 miles from Nome).

SISTERS of CHARITY of PROVIDENCE
Harrison (est. Holy Cross Hospital at Nome in 1903; 42 patients first year, 286 the second). The Sisters now administer Providence Hospital in Anchorage.

SISTERS of ST. ANN
Alaska Sportsman, March, '42 (Holy Cross, 1888; 3 sisters); Apr., '57 (burning of St. Mary's Hospital at Dawson); *Alaska-Yukon Magazine*, Sept., '08 (photo, St. Mary's, Dawson); Yorke (*Catholic World*, 1893); see also Calasanz and Savage. See also Holy Cross.

SISTERS, URSALINE
Llorente (Akulurak); O'Connor (Akulurak); Santos (Akulurak). See also Akulurak.

SITKA
Adams (photo, plaque, battle of Sitka); *Alaska Almanac* (photo); *Alaska Sportsman*, see Index; *Alaska Magazine*, Jan., '27; *Alaska Monthly*, July, '07; *Alaskan*, Fall, '49; *Alaska Weekly*, Oct., '50; Feb., '51; March, '51; *Alaska-Yukon Magazine*, Oct., '07 (bust of Baranov; numerous articles); Oct., '08 (articles, photo); Nov., '10; Anderson (*Proc.*, Iowa Acad. of Sci., 1916, 1918); Andreev; Andrews; Arctander; Auldridge (*Alaska Life*, May, '47); Badlam (old photo); Baer (see the Arctic Bibliography); Baker; Ballou; Baranov; Bancroft; Barbeau; Barber; Bartoshevich (see the Arctic Biblio.); Beach; Beardslee; Blake, T.; Bloodgood (*Overland*, Feb., 1869); Brevig (Baranov imported needed artisans from Scandinavia, allowing them to attend Lutheran services in the first Protestant church in Alaska); Bright; Broke; Brooks; Browne; Bruce (*Bulletin*, USGS, 1913); Burchard; Burroughs (Harriman); Butler and Dale; Caldwell; Callan (*Alaska Life*, Jan., '47); Calvin; Carpenter; Chaffee; Chase; Cheney; Clark, H.; Clark, S.; Chevigny; Colby; Collis; Cook; Corser (Sitka-Wrangel feud); Couch (post office from 1867); Crain (*Proc.*, US Naval Inst., Feb., '55); Dall; Davidson (photos); Davis; DeArmond (*Alaska Life*, Nov., '45; Jan., '47); Denison; Dole; Downes; D'Wolf; Elliott; Erman; Faris (Jackson's arrest at Sitka); Fedorova; Field; Fitzgerald; Franck; Frede; Georgeson;

Greely; Golovnin; Greenhow; Grinnel; Gruening; Halleck; Hallock; Harford (*Ann. Rept.*, US C&GS, 1867); Harriman; Hart; Hayes; Hellenthal; Henderson; Herron; Higginson; Hilscher; Holbrook; Hough; Howard, O. (in *Compilation of Narratives*; in *St. Nicholas*, May, '08 [W-1590]); Hulley; Jackson; Jacobin; James; Jenkins; Kashevaroff; Kellogg; Kinscella; Kittlitz; Knopf (USGS, 1912); Kotzebue; Kuehnelt-Leddihn; Kuppfer (see the Arctic Bibliography); L'Amour; Langsdorff; Lazarev (in Russian); Lazell; Lindberg (*Ak. Sportsman*, July, '49); Lisiansky; Lutke; Manning; Martin; Mayberry; Menzel (sorcery trial); Morris (old photo of Russian buildings); Nevskii; Nichols; Nozikov; Perkins; Petrof; Pilder; Pilgrim; Pilz; Poniatowski (in French); Powell; Ravenstein; Rickard; Roche; Rogers; Rossiter; Rousseau; Schwatka; Scidmore; Seward; Shepard; Sherman; Shiels; Simpson; Sokolov (in Russian); Speck; Stefansson; Stewart, R.; Stuck; Stromstadt (W-1599); Swanton; Swarth; Swineford; Sundborg; Tarsaidze; Taylor; Tewkesbury; Thomas, E.; Tompkins; Tuttle; Underwood; US Customs Service : W-7618); US Dept. of Justice (W-7618); US Senate (W-9706, W-9819, W-9820); US House (W-10054, W-10249); US Treasury (W-7393, W-7398, W-7406, W-7424, W-7506, W-7527); Vancouver; Wagner; Walden; Ward; Wardman; Wead; Webster, J. (*Condor*, 1941); Whymper; Wickersham; Williams, H.; Willard; Willett; Williamson; Willoughby; Winslow; Wolfenden & Hamilton; Woollen; Wright; Young. See also Baranov, Baranov Castle; Pioneer's Home, Sheldon Jackson College; Sitka Hot Springs; Sitka Jack; Sitka National Monument.

SITKA HOT SPRINGS
Alaska Sportsman, Aug., '38; *Alaska-Yukon Magazine*, Jan., '08; Andrews (Dr. Goddard); Baker; Colby; Franck.

SITKA JACK
Andrews (great potlatch of 1877); Beardslee; Gruening; Howard; Morris; Pilgrim; Scidmore; Schwatka; Willard; Winslow; Wright (orator chief).

SITKA NATIONAL MONUMENT
Alaska Life, Dec., '43; *Alaska Sportsman*, Feb., '36 (has Russian graves from 1804); Dec., '40; Andrews, Browne; Colby; Henderson; Pilgrim; Underwood; US Nat. Park Serv. (Sitka National Monument; numerous editions); US President (proclamation, 1910); Winslow.

SKAGWAY
Alaska Life, Aug., '39; Nov., '39 (murder of Horton, 1900, by Indians); Aug., '40 ("Skagway" Bill Fonda); Nov., '41; March, '43 (Skagway in wartime); Jan., '44; Aug., '46 (initially Mooresville after William Moore's 1888 wharf); *Alaska Sportsman*, see Index; *Alaska Weekly*, Nov., '50; Jan., '51; Feb., '51; March, '51; Oct., '51 (highway to Carcross); *Alaska-Yukon Gold Book* (photos, Jack Newman, Horse Memorial, Molly Walsh, Dyea, the Scales; stories on Newman, Soapy Smith, Sheep Camp slide); *Alaska-Yukon Magazine*, Nov., '11; Andrews; Anzer; Baker; Bankson; Barker (*Spirit of Missions*, 1898); Beach; Becker; Berton; Bright;

Brooks; Burg; Burroughs; Caldwell; Cameron; Carpenter; Castner; Chase; Clark; Clevenger (*Baptist Home Missions Monthly,* Jan., '01); Cody (*Canadian Magazine,* '07); Colby; Collier and Westrate; Corser; Couch; Davis; Denison; Dole; Fletcher & Hayne (W-1600); Fonda; Franck; Garland; Good (*Assembly Herald,* '09); Greely; Griffin; Gruening; Hart; Harris; Hawthorne; Hellenthal; Henderson; Higginson; Hilscher; Hulley; Hunt; Itjen; Jacobin; Jenkins; Judge; Latourette (*Baptist Home Missions Monthly,* 1898); Lazell; Lung-Martinsen; Meals; Miller, J.; Morehouse (*Baptist Home Missions Monthly,* 1899); Morgan, E.; Morgan, L.; Nichols; O'Connor; Ogilvie; Pilgrim; Powell; Rickard; Rogers; Rossiter; Rutzebeck; Santos; Schwatka; Scidmore; Service; Shand; Shiels; Stephenson; Sullivan; Sundborg; Swineford; Stuck; Tewkesbury; Tuttle; Underwood; Whiting; Wickersham; Williams, J.; Williamson; Winslow; Young. See also Chilkoot Pass, Dyea, Klondike, Smith, White Pass.

SKARLAND, IVAR and CHARLES J. KEIM
"Archaeological Data on the Denali Highway," *Anthrop. Papers,* University of Alaska, May, 1958.

SKELTON, RALEIGH ASHLIN
Captain James Cook after Two Hundred Years. London: British Museum, 1969. 32 pp.
"Captain James Cook as Hydrographer," *Mariner's Mirror,* 1954.
Charts and Views drawn by Cook and his Officers. Cambridge: Cambridge University Press, 1955.
Explorer's Maps: Chapters in the Cartographic Record of Geographical Discovery. London: Routledge & Paul, 1958. 447 pp.
Marine Surveys of James Cook in North America, 1758-68. London: Map Collectors Circle, 1967. 34 pp.

SKEWES, JOSEPH HENRY
Sir John Franklin: The True Secret of the Discovery of his Fate. London: Bemrose & Sons, 1889. 243 pp.

SKINNER, CONSTANCE LINDSAY
The Search Relentless. New York: Howard-McCann, 1928. 252 pp. Goldrush.

SKUD, BERNARD EINAR
Statistics of the Alaska Herring Fishery, 1878-1956. Wn.DC: US F&WS, 1960. 21 pp.

SLAVIN, S. V.
"American Expansion in Northeastern Russia in the Beginning of the 20th Century," *Letopis Severa,* 1940 (in Russian). Commercial relations; Siberian-Bering tunnel; Northeastern Siberian Co.

SLAVINSKII, NIKOLAI
Letters about America and Russian Colonies. See Tompkins.

SLAYDEN, THELMA THOMPSON
Miracle in Alaska. New York: Frederick Fell, 1963. 260 pp.

SLEATOR, WILLIAM
The Angry Moon. Boston: Little, Brown, 1970. 45 pp. Tlingit legend.

SLEVIN, JOSEPH RICHARD (b. 1881)
The Amphibians of Western North America. San Francisco: Calif. Acad. of Sci., 1928. 152 pp.

SLIJPER, EVERHARD JOHANNES
Whales. Trans., A.J. Pomerans. London: Hutchinson & Co., 1962. 475 pp.

SLIUNIN, NIKOLAI VASILEVICH (b. 1850)
See the Arctic Bibliography.

SLODKEVICH, VSEVOLOD SERGEEVICH
See the Arctic Bibliography.

SLOTNICK, HERMAN E.
"The Ballinger-Pinchot Affair in Alaska," *Journal of the West,* April, 1971.
"The 1958 Election in Alaska," *Western Political Q.,* June, 1963.
"The 1960 Election in Alaska," *Western Political Q.,* March, 1961.
"The 1964 Election in Alaska," *Western Political Q.,* June, 1965.
"The 1966 Election in Alaska," *Western Political Q.,* June, 1967.

SLOVTSOV, PETR ANDREEVICH (1767-1843)
See the Arctic Bibliography.

SMALL, MARIE
Four Fares to Juneau. New York: McGraw-Hill, 1947. 237 pp. Autobiog.

SMILEY, CHARLES HUGH
"Atmospheric Refraction at Low Altitudes," *Papers,* Royal Meteorological Soc., Canada, 1950.

SMITH, ALEXANDER MALCOLM (ca. 1859-1958)
Alaska Life, Apr., '43 ("Captain Sandy"); *Alaska Sportsman,* Jan., '56; Couch (postmaster, Almalcolm camp, Yukon, 1915-17); Willoughby. Legendary-like prospector.

SMITH, ARTHUR MAXSON
On to Alaska with Buchanan. Los Angeles: Ward Ritchie Press, 1937. 124 pp. B. George Buchanan of Detroit brought boys (and later girls) to Skagway and Whitehorse in summers as a character building experience.
Alaska Weekly, Oct., 1951. See also Stearne.

SMITH, BARBARA SWEETLAND
Preliminary Survey of Documents in the Archive of the Russian Orthodox Church in Alaska. Boulder, Colorado: Western Interstate Commission for higher Education, 1974. 135 pp. Bibliography, chronology, glossary. Very valuable.

SMITH, BEVERLY
"Tokyo Turnpike," *Americana,* March, 1943.

SMITH, B. WEBSTER
The Fram. London: Blackie, 1940. 223 pp. Nansen's polar vessel.

SMITH, CHARLES EDWARD
From the Deep of the Sea. London: Black, 1922. 288 pp. Diary. Smith was surgeon on the whaler *Diana of Hull.*

SMITH, CHARLES N.
"Hunting Big Game in Alaska," *Overland Monthly,* March, 1913.

SMITH, CHARLES WESLEY (b. 1877)
Check-List of Books and Pamphlets relating to the History of the Pacific Northwest to be in Representative Libraries of that Region. Olympia: Washington State Library, 1909. 191 pp.
Pacific Northwest Americana: A Checklist of Books and Pamphlets relating to the History of the Pacific Northwest. New York: H.W. Wilson, 1921. 329 pp. Third Edition, revised by Isabel Mayhew. Portland: Binfords and Mort, 1950. 381 pp.
Special Collections in Libraries of the Pacific Northwest. Seattle: University of Washington Press, 1927. 20 pp.
A Union List of Manuscripts in Libraries of the Pacific Northwest. Seattle: University of Washington Press, 1931. 57 pp.

SMITH, COURTNEY M.
"Wartime Public Health in Alaska," *Am. J. of Public Health,* Sept., 1942.

SMITH, DARRELL HEVENOR
The Bureau of Education: Its History, Activities and Organization. Baltimore: Johns Hopkins Press, 1923. 157 pp.

SMITH, DAVID MURRAY
Arctic Expeditions. London: Fullerton and Jack, 1880. 824 pp.

SMITH, FRANCES C.
Men at Work in Alaska. New York: Putnam, 1967. 127 pp.
The World of the Arctic. Philadelphia: Lippincott, 1960. 126 pp. Juvenile.

SMITH, FRANCIS E.
Achievements of Captain Robert Gray. Tacoma: n.p., 1922. 12 pp. 2nd ed., Tacoma: Barrett-Redfield, 1923. 16 pp.

SMITH, HARLAN I.
"Stone Hammers or Pestles of the Northwest Coast," *Amer. Anthrop.,* Apr., 1899.
"Archeological Remains on the Coast of Northern British Columbia and Southern Alaska," *Amer. Anthrop.,* Oct., 1909.
"A Visit to the Indian Tribes of the Northwest Coast," *Amer. Museum J.,* Feb., 1910.
"Canoes of the North Pacific Indians," *Amer. Museum J.,* Aug., 1910.

SMITH, HERBERT B.
"Some Observations of Christian Work in Alaska," *Missionary Review of the World,* Jan., 1930.

SMITH, HUGH M.
"America's Most Valuable Fishes," *Nat. Geog.,* May, 1912.

"America's Surpassing Fisheries," *Nat. Geog.,* June, 1916.
"Making the Fur Seal Abundant," *Nat. Geog.,* Dec., 1911.

SMITH, JEFFERSON RANDOLPH ("Soapy")
Alaska Life, Apr., '42; June, '43; June, '49 (Sid Marquis); *Alaska Sportsman,* see Index; *Alaska-Yukon Gold Book; Alaska-Yukon Magazine,* Dec., '07; Jan., '08 ("Correspondence of a Crook"); Andrews; Anzer; Bankson; Becker; Berton; Cameron; Carpenter; Clark; Colby; Collier & Westrate; Davis; Denison; DeVere (*Ak.-Yukon Mag.,* '08); Franck; Hawthorne; Hellenthal; Higginson; Jones; O'Connor; Powell; Rickard; Robertson & Harris; Shea & Patten (W-1606); Shiels; Steffa (W-671); Suydam (W-1607); Underwood; Walden; Whiting; Williamson; Wickersham; Willoughby; Winslow.

SMITH, JOSEPH P.
Alaska: Handbook No. 86. Wn.DC: Bureau of American Republics, 1897. 133 pp.

SMITH, KATHERINE L.
"Interesting Westerners," *Sunset,* Sept., 1917. Wm. Duncan.
"Sitka," *World Traveler,* July, 1925.

SMITH, MARY E. E.
Eskimo Stories. Chicago: Flanagan, 1902. 189 pp. Juvenile.

SMITH, MAUDE PARSON
Alaska. Hartford: Church Missions Pub. Co., 1910. 89 pp.

SMITH, PAUL
"The Submarine Topography of Bogoslof Island," *Geog. Rev.,* Oct. '37.

SMITH, PHILIP SIDNEY (1877-1949)
"Notes on the Recent Changes in the Bogoslof Islands," *Science,* May, 1908.
The Gold Placers of Parts of Seward Peninsula. Bulletin, USGS, 1908.
"Explorations of Northwestern Alaska," *Geog. Rev.,* 1925. US Naval Pet. Res. No. 4.
"The Gold Resources of Alaska," *Econ. Geol.,* 1930.
Geology and Mineral Resources of Northwestern Alaska. Bulletin, USGS, 1930.
"Areal Geology of Alaska," USGS Prof. Pap., 1939.
"Occurrences of Molybdenum Minerals in Alaska," USGS *Surv. Bulletin,* 1942.
"Possible Future Oil Provinces in Alaska," *Bulletin,* Amer. Assn. of Pet. Geol., 1941.
"Past Placer-Gold Production from Alaska," USGS *Bulletin,* 1934.
"Past Lode Production from Alaska," *Surv. Bulletin,* 1942. USGS.
"Lake Clark-Central Kuskokwim Region, Alaska," USGS, *Surv. Bulletin,* 1917.
See also the Arctic Bibliography; see also a full index of USGS publications on Alaska.

SMITH, RICHARD AUSTIN
The Frontier States: Alaska, Hawaii. New York: Time-Life Books, 1968. 192 pp.

SMITH, THOMAS G.
"The Treatment of the Mentally Ill in Alaska, 1884-1912: A Territorial Study," *Pacific Northwest Q.*, Jan., 1974.

SMITH, THOMAS VESEY
"Middleton Island" Smith. See Underwood. Smith established a fox farm on Middleton Island in 1903 where he stayed for 10 years.

SMITH, W. W.
Alaska, the Eldorado of the North. Hartford, 1910. 3v.

SMITH, WALTER R.
"Geology and Oil Developments in the Cold Bay District," USGS, *Surv. Bulletin*, 1926.

SMITH, WALTER S.
Heredity and Environment: A Novel of Alaska and the North. Boston: Meador, 1930. 125 pp.

SMITH, WILFRID ROBERT (b. 1869)
Under the Northern Lights. Portland: Columbia Printing Co., 1916. 95 pp. "Platinum Bill" Smith.

SMITH, WILLIAM D.
Northwest Passage: Historic Voyage of the SS Manhattan. New York: American Heritage Press, 1970. 204 pp.

SMITHSONIAN INSTITUTION
See the Arctic Bibliography. See also Sherwood, and J. James. See as well Kennicott, Dall, Baker, Bannister, etc. See U.S. Smithsonian Institution.

SMITTER, WESSEL (b. 1894)
Another Morning. New York: Harper, 1941. 355 pp. Matanuska valley.

SMOOKLER, IDAIR
Copper in Alaska: Selected List of Official Publications. Wn.DC: GPO, 1943. 6 pp. US Office for Emergency Management.

SMUCKER, SAMUEL M.
Life of Dr. Elisha Kent Kane. Philadelphia: Lippincott, 1858. 406 pp.
Arctic Explorations and Discoveries during the 19th Century. New York: Miller and Orton, 1857. 517 pp. 2nd ed., New York: W. Allison, 1886. 640 pp.

SMYTH, NATHAN A. and AMOS PINCHOT
Brief on the Cunningham Coal Entries in Alaska. N.p., 1912. 127 pp.

SNELL, ROY JUDSON (b. 1878)
Eskimo Legends. Boston: Little, Brown, 1925. 203 pp.
The Walrus and His Hunters. Repr., *Alaska-Yukon Magazine*, Nov., '09.
Little White Fox and His Arctic Friends. Boston: Little, Brown, 1916. 130 pp.
An Eskimo Robinson Crusoe. Boston: Little, Brown, 1917.
Captain Kituk. Boston: Little, Brown, 1918. 225 pp.

Arctic Stowaways. Chicago: Rand McNally, 1935. 180 pp.
On the Yukon Trail. Chicago: Rand McNally, 1922. 322 pp.
Told Beneath the Northern Lights. Boston: Little, Brown, 1925. 238 pp.

SNIDER, GERRIT "Heinie"
Centennial: One Hundred Stories of Alaska. Anchorage: Color Art Printing Co., 1966. 192 pp.
Mink Raising in Alaska. Anchorage: The Time Publishing Co., 1929. 51 pp.
So Was Alaska. Anchorage: Color Art Printing Co., 1961. 95 pp.

SNIFFEN, MATTHEW K.
Conditions among Certain Native Tribes of Alaska. Paper, Annual Meeting, Lake Mohonk Conference, 1914.

SNIFFEN, MATTHEW K. and THOMAS SPEES CARRINGTON
The Indians of the Yukon and Tanana Valleys. Philadelphia: Indian Rights Association, 1914. 35 pp.

SNODGRASS, JEANNE O.
American Indian Painters: A Biographical Directory. New York: Museum of the American Indian, 1967.

SNOW, ALBERT S.
See note in Baker. Snow commanded the *Patterson* (US C&GS) in 1886 and 1887.

SNOW, C. K.
"The Mis-naming of Alaska's Mt. Ararat," *Alaska-Yukon Magazine*, Aug., '10.

SNOW, CHARLES W. and EWEN MacLENNAN
Songs of the Neukluk. Council, Alaska: the Author, 1932. 30 pp.

SNOW, EDWARD ROWE
Famous Lighthouses of America. New York: Dodd, Mead, 1955. 314 pp.

SNOW, HENRY JAMES (b. 1848)
In Forbidding Seas. London: Arnold, 1910. 303 pp. Sea-otter hunting in the Kuriles.

SNOW, WILLIAM PARKER (1817-1895)
Voyage of the Prince Albert. London: Longmans, 1851. 416 pp.

SNYDER, HOWARD
"Stepping Stones to Japan," *Our Navy*, Feb., '43.

SNYDER, LESTER LYNNE (b. 1894)
The Birds of Wrangell Island. Toronto: University of Toronto Library, 1926. 20 pp.

SOCIETY for PROMOTING CHRISTIAN KNOWLEDGE
See the Arctic Bibliography, and T-4230 ff.

SOKOLOV, ALEKSANDR P.
See the Arctic Bibliography. None of Sokolov's many works on the history of Russian activity are in English translation.

SOKOLOV, D.
A Manual of the Orthodox Church's Divine Services. New York: Wynkoop Hallenbeck Co., Printers, 1899. 166 pp.

SOLA, A. E. IRONMONGER (b. 1868)
Klondyke: Truth and Facts of the New El Dorado. London: Mining and Geographical Institute, 1897. 92 pp. Incl. natives, geog. descr. etc.

SOLECKI, RALPH STEFAN (b. 1917)
"Archaeology and Ecology of the Arctic Slope of Alaska," *Annual Report,* Smithsonian Institution, 1950.

SOLIDAY, GEORGE W. (1869-1950)
The George W. Soliday Collection of Western Americana: A Checklist, Descriptive and Priced. New York: Peter Decker, 1940-45. Also Antiquarian Press, 1960. 682 pp. 7500 items.

SOLKA, PAUL, Jr.
"Wrong Font Thompson," *Alaska Journal,* Spring, 1974.

SONNENFELD, J.
"Arctic Reindeer Industry: Growth and Decline," *Geog. Rev.,* Jan., 1959.

SONNTAG, AUGUST
Professor Sonntag's Thrilling Narrative of the Grinnell Exploring Expedition to the Arctic Ocean in the Years 1853-1855 in Search of Sir John Franklin. Philadelphia: J.T. Lloyd, 1857. 176 pp. This was an imposture done by Charles C. Rhodes, based on a brief ms. of Sonntag's who repudiated authorship. See the Arctic Bibliography.

SORELLE, VIVIAN
"Vacation in the Land of Lonesome Men," *Delineator,* 1936.

SOULE, SIDNEY HOWARD
The Rand McNally Guide to the Great Northwest. Chicago: Rand McNally, 1903. 365 pp.

SOUTHEASTERN ALASKA
See particularly George Rogers.

SPANISH VOYAGES
See Spanish explorers under the general heading Explorations.

SPARKS, JARED (1789-1866)
The Life of John Ledyard. Cambridge, Mass.: Hilliard and Brown, 1828. 325 pp.
Memoirs of the Life and Travels of John Ledyard. London: H. Colburn, 1828. 428 pp.
Travels and Adventures of John Ledyard. London: H. Colburn, 1834. 428 pp. With Cook on the third voyage.

SPAULDING, ALBERT C.
Archaeological Investigations on Agattu. Ann Arbor: University of Michigan Press, 1962. 79 pp.

SPAULDING, PHILIP TAFT
"McKinley: A Study in Survival," *Farthest North Collegian,* 1948. Account of University of Alaska McKinley Expedition of 1948.

SPECK, GORDON
Northwest Explorations. Portland: Binfords and Mort, 1954. 394 pp.
Samuel Hearne and the Northwest Passage. Caldwell: Caxton Printers, 1963. 337 pp.

SPENARD
Alaska Life, Jan., '46; *Alaska Sportsman,* Feb., '58 (founded in 1916 by Joseph Spenard on Jeter Lake); Colby; Couch (post office from 1949).

SPENCE, SYDNEY ALFRED
Captain James Cook, R.N., 1728-1779. Mitcham, England: the Author, 1960. 50 pp. Bibliography.

SPENCER, ARTHUR COE
The Geology and Mineral Resources of a Portion of the Copper River District. With F. Schrader. Wn.DC: GPO, 1901. 94 pp. 56th Cong., House Doc. No. 546 (2nd Sess.).
The Juneau Gold Belt, Alaska. Wn.DC: GPO, 1906. USGS.

SPENCER, ROBERT FRANCIS (b. 1917)
"Eskimo Polyandry and Social Organization," *Proc.,* Internat. Congress of Americanists. Copenhagen, 1956.
The North American Eskimo: Ecology and Society. Wn.DC: Smithsonian Institution, 1959. 490 pp.

SPENCER, ROBERT and JESSE D. JENNINGS
The Native Americans. New York: Harper and Row, 1965. 593 pp.

SPICER, GEORGE WASHINGTON (b. 1897)
The Constitutional Status and Government of Alaska. Baltimore: Johns Hopkins Press, 1927. 121 pp. Excellent summary.

SPIRIT of MISSIONS
Periodical, published monthly by the Protestant Episcopal Church.

SPOKANE CHAMBER OF COMMERCE
See T-4265.

SPRAGUE, RODERICK
See the Arctic Bibliography.

SPRAY, LAFE E.
"Tom Nestor, the Man that Knows, Talks Iditarod," *Alaska-Yukon Magazine,* May, 1911. "A. Sauerdo"
"Fairbanks: Alaska's Golden Heart," *Alaska-Yukon Magazine,* July, 1912.
"Skagway: Gem of Alaska," *Alaska-Yukon Magazine,* Nov., 1911.
For further bibliography see the Wickersham bibliography.

SPRING, NORMA
Alaska: Pioneer State. Camden: T. Nelson, 1967. 234 pp.
Alaska: The Complete Travel Book. New York: Macmillan, 248 pp.

SPRING, ROBERT (b. 1918)
High Worlds of the Mountain Climber. Seattle: Superior Publishing Co., 1959. 142 pp. Photography.

SPRINGER, JOHN A.
Innocent in Alaska: The Story of Margaret Knudsen Burke. New York: Coward-McCann, 1963. 319 pp.

SPROAT, GILBERT MALCOLM
Scenes and Studies of Savage Life. London: Smith, Elder and Co., 1868. 317 pp. *Boston* at Nootka Sound.

SPURR, JOSIAH EDWARD (1870-1950)
Through the Yukon Gold Diggings. Boston: Eastern Pub. Co., 1900. 276 pp. Summer, 1896, with Schraeder and Goodrich.
"From the Coast to the Golden Klondike," *Outing*, Sept., 1897.
"Geology of the Yukon Gold District, Alaska," *Annual Rpt.*, USGS, 1896.
"A Reconnaissance in Southwestern Alaska in 1898," *Annual Report*, USGS, 1898, Part VII. Tyonek on Cook Inlet, over the Tordrillo Range, down the Kuskokwim, to the Nushagak, to Katmai, and the *Dora*. See also Baker.
"Report of the Kuskokwim Expedition," *Maps and Descr.*, Explorations in Alaska, 1898. 55th Cong., 3rd Sess., Sen. Doc. No. 172. 138 pp.
Mt. Spurr in the Alaska Range 75 miles west of Anchorage was named for Josiah Spurr. On July 9, 1953 an eruption of Mt. Spurr covered Anchorage and part of the Kenai Peninsula with several inches of volcanic ash, and obscured the sun.

STAEHLIN von STORCKSBURG, JAKOB (1710-1785)
An Account of the New Northern Archipelago, lately discovered by the Russians in the Seas of Kamtschatka and Anadir. Trans. C. Heydinger. London: C. Heydinger, 1774. 138 pp. Commercial voyages in the Aleutians, and Russians cast away on East Spitzbergen, 1743-49. See also the Arctic Bibliography.

STAENDER, GILBERT and VIVIAN STAENDER
Adventures with Arctic Wildlife. Caldwell: Caxton Printers, 1970. 260 pp.

STALEY, W. W. and R. H. STORCH
"Choosing a Mining Method for Gold-bearing Gravels," *Eng. and Mining J.*, July, 1937.

STANFORD RESEARCH INSTITUTE
"Blasting Secrets from a Glacier," *Research for Industry*, September, 1949.

STANIUKOVICH, MIKHAIL NIKOLAIEVICH
See the Arctic Bibliography.

STANLEY, WILLIAM M.
A Mile of Gold. Chicago: Laird and Lee, 1898. 219 pp. The Klondike gold rush in 1896.

STANLEY-BROWN, JOSEPH (1858-1941)
"Geology of the Pribilof Islands," *Bulletin*, Geol. Soc. of Amer., 1892.
"Report on Auriferous Sands from Yakutat Bay," *National Geographic*, 1891.
"Past and Future of the Fur Seal," *Bulletin*, US Fish Commission (US F&WS), 1893. Stanley-Brown was a US Special Treasury Agent in the Pribilofs. His maps were used in the pelagic sealing controversy of the 1890's.

STANSBURY, CHARLES FREDERICK (1854-1922)
Klondike: Land of Gold. New York: F.T. Neely, 1897. 190 pp.

STANTON, STEPHEN BERRIEN (b. 1864)
The Behring Sea Dispute. New York: A.B. King, 1889. 58 pp.

STANTON, WILLIAM J.
"Purpose and Source of Seasonal Migration to Alaska," *Econ. Geog.*, April, 1955.

STANWELL-FLETCHER, THEODORA C.
Driftwood Valley. Boston: Little, Brown, 1957. 222 pp. Northern BC.

STAPLETON, AUGUSTUS G.
Political Life of the Right Honourable George Canning, 1822-27. Rev. Ed. 3v. London: Longmans, 1831.

STAPLETON, EDWARD J.
Some Official Correspondence of George Canning, 1821-27. London: Longmans, 1887, 2v.

STARBUCK, ALEXANDER
History of the American Whale Fishery. Waltham, Mass.: 1878. 767 pp. Also New York: Argosy-Antiquarian, 1964. 2v.

STARK, CHARLES RATHBONE, Jr. (b. 1885)
The Bering Sea Eagle. Caldwell: Caxton Printers, 1957. 170 pp. Harry L. Blunt, Bush Pilot.

STARR, WALTER AUGUSTUS
My Adventures in the Arctic, 1898-1900. San Francisco: the Author, 1960. 68 pp.

STATON, FRANCES M. and MARIE TREMAINE
A Bibliography of Canadiana. Toronto: Public Library, 1935. 828 pp.

STEARNS, MYRON M.
"On to Alaska with Buchanan," *Reader's Digest*, 1938.

STECKLER, GERARD G., S. J.
"The Diocese of Juneau," *Historical Studies and Records* (US Catholic Historical Society), 1959.
"The Case of Frank Fuller: The Killer of Alaska Missionary Charles Seghers", *Pacific NW Q.*, 1968

STEEL, HARRY G.
Editor of several early Alaska newspapers: *Dawson News, Seward Gateway*, and others. See the Wickersham bibliography.

STEEL, WILL A.
Home Rule Measure for Alaska. Juneau: Alaska Territory, 1927. 11 pp. Will Steel was an early Alaska newspaper editor, often with his brother Harry Steel. His papers included the *Cordova Daily Alaskan* and the *Chitina Leader* (published at Cordova).

STEELE, GEORGE P.
Seadragon: Northwest under the Ice. New York: Dutton, 1962. 255 pp. *Seadragon's* discovery of an underwater northwest passage.

STEELE, HARWOOD ELMES ROBERT (b. 1897)
Policing the Arctic. London: Jarrolds, 1936. 390 pp. RCMP.

STEELE, J. L.
"Alaska Coal and Oil Resources," *Pan Pacific Progress*, Alaska issue, 1930.
"American Mining Congress," *Alaska-Yukon Magazine*, 1909.

STEELE, JAMES WILLIAM
See T-4294 ff.

STEELE, SAMUEL BENFIELD (b. 1849)
Forty Years in Canada. London: H. Jenkins, 1915. 428 pp.

STEESE, JAMES GORDON (d. 1958)
"Across Alaska by Automobile," *Amer. Motorist*, 1923.
"The Alaska Road Commission," *Michigan Technic*, 1923.
"The Alaska Railroad," *Michigan Technic*, 1923.
See also Wickersham's bibliography. General Steese was a president of the Alaska Road Commission, building what is now the Steese Highway, 1922-27.

STEESE, JAMES and JOHN NOYES
"Communications in Alaska," *Geography* (England), 1934.

STEFANSSON, EVELYN BAIRD (1913-1962)
Here is Alaska. New York: Scribner's, 1943. 154 pp. Mostly Arctic.
Within the Circle. New York: Scribner's, 1945. 160 pp. Arctic.
Here is the Far North. New York: Scribner's, 1957. 154 pp.
"A Bibliographical Exploration of Alaska," *Library Bulletin*, 1958.

STEFANSSON, VILHJALMUR (1879-1962)
"Underground Ice in Northern Alaska," *Bulletin*, Amer. Geog. Soc., 1910.
My Life with the Eskimo. New York: Macmillan, 1913. 538 pp. Stefansson-Anderson expedition of the American Museum of Natural History, 1908-12.
The Stefansson-Anderson Arctic Expedition. New York: American Museum of Natural History, 1914. 395 pp. Also 1919; 475 pp.
"The Technique of Arctic Winter Travel," *Bulletin*, Amer. Geog. Soc., 1912.
The Friendly Arctic: The Story of Five Years in the Polar Regions. New York: Macmillan, 1921. 784 pp. Narrative of the Canadian-Arctic Expedition, 1913-18. Nome, the *Karluk*, etc.
Canadian Arctic Expedition, 1913-18. Ottawa: King's Printer, 1919-46. 14v.
Hunters of the Great North. New York: Harcourt, Brace, 1922. 301 pp. Leffingwell-Mikkelsen Expedition of 1906-07, Stefansson's first Arctic expedition.
The Northward Course of Empire. New York: Harcourt, Brace, 1922. 274 pp.
The Adventure of Wrangel Island. New York: Macmillan, 1925. 424 pp. Stefansson pushed the British claim to Wrangel Island, but the Canadian government would not support him. After the death of four volunteers, the Russian ship *Red October* landed at the island in 1924 and removed the remaining British and their furs.

Unsolved Mysteries of the Arctic. New York: Macmillan, 1938. 381 pp.
Ultima Thule: Further Mysteries of the Arctic. New York: Macmillan, 1940. 383 pp.
Arctic Manual. New York: Macmillan, 1944. 556 pp. This was issued by the US Army Air Corps.
Not By Bread Alone. New York: Macmillan, 1946. 339 pp. Arctic diet.
The Fat of the Land. New York: Macmillan, 1956. 339 pp. Revised edition of the above work.
"Causes of Eskimo Birthrate Increase," *Nature*, 1956.
Greenland. Garden City: Doubleday, Doran, 1942. 338 pp.
"Was the Diomede Scare a Japanese Plot?" *Alaska Life*, 1941.
"An Eskimo Discovery of an Island North of Alaska," *Geog. Rev.*, 1934. On the *Takpuk*, near 70°20'N, 145°30'W, in Sept. 1931.
"The Stefansson Library," *Arctic Circular*, 1952. See the Arctic Bibliography.
"Alaska: American Outpost No. 4," *Harper's*, 1941.
"American Far North," *Foreign Affairs*, 1939.
"Untapped Wealth of Alaska," *Sci. Digest*, 1942.
Discovery: The Autobiography of Vilhjalmur Stefansson. New York: McGraw-Hill, 1964. 411 pp.
Northward Ho! New York: Macmillan, 1925. 181 pp. Juvenile.
Northwest to Fortune. New York: Duell, Sloan and Pearce, 1958. 356 pp.
Prehistoric and Present Commerce among the Arctic Coast Eskimo. Ottawa: Canada National Museum, 1914. 29 pp.
The American Far North. Repr. from *Foreign Affairs.*
The Arctic in Fact and Fable. New York: Foreign Policy Association, 1945. 96 pp.
See also the following:
Bartlett, R.; Berry; Fletcher; Hanson; Holden; Irwin; Masik; Montgomery; Myers; Noice; Peary; Thomas, L.; Weigert; Whelen; Wissler. See as well Wead, and Le Bourdaus.

STEFFENS, J. LINCOLN
"Life in the Klondike Gold Fields," *McClure's*, 1897.

STEGNER, WALLACE EARLE (b. 1909)
The Big Rock Candy Mountain. New York: Duell, Sloan and Pearce, 1943. 515 pp. Alaska and the West.

STEIN, ROBERT
Can a Nation Be a Gentleman? Wn.DC: Judd & Detweiler, 1911. 11 pp.
The Defense of Alaska. Wn.DC: Judd & Detweiler, 1910. 23 pp.
"The Gold Fields of Alaska," *Review of Reviews*, 1896.

STEJNEGER, LEONHARD HESS (1851-1943)
"Contributions to the Natural History of the Commander Islands," *Proc.*, US National Museum, 1883.
"Investigations Relating to the Date of the Extermination of Steller's Sea-cow," *Proc.*, US National Museum, 1884.
"On the Extermination of the Great Northern Sea-cow," *Journal*, Amer. Geog. Soc., 1886.
"How the Great Northern Sea-cow became Exterminated," *Amer. Naturalist*, 1887.

"Skeletons of Steller's Sea-cow Preserved in Various Museums," *Science*, 1893.

"Results of Ornithological Explorations in the Commander Islands and Kamtschatka," *Bulletin*, US National Museum, 1885.

"Analecta Ornithologica," *Auk*, 1884-85.

"Revised and Annotated Catalogue of the Birds Inhabiting the Commander Islands," *Proc.*, 1887.

The Asiatic Fur-Seal Islands and Fur-Seal Industry. Wn.DC: GPO, 1899. 384 pp.

"The Russian Fur-Seal Islands," *Bulletin*, US Fish Commission, 1896.

"Report on the Rookeries of the Commander Islands, Season of 1897," US Treasury Document No. 1997. 1897.

"Observations on the Fur Seals of the Pribilof Islands," US Treasury Document No. 1913. 1898.

"Aleut Baidarkas in Kamchatka," *Science*, 1895.

"The Fur Seal Industry of the Commander Islands," *Bulletin*, US Bur. of Fisheries, 1925.

Steller's Journal of the Sea Voyage from Kamchatka to America and Return on the Second Expedition, 1741-42. In Golder's *Bering's Voyages*, Vol. II.

"An Early Account of Bering's Voyages," *Geog. Rev.*, 1934.

"Vitus Jonassen Bering," *Amer. Scandinavian Rev.*, 1941.

"Unsolved Problems in Arctic Zoogeography," in *Problems of Polar Research* (New York: Amer. Geog. Soc., 1928).

"Who was J.L.S.?" *Library Quarterly* (Chicago), 1934. "Neue Nachrichten" in 1776: Johann Lorenz Stavenhagen.

Georg Wilhelm Steller, The Pioneer of Alaskan Natural History. Cambridge: Harvard University Press, 1936. 623 pp.

STELLER, GEORG WILHELM (1709-1746)
See the Arctic Bibliography; see also T-4331 ff.
See as well the following:
Barbeau; Beckmann (see Golder's *Bering's Voyages*); Bell; Ford, C. (T-1599); Gmelin; Gruening; Golder; Pallas (see Golder); Stejneger; Sutton (T-4407); Wendt; Wotte.

STEPHEN, PAMELA
Winged Canoes at Nootka. Toronto: J. Dent, 1955. 227 pp.

STEPHENSON, WILFRED S.
A Collection of Pen Sketches and Tinted Wash Drawings of Sailing Ships, Passenger Liners and War Ships Familiar in Pacific Coast and Alaskan Ports. Vancouver, Wn.: Ben Kreis Agency, 1947. 25 pp.

STEPHENSON, WILLIAM B., Jr. (b. 1880)
The Land of Tomorrow. New York: Doran, 1919. 240 pp.

STERLING, HAWLEY
"Alaska Through a Windshield," *Christian Science Monitor*, June, 1941.

STERNBERG, LEO
See Chester S. Chard.

STERRETT, J.
"Vacationing in Alaska," *Sunset*, 1932.

STEVENS VILLAGE
Alaska Sportsman, see Index; Baker (Stevens Creek); Colby (near the mouth of the Dall River); Couch (post office from 1936); Stuck.

STEWART, CHARLES LOCKWOOD
"Martinez and Lopez de Haro on the Northwest Coast, 1788-89," unpublished doctor's thesis, University of California, 1936.

STEWART, ELIHU (b. 1844)
Down the Mackenzie and Up the Yukon in 1906. London: John Lane, 1913. 270 pp.

STEWART, ETHEL
"Early Days at Fort McPherson," *Beaver*, 1954. First Hudson's Bay Co. on the Peel River; Loucheux Indians.

STEWART, GEORGE RIPPEY (b. 1895)
Names on the Land. Boston: Houghton Mifflin, 1945. 511 pp. Rev. 1958.
"The Name 'Alaska' ", *Names*, 1956. On this subject see Alaska, and also Geoghegan.
N.A. 1: The North-South Continental Highway. Boston: Houghton Mifflin, 1957. 176 pp.

STEWART RIVER (Yukon Territory)
Alaska Sportsman, Feb., '44 (Margaret Shand); Oct., '52 (photo, Stewart City); Brooks (four men found gold here in 1883); Cameron (river discovered by James G. Stewart, Campbell's clerk, 1849); Colby; Davis; Denison-Mahoney (Jack London); Hulley; Ogilvie (boom 1882, 1885-86); Shand (hotel); Schwatka (Indian name, Na-chon-de, meant mouth obscured by islands); Stuck; Wickersham.

STEWART, ROBERT LAIRD (1840-1916)
Sheldon Jackson, Pathfinder and Prospector of the Missionary Vanguard in the Rocky Mountains and Alaska. New York: Revell, 1908. 488 pp. Solid biography.

STEWART, THOMAS DALE (b. 1901)
"The Life and Writings of Dr. Ales Hrdlicka, 1869-1939," *Amer. Journ. of Physical Anthrop.*, 1940. See also T-1600.

STEWART, T.
"The Meaning of Statehood to Alaska," *State Government*, 1958.

STIKINE RIVER
Alaska Life, June, '40 (gold on the Iskut); Oct., '41; Feb., '42 (Barringtons); Apr., '45 (Peter Skene Ogden); Apr., '46; Apr., '48 (photos of the Barrington boats); June, '49 *Alaska Sportsman*, Aug., '37 (Barringtons on the river from 1916); March, '43 (Stikine and Teslin trails); Sept., '47 (history); Aug., '49 (*Hazel B. III*); Sept., '49; Apr., '58 (Tlingits controlled the river to a canyon 7 miles above later Telegraph; from there controlled by Tahltans); June, '60 (Glenora); Andrews (Ogden and Zarembo); Bancroft (Ogden; Dionysius; Blake); Barbeau (Shaiks); Barrow; Blake, W.; Chase, B.; Colby; Corser; Dall (discovery by the *Atahualpa* of Boston; Dryad); Dole (means great river); Garland (descent on the *Strathcona* from Glenora in 1898); Gray (*New Dominion*, 1878); Greenhow (*Atahualpa* discovery by hearsay);

Hulley; Muir; Morris; Pilgrim; Scidmore (no boats on the river in 1884); Tompkins (*Dryad*); Underwood; Vancouver; Willoughby; Young. See also Wrangel, and Telegraph Creek.

On the Stikine River Indians ("Stick" Indians) see the following:

Jenkins (Chilkoots would not allow Stikines to cross the summit; instead they traded at Tahkeesh House); Morris; Schwatka (regarded nearly as slaves by the Chilkats; dejected and docile); Underwood; Wickersham (actually the Tena; called by the miners the Wood or Forest Indians; gold rush ended Chilkat domination); Willard; Wright; Young (distinguishes between Stickeen and Stick Siwashes [Tena]).

STIMPLE, BERT
Fun on the Farm in Alaska. New York: Carlton Press, 1962. 165 pp. Tanana Valley, 1930's.

STIRLING, MATTHEW W.
"Nomads of the Far North," *Nat. Geographic,* 1949.
"Indians of the Far West," *Nat. Geographic,* 1948.
"Indians of Our North Pacific Coast," *Nat. Geog.,* 1945.
Indians of the Americas. Wn.DC: Nat. Geog. Soc., 1965. 423 pp. 7th printing.

STOCK, EUGENE (1836-1928)
Metlakahtla and the North Pacific Mission. London: Church Missionary House, 1880. 130 pp.

STOCKTON, CHARLES HERBERT
"The Arctic Cruise of the *USS Thetis* in the Summer and Autumn of 1889," *National Geographic,* 1890. Sealing and Whaling Patrol. See Baker.

STODDARD, CHARLES WARREN (1843-1909)
Over the Rocky Mountains to Alaska. St. Louis: B. Herder, 1899. 168 pp.

STODDARD, GORDON ANTHONY
Go North, Young Man: Modern Homesteading in Alaska. Portland: Binfords and Mort, 1957. 239 pp. Kenai Peninsula.

STOECKL, Baron EDOUARD de
"The Projected Purchase of Alaska, 1859-60," *Pacific Historical Review,* 1934. Trans. H. McPherson.

STOFFEL, KARL
"Alaska: Outpost of the Pacific," *Scribner's Commentator,* 1941.

STONE, ANDREW JACKSON (b. 1859)
Saw-tooth Power! San Francisco, 1914. 83 pp. Alaska economic conditions.
See the Arctic Bibliography for works on natural history.

STONE, IRVING
Sailor on Horseback: The Biography of Jack London. Boston: Houghton Mifflin, 1938. 338 pp.

STONE, KIRK HASKIN (b. 1914)
"Land Tenures and Sequent Occupance in the Matanuska Valley," *Annals,* Assn. of Amer. Geographers, 1942.

"Some Geographic Bases for Planning New Alaskan Settlement," *Alaskan Science Conference,* 1950.
"Alaskan Problems and Potentials," *Journ. of Geog.,* 1951.
"Populating Alaska," *Geog. Rev.,* 1952.

STONE, RALPH WALTER
"Abstract of Alfred G. Maddren's 'Sulphur on Unalaska and Akun Islands and near Stepovak,' " *Journ.,* Acad. of Sci., 1919. See also Baker.

STONEY, GEORGE MORSE (d. 1905)
"Naval Explorations in Alaska," *Proc.,* US Naval Institute, 1899. Kobuk River, and the Noatak, Etivluk, Colville, Chipp, Selawik Rivers.
Explorations in Alaska: Extracts. Seattle: Shorey Book Store, 1965. Facs. 102 pp.
Stoney first went to the Arctic on the *Rodgers,* and was treated with extreme kindness by Siberian natives after it wrecked. When in the Arctic on the *Corwin* he took these natives presents. He discovered the mouth of the Kobuk.

STORCH, R. H.
See W.W. Staley.

STOREY, MOORFIELD
Charles Sumner. Boston: Houghton Mifflin, 1900. 466 pp.

STORKERSON, STORKER T.
"Drifting in the Beaufort Sea," *MacLean's Magazine,* 1920.

STORY, ISABELLE F.
"Here Alaska's Destiny was Set," *Mentor,* 1925.

STOUT, ARTHUR B.
"Ethnology: A Contribution to the History of the Aleutian Isles, or Aleutia," *Kansas City Review of Science and Industry,* 1881.

STOW, NELLIE
The Russians in California. San Francisco: Calif. Hist. Soc., 1933. 88 pp.

STOWELL, DAVID
"A History of Alaskan Weather Observations," *Alaskan Science Conference,* 1951. Omits Bannister.

STRALENBERG, P. J. von (1676-1747)
A Historico-Geographical Description of the North and Eastern Parts of Europe and Asia. London, 1738.

STRANGE, JAMES (1753-1840)
James Strange's Journal and Narrative of the Commercial Expedition from Bombay to the North-west Coast. Madras: Gov't. Press, 1928. 63 pp. 1785-86. Nootka, and Prince William Sounds.

STRATEMEYER, EDWARD (1862-1930)
To Alaska for Gold. Boston: Lee and Shepard, 1899. 248 pp.
The Rover Boys in Alaska. New York: Grosset and Dunlap, 1914. 285 pp.

STRAUSS, HILDEGARD
"History of Alaska Transportation," *Alaska Life,* 1941. Marine history, incl. whaling.

STREETER, DANIEL WILLARD
An Arctic Rodeo. New York: Putnam's, 1929. 356 pp. Capt. Bob Bartlett.

STREETT, St. CLAIR
"The First Alaskan Air Expedition," *Nat. Geog.*, 1922.
"Alaskan Flying Expedition," *Soc. Auto. Eng. J.*, 1921. The four DeHavilands, from New York to Nome.

STRESEMANN, ERWIN
"Birds Collected in the North Pacific Area during Capt. James Cook's last Voyage, 1778-1779," *Ibis*, Apr., '49.

STRINGER, ARTHUR J. A.
"Red-plush Pioneers," *Sat. Eve. Post*, 1935. The Matanuska Colony.
The Lamp in the Valley: A Novel of Alaska. Indianapolis: Bobbs-Merrill, 1938. 314 pp.

STRINGER, ISAAC O.
Alaska Sportsman, Sept., '56 (Laura Berton; Stringer on Herschel Island in 1896, then to Dawson); *Alaska-Yukon Magazine*, Sept., '08 (photos); Stuck (first Bishop of Selkirk, then Yukon Territory).

B. STEPHEN STRONG
"An Economic History of the Athabaskan Indians of the Upper Copper River", unpub. master's thesis, McGill University, 1972.

STROMSTADT, DAZIE M.
See T-4365 ff.

STRONG, CHARLES S.
"Cameraloguing Alaska and the Canadian Northwest," *Photo-Era*, 1931.
King Ram: A Novel. New York: John Day Co., 1961.

STRONG, JOHN F. A. (d. 1929) (Governor of Alaska, 1913-1917)
Annual Reports to the Secretary of Interior, 1913-1917.
"Katalla," *Alaska-Yukon Magazine*, Aug., '07.
"The Development of Alaska," *Alaska-Yukon Magazine*, May, '10.
See also the following:
Gruening; Harrison ("magnetic personality"); Hulley; Sommers (W-2222); Stuck; Teck (*Sunset*, May, 1915); Wickersham; Young; see also *Alaska Sportsman*, Nov., 1947.

STRUVE, OTON VASILEVICH
See the Arctic Bibliography.

STUART-STUBBS, B.
Maps relating to Alexander Mackenzie. Vancouver: University of British Columbia Press, 1968.

STUCK, HUDSON (1863-1920)
The Ascent of Denali. New York: Scribner's, 1914. 188 pp. First ascent of the South Peak, taller than the North Peak.
"Ascent of Denali," *Scribner's*, 1913.
"On Denali," *Spirit of Missions*, Jan., 1914.

Ten Thousand Miles with a Dog Sled: A Narrative of Winter Travel in the Interior of Alaska. New York: Scribner's, 1914. 420 pp. Stuck's best known work: Indians, Eskimos, dogs, etc. Travel over a period of 8 years as Episcopal archdeacon.
Voyages on the Yukon and Its Tributaries: A Narrative of Summer Travel in the Interior of Alaska. New York: Scribner's, 1917. 397 pp. On the *Pelican*, Stuck's mission boat, on the Yukon between St. Michael and Yukon Flats, and on the Porcupine, Chandalar, Tanana, Koyukuk, Innoko and Iditarod Rivers and Shageluk Slough.
A Winter Circuit of our Arctic Coast: A Narrative of a Journey with Dogsleds around the Entire Coast of Alaska. New York: Scribner's, 1920. 360 pp. Trip in the winter of 1917-18 from Ft. Yukon to the Kobuk, Point Hope, Barrow, the headwaters of the Porcupine, and back to Ft. Yukon, with Walter Harper, incl. a meeting with Stefansson.
"Journey round the Whole Arctic Coast of Alaska," *Royal Geographic Society Journal*, 1918.
The Alaskan Missions of the Episcopal Church: A Brief Sketch, Historical and Descriptive. New York: Domestic and Foreign Missionary Society, 1920. 179 pp.
"Round of the Creeks," *Spirit of Missions*, 1907.
"Archdeacon Stuck writes from Tanana on April 3rd," *Spirit of Missions*, 1911.
"Johnny and the Sugar," *Spirit of Missions*, 1914.
On Hudson Stuck see the following:
Alaska Sportsman, Jan., '54 (photo); Sept., '54; Burke; Cameron ("brilliant, refined gentleman"); Chitty; Colby; Franck (grave at Ft. Yukon); Gruening; Holden (T-2148); Jenkins (died of bronchial pneumonia; not liked by clergy); Kitchener; Pearson (T-3509 ff); Wickersham; Wood (*Living Church*, 1920). See also Dean, David.

STURDEVANT, CLARENCE LYNN (b. 1885)
"The Alaska Military Highway," *Eng. Journal*, 1943.
"The Alcan Military Highway: Its History, Organization, and Progress," *Civil Engineering*, 1943.
"US Army's First Official Story of the Alaska Highway," *Roads and Bridges*, 1943.
"The Military Road to Alaska: Organization and Administrative Problems," *Military Engineer*, 1943.

STURDZA, ALEXANDER
See the Arctic Bibliography, and T-4376 ff.

STURMER, ROMAN
"Background Information on the Russian Orthodox Church in Kodiak," *Glad Tidings*, 1956.

STURSBERG, PETER
Journey into Victory. London: Harrap & Co., 1944. 160 pp. WW II.

SUE, EUGENE
The Wandering Jew. New York: Random House, 1933. 485 pp.

SULLIVAN, EDWARD DEAN
The Fabulous Wilson Mizner. New York: Henkle Co., 1935. 324 pp. The Mizners were a well known fixture at Dawson during the gold rush.

SULLIVAN, MAY KELLOGG (b. ca. 1870)
A Woman who went to Alaska. Boston: J.H. Earle, 1902. 392 pp. Gold rush in Dawson, Nome and less spectacular camps.
The Trail of a Soudough: Life in Alaska. Boston: R.G. Badger, 1910.
"A New Klondike," *Alaska-Yukon Magazine,* Apr., '07.
"Eyllen's Water Witch," *Alaska-Yukon Magazine,* May, '07.
"Estella, the Eskimo," *Alaska-Yukon Magazine,* June, '07.
"The Old Stone House," *Alaska-Yukon Magazine,* Nov., '07.
"Eskimo Graves," *Alaska-Yukon Magazine,* Apr., '08.

SULLIVAN, ROBERT JEREMIAH (b. 1912)
The Tena Food Quest. Wn.DC: Catholic University Press, 1942. 142 pp.

SULZER, CHARLES A. (d. 1919)
Testimony on Opening Alaska's Coal and Oil Resources. 65th Cong., 1st Sess., US Senate, Hearings (W-9412).
Statement on Fish and Fish Hatcheries. Hearings, US House, 1918. (W-9803).
Sulzer opposed Wickersham in the elections of 1916 and 1918 for delegate to Congress. He was elected by canvassing boards in Alaska, but Wickersham carried the election to Congress on each occasion. Sulzer served in the 2nd and 3rd territorial legislatures. He operated a copper mine at Sulzer, on the west coast of Prince of Wales Island. See Gruening, and Shiels.

SULZER, WILLIAM (b. 1863)
Statement on Territorial Government. US House, 58th Cong., 2nd Sess. (W-9846).
Statement on Alaska Representative. US House, 59th Cong., 1st Sess. (W-9848).
"What Alaska Needs," *Alaska-Yukon Magazine,* May, '11.
"The Preservation of the Fur Seals," *Editorial Review,* 1912. See also the Wickersham bibliography. See Gruening; Nichols, and Underwood.

SUMDUM
Baker (in Sanford Cove, Endicott Arm, Holkham Bay; name is native "boom boom"); Colby; Couch (post office 1897-1942); Dole (White on the *Wayanda*); Higginson; Howard; Muir; Scidmore (mining camp emptied at word of Harris' find); Winslow; Young.

SUMNER, CHARLES (1811-1874)
Speech of the Honorable Charles Sumner, of Massachusetts, on the Cession of Russian America to the US. Wn.DC: Congressional Globe Office, 1867. 48 pp. Numerous other editions. The printed speech is not the one delivered, there being no reporters present, and Sumner speaking almost extemporaneously from notes on the back of an envelope, for three hours. Much of his information came from Robert Kennicott and Henry Bannister of the Scientific Corps of the Western Union Russian-American Overland Telegraph Expedition. See Sherwood, and J. James.
Memoirs and Letters of Charles Sumner, 1860-1874. Boston: Roberts, 1893.
Works. Boston: Lee & Shepard, 1870-1883. 15v.

See also the following:
Brindley (*Alaska-Yukon Magazine,* Apr., '07); Brooks; Gruening; Higginson; James; Morris (speech attacked Elliott); Pierce, E. (T-3579); Shiels (*Purchase of Alaska*); Stewart; Storey (T-4355). See also Purchase of Alaska.

SUMNER, LOWELL
"Magnificent Katmai," *Sierra Club Bulletin,* 1952.
"Your Stake in Alaska's Wildlife and Wilderness," *Sierra Club Bulletin,* 1956.

SUNDBORG, GEORGE (b. 1913)
Opportunity in Alaska. New York: Macmillan, 1945. 302 pp. Deals primarily with economic opportunity for the individual migrant, particularly in agriculture and mining.
Agricultural Development in Alaska: Further Possibilities and Problems. Portland: North Pacific Planning Project, 1944. 46 pp.
International Fisheries Cooperation between Canada and the United States in the North Pacific. Portland: North Pacific Planning Project, 1943. 68 pp.
Shipping Services in the American North Pacific. Portland: North Pacific Planning Project, 1944. 92 pp.
Statehood for Alaska: The Issues Involved and the Facts about the Issues. Anchorage: Alaska Statehood Association, 1946. 35 pp.
Valdez Industrial Report. Juneau: Alaska Development Board, 1955. 36 pp.
"The North Pacific Plans," *Alaska Life,* July, 1943.

SUNDERMAN, JAMES F.
World War II in the Air. New York: Franklin Watts, 1962. 306 pp.

SUN-DOGS
Alaska Sportsman, June, '38 (photo); Davis; Henderson; James; Romig; Stuck; see also Schwatka (*Summer*).

SUNRISE
Alaska Sportsman, Jan., '46; Nov., '46; Jan., '47 (4 parts on prospecting); *Alaska-Yukon Magazine,* Sept., '09 (photo); Berry; Colby; Castner (*Compilation of Narratives*); Chase (gold in 1904; encouraged activity in the Susitna Basin and Talkeetna Mts. [yielded mostly coal]); Corbett (1898); Couch (post office 1899-1918); Kitchener (NC Co.); Learnard (*Compilation of Narratives*).

SUNSET MAGAZINE
Alaska. Menlo Park, Calif.: Lane Book Co., 1963. 79 pp.

SUR, FOREST JOHN
Placer Gold Mining and Prospecting. Hollywood: Stanley Rose, 1934. 116 pp.

SURBER, ROSALIND
"Aleutian Honeymoon," *Alaska Life,* Aug., '42. Three parts on fur trapping on Amatignak, near Kiska.

SURIA, TOMAS de
Journal. Trans., Henry Wagner. Repr. from *Pacific Historical Review,* Sept., 1936. Suria was a painter with Malaspina in 1791. The journal breaks abruptly at Nootka.

SUSHKOV, BORIS ALEKSANDROVICH
See T-4404.

SUSITNA RIVER
Alaska Sportsman, Oct., '38; July, '52; Apr., '54 (photo); *Alaska-Yukon Magazine*, Sept., '09; Jan., '11 (Andrews on exploration; Malakov explored the Susitna in 1834); Baker; Brooks (1845 Russians had rough map of the entire river); Dickey (*National Geographic*, 1897); Hulley; US Congress (*Compilation of Narratives*: Abercrombie; Glenn; Learnard); see also Spurr, and the Arctic Bibliography.

SUTHERLAND, DAN A. (Ter. Sen., 1913-19; Ter. Del., 1921-31)
Judicial Railroading in Alaska. Speech (extracts), Alaska Territorial Senate. W-3868. See also W-10366-10368. See also the following:
W-9892 (Congressional testimony); W-9809 (fisheries).

SUTHERLAND, HOWARD V.
Bigg's Bar and Other Poems. Philadelphia: Biddle, 1901. 78 pp.
Out of the North. New York: Desmond FitzGerald, 1913. 20 pp.

SUTHERLAND, MASON
"A Navy Artist Paints the Aleutians," *National Geographic*, 1943.

SUTIL and MEXICANA
Spanish Voyage to Vancouver and Northwest Coast of America. Trans., Cecil Jane. London: Argonaut Press, 1930. 156 pp. A journal by a member of the expedition, anonymous. 1792.
See also the Arctic Bibliography.

SUTTER, JOHN AUGUSTUS (1803-1880)
Sutter: Rascal and Adventurer. New York: Random House, 1949. 382 pp. Marguerite Wilbur.
Sutter's Own Story. New York: the Author, 1936. 254 pp. E.G. Gudde.
Sutter: The Man and his Empire. New York: Macmillan, 1939. 394 pp. James Zollinger.
See also the following:
Dall (Ross sold to Sutter for $30,000); Rickard (Sutter unable to pay until 1850, after the gold strike); Tompkins; Willoughby (story of meeting of von Wrangel and Sutter).

SUTTON, ANN and MYRON SUTTON
Steller of the North. Chicago: Rand McNally, 1961. 231 pp.
The Endless Quest: Life of John Franklin. London: Constable Young, 1965. 244 pp.

SUTTON, GEORGE MIKSCH (b. 1898)
Eskimo Year. New York: Macmillan, 1934. 321 pp. Southampton Island, 1929-30.
"Notes on the Winter Birds of Fairbanks," *Condor*, 1945.
"Notes on the Winter Birds of Attu," *Condor*, 1946.
See also the Arctic Bibliography.

SVENSKA MISSIONSFORBUNDET I AMERIKA
See the Arctic Bibliography, and T-4409.

SVERDRUP, HARALD ULRIK (b. 1888)
See the Arctic Bibliography, and T-4410 ff.

SVERDRUP, OTTO NEWMANN (1854-1930)
New Land: Four Years in the Arctic Regions. London: Longmans, Green, 1904. 2v. The second *Fram* expedition, 1898-1902 for the North Pole.

SWADESH, MORRIS (b. 1909)
"Time Depths of American Linguistic Groupings," *Amer. Anthrop.*, June, 1954.

SWAINE, CHARLES
An Account of a Voyage for the Discovery of a Northwest Passage. London: Jolliffe, 1748-49. 2v. California, 1746-47, Capt. Francis Smith.
The Great Probability of a Northwest Passage. London: Jefferys, 1768. 153 pp. de Fonte.

SWAN, JAMES GILCHRIST (b. 1818)
British Columbia. Victoria: Wolfenden, 1884. 10 pp.
The Northwest Coast. New York: Macmillan, 1857. 345 pp.
Official Report, Centennial Exposition: Cruise of the *Wolcott*. Repr. from *Report*, Customs District, W.G. Morris, 1879. This report favors private mission activity among the Indians.
"The Eulachon or Candle-fish of the Northwest Coast," *Proc.*, US National Museum, 1880.
"Tattoo Marks of the Haida Indians of Queen Charlotte Islands and the Prince of Wales Archipelago," *Fourth Ann. Report*, US Bur. of Amer. Ethnology, 1882.

SWANTON, JOHN REED (b. 1873)
"The Development of the Clan System and of Secret Societies among the Northwestern Tribes," *Amer. Anthrop.*, 1904.
"Explanation of the Seattle Totem Pole," *J. Amer. Folklore*, 1905.
"Types of Haida and Tlingit Myths," *Amer. Anthrop.*, 1905.
Contributions to the Ethnology of the Haida. New York: Stechert, 1905. 300 pp. Jessup North Pacific Expedition; Skidegate, Masset, Kaigani.
"Haida Texts: Masset Dialect," *Publications*, Jessup North Pacific Expedition, 1908.
"Haida Texts and Myths: Skidegate Dialect," *Bulletin*, US Bur. of Amer. Ethn., 1905.
"Social Conditions, Beliefs, and Linguistic Relationships of the Tlingit Indians," *26th Ann. Rept.*, US bur. of Amer. Ethn., 1904.
Haida Songs. Leyden: E.J. Brill, 1912. 284 pp.
"Tlingit Myths and Texts," *Bulletin*, Smithsonian Institution (US Bur. Amer. Ethn.), 1909.
Indian Tribes of Alaska and Canada. Seattle: Shorey Book Store, 1965. Fasc.
The Indian Tribes of North America. St. Clair Shores, Mich.: Scholarly Press, 1968. Repr. of US Bur. Amer. Ethn. *Bulletin*, 1952.

SWARTH, HARRY SCHELWALD (b. 1878)
Birds and Mammals of the 1909 Alexander Alaska Expedition. Berkeley: University of California Press, 1911. 163 pp.
Birds and Mammals from Vancouver Island. Berkeley: University of California Press, 1912. 124 pp.
Birds and Mammals of the Stikine River Region. Berkeley: University of California Press, 1922.
Birds and Mammals of the Skeena River Region.

Berkeley: University of California Press, 1924.
Birds and Mammals of the Atlin Region, Northern BC. Berkeley: University of California Press, 1926.
"Occurrence of some Asiatic Birds in Alaska," *Proc.,* California Academy of Science, 1928.
Birds of Nunivak Island, Alaska. Los Angeles: Cooper Ornithological Club, 1934. 64 pp.
See also the Arctic Bibliography.

SWAYZE, NANSI
The Man Hunters: Jenness, Barbeau, Wintemberg. Toronto: Clarke, Irwin, 1960. 180 pp.

SWENSON, MARGARET C.
Kayoo, the Eskimo Boy. New York: Scribner's, 1939. 112 pp.

SWENSON, OLAF (b. 1883)
Northwest of the World: Forty Years of Trading and Hunting in Northern Siberia. New York: Dodd, Mead, 1944. 270 pp. Seattle trader in the area of the Kamchadales and Chukchis, from before 1900 to 1930.

SWERDLOFF, HERMAN G.
Yarns of the Yukon. Perth Amboy: Yukon Press, 1966. 232 pp.

SWIFT, HILDEGARDE
Edge of April: A Biography of John Burroughs. New York: William Morrow, 1957. 290 pp.
From the Eagle's Wing: A Biography of John Muir. New York: William Morrow, 1962. 287 pp.

SWIFT, JONATHAN (1667-1745)
Gulliver's Travels. London: Benjamin Motte, 1727 (2nd ed.) Swift set the story of Gulliver on the Northwest Coast of North America.

SWINEFORD, ALFRED P. (Governor of Alaska, 1885-1889)
Alaska: Its History, Climate and Natural Resources. Chicago: Rand McNally, 1898. 256 pp. Primarily descriptive.
On Swineford see the following:
Alaska-Yukon Magazine, Nov., '09 (d. 1909, Juneau, age 73); Gruening (annual reports are classics; bitter on the AC Co.); Hulley; Kitchener (intermittent criticism of AC Co.); Nichols (apostle of territorial government); Stuck (need of medical aid for natives); Young. See also Wickersham's bibliography.

SWINEHART, GEORGE
See the Arctic Bibliography. Swinehart was an editor of early gold rush newspapers: *Alaska Mining Record,* Juneau, 1894-95; *Caribou Sun,* Caribou Crossing (Carcross, Y.T.); *Midnight Sun,* Dawson, 1898; *Arctic Weekly Sun,* Nome, 1900.

SYND, Lt. JOHANN (d. 1779)
Bancroft (served under Bering on the *St. Peter*; stayed in Okhotsk, dying there in 1779; various voyages); Brooks (discovered St. Matthew Island); Coxe (on Synd on the coast of the Seward Peninsula); Hulley (1767 map distorted); Kitchener (first to sight Pribilofs in 1767); Staehlin; Tompkins (Ismailov accompanied Synd, and gave an account to Cook in 1778).

SYNGE, MARGARET BERTHA
A Book of Discovery. Edinburgh: Nelson, 1962. Cook's 3rd voyage.
Captain Cook's Voyages round the World. London: T. Nelson & Sons, 1897. 163 pp.
Cook's Voyages. London: Rivington, Perceval, 1894.

SZECHENYI, ZSIGMOND (b. 1898)
See the Arctic Bibliography, and T-4440.

T

TABER, RALPH G.
Stray Gold: A Rambler's Clean-up. St. Paul: St. Paul Book and Stationary Co., 1915. 191 pp. Poetry.

TABER, STEPHEN (b. 1882)
See the Arctic Bibliography.

TAFT, WILLIAM HOWARD (1857-1930)
Alaska-Yukon Magazine, Sept., '09 (frankly opposed to a legislative assembly for Alaska); Feb., '10 (favors gov't. by commission); Gruening (conservatism; speech at Alaska-Yukon-Pacific Exposition, 1909); Hulley (defeat of the Beveridge bill); Nichols (did not understand frontier man).

TAGISH CHARLIE
Becker (Carmacks' brother-in-law; drowned at Carcross); Cameron; Davis (employed by Ogilvie in the 1880's); Franck; Higginson (with "Skookum Jim" and Carmacks on the Klondike); Ogilvie (often called "cultus," meaning "no-good;" packer on the Chilkoot Pass trail, 1887).

TAHLTAN INDIANS
Alaska Sportsman, May, '55 (photo on Tahltan River); Nov., '57 (photos, notes); Apr., '58 (lived north of Telegraph Creek); Emmons. See also Stikine River.

TAKOTNA RIVER and TAKOTNA
Alaska Sportsman, Oct., '46 (descr. village); Aug., '48; May, '50 (photo, store); *Alaska Weekly,* Aug., '51 (new constr.; lawless conditions); *Alaska-Yukon Magazine,* Nov., '10 (photos); Jan., '11 (photo, freighting, Kuskokwim valley); Colby (river joins Kuskokwim at McGrath; village is mining camp); Couch (post office from 1914); Kitchener (NC Co. here 1923-28); Hulley (Zagoskin); Lipke (Berrys and Cloughs).

TAKU
Alaska Life, Feb., '47 (legend of Taku Glacier); May, '48; *Alaska Sportsman,* Jan., '38 (Taku Glacier Survey); June, '40 (glacier photos); Dec., '40; Oct.,

'41; Sept. '47; May, '52 (storm on Taku Inlet); Jan., '53; July, '53; Aug., '54 (photo, Indian dugout, upper Taku River); Nov., '54 (lodge); Feb., '54 (descr. of wind); Sept., '56; Feb., '57; Feb., '58 (deVigne built lodge in the 1920's); Apr., '58; *Alaska Weekly*, Aug., '50 (Rutgers University glacier study); *Alaska-Yukon Magazine*, Sept., '07 (Indian legend: Klosch drowned his brother in the river); Aug., '08 (photo, tourists); Nov., '10; Jan., '11 (river disc. by Kuznetsov, 1834, surveyed by Zarembo, 1838, ascended by Douglas of H.B. Co., 1840); Cameron; Baker; Colby (Klumma Gutta in Indian name of the glacier); Couch (post office at Taku Harbor, 1907-49); now Taku Inlet); Corser (notes on name); Franck; Higginson; Lipke (Taku wind); Morris (Taku Indian attempts murder of policeman at Wrangell); Potter; Rickard; Schwatka; Scidmore; Vancouver; see also Dall (Douglas ascended river 35 miles in 1840); Dole (Taku Indians keen traders, mercenary). See as well Hubbard, Harriman; Underwood; Willoughby.

TALKEETNA

Alaska Sportsman, May, '50 (river takes two blocks of Main Street); June, '50; Apr., '53 (photo; names means river of plenty); July, '53; March, '56; Sept., '56, and Index; Baker; Colby (meeting of Talkeetna, Chulitna, and Susitna); Couch (post office from 1916); Hulley (Matanuska valley separates Talkeetna from Chugach mountains); see also Bagg, Griffiths, Learnard, Mathys and Yanert in *Compilaton of Narratives*.

TANACROSS

Alaska Sportsman, Aug., '45 (photos, story; first white visitor, E.H. Wells, 1890, with *Leslie's Illustrated*); Baker (telegraph station); Couch (installation of wireless at Eagle in 1910 led to abandonment of telegraphy station; St. Timothy's post office, 1920-27, 1931-34, changed to Tanacross, 1934); Poor (army post); Stuck.

TANANA

Alaska Citizen, Oct., '14; *Alaska Life*, Sept., '40; *Alaska Sportsman*, July, '41 (photo, Tower House); Dec. '48 (half of the buildings empty); Sept., '53 (photo, log church); June, '55 (NC Co. store burns; town founded by Kensley and Mayo, 1874, as Fort Adams—changed to Tanana in 1896); March, '57 (photos); *Alaska-Yukon Magazine*, Nov., '08 (photo); Baker (in order upstream: Ft. Gibbon, Weare, Tanana Station, St. James Station); Andrews (Weare est. by N. Amer. Transp. and Trading Co.; NC Co. post called Tanana); Cameron (on Ft. Jette and Hudson Stuck); Colby (some Ft. Gibbon buildings remain); Couch (post office from 1898, called Ft. Gibbon 1907-08); Dole; Helmericks; Henderson (Prevost here); Higginson; Hrdlicka (descr. potlatch); Kitchener (full history: Nuklukayet was a clearing, 2 miles below mouth of the Tanana on "right" bank; Weare named for Charles A., Portus B. and Ely A. Weare; Army left Ft. Gibbon in 1922); Prevost (3 articles in *Spirit of Missions;* see W-1138 ff.); Rickard (one settlement with 3 names); Santos (chapel descr., priests named, 1904-31); Schwatka (photos; Nuklakayet trading station here in 1883, Harper and McQuesten as agents for AC Co.; it was a trading station in an earlier period for exchange between English above and Russians below); Stuck

(original name was Nu-cha-la-woy-ya, meaning between the rivers); Wickersham (first printing press on the Yukon).

TANANA INDIANS

Alaska Sportsman, Sept., '53 (photo, Chief Thomas and family; dwelled south and west of Circle City); Dall (Tena and Kutchin were people of the mountains, or Gens des Buttes); Hulley (now fewer than one thousand Yukon and Tanana Indians remaining); Kitchener (two fierce tribes, highlanders and lowlanders); Schwatka (traded at Ft. Selkirk prior to 1851; Tananas were feared); Sniffen and Carrington; Stuck (Gens de Montagne). See also the Arctic Bibliography.

TANANA RIVER and VALLEY

For material on agriculture, see the following, and the Arctic Bibliography:

Aamodt and Savage (cereal, forage and range); Bennett, H. and Thomas (soil reconnaissance); Gasser; Hodgson (clover); Johnson (farming); Kellogg and Nygard (soils); Miller, E. (interior Alaska agriculture); Miller, O. (Matanuska valley); Pewe, T. (silt origin); Sundborg; Weston (in *Alaska Sportsman*, 1939).

See also the following:

Alaska Sportsman, July, '41 (photo); Aug., '42; Feb., '43; Dec., '48 (river boat); June, '52 (Nenana ice); Oct., '56 (*Mosquito*); *Alaska-Yukon Magazine*, Feb., '08; Jan., '09 (special Tanana issue); Allen (1885); Andrews (gold); Cameron; Colby; Dall; Davis; Fraser (gold); Friend; Glenn; Gordon; Helmericks; Hulley; Moffit (USGS); Mills; Pilgrim; Powell; Rainey (archaeology); Schwatka; Sniffen and Carrington (1914); Stuck; US Adj-Gen Office (*Reports of Explorations* [Wn.DC: GPO, 1899; 464 pp.] [Cook Inlet, Susitna, Copper River, Tanana River]); US Army (Allen); Corps of Engineers 1955; USGS; Wickersham. See also Fairbanks.

TANANA VALLEY RAILROAD

Alaska Sportsman, Feb., '58 (built 1903-05, operated by US gov't. 1917-1930, then became part of Alaska Railroad, Chena to Chatanika); *Alaska-Yukon Magazine*, March '07 (photo, depot); Dec., '07; Feb., '08 (photo); Jan., '09 (Joslin); Andrews; Gruening; Joslin (president of road; see Wickersham's bibliography); Hulley; Kitchener; Koenig; Powers; Rickard.

TANNER, ZERA LUTHER (1835-1906)

Explorations of the Fishing Grounds of Alaska, Washington Territory and Oregon during 1888. *Bulletin*, US Fish Comm. 1888. Soundings, navigation perils, sea otter hunting, Unalaska to Middleton Island, *Albatross*.

"Deep-sea Exploration: Description of the Steamer *Albatross*," *Bulletin*, US Fish Commission, 1896.

See also Baker, and the Arctic Bibliography.

TANSILL, CHARLES CALLAN

Canadian-American Relations, 1875-1911. New Haven: Yale University Press, 1943. Bering Sea controversy.

The Foreign Policy of Thomas F. Bayard, 1885-1897. New York: Fordham University Press, 1940.

TARR, RALPH STOCKMAN (1864-1912) **and LAWRENCE MARTIN**
Alaskan Glacier Studies of the National Geographic Society. Wn.DC: Nat. Geog. Soc., 1914. 498 pp. Yakutat Bay, Prince William Sound, Copper River.

TARR, RALPH STOCKMAN and BERT S. BUTLER
"The Yakutat Bay Region, Alaska: Physiography and Glacial Geology," USGS Professional Paper, 1909. Previous explorations.
See also *Alaska-Yukon Magazine*, Apr., '09, on earthquake activity.

TARR, RALPH STOCKMAN
"The Malaspina Glacier," *Bulletin*, Amer. Geog. Soc., 1907.
"The Theory of Advance of Glaciers in Response to Earthquake Shaking," *Zeitschrift fur Gletscherkunde*, 1910.
"Glaciers and Glaciation of Alaska," *Annals*, Assn. of Amer. Geographers, 1912.

TARSAIDZE, ALEXANDRE (b. ca. 1898)
Czars and Presidents: the Story of a Forgotten Friendship. New York: McDowell Obolensky, 1958. 383 pp. Primarily the American Civil War and the Alaska Purchase.

TATE, CHARLES MONTGOMERY (1852-1933)
Chinook as Spoken by the Indians of the Pacific Coast. Victoria: T.R. Cusack, 1914. 48 pp.

TATEWAKI, MISAO and YOSHIO KOBAYASHI
"A Contribution to the Flora of the Aleutian Islands," *Journal of the Faculty of Agriculture*, Hokkaido Imperial University, 1934.

TAVERNER, PERCY ALGERNON (1875-1947)
Birds of Western Canada. Ottawa: King's Printer, 1926. 380 pp.
Birds of Canada. Toronto: Musson Book Co., 1938. 455 pp.
See also the Arctic Bibliography.

TAWRESEY, ALFRED
"Sea-going Indians," *Proc.*, US Naval Institute, 1937. Early history, Aleutian Islands.

TAX, SOL
Indian Tribes of Aboriginal America: Selected Papers from the 29th International Congress of Americanists. Chicago: Rand McNally, 1952.

TAXAY, DON
Money of the American Indians and Other Primitive Currencies of the Americas. New York: Nunmus Press, 1970. 158 pp.

TAYLOR, BARBARA A.
Alaska: Last Frontier. New York: Carlton Press, 1963. 174 pp.

TAYLOR, CHARLES MAUS (b. 1849)
Touring Alaska and the Yellowstone. Philadelphia: G.W. Jacobs, 1901. 388 pp.

TAYLOR, ELIZABETH (1856-1932)
See *Alaska Life*, July, 1949; letters and biog. notes.

TAYLOR, FRANK J.
High Horizons: Daredevil Flying Postman to Modern Magic Carpet. New York: McGraw-Hill, 1951. 198 pp.

TAYLOR, K. A.
"Shadow of the Arctic Circle," *Sunset*, 1929.

TAYLOR, L. D.
Ice Structures, Burroughs Glacier. Columbus: University of Ohio Press, 1962. 106 pp.

TAYLOR, RAYMOND FRANK (b. 1897)
Pocket Guide to Alaska Trees. Wn.DC: GPO, 1929. 39 pp. US Forest Service.
See also the Arctic Bibliography.

TCHILINGHIRIAN, S. D. and WILLIAM S. E. STEPHEN
Stamps of the Russian Empire Used Abroad. Repr. from work of same title, British Society of Russian Philately.

TEAL, JOHN J., Jr.
See George Kimble.

TEBENKOV, MIKHAIL DMITRIEVICH (d. 1872)
See the Arctic Bibliography, and T-4474. Tebenkov was Chief Manager of the Russian-American Co., 1845-50. In 1831 he visited Norton Sound, and in 1833 Wrangel sent him to establish a trading post at St. Michael. In the 1850's charts drawn by Tebenkov, who was a surveyor by training, were engraved and printed at Sitka, then sent to St. Petersburg for binding, and the addition of title pages. In the 1870's Baker wrote that Tebenkov's charts were the most valuable Russian contribution to science. Several copies of Tebenkov's *Atlas of the Northwest Coast of America* are available at libraries in Alaska.

TEICHMANN, EMIL (1845-1924)
A Journey to Alaska in the Year 1868. Kensington: Cayme Press, 1925. 272 pp.

TEIT, JAMES
"Two Tahltan Traditions," *Journal of Amer. Folklore*, 1909. See also the Arctic Bibliography.

TEKESKY, PAULINE
Seward's Folly: The Story of Alaska. Chapel Hill: University of North Carolina Press, 1960. 32 pp. Bibliography.

TELEGRAPH CREEK, BC
Alaska Life, Feb., '42 (photo); *Alaska Sportsman*, Aug., '37 (photos); Aug., '38 (photos, Indian graves); Sept., '47 (descr.); Feb., '49 (Ball Ranch); July, '49 (Ball Ranch); July, '54 (photo); Nov., '57 (photo; founded as supply point for Overland Telegraph line); Chase (named by Western Union explorers in 1866); Garland (telegraph planned to cross the Stikine here); Hulley; Willoughby (River House); Winslow. See also Stikine River.

TELEGRAPH LINE, MILITARY (Valdez-Eagle, 1900)

Alaska Sportsman, Feb., '45 (100 horses and mules kept at Ft. Liscum to supply line); Feb., '53 (new line completed between Anchorage and Tok); Nov., '55 (on Nahlin Station, Yukon Telegraph line); Jan., '57 (much of original line used by rural communications system); Jan., '58; Apr., '58 (on now abandoned Yukon Telegraph line); *Alaska-Yukon Magazine*, July, '07 (on history, from 1901, of the military cable and telegraph system); July, '07 (wireless stations successful at Safety and St. Michael; plans for Cape Flattery and Nome); Nov., '08 (Alaska military wireless stations at Fairbanks, Nome, Ft. Gibbon, Ft. Egbert, and Circle City); May, '09; Couch (line crossed Tanana at Tanacross; line abandoned in 1910 when wireless station established at Eagle); Gruening (Greely was chief signal officer, with William Mitchell as assistant; telegraph system linked to states in 1905, Canadian line to Dawson following the old Overland Telegraph route); Kitchener (line completed to Eagle on October 29, 1900); Potter (sound); Stuck (stations every 40-50 miles; shelter cabins half-way between; line and Ft. Egbert abandoned [1914]); Underwood (winter mail carriers use telegraph stations, which also serve as rescue stations); Wickersham (sent first telegram from Eagle on October 19, 1900; system Valdez to Eagle, and from Eagle over the Canadian line "outside" working well in 1903).

TELLER

Alaska Sportsman, March, '37; June, '39; Allan; Baker (reindeer station est. by Sheldon Jackson in 1892 at Grantley Harbor, Seward Peninsula; named in honor of Sec. of the Interior, Henry Moore Teller; settlement moved to north shore of Port Clarence; post office est. Apr., 1900); Brevig (full descr.); Colby (171 reindeer on July 4, 1892); Couch (first postmaster was Tollef Brevig); Denison (descr. by Klondike Mike; Byrd landed here after polar flight across pole); Gruening (Sen. Teller favored introduction of reindeer); Harrison (Teller of Colorado was one of the few to advocate reindeer; railroad proposed between Nome and Teller); Kitchener (not quite abandoned); Miller, M. (film "Eskimo" made here; *Norge* landed here 1926; Teller Mission across bay from Teller); Thompson (in *Washington Magazine*, 1906); Wead; Wickersham; Young. See also Port Clarence.

TEMPLETON, GEORGE

The Man from Alaska. New York: Grossett and Dunlap, 1936. 256 pp.

TENAKEE SPRINGS

Alaska Sportsman, July, '42 (Ed Snyder); Baker (eastern shore, Tenakee Inlet, Chichagof Island); Colby (canning center with two general stores); Couch (Tenakee post office here 1902-28; Tenakee Springs from 1928).

TERHUNE, H. W.

See Frank Heintzleman.

TERMINAL PUBLISHING CO.

See T-4478 ff.

TERNAUX-COMPANS, HENRI

See the Arctic Bibliography; see also the *Pacific Northwest Quarterly*, April, 1959. This is an account of the first extended exploration into the interior of Alaska, by Glazunov.

TEWKESBURY, DAVID B. and **WILLIAM TEWKESBURY**

Tewkesbury's Who's Who in Alaska and Alaska Business Index. Seattle: Lowman and Hanford, 1947. 320 pp. 659 short biographies of Alaskans of prominence.

Alaska Highway and Travel Guide, Business Directory and Almanac. Seattle: Lowman and Hanford, 1950. 712 pp. Generally descriptive; well illustrated.

Alaska Business Directory, Travel Guide and Almanac with Homestead Laws, Hunting, Living Costs, Etc. Seattle: Tewkesbury Publ. Co., 1948. 518 pp.

THALBITZER, WILLIAM CARL (b. 1873)

A Phonetical Study of the Eskimo Language. Copenhagen: B. Luno, 1904. 405 pp.

"Eskimo," *Handbook of American Indian Languages*, Boas. Bulletin, Bur. of Amer. Ethn., 1911.

"The Aleutian Language compared with Greenlandic," *Internat. J. of Amer. Ling.*, 1922.

"Eskimo Place Names in Alaska and Greenland in the Light of Archeology," *Geografisk Tidsskrift* (Copenhagen), 1932.

See also the Arctic Bibliography.

THANE

Alaska Sportsman, June, '41 (ghost mining camp south of Juneau; Alaska-Gastineau Mine); *Alaska-Yukon Magazine*, Sept., '07 (photo, Bart Thane); Colby; Couch (post office from 1914 to circa. 1924); DeArmond (history; Thane was gen. manager of the Alaska-Gastineau Mining Co.; mine closed 1921; post office closed 1936; to 1914 Thane was called Sheep Creek); Hurja (*Sunset*, 1916); Underwood.

THIBERT, ARTHUR

English-Eskimo and Eskimo-English Dictionary. Ottawa: University of Ottawa, 1954. 171 pp.

THE THLINGET

Monthly periodical published at the Sitka Training School, 1908-12.

THIERY, MAURICE

See the Arctic Bibliography, and T-4484 ff (for translations).

THOMAS BAY

Baker (named for Lt. Commander Charles Mitchell Thomas who surveyed the bay in 1887); Colp (haunted); Gruening; Scidmore; Vancouver.

THOMAS, BENJAMIN PLATT

Russo-American Relations, 1815-1867. Baltimore: Johns Hopkins University Press, 1930. 185 pp. Treaty of 1824, commercial treaty of 1832, Crimean War, American Civil War, Purchase of Alaska.

THOMAS, CHARLES MITCHELL

"Surveys in Southeastern Alaska," *Coast and Geodetic Survey Reports*, 1888, 1889. See also Baker. Thomas conducted many important early surveys.

THOMAS, CHARLES W.
Ice is Where you Find It. Indianapolis: Bobbs-Merrill, 1951. 378 pp.

THOMAS, EDITH LUCRETIA RICHMOND
A Night in Sitka. New York: Harbinger House, 1948. 84 pp.

THOMAS, EDWARD HARPER (b. 1868)
Chinook: A History and Dictionary of the Northwest Coast Trade Jargon. Portland: Metropolitan Press, 1935. 179 pp.

THOMAS, JOHN HUNTER
"The Vascular Flora of Middleton Island, Alaska," *Taxonomic Notes,* Stanford University, 1957.

THOMAS, LOWELL JACKSON (b. 1892) **and LOWELL THOMAS, Jr.**
Famous First Flights that Changed History. Garden City: Doubleday, 1968. 340 pp.

THOMAS, LOWELL J.
Kabluk of the Eskimo. Boston: Little, Brown, 1932. 276 pp.
Lowell Thomas' Book of the High Mountains. New York: Julian Messner, 1964. 512 pp.
Sir Hubert Wilkins: His World of Adventure. New York: McGraw-Hill, 1961. 296 pp.
The First World Flight. Boston: Houghton Mifflin, 1925.
Woodfill of the Regulars. New York: Doubleday Doran, 1929. 325 pp.

THOMAS, LOWELL J. Jr.
The Trail of '98: An Anthology of the Klondike. New York: Duell, Sloan and Pearce, 1962. 191 pp.

THOMAS, MARY (Tay)
Only in Alaska. Garden City: Doubleday, 1969.
Cry in the Wilderness. Anchorage: Color Art Printing, 1967. 125 pp.
Follow the North Star. Garden City: Doubleday, 1960. 165 pp.

THOMAS, WILLIAM S. (b. 1858)
Trails and Tramps in Alaska and Newfoundland. New York: Putnam's, 1913. 330 pp.

THOMPSON, ARTHUR RIPLEY (b. 1872)
Gold-Seeking on the Dalton Trail. Boston: Little, Brown, 1902. 352 pp.

THOMPSON, BEN H.
See George M. Wright.

THOMPSON, DONNIS STARK
The Loon Lake Mystery: An Alaskan Tale. New York: Criterion Books, 1966. 144 pp. Juvenile.

THOMPSON, DOROTHY J.
The Eskimo Woman of Nome, Alaska. Repr. from *Proc.,* Alaskan Science Conf., 1951.

THOMPSON, DOROTHY TOSTLEBE
"Two Eskimo Geographers," *J. of Geog.,* 1951.

THOMPSON, EDGAR T. and EVERETT C. HUGHES
Race, Individual and Collective Behavior. Glencoe, Illinois: Free Press, 1958. 619 pp.

THOMPSON, J. WALTER CO.
The Alaskan Market, 1958. New York: J. Walter Thompson Co., 1958. 39 pp.

THOMPSON, HOLLAND
Lands and Peoples. New York: Grolier, 1956. 400 pp.

THOMPSON, PAUL W.
"Alcan," *Infantry Journal,* 1942.

THOMPSON, RAYMOND and LOUISE H. FOLEY
The Siberian Husky. Alderwood Manor, Wn.: Raymond Thompson Co., 1962. 69 pp.

THOMPSON, ROBERT
The Russian Settlement in California. Santa Rosa, Calif.: Sonoma Democrat, 1896. 34 pp.

THOMPSON, SETON HAYES (b. 1906)
"Salmon-tagging Experiments in Alaska, 1929," *Bulletin,* US Bur. of Fisheries, 1930.
"Conditions of Razor Clam Fishery in Vicinity of Cordova, Alaska," *Bulletin,* US Bur. of Fisheries, 1935.

THOMPSON, STITH
Tales of the North American Indians. Cambridge: Harvard University Press, 1929. 386 pp.

THOMPSON, THOMAS GORDON
See the Arctic Bibliography, and T-4510 ff.

THOMPSON, WILLIAM FRANCIS
See the Arctic Bibliography, and T-4512 ff.

THOMPSON, WILL FRANCIS, Jr.
"Observations in Kamishak, Alaska," *Geog. Rev.,* July, 1949.

THOMPSON, WILLIAM F. ("Wrong Font")
"First Account of Conquering Mt. McKinley," Sunday Magazine, *New York Times,* June, 1910. Thompson edited the Fairbanks *News-Miner* from 1908. He was strongly opposed to James Wickersham. See P. Solka.

THOMSON, JAY EARLE
Our Pacific Possessions. New York: Scribner's, 1931. 264 pp.

THORBURN, LOIS, and DON THORBURN
No Tumult, No Shouting: The Story of the PBY. New York: Holt, 1945. 264 pp. Navy Air Force in the Aleutians.

THOREN, RAGNAR
Picture Atlas of the Arctic. New York: American Elsevier Publishing Co., 1969. 475 pp.

THORNE, JAMES FREDERIC (b. 1871)
In the Time That Was. Seattle: the Raven, 1909. 28 pp. Chilkat legend.

THORNTON, HARRISON ROBERTSON (1858-1893)
Among the Eskimos of Wales, Alaska, 1890-93. Baltimore: Johns Hopkins Press, 1931. 268 pp.

For further information on Rev. Thornton see the following: Hayes; Henderson; Miller (killed, 1893); Stuck (shot by drunken Eskimo); Wead.

THULAND, C. M.
See the Arctic Bibliography.

THUMAN, WILLIAM
See T-4530 ff, and the Arctic Bibliography.

TIBER, B. M.
"Beyond the Arctic Circle," *Public Health Nursing*, 1935.
"Leaves from an Alaska Logbook," *Public Health Nursing*, 1941.

TICHY, HERBERT (b. 1912)
See the Arctic Bibliography, and T-4532.

TICKASOOK
See T-4534, and the Arctic Bibliography.

TIGERT, JOHN J.
"Alaskan Natives' Health Improved by Government Efforts," *Nation's Health*, 1926.

TIKHMENEV, PETR ALEKSANDROVICH (d. 1888)
Historical Review of the Organization of the Russian American Co. Trans. D. Krenov. Seattle: WPA, 1939-40. Ms., University of Washington Library. Original published in St. Petersburg, 1861-63. Contains many valuable early documents.
See also the Arctic Bibliography. Tikhmenev's *Historical Review* has been called the most important early attempt at a history of the Russian-American Company.

TIKHON, Bishop
See the Arctic Bibliography, and T-4538 ff. See also B. Smith, *Preliminary Survey*.

TILTON, GEORGE FRED
Cap'n George Fred Himself. Garden City: Doubleday Doran, 1929. 295 pp. Alaskan Whaling.

TINGLE, GEORGE R.
See Wickersham's bibliography for listings of Senate testimony. Tingle was an expert on fisheries in the 1880's.

TLINGIT
See Indians.

TODD, A. L.
Abandoned. New York: McGraw-Hill, 1961. 323 pp. A.W. Greely in the Canadian Arctic in 1881-84.

TODD, JOHN W., Jr.
"Reflections of an Antiquarian Bookseller," *Puget Soundings*, December, 1960. Alaskan books.

TOKAREVA, T.
"Some Materials on the Craniology of the Aleuts," *Anthro. Ahurnal* (Moscow), 1937.

TOLAND, J.
Ships in the Sky: The Story of the Great Dirigibles. New York: Holt, 1957. 352 pp.

TOLLEMACHE, STRATFORD HALIDAY ROBERT LOUIS (b. 1864)
Reminiscences of the Yukon. London: Longmans, 1911. 316 pp.

TOLMACHOFF, INNOKENTY PAVLOVICH (1872-1950)
"Carcasses of the Mammoth and Rhinoceros Found in the Frozen Ground of Siberia," *Bulletin*, Geol. Soc. of Amer., 1928. Some history of finds. See also *Trans.*, Amer. Phil. Soc., 1929.
"The Use of the Divining Rod in Gold Prospecting in Alaska," *Science*, 1931.
Siberian Passage: An Explorer's Search into the Russian Arctic. New Brunswick: Rutgers University Press, 1949. 238 pp.
See also the Arctic Bibliography.

TOLMAN, STELLA W., et alii
Around the World. New York: The Morse Co., 1897-1901. 3v.

TOMASEVICH, JOZO
International Agreements on Conservation of Marine Resources. Palo Alto: Stanford University Press, 1943. 297 pp.

TOMLINSON, EVERETT TITSWORTH (b. 1859)
Three Boys in Alaska. New York: D. Appleton, 1928. 224 pp.

TOMPKINS, STUART RAMSAY (b. 1886)
Alaska: Promyshlennik and Sourdough. Norman, Okla.: University of Oklahoma Press, 1945. 350 pp.
Let's Read About Alaska. Grand Rapids: Fideler Co., 1949. 112 pp.
Life in America: Alaska. Grand Rapids: Fideler Co., 1958. 128 pp.
"Drawing the Alaska Boundary," *Canadian Historical Review*, 1945.
"Russia's Approach to America," *BC Hist. Q.*, 1949.
"The Klondike Gold Rush: A Great International Adventure," *BC Hist. Q.*, 1953.
"After Bering: Mapping the North Pacific," *BC Hist. Q.*, 1955.

TONGASS
Alaska Sportsman, March, '52 (last Tongass Indian dies); Jan., '54 (history of Ft. Tongass); July, '56 (last island resident dies); Aug., '56 (forest divided); Apr., '58 (Narrows); Baker (4 miles east of Cape Fox, Dixon Entrance; Tongass Island was Kut-tuk-wah in 1869); Bancroft (Ft. Tongass was first military post in Alaska); Dall (8' yellow cedars felled for Ft. Tongass in 1867); Gruening; Morris (history of Tongass natives); Smith, C.G.; Vancouver; Young (decimation of Tongass natives by smallpox and war with Haidas).

TOPHAM, HAROLD W.
"An Expedition to Mt. St. Elias," *Alpine Journal*, 1889.
"A Visit to the Glaciers of Alaska and Mt. St. Elias," *Proc.*, Royal Geog. Soc., 1889.

TORRES, CAMPOS, RAFAEL (1853-1904)
See the Arctic Bibliography.

TORRUBIA, JOSE (F. GIUSEPPIO)
See the Arctic Bibliography.

TOTEMS; TOTEM POLES
Alaska Life, March, '41; May, '41; July, '45 ("Talking Totems"); Nov., '47; *Alaska Sportsman*, see Index; *Alaska Weekly*, Nov., '50 (opposition to sale); Apr., '51 (Truman-Stalin totem); *Alaska-Yukon Magazine*, July, '07 (Pioneer Square, Seattle, totem); Apr., '08; Nov., '09; Oct., '11; Arctander (Duncan on social implications); Badlam (Wrangell); Barbeau (see the Arctic Bibliography); Belcher; Boas; Bright; Burroughs (Harriman: five or six taken from Tongass Island); Cameron; Campbell-Johnston; Carpenter (photo, grave totems); Chase; Clark; Cleveland; Colby; Collis (horrid); Corser; Crane; Dall (Yukon Indians); Davis; Deans; Denison; Dixon; Dorsey (*Popular Science*, 1898); Drucker; Eifert; Emmons; Franck; Farb; Frazer; Frobese; Garfield and Forrest; Garfield; Goddard; Goldenweiser (*J. Amer. Folklore*, 1910) (W-6405); Green, J.S.; Grinnell; Hambleton (see the Arctic Bibliography); Hawthorne (Bella Bella); Higginson; Hopkins (Ann. Rept., Smithsonian, 1918); Hulley; Inverarity; Jacobin; Jenness; Jewitt; Judson; Keithahn; Kintinnok (see Higginson); Kotzebue; Krause; Krieger; Langsdorff; LaPerouse; Lipke; Lisiansky; MacDowell; MacKenzie; Malaspina; Marchand; Maurelle; Mayol; Meares; Milacsek (see the Arctic Bibliography); Morris (Ft. Simpson Indians take down images; Rev. Crosby has totems burned; explanation of non-sale); Muir (Kadashan tells archaeologist he has committed sacrilege by cutting down totem); Niblack; Paul, F.L. (see Jacobin's *Guide*); Phillips, W.; Pilgrim; Potter (fed. gov't., not Alaska, restored totems); Pond (*Alaska Monthly*, 1906); Portlock; Raley; Ravenhill; Rickard; Rogers; Roquefeuil; Rossiter; Schmidt (*Anthropos*, 1914); Schwatka; Scidmore; Shelton; Shotridge; Simpson; Smith, C.W.; Smith, Harlan (*Amer. Mus. J.*, 1911); Stuck; Sundborg; Swanton; Tewkesbury; Underwood; Vancouver; Wickersham (*Sunset*, 1924); Willoughby; Wingert; Winslow; Winter and Pond (W-6424); Young (on the significance of women).

TOWER, W.
A History of the American Whale Fishery. Philadelphia: Lippincott, 1907. 245 pp.

TOWNLEY, SIDNEY DEAN and M. W. ALLEN
Descriptive Catalogue of Earthquakes on the Pacific Coast of the United States, 1769-1928. Berkeley: University of California Press, 1939. 297 pp.

TOWNSEND, CHARLES HASKINS (1859-1944)
"Notes on the Natural History and Ethnology of Northern Alaska," *Rept. of the Corwin*, 1885.
"Dredging and Other Records of Fish Commission Steamer *Albatross*," *Fish Commission Report*, 1900.
"Fur-seal and Seal Fisheries," *Bulletin*, Bur. of Fisheries, 1908.
"The Distribution of Certain Whales as Shown by Logbook Records of American Whales," *Zoologica*, 1935.

TOWNSEND, JOAN B. and SAM-JOE
"Archaeological Investigations at Pedro Bay, Alaska," *Anthrop. Papers*, University of Alaska, 1961. Lake Iliamna excavations, 1960.

TRACY ARM
Alaska Sportsman, Oct., '41; Aug., '46; July, '55; Oct., '56 (Ford's Terror Wilderness Area); Baker (named by Lt. Cmdr. Henry B. Mansfield, 1889, for Sec. of Navy Benj. Tracy); *Nat. Geog.*, 1947.

TRANTER, GLADDIS JOY (b. 1902)
Plowing the Arctic. London: Hodder and Stoughton, 1944. 256 pp.

TRATMAN, E. E. R.
"Alaska Highway," *Engineer*, 1943.

TREADGOLD, ARTHUR NEWTON CHRISTIAN
Report on the Goldfields of the Klondike. Toronto: Morang, 1899. 94 pp.

TREADWELL MINES
Alaska Sportsman, June, '46; July, '55 (actually 4 mines); *Alaska-Yukon Magazine*, Sept., '07; Burroughs; Christoe; Collis; Dole; Gruening (1917 disaster; US Sen. J. Jones [Nevada] stockholder); Higginson; Hulley (Jones secured Kinkead's appointment); Rickard; Scidmore; Underwood; Wickersham. See also James Foster ("The Western Federation Comes to Alaska" [*Pac. NW Q.*, October, 1975]).

TREES
See Arctic Bibliography.

TRELAWNEY-ANSELL, EDWARD CLARENCE
I Followed Gold. New York: Lee Furman, 1939. 321 pp. Gold rushes.

TRENCHARD, JOHN C.
"The Cliff Dwellers of King Island," *Pacific Horizons*, 1939.

TREZONE, C. E.
Cape Nome and the Northern Placer Mines. Seattle: Denny-Coryell, 1900. 45 pp.

TROUT
See Arctic Bibliography.

TROUT, PETER L.
My Experiences at Cape Nome, Alaska. Seattle: Lowman and Hanford, 1899. 42 pp.
New Theory Concerning the Origin and Deposition of Placer Gold. Seattle: Piggott, 1901. 82 pp.
"Reminiscences of John Muir," *Alaska-Yukon Magazine*, 1907.

TROUTMAN, ARTHUR
The Alaska Oil and Gas Handbook. Austin: Oil Frontiers Pub. Co., 1958. 76 pp.

TROY, JOHN WEIR (1868-1942) Governor of Alaska, 1933-39
Alaska Life, Oct., '39 (photo, notes); Aug., '40; *Alaska Sportsman*, June, '35 (photo); Dec., '39 (biog.); *Alaska Weekly*, May, '51 (Mt. Troy); Gruening (customs collector during Wilson administration; appointed by FDR); Hulley (came to Skagway during gold rush); Pilgrim; Shiels (delegate Dimond recommended appointment as governor); see also Wickersham's bibliography.

TRUMAN, BENJAMIN C.
Occidental Sketches. San Francisco: SF News Co., 1881. 212 pp. Summer in Alaska, 1869, on *Fideliter* with Capt. Kohl.

TRUSLER, JOHN
The Habitable World Described. London: the Author, 1787-1797. 20v. Vol. 5 descr. Aleutian Islands.
A Descriptive Account of the Islands Lately Discovered in the South Seas. London: 1778. Inc. Kamchatka.

TRUSLOW, FREDERICK KENT ·
"Return of the Trumpeter," *National Geographic,* 1960.

TUCK, RALPH (b. 1904)
See the Arctic Bibliography; USGS Bulletins on Moose Pass-Hope, Curry, Kashwitna-Willow Creek, Eska Creek, and Valdez Creek.
"Asymmetrical Topography in High Latitudes," *J. of Geol.,* 1935.
"The Loess of the Matanuska Valley," *J. of Geol.,* 1938.
"Origin of the Muck-silt Deposits at Fairbanks," *Bulletin,* Geol. Soc. of Amer., 1940.

TUCKER, EPHRAIM W.
Five Months in Labrador and Newfoundland. Concore: Boyd and White, 1839. 156 pp. Summer, 1838.
History of Oregon. Buffalo: A.W. Wilgus, 1844. 84 pp.

TUCKER, S.
"The Rainbow in the North," in *Rainbow of the North.* London: Nisbet, 1854. 222 pp. Episcopal Church in the Canadian Arctic.

TUPPER, CHARLES
Political Reminiscences. London: 1914.
Recollections of Sixty Years. New York: Cassell & Co., 1914.

TURNAGAIN ARM
Alaska Sportsman, March, '44 (photo; tides); March, '52; Dec., '52 (photo); Feb., '53; Feb., '56 (bore tide); Jan., '58; Apr., '58, and Index; Baker (former names); Cook; Learnard (*Compilation of Narratives*); Vancouver.

TURNER, JOHN HENRY (d. 1893)
"The Boundary North of Fort Yukon," *National Geog.,* 1893. See Baker.
"Results of Magnetic Observations at Stations (5) in Alaska," *Ann. Rept.,* US C&GS, 1892.

TURNER, LUCIEN McSHAN
"Notes on the Birds of the Nearest Islands," *Auk,* 1885.
Contributions to the Natural History of Alaska. Wn.DC: GPO, 1886. 226 pp. US Army Signal Corps, Yukon delta.
See also the Arctic Bibliography.

TURNER-TURNER, J.
Three Years' Hunting and Trapping in America. London: McClure & Co., 1888. 182 pp. Repr. New York: Arno Press, 1967.

TUSSING, ARLON R.
Fisheries Policy. College: University of Alaska, ISEGR, 1972. 344 pp.
Alaska Pipeline Report. College: University of Alaska, ISEGR, 1971. 237 pp.
See also State of Alaska.

TUTEIN, PETER
The Sealers. New York: Putnam's, 1938. 247 pp. Trans. from Danish, Eugene Gay-Tiffit.

TUTTLE, CHARLES RICHARD (b. 1848)
The Golden North: A Vast Country of Inexhaustible Gold Fields and of Illimitable Cereal and Stock Raising Capabilities. Chicago: Rand McNally, 1897. 307 pp.
Alaska: Its Meaning to the World, Its Resources, Its Opportunities. Seattle: Shorey & Co., 1914. 318 pp. Seattle C. of C. Appendix lists all newspapers and government officials.
See also the Arctic Bibliography.

TUTTLE, FRANCIS
Report of the Cruise of the Bear, 1896-98. Wn.DC: GPO, 1899. See also *Bear.*

TWEEDDALE, GEORGE WITEMAN (b. 1883)
North of 62°; A Story of Adventure. Buffalo: Foster and Stewart, 1946. 235 pp.

TWEEDSMUIR, Lord
Hudson's Bay Trader. New York: W.W. Norton, 1951. 195 pp. 1938-39.

TWENHOFEL, WILLIAM STEPHENS (b. 1918)
"Recent Shore-line Changes along the Pacific Coast of Alaska," *Amer. J. of Science,* July, 1952.

TWISS, Sir TRAVERS (1809-97)
The Oregon Question. London: Longman, 1846. 391 pp.
The Oregon Territory. New York: Appleton, 1846. 264 pp.

TYDINGS, MILLARD
Copper River and Northwestern Railway Company: Report. US Congress, Senate (77th Cong., 1st Sess.), 1941. On conveyance of the CR&NW RR right-of-way.

TYLER, ALICE FELT
The Foreign Policy of James G. Blaine. Minneapolis: University of Minnesota Press, 1927. Bering Sea controversy.

TYLER, CHARLES MARION
The Island World of the Pacific Ocean. San Francisco, 1887. 387 pp.

TYRRELL, JOSEPH BURR
Documents Relating to the Early History of Hudson Bay. Toronto: Tyrrell, 1931. 419 pp.
"The Gold of the Klondike," *Trans.,* Royal Soc. of Canada, 1912.
"The Basin of the Yukon River in Canada," *Scottish Geog. Magazine,* 1900.

TYTLER, PATRICK FRASER
Historical View of the Progress of Discovery of the More Northern Coasts of America. New York: Harper, 1836. 360 pp.

TYZHNOV, IL'IA
See the Arctic Bibliography, and T-4600 ff.

U

UDALL, STEWART L.
The Quiet Crisis. New York: Holt, Rinehart & Winston, 1963. 209 pp.

ULLMAN, JAMES R.
High Conquest: The Story of Mountaineering. Philadelphia: Lippincott, 1945. 427 pp.

UMNAK ISLAND
Alaska Life, March, '41 (teacher's article); Aug., '48 (photo, volcano); *Alaska Sportsman,* Jan., '39; Apr., '39; July, '39; March, '40 (sheep); Apr., '40; May, '40 (photo, village); Feb., '41 (shipwreck); June, '43; Dec., '45; June, '46 (secret air base); May, '49 (hay for Nikolski Bay cattle); Aug., '49; Apr., '54 (photo, Nikolski village); June, '56 (wool to Seattle); May, '57; Oct., '57 (reindeer); March, '58, and Index; Andreev (discovered, 1758-59); Baker; Bancroft; Colby; Cook; Coxe; Dall (great earthquake, 1817); Hulley (Glottov reached in 1759); Kitchener; Krenitsyn and Levashev; Masterson; Petrof (*Compilation of Narratives:* originally 11 villages, but population of 120 in 1880; volcanic eruptions in 1878 and 1880); Sauer; Tompkins.

UNALAKLEET (Unalaklik)
Alaska Sportsman, Sept., '46 (potatoes); Jan., '47 (photo, Eskimos); July, '47 (Degnan to Juneau); March, '48 (home grown vegetables); Feb., '50; Dec., '50 (photo); Dec., '51; May, '54 (opposition to reservation); Feb., '56 (photo); Sept., '56 (salmon derby); and Index; Allen; Baker; Carrighar; Colby; Couch (post office from 1901); Dall (trading post built at mouth of Unalaklik River, 1840); Hulley (Unalaklik River was portage route, Norton Sound to Yukon); James (small Russian fort, large native village); Machetanz (uncle was trader here); Moore (missionary Karlson); Poor; Stefansson; Stuck; Swineford; Whymper.

UNALASKA
Alaska Sportsman, Feb., '38 (photo, both sides of bay); July, '39 (photo); June, '40; Apr., '41 (port closed to foreign shipping, Jan., '41); Jan., '43 (photo, church); May, '43 (photo); Apr., '46; March, '55 (Fr. Baranoff); and Index; *Alaska Weekly,* July, '51; Sept., '51 (deputy marshal office

moved to Cold Bay); Andreev (discovered 1758-59); Andrews (Jesse Lee Home founded 1890); Baker (also Iliuliuk, founded by Soloviev between 1760 and 1770); Bancroft; Calasanz (Unalaska in 1888); Campbell; Chevigny; Colby; Cook (conferred here with Russians); Couch (post office: Unalaska, 1874; Ounalaska, 1888-98; Unalaska from 1898); Coxe (descr. natives; 16 huts in 1769; population of over 1000 reduced by famine, 1762); Dall; Dole; Davidson (weather data, Veniaminov, 1825-34); Elliott (Aleuts; Glottov, 1757); Gruening; Harriman (Burroughs); Hayes (Mt. Newhall); Henderson; Higginson; Hubbard; Hulley; Judge (photo; 200 pop., 1890); Kitchener (Chirikov sighted; Glottov here 1758; log church 1808; Veniaminov mission, 1825; Niebaum est. Alaska Comm. Co. store in 1868; hotel for transients, 1896; bombing, 1942); Krenitsyn and Levashev; Krusenstern; Ledyard; Lutke; Masterson; Miller; Morgan; Morris; Muir (*Corwin*); Ogilvie; Oliver; Petrof; Schwatka; Scidmore (mail route from Sitka, 1891, tourist route 1893); Shepard; Stuck; Swineford; Wead (gold rush conditions); Wickersham; Winchell; see also the Arctic Bibliography. See as well Veniaminov.

UNDERHILL, RUTH
Indians of the Pacific Northwest. Wn.DC: GPO, 1936. 232 pp. Education Division, US Office of Indian Affairs, Dept. of Interior.

UNDERWOOD, JOHN JASPER (b. 1871)
Alaska: An Empire in the Making. New York: Dodd, Mead, 1913. 440 pp. Underwood was at Dawson in 1899, and founded *Council City News* in 1902. General coverage. See also Wickersham's bibliography, and the Arctic Bibliography.

UNGA ISLAND
Alaska Sportsman, Feb., '38 (photo); July, '40 (cod fishing); Oct., '40; Feb., '49 (Apollo Mine, 1890-1906, yielded $3 million; lead and zinc prospects); Sept., '50; May, '57 (petrified tree stumps below water line, treeless island); Baker; Brooks (gold lode discovered 1884); Colby (Russian sea otter station); Couch; Dall (many lost in 1788 tidal wave); Dole; Golder (folklore); Hayes; Henderson; Higginson; Jackson; Kitchener; Petrof (frame buildings erected by prosperous sea otter hunters); Pinart (Aleut burial cave, 1871); Scidmore (cod fishery); Swineford (school erected at native expense); Whymper.

UNIMAK ISLAND
Alaska Sportsman, June, '46 (Scotch Cap Light destroyed by tidal wave, 5 lost); Dec., '46 (photos, Scotch Cap); Aug., '49 (Mt. Pogromni); Jan., '51 (*SS Mt. McKinley*); Oct., '57; *Alaska Weekly,* June, '51 (sulphur); Baker (Pogromni named by Sarychev; Cape Sarichef named by Lutke, 1828 for Gavrill Andreevich Sarychev); Chase (Fred Hardy); Colby; Dall (tidal wave, earthquake, volcanic eruption, 1827); Franck; Gibbs; Hubbard (buried aboriginal villages); Harrison; Hulley (Cook discovered Unimak Pass); Miller; Petrof; Scidmore; Snow; Swineford; Wickersham (Fred Hardy).

UNION BOOK and PUBLISHING CO.
Alaska and the Yukon Territory. Chicago, n.d. 16 pp.

UNION DIESEL ENGINE CO.
See T-4611.

UNION PACIFIC RAILROAD CO.
See T-4612 ff.

UNITED STATES [US]
In addition to those sources listed here, the student and researcher is advised to check the government records depository section of the nearest major library for more current materials. A very valuable repository is the Alaska Resources Library in Anchorage, with publications of federal agencies operating in Alaska. See US Nat. Archives.

US ADJUTANT-GENERAL'S OFFICE, MILITARY INFORMATION DIVISION
Reports of Explorations in the Territory of Alaska, 1898. Glenn and Abercrombie. Wn.DC: GPO, 1899. 464 pp. Includes the following: Abercrombie (Valdez); Brookfield (Valdez Glacier); Brown (Valdez miners); Cleave (Copper River); Glenn (Cook Inlet); Heinden (Lowe River to Copper River); Koehler (Copper River); Learnard (Portage to Turnagain Arm); Lowe; Preston (Valdez Glacier); Rafferty (Copper River); Yanert (Chunilna and Susitna Rivers).
Explorations in Alaska, 1899. Wn.DC: GPO, 1901. 77 pp. Herron, 1899, route for all-American overland route from Cook Inlet to the Yukon.

US AGRICULTURAL RESEARCH ADMINISTRATION
Alaska Insect Control Project. Wn.DC: GPO, 1947. 132 pp. Anchorage, Fairbanks, Valdez: mosquitoes, blackflies, no-see-ums, horseflies, deerflies.
Report on Exploratory Investigations of Agricultural Problems of Alaska. Wn.DC: GPO, 1949. 185 pp.

US AIR FORCE
Survival: Training Edition. AF Manual 64-3; Subsequent revisions, editions. Wn.DC: GPO, 1956. 373 pp.

US AIR FORCE, AIR WEATHER SERVICE
"The Automatic Weather Station takes over a Dreary Job," *Air Force Bulletin*, Nov., '52.
Report on Project Red Fang. Wn.DC: GPO, 1953. 20 pp. Amchitka Island automatic weather reporting station.
Climatology of the Arctic Regions. Wn.DC: GPO, 1946. 3v.
"Juneau Icefield Research Project," *Air Force Bulletin*, 1951.

US AIR FORCE, ALASKAN AIR COMMAND
See the Arctic Bibliography, and Air University, Maxwell AFB.

US AIR FORCE, ARCTIC WEATHER CENTRAL
Climate, Weather, and Flying Conditions of Alaska and Eastern Siberia. Elmendorf AFB, 1950. 52 pp.

US AIR FORCE, DIRECTORATE of INTELLIGENCE
Photo Interpretation of Arctic Territories. Wn.DC: GPO, 1951. 252 pp.

US AIR UNIVERSITY
Ice Fog and Air Base Location. Maxwell AFB, 1949. 19 pp. Numerous publications on various aspects of Air Force activity in Alaska; see library card index.

US ALASKA RAILROAD COMMISSION
Railway Routes in Alaska. Wn.DC: GPO, 1913. 172 pp. Commission, composed of J.J. Morrow, A.H. Brooks, L.M. Cox, and C.M. Ingersoll, appointed by Taft, examined the following routes: White Pass and Yukon RR; Haines-Fairbanks; Katalla and Controller Bay; Cordova-Fairbanks; Valdez-Fairbanks; Seward-Fairbanks; Iliamna-Kuskokwim. See Wickersham's bibliography, and the Arctic Bibliography for material on the Alaska Engineering Commission (railroad construction), Alaska Railroad, Alaska Railroad Commission, and Alaska Railroad Company. See Alaska Railroad.

US ALASKA RAILROAD RECORD
Published by the Alaska Railroad (Alaskan Engineering Commission) at Anchorage 1916-20. Official publication of the Commission.

US ALASKA RESOURCES LIBRARY
[Anchorage]
This valuable government repository is maintained by the US Interior Department, but houses a wide variety of current and occasional government (federal) publications. The collection is especially useful for materials on native claims settlement, on oil development, on other natural resource development and management, and on federal and state land use planning.

US ALASKA ROAD COMMISSION
Reports: 1905-1942. Issued irregularly. Original name was the US Board of Road Commissioners for Alaska. The commission was initially under the US Army. It is sometimes confused with the Alaska Territory Board of Road Commissioners, and the US Bureau of Roads under the jurisdiction of the Forest Service, Agriculture Department. In 1927 the US Army, Alaska Road Commission, was transferred to the US Dept. of Interior.

US ALASKAN ENGINEERING COMMISSION
Many records of the AEC are housed at the Alaska Railroad offices in Anchorage. These records cover the first 5 years of Anchorage town government.

US ALASKAN INTERNATIONAL HIGHWAY COMMISSION
Message from the President of the US. Wn.DC: GPO, 1940. 33 pp. History, routes, Alaska military highway.

US, AMERICAN and BRITISH CLAIMS ARBITRATION
Arbitration of Outstanding Claims between Great Britain and the US: The Favorite. Vancouver: Western Specialty, Printers, 1913. 28 pp. See the Wickersham bibliography.

US ARCTIC, DESERT, TROPIC INFORMATION CENTER
Glossary of Arctic and Subarctic Terms. Maxwell AFB, 1955. 90 pp.

US ARCTIC HEALTH RESEARCH CENTER
Activities Report. Wn.DC: GPO, 1951. 87 pp. Public Health Service, Bureau of State Services. See also the Arctic Bibliography.

US ARMY
Cold Facts for Keeping Warm. Wn.DC: GPO, 1952. 46 pp.
Building Alaska with the US Army, 1867-1958. Ft. Richardson, 1958. 168 pp.
The Army's Role in Building Alaska. Ft. Richardson, 1969. See Garfield, Driscoll, Potter, and Marston.

US ARMY, AIR CORPS
Arctic Manual. Wn.DC: GPO, 1940. 2v. Prepared by Vilhjalmur Stefansson.
Report of Cold Weather Detachment, 1942-43. Ladd Field, 1943. 2v. Includes laboratory reports.

US ARMY, CORPS of ENGINEERS
Harbors and Rivers in Alaska. Wn.DC: GPO, 1954. 98 pp. Reports on 75 localities, with notes on hydroelectric power incl.
Permafrost Reference Bibliography. Boston: Arctic Constr. and Frost Effects Lab., 1953. 195 pp.
Southeastern Alaska. Wn.DC: GPO, 1954.
Tanana River Basin, Alaska. Wn.DC: GPO, 1955. 88 pp.
Comprehensive Report: Investigation of Military Construction in Arctic and Subarctic Regions. Wn.DC: GPO, 1950. 68 pp.
Engineering Problems and Construction in Permafrost Regions. Wn.DC: GPO, 1956. 53 pp.

US ARMY, CORPS of ENGINEERS, CANADIAN ARMY ENGINEERS
Digest of Current Information on Permafrost. Alaskan Air Command, 1957. 57 pp.

US ARMY, CORPS OF ENGINEERS SNOW, ICE and PERMAFROST RESEARCH EST.
Some Aspects of Snow, Ice and Frozen Ground. Wilmette, Ill.: 1953. 32 pp.

US ARMY, DEPARTMENT of the COLUMBIA
Report of a Military Reconnaissance in Alaska. Wn.DC: GPO, 1885. 121 pp. Schwatka, 1883. See also Schwatka.
Report of an Expedition to the Copper, Tanana and Koyukuk Rivers. Wn.DC: GPO, 1887. 172 pp. Allen, 1885. See also Allen.

US ARMY MAP SERVICE
See the Arctic Bibliography.

US ARMY SERVICE FORCES, SPECIAL SERVICE DIVISION
A Pocket Guide to Alaska. Wn.DC: GPO, 1943. 52 pp.

US ARMY, SURGEON GENERAL'S OFFICE
"Frostbite," *Army Medical Bulletin*, 1943.
"Immersion Foot," *Army Medical Bulletin*, 1943.
"Trench Foot," *Army Medical Bulletin*, 1944. See also the Arctic Bibliography.

US BERING SEA CLAIMS COMMISSION
Fur Seal Arbitration: Proceedings. Wn.DC: GPO, 1895. 16v. The legal points having been established at Paris in 1893 through arbitration, the task of this commission was to investigate the facts and award claims on the basis of the law established. Sessions were held at Victoria in 1896 and 1897. See also the Arctic Bibliography and Wickersham's bibliography.

US BOARD on GEOGRAPHIC NAMES
Sixth Report, 1890-1932. Wn.DC: GPO, 1933. 834 pp.
"Orthography of Bering," *Bulletin*, Smithsonian Institution, 1890. Marcus Baker.
Decisions of the Board, 1919: Report of Subcommittee on System for Transliterating Russian Alphabetic Characters. See W-9379.
See also the Arctic Bibliography, and Catalog of Publications and Indexes to Decisions of the Board on Geographic Names.

US, BUREAU OF AMERICAN ETHNOLOGY, SMITHSONIAN INSTITUTION
Annual Reports. From 1881.
Bulletins. From 1887.

US BUREAU OF BIOLOGICAL SURVEY, DEPARTMENT OF AGRICULTURE
Biological Survey of the Pribilof Islands. Wn.DC: GPO, 1923. 255 pp.
Federal Laws relating to Wild Life in Alaska. Wn.DC: GPO, 1933. 12 pp.
Distribution of Game and Fur-Bearing Animals in Alaska, 1938. Wn.DC: GPO, 1939. 1 p., 25 maps.
Status of the American Bison in the US and Alaska. Wn.DC: GPO, 1939. 10 pp.

US BUREAU OF COMMERCIAL FISHERIES
Progress Report on Alaska Fishery Management and Research. Wn.DC: GPO, 1958-59. 2v. US F&WS.

US BUREAU OF CUSTOMS
Alaska Commerce in 1929. Wn.DC: GPO, 1930. 10 pp. Report of the Collector of Customs of Juneau, Alaska, relative to the shipment of gold and silver and merchandise from Alaska.

US BUREAU OF EDUCATION, DEPARTMENT OF THE INTERIOR
Annual Reports. From 1870.
Annual Reports on the Introduction of Domestic Reindeer into Alaska. 1890-1906.
English-Eskimo and Eskimo-English Vocabularies. Wn.DC: GPO, 1890. 72 pp. Bureau Information Circular.
Medical Handbook. Wn.DC: GPO, 1913. 179 pp. Bureau of Education, Alaska School Service.
See also US Office of Education; Arctic Bibliography; Wickersham's bibliography. See Education.
See also Bureau of Indian Affairs. See as well Sheldon Jackson. Education and medical services for Alaska natives were administered by the US Bureau of Education from 1884 until 1930 when they were transferred to the Bureau of Indian Affairs, which administered them through the Alaska Native Service. See D.H. Smith.

US BUREAU OF FISHERIES, DEPARTMENT OF COMMERCE
Reports of the US Commissioner of Fisheries,

1911-1945. Wn.DC: GPO, 1912-1948. Legislation, patrols, count, methods, etc.

Dredging and Hydrographic Records of the US Fisheries Steamer Albatross for 1906. Wn.DC: GPO, 1907. 49 pp. Dutch Harbor, Western Aleutians, Bering Sea, Petropavlovsk, Kurile Islands, Japan.

Statistical Review of the Alaska Salmon Fisheries. Wn.DC: GPO, 1928-33. Issued in four parts: Bristol Bay and the Alaska Peninsula; Chignik to Resurrection Bay; Prince William Sound, Copper River, Bering River; Southeast Alaska.

See also the Arctic Bibliography; see as well Baker for notes on the work of the Commission. See also US Fish and Wildlife Service.

US BUREAU OF FOREIGN AND DOMESTIC COMMERCE
Statistical Abstract of the US, 1941. Wn.DC: GPO, 1942. 1017 pp.

US BUREAU OF INDIAN AFFAIRS
Annotated Bibliography on Alaska. Juneau District Office: BIA, 1960. 50 pp. See also the Arctic Bibliography.

See US Bureau of Education. See Education. See also Alaska Natives. For original records see US National Archives.

US BUREAU OF INSULAR AFFAIRS, WAR DEPARTMENT
Compilation of Acts of Congress and Treaties relating to Alaska from March 30, 1867 to March 3, 1905. Wn.DC: GPO, 1906. 496 pp.

See also the Arctic Bibliography.

US BUREAU OF LAND MANAGEMENT
Agricultural Settlement Opportunities in Alaska: Anchorage. Wn.DC: GPO, 1947. 27 pp.

Areas Suitable for Group Agricultural Settlement in Alaska. Wn.DC: GPO, 1947. 5 pp.

Alaska: Information Relative to the Disposal and Leasing of Public Lands. Wn.DC: GPO, 1948. 24 pp.

Land Settlement and Resource Development along the Alaska Highway. Wn.DC: GPO, 1948. 7 pp.

Alaska Federal Land Withdrawals and Reservations. Wn.DC: GPO, 1958. 60 maps. See also the Arctic Bibliography, and Joint Federal-State Land Use Planning Commission est. under the 1971 Alaska Native Claims Settlement Act.

Orders Affecting Public Lands in Alaska, as of June 30, 1958. Wn.DC: GPO, 1959. 147 pp.

US BUREAU OF LIGHTHOUSES, DEPARTMENT OF COMMERCE
Light List, Incl. Fog Signals, Pacific Coast, US, Canada, Hawaiian and Samoan Islands. Wn.DC: GPO, 1912-41.

Pacific Coast of the US: Buoy List. Alaska: 16th Lighthouse District. Wn.DC: GPO, 1913-31. 18v. See also the Arctic Bibliography. See also Alaska Dept. of Parks.

US BUREAU OF MINES, DEPARTMENT OF THE INTERIOR
Annual Reports. 1917-23. Wn.DC: GPO, 1917-24. Reports of Mine Inspectors. See also the Arctic Bibliography.

Minerals Yearbook. Wn.DC: GPO, 1934-49. 15v.

US BUREAU OF PRISONS
Social Service Resource Directory: Alaska. Wn.DC: GPO, 1938. 33 pp.

US BUREAU OF PUBLIC HEALTH SERVICE;
see US TREASURY DEPARTMENT

US BUREAU OF RECLAMATION
Eklutna Project, Alaska. Juneau, 1948. 97 pp.

Eklutna Dam, Power Plant and Tunnel. Wn.DC: GPO, 1958. 254 pp.

Alaska: A Reconnaissance Report on the Potential of Water Resources. Wn.DC: GPO, 1952. 287 pp. See also the Arctic Bibliography.

US BUREAU OF SHIPS
"Ships against Ice," *Journal,* US Bur. of Ships, Aug., 1954. Ice-breaker operations: *Glacier, Atka, Burton Island, Northwind.*

US BUREAU OF STANDARDS
"Alaskan Eclipse Expedition," *Journal,* Franklin Inst., April, 1951. US Naval Res. Lab. exped. to Attu, 1950.

US BUREAU OF STATISTICS, DEPARTMENTS OF COMMERCE AND LABOR
"Commercial Alaska, 1867-1903," *Summary of Commerce and Finance,* 1903.

US BUREAU OF STATISTICS, TREASURY DEPARTMENT
Commercial Alaska in 1901. Repr. from *Summary of Commerce and Finance.* See above.

US BUREAU OF THE CENSUS, DEPARTMENT OF COMMERCE
Tenth Census: Alaska. 47th Cong., 1st Sess., House Misc. Doc. 64, Part 2. Ivan Petrof.

Report of Population, Industries, and Resources of Alaska. Wn.DC: GPO, 1884. 189 pp.

Eleventh Census: Alaska. 52nd Cong., 1st Sess., House Misc. Doc. 340, Part 7. Scidmore, Applegate, Schanz, Greenfield, Woolfe, et alii.

"Population of Alaska (Natives)," *Bulletin,* 11th Census. 7 pp. J.W. Kelly, Capt. M.A. Healey. 1891.

"Fish and Fisheries: Marine Mammalia," *Bulletin,* 11th Census.

"The Census of Alaska," *Bulletin,* 11th Census. 6 pp. Petrof.

Wealth and Resources of Alaska. Repr. from *Bulletin,* 11th Census. Ivan Petrof.

Alaska: Statistics of Population, 1890. Repr. from *Bulletin,* 11th Census. 9 pp. Petrof, Bruce, Boursin.

Twelfth Census: Alaska. Population by Districts and Minor Civil Divisions. 56 Cong., 1st Sess., House Misc. Doc. 26, 1901. See the Arctic Bibliography.

Report on the Cape Nome Mining Region. 56th Cong., 1st Sess., Sen. Doc. 357. 12 pp.

Thirteenth Census: Statistics for Alaska. Repr. of Supplement. Wn.DC: GPO, 1913. 71 pp.

Indian Population in the US and Alaska. Wn.DC: GPO, 1915. 285 pp.

Population: Alaska. *Bulletin,* 1912. 5 pp. by judicial districts.

Fourteenth Census: Population, Alaska. Wn.DC: GPO, 1921. 4 pp.

Population: Alaska. Occupational Statistics.

Wn.DC: GPO, 1921. 9 pp.

Population: Alaska. Composition and Characteristics of the Population. Wn.DC: GPO, 1921. 13 pp.

Population of Outlying Possessions. Wn.DC: GPO, 1921. 11 pp.

Fourteenth Census of the US: Instructions to Special Agents. Wn.DC: GPO, 1919. 24 pp.

Fifteenth Census, 1930. Number and Distribution of Inhabitants, Composition and Characteristics of the Population, Occupations, Unemployment, and Agriculture. Wn.DC: GPO, 1930.

Outlying Possessions: Number and Distribution of Inhabitants. Wn.DC: GPO, 1932. 338 pp.

The Indian Population of the US and Alaska. Wn.DC: GPO, 1937. 238 pp.

Population — Agriculture: Final Bulletin. Wn.DC: GPO, 1931. 24 pp.

Sixteenth Census. Wn.DC: GPO, 1941. 7 pp. Alaska.

Population Characteristics. Wn.DC: GPO, 1943. 20 pp.

Territory of Alaska: Population, Composition and Characteristics. Wn.DC: GPO, 1941. 35 pp.

Agriculture: Territories and Possessions, etc. Wn.DC: GPO, 1943. 306 pp.

16th Census of the US: 1940. Census of Business: 1939. Alaska, Hawaii and Puerto Rico. Wn.DC: GPO, 1943. 42 pp.

Seventeenth Census: Census of Population, 1950. Number of Inhabitants, Alaska. Wn.DC: GPO, 1952. 8 pp.

Census of Population: General Characteristics. Wn.DC: GPO, 1952. 48 pp.

Census of Population, 1950: Detailed Characteristics. Wn.DC: GPO, 1952. 60 pp. Age, race, sex, non-native and aboriginal.

Eighteenth Census, 1960: Census of Population. Wn.DC: GPO, 1960. 19 pp.

Nineteenth Census, 1970: Census of Population. Wn.DC: GPO, 1970. 28 pp.

See the Arctic Bibliography.

US BUSINESS AND DEFENSE SERVICES ADMINISTRATION, OFFICE OF DISTRIBUTION

Alaska: Its Economy and Market Potential. Wn.DC: GPO, 1959. 61 pp.

US CIVIL AERONAUTICS ADMINISTRATION

Alaska Flight Information Manual. Wn.DC: GPO, 1954. 47 pp.

US CIVIL AERONAUTICS BOARD

Territorial Air Routes of US Carriers. Maps. Wn.DC: GPO, 1953. See also the Arctic Bibliography.

Alaska Air Transportation Investigation. Wn.DC: GPO, 1941. 27 pp. Examiner's Report.

See also reports on accidents, Arctic Bibliography. See also Nat. Air Transp. Safety Board.

US CIVIL SERVICE COMMISSION

See the Arctic Bibliography.

US COAST AND GEODETIC SURVEY

Coast Pilot of Alaska. From Southern Boundary to Cook's Inlet. George Davidson. Wn.DC: GPO, 1869. 251 pp. This is the first part; the second part did not appear until 1916.

Pacific Coast Pilot. Alaska. Part I, 2nd Ed. Dixon Entrance to Yakutat Bay. Dall and Baker. Wn.DC: GPO, 1883. 333 pp.

Pacific Coast Pilot. Coast and Islands of Alaska. 2nd Series. Wn.DC: GPO, 1879. 375 pp. Actually an appendix to the 2nd Edition. William Dall.

Pacific Coast Pilot. Alaska. Part I. 3rd Ed. Dixon Entrance to Yakutat Bay. Henry E. Nichols. Wn.DC: GPO, 1891. 243 pp.

US Coast Pilot. Pacific Coast. Alaska. Part I. 4th Ed. Graves and Francis. Wn.DC: GPO, 1901. 246 pp. See Baker.

US Coast Pilot. Pacific Coast. Alaska. Part I. 5th Ed. Graves. Wn.DC: GPO, 1908. 239 pp.

There have been numerous subsequent editions of the first part of the coast survey. See the Arctic Bibliography.

US Coast Pilot. Pacific Coast. Alaska. Part II. 1st Ed. Yakutat Bay to Arctic Ocean, including Aleutian Islands. R.S. Patton and A.L. Giacomini. Wn.DC: GPO, 1916. 303 pp.

For subsequent editions see the Arctic Bibliography.

See also the following:

"Report on the Method, Scope, and Completion of a History of Maritime Discovery and Exploration of the Western Coast of the US," *US Coast Survey Report,* 1857. Appendix 52. J.G. Kohl.

"History of Discovery and Exploration on the Coast of the United States," *Annual Report,* US C&GS, 1884.

"An Examination of Some of the Early Voyages of Discovery and Exploration on the Northwest Coast of America from 1539 to 1603," *Annual Report,* US C&GS, 1886. George Davidson.

Coast and Geodetic Survey: Its History, Activities and Organization. Baltimore: Johns Hopkins University Press, 1923. 107 pp. Gustavus Weber.

The Coast and Geodetic Survey, 1807-1957: 150 Years of History. Wn.DC: GPO, 1957. 89 pp. Joseph Wraight and Elliott B. Roberts.

Safeguard the Gateways of Alaska: Her Waterways. Wn.DC: GPO, 1918. 41 pp.

Earthquake History of the US. Wn.DC: GPO, 1938. 85 pp. See also Alaska Earthquakes. This volume contains a chronological list of disturbances, 1788-1937.

See also the Arctic Bibliography for more recent publications on concerns of the Coast and Geodetic Survey. See the Arctic Bibliography also for materials on charts, manuals, tables, etc.

US COAST GUARD

"The Coast Guard in Northern Waters," *Proc.,* US Naval Inst., January, 1950.

Complete List of Lights and Other Marine Aids. Vol. I-V, corrected to Jan. 1, 1955. Wn.DC: GPO, 1955. 288 pp.

Lighthouses and Lightships of the US. Boston: Houghton Mifflin, 1917. 308 pp. George R. Putnam.

US COMMISSION, ALASKA EXHIBIT, LOUISIANA PURCHASE EXPOSITION, 1904

The Exhibition of the District of Alaska. St. Louis: Woodward and Tiernan, 1904. 55 pp.

US COMMISSION to STUDY the PROPOSED HIGHWAY to ALASKA

Report of the Commission, 1933. Wn.DC: GPO, 1933. 116 pp.

US CONGRESS, JOINT COMMITTEE HEARINGS

Misc. matters, incl. Cunningham coal claims and charges by Glavis. See W-9387-91. 1910-1911.

US CONGRESS, HOUSE, COMMITTEE ON AGRICULTURE

Reindeer; Agricultural Experiment Stations; Wildlife Protection. See W-9775; W-9919-22; Fuller 1008 ff.

US CONGRESS, HOUSE, COMMITTEE ON APPROPRIATIONS

W-9776-78, Hearings, 1915-1919; W-9924-27, Reports, 1896, 1911-15 (railroad, Coast Guard, mineral resources, boundary, influenza, public buildings).

US CONGRESS, HOUSE, COMMITTEE ON INTERSTATE AND FOREIGN COMMERCE

W-9793-94, Hearings, 1915, 1924; W-9966-88, Reports, 1898-1916, 1924 (Revenue Cutter Service [new vessels]; Coast Guard; Lighthouse Service; bridges).

Report. H. Res. 11019 (medals for Jarvis, Ellsworth Bertholf and Call); 57th Cong., 1st Sess., House Report 2336.

Hearing. H. Res. 4520 and H. Res. 5926 (amendment to the Civil Aeronautics Act of 1938); Wn.DC: GPO, 1957. 59 pp.

Report. The International Geophysical Year: the Arctic, Antarctica. 85th Cong., 2nd Sess., House Report No. 1348. Wn.DC: GPO, 1958. 182 pp. Dr. H. Odishaw. See also *Science*, January, 1958.

US CONGRESS, HOUSE, COMMITTEE ON JUDICIARY

W-9795-98, Hearings, 1911, 1921-24; W-9990-10007, Reports, 1898-1911, 1920-24 (coal fraud cases, unlawful sealing, Bering Sea controversy claims, court organization, business and commercial taxes).

Report. H. Res. 24747; 59th Cong., 2nd Sess., House Report 6748 (court appeals procedure), 1907.

Report. S. 4205, 66th Cong., 2nd Sess., House Report, 968 (judicial district boundaries), 1920.

US CONGRESS, HOUSE, COMMITTEE ON LABOR

Report. H. Res. 9021; 76th Cong., 3rd Sess., Serial No. 10442 (wage rates, public works projects), 1940.

US CONGRESS, HOUSE, COMMITTEE ON MERCHANT MARINE AND FISHERIES

W-9799-9809, Hearings, 1910-24; W-10009-27, Reports, 1888-1924 (protection and regulation of fisheries, shipping conditions, Merchant Marine, sealing).

Report. Investigation of the Fur-seal and other Fisheries of Alaska. H. Res. 12432; 50th Cong., 2nd Sess., House Report No. 3883 (incl. testimony of H.W. Elliott, his map showing AC Co. posts; Ed Schieffelin and various natives' testimony re: AC Co. operations), 1889.

Hearings. Fish Traps in Alaskan Waters. H. Res. 4254 and H. Res. 8213; 74th Cong., 2nd Sess.; Wn.DC: GPO, 1936. 288 pp.

Hearings. Alaskan Fisheries. H. Res. 5476; 76th Cong., 3rd Sess.; Wn.DC: GPO, 1940. 158 pp. Est. Alaska Fisheries Commission.

Hearings. Alaska Fisheries. H. Res. 162; 76th Cong., 3rd Sess. (transfer of control of Alaska fisheries from the federal government to the territorial legislature, abolition of fish traps); Wn.DC: GPO, 1939-40. 4 parts.

Report. Giving Effect to the Provisional Fur Seal Agreement of 1942. H. Res. 2924; 78th Cong., 1st Sess., House Report No. 746 (Japanese abrogation of the agreement); Wn.DC: GPO, 1943. 30 pp.

Report. Merchant Marine and Fisheries Problems, Alaska. Also *Hearings.* 85th Cong., 1st Sess. Wn.DC: GPO, 1957. 322 pp.

Hearings. Misc. Fish and Wildlife Legislation. 86th Cong., 1st Sess. Wn.DC: GPO, 1960. 294 pp. Also proposed Arctic Wildlife Range.

See also the Arctic Bibliography; see also Fuller's bibliography, esp. for material between 1930-40.

US CONGRESS, HOUSE, COMMITTEE ON MILITARY AFFAIRS

W-10028-32, Reports, 1842, 1886-1912 (est. post; exploration).

Report. Relief of People in the Yukon River Country. 55th Cong., 3rd Sess., House Doc. No. 244. Wn.DC: GPO, 1899. 123 pp. Contains correspondence of Capt. P.H. Ray re: Sheldon Jackson; also correspondence of Ray and Richardson re: conditions at Ft. Yukon, Circle City, etc.

Hearings. Roads and Trails in Alaska. 64th Cong., 1st Sess. Wn.DC: GPO, 1917. 16 pp. Incl. statements of Wickersham and Richardson.

Report. Amendment to Sect. 40, National Defense Act. H. Res. 9391; 76th Cong., 3rd Sess. (ROTC, Univ. of Alaska); House Report No. 2510.

Report. Military Code for Alaska. H. Res. 5822; 77th Cong., 1st Sess., 1941.

US CONGRESS, HOUSE, COMMITTEE ON CLAIMS

W-9779-81, Hearings, 1910, 1916; W-9929-36, Report, 1904-16; 1923-24 (Wales Island Packing Co., fur seal investigations, victims of wreck of cutter *Tahoma*, AC Co.).

US CONGRESS, HOUSE, COMMITTEE ON COMMERCE

W-9937-41, Reports, 1861, 1884-90 (Perry McD. Collins; refuge stations near Pt. Barrow).

US CONGRESS, HOUSE, COMMITTEE ON EDUCATION

W-9942-43, Reports, 1891, 1908 (experiment station in SE Alaska; compulsory education for Alaska natives).

US CONGRESS, HOUSE, COMMITTEE ON ELECTIONS

W-9782-84, Hearings, 1918-20; W-9944-48, 1882-83, 1918-21 (petition for M. Ball; contested election, Wickersham and Sulzer/Grigsby).

US CONGRESS, HOUSE, COMMITTEE ON EXPENDITURES IN THE DEPARTMENT OF COMMERCE AND LABOR

W-9785-88, Hearings, 1912-13; W-9949-51, Reports, 1913-14 (fur seal industry).

US CONGRESS, HOUSE, COMMITTEE ON EXPENDITURES IN THE INTERIOR DEPARTMENT

W-9789, Hearings, W-9952, Report, 1911 (Chugach National Forest).

US CONGRESS, HOUSE, COMMITTEE ON EXPENDITURES IN THE WAR DEPARTMENT

Report on Return of Salmon to Packers. March 2, 1921. 14 pp. Mr. Graham of Illinois. W-9953.

US CONGRESS, HOUSE, COMMITTEE ON FOREIGN AFFAIRS

W-9790 ff, Hearings, 1908, 1912 (Canadian boundary; bill to approve convention, fur seals and otters).

W-9956-63, Reports, 1893-1914 (fur seals, seizures, convention).

Transmitting Information Concerning the Treaty with Russia. W-9954. See also National Archives and Record Service microfilm on documents relating to the transfer.

Favoring Passage of a Bill Making Appropriations. W-9955.

US CONGRESS, HOUSE, COMMITTEE ON GOVERNMENT OPERATIONS

Observations and Findings of the Subcommittee to make studies in Alaska and the Far East. 81st Cong., 1st Sess. Wn.DC: GPO, 1949. 28 leaves.

Alaska Native Loan Program: 25th Report. Wn.DC: GPO, 1958. 40 pp. 4 communities in SE Alaska related to canneries. Majority and minority reports. BIA.

US CONGRESS, HOUSE, COMMITTEE ON INTERIOR AND INSULAR AFFAIRS

Alaska. Hearings before the Subcommittee on Territorial and Insular Possessions of the Committee on Public Lands. 80th Cong., 1st Sess., House Resolution 93. Aug., '47. Wn.DC: GPO, 1948. 420 pp.

Report. Authorizing a Program of Useful Public Works for the Development of the Territory of Alaska. S.855. Wn.DC: GPO, 1949. 9 pp.

Alaska's Vanishing Frontier. Subcommittee on Territories and Insular Possessions. William H. Hackett, staff consultant. Wn.DC: GPO, 1951. 88 pp.

Report. H. Res. authorizing Committee on Interior and Insular Affairs to conduct an Investigation of the Bureau of Indian Affairs. Wn.DC: GPO, 1953. 1594 pp. House Report No. 2503, 82nd Cong., 2nd Sess. A basic reference on Alaska natives. Contains BIA's own report of its activities. Statistical data on natives.

Alaska. Hearings, H. Res. 30. 1955. Social and economic conditions in Alaska. Wn.DC: GPO, 1956. 5 parts.

Statehood for Alaska. Hearings, H. Res. 50. Wn.DC: GPO, 1957. 499 pp.

Report. Providing for the Admission of the State of Alaska into the Union. H. Res. 7999. Wn.DC: GPO, 1957. 499 pp. See also the bibliography in Naske's Interpretive History of Statehood.

Report. Transport Requirements for the Growth of Northwest North America. Report of the Alaska International Rail and Highway Commission. Battelle Memorial Inst. Wn.DC: GPO, 1961. 3v.

Known popularly as the Battelle Report. 87th Cong., 1st Sess., House Doc. No. 176.

See the Arctic Bibliography for further reports and hearings associated with the Committee on Interior and Insular Affairs, particularly those dealing with oil exploration and development, with the nomination of Walter Hickel as Secretary of Interior, and with the Alaska Native Claims Settlement Act of 1971. See also Government Documents depository, nearest major library. See United States.

US CONGRESS, HOUSE, COMMITTEE ON MINES AND MINING

W-9811-13, Hearings, 1910-24; W-10033-35, Reports, 1914-25. Safety measures, mining code.

US CONGRESS, HOUSE, COMMITTEE ON NAVAL AFFAIRS

W-9814-16, Hearings, 1899-1913 (Alaska coal as fuel for US Navy).

Report. Jeanette Inquiry. 48th Cong., 1st Sess., House Misc. Doc. No. 66 (unfair treatment of Jerome J. Collins by Lt. G. deLong on the Jeannette, with commentary on conditions, and search in the Lena delta, 1882); Wn.DC: GPO, 1884. 1046 pp.

US CONGRESS, HOUSE, COMMITTEE ON POST OFFICE AND CIVIL SERVICE

Hearing. Fourth-class Mail Matter in Alaska and Hawaii. H. Res. 9873, H. Res. 9892, S. 2869 (restoration of previous regulations); 86th Cong., 2nd Sess., 1960.

US CONGRESS, HOUSE, COMMITTEE ON POST OFFICES AND POST ROADS

W-10036-37, Reports, 1913, 1924 (use of air routes for mail). See also Fuller 1155-61.

US CONGRESS, HOUSE, COMMITTEE ON PRINTING

W-10038-53, Reports, 1886 (L.M. Turner), 1884, 1885 (Corwin), 1890 (courts in Alaska), 1892 (Paris tribunal), 1896 (fur seals, salmon), 1897 (Governor's Report), 1900 (Bear), 1900, 1901 (agricultural investigations), 1898 (further civil government), 1901, 1911 (copies of Copper River reports), 1913 (laws applicable to the territory).

US CONGRESS, HOUSE, COMMITTEE ON PUBLIC BUILDINGS AND GROUNDS

W-9817-21, Hearings, 1914-21; W-10054-58, Reports, 1882, 1914-22 (public buildings at Juneau, Fairbanks, Cordova, Nome; transfer of Sitka building to Presbyterian mission).

US CONGRESS, HOUSE, COMMITTEE ON PUBLIC EXPENDITURES

Report. Allegations in Connection with the Purchase of Alaska. 40th Cong., 3rd Sess., 1869. 41 pp. C.T. Hulburd.

US CONGRESS, HOUSE, COMMITTEE ON PUBLIC LANDS

W-9822-38, Hearings, 1902-17, 1924; W-10060-10123, Reports, 1877, 1890-1924 (agricultural and oil lands, coal lands, timber, railroads, townsites, school, park and commercial uses, Cordova and Controller Bay, extension of land laws, mining claims, homesteads).

Hearings. H. Res. 13113; Leasing of Coal and Coal Lands in Alaska. 62nd Cong., 2nd Sess. Wn.DC: GPO, 1912. 74 pp.

Hearings. Alaska Coal Leasing Bill. H. Res. 13137 (testimony incl. Wickersham, Franklin K. Lane, A.H. Brooks, Falcon Joslin); 63rd Cong., 2nd Sess., 2 parts (267 pp.).

Hearings. To Establish Mt. McKinley National Park. H. Res. 14775; 64th Cong., 1st Sess., 1916. 39 pp.

Report. Mt. McKinley. S. 5716. W-10110. 2 pp.

Report. Abolition of 80-rod Reserved Shore Spaces between Claims on Shore Waters in Alaska. 66th Cong., 2nd Sess., 1920. 6 pp. See also Gruening.

Report. Reorganizing the System of Land Offices and Districts in Alaska. H. Res. 6601; 77th Cong., 2nd Sess. Wn.DC: GPO, 1942. 4 pp.

Hearings. Alaska Veterans' Homesteading Act, 1947. H. Res. 868, H. Res. 4059, H. Res. 4060; 80th Cong., 1st Sess. Wn.DC: GPO, 1947. 260 pp. Lemke and Peden bills.

Report. Compilation of Material Relating to the Indians and the Territory of Alaska, including certain laws and treaties affecting such Indians. H. Res. 66; 81st Cong., 2nd Sess. Wn.DC: GPO, 1950. 1110 pp. Statistical and General Information. Incl. data on 155 villages. See also US Congress, House, Committee on Interior and Insular Affairs.

US CONGRESS, HOUSE, COMMITTEE ON REVISION OF LAWS

W-10124-28, Reports, 1898-1902 (criminal law codification, further provisions for civil government, formation of private corporations).

US CONGRESS, HOUSE, COMMITTEE ON RIVERS AND HARBORS

W-9839-40, Hearings, 1904, 1922 (river mouth improvement, Nome, Wrangell).

W-10129, Report, 1904 (amend S. 3844, Snake River mouth, Nome).

Hearings. Improvement of Petersburg Harbor. Wn.DC: GPO, 1933. 10 pp. 72nd Cong., 2nd Sess. (This selection is representative only.)

US CONGRESS, HOUSE, COMMITTEE ON ROADS

Hearings. Roads. H. Res. 4442, H. Res. 8368 (constr. of highway to connnect northwest US with BC, YT, and Alaska); 71st Cong., 2nd Sess. Wn.DC: GPO, 1930. 18 pp.

Hearing. Survey, Location, Construction of Highway to Alaska. S. 1374; Wn.DC: GPO, 1935. 9 pp. 74th Cong., 1st Sess.

Hearings. Proposed Highway to Alaska. H. Res. 3095; 77th Cong., 2nd Sess. Wn.DC: GPO, 1942. 131 pp.

Report. The Alaska Highway. H. Res. 255; 79th Cong., 2nd Sess. Wn.DC: GPO, 1946. 323 pp.

US CONGRESS, HOUSE, COMMITTEE ON RULES

W-10130-36, Reports, 1900-19 (salaries of officers in Alaska; railroad construction; Alaska Central RR; Ballinger reports; Alaska Engineering Commission).

US CONGRESS, HOUSE, COMMITTEE ON THE CIVIL SERVICE

Hearings. The Alaska Railroad. H. Res. 5736 (re-tirement); 74th Cong., 2nd Sess. Wn.DC: GPO, 1936. 49 pp.

Report. Retirement, Employees, Alaska Railroad. S. 2293; 74th Cong., 2nd Sess., House Report 3011. Wn.DC: GPO, 1936. 7 pp.

Report. Alaska Railroad Retirement. H. Res. 8046; 76th Cong., 3rd Sess., House Report 2343. Wn.DC: GPO, 1940. 5 pp.

US CONGRESS, HOUSE, COMMITTEE ON THE TERRITORIES

W-9841-9909, Hearings, 1902-24; W-10138-10250, Reports, 1880-1924 (coal leases; agricultural development; fishing; care of insane; non-native indigent assistance; liquor prohibition; incorporation of cities; Territory of Alaska; M.D. Ball; delegate; legislative assembly; civil government; Alaska Pacific Railroad; Valdez, Marshall Pass and Northern RR; Alaska Short Line RR; Council City and Solomon River RR; Copper River and Northwestern RR; Alaska Northern RR; Nome to Kuguruk RR).

Hearings. Territory of Alaska. H. Res. 30; 58th Cong., 2nd Sess. Wn.DC: GPO, 1904. 24 pp.

Hearings. Conditions in Alaska. 62nd Cong., 2nd Sess. Wn.DC: GPO, 1912. 197 pp. Incl. testimony of Wickersham, Bishop Rowe, Gov. Walter Clark, J.J. Underwood.

Hearings. Transportation. 62nd Cong., 2nd Sess. Wn.DC: GPO, 1912. 173 pp.

Hearings. The Building of Railroads in Alaska. H. Res. 1739, H. Res. 1806, H. Res. 2145; 63rd Cong., 1st Sess. Wn.DC: GPO, 1913. 467 pp.

Hearings. Commission Form of Government in Alaska. H. Res. 15763. 63rd Cong., 2nd Sess. Wn.DC: GPO, 1914. 95 pp.

Hearings. Construction of Alaska Railroad. H. Res. 7417; 66th Cong., 1st Sess. Wn.DC: GPO, 1919. 201 pp. Increase of appropriated funds.

Hearings. Bill to Repeal law allowing Territory of Alaska to Tax the Fisheries. H. Res. 9527; 64th Cong., 1st Sess. Wn.DC: GPO, 1916. 5 parts.

Hearings. Nome-Shelton-Kuguruk River-Keewalik Project. H.J. Res. 60; 68th Cong., 1st Sess. 14 pp.

Report. Penal Colonies in Alaska. 49th Cong., 1st Sess., House Report 1685. 1 pp. C.S. Baker.

Report. Care of Insane. S. 3035; 58th Cong., 2nd Sess., House Report 2743. 1 pp.

Report. Donate Ft. Davis Buildings to Women's Home Missionary Society for the Methodist Episcopal Church, for a hospital at Nome. H.J.Res. 249; 67th Cong., 2nd Sess., House Report 560. 2 pp.

Hearing. Road, Trail and Tramway Construction, Seward Peninsula. H.J. Res. 48; 70th Cong., 1st Sess. Wn.DC: GPO, 1928. 22 pp.

Hearings. Repeal of Certain Dry Laws. H. Res. 499; 72nd Cong., 1st Sess. Wn.DC: GPO, 1932. 70 pp.

Report. Prohibit Manufacture and Sale of Alcoholic Liquors. S. 2729; 73rd Cong., 2nd Sess. Wn.DC: GPO, 1934. 4 pp.

Report. Referendum on One-House Legislature for Alaska. H. Res. 6651; 75th Cong., 1st Sess., House Report 1210. Wn.DC: GPO, 1937. 2 pp.

Hearing. Alaska Legislation. H. Res. 5126 (reindeer); 75th Cong., 1st Sess. Wn.DC: GPO, 1937. 33 pp.

Report. Reindeer Industry in Alaska. S. 1722; 75th Cong., 1st Sess., House Report 1188. Wn.DC: GPO, 1937. 8 pp.

Hearing. Tax on Freight and Passenger Transportation in Alaska. S. 2254; 75th Cong., 1st Sess. Wn.DC: GPO, 1937. 30 pp.

Report. License Tax on Alaska. S. 2254; 75th Cong., 1st Sess., House Report 1137. Wn.DC: GPO, 1937. 6 pp.

Report. Preventing Aliens from Fishing in the Waters of Alaska. H. Res. 10432; 75th Cong., 3rd Sess., House Report 2243. Wn.DC: GPO, 1938. 4 pp.

Report. Convey Tract of Land to the University of Alaska. H. Res. 9912 (fromthe Tongass National Forest for experimentation); 75th Cong., 3rd Sess., House Report 2225. Wn.DC: GPO, 1938. 2 pp.

Hearings. H. Res. 4868; H. Res. 2413; H. Res. 161 (hotel, Mt. McKinley; water supply, Ketchikan; homestead, Hawaii); 76th Cong., 1st Sess. 17 pp.

Hearings. Slum Clearance and Low-cost Housing, Alaska. H. Res. 8884; 76th Cong., 3rd Sess. Wn.DC: GPO, 1940. 11 pp.

Report. Slum Clearance in Alaska. H. Res. 8884; 76th Cong., 3rd Sess., House Report 2027. Wn.DC: GPO, 1940. 2 pp.

Report. Authorizing Legislature of Alaska to Create Corporate Authority to Undertake Slum Clearance. H. Res. 93; 77th Cong., 1st Sess., House Report 504.

Report. Protection of Walruses in Alaska. H. Res. 1606; 77th Cong., 1st Sess., House Report 883.

Hearing. Alaska Legislation. S. 1289 (conveyance of Copper River and Northwestern RR); 77th Cong., 1st Sess. Wn.DC: GPO, 1941. 10 pp.

Report. Care of Insane. S. 2248; 77th Cong., 2nd Sess., House Report 2364. Wn.DC: GPO, 1942. 5 pp.

Hearings. Geophysical Institute, University of Alaska. H. Res. 4785, H. Res. 6431, H. Res. 6486; 79th Cong., 2nd Sess. Wn.DC: GPO, 1946. 60 pp.

Hearings. Study and Investigation of the Various Questions and Problems relating to the Territory of Alaska. H. Res. 236; 79th Cong., 1st Sess. Wn.DC: GPO, 1946. 236 pp. Statehood; Highway construction; Municipality financing; Election of governor; Interior control of natives; Fisheries; Land withdrawals; Timber permits; Public health, education, power; Individual and local problems.

Report. Study and investigation, Territory of Alaska. H. Res. 236; 79th Cong., 2nd Sess., House Report 1583. Wn.DC: GPO, 1946. 31 pp.

Reports, Hearings. Bibliography: Alaska: Politics and Government, 1900-1959. Compiled by the Library of Congress. W.A. Cathcart. Wn.DC: GPO, 1959. 246 pp.

See the Arctic Bibliography, and bibliographies prepared by various federal agencies as well as listings under specific categories for further information. See also the annual index of the *Congressional Quarterly* under Alaska, and various related headings, particularly for material since 1960.

US CONGRESS, HOUSE, COMMITTEE ON WAYS AND MEANS

W-9910-17, Hearings, 1896-1921; W-10251-65, Reports, 1876-1915 (fur seals, reindeer meat, AC Co., customs, trade statistics, fur population extinction).

Report. Alaska Commercial Company. 44th Cong., 1st Sess., House Report 623. Wn.DC: GPO, 1876. 143 pp. Following this report, favorable to AC

Co., the fur seal lease on the Pribilof Islands was granted to the company. The report includes testimony.

Hearings. Fur Seals of Alaska. H. Res. 13387; 57th Cong., 1st Sess. Wn.DC: GPO, 1902. 19 pp. H.W. Elliott. Terms of the new lease given the North American Commercial Co.

Hearings. Tariff, Reindeer Meat. 66th Cong., 3rd Sess. Statement and Brief of Carl J. Lomen. Wn.DC; GPO, 1921. 25 pp.

US CONGRESS, HOUSE, COMMITTEES ON CONFERENCE

W-10266-84, Reports, 1906-24 (delegate election; alien fishermen; judicial districts; public lands; agricultural entries on coal lands; legislative assembly; convention of 1911; assistance to indigents; railroad construction; coal land leases; aids to navigation; Lighthouse Service; fisheries protection).

US CONGRESS, HOUSE, SPECIAL COMMITTEE ON CONSERVATION OF WILD LIFE RESOURCES

Hearings. Conservation of Wildlife. H. Res. 65 (Resolution to investigate all matters pertaining to the replacement and conservation of wild animal life); 76th Cong., 3rd Sess. Wn.DC: GPO, 1940. 429 pp.

Report. Conservation of Wildlife. H. Res. 65; 76th Cong., 3rd Sess. Wn.DC: GPO, 1941. 64 pp.

Hearings. Conservation of Wildlife. H. Res. 49; 77th Cong., 1st Sess. Wn.DC: GPO, 1942. 283 pp.

Hearings. Conservation in Alaska. 77th Cong., 2nd Sess. Wn.DC: GPO, 1943. 204 pp.

Report. Conservation in Alaska. 77th Cong., 2nd Sess., House Report 2746. Wn.DC: GPO, 1943. 24 pp.

US CONGRESS, HOUSE, SELECT COMMITTEE ON THE ESTABLISHMENT OF A MILITARY POST AT THE MOUTH OF THE COLUMBIA RIVER

Report. Establishment of a Military Post at the Mouth of the Columbia River, and the Expediency of Providing for the More Perfect Exploring of the Northwest Coast of America. 19th Cong., 1st Sess., House Report 213. Wn.DC: GPO, 1826. 22 pp. William Baylies.

US CONGRESS, HOUSE, DOCUMENTS

W-10285-97, Documents, 1898-1920 (Criminal laws; Grand Jury Reports on paupers, indigent and insane; fox propagation; construction of capitol building at Juneau [1904]; report, Internat. Geog. Conf.; contested election [Wickersham-Sulzer]).

Report. International Geographic Conference (8th Congress). 58th Cong., 3rd Sess., House Doc. 460 (1904). This report includes the following: A.H. Brooks, Geography of Alaska, with Geomorphology; Middleton Smith, Habits and Northern Range of the Resident Birds of Point Barrow; F.A. Cook, Results of a Journey around Mt. McKinley; A.H. Brooks, The Exploration of Alaska.

A Digest of International Law. Wn.DC: GPO, 1906. 8v. 56th Cong., 2nd Sess., House Doc. 551.

US CONGRESS, HOUSE, MISCELLANEOUS DOCUMENTS

W-10298-10307, Resolutions, Minor, 1871-1890.

Memorial, Luis Goldstone. Alaska Seal Fishery. 42nd Cong., 1st Sess., House Misc. Doc. No. 5 (1871).

US CONGRESS, HOUSE, SPEECHES

W-10308-68, 1868-1924 (Wickersham, Sutherland, et alii).

Treaty between US and Russia for the Transfer of Alaska. March 2, 1868. Hon. William Higby.

Is Alaska a Territory? Status of the Alaskan Indians. February 22, 1910. Hon. James Wickersham.

Power of Attorney and Association Placer Mining Claims in Alaska. February 6, 1911. Hon. James Wickersham.

A National Coal Monopoly in Alaska. February 23, 1911. Hon. James Wickersham.

Legislature for Alaska. April 24, 1912. Hon. James Wickersham.

The Alaska Railway Bill. January 14, January 28, 1914. Hon. James Wickersham.

The Full Territorial Form of Government for Alaska. July 25, 1916. Hon. James Wickersham.

Decline of Population and Industry in Alaska. January 9, 1922. Hon. Dan Sutherland.

US CONGRESS, SENATE COMMITTEE ON AGRICULTURE AND FORESTRY

Report. Alaska Game Commission. S. 2559; 68th Cong., 1st Sess., Senate Report 480. Wn.DC: GPO, 1924. 5 pp.

Report. S.J.R. 127 (Transfer of Wild Game Protection Laws from Governor of Alaska to Department of Agriculture); 68th Cong., 1st Sess., Senate Report 573. Wn.DC: GPO, 1924. 3 pp.

US CONGRESS, SENATE, COMMITTEE ON APPROPRIATIONS

W-9392, Hearings, 1919; W-9428-29, Reports, 1913 (influenza; Juneau public building).

Hearings. Influenza in Alaska. S.J.R. 199; 65th Cong., 3rd Sess. Wn.DC: GPO, 1919. 21 pp.

US CONGRESS, SENATE, COMMITTEE ON ARMED SERVICES

Report. Alaskan Task Force (7th Rept.). Sen. Res. 18 (preparedness); 82nd Cong., 1st Sess. Wn.DC: GPO, 1951. 120 pp.

US CONGRESS, SENATE, COMMITTEE ON CLAIMS

W-9430-41, Reports, 1904-25 (Wales Island Packing Co.; North American Transportation and Trading Co.; Alaska Steamship Co.; wharf damage, Dutch Harbor, Alaska Commercial Co. [1920]).

US CONGRESS, SENATE, COMMITTEE ON COMMERCE

W-9393-94, Hearings, 1920-26; W-9442-95, Reports, 1896-1924 (water transportation; protection of fur seals; revenue cutter service; lighthouses; fog signal stations; life-saving station at Nome; bridge at Nome; trestles on Controller Bay; Copper River bridge; Pribilof Islands fun; Coast Guard).

Fuller-958-64, Reports, 1926-40 (fur seals; fisheries; protection of oyster culture; closed season on salmon trolling).

Report. S.J.R. 205 (appreciation, officers and crew, Alaska Steam vessel *Cordova*, for heroic services in rescuing 56 from the Revenue Cutter

Tahoma); 63rd Cong., 3rd Sess., Senate Report 1013 (1915).

Hearings. Alaska Water Transportation. S. 4012 (rates); 66th Cong., 2nd Sess. Wn.DC: GPO, 1920. 183 pp.

Hearings. Alaska Fur Seals. S. 3679 (conservation); 69th Cong., 1st Sess. Wn.DC: GPO, 1926. 84 pp. Incl. testimony of H.W. Elliott on fur seal conservation on the Pribilof Islands. Testimony on the original bill for this purpose was heard in 1922-23, S. 3731.

US CONGRESS, SENATE, COMMITTEE ON CONSERVATION OF NATURAL RESOURCES

W-9395-96, Hearings, 1910; W-9496, Report, 1910 (protection of fur seals).

US CONGRESS, SENATE, COMMITTEE ON EDUCATION AND LABOR

Report. Wage Rates, Federal Public Works, Alaska and Hawaii. S. 3650; 76th Cong., 3rd Sess. Senate Report 1550. Wn.DC: GPO, 1940. 1 pp.

US CONGRESS, SENATE, COMMITTEE ON FINANCE

W-9497-9501, Reports, 1914-20 (tax on railroads, relief for Copper River and Northwestern RR).

US CONGRESS, SENATE, COMMITTEE ON FISHERIES

W-9397-98, Hearings, 1912, 1916, 1917; W-9502-10, Reports, 1889-1916 (fur seal protection; whales; private salmon hatcheries; fishery experiment station).

US CONGRESS, SENATE, COMMITTEE ON FOREIGN RELATIONS

W-9511-24, Reports, 1888-1916 (protection of fur bearing animals; loss compensation, pelagic sealing; fisheries treaty; 1911 convention).

Hearings. Alaska Highway. S. Res. 253 (inquiry on location); 77th Cong., 2nd Sess. Wn.DC: GPO, 1942. 94 pp.

US CONGRESS, SENATE, COMMITTEE ON FOREST RESERVATIONS AND ON THE PROTECTION OF GAME

W-9526-27, Reports, 1895, 1902 (protection of game, eggs of wild fowl).

US CONGRESS, SENATE, COMMITTEE ON INDIAN AFFAIRS

Hearings. Tlingit and Haida Jurisdictional Act. S. 1196; 72nd Cong., 1st Sess. Wn.DC: GPO, 1932. 29 pp.

Report. Tlingit and Haida Jurisdictional Act. S. 1196 (land claims); 72nd Cong., 1st Sess., Senate Report 462. Wn.DC: GPO, 1932. 4 pp.

Hearings. Survey of Conditions of the Indians of the US. Parts 35 and 36: Metlakahtla Indians; Alaska, including the reindeer industry. 72nd Cong., 1st Sess., and beyond. Part 35—Wn.DC: GPO, 1939. 1348 pp. Part 36—Wn.DC: GPO, 1939. 742 pp.

Report. Alaska Reindeer Industry. S. 1722; 75th Cong., 1st Sess., Senate Report 474. Wn.DC: GPO, 1937. 4 pp.

US CONGRESS, SENATE, COMMITTEE ON INDUSTRIAL EXPOSITIONS

W-9528-30, Reports, 1908-09 (Alaska-Yukon-Pacific Exposition, Seattle, 1909).

US CONGRESS, SENATE, COMMITTEE ON INTERIOR AND INSULAR AFFAIRS

Hearings. Repeal Act authorizing Indian Reservations. S. 2037, and S.J.R. 162; 80th Cong., 2nd Sess. Wn.DC: GPO, 1948. 606 pp. The primary issue in the hearings was apparently the effect of further reservations on land claims by Alaska natives, and also the exploitation of natural resources by whites, especially those providing subsistence to natives. Witnesses testifying included V. Stefansson (gov't. policies re: Eskimos), William Warne (schools at Unalakleet, Kake, Hydaburg), Don C. Foster (Alaska school system, mistreatment of Eskimos, jade mining at Shungnak), Fredericka Martin (social conditions of Aleuts under Russian administration).

Hearing. Alaska Indian Reservations. 81st Cong., 2nd Sess. Wn.DC: GPO, 1950. 50 pp. This hearing, ordered by Sec. of Interior Julius A. Krug, incl. testimony by Gov. Gruening and Delegate Bartlett on social, economic and political discrimination suffered by Alaska natives.

Report. Russian Administration of Alaska and the Status of the Alaska Natives. See Vladimir Gsovski.

Hearings. Alaska Statehood. H. Res. 331, S. 2036 (admission); 81st Cong., 2nd Sess. Wn.DC: GPO, 1950. 531 pp.

Report. Admission into the Union. H. Res. 331; 81st Cong., 2nd Sess., Senate Report 1929. Wn.DC: GPO, 1950. 42 pp.

Report. Admission into the Union. S. 50; 82nd Cong., 1st Sess. Wn.DC: GPO, 1951. 54 pp.

Hearings. Alaska Statehood and Elective Governorship. S. 50, S. 224; 83rd Cong., 1st Sess. Wn.DC: GPO, 1953. 504 pp. Testimony received at Ketchikan, Juneau, Fairbanks, Anchorage.

Report. Admission into the Union. S. 50; 83rd Cong., 2nd Sess., Senate Report 1028. Wn.DC: GPO, 1954. 45 pp.

Hearings. Alaska Statehood. S. 50; 83rd Cong., 2nd Sess. Wn.DC: GPO, 1954. 364 pp.

Hearings. Alaska-Hawaii Statehood. S. 49, S. 399; S. 402 (commonwealth status); 84th Cong., 1st Sess. Wn.DC: GPO, 1955. 188 pp.

Report. Alaska Mental Health. H. Res. 6376; 84th Cong., 2nd Sess., Senate Report 2053. Wn.DC: GPO, 1956. 34 pp.

Hearings. Alaska Statehood. S. 49; 85th Cong., 1st Sess. Wn.DC: GPO, 1957. 154 pp.

Report. Admission into the Union. S. 49; 85th Cong., 1st Sess., Senate Report 1163. Wn.DC: GPO, 1957. 2 parts.

Hearings. Alaska Submerged Lands. H. Res. 8054 (lease of oil and gas deposits beneath navigable waters); 85th Cong., 2nd Sess. Wn.DC: GPO, 1959. 149 pp.

Report. Alaska Omnibus Bill. S. 1541; 86th Cong., 1st Sess. Wn.DC: GPO, 1959. 60 pp.

Hearing. Alaska Mineral Leasing. S. 1855, S. 1723, S. 1412; 86th Cong., 1st Sess. Wn.DC: GPO, 1959. 63 pp.

Hearing. Mineral Rights for Alaska Homesteaders. S. 1670 (quitclaiming oil and gas rights); 86th Cong., 1st Sess. Wn.DC: GPO, 1959. 91 pp.

Hearings. Hydroelectric Requirements and Resources in Alaska. 86th Cong., 2nd Sess. Wn.DC: GPO, 1960. 259 pp.

See the Arctic Bibliography for more recent listings, and the *Congressional Quarterly* annual index. See also the government records depository of the nearest major library for material on Alaska Native Claims and the nomination of Walter Hickel as Secretary of Interior. See Alaska Resources Library (United States).

US CONGRESS, SENATE, COMMITTEE ON INTERSTATE AND FOREIGN COMMERCE

Hearings. Air Carrier Certificates. H. Res. 9252, H. Res. 9253; 84th Cong., 2nd Sess. Wn.DC: GPO, 1956. 154 pp.

Hearing. Certification for Airlines. S. 3163, S. 3164; 84th Cong., 2nd Sess. Wn.DC: GPO, 1956. 107 pp.

Report. Transportation Problems of Alaska and the Pacific Coast States. S. Res. 13 and S. Res. 163; 84th Cong., 2nd Sess., Senate Report 2802. Wn.DC: GPO, 1956. 10 pp.

Hearings. Alaska and West Coast Transportation Problems. S. Res. 13 and S. Res. 163; 84th Cong., 2nd Sess. Wn.DC: GPO, 1956. 407 pp.

Hearings. Pacific Coast and Alaska Fisheries. S. Res. 13; 84th Cong., 2nd Sess. Wn.DC: GPO, 1956. 651 pp.

Report. Pacific Coast and Alaska Fisheries. S. Res. 13, S. Res. 163; 84th Cong., 2nd Sess., Senate Report 3801. Wn.DC: GPO, 1956. 40 pp.

Report. Rehabilitation of Alaska Salmon Fisheries. 84th Cong., 2nd Sess. Wn.DC: GPO, 1956. 14 pp. Magnuson.

Hearing. Water Transportation of Freight, Alaska and US Ports. S. 1798; 85th Cong., 1st Sess. Wn.DC: GPO, 1957. 42 pp.

Hearings. Alaskan Transportation. S. 1448 (restriction of discrimination); 85th Cong., 1st Sess. Wn.DC: GPO, 1958. 104 pp.

Hearings. Alaska Transportation Legislation. S. 1507, S. 1508, S. 1509; 86th Cong., 1st Sess. Wn.DC: GPO, 1959. 283 pp.

Hearing. Federal Airport Act, Alaska. S. 2208; 86th Cong., 1st Sess. Wn.DC: GPO, 1959. 29 pp.

Hearing. Arctic Wildlife Range. S. 1899; 86th Cong., 1st Sess. Wn.DC: GPO, 1960. 457 pp.

Hearings (Joint). Alaskan and Hawaiian Transportation. S. 1507; 86th Cong., 1st Sess. Wn.DC: GPO, 1961. 508 pp.

US CONGRESS, SENATE, COMMITTEE ON JUDICIARY

W-9399-9402, Hearings, 1906-09; W-9532-37, Reports, 1902-20 (district judges, judicial districts).

Report. Wickersham, District Judge, Third Division, Alaska. 59th Cong., 1st Sess., Senate Executive Document No. 7. Wn.DC: GPO, 1906. 104 pp.

US CONGRESS, SENATE, COMMITTEE ON MILITARY AFFAIRS

W-9538-45, Reports, 1862-1912 (est. military post in the interior; exploration of the Yukon; compilation of narratives [see below]); leave of absence for nurses).

Report. Memorial, Perry McD. Collins. S. 205; 37th Cong., 2nd Sess. Wn.DC: GPO, 1862. 9 pp.

Report. Compilation of Narratives of Explorations in Alaska. 56th Cong., 1st Sess., Senate Report 1023.

Wn.DC: GPO, 1900. This is one of the most valuable compilations of documents for the exploration of Alaska. The reports included are as follows:

Raymond   —Yukon reconnaissance, 1869
Howard   —Visit to Alaska, 1875
Petrof   —Population and Resources, 1880
Schwatka   —Yukon reconnaissance, 1883
Ray   —International Polar Exped.,
                 Pt. Barrow, 1881-84
Abercrombie—Copper River, 1884
Allen   —Copper, Tanana and Koyukuk Rivers,
                 1885
Ray   —Destitute Relief, Gold Fields, 1897
Abercrombie—Copper River, 1898
Glenn   —Trip to Tanana, 1898
Wells   —Yukon, 1897
Ray   —Destitute Relief, 1898
Glenn   —Cook Inlet, 1899
Richardson —Yukon, 1899
Abercrombie—Military Road, 1899

Report. ROTC, University of Alaska. S. 3768; 76th Cong., 3rd Sess., Senate Report 1786. Wn.DC: GPO, 1940. 2 pp.

Report. Military Code for Alaska. H. Res. 5822; 77th Cong., 1st Sess. Wn.DC: GPO, 1941. 3 pp.

US CONGRESS, SENATE, COMMITTEE ON MINES AND MINING

W-9546-53, Reports, 1901-19 (mining laws, coal land laws).

Report. Amend Mining Laws. S. 5589 (incl. poem "Lament of a Sourdough," Samuel C. Dunham); 56th Cong., 2nd Sess., Senate Report 2414). Wn.DC: GPO, 1900. 65 pp.

US CONGRESS, SENATE, COMMITTEE ON NAVAL AFFAIRS

W-9554-55, Reports, 1916-19 (radio on Unga Island).

Report. Alaskan Aerial Survey Expedition. H. Res. 3801; 71st Cong., 2nd Sess., Senate Report 807. Wn.DC: GPO, 1930. 7 pp.

US CONGRESS, SENATE, COMMITTEE ON POST OFFICE AND POST ROADS

W-9556, Report, 1925; Fuller-488, 1170-73, Reports, 1937, 1939, 1940. (Administrative matters).

US CONGRESS, SENATE, COMMITTEE ON PRINTING

W-9557-72, Reports, 1888-1913 (fishery documents; *Corwin;* Paris arbitration tribunal).

US CONGRESS, SENATE, COMMITTEE ON PUBLIC BUILDINGS AND GROUNDS

W-9573-74, Reports, 1912 (residence for the Governor of Alaska, Alaska Historical Library and Museum).

US CONGRESS, SENATE, COMMITTEE ON PUBLIC LANDS

W-9575-9626, Reports, 1912-23 (coal land laws; surveys; homesteading; coal for the US Navy; grazing lands; Mt. McKinley; water power; public park at Skagway).

US CONGRESS, SENATE, COMMITTEE ON PUBLIC WORKS

Hearings. Alaska Public Works. S. 855 (authorize a program of useful public works); 81st Congress. Wn.DC: GPO, 1949. 123 pp.

Report. Useful Public Works. S. 855; 81st Cong., 1st Sess., Senate Report 749. Wn.DC: GPO, 1949. 10 pp.

Hearing. Highways in Alaska. S. 2976; 86th Cong., 2nd Sess. 1960.

US CONGRESS, SENATE, COMMITTEE ON TERRITORIES

W-9413-25, Hearings, 1907-17 (telegraph and telephone lines; legislative council and assembly; general conditions; railroads; Mt. McKinley National Park; alcoholic liquor prohibition).

W-9628-9707, Reports, 1880-1925 (railroad construction; telephone and telegraph lines; town incorporation).

Report. Civil Government for Alaska. S. 1153; 47th Cong., 1st Sess., Senate Report 457. Wn.DC: GPO, 1882. 45 pp. Incl. statements of M.D. Ball, Sheldon Jackson and Ivan Petrof.

Report. Code of Criminal Procedures. H. Res. 8571; 55th Cong., 3rd Sess., Senate Report 1651. 1899. 1 p.

Report. Delegate Bill. H. Res. 9865 (amendment); 57th Cong., 2nd Sess., Senate Report 3298. 1903. 2 pp.

Report. Conditions in Alaska. 58th Cong., 2nd Sess., Senate Report 282. Wn.DC: GPO, 1904. 308 pp.

Report. Civil Government. S. 3035 (care of insane); 58th Cong., 2nd Sess., Senate Report 1684. Wn.DC: GPO, 1904. 2 pp.

Hearings. Railroad, and Telegraph and Telephone Lines. S. 6937, S. 6980, S. 191, H. Res. 18891; 59th Cong., 1st Sess. Wn.DC: GPO, 1907. 144 pp.

Report. Care of Persons Judged Insane. S. 4712; 60th Cong., 1st Sess., Senate Report 310. 1908. 2 pp.

Report. Government of Alaska. S. 5436; 61st Cong., 2nd Sess., Senate Report 259. Wn.DC: GPO, 1910. 159 pp.

Hearings. Civil Government in Alaska. S. 1647; 62nd Cong., 1st Sess. Wn.DC: GPO, 1911. 60 pp.

Report. Compulsory Education. 62nd Cong., 2nd Sess., Senate Report 504. Wn.DC: GPO, 1912. 1 p.

Hearings. Conditions in Alaska. 62nd Cong., 2nd Sess. Wn.DC: GPO, 1912. 54 pp.

Hearings. Railroads for Alaska. 62nd Cong., 2nd Sess. Wn.DC: GPO, 1912. 32 pp.

Hearings. Legislative Assembly. 62nd Cong., 2nd Sess. Wn.DC: GPO, 1912. 24 pp. Incl. statements of Gifford Pinchot and James Wickersham.

Hearings. Construction of Railroads in Alaska. S. 48, S. 133 (authorization for President to build); 63rd Cong., 1st Sess. Wn.DC: GPO, 1913. 718 pp.

Hearings. The Building of Railroads in Alaska. H. Res. 1739, H. Res. 1806, H. Res. 2145; 63rd Cong., 1st Sess. Wn.DC: GPO, 1913. 467 pp.

Hearings. Mt. McKinley National Park. S. 5716; 64th Cong., 1st Sess. Wn.DC: GPO, 1916. 20 pp.

Report. Mt. McKinley National Park. S. 5716; 64th Cong., 1st Sess. Wn.DC: GPO, 1916. 2 pp.

Hearings. Prohibition of Liquor. S. 7963; 64th Cong., 2nd Sess. Wn.DC: GPO, 1917. 13 pp.

Report. Railroad Construction. H. Res. 7417; 66th Cong., 1st Sess., Senate Report 189. Wn.DC: GPO, 1919. 3 pp.

Report. Donation of Ft. Davis Lands (abandoned). H.J.R. 249; 67th Cong., 2nd Sess., Senate

Report 583. Wn.DC: GPO, 1922. 1 p.

Report. Establish Industrial Schools, Alaska Native Children. H. Res. 4825; 68th Cong., 2nd Sess., Senate Report 954. Wn.DC: GPO, 1925. 4 pp.

US CONGRESS, SENATE, COMMITTEE ON TERRITORIES AND INSULAR AFFAIRS

Report. Referendum on One-House Legislature. H. Res. 6651; 75th Cong., 1st Sess., Senate Report 1045. Wn.DC: GPO, 1937. 2 pp.

Report. Prohibition in Alaska. S. 2729 (repeal of Alaska prohibition); 73rd Cong., 2nd Sess., Senate Report 291. Wn.DC: GPO, 1934. 1 p.

Report. Crime and Criminal Procedure in Alaska. S. 2254 (to tax Alaska shipping and amend the criminal code); 75th Cong., 1st Sess., Senate Report 510. Wn.DC: GPO, 1937. 3 pp.

Report. Alien Fishing. H. Res. 10432; 75th Cong., 3rd Sess., Senate Report 2066. Wn.DC: GPO, 1938. 5 pp.

Report. Fur Farm Experiment Station. S. 3894; 75th Cong., 3rd Sess., Senate Report 1677. Wn.DC: GPO, 1938. 2 pp.

Hearings. Settlement and Development of Alaska. 76th Cong., 3rd Sess. Wn.DC: GPO, 1940. 254 pp. Contains text of a bill providing for the incorporation of development corporations, and statements by 27 witnesses. Testimony incl. railroad's development role, status of various industries, and suspension of immigrant restrictions (anti).

Report. Territorial Housing Corporation Authority. S. 3686; 76th Cong., 3rd Sess., Senate Report 1582. Wn.DC: GPO, 1940. 2 pp.

Report. Territorial Housing Corporation Authority. H. Res. 93; 77th Cong., 1st Sess., Senate Report 504. Wn.DC: GPO, 1941. 4 pp.

Report. Conveyance of CR&NW RR Properties. S. 1289; 77th Cong., 1st Sess., Senate Report 375. Wn.DC: GPO, 1941. 4 pp.

Report. Care of Insane. S. 2248; 77th Cong., 2nd Sess. Wn.DC: GPO, 1942. 5 pp.

For further citations of Senate reports and hearings concerning Alaska, see the Arctic Bibliography, and the *Congressional Record.* See also the *Congressional Quarterly,* esp. the annual index. See O. Miller for material on settlement and the Matanuska Colony. See C. Naske for material on statehood. See also the subjects Oil, and Natives.

US CONGRESS, SENATE, DOCUMENTS

W-9708-9747 (seals, criminal code, courts, civil government, gold mining, education, boundary, natives, mineral resources, coal lands, compiled laws, influenza epidemic, water power, etc.).

Memoir, Historical and Political, of the Northwest Coast. Robert Greenhow. 26th Cong., 1st Sess., Senate Doc. No. 174.

Special Report. Commission to Codify and Revise Criminal and Penal Laws. 55th Cong., 2nd Sess., Senate Doc. No. 60. Wn.DC: GPO, 1898. 144 pp.

Notes on Conferences. H. Res. 8571 (Define and Punish Crimes in Alaska [codification]); 55th Cong., 3rd Sess., Senate Doc. No. 122. Wn.DC: GPO, 1899. 22 pp.

History of the Discovery of Gold at Cape Nome. See H.L. Blake.

Petition, Alaska C. of C. 57th Cong., 1st Sess., Senate Doc. No. 238. Wn.DC: GPO, 1902. 5 pp.

Asks representation in Congress, retention of license taxes, change location of capital, homestead surveys, lighthouses.

Alaska Boundary. J.W. Foster. See *National Geographic,* November, 1899.

Proposed Restoration of Prohibition in Alaska. S. 6944; 57th Cong., 2nd Sess., Senate Doc. No. 85. Wn.DC: GPO, 1903. 14 pp.

Report. Conditions and Needs, Alaska Natives. G.T. Emmons. 58th Cong., 3rd Sess., Senate Doc. No. 106. Wn.DC: GPO, 1905. 23 pp.

Compiled Laws of the Territory of Alaska. Compiled, codified, arranged and annotated under authority of the Joint Committee on Territories. 62nd Cong., 3rd Sess., Senate Doc. No. 1093. Wn.DC: GPO, 1913. 924 pp.

Letter from the Chief of Office of the Isthmian Canal Comm., 63rd Cong., 2nd Sess., Senate Doc. No. 258. On transmittal of railroad material from the Panama Canal project to Alaska.

US CONGRESS, SENATE, MISCELLANEOUS DOCUMENTS

W-9748-9767, 1848-1902 (Asiatic relations, P.M. Collins' Overland Telegraph Expedition, reports on Alaska by L.M. Turner and E.W. Nelson, fur seal lease, importation of reindeer, Bering Sea claims, Noyes case at Nome, administration).

Memoir, Geographical, Political and Commercial, Siberia, Manchuria, and the Asiatic Islands on the Northern Pacific Ocean. A.H. Palmer. 30th Cong., 1st Sess., Senate Misc. Doc. No. 80. Wn.DC: GPO, 1848. 81 pp.

Memorial. Perry McDonough Collins. Asking aid for Russian-American Western Union Overland Telegraph Expedition. 38th Cong., 1st Sess., Senate Misc. Doc. No. 98. 1864. 2 pp.

Resolutions, Minnesota Legislature. Asks Congress to confirm by requisite legislation the annexation of Alaska to the Dominion of Canada. 40th Cong., 2nd Sess., Senate Misc. Doc. No. 58. 1868, 2 pp.

Petition. Survey railroad through BC to Alaska. J.A. Lynch. 49th Cong., 1st Sess., Senate Misc. Doc. No. 84. 1886. 3 pp.

The Case of Judge Arthur H. Noyes in the Senate of the US Cong. Rec., Feb. 5, 1902.

US CONGRESS, SENATE, SPEECHES

W-9768-9774, 1896-1916 (Alaska boundary, mining locations, fur seals, railroads).

Alien Mining Locations in Alaska: The Scandinavian segregated from the Laplander. Hon. H.C. Hansbrough, N.D. April 30, 1900. 15 pp. Re: Nome Noyes case.

Alaska Railroad to the Bering Coal Fields. Hon. W.L. Jones. April 19, 1916. 8 pp.

See Charles Sumner.

US DEPARTMENT OF AGRICULTURE

W-8440-8607, to 1924. See also the Arctic Bibliography. See also US Agricultural Research Administration, US Bureau of Biological Survey, US Forest Service, US Weather Bureau and related agencies.

"Botany of Yakutat Bay, Alaska," *Contributions,* Div. of Botany, US National Herbarium, 1895. Frederick Funston. See W. Hunt.

Soil Reconnaissance in Alaska. Hugh Bennett and Thomas Rice. Bureau of Soils. Wn.DC: GPO, 1914. 212 pp.

Report. Reconnaissance of Soils, Agriculture and other Resources of Kenai Peninsula Region. Hugh Bennett. Bureau of Soils. Wn.DC: GPO, 1918. 142 pp.

Annual Reports. Secretary of Agriculture. Misc. material related to Alaska. See individual editions.

Report on Agriculture in Alaska. Annual from 1897. See also the reports and data of the Agriculture Experiment Stations, esp. those by C.C. Georgeson. See also Orlando Miller, *The Frontier in Alaska and the Matanuska Colony*. See also W-8558-8591.

Information for Prospective Settlers in Alaska. First issued in 1916, revised periodically. C.C. Georgeson. See also the Interior Department's *Mid-Century Alaska*. See as well O. Miller.

"Fur Industry of the Pribilof Islands," *Fur Resources of the US*. Wn.DC: GPO, 1930. 51 pp.

Insects of Agricultural and Household Importance in Alaska. J.C. Chamberlin. Wn.DC: GPO, 1949. 59 pp. Agr. Res. Admin., Ak. Agr. Exp. Sta.

Markets for the Products of Cropland in Alaska. Wn.DC: GPO, 1950. 50 pp. Bur. Agr. Econ.

Some Economic Aspects of Farming in Alaska. Wn.DC: GPO, 1950. 89 pp. Bur. Agr. Econ.

See O. Miller.

US DEPARTMENT OF THE AIR FORCE

Dependent's Information. Wn.DC: GPO, 1955. 16 pp.

Survival: Training Edition. Wn.DC: GPO, 1956. 373 pp. Food and accident treated in detail.

US DEPARTMENTS OF THE ARMY AND THE AIR FORCE

Arctic Construction. Wn.DC: GPO, 1952. 464 pp.

US DEPARTMENT OF COMMERCE

W-8608-9038 (C&GS, census, fisheries and fur seals, foreign commerce, fox farms, Klondike, mining and prospecting, monthly summaries of commerce and finance, and annual reports to the secretary, steamboat inspection service).

Alaska Fur Seal Skins. 69th Cong., 1st Sess., Senate Report 73. Wn.DC: GPO, 1926. 32 pp.

Pulpwood Supply in Alaska. 71st Cong., 2nd Sess., Senate Doc. 120. Wn.DC: GPO, 1930. 335 pp.

Laws and Regulations for Protection of Commercial Fisheries. Wn.DC: GPO, 1940. 50 pp. Also additional editions.

US DEPARTMENT OF DEFENSE

Arctic Bibliography. Prepared for and in cooperation with the US Department of Defense under direction of the Arctic Institute of North America. From 1953. See Arctic Institute of North America, and Arctic Bibliography.

A Pocket Guide to Alaska. Wn.DC: GPO, 1954. 68 pp.

The Arctic. Wn.DC: GPO, 1958. 14 pp. Defense.

US DEPARTMENT OF JUSTICE

W-7855-7888, 1884-1917 (Reports to the President, receipts of licenses, letters to Congress, codification, Fuller, administration, instructions to judges, marshals and others, attorney-general opinions, special Alaska cases).

Compilation of Laws Applicable to Duties of Governor, Attorney-General, Judge, Clerk, Marshal and Commissioners of Alaska. Wn.DC: GPO, 1884. 60 pp.

Annual Reports. Attorney General of the US. From 1898. Misc. material concerning the district courts in Alaska.

Letter. Transmits special report on revision and codification of criminal and penal laws of the US relating to Alaska. 55th Cong., 2nd Sess., Senate Doc. 60. Wn.DC: GPO, 1898. 144 pp.

Letter. Transmits report of the work of the commission to codify the laws other than criminal of the district of Alaska. 55th Cong., 3rd Sess., House Doc. 99. Wn.DC: GPO, 1898. 353 pp.

US Circuit Court of Appeals, 9th Circuit. *Records in the Matter of the Contempt Case of Alexander McKenzie*. San Francisco: Filmer Brothers Printing, 1901. 3v. Circuit Judges Gilbert, Ross and Morrow.

US Circuit Court of Appeals, 9th Circuit. *Records in the Contempt Case In Re Arthur H. Noyes, Thomas J. Geary, Joseph K. Wood and C.A.S. Frost*. San Francisco: Filmer Brothers Printing, 1901. 14v.

Instructions to US Judges, Marshals, Attorneys, Clerks and Commissioners for the District of Alaska. Wn.DC: GPO, 1910. 317 pp.

Catalogue. Dept. of Justice, Alaska-Yukon-Pacific Exposition, Seattle, 1909. 32 pp.

Brief. Cunningham Coal Entries in Alaska. Submitted on behalf of Gifford Pinchot. 1911. 127 pp.

US Circuit Court of Appeals, 9th Circuit. *Alaska Coal Land Cases*. 62nd Cong., 1st Sess., Senate Doc. No. 8. Wn.DC: GPO, 1911. 10 pp.

Territory of Alaska, Petitioner, v. Annette Island Packing Co. Wn.DC: GPO, 1923. 9 pp.

See Alaska, State, Court System. See also Spicer, G.W.

US DEPARTMENT OF LABOR

W-9039-49, 1875-1916 (Alaska Railroad strike [1916], labor laws, proposed Icelandic immigration, opportunities in agriculture and mining, child labor legislation).

Report. Icelandic Committee from Wisconsin on the Character and Resources of Alaska. Jon Olafsson. Wn.DC: GPO, 1875. 6 pp.

Child Labor Legislation in the US. Wn.DC: GPO, 1915. 1131 pp. Helen Sumner and Ella Merritt. US Dept. of Labor, Children's Bureau.

"The Alaskan Gold Fields and the Opportunities They Offer for Capital and Labor," in *Bulletin*, US Dept. of Labor, May, 1898.

"The Yukon and Nome Gold Region," in *Bulletin*, US Dept. of Labor, 1900.

US DEPARTMENT OF STATE

W-7324-7360, 1824-1912 (Collins' Overland Telegraph Expedition, Bering Sea controversy, boundary, Wales Island Packing Co. claims, Russian-American relations, purchase, Blake's excursion on the Stikine, conventions with Britain).

American State Papers, Vol. 4: Claims of Great Britain and Russia to the Northwest Coast. J.Q. Adams, R. Rush, et alii. Objection to the Ukase of 1821 (100 mile limitation).

Letter. Perry McDonough Collins; 35th Cong., 1st Sess., House Exec. Doc. No. 98. Wn.DC: GPO, 1858. 67 pp.

Purchase of the Russian Possessions. Papers relating to the Value and Resources of the Country; 40th Cong., 2nd Sess., House Exec. Doc. No. 177. 5 pp.

Letter. Perry McDonough Collins; 35th Cong., 2nd Sess., House Exec. Doc. No. 53. 16 pp.

Communication from William H. Seward, Secretary of State, on the subject of an International Telegraph connecting the eastern and western hemispheres by way of Bering Strait. 38th Cong., 1st Sess., Senate Misc. Doc. No. 123. 25 pp.

Geographical Notes upon Russian America. 40th Cong., 2nd Sess., House Exec. Doc. No. 177, part 2. 19 pp.

Diplomatic Correspondence of US and Russia relative to the Purchase of Alaska. 40th Cong., 2nd Sess., House Exec. Doc. No. 1. See also microfilm, Nat. Archives and Fed. Records Service.

Letter. Transmits memorial of Wales Island Packing Co.; 58th Cong., 2nd Sess., House Doc. No. 510.

"US, Canada, Japan, and USSR sign Fur Seal Convention," *Bulletin*, Dept. of State, March 4, 1957.

See also Alaska Diplomacy.

US DEPARTMENT OF THE INTERIOR

W-7946-8439 (annual reports to the President by the Sec. of the Interior, letters to Congress transmitting reports etc. regarding condition of natives, fur seal, education, railroads and care of the insane, etc.

Alaska, 1952/53. Wn.DC: GPO, 35 pp. Office of Territories. Subsequent editions to 1958. Also a revised edition submitted to the Sec.-Gen. of the UN, pursuant to charter, 1947.

The Alaska Flag. Wn.DC: GPO, 1931. 4 pp.

Home Care of Tuberculosis in Alaska. Lawrence, Kansas: BIA, 1947. 117 pp. Alaska Native Service.

Alaska Native Service. Report for Teachers and Medical Workers. Wn.DC: GPO, 1946. Survey of schools, villages, etc. Miss Byrdie McNeil.

Alaska Native Service. Wn.DC: GPO, 1957. 26 pp.

Alaska School Service: Medical Handbook; see Romig.

Annotated Bibliography on Alaska. Juneau: BIA (Dist. Off.), 1960. 50 pp.

Alaska: The Land of Yesterday, Today and Tomorrow. Chicago: Horner Printing Co., 1936. 24 pp.

The Exhibition of the District of Alaska at the Lewis and Clark Exposition, Portland, Oregon, 1905. Portland: Irwin-Hodson Printers, 1905. 65 pp.

General Information Regarding the Territory of Alaska. Wn.DC: GPO, 1912. 24 pp. And numerous subsequent editions.

Letter. Transmits Report of Vincent Colyer, Special Agent, concerning the Indian Village of Wrangell, showing conditions previous to bombardment by US troops. 41st Cong., 2nd Sess., Senate Exec. Doc. No. 68. 1870. 23 pp.

Letter. Transmits Report of Sheldon Jackson on the Condition of Education in Alaska. 47th Cong., 1st Sess., Senate Exec. Doc. No. 30. 1881. 28 pp.

Letter. Transmits Report of the Governor of Alaska relative to Outrages upon Indian Women in Alaska. 50th Cong., 2nd Sess., Senate Exec. Doc. No. 141. 1889. 24 pp.

Mid-Century Alaska. Wn.DC: GPO, 1951, 1952, 1957. 155 pp. General compendium, authoritative.

Population and Resources of Alaska. Ivan Petrof. Wn.DC: GPO, 1881. 86 pp. 46th Cong., 3rd Sess., House Exec. Doc. No. 40.

The Problem of Alaska Development. Wn.DC: GPO, 1939. 94 pp.

Progress in Alaskan Administration. Wn.DC: GPO, 1931. 9 pp.

Regulations Governing Coal-land Leases in the Territory of Alaska. Wn.DC: GPO, 1916. 86 pp.

Report. Care of Insane in Alaska. 69th Cong., 1st Sess., House Doc. No. 432. Wn.DC: GPO, 1926. 43 pp. See also Thomas Smith.

Report. Settlement of Possessory Claims in Alaska. H. Res. 1921; 83rd Cong., 2nd Sess. Wn.DC: GPO, 1953. 10 pp.

Reports: Depts. of Justice, Agriculture, Interior. H. Res. 1921 (Possessory Claims in Alaska); 84th Cong., 1st Sess.

Reports. Condition of Educational and School Service and Management of Reindeer Service. Frank C. Churchill. 59th Cong., 1st Sess., Senate Doc. No. 483. Wn.DC: GPO, 1906. 176 pp.

Report. Snettisham Project. 87th Cong., 1st Sess., House Doc. No. 40. Wn.DC: GPO, 1961. 84 pp.

Water Resources of Alaska. 86th Cong., 2nd Sess. Wn.DC: GPO, 1960. 21 pp.

See also listings under specific agencies, e.g., US Bureau of Land Management, US Office of Education. See also the government records depository of the nearest major library. See also Alaska Task Force. See as well Alaska Resources Library (United States).

US DIVISION OF TERRITORIES AND ISLAND POSSESSIONS

General Information, Territory of Alaska; see US Dept. of Interior.

US ENGINEER SCHOOL

Alaskan Railroads: A Selected List. Ft. Belvoir, Va. December, 1947. Bibliography.

US ENGINEER DEPARTMENT

Juneau and Douglas Harbors. 75th Cong., 1st Sess., House Doc. No. 249. Wn.DC: GPO, 1937. 19 pp.

Similar surveys of the following harbors were made: Kodiak Harbor (1932, 1939); Nome Harbor (1930); Petersburg Harbor (1932, 1939); Seldovia Harbor (1940); Sitka Harbor (1927); Salmon River (1930, 1932); Sitka Harbor, Inner (1929, 1937, 1938); Skagway Harbor (1938); Unalaska Harbor (1938); Wrangell Harbor (1932, 1939); Wrangell Narrows (1930); see also Fuller 1179-96.

US FEDERAL COMMUNICATIONS COMMISSION

List of Radio Stations in Alaska. Wn.DC: GPO, 1943. 67 pp.

Rules and Regulations: Alaska. Wn.DC: GPO, 1942. 7 pp.

US FEDERAL HOUSING AUTHORITY

Minimum Construction Requirements. Wn.DC: GPO, 1940, 24 pp.

US FEDERAL POWER COMMISSION

Water Power, Southeast Alaska, 1947. Wn.DC: GPO, 1947. 168 pp. With the US Forest Service, Dept. of Agriculture.

Alaska Power Market Survey. San Francisco: GPO, 1950. 104 pp.

See also US Army, Corps of Engineers.

US FISH AND WILDLIFE SERVICE, DEPARTMENT OF THE INTERIOR

Reports. Alaska Fishery and Fur-seal Industries. From 1893. Initial publication was by the US Treasury Department, Special Agents Division. Reports for 1903-05 were issued by the Dept. of Commerce and Labor, Division of Alaskan Fisheries; 1906-37 by the Bureau of Fisheries. From 1940 the reports were issued by the US Fish and Wildlife Service. Reports include legislation, reserves, patrols, details of catch and canning as well as statistics on salmon, herring, halibut, cod, whales, clams, shrimp, crab, etc.

Pacific Salmon. Chicago, 1943. See Fuller 977.

Laws for Protection of the Commercial Fisheries. Wn.DC: GPO, 1951. 61 pp.

Migration of Some North American Waterfowl. Wn.DC: GPO, 1949. 48 pp. Special Scientific Report. US F&WS.

Alaska Fisheries, 1953. Wn.DC: GPO, 1954. 5 pp. Subsequent editions.

Waterfowl Populations and Breeding Conditions, Summer, 1953. Wn.DC: GPO, 1954. 250 pp. Special Scientific Report. US F&WS. Previous editions.

Administration of Alaska Commercial Fisheries. Juneau: US F&WS, 1956. 34 pp. Conditions and trends.

Utilization of Alaskan Salmon Cannery Waste. Wn.DC: GPO, 1947. 89 pp. Fishery Products Laboratory, Ketchikan.

Alaska's Fish and Wildlife. Wn.DC: GPO, 1953. 60 pp. Clarence J. Rhodes and Will Barker.

Report of the Alaska Crab Investigation. Wn.DC: GPO, 1942. 108 pp. King Crab in the Bering Sea, south side of the Alaska Peninsula, Kodiak Island and lower Cook Inlet.

Report. Alaska Exploratory Fishing Expedition. Wn.DC: GPO, 1949. 25 pp. Northern Bering Sea.

Harbor Seals and Sea Lions in Alaska. Wn.DC: GPO, 1947. 23 pp.

Literature on the Natural History of the Arctic Region. Wn.DC: GPO, 1949. 48 pp. Hartley Harrad, Thompson Jackson.

Vitamin A in Liver of the Alaska Fur Seal. Repr. from *Comm. Fisheries Review*, April, 1949.

Health and Growth of Aleut Children. Wn.DC: GPO, 1949. 17 pp.

"The Return of the Musk Ox," *Annual Report*, US F&WS, 1941. Nunivak Island.

See also the Arctic Bibliography. See as well Alaska Resources Library (US).

US FOREST SERVICE, DEPARTMENT OF AGRICULTURE

W-8470-8514, 1970-24 (use of forest reserves, water power, wood pulp production).

Reports. Forester to the Sec. of Agriculture. From 1917.

Sitka Spruce. Bulletin, 1922. 38 pp.

Report to the Federal Power Commission. Wn.DC: GPO, 1924. 172 pp. Southeastern Alaska.

"The Western Range," in *US Forest Service*, 1936. 74th Cong., 2nd Sess., Senate Doc. No. 199.

Tongass National Forest, Alaska. Wn.DC: GPO, 1940. 46 pp.

Review of Forest Service Activities in Alaska. Wn.DC: GPO, 1958. 40 pp. Report to the Congress of the Comptroller General of the GAO.

US GENERAL LAND OFFICE, DEPARTMENT OF THE INTERIOR

W-7994-8085, 1868-1924 (regulations for public lands, use, timber rights, coal lands, instructions to land office employees, native rights, mining laws, homesteads).

Annual Reports. Commissioner of the General Land Office. From 1868.

Letter. Purchase of Alaska. Hon. N.P. Banks. W-7994.

The Public Domain. 47th Cong., 2nd Sess., House Misc. Doc. No. 45. Wn.DC: GPO, 1880. Also 1881, 1884.

Circular from the Gen. Land Office. Wn.DC: GPO, 1898. 26 pp. Homestead Act in Alaska.

Report. Agricultural Prospects, Natives, Salmon Fisheries, Coal Prospects, Timber Development, Alaska. Wn.DC: GPO, 1904. 95 pp. James W. Witter.

Annual Reports. Surveyor General of Alaska, 1893-1904. In *US General Land Office Reports.*

The Cunningham Claims. Coal Entries, Alaska Series. *US v. Andrew L. Scofield, et alii.* Wn.DC: GPO, 1911. 66 pp.

Report. Reduction of Area of Homesteads in Alaska. Wn.DC: GPO, 1915. 18 pp.

Circular of Instructions. Acquisition of title to Public Lands, Alaska. Wn.DC: GPO, 1916. 89 pp. Subsequent editions.

Alaska. Information relative to the Disposal and Leasing of Public Lands. Wn.DC: GPO, 1939. 10 pp. Subsequent editions. See also the Arctic Bibliography, and O. Miller.

US GEOGRAPHIC BOARD; see US Board on Geographic Names

US GEOLOGICAL SURVEY, DEPARTMENT OF THE INTERIOR

W-8200-8396, 1868-1925 (economic geology, mineral resources, coal and tin deposits, mineral springs, glaciers, earthquakes, petroleum fields, water supply, volcanoes, fossils, geographic names, etc.).

For a full listing of USGS publications contact the Alaska district office library in Anchorage. There are several full collections of USGS Alaska publications in Alaska, at the USGS district office, at the University of Alaska, and at the State Historical Library at Juneau. On the relationship between the USGS and other agencies in exploration and reconnaissance of Alaska, see particularly Morgan Sherwood's *Exploration of Alaska.*

US HYDROGRAPHIC OFFICE, NAVY DEPARTMENT

W-7927-32, 1886-1900 (deep sea soundings, notices to mariners, ice movement, etc.).

Report of Ice and Ice Movements in the Bering Sea. Wn.DC: GPO, 1890. 25 *Thetis*, summer, 1889.

Ice and Ice Movements in the Bering Sea. Wn.DC: GPO, 1900. 19 pp.

Naval Air Pilot, Alaska Peninsula, Southern & Southeastern Alaska. Wn.DC: GPO, 1934. 236 pp. Subsequent editions. See also FAA.

Weather Summary, Alaska Area. Wn.DC: GPO, 1944. 279 pp.

References to the Physical Oceanography of the Western Pacific. Wn.DC: GPO, 1946. 174 pp.

Manual of Iceseamanship. Wn.DC: GPO, 1950. 128 pp. Procedures of operation.

A Functional Glossary of Ice Terminology. Wn.DC: GPO, 1952. 88 pp.

Sailing Directions for British Columbia. Wn.DC: GPO, 1952. 262 pp.

List of Lights and Fog Signals. Wn.DC: GPO, 1953. 671 pp.

Navigation Dictionary. Wn.DC: GPO, 1956. 253 pp.

US INTERNATIONAL BOUNDARY COMMISSION
W-9368-75, 1898-1918. See also Alaska Boundary Tribunal, and International Boundary Commission.

US INTERSTATE COMMERCE COMMISSION
Alaska Transportation Problems. Wn.DC: GPO, 1957. 10 pp.

US LAWS, STATUTES
W-10369-80 (Alaska Court Rules); W-183-7 (Territory of Alaska, Attorney-General), W-223-67 (Governor of Alaska), W-272-307 (Territory of Alaska, Legislature: session laws, journals), W-169-359 (Public Documents: Territorial agencies), W-343-51 (Secretary of Alaska), W-4449-77 (Laws and decisions: bar association, mining laws, Wickersham's *Alaska Reports*, articles), W-3812-77 (government: articles on law and government problems), W-7850-53 (US Bureau of Insular Affairs: Compilation of Acts of Congress, Supreme Court cases), W-7865-66, W-9711-12, W-9737, W-10286 (US Dept. of Justice, Codes), W-7873-83 (US Dept. of Justice, General publications: laws applicable to Governor, Marshals, Comissioners, etc.).

The Laws of Alaska. Chicago: Callahan & Co., 1900. 553 pp. Thomas H. Carter. This is one of the most useful compendia on Alaska (Congressional) legislation, containing all bills of significance to 1900.

Compilation of the Acts of Congress and Treaties relating to Alaska. Wn.DC: GPO, 1906. 496 pp. Fred F. Barker. 59th Cong., 1st Sess., Senate Document No. 142. See also additional editions, 1907, 1909, and 1914.

The Compiled Laws of the Territory of Alaska, 1913. Wn.DC: GPO, 1913. 924 pp. 62nd Cong., 3rd Sess., Senate Document No. 1093.

Compiled Laws of Alaska: Annotated. San Francisco: Bancroft-Whitney Co., 1948. 3v. 2750 pp.

For specific acts see the various editions of compilations, esp. the *Compiled Laws of Alaska: Annotated.* Session Laws were published from 1949-59.

See also Government of Alaska, and US Department of Justice. See Spicer, G.W.

US LIBRARY OF CONGRESS
W-9380-82, 1898-1914 (maps of Alaska).
Alaska and the Northwest Part of North America,

1588-1898. Wn.DC: GPO, 1898. 119 pp. Philip Lee Phillips.

Monthly Check List of State Publications. From 1919. Wn.DC: GPO, See Alaska in Index.

References on Aeronautics in Alaska, 1926-37. Div. of Aeronautics. Libr. of Congress, 5 pp. Typescript. 1937. See also supplements, 1941-1943.

State Law Index. Wn.DC: GPO, 1929-41. 8v. Check topical headings. See also supplements.

Alaska: A Selected List of References. See Grace Fuller.

Aleutian Islands: A Selected List of References. See Grace Fuller.

Russian Administration in Alaska and the Status of Alaska Natives. See Vladimir Gsovski.

Annotated Bibliography on Snow, Ice and Permafrost. Wn.DC: GPO, 1951-52. 2v. See the Arctic Bibliography for subsequent editions.

The Polar Bibliography. Wn.DC: GPO, 1956. 223 pp. Unpublished documents, reports, staff studies, memoranda, manuals, by US military and contractors.

See the Library of Congress List of Publications, and the Arctic Bibliography. For manuscript holdings, see Frederick, R., and Smith, B.S.

US MEDICAL NUTRITION LABORATORY
Final Report of Survival in the Cold. Chicago: 1948. 78 pp.

US MILITARY SEA TRANSPORTATION SERVICE, US NAVY
See the Arctic Bibliography.

US NATIONAL ACADEMY OF SCIENCES
Catalogue of the Meteorites of North America to 1909. Repr. from *Memoirs*, Nat. Acad. of Sci., 1915.

US NATIONAL ARCHIVES
Contact the National Archives and Federal Records Service, Region 10, Seattle, for a listing of Alaska materials at the Region 10 Center, and in the National Archives, Wn.DC. There are a number of significant collections available on microfilm, incl. portions of the Alaska Governor's Office papers (territorial), now housed in Juneau. The records of government agencies (federal, including Territory of Alaska to 1958) operating in Alaska which have been declared historical are stored at Seattle in many, but not all cases. Contact the director. Many current materials are collected and deposited at the Alaska Resources Library, Anchorage, administered by the Interior Dept., but maintaining a variety of records. See R. Frederick.

US NATIONAL MUSEUM, SMITHSONIAN INSTITUTION
W-9090-9185, 1878-1926 (natural history, natives).

See the Arctic Bibliography, esp. under the names of known scholars in the field of natural history, ethnology, ethnography, anthropology, etc. See also Sherwood.

US NATIONAL PARK SERVICE, DEPARTMENT OF THE INTERIOR
W-8404-06, 1917-25 (bibliography, Mt. McKinley).

"Bibliography of Books, Government Reports and

Magazine Articles on Mt. McKinley National Park," in *Reports*, Dept. of the Interior, 1917. 65th Cong., 2nd Sess., House Doc. No. 915.

Proceedings, National Park Service. From 1912.

Reports. Director, National Park Service. From 1917.

The National Parks Portfolio. Wn.DC: GPO, 1931. 274 pp. Subsequent editions.

Economic Aspects of Recreation in Alaska. Wn.DC: GPO, 1953. 191 pp.

Analysis of Passenger Travel to Alaska. Seattle: University of Washington, 1953. 96 pp. Data survey, Wm. J. Stanton.

Recreation in Anchorage. Wn.DC: GPO, 1954. 35 pp.

A Recreation Program for Alaska. Wn.DC: GPO, 1955. 102 pp.

Various brochures for Mt. McKinley National Park, Katmai National Monument, Glacier Bay National Monument, Sitka National Monument.

See also the environmental impact statements produced for 28 proposed withdrawals of land in Alaska by the federal government, 1973-74. See as well Alaska Task Force. See also Alaska Resources Library (US).

US NATIONAL RESOURCES COMMITTEE

Alaska: Its Resources and Development. Wn.DC: GPO, 1938. 213 pp. 75th Cong., 3rd Sess., House Doc. No. 485.

Bibliography and Abstracts on the Subject of Agriculture in Alaska. Juneau: Nat. Res. Planning Board, 1942. 139 pp. George Sundborg.

See also the Arctic Bibliography.

US NATIONAL SCIENCE FOUNDATION

A Bibliography for the International Geophysical Year. Wn.DC: GPO, 1957. 51 pp.

US NAVAL INSTITUTE

See the *Proceedings* (Index) from 1950.

US NAVAL PHOTOGRAPHIC CENTER

Cold Weather Photography. Wn.DC: GPO, 1955. 118 pp.

US NAVY DEPARTMENT

Instructions for the Expedition toward the North Pole. Wn.DC: GPO, 1871. 36 pp. *Polaris*, 1871-73.

Polaris Investigation. Wn.DC: GPO, 1873. 184 pp.

Report of the Secretary 1873. Wn.DC: GPO, 1873. 628 pp.

Report to the President of the US of the Action of the Navy in the Matter of the Disaster to the US Exploring Expedition. Wn.DC: GPO, 1873. 154 pp.

Narrative of the North Polar Expedition, US Ship Polaris, Capt. Charles F. Hall, Commanding. Wn.DC: GPO, 1876. 696 pp.

Reports of Commander L.A. Beardslee. Wn.DC: GPO, 1880. 34 pp. 46th Cong., 2nd Sess., Senate Exec. Doc. No. 105.

Reports of Capt. L.A. Beardslee, US Navy, Relative to Affairs in Alaska. Wn.DC: GPO, 1882. 198 pp. 47th Cong., 1st Sess., Senate Exec. Doc. No. 71.

Reports of US Naval Officers Cruising in the Waters of Alaska. Wn.DC: GPO, 1882. 52 pp. 47th Cong., 1st Sess., House Exec. Doc. No. 81.

Letters on Surveying Expedition to the North Pacific Ocean. Ms., 2v., 1855, Bering Strait, China Sea. US Navy Dept.

Report. Winfield S. Schley, commanding the Greely Relief Expedition of 1884. Wn.DC: GPO, 1887. 75 pp. *Bear, Thetis* and *Alert*.

US NAVY, BOARD ON SUBMARINE, DESTROYER, MINE, AND NAVAL AIR BASES

Report. Need of Additional Naval Bases to Defend the Coasts of the US. Wn.DC: GPO, 1939. 39 pp. 76th Cong., 1st Sess., House Doc. No. 65.

US NAVY, BUREAU OF DOCKS AND YARDS

Arctic Engineering. Wn.DC: GPO, 1955. 4 parts. With the cooperation of the Dept. of Commerce, Office of Tech. Servs.

US NAVY, BUREAU OF MEDICINE AND SURGERY

Edible Plants of the Arctic Region. Wn.DC: GPO, 1943. 49 pp.

Alaska Insect Control Project. Wn.DC: GPO, 1947. 132 pp.

Fundamentals of Arctic and Cold Weather Medicine and Dentistry. Wn.DC: GPO, 1949. 204 pp. Wn. Research Division.

US NAVY, CIVIL ENGINEERS CORPS

Cold Weather Engineering. Wn.DC: GPO, 1948. 109 pp.

Permafrost Must Be Respected. Repr. from US Navy Civil Engineer Corps, *Bulletin*, May, 1948.

US NAVY, PACIFIC FLEET

Report of the 1948 Point Barrow Supply Expedition. Wn.DC: GPO, 1948. 128 pp.

Report of the Bering Sea Expedition, Winter, 1953. Wn.DC: GPO, 1953. 164 pp.

See also Elisha Kent Kane.

US OFFICE OF BUSINESS ECONOMICS

Income in Alaska. Wn.DC: GPO, 1960. 35 pp.

US OFFICE OF EDUCATION, DEPARTMENT OF THE INTERIOR

Annual Report on the Introduction of Domestic Reindeer into Alaska. See Sheldon Jackson.

Public Education in Alaska. Wn.DC: GPO, 1936. 56 pp. See also US Bureau of Education. See Education.

US OFFICE OF INDIAN AFFAIRS

W-8086-94, 1868-1924 (bombardment of Wrangell, Metalaktla Indians, census, Sitka Training School, etc.).

Bombardment of Wrangell, Alaska. Wn.DC: GPO, 1870. 23 pp. Report of the Secretary of War, Secretary of Interior, and letter to the President. Vincent Colyer.

"The Contract School at Sitka," in *Annual Report*, Comm. of Indian Affairs, 1885. 49th Cong., 1st Sess., House Exec. Doc. No. 1, Part 5.

Reports. Commissioner of Indian Affairs. From 1867.

See also the Arctic Bibliography, and also Fuller-75-82. See as well Bureau of Indian Affairs. See Education. See Alaska Natives.

US OFFICE OF NAVAL OPERATIONS
Cold Weather Medicine. Wn.DC; GPO, 1954. 32 pp.
Low Temperature Sanitation. Wn.DC: GPO, 1954. 89 pp.
The Dynamic North. Wn.DC: GPO, 1956. 2v. Stefansson.

US OFFICE OF NAVAL RESEARCH
Across the Top of the World: A Discussion of the Arctic. Wn.DC: GPO, 1947. 71 pp. Bibliography by Stefansson.
Arctic Research Laboratory. Wn.DC: GPO, 1955. 34 pp. Est. at Barrow in 1948 the Naval Research facility has at times been operated under contract to the University of Alaska.

US OFFICE FOR EMERGENCY MANAGEMENT
Copper in Alaska: A Select List of Official Publications. Wn.DC: GPO, 1943. 6 pp.

US PAN-AMERICAN UNION
W-9383-9386, 1897-1914 (furs, forests).

US POST OFFICE DEPARTMENT
W-7889-7913, 1885-1925 (annual reports of the Postmaster General, appropriations, mail contracts, advertisements, railway mail service).
Annual Reports. Postmaster General; from 1909.

US PRESIDENT
W-6832-7323, 1822-1925 (Messages, Proclamations, Executive Orders).
Message. Transmits information, Feb., 1822, on US territorial claims north of the 42nd parallel. 17th Cong., 1st Sess., House Doc. No. 112. Wn.DC: GPO, 1822. 38 pp. See Tompkins; see also Alaska Diplomacy.
Message. Bering Sea Controversy, Dec., 1838. 25th Cong., 3rd Sess., House Exec. Doc. No. 2.
Special Message. Treaty, Alaska. March 30, 1867.
Message. Transmits Alaska Purchase Treaty. July, 1867. 40th Cong., 1st Sess., Senate Exec. Doc. No. 17.
Special Message. Interference of Russian Naval Vessels with American Whalers. Jan., 1868. 40th Cong., 2nd Sess.
Message. Transfer of Territory. Jan., 1868. 40th Cong., 2nd Sess., House Exec. Doc. No. 125.
Message. Response to Resolution of the House: Transmits correspondence re: Russian America. 40th Cong., 2nd Sess., House Exec. Doc. No. 177, Part 1.
The reports incl. in this message are the following:

Geography and Geology	Wm. P. Blake
Report, with Misc. Papers	Wm. H. Seward
Letter	P. McD. Collins
Letter (re: Kennicott)	J.P. Kirtland
Report, Sec. Treas.	Hugh McCulloch
Report, Ascent of Mt. Makushin	Lt. Hodgedon
Report, Botany	Dr. Kellogg
Report	George Davidson
Report, Geology	Theo. A. Blake
Report, Conchology	Harford

Vocabulary of Native Languages
Meteorological Data, Sitka and Unalaska
Meterology, Cruise of the *Lincoln*
Message. Response to Resolution of the House. Digest of above.

Annual Message. Andrew Johnson. Dec. 9, 1868.
Proclamation: Treaty of Cession. US Stat. L., Vol. XV.
Annual Message. Grover Cleveland. *Dec. 6, 1886.* On Chinese mistreatment.
Message. Transmits report on the Boundary. March, 1889. 50th Cong., 2nd Sess., Senate Exec. Doc. No. 146.
Annual Message. Theodore Roosevelt. Dec., 1906. Fur seal depletion.
Annual Message. Wm. Howard Taft. Dec., 1909. Fur seal protection.
Annual Message. Wm. Howard Taft. Dec., 1910. Commission to govern Alaska (migratory Alaskans).
Special Message. Transmits session laws, Alaska Territory. 1923. See other editions, other years.
For other presidential messages see the Arctic Bibliography, and Wickersham's bibliography.

US PUBLIC HEALTH SERVICE; see US Treasury Department.

US QUARTERMASTER TECHNICAL TRAINING SERVICE
Cold Weather Clothing. Wn.DC: GPO, 1951. 105 pp.

US REVENUE CUTTER SERVICE, US TREASURY DEPARTMENT
W-7589-7608, 1867-1904 (reports of various captains).
Report. Botany of the Cruise of the *Lincoln.* 40th Cong., 2nd Sess., House Exec. Doc. No. 177. Albert Kellogg.
Report. Cruise of the *Wyanda.* 41st Cong., 2nd Sess., House Misc. Doc. No. 161. 1868. J.W. White.
Report. Cruise of the *Walcott.* 1875. James Swan. See Swan.
Report upon Alaska and its People. Wn.DC: GPO, 1880. 52 pp. George W. Bailey, US Revenue Marine.
Report. Cruise of the *Corwin*, 1880. C.L. Hooper. See Hooper.
Report. Shelling of Villages by the *Corwin.* 47th Cong., 2nd Sess., House Exec. Doc. No. 9, Parts 1-4. 1883.
Report. Cruise of the *Corwin*, 1881. C.L. Hooper. See Hooper.
Report. Cruise of the *Corwin*, 1884. M.A. Healy. See Healy.
Report. Cruise of the *Corwin*, 1885. M.A. Healy. See Healy.
Report. Cruise of the *Bear*, and Overland Expedition for relief of Whalers. Wn.DC: GPO, 1899. 144 pp.
Report. Cruise of the *Nunivak*, Yukon River, 1899-1901. J.C. Cantwell.
Annual Reports. Life Saving Service. From 1890.

US SMITHSONIAN INSTITUTION
W-9061-89 (Annual Reports), W-9090-9185 (National Museum), W-9186-9201 (Bureau of American Ethnology), W-9202 (Contributions to North American Ethnology), W-9203 (Harriman Alaska Series), W-9204-9232 (miscellaneous publications).
"A Journey to the Youcan, Russian America," in *Annual Report*, Smithsonian Inst., 1864. 38th Cong., 2nd Sess., House Misc. Doc. No. 55. W.W. Kirby. Kennicott. See Sherwood.

"The Aurora Borealis," in *Annual Report*, Smithsonian Inst., 1865. Elias Loomis.

"Notes on the Tinneh or Chipewyan Indians," *Annual Report*, Smithsonian Inst., 1866.

Atnatanas: Natives of the Copper River. See Allen.

"Bogoslof Volcanoes," *Annual Report*, Smithsonian Inst., 1901. C.H. Merriam.

"Reindeer in Alaska," *Annual Report*, Smithsonian Inst., G.H. Grosvenor.

"The Klondike and Yukon Goldfields in 1913," *Annual Report*, Smithsonian Inst., 1914.

"The Background of Totemism," *Annual Report*, Smithsonian Inst., 1918. E.W. Hopkins.

A Catalogue of Earthquakes on the Pacific Coast, 1769-1897. Wn.DC: GPO, 1898. 253 pp. Smithsonian Inst.

See also Smithsonian Institution.

US SUPERINTENDENT OF DOCUMENTS
W-9050-60, as follows:

Partial Reference List of US Gov't. Publications on Alaska. Wn.DC: GPO, 1898. 37 pp. US Documents Office.

US Public Documents Relating to Noncontinuous Territory. Wn.DC: GPO, 1911. 112 pp.

US Government Publications, Monthly Catalog. This monthly listing is an invaluable reference for the researcher. It is a continuing publication of the US Documents Office. See also the various catalogs of documents and microfilm published by the National Archives and Records Service.

Fishes and Wildlife. Wn.DC: GPO, 1943 and other editions. 27 pp.

US TREASURY DEPARTMENT
W-7361-7676, as follows:

W-7361-7528 (Letters to Congress, 1868-1924, re: customs collectors' reports, fur-seal fisheries, public bldgs., education, lighthouses, boundary, insane persons, road construction, resource survey, telegraph, railroads); W-7529-73, 1881-1925 (Director of the Mint, reports on production of precious metals); W-7574-88, 1880-1916 (Bur. Publ. Health Serv., care of seamen, educ. and relief work in Alaska, sanitation); W-7589-7608, 1867-1924 (Revenue Cutter Service, reports of captains); W-7609-22, 1876-1924 (Customs Service); W-7623-7660, 1869-1905 (fur seal fisheries); W-7661-64, 1922-25 (Bur. Budget, care of insane, governor's residence, fisheries protection, Alaska Railroad); W-7665-76, 1879-1924 (customs service, fisheries regulation, sea-otter hunting, public bldgs., telegraph, report of William Gouvernor Morris).

Letter. May, 1868; Capt. J.W. White. *Wyanda.* 3 pp. 40th Cong., 2nd Sess., House Misc. Doc. No. 161.

Survey, Alaska and Aleutian Islands. 41st Cong., 2nd Sess., House Exec. Doc. No. 255. 7 pp. 1870.

Letter. Transmits Report, Special Agent H.H. McIntyre. 41st Cong., 2nd Sess., House Exec. Doc. No. 36; Wn.DC: GPO, 1870. 18 pp.

Letter. Lease, Alaska seal fisheries. 41st Cong., 3rd Sess., House Exec. Doc. 108; Wn.DC: GPO, 1871. 24 pp.

Report. Pribilof Island Group. Henry W. Elliott. Wn.DC: GPO, 1873. 125 pp. Treasury Department.

Report. Condition of Affairs in the Territory of Alaska. Henry W. Elliott. Wn.DC: GPO, 1875. 277 pp. Treas. Dept.

Letter. Transmits information of seal fisheries. 44th Cong., 1st Sess., House Exec. Doc. No. 83; Wn.DC: GPO, 1876. 478 pp.

Report. William Gouvernor Morris, 1879. See Morris.

Letter. Response to Sen. Res. re: Alaska conditions and resources. 46th Cong., 2nd Sess., Sen. Exec. Doc. No. 192; Wn.DC: GPO, 1880. 6 pp.

Report. Seal Islands of Alaska. Henry W. Elliott. Wn.DC: GPO, 1880. 185 pp. US Bur. of Census.

Letter. Response to House Res. re: shelling of two villages in Alaska. 47th Cong., 2nd Sess., House Exec. Doc. No. 9; Wn.DC: GPO, 1882. 2 pp.

Record of Investigations at Neah Bay, Wn. 48th Cong., 1st Sess., House Misc. Doc. No. 11.

Habits of Fur Seals. H.W. Elliott. *Natural History of Seals.* J.A. Allen. 47th Cong., 1st Sess., Senate Misc. Doc. No. 124.

Reports. Special Agents A.W. Williams, A.W. Lavender, J. Murray, J. Stanley-Brown and W.H. Williams on condition of seal islands for 1891. 52nd Cong., 2nd Sess., Senate Exec. Doc. No. 107; Wn.DC: GPO, 1893. 140 pp.

Reports of Agents. 54th Cong., 1st Sess., Senate Doc. No. 137; Wn.DC: GPO, 1895. 533 pp. C.S. Hamlin, J.B. Crowley, Joseph Murray. Also C.H. Townsend and F.W. True.

Report. Henry W. Elliott. Fur Seal Fisheries. 54th Cong., 1st Sess., House Doc. No. 175; Wn.DC: GPO, 1896. 240 pp.

Observations on the Fur Seals. David Starr Jordan. Treas. Dept. Doc. No. 1913. Wn.DC: GPO, 1896. 69 pp.

Letter. Transmits report of Henry W. Elliott, 1896. 54th Cong., 1st Sess., House Doc. No. 175; Wn.DC: GPO, 1896. 240 pp.

Report on Alaska. Ivan Petrof. Repr. from *Rept. on Internal Commerce*, Treas. Dept., 1890.

Regulations. Entry and Transportation of Merchandise for Klondike Region and Northwest Territory of British Columbia via the subports of Juneau, Dyea, and Skagway or other customs ports. Wn.DC: GPO, 1898. 3 pp.

Seal and Salmon Fisheries and General Resources of Alaska, 1898. 55th Cong., 1st Sess., House Doc. No. 92; Wn.DC: GPO, 1899. 4v. Vol. 1: Reports by Special Treasury Agents, 1868-1895 (D.S. Jordan); Vol. 2: Reports, 1895-96 re: pelagic sealing (D.S. Jordan); Vol. 3: Reports, H.W. Elliott and Lt. W. Maynard, with commentary by D.S. Jordan; also on education in Alaska by Sheldon Jackson; Vol. 4: Reports, C.H. Townsend, F.W. True, and J.J. Brice, with commentary by D.S. Jordan; also reports of W.G. Morris, Ivan Petrof and Leonhard Stejneger.

The Fur Seals and the Fur Seal Islands of the North Pacific Ocean. See Jordan.

A History of Public Buildings under the Control of the Treasury Department. Wn.DC: GPO, 1901. 648 pp.

Letter. Transmits Communication from Attorney-General re: Alaska public buildings. 57th Cong., 1st Sess., House Doc. No. 669; Wn.DC: GPO, 1902. 2 pp.

Annual Statements. Commerce and customs business of Alaska. From 1904. The information is also available in the annual reports of the Governor of

Alaska. Statements for 1912 and 1913 were printed at Juneau; after that at Washington, DC.

Letter. Transmits data re: *Ameria,* wrecked May, 1912. 62nd Cong., 3rd Sess., House Doc. No. 1393.

See also US Revenue Cutter Service.

US TREATIES

Treaty concerning the Cession of Russian Possessions in North America. Wn.DC: GPO, 1867. 9 pp.

Message. Transmits Convention between US and Great Britain re: seal fisheries of the Bering Sea. Wn.DC: GPO, 1892. 102 pp.

Convention between US and Great Britain for Joint Survey of Territory Adjacent to the Boundary Line. Wn.DC: GPO, 1892.

Proclamation. Announces agreement with Great Britain re: Alaskan boundary. Wn.DC: GPO, 1906.

Compilation of the Acts of Congress and Treaties relating to Alaska. To 1913. Wn.DC: GPO, 1914.

Message. Transmits Convention looking to the Protection and Preservation of Fur Seals and Sea Otters. Wn.DC: GPO, 1911.

Proclamation. Announces Treaty between US and Great Britain for Fur Seal Protection. Wn.DC: GPO, 1911.

Convention. US and Other Powers, Preservation and Protection of Fur Seals. Wn.DC: GPO, 1911.

Report. Convention for Mutual Protection of Migratory Birds. Sen. Res. 25; Senate Committee on Foreign Relations. 1913. W-9522.

Agreement. Radio Communication between Alaska and British Columbia. Wn.DC: GPO, 1939. 9 pp. Dept. of State Publ. 1306.

Agreement. Fur Seals Research Program. Canada, Japan, US. Wn.DC: GPO, 1953. Dept. of State Publ. 4758.

Interim Convention. North Pacific Fur Seals. US, Canada, Japan, USSR. Wn.DC: GPO, 1958. 59 pp.

US WAR DEPARTMENT

W-7677-7718, 1867-1924 (Alaska formed, military department; Dept. of Alaska for short periods, under Dept. of Columbia 1870-1913, superseded by the Western Department. Maj. Gens. Halleck, Davis, Thomas, Canby, Howard and others prepared annual reports for the President on exploration, telegraph, supply, subsistence, road construction, Indians, etc.); W-7719-66 (Letters: military affairs, bombardment of Wrangell, liquor traffic, colonization by Icelanders, exploration, gold fields, relief of miners, road construction, harbor and navigational engineering, telegraph and cable system); W-7767-75 (Adj. Gens. reports on reconnaissance, gold fields, relief of miners, special orders, general orders); W-7776-95 (Judge-Advocate Gen., Quartermaster Gen., Surgeon Gen., Chief of Engineers); W-7796-7854 (Board of Road Commissioners, Board of Engineers for Rivers and Harbors, Chief Signal Officer, Bureau of Insular Affairs).

Report. Maj. Gen. Halleck. 40th Cong., 2nd Sess., House Exec. Doc. No. 1. In Report of the Sec. of War for 1867.

Report. Maj. Gen. Davis. 40th Cong., 3rd Sess., House Exec. Doc. No. 1. In Report of the Sec. of War for 1868.

Report. Maj. Gen. Thomas. 41st Cong., 2nd Sess., House Exec. Doc. No. 1. In Report of the Sec. of War for 1869.

Report of a Tour of Alaska in 1875. See O.O. Howard.

Letter. Transmits report of Maj. Gen. Davis re: bombardment of Indian villages. 41st Cong., 2nd Sess., Senate Exec. Doc. No. 67; Wn.DC: GPO, 1870. 10 pp.

Official Report of Lt. Schwatka. See Schwatka.

Report. Capt. P.H. Ray and Lt. W.P. Richardson re: Condition of Affairs in Alaska Gold Fields. See Ray.

Report. Copper River Expedition. See Allen.

Report. Explorations, Cook Inlet, Susitna, Copper and Tanana Rivers. See Abercrombie, and Glenn.

Report. Relief Action, Yukon River Country. See Ray, Richardson, and Jackson.

Report. Copper River Exploring Expedition. See Abercrombie.

Report. Explorations in Alaska, 1899, for an all-American overland route from Cook Inlet to the Yukon. See Herron.

Report. Reconnaissance of the Yukon River, 1869. See Raymond.

Report. International Polar Expedition to Point Barrow, 1885. See Ray, and Murdoch.

Contributions to the Natural History of Alaska, 1874-81. See Turner.

Report. Natural History Collections, Alaska, 1877-81. See E.W. Nelson.

Compilation of the Acts of Congress and Treaties relating to Alaska. See US Treaties. Bureau of Insular Affairs.

Operations in snow and extreme cold. Wn.DC: GPO, 1941. 82 pp.

Arctic Manual. Wn.Dc: GPO, 1942. 74 pp. See the Arctic Bibliography.

A Pocket Guide to Alaska. Wn.DC: GPO, 1943. 62 pp. Special Service Division, Army Air Corps.

Dog Team Transportation. Wn.DC: GPO, 1944. 139 pp.

The Capture of Attu. Wn.DC: GPO, 1944. 217 pp. Personal recollections.

"Extracts from a Diary found on the Body of a Japanese Officer on the Island of Attu," *Explorers' Journal,* Spring, 1944.

Constr. of Runways, Roads and Bldgs. on Frozen Ground. Wn.DC: GPO, 1945. 64 pp.

See also US Army Alaska, US Air Force Alaska Air Command, and Alaska Command (unified command of the US Forces in Alaska, discontinued, 1975). See also US Congress, Senate, Committee on Military Affairs, *Compilation of Narratives;* see as well Sherwood.

US WEATHER BUREAU, DEPARTMENT OF AGRICULTURE (now Dept. of Commerce)

W-8444-61, 1895-1926 (misc. articles in *Monthly Weather Review,* US Weather Bureau).

Climatological Data, Alaska. Monthly publication of the US Weather Bureau, from 1915.

Data from Aerological Soundings at Fairbanks, 1936-38. Wn.DC: GPO, 1940. 35 pp.

Air Routes, Alaska to Siberia. Wn.DC: GPO, 1942. 99 pp.

Climatology of the Arctic Regions. Wn.DC: GPO, 1946. 3v.

Temperatures at Selected Stations in the US. Wn.DC: GPO, 1948. 20 pp.

US WORK PROJECTS ADMINISTRATION
Compilation of Sources of Information on the Territories and Outlying Possessions of the US. New York: WPA, 1937. Mimeographed. The cards prepared in the Library of Congress on Alaska references were photocopied, averaging four to a page, and the pages bound into several volumes. A copy of each of the volumes is available in the Alaska Collection of Alaska Methodist University. Although Fuller (No. 8) reports that the Alaska number of this series was to be microfilmed by the College of the City of New York, apparently no such film has ever been prepared.
Annotated Bibliography of the Polar Regions. New York: WPA, 1938. 2v. 68 pp. Mimeographed.
A Guide to Alaska. See Merle Colby.

UNIVERSITY OF ALASKA
See the lists of publications prepared by the various institutes and centers of the University, e.g., the Institute for Social, Economic and Government Research, the Center for Northern Educational Research, etc. See also the various publications of the Rasmuson Library, especially those describing new acquisitions to the several historical collections. See also the publications describing acquisitions and collections of the Archive of the University at Fairbanks.
Alaska History Research Project: Alaska Church Documents. See Alaska History Research Project.
A Bibliography of Alaskan Literature. See Wickersham.
Anthropological Papers. Entered in this bibliography under the authors' names. Contact the Dept. of Anthropology.
A Program of Education for Alaska Natives: Research Report. College: University of Alaska, 1959. 303 pp.
For material on the University of Alaska see the following: *Alaska Life*, Apr., '47 (G.I. Bill); July, '48; *Alaska Sportsman*, see Index; *Alaska Weekly*, March, '51 (Erskine library); May, '50; Aug., '50 (Andrew Nerland); Sept., '50 (Minnie Wells); Oct., '50 (Duckering); numerous other incidental articles; Andrews; Cashen; Chase (history); Colby; Davis; Denison; Franck; Gruening; Hart (excellent summary); Hayes; Hilscher; Hulley; Kitchener (Erskine library); Pilgrim; Potter; Underwood; Winslow.

UNIVERSITY PEAK
Alaska Sportsman, July, '55 (ascents of 1954 and 1955). Until its ascent in 1955 this was the highest unclimbed peak in N. America. Lying in the Skolai Range of the Wrangells, it was discovered in 1930 and named by Terris Moore in 1953 in honor of the University of Alaska.

UNUK RIVER
Alaska Sportsman, Apr., '35; Jan., '37; Baker (Burroughs Bay, Revillagigedo Island); Couch (post office from 1949 to 1950).

URANIUM
Alaska Sportsman, Oct., '55 (Prince of Wales Island); Nov., '55; Apr., '56; Dec., '57 (ore shipped).

URSULINE SISTERS
Life of the Rev. Mother Amadeus of the Heart of Jesus. New York: Paulist Press, 1923. 226 pp. Mother Amadeus was Ursuline Provincial in Alaska at the turn of the century.
See also Santos.

USHIN, STEPHEN M.
Journal. Extracts appear in Alaska Church Documents (Alaska History Research Project). The original is apparently with the Russian Orthodox Church Collection in the Library of Congress. See Russian Orthodox Church. See also Hulley.

USOV, P.
See the Arctic Bibliography.

UTKIAVIK
See Barrow.

UYAK
Baker (village, bay and cape on Kodiak Island); Colby (pop. 17); Couch (post office 1900-14, and 1916-33); Heizer; Higginson (cannery village).

UYEDA, CLIFFORD
The Deer Mountain. New York: Exposition Press, 1959. 163 pp.

V

VACHON, ANDREW WILLIAM
Ketchikan Sketchings. Seattle: R.D. Seal, 1959. 129 pp.
Fish Without Chips. Juneau: Men of the Cathedral, 1960. 256 pp.

VAETH, J. GORDON
To the Ends of the Earth: Explorations of Roald Amundsen. New York: Harper & Row, 1962. 219 pp.

VAGIN, IRENE
"Lay Missionary for Alaska," *Russian Orthodox Journal*, May, 1959.

VAHL, JENS (1828-1898)
Alaska: Folket og Missionen. Kobenhavn: G.E.C. Gad Boghandel, 1872. 108 pp. Russian period, native peoples.
Lapperne og den Lapske Mission. Kobenhavn: G.E.C. Gad Bohandel, 1866. 2v.

VAIL, ISAAC NEWTON
Alaska: Land of the Nugget. Pasadena: Press of G.A. Swerdfiger, 1897. 68 pp.

VAKHTIN, V. (1840-1912)
See the Arctic Bibliography, and T-4630.

VALAAM MONASTERY

K Stolietnemu Jubileiu Pravoslaviia v Amerikie (1794-1894). St. Petersburg: M. Merkushev, 1894. 292 pp. This centenary history of the Orthodox missionaries in Alaska is a valuable contribution to Alaska history. See the bibliographical note in Barbara Smith's *Preliminary Survey.* See also Chevigny; Fedorova; Tompkins. See also the Arctic Bibliography, and T-4632.

VALDES, CAYETANO

Baker (according to Vancouver, Port Valdez named by Fidalgo in 1790 for Valdes, who was on the Northwest coast, 1789-92); Galiano (on the 1792 voyage Galiano commanded the *Sutil* and Valdes the *Mexicana*); Espinosa y Tallo (Espinosa's account of the voyage was probably written by Valdes, according to Wagner); Wagner.

VALDEZ

Abercrombie; *Alaska Life,* Jan., '44; *Alaska Sportsman,* see Index; *Alaska-Yukon Magazine,* July, '07 (photo); Oct., '07 (Home Railway); June, '09; Feb., '10; Nov., '10 (gold discoveries); Apr., '11 ("hangman's tree"); Dec., '11; July, '12; *Alaska Weekly,* Feb., '50; Feb., '51 (weather, ice); Aug., '51; Andrews; Baker (on name, for Cayetano Valdes, captain of the *Mexicana,* or Antonio Valdes y Bazan, Minister of Marine in Spain, by Fidalgo in 1790); Beach (*Iron Trail*); Brookfield (in *Compilation of Narratives;* 3000 prospectors landed at Port Valdez in 1898); Brown, Chas. (in *Compilation of Narratives:* hardships of inexperienced prospectors); Carpenter (Keystone Canyon); Cleave (in *Compilation of Narratives*); Colby; Couch (post office from 1899); Denison; Denison-Mahoney (Klondike Mike with body of Judge Humes); Fidalgo (naming of Valdez); Foster, Wm. (*Amer. City,* Jan., '55); Franck; Gillette (in *Compilation of Narratives*); Glenn (in *Compilation of Narratives*); Greely (telegraph trail); Gruening; Hart; Herron (on Anthony Dimond); Higginson; Hulley; Jacobin; Johnson, B. (Wn. Acad. of Sci., Journ., 1918); Kuehnelt-Leddihn (1945 economic data); Moffitt (USGS, 1913); Nichols (political); Pilgrim; Potter (Canadian annexation); Remington; Rossiter; Santos; Sherman; Stuck; Sundborg; Tewkesbury; Tompkins (on Abercrombie); Tuck (*Mineral Resources of Alaska,* 1936, USGS); Valdes; Vancouver; Wagner; Wickersham; Winslow. See also Klondike; Richardson Highway; Oil; Valdez Glacier; Earthquake.

VALDEZ GLACIER

Alaska Sportsman, Nov., '40 (photos); July, '42 (photo); July, '56 (photo); Abercrombie (in *Compilation of Narratives*); Brookfield (in *Compilation of Narratives*); Brooks (on the 1898-99 attempt to cross the glacier; Brown, Chas. (in *Compilation of Narratives*); Colby; Koehler (over glacier in 1898); Lowe (1898); Margeson (1898); Preston (in *Compilation of Narratives*); Rafferty (in *Compilation of Narratives*); Remington; Rice (in *Compilation of Narratives:* Abercrombie's relief station at the summit); Schrader; Tompkins; Wentworth and Ray (see the Arctic Bibliography).

VALLEY of TEN THOUSAND SMOKES

See Katmai National Monument.

VAN BUSKIRK, PHILIP CLAYTON (b. 1834)

An Excursion to Wrangell in 1896; see Monroe.

VAN CAMPEN, HELEN (ca. 1880-1960)

"I'll See you in Alaska," in Jacobin's *Guide to Alaska,* 1946.
On Mrs. Van Campen, a celebrated Seward and Fairbanks pioneer, see the following: *Alaska Life,* June, '40; *Alaska Sportsman,* Nov., '60.

VAN CLEVE, H.

See T-2858.

VAN CLEVE, RICHARD

See T-2889, T-4511, and T-4517.

VANCOUVER, GEORGE (1757-1798)

A Voyage of Discovery to the North Pacific Ocean. London: G.G. and J. Robinson, 1798. 3v. and atlas. Other editions.
A Voyage of Discovery to the North Pacific Ocean and Round the World. London: J. Stockdale, 1801. 6v. Same as the above work in smaller format.
Narrative or Journal of a Voyage of Discovery to the North Pacific Ocean and Around the World. London: Lee, 1802. 80 pp.
Short Abstract of a Voyage of Discovery to the North Pacific Ocean. Edinburgh, 1798.
There are as well numerous translations of Vancouver's account. See also the following on Vancouver:
Alaska Life, Oct., '41; *Alaska Sportsman,* Aug., '40; Anderson, B.; Baker; Bancroft; Barbeau; Barry, J. (*Oreg. Hist. Q.,* Dec., '34, on Broughton on the Columbia River; *Oreg. Hist. Q.,* June, '38, on discovery of the Columbia River; *Wn. Hist. Q.,* Jan., '30, on Broughton in the San Juans); Bell, E. (*Journal;* see extracts in *Oreg. Hist. Q.,* March and June, '32, and in the *Wn. Hist. Q.,* Oct., '14); Boit (log of the *Columbia*); Boone; Brooks (Vancouver missed the mouths of the Columbia, Fraser, Stikine, Copper and Susitna); Burney (history of voyages); Burrard (*BC Hist. Q.,* Apr., '46: naming of Burrard Inlet); Caamano (Journal); Carr and Salazar (see the Arctic Bibliography); Clowes (*The Royal Navy* [Boston: Little, Brown, 1899-1903. 7v]); Cook and King (Vancouver was a member of Cook's crew on the 1776-1780 voyage); Craig (*Pac. NW Q.,* Oct., '53: letter from the Vancouver expedition); Cotterill (lengthy Vancouver quotes on Puget Sound exploration); Davidson, G.; Denton (4 chapters); Dillon (*BC Hist. Q.,* July-Oct., '51 [Archibald Menzies' trophies]; *Pac. NW Q.,* Oct., '50 [Charles Vancouver's plan]); Haig-Brown; Godwin; Greenhow (highly favorable comment on character of the journal); Gunther (*Pac. NW Q.,* Jan., '60); Higginson (on Vancouver's lack of imagination); Howay; Laut; Manby (officer on the *Chatham:* Ms. journal in Public Records Office, London); Manning; Marshall; Meany; Menzies (Ms. journal in the British Museum; see Menzies); Roper (see Bromberg); Scidmore; Shaw (S-9377); Speck; Wagner; Walbran (*BC Coast Names* [Ottawa: GPB, 1909]); Whitebrook (*Pac. NW Q.,* July, '53); Wilbur; Woollen; see also Anderson for information on unpublished ms. sources; see also the Arctic Bibliography.

VANDERCOOK, JOHN WOMACK

Great Sailor: A Life of the Discoverer Captain James Cook. New York: Dial Press, 1951. 339 pp.

VAN DEUSEN, GLYNDON G.
William Henry Seward. New York: Oxford University Press, 1967. 224 pp.

VAN DYKE, EDWIN COOPER
The Coleoptera Collected by the Katmai Expeditions. Wn.DC: GPO, 1941. 26 pp. National Geographic Society. See also T-3879.

VAN HISE, C. R. and L. HAVEMEYER
Conservation of Our Natural Resources. New York: Kraus Reprints, 1970. Original publication, 1930.

VAN LOON, DIRK
Papeek. Philadelphia: Lippincott, 1970. 93 pp.

VAN STEENSEL, M.
People of Light and Dark. Ottawa: Queen's Printer, 1966. 156 pp. Radio broadcast essays.

VANSTONE, JAMES W.
Eskimos of the Nushagak River: An Ethnographic History. Seattle: University of Washington Press, 1967. 192 pp.
Point Hope: An Eskimo Village in Transition. Seattle: University of Washington Press, 1962. 177 pp.
V.S. Khrohchenko's Coastal Explorations in Southwestern Alaska, 1822. Ed. Seattle: University of Washington Press, 1973. 224 pp.
"Ethnohistorical Research in Alaska," *Alaska Review*, Fall, 1967.
"Carved Human Figures from St. Lawrence Island," *Anthrop. Papers*, Univ. of Alaska, 1953.
"Archaeological Excavations at Kotzebue," *Anthrop. Papers*, Univ. of Alaska, 1955.
"An Archaeological Reconnaissance of Nunivak Island," *Anthrop. Papers*, Univ. of Alaska, 1957.
"An Eskimo Community and the Outside World," *Anthrop. Papers*, Univ. of Alaska, 1958.
"An Early Account of the Russian Discoveries in the North Pacific," *Anthrop. Papers*, Univ. of Alaska, 1959.
"Notes on the Economy and Population Shifts of the Eskimos of Southampton Island," *Anthrop. Papers*, Univ. of Alaska, 1960.
"Three Eskimo Communities (Napaskiak, Point Hope, and Eskimo Point)," *Anthrop. Papers*, Univ. of Alaska, 1960.
"Tikchik Village: A Nineteenth Century Riverine Community in Southwestern Alaska," *Fieldiana*, 1967.
"An Annotated Ethnohistorical Bibliography of the Nushagak River, Alaska," *Fieldiana*, 1968.
"Akulivichuk: A Nineteenth Century Village on the Nushagak River, Alaska," *Fieldiana*, 1970.
"Ethnohistorical Research in Southwestern Alaska: A Methodological Perspective," in *Ethnohistory in Southwestern Alaska and the Southern Yukon: Method and Content*, Margaret Lantis.
"Nushagak: An Historic Trading Center in Southwestern Alaska," *Fieldiana*, 1972.
"Exploring the Copper River Country," *Pac. NW Q.*, Oct., 1955. Russian and American expeditions to Taral at the confluence of the Copper and Chitina Rivers.

"Russian Exploration in Interior Alaska," *Pac. NW Q.*, June, 1956. Andrei Glazunov.
"Notes on Kotzebue Dating," *Tree-Ring Bulletin*, July, 1953.
See also the Arctic Bibliography.

VAN VALIN, WILLIAM B. (b. 1878)
Eskimoland Speaks. Caldwell: Caxton Printers, 1941. 242 pp.

VAN WAGENEN, JAMES H.
"International Boundary Commission: US, Alaska and Canada," *Amer. For. Serv. Journ.*, Apr., 1935.

VASILIEV, IVAN F.
See the Arctic Bibliography.

VASILIEV, MIKHAIL NIKOLAIEVICH (d. 1847)
See the Arctic Bibliography.

VATER, JOHANN SEVERIN
See the Arctic Bibliography, and T-4657 ff.

VAUDRIN, BILL
Tanaina Tales from Alaska. Norman: University of Oklahoma Press, 1969. 133 pp.

VAUGHAN, ELIZABETH
Statistical Review of Pink Salmon Trap Fishery of Southeastern Alaska. Wn.DC: GPO, 1942. 237 pp. US F&WS.

VAUGHAN, TOM
Krasheninnikov's Explorations of Kamchatka. Ed., and Trans. Portland: Oregon Historical Soc., 1972.

VAUGONDY, DIDIER ROBERT de
See the Arctic Bibliography, and T-4660 ff.

VAURIE, CHARLES
See the Arctic Bibliography, and T-4663 ff.

VENIAMINOF, MT.
Alaska Sportsman, Aug., '39 (recent eruption); March, '54 (photo of eruption); Sept., '55; Colby; Davidson (*Trans.*, Geog. Soc. of the Pacific, 1892); Dall.

VENIAMINOV, IVAN EVSIEEVICH POPOV (1797-1879)
" 'The Condition of the Orthodox Church in Russian America,' Innokentii Veniaminov's History of the Russian Church in Alaska," *Pac. NW Q.*, April, 1972. Nichols and Croskey.
Few of Fr. Veniaminov's works have been published or translated. See the Arctic Bibliography and T-4670 ff for a complete listing of works in Russian. See the following for information on Veniaminov (Bishop Innocent, Metropolitan of Moscow):
Alaska Life, March, '43 (by Andrews); *Alaska-Yukon Magazine*, Oct., '07 (photo); Baker; Bancroft; Barsukov (trans.: San Francisco: Cubery & Co., 1897. 23 pp.); Colby; Hale (1877); Henri, V. (T-2071); Higginson; Kashevaroff (*Alaska Mag.*, Jan., '27); Martin, F.; Pfizmaier (T-3565); S.Z. (T-3934); Schott (see the Arctic Bibliography); Shenitz (*Russian Orthodox Journal*, 1957); Shiels (*BC*

Hist. Q., Oct., '47); Stepanova (see the Arctic Bibliography); Vdovin (T-4667); see also Barbara Smith's *Preliminary Survey*.

VERHOEVEN, L. A.
A Report to the Salmon Fishing Industry of Alaska. Seattle: University of Washington Press, 1952. 71 pp.

VERNE, JULES
See T-4685 ff.

VERNON, FRANCIS V.
Voyages and Travels of a Sea Officer. Dublin: Wm. M'Kenzie, 1792. 306 pp.

VER WIEBE, W.A.
Oil Fields in North America. Wichita: Edwards Bros., 1949. 251 pp.

VERRIER, CHARLES
"The Collins Overland Line and American Continentalism," *Pacific Historical Review*, 1959.

VERSTOVIA, MT.
Alaska-Yukon Magazine, Oct., '07 (photo); Baker (named by Vasiliev in 1809); Colby; Rickard (photo); Scidmore; see also Sitka.

VESANEN, EIJO
On Alaska Earthquakes. Helsinki, 1947. 21 pp.

VIANA, FRANCISCO JAVIER de
See the Arctic Bibliography, and T-4696.

VICTOR, PAUL EMILE
My Eskimo Life. Toronto: Musson, 1938. See also the Arctic Bibliography.

VICTOR, RALPH
The Boy Scouts of the Yukon. New York: Chatterton, 1912. 194 pp.

VICTORIA
Alaska Sportsman, Feb., '35 (Mrs. Plaut, photo); May, '41 (Johnny O'Brien); Nov., '41 (photo at Nome); Oct., '54; June, '57 (full history); *Alaska Weekly*, June, '50; July, '50 (80 years old); March, '51); Aug., '56; *Alaska-Yukon Magazine*, Dec., '07 (photo).

VIDAL, GORE (b. 1925)
Williwaw. New York: Dutton, 1946. 222 pp. Aleutians.

VIERECK, PHILLIP
Eskimo Island: A Story of the Bering Sea Hunters. New York: John Day, 1961. 160 pp.

VIKSTEN, ALBERT (b. 1889)
See the Arctic Bibliography, and T-4700.

VILLARD, HENRY
A Journey to Alaska. New York: Putnam's, 1899. 48 pp.

VILLIERS, ALAN JOHN
Captain Cook: The Seaman's Seaman. London: Hodder and Stoughton, 1967. 266 pp.

Captain James Cook. New York: Scribner's, 1967. 307 pp.
Pioneers of the Seven Seas. London: Routledge & Kegan Paul, 1956. 354 pp.

VINCENT, LEON S.
"The Top of the World," *Alaska Sportsman*, 1944.
"Tundra Tractor Train," *Alaska Sportsman*, 1955.
"King of the Arctic," *Alaska Sportsman*, 1959.
Vincent was an Alaska school teacher, and served in numerous other capacities before his death in 1957.

VINIGG, EDWARD PAYSON (1847-1920)
An Inglorious Columbus. New York: D. Appleton, 1885. 788 pp. 5th century discovery of America.

VISHNEVSKII, BORIS NIKOLAEVICH
See the Arctic Bibliography, and T-4706.

VIZE, VLADIMIR IUL'EVICH
See the Arctic Bibliography, and T-4709.

VOBLOV, I. K.
"Eskimo Ceremonies," trans. C.C. Hughes, *Anthrop. Papers*, Univ. of Alaska, 1959.

VOEGELIN, C. F. and Z. S. HARRIS
Index to the Franz Boas Collection of Material for American Linguistics. Baltimore: Waverly Press, 1945. 43 pp.

VOEGELIN, C. F. and F. M. VOEGELIN
Languages of the World: Native American Fascicle One. Bloomington: University of Indiana Press, 1964. 149 pp.

VOICE of the YUKON
As Heard by some who "Mushed" the Great Stampede to the River Thron Diuck for the gathering of Gold in the year 1898. Vancouver: Wrigley, 1930. 45 pp.

VOIGTLANDER, O.
See the Arctic Bibliography, and T-4713.

VOLCANOES and VOLCANOLOGY
Alaska Life, Aug., '44 (photos); *Alaska Sportsman*, see Index; Becker (USGS Ann. Rept., 1896); Byers and Brannock (*Trans.*, Amer. Geophys. Union, 1949); Capps (USGS Prof. Paper, 1916: ancient eruption, upper Yukon basin); Coats (USGS Bulletin, 1950: Aleutian Arc); Coats (USGS Bulletin, 1956: Adak); Cordeiro ("Volcanoes of Alaska," *Appalachia*, July, 1910); Dall; Davidson (*Science*, 1884: St. Augustine); Finch (Arctic Biblio.); Freiday (*Nat. Hist.*, 1945: Aleutians); Grewingk (survey of all volcanoes, and listing); Hanson (*Proc.*, Pac. Sci. Conf., 1933: Unuk and Pelly River areas); Hubbard (Aniakchak, Shishaldin, Bogoslof, Veniaminof, Makushin, Pogromni, Akun Head, Akutan Crater, Katmai); Jaggar (Arctic Biblio.); Keller (*Ak. Sports.*, Aug., '49); Lowney (*Ak. Life*, Apr., '46); Matschinski (Arctic Biblio.); Perrey (Arctic Biblio.); Powers (*Proc.*, Pac. Sci. Conf., 1953: Alaska volcanoes, 1949-53); Robinson (USGS Rept., 1947); Silk (*Ak. Life*, Sept., '44: tragedy on Chuginadak); Simons and Mathewson (USGS Bulletin, 1955: Gt. Sitkin Is.); Smithsonian

Inst. (Arctic Biblio.); Snyder (USGS Circular, 1954: Katmai); Underwood; USGS (see Index); Wickersham (see the bibliography); Willoughby (Fr. Hubbard); Wolff (Arctic Biblio.). See the Arctic Bibliography on this complex and technical subject.

VON BERNEWITZ, M. W
Handbook for Prospectors. New York: McGraw-Hill, 1926. 319 pp.

VOYAGE of the CHELYUSKIN
By members of the Expedition. New York: Macmillan, 1935. 325 pp. Trans. Alex Brown.

VOYAGES; see Exploration.

VRANGEL, FERDINAND PETROVICH
See Wrangel.

VROOMAN, C. W., et alii
Some Potentials and Problems of Cattle Raising on Kodiak Is. Palmer: Agri. Exp. Sta., 1956. 32 pp.

VSEMIRNYI, TRUD
See the Arctic Bibliography.

VYVYAN, CLARA COLTMAN
Arctic Adventure. London: Owen, 1961. 172 pp.

WACHEL, PAT
Oscar Winchell: Alaska's Flying Cowboy. Minneapolis: T.S. Denison & Co., 1967. 210 pp.

WACHUSETT
Gruening (Glass on the *Jamestown* was succeeded by Lull on the *Wachusett*); Scidmore (arrived 1881); Willard (relieved by the *Adams* in 1882).

WACKER
Alaska Sportsman, May, '50 (founded by Eugene Wacker, 1907); July, '52 (pulp mill); Colby; Couch (post office from 1920; name changed to Ward's Cove in 1951).

WADA, JUJIRO (Frank Wada)
Alaska Life, Apr., '43 (most active, 1902-03); *Alaska-Yukon Magazine,* Jan., '09 (almost hanged at Fairbanks); Chase; Davis (Wada, a Japanese boy from Barnette's stranded boat); Rickard; Underwood (historic dog run from Chandalar River to Arctic Coast, thence to the Mackenzie, and the Rat and down the Porcupine, 1907).

WAGNER, ELBE
Partners Three. New York: Crowell, 1928. 295 pp.

WAGNER, HARR (1857-1936)
Joaquin Miller and His Other Self. San Francisco: Harr Wagner Publ. Co., 1929. 312 pp. See J. Miller.

WAGNER, HENRY RAUP (1862-1957)
Bibliography of Printed Works in Spanish relating to those Portions of the US belonging to Mexico. Santiago de Chile, 1917.
California Voyages, 1539-41. San Francisco, 1924.
"Quivira, A Mythical California City," *Calif. Hist. Soc. Q.,* 1924.
"The Voyage to California of Sebastian Rodriguez Carmeno in 1595," *Calif. Hist. Soc. Q.,* April, 1924.
Sir Francis Drake's Voyage around the World. San Francisco, 1926. 554 pp.
"Some Imaginary California Geography," *Proc.,* Amer. Antiq. Soc., April, 1926.
Spanish Voyages to the Northwest Coast of America in the Sixteenth Century. San Francisco: Calif. Hist. Soc., 1929. 571 pp.
"Fray Benito de la Sierra's Account of the Hezeta Expedition in 1775," *Calif. Hist. Soc. Q.,* Sept., '30.
"Apocryphal Voyages to the Northwest Coast of America," *Proc.,* Amer. Antiq. Soc., Apr., '31.
"The Manuscript Atlases of Battista Agnese," *Papers,* Biblio. Soc. of Amer., 1931.
"The Last Spanish Exploration of the Northwest Coast and the Attempt to Colonize Bodega Bay," *Calif. Hist. Soc. Q.,* Dec., '31.
"A Map of Cabrillo's Discoveries," *Calif. Hist. Soc. Q.,* 1932.
"The Names of the Channel Islands," *Publications,* Hist. Soc. of So. Calif., 1933.
Spanish Explorations in the Strait of Juan de Fuca. Santa Ana, Calif.: Fine Arts Press, 1933. 323 pp.
"An Exploration of the Coast of Southern California," *Q.,* Hist. Soc. of So. Calif., Dec., 1935.
Cartography of the Northwest Coast of America to the Year 1800. Berkeley: University of California Press, 1937. 2v.
Journal of Tomas de Suria of His Voyage with Malaspina to the Northwest Coast of America in 1791. Glendale, 1936. See also *Pacific Hist. Rev.,* Sept., 1936.
Wagner was a scholarly mining engineer. Professionally engaged in Mexico, he learned Spanish and became deeply interested in the contribution of the Spanish to the history and culture of the northwest coast. His was the first systematic investigation of the journals and other records of Spanish exploration there, it not having been the policy of the Spanish government to encourage their publication. In his *Cartography* he furnishes copies of the charts produced by these explorations, along with very valuable summaries of the voyages up to the time of Vancouver, 1794, including Russians, British and Americans. Wagner did a great deal of his own publishing, and usually in limited editions, so his works are not as readily available as they might otherwise be.

WAHRHAFTIC, CLYDE (b. 1919)
Quaternary and Engineering Geology in the Central Part of the Alaska Range. USGS Prof. Paper, 1956. 118 pp.

"The Alaska Range: Its Geological Evolution," in Howell Williams' *Landscapes of Alaska*.

WAID, EVA CLARK
  Alaska: Land of the Totem. New York: Woman's Board of Home Missions of the Presbyterian Church, 1910. 127 pp.

WAINWRIGHT
  Alaska Sportsman, 5 articles by J. Lester Minner, see Index; Andrews (Andrews was a teacher there); Aldrich; Baker (named by Beechey in 1826 for one of his officers, Lt. John Wainwright); Colby; Couch (post office in 1904, and from 1916); Forrest (teachers, 1915-18); Hayes (Percy Ipalook); Poor; Richards (best on Wainwright); Rossman, Stuck.

WAITE, WILMA
  A Bibliographical Study of US Explorations in Alaska, 1869-1900. Unpublished master's thesis, University of California, 1944. See also Sherwood.

WALBRAN, JOHN T.
  British Columbia Coast Names, 1592-1906. Ottawa: GPB, 1909. 253 pp.

WALCUTT, C. C.
  Jack London. Minneapolis: University of Minnesota Press, 1966. 48 pp.

WALDEN, ARTHUR TREADWELL (b. ca. 1872)
  A *Dog-Puncher on the Yukon*. Boston: Houghton Mifflin, 1928. 289 pp.
  Leading a Dog's Life. Boston: Houghton Mifflin, 1931. 279 pp.

WALDEN, JANE BREVOORT
  Igloo. London: G.P. Putnam's Sons, 1931. 211 pp. Dog story.

WALES
  Alaska Sportsman, Jan., '37 (photo); Apr., '42 (reindeer); Nov., '54 (photo, walrus); Jan., '55 (village photos); Feb., '55; Aug., '55 (birthplace, Robert Mayokok), and Index; Albee (good picture of village life); Aldrich (Gilley affair: attacking natives killed by whalers, 1878); Baker (native village in Kingegan, pop. 488 in 1890); Beechey (King-a-ghen, 1827); Colby; Couch (post office from 1902); Dole (Cong. mission est. 1890; missionary murdered, 1894); Hulley; Miller; Poor (Tin City); Stuck; Swineford; Sundborg; Thornton; Underwood (Gilley affair; Lopp). See also D. Ray.

WALFORD, LIONEL ALBERT (b. 1905)
  Marine Game Fishes of the Pacific Coast from Alaska to the Equator. Berkeley: University of California Press, 1937. 205 pp.

WALKER, FRANKLIN
  Jack London and the Klondike. San Marino: The Huntington Library, 1966. 142 pp.

WALKER, ROBERT J. (1801-69)
  Letter. Wn.DC: Chronicle Printing, 1868. 11 pp.

WALKER, THEODORE J.
  Whale Primer. San Francisco: Cabrillo Hist. Soc., 1962. 58 pp.

WALLACE, IRMA L.
  "Food from the Snows is Building New Industry," *Industrial Digest*, 1928. Reindeer meat.

WALRUS
  See the Arctic Bibliography, and also the Institute of Marine Biology, University of Alaska. See also the following:
  Alaska Life, Nov., '42; *Alaska Sportsman*, see Index; *Alaska-Yukon Magazine*, Nov., '09; Allen, J.A. (see the Arctic Bibliography); Baer (Arctic Bibliography); Bailey and Hendee (*J. of Mammalogy*, Feb., '26); Bee and Hall; Belopolskii (Arctic Bibliography); Bernard (*J. of Mammalogy*, May, '25); Borden; Brooks, J. (Arctic Bibliography); Carrighar; Cameron; Clark, A.H.; Cobb (*Proc.*, Zoolog. Soc. of London, 1933); Collins (*J. of Mammalogy*, May, '40); Cook, J.; Davies (*Geog. Rev.*, Oct., '58); Dole; Dufresne; Darling (New York: Morrow, 1955); Dunbar (Ottawa: Fisheries Res. Bd., 1949); Elliott; Fay (*Trans.*, 22nd N. Amer. Wildlife Conf., 1957); Gilder; Gruening (est. 100,000 killed in the 1870's); Hanna, G.D. (*J. of Mammalogy*, 1920); Higginson; Leopold and Darling; Lincoln (*Oryx*, 1958); McCracken; Madsen; Miller, M.; Murie, J. (*Trans.*, Zoolog. Soc. of London, 1871); Pennant; Preble; Scheffer; Schiller (*J. of Mammalogy*, 1954); Spencer (*Pac. Discovery*, 1953); Stejneger (*Proc.*, Biol. Soc. of Wn., 1914); Stuck; Wrangel.

WALSH, JAMES J.
  American Jesuits. New York: Macmillan, 1934. 336 pp.

WALSH, MOLLIE (d. 1902)
  Alaska Sportsman, Aug., '39 (monument in Skagway); Feb., '57 (photo, monument); *Alaska-Yukon Gold Book* (Jack Newman); Franck. Mollie Walsh operated a cook tent on the gold rush trail. She was apparently murdered by a drunken husband.

WALTON, W. B.
  Eskimo or Innuit Dictionary. Seattle: Metropolitan Printing Co., 1901. 32 pp.

WAMBHEIN, H. G.
  Ben: The Life Story of Carl Ben Eielson. Hatton, N.D.: n.p., 1930. 40 pp.

WARD COVE
  Alaska Sportsman, Oct., '54 (pulp mill); Aug., '55 (pulp mill photo); Couch (post office known as Wacker 1920-51, Ward Cove).

WARD and ASSOCIATES
  The Ward Index of Consumer Prices in Five Alaskan Cities. Seattle: 1956. Mimeo. 66 pp.

WARDMAN, GEORGE
  A *Trip to Alaska*. Boston: Lee & Shepard, Publishers, 1884. 237 pp. Wardman was an agent of the US Treasury Dept. This work relates his voyage on the *Rush* in 1879.

WARE, KAY and L. SUTHERLAND
  Let's Read About Alaska. St. Louis: Webster Publ. Co., 1960. 32 pp.

WARING, GERALD ASHLEY (b. 1883)
Mineral Springs of Alaska. Wn.DC: GPO, 1917. 114 pp. USGS.

WARNER, DONALD F.
The Idea of Continental Union: Agitation for the Annexation of Canada to the US, 1849-93. Lexington: University of Kentucky Press, 1960. 276 pp.

WARNER, GERTRUDE CHANDLER
Windows into Alaska. New York: Friendship Press, 1928. 104 pp.

WARNER, OLIVER MARTIN WILSON
English Maritime Writing. London: Longmans, Green, 1958.
Great Seamen. London: G. Bell, 1961. 226 pp.

WASHBURN, BRADFORD (Henry Bradford Washburn) (b. 1910)
A Tourist Guide to Mt. McKinley. Anchorage: Alaska Northwest Publishing Co., 1974.
Mt. McKinley and the Alaska Range. Boston: Museum of Science, 1951. 88 pp.
Bradford on Mt. Fairweather. New York: Putnam's, 1930. 127 pp.
"The Ascent of Mt. St. Agnes," *Amer. Alpine J.,* 1939.
"The Ascent of Mt. Bertha," *Amer. Alpine J.,* 1941.
"The Ascent of Mt. Hayes," *Amer. Alpine J.,* 1942.
"Alaska and the War," *Amer. Alpine J.,* 1944.
"Mt. McKinley from the North and West," *Amer. Alpine J.,* 1947.
"Operation White Tower," *Amer. Alpine J.,* 1948.
"Mt. McKinley: The West Buttress," *Amer. Alpine J.,* 1951.
"Mt. McKinley via the West Ridge: A Proposed Ascent," *Amer. Alpine J.,* 1953.
"Mapping McKinley's Southeast Approaches," *Amer. Alpine J.,* 1956.
"Mt. Hunter via the West Ridge," *Amer. Alpine J.,* 1954.
"Doctor Cook and Mt. McKinley," *Amer. Alpine J.,* 1958. Disputes Cook's claim as forwarded by his daughter.
"Snow Blindness," *Amer. Alpine J.,* 1958.
"The Ascent of Mt. St. Agnes, Chugach Range," *Alpine J.,* 1939.
"The Ascent of Mt. Lucania," *Alpine J.,* 1938.
"The Harvard-Dartmouth Alaskan Expedition, 1933-34," *Geog. J.,* 1936.
"A Preliminary Report on Studies of the Mountains and Glaciers of Alaska," *Geog. J.,* 1941.
"Conquest of Mt. Lucania," *Can. Geog. J.,* 1938.
"The Practical Igloo," *Can. Geog. J.,* 1949.
"Back-Packing to Fairweather," *Alaska Sportsman,* 1931.
"Morainic Bandings of Malaspina and other Alaskan Glaciers," *Bull.,* Geog. Soc. of Amer., 1935.
"Movement of the South Crillon Glacier, Crillon Lake, Alaska," *Bull.,* Geog. Soc. of Amer., 1937.
"Aerial Exploration of the Great Glaciers of the Alaskan Coast and Interior," *Bull.,* Geog. Soc. of Amer., 1941.
"Photographs of Mt. McKinley," *Sierra Club Bull.,* 1950.

"The First Ascent of Mt. Deception," *Sierra Club. Bull.,* 1944.
"Mapping Mt. McKinley," *Scientific American,* 1949.
"The Conquest of Mt. Crillon," *Nat. Geog.,* 1935.
"Exploring Yukon's Glacial Stronghold," *Nat. Geog.,* 1936.
"Over the Roof of our Continent," *Nat. Geog.,* 1938.
"Mt. McKinley Conquered by a New Route," *Nat. Geog.,* 1953.
"Advancing Glaciers in Alaska," *Science,* 1934.
"Arctic Mineral Domain," *Explosives Engineer,* 1942.
"McKinley Weather Experiences," *Weatherwise,* 1952.
"Mt. McKinley," *Pacific Discovery,* 1953.
"On-the-Spot Photographs Expedite Mt. McKinley Survey," *Civil Engineering,* 1954.
"The South Buttress of Mt. McKinley," *Appalachia,* 1954.
"Mt. McKinley, Alaska," *Mountain World,* 1956.
"Alaska's Hochgebirge," *Atlantis,* 1955.
See also photographs in Howell Williams' Landscapes.
See also the following:
Alaska Sportsman, Jan., '42 (Mt. Hayes, with wife); *Alaska Weekly,* May, '51 (photo); Aug., '51; Colby (Harvard instr.); Franck (Bob Reeve); Hanna (in *Pacific Discovery,* 1953); Potter (Bob Reeve); Wahrhaftig (*Proc.,* Alaskan Science Conf., 1951); Washburn (Bibliography; *Mt. McKinley and the Alaska Range*).

WASHBURN, M. L. (ca. 1850-1911)
"Fox Farming in Alaska," in Harriman's Alaska. See Kitchener. Washburn was an employee of the Alaska Commercial Co., managing the operation at Kodiak from 1877, and eventually becoming vice-president and general manager of the Northern Commercial Co. and the Northern Navigation Co. He founded the first fox farm in Alaska, and chaperoned the Harriman's on their 1899 Kodiak visit.

WASHBURN, WILLIAM S.
"Aleutian Islands," in *Chamber's Encyclopedia* (1888).

WASHINGTON, JOHN
Eskimaux and English Vocabulary. London: John Murray, 1850. 160 pp.

WASILLA
Alaska Sportsman, see Index; *Alaska Weekly,* May, '50; Baker (Glenn named Lucile Lake in 1898, possibly from Wassilla, Knik Indian chief); Colby; Couch (post office from 1917); Learnard (in *Compilation of Narratives*).

WASKEY, FRANK HINMAN (b. 1875)
Memories of Nelson Island. Typewritten ms., Alaska Historical Library.
See the following:
Alaska Monthly, Sept., '06; *Alaska Weekly,* Aug., '51 (Tin City, Nome); *Alaska-Yukon Magazine,* March, '07 (photo); May, '08 (photo); March, '09 (photo; pres., Nome Bank and Trust; home: Bal-

lard, Seattle); Gruening; Hulley (suggests Waskey was a peoples' candidate, Hoggatt, et al., rep. big business); McCollom (*Alaska Journal*); Nichols (elected over Swineford); Stuck; Underwood (miner walked 60 miles to vote for Waskey); Wickersham.

WATERMAN, THOMAS TALBOT
"Houses of the Alaskan Eskimo," *Amer. Anthrop.*, Apr., '24.

WATERMAN, THOMAS T. and RUTH GREINER
Indian Houses of Puget Sound. New York: Museum of the Amer. Indian, 1921. 59 pp.

WATERMAN, THOMAS T., et alii
Native Houses of Western North America. New York: Museum of Amer. Indian, 1921. 97 pp.

WATERMAN, THOMAS T. and GERALDINE COFFIN
Types of Canoes on Puget Sound. New York: Museum of Amer. Indian, 1920. 43 pp.

WATSON, ARTHUR CHACE
The Long Harpoon: A Collection of Whaling Anecdotes. New Bedford: G.H. Reynolds, 1929. 165 pp.

WAXELL, SVEN LARSSON (1701-62)
The American Expedition. London: William Hodge & Co., 1952. 236 pp.
Report on the Voyage of the St. Peter. In Golder, *Bering's Voyages*.
A Letter from a Russian Sea-Officer. London: A. Linde, 1754. 83 pp.
See the Arctic Bibliography for a list of works in Russian; see also T-4758 ff.

WEAD, FRANK WILBUR (b. 1895)
Gales, Ice and Men: A Biography of the Steam Barkentine Bear. New York: Dodd, Mead, 1937. 272 pp. See *Bear*.

WEARE
Alaska Sportsman, June, '55 (named for Charles A., Ely A., and Portus B. Weare, officials of the North American Transportation and Trading Co. of Chicago); Baker (trading station on north bank of the Yukon near Tanana); Couch (post office, 1897-98); Henderson; Judge; Kitchener.

WEARE
Alaska Life, Dec., '41 (wrecked off St. Michael, 1900); Davis (on the Yukon from 1892); Henderson (brought out a million and a half in gold); Judge; Kitchener; Ray (in *Compilation of Narratives*); Richardson (in *Compilation of Narratives*).

WEARE, PORTUS B.
Henderson (paid for the education of an Aleut girl; formed mineral collection); Judge (great "corn king" of Chicago); Moore (partner of J.J. Healy); Kitchener.

WEATHER
See the Arctic Bibliography.

WEBB, NANCY M.
Aguk of Alaska. Englewood Cliffs: Prentice-Hall, 1963. 64 pp.

WEBB, WILLIAM SEWARD (1851-1926)
California and Alaska. New York: Putnam's, 1891. 268 pp.

WEBER, GUSTAVUS A.
The Coast and Geodetic Survey: Its History, Activities and Organization. Baltimore: Johns Hopkins Press, 1923. 107 pp. See also Sherwood.

WEBSTER, DONALD HUMPHRY
See T-4767 ff.

WEBSTER, FRANK V.
See T-4776 ff.

WEBSTER, J. DAN
"Notes on the Birds of Sitka and Vicinity," Condor, 1941.

WEED, ALBERTA L.
Grandma Goes to the Arctic. Philadelphia: Dorrance, 1957. 279 pp.

WEED, WALTER H.
The Copper Mines of the World. New York: Hill Publ. Co., 1907. 375 pp.

WEEKS, TIM and RAMONA MAHER
Ice Island: Polar Science and the Arctic Research Laboratory. New York: John Day, 1965. 220 pp.

WEEMS, CARRINGTON
The Bishop of the Arctic. New York: 1912. 11 pp. Rowe.

WEIGERT, HANS WERNER and VILHJALMUR STEFANSSON
Compass of the World: A Symposium on Political Geography. New York: Macmillan, 1944. 466 pp. Also 1949.

WEINLAND, WILLIAM H.
Kitchener (accompanied H. Hartmann to the lower Kuskokwim in 1884; est. Moravian mission at Mumtrekhlagamute [Bethel]); Schwalbe (served at Bethel 1885-87); see also Moravian Church.

WEISS, E. J.
"Opportunities in Chemical Industry in Alaska," *Chemical and Metallurgical Eng.*, 1941.

WELLCOME, Sir HENRY SOLOMON (ca. 1853-1936)
The Story of Metlakahtla. London: Saxon & Co., 1887. 483 pp. Numerous other editions. In defense of William Duncan.

WELLING, JAMES CLARKE
The Bering Sea Arbitration. Wn.DC: The University Press (Columbia University), 1893. 18 pp.

WELLINGTON, JOHN L.
The Gold Fields of Alaska. Cripple Creek, Colo.: Buckner Printing Co., 1896. 72 pp.

WELLS, E. HAZARD
"The Frank Leslie Expedition to Alaska," *Frank Leslie's Illus.*, 1890-91. See Leslie.

Up and Down the Yukon. In *Compilation of Narratives.*

Report. Relief of People in the Yukon Country. 55th Cong., 3rd Sess., House Doc. No. 244.

"Down the Yukon and Up the Fortymile," *Alaska Journal*, 1974.

WELLS, HARRY LAURENZ (b. 1854)
Alaska and the Klondike. Portland: the Author, 1897. 72 pp.
Alaska: The New Eldorado. Portland: J.K. Gill Co., 1897. 88 pp.

WELLS, ROGER, Jr. and JOHN W. KELLY
English-Eskimo and Eskimo-English Vocabularies. Wn.DC: GPO, 1890. 72 pp. US Bur. of Educ.

WELZL, JAN (b. 1870)
The Quest for Polar Treasures. New York: Macmillan, 1933. 352 pp. Trans. M. and R. Weatherall.
Thirty Years in the Golden North. New York: Macmillan, 1932. 336 pp. Trans. Paul Selver.
Welzl is said to have repudiated these works which are fantastic in nature.

WENDT, FLORENCE
Life along the Yukon in 1935 as seen by a Tourist. Madison, Wisc.: the Author, 1936. 118 pp.

WENTWORTH, ELAINE
Mission to Metlakatla. Boston: Houghton Mifflin, 1968. 192 pp.

WEST, ELLSWORTH LUCE and ELEANOR RANSOM MAYHEW
Captain's Papers: Log of Whaling and Other Sea Experiences. Barre, Mass.: Barre Publishers, 1965.

WEST, FREDERICK HADLEIGH
"On the Distribution and Territories of the Western Kutchin Tribes," *Anthrop. Papers*, Univ. of Alaska, 1959.

WESTERN UNION TELEGRAPH COMPANY
To the Stockholders: Statement of the Origin, Organization and Progress of the Russian-American Telegraph Western Union Extension, Collins' Overland Line. Rochester, New York: Evening Express Book and Job Printing Office, 1866. 165 pp.
See also the following:
Andrews (*Alaska Life*, Sept., '45); Bannister; Bulkley (Journal, Portland Public Library); Bush; Colby; Collins; Dall; *Esquimaux*; Franck; Garland; Herron; Higginson; Hulley; James; Kennan; Kennicott; Mahoney; Neuberger (*Alaska Life*, March, '43); Ogilvie; Petrof (*Compilation*); Raymond (*Compilation*); Rickard; Scammon; Seward; Sherwood; Shiels; Whymper; Wickersham.

WESTGATE RICHARD S. and VICTOR FISCHER
Recreation in Anchorage. Wn.DC: GPO, 1954. 35 pp. NPS.

WETMORE, ALEXANDER
"The Eagle, King of Birds, and His Kin," *Nat. Geog.*, 1933.
"Birds of the Northern Seas," *Nat. Geog.*, 1936.

WEYER, EDWARD MOFFAT, Jr.
"An Aleutian Burial," *Anthrop. Papers*, Amer. Mus. of Nat. History, 1929.
The Eskimos. New Haven: Yale University Press, 1932. 491 pp.
"Archaeological Material from the Village Site of Hot Springs, Port Moller, Alaska," *Anthrop. Papers*, Amer. Mus. of Nat. History, 1930.
"Day and Night in the Arctic," *Geog. Rev.*, 1943.

WHALES and WHALING
Alaska Life, Nov., '45 (history); *Alaska Sportsman*, May, '37 (photo); Akutan and Port Hobron [Sitkalidak Is.]); March, '38; Apr., '42 (328 taken in Queen Charlottes); July, '43 (best baleen baskets are from Barrow); Feb., '44; Aug., '44; Apr., '45; May, '45; Nov., '46 (attacking a baleen whale); Feb., '47 (Akutan, Port Hobron and Port Armstrong stations closed during the war); March, '47 (Point Hope); Oct., '48 (Kasaan Bay); Dec., '48; Feb., '49; May, '49; Jan., '49 (Hinchinbrook Island); Oct., '49; Jan., '50 (Cleveland Pen.); July, '50 (insulin); Sept., '50; July, '51; Aug., '51 (Prince of Wales Island); Sept., '51 (most whaling now done in the Antarctic); Nov., '51 (Cape Bartolome); June, '52 (Coal Harbor, Vancouver Island); Nov., '52; Dec., '52; July, '53 (Barrow); Nov., '55 (King Island whaling headquarters in 1880); Jan., '56; Feb., '57 (a beaked Baird at Dry Bay); March, '57; and Index; *Alaska-Yukon Magazine*, Dec., '08 (1897 disaster); Aldrich (*Lucretia* mutiny, 1883; *Shenandoah* raid; "wreck" season of 1871, and 1876); Andrews (*Wn. Hist. Q.*, 1918); Andrews, Roy (*World's Work*, 1908 ["Whale Hunting"]; *Bul.*, Amer. Mus. Nat. Hist., 1909 [finback and humpback]; *Amer. Mus. J.*, ["summer with Pac. Coast Whalers"]; *Nat. Geog.*, 1911 ["Shore Whaling"]; *Memoirs*, Amer. Mus. Nat. Hist., 1914 ["Calif. Gray Whale"]; *Memoirs*, Amer. Mus. Nat. Hist., 1916 ["The Sei Whale"]); Andrews, Ralph; Bailey and Hendee (*J. of Mammalogy*, 1926); Barbeau; Bertholf (Barrow relief, 1897); Birkeland (Akutan); Blond; Bodfish; Borden (Nootka); Brandt (Arctic Bibliography); Brass (*J.*, Royal Asiatic Soc., 1897); Brower (Barrow life) Burns (Bering and Chukchi Seas); Cameron (whalebone); Carrighar; Chamisso (W-6703); Clark, A. (in Goode); Clarke (Arctic Bibliography); Clock (*Pacific Monthly*, 1910 [shanghaied whalemen]); Cook, John A.; Colby (Akutan, Pt. Hope); Crisp (*The Adventure of Whaling* [London: Macmillan, 1954]); Dall (Capt. Roys first through Bering Strait, 1848; Russian gov't. organized company, 1850); Deason (*Trans.*, N. Amer. Wildlife Conf., 1946); Denmead and Dodd (*Proc.*, Pac. Sci. Conf., 1939); Dole (Russo-Finland Whaling Co., Crimean War; Killisnoo, 1880); Drewance (*Ak. Sports.*, 1941 [*Bear* at Barrow]); Dufresne (14 species); Dulles, F. (1871 disaster); Faber (Arctic Bibliography); Federal Writers' Project (Whaling Masters); Franck (Arctic coast, 1848-90); Fraser and Purves (*Nature*, Dec., '55); Gawn (*Nature*, Jan., '48); Gilmore (*Pac. Discovery*, July, '56; *Sci. Amer.*, Jan., '55); Gruening (whalers reduce Eskimos to hardship); Hadley (*Bul.*, Amer. Geog. Soc., 1915 [journal excerpts, Jack Hadley: ships lost in Beaufort Sea; boom at Herschel Is.]); Hanna (*Proc.*, Biol. Soc. of Wn., 1914; *J. of Mammalogy*, May, 1920, Nov., 1923); Harrison; Heizer (*Bul.*, US Bur. of Amer. Ethnology, 1943 [aconite poison whaling]; *Amer. Anthrop.*, Jan., '43

[Eskimo poison lances]); Henderson; Holmes (wreck of the *Citizen*, 1852); Hulley; Jellison (*J. of Mammalogy*, May, 1953); Jenkins (*History of the Whale Fisheries* [London: Witherby, 1921]); Jones (*Albatross*); Jorpes (Arctic Bibliography); Kawakami (Arctic Bibliography); King (*Circulation*, Sept., '53); Lantis (Alaska Whale Cult); Larson (*Think: art*); Mackintosh (*Nature*, March, '52; *Ann. Rept.*, Smithsonian, 1946); Marsh (*Can. Geog. J.*, July, '50); Melville; Miller & Kellogg (basic); Miller, M. (notes on disasters); Morison; Munro; Murdoch (Pt. Barrow; *Pop. Sci. Monthly*, Apr., '91); Nishimoto (Arctic Bibliography); Oliver (Akutan); Omura (Arctic Bibliography); Ottestad (Arctic Bibliography); Palmer (*Nature*, Jan., '56); Pedersen (*Beaver*, Sept., '52); Pedersen, T. (Russo-Finland Whaling Co.); Petrof; Pinart; Preble; Rabot (*Ann. Rept.*, Smithsonian, 1913); Ray, P. (*Compilation of Narratives*); Sanderson (*Follow the Whale* [Boston: Little, Brown, 1956]); Sanford (*Comm. Fish Rev.*, 1967); Scammon; Scidmore; Scoresby; Smith, C.; Stefansson; Strauss; Stuck; Swanson (*Pac. NW Q.*, Apr., '56 [southern reach of Eskimo whaling influence]); Swineford (on whale captains); Tower (history); Townsend; Turner; Underwood; (US F&WS: *Bibliography of Whales and Whaling Industry* [Wn.DC: GPO, 1921]); US Rev. Cutter Serv.; VanStone (*Pac. NW Q.*, Jan., '58: Arctic coast whaling, 1848-1914); Wead (many Negro whalemen); Whymper (Russian and American fur competition); Wickersham; Wyrick (*J. of Mammalogy*, Nov., '54); Zenkovich (Arctic Bibliography). On this large subject see the Arctic Bibliography.

WHALEY, FRANK H.
Alaska Life, Jan., '42; *Alaska Sportsman*, July, '56; Aug., '57; Jan., '58; Feb., '58; Mr. Whaley was associated with the beginnings of the Alaska Visitors' Association.

WHALEY, NEVA
Alaska Sportsman, June, 1942; *Alaska Life*, July, 1942.

WHARTON, DAVID
The Alaska Gold Rush. Bloomington: Indiana University Press, 1972. 274 pp.
"Stampede Towns of the Upper Yukon," *Journal of the West*, Nov., 1967.

WHEATON, HELEN
Prekaska's Wife: A Year in the Aleutians. New York: Dodd, Mead, 1945. 251 pp. 1933-34 on Atka. Interesting from the point of view of native life, one of superiority.

WHEELER, DOROTHY D.
"Wintering in Alaska," *Country Life*, 1936.

WHEELER, JAMES COOPER (b. 1849)
Captain Pete in Alaska. New York: Dutton, 1910. 302 pp.

WHEELER, JOHN OLIVER
"Evolution and History of the Whitehorse Trough," unpublished master's thesis, Columbia University, 1956.

WHEELER, KEITH
Eight articles on the Aleutians in the Washington *Evening Star*, July, 1942.

WHEELER, OLIN DUNBAR (b. 1852)
Wonderland '98. Chicago: Rand McNally, 1898. 103 pp.

WHELEN, TOWNSEND
Hunting Big Game. Harrisburg: Military Service Publ. Co., 1946. 282 pp.

WHERRY, JOSEPH H.
Indian Masks and Myths of the West. New York: Funk & Wagnalls, 1969. 273 pp.
The Totem Pole Indians. New York: Funk & Wagnalls, 1965. 152 pp.

WHISHAW, LORNA
As Far as You'll Take Me. New York: Dodd, Mead, 1958. 216 pp.

WHITE ALICE SYSTEM
Alaska Sportsman, May, '57; see also the Arctic Bibliography.

WHITE, DAPHNE MILBANK
"May this House be Free from Bears," *Puget Soundings*, Dec., '60.

WHITE, ELMER JOHN ("Stroller") (1859-1930)
Stroller's Weekly, published at Juneau, 1921-1930.
Tales of a Klondike Newsman. Vancouver: Mitchell Press, 1969. 182 pp. Comp., R. DeArmond.
See also the following:
Alaska Sportsman, Oct., '47; *Alaska-Yukon Magazine*, Aug., '07 (Noah's Ark story); Chase (Skagway); Colby (ice worm inventor); Hulley; Willoughby (role in territorial legislature).

WHITE, HELEN A.
Alaska Big Game Animals. Anchorage: Anchorage Printing Co., 1961. 20 pp.
Alaska Wildberry Trails. Anchorage: Anchorage Printing Co., 1959. 48 pp.
Bird Sampler. Anchorage: Anchorage Printing Co., 1963. 51 pp.
It's True about Alaska. Anchorage: Anchorage Printing Co., 1962. 12 pp.
Landscaping for Alaskans. Anchorage: Anchorage Printing Co., 1962. 31 pp.
More about Alaska Wildflower Trails. Anchorage: Anchorage Printing Co., 1962. 48 pp.
What's Cookin' in Alaska. Anchorage: Anchorage Printing Co., 1961. 51 pp.
More about What's Cookin' in Alaska. Anchorage: Anchorage Printing Co., 1962. 44 pp.
"The Alaska-Yukon Wild Flowers Guide," *Alaska Geographic*, 1974.

WHITE, JAMES (1863-1928)
Boundary Disputes and Treaties. Toronto: Brook and Co., 1914. 958 pp.
Treaty of 1825: Correspondence. Ottawa: Royal Society of Canada, 1915. 10 pp.
"The Geographical Work of the Canadian Arctic Expedition," *Geog. Journal*, June, 1924.

WHITE, JAMES T.
See US Revenue Cutter Service.

WHITE, JOHN W.
See US Revenue Cutter Service; see also the Arctic Bibliography.

WHITE MOUNTAIN
Colby; Couch (post office from 1932; ANS school); Harrison (Wild Goose Mining and Trading Co., photo); Hulley; Kitchener; Tewkesbury.

WHITE PASS
Alaska Sportsman, June, '53 (photo); Nov., '54 (2900 feet, 20 miles from Skagway); May, '57 (Dead Horse Gulch); Feb., '58; July, '57; and Index; *Alaska-Yukon Magazine*, Nov., '08; Andrews (map of trail); Anzer (Brackett freight camp); Baker (named by Ogilvie, 1887, for Thomas White, Canadian minister of interior); Bankson; Becker; Berton; Brooks (wagon road); Burg; Burroughs (in Harriman); Cameron (easier than the Chilkoot); Colby; Davis; Franck; Harris (opened for travel July 16, 1897); Hawthorne; Higginson (first explored and surveyed by Capt. Moore of Ogilvie's survey, June 1887); Hunt (anecdotal); Lung; Morgan; Ogilvie (with Tagish Jim); Rickard; Sherman; Sullivan; Walden; Wells (*Compilation of Narratives*); Young (no leadership; 3000 horses killed).

WHITE PASS & YUKON RAILWAY
Alaska Life, Feb., '44; May, '44; Aug., '44; Aug., '45; *Alaska Sportsman*, Nov., '39 (Minnesota interests surveyed pass in 1896 but failed to get franchise for railroad from Can. gov't.); May, '44 (blizzard blocks line for 15 days); Jan., '46; Aug., '47; Feb., '52; May, '53 (robbery of Whitehorse office); Nov., '53; Nov., '54; Dec., '54 (the "Dutchess"); Jan., '55; Sept., '55; Nov., '55; May, '56 (road begun April, 1898, completed July, 1900); Sept., '56; June, '57; Apr., '58, and Index; *Alaska Weekly*, July, '50 (first train June 8, 1900); *Alaska-Yukon Magazine*, Nov., '08; May, '09 (photo); Anzer; Becker (photo, first train); Berton, L.; Berton, P.; Cameron (1919); Castner; Colby (financed by the Close Brothers, London; built by M.J. Heney and E.C. Hawkins); Cory, T. (*The White Pass & Yukon Railway* [Seattle, 1901, 144 pp.]); Davis; Denison; Dole (30 fatalities during const.); Franck; Graves (president); Griffin; Gruening (taxes on the American section); Hart; Gillette (technical data; compares route with that out of Valdez which Gillette preferred); Hewetson (*Can. J. of Econ. & Pol. Sci.*, 1945; also in C.A. Dawson's *New Northwest* [Toronto: Univ. of Toronto Press, 1947]); Higginson; Hulley; Kitchener (in 1914 WP&YR bought entire business of Northern Nav. Co., incl. steamboats and barges, ending White Pass steamer excursions); Rickard (excellent photos); Stuck (monopoly secured by 1914 purchase, Skagway to St. Michael); Tewkesbury; Tompkins; Underwood; Walden; Whiting (best); Wickersham; Winslow. See also Skagway, White Pass, White Pass City, Klondike, etc. See also T-4828 ff.

WHITE PASS CITY
Becker (photo); Hawthorne; Rickard (on Brackett Rd., 10 miles from Skagway).

WHITE PASS ROYAL MAIL STAGES
Alaska-Yukon Magazine, Aug., '07.

WHITE RIVER
Alaska Sportsman, May, '40 (photo); Oct., '40; Baker (disc. by Robt. Campbell, 1850, named by him for water color); Ogilvie (contains much volcanic ash; Chilkat name means Sand River); Schwatka (called by Stick Indians Yukokon); Stuck.

WHITE, STEWART EDWARD (1873-1946)
Wild Geese Calling. Garden City: Doubleday Doran, 1940. 577 pp. Southeast logging.
Call of the North. Garden City: Doubleday Doran, 1941. 260 pp.
Pole Star. Garden City: Doubleday Doran, 1935. 452 pp. with Harry DeVighne. Baranov and the Russian fur trade.
Silent Places. Garden City: Doubleday Doran, 1919. 304 pp. Hudson's Bay.
"The Case against Ballinger Cleared Up," *Amer. Mag.*, 1910.
"Sanctuary for the Alaskan Bear," *Sierra Club Bul.*, 1932.

WHITE, TRUMBULL
"Coming Storm over Alaska," *New Outlook*, Aug., '33. Native claims.

WHITE, WILLIS BOYD
The Gold Hunters of Alaska. Boston: Little, Brown, 1889. 348 pp.

WHITEHEAD, ROBERT
The First Book of Bears. New York: Franklin Watts, 1966. 54 pp.

WHITEHEAD, R. F.
"Problems of Aerial Photography," *Aviation*, 1930.

WHITEHORSE
Alaska Life, Aug., '44; June, '45; *Alaska Sportsman*, see Index; *Alaska-Yukon Magazine*, Nov., '08; *Alaska Weekly*, June, '50; May, '50 (faked film footage); Dec., '50 (museum proposal); Feb., '51 (Mrs. G. Black); Jan., '51; June, '51; Cameron (1919); Colby; Dole (copper mines); Franck (no town before 1898); Higginson; Hulley (Norman Wells); Illingworth (capitol moved to Whitehorse, 1952); Kitchener (NC Co. bought store here in 1927); Griffin; Jacobin (original name, Closeleigh, honored the London bankers who built the White Pass and Yukon Railway; river steamers ceased operation in 1955; Sam McGee); Rickard (named for crests of waves in Whitehorse Rapids); Service (autobiography); *Whitehorse Star*.

WHITEHORSE RAPIDS
Alaska Sportsman, Aug., '42 (photo); May, '55 (tramway); Sept., '56; Oct., '56; *Alaska Weekly*, Oct., '50; *Alaska-Yukon Magazine*, May, '09 (photo); Brooks (loss of life insignificant: 7080 boats with 28,000 passengers in 1898, only 23 persons drowned, 18 in Miles Canyon); Chase; Colby; Davis; Franck; Hawthorne; Higginson; Jacobin (Indian name Whitehorse for drowned chief); Ogilvie; Rickard; Stuck; Schwatka; Underwood; Walden.

WHITEHOUSE, STUART
"Patrol Squadron 41," *Alaska Life*, Nov., '42. Aleutians, WW II.

WHITING, FENTON BLAKEMORE (1866-1936)
Grit, Grief and Gold: A True Narrative of an Alaska Pathfinder. Seattle: Peacock Publ. Co., 1933. 247 pp. Story of building of the White Pass and Yukon Railway, and activities as Chief Surgeon on the building of the Copper River and Northwestern Railway. Dr. Whiting performed the autopsy on Soapy Smith at Skagway in 1898.

WHITNAH, D. R.
A History of the US Weather Bureau. Urbana: University of Illinois Press, 1961. 366 pp.

WHITNEY, ELLIOTT (pseud., Harry L. Sayler)
The Black Fox of the Yukon. Chicago: Reilly & Britton Co., 1917. 272 pp.
The King Bear of Kodiak Island. Chicago: Reilly & Lee Co., 1912. 268 pp.
The Bully of the Frozen North. Chicago: Reilly & Lee, Publ., 1936. 268 pp.

WHITNEY, ROGER S.
"An Attempt on Mt. Hayes," *Can. Alpine J.*, 1937.

WHITAKER, JAMES W.
"Mount McKinley," *Puget Soundings*, Dec., 1960.

WHITTIER
Alaska Life, Dec., '44; *Alaska Sportsman*, Nov., '41 (named for Whittier Glacier, which was named for the American poet John Greenleaf Whittier); Nov., '55 (collapse of gull nesting ground); June, '58 (largest structures in Alaska built by Army at Whittier); Jan., '43 (tunnel, 13,000); *Alaska Weekly*, July, '50; March, '51; Couch (post office from 1946); Fitch (Alaska Railroad); Gruening; Kitchener (1895 petition for Prince William Sound boat service and portage to Turnagain Arm); Tewkesbury; see also the Arctic Bibliography. The US Army developed Whittier as a supply depot and point of entry for Alaska bases during WW II. The Army abandoned the post in 1950. Numerous proposals for abandonment of the ARR line south of Portage to Seward have been advanced, but have never met with success. See Fitch.

WHYMPER, FREDERICK (b. 1838)
Travel and Adventure in the Territory of Alaska. London: J. Murray, 1868. 331 pp. This is one of the best works produced on the Russian-American Overland Telegraph Expedition of 1865-66. Whymper joined the expedition at Vancouver, sketching and recording his experiences at Sitka, St. Michael, Petropavlovsk, Anadyr River, and at Nulato and on the Yukon. Whymper's account, and his artwork, constitute one of the more significant contributions to Alaska description of this period.
A Journey from Norton Sound, Bering Sea, to Ft. Yukon. London: W. Clowes & Son, 1868. 19 pp.
The Heroes of the Arctic and Their Adventures. London: Society for Promoting Christian Knowledge and New York: Pott, Young, & Co., 1875. 302 pp.
"Russian America, or 'Alaska:' the Natives of the Yukon River and Adjacent Country," *Trans.*, Ethno-

logical Society of London, 1869.
See also the following:
Alaska Sportsman, Aug., '39 (7 drawings); Baker (Whymper Creek, Whymper Point); Morris; Raymond; Wickersham.

WHYTFLIET, CORNELIUS
See the Arctic Bibliography.

WICK, CARL IRVING
Ocean Harvest: The Story of Commercial Fishing in Pacific Coast Waters. Seattle: Superior Publ. Co., 1946. 185 pp.

WICKERSHAM, JAMES (1857-1939)
A Bibliography of Alaskan Literature, 1724-1924. Fairbanks: Alaska Agricultural College and School of Mines, 1927. 635 pp. One of the most valuable sources for Alaska historical material, this comprehensive work includes a thorough listing of government documents to 1924. Wickersham and his assistants collected Alaskana for many years before publication of this work, which also contains a brief sketch of Alaska history.
Old Yukon: Tales, Trails and Trials. Wn.DC: Washington Law Book Co., 1938. 514 pp. One of the premier works on Alaska, for its treatment of the Yukon, often compared with Ogilvie's *Early Days on the Yukon*.
Alaska Reports. St. Paul: West Publ. Co., 1903-36. 8v. Alaska district judge decisions, 1884-1935.
Address at the Driving of the Golden Spike and Completion of the Tanana Mines Railway. Fairbanks, 1905. 9 pp.
An Address Delivered at the Laying of the Cornerstone of the Alaska Agricultural College and School of Mines. Fairbanks, 1915. 7 pp.
Alaska: Its Resources, Present Condition, and Needed Legislation. Tacoma: Allen & Lamborn Printing, 1902. 15 pp.
Speech of the Hon. James Wickersham, Delegate to Congress, delivered for a Joint Session of the First Alaska Territorial Legislature. Juneau, 1913. 8 pp.
The Organization of Territorial Government in Alaska: An Appeal to Alaskans. Juneau, 1927. 32 pp.
Alaska's Trade Value to the US, at the Dedication of the Federal and Territorial Building at Juneau. 71st Cong., 3rd Sess., in the *Cong. Record*, Feb. 9, 1931.
Extension of Remarks (above) in the House. 72nd Cong., 1st Sess., in the *Cong. Record*, May 18, 1932.
Statement. Committee on Territories, May, 1911. 62nd Cong., 1st Sess. Wn.DC: GPO, 1911. 108 pp. Alaska Home Rule bill.
"Slaughter of the 'Silver Horde'. . .Huge Profits for the Packers, but not a Penny for the People," *Amer. Conservation*, Aug., 1911.
"The Oldest and Rarest Lincoln Statue," *Sunset*, Feb., 1924.
"The Creation of Denali, by Yako, the Athabaskan Indian," *Alaska Magazine*, Jan., 1927.
"The Glacial Age in Alaska," *Alaska Magazine*, Feb., 1927.
See also the following:
Alaska Life, Dec., '39 (photo, obituary); Dec., '43 (by C. Andrews); *Alaska Sportsman*, Apr., '51 (Wickersham at one time advocated the division of Alaska into four separate states: Sitka [capital at Juneau],

Alaska [capital at Valdez], Seward [capital at Nome], Tanana [capital at Fairbanks]); May, '58; *Alaska-Yukon Magazine*, Nov., '07 (by E.S. Harrison); July, '12; Calasanz ($150 donation to Holy Cross Mission); Chase (photos); Colby (US District Judge [Alaska], 1900-07; Alaska Delegate to Congress, 1909-21, 1931-33); Fink (W-3826); Gruening; Harrison; Hulley (T. Roosevelt kept Wickersham in office with 5 recess appointments; he was never confirmed by the Senate); Kitchener (Barnette proposed the naming of Fairbanks at Wickersham's suggestion); Nichols; Rowe (see Jenkins); Shiels (on Sulzer and Grigsby); Tewkesbury (biog. Grace Wickersham); Wickersham.

WIEDEMANN, THOMAS, Sr. (b. ca. 1879)
Cheechako into Sourdough. Portland: Binfords & Mort, 1942. 266 pp. Sailing the *Eliza Anderson* in 1897, Wiedemann and his passengers were forced to abandon her at Unalaska due to her decrepit status. Some, including Wiedemann went on to St. Michael on the *Baranof*, a whaler. Taking the *W.K. Merwin* on the Yukon, they were overtaken by freeze-up, and wintered in a slough opposite the Eskimo village of Nunabislogarth, which Wiedemann describes thoroughly. He subsequently worked a claim in Dawson successfully.
See also four articles in *Alaska Life:*
"Benson's Bar Gold Stampede of Oct., 1897," May, '42; *"Eliza Anderson* Expedition," Sept., '43; "An Eskimo Rescue," June, '46; "More on the Last Russian Steamer built in Alaska," March, '47. See also C.L. Andrews in *Alaska Life*, Jan., '47, on this steamer, the *Politofski.*
"A Stranger Came Aboard," *Alaska Sportsman*, Apr., '56.
"Within Minutes of Death," *Alaska Sportsman*, July, '56.

WIEDEMANN, THOMAS and LUTHER NORRIS
The Saga of Alaska. Prairie City, Ill.: Press of James A. Decker, 1946. 85 pp.

WIEN, NOEL (b. 1899)
Harkey; also Potter; see Aviation.

WIEN, SIGURD (b. 1903)
See Potter; see also Kennedy; see Aviation. See also Fritz, Harold and Ralph Wien.

WIEN AIR ALASKA
Also Wien Alaska Airlines, and Wien Consolidated Airlines. *Alaska Sportsman*, Apr., '41; Nov., '55; July, '56; July, '57; Nov., '57 (group photo); and Index; *Alaska Weekly*, May, '50 (instrument training for Noel Wien in Seattle); Denison; Harkey; Hart; Hulley; Jeffery; McGarvey; Potter; Savage (fatal crash of Ralph at Kotzebue in 1930; two priests killed with him); Tewkesbury.

WIGAN, S. O. and W. R. H. WHITE
Tsunami of March 27-29, 1964: West Coast of Canada: Ottawa: GPB, 1964. 12 pp. Dept. of Mines and Technical Services. See also Earthquake, Alaskan Earthquakes.

WIGGINS, IRA LOREN (b. 1899)
Current Biological Research in the Alaskan Arctic. Stanford: Stanford University Press, 1953. 55 pp.

Incl. paper on the organization of the Arctic Research Lab. at Barrow.
"North of Anaktuvuk," *Pac. Discovery*, May, 1953.

WIGGINS, IRA LOREN and JOHN H. THOMAS
A Flora of the Alaskan Arctic Slope. Toronto: University of Toronto Press, 1962. 425 pp. Arctic Institute of N. Amer.

WIKSTROM, ROBERT (b. 1922)
Alaska Oddities. Seattle: R.D. Seal, 1958. 80 pp.

WILBUR, RAY LYMAN
Progress in Alaskan Administration. Wn.DC: GPO, 1931. 9 pp.
"A New Alaska in the Making," *Current History*, Oct., 1931. Mr. Wilbur was Secretary of the Interior, 1929-33.

WILCOXEN, J. M.
History of the Arctic Brotherhood. Authorized. Seattle: White and Davis, 1906. 53 pp.

WILD GOOSE MINING & TRADING CO.
Alaska Sportsman, Oct., '53 (Charles D. Lane, of Missouri, capitalized the company at Nome with a million dollars); Brooks (implicated in the Noyes-McKenzie affair); Fitz (did not interfere with claim jumping; built a few miles of railroad); Harrison (photo; biog.); Hines (worked for company); Hulley; Rickard; Wickersham (photo; notes).

WILD GOOSE RAILROAD
See Seward Peninsula Railroad.

WILDLIFE
See the Arctic Bibliography.

WILEY, S. C.
Colonization and Settlement in the Americas: A Selected Bibliography. Ottawa: GPB, 1960. 68 pp. Dept. of Mines and Technical Surveys.

WILEY, WILLIAM HALSTED (1842-1925) and **SARA KING WILEY** (1871-1909)
The Yosemite, Alaska, and the Yellowstone. London, and New York: Wiley & Sons, 1893. 230 pp.

WILIMOVSKY, NORMAN J.
See the Arctic Bibliography.

WILKERSON, ALBERT SAMUEL (b. 1897)
Some Frozen Deposits in the Goldfields of Interior Alaska. New York: American Museum of Natural History, 1932. 22 pp.
"Fairbanks, Alaska: A Study of its People and their Environment," *Bulletin*, Geog. Soc. of Philadelphia, 1933.

WILKES, CHARLES
Narrative of the US Exploring Expedition of 1838-42. Philadelphia: Lippincott, 1844. Around Cape Horn to the Columbia River and the Strait of Juan de Fuca.

WILKINS, GEORGE HUBERT (1888-1958)
"Flights North of Point Barrow: An Abstract from the Report on the Detroit News-Wilkins Expedition of 1927," *Geog. J.*, 1928. With Carl Ben Eielson.

"Captain Wilkins' Arctic Expeditions, 1926-28: A Summary Statement," *Geog. Rev.*, 1928. Detroit Arctic Expedition of 1926; Detroit News-Wilkins Expedition of 1927; Wilkins Alaska-Spitzbergen flight of 1928.

"The Flight from Alaska to Spitzbergen, 1928," *Geog. Rev.*, 1928.

Flying the Arctic. New York: G.P. Putnam, 1928. 336 pp.

"Polar Exploration by Airplane," *Problems of Polar Research.* New York: Amer. Geog. Soc., 1928.

"In Polar Lands," *Can. Geog. J.*, 1931.

Under the North Pole. New York: Brewer, Warren and Putnam, 1931. 347 pp.

"Our Search for the Lost Aviators," *Nat. Geog.*, 1938. The Levanevskii Party.

Thoughts Through Space. New York: Creative Age Press, 1942. 421 pp.

"Lincoln Ellsworth, 1880-1951," *Arctic*, 1951.

See also the Arctic Bibliography. See also the following:

Alaska Sportsman, June, '50; Nov., '57 (photo, Eielson dedication); Colby; Grierson; Stefansson; Supf (T-4401); Thomas, L.; Wead (last voyage of the *Bear*).

WILLARD, CAROLINE McCOY WHITE (1853-1916)

Life in Alaska. Philadelphia: Presbyterian Board of Publication, 1884. 384 pp. Haines (named for F.E.H. Haines, Sec. of the Women's Committee of Home Missions [see Stewart]; information on naval rule of Alaska).

Children of the Far North. New York: Women's Board of Home Missions of the Presbyterian Church, n.d. 12 pp.

Kin-da-shon's Wife: An Alaskan Story. New York: Ravell, 1892. 281 pp.

WILLARD, FREDERICK EUGENE AUSTIN (b. 1882)

"Notes from the Arctic," *Alaska-Yukon Magazine*, March, 1909. Porcupine River.

"They Also Serve," *Alaska Life*, Jan., 1946.

" 'Big Rain' explains 'Assassination,' " *Alaska Life*, Aug., '49.

WILLEY, GEORGE FRANKLYN

"Lady Luck and the Cold Deck," *Alaska Sportsman*, Oct., '54.

WILLIAMS, FRANCES

I Asked for It. Philadelphia: Dorrance, 1954. 140 pp. Alaska Highway.

WILLIAMS, GLYNDWR

The British Search for the Northwest Passage in the 18th Century. London: Longmans, 1962. 306 pp.

WILLIAMS, HAROLD

One Whaling Family. Boston: Houghton Mifflin, 1964. 401 pp. Diary, Eliza Williams, whaler *Florida*, 1858-61; William Williams, whaler *Florence*, 1873-74.

WILLIAMS, HENRY LLEWELYN

History of the Adventurous Voyage and Terrible Shipwreck of the US Steamer Jeannette in the Polar Seas. New York: A.T.B. DeWitt, 1882. 95 pp.

WILLIAMS, HOWELL (b. 1893)

Landscapes of Alaska: Their Geologic Evolution. Berkeley: University of California Press, 1958. 148 pp. Williams edited this volume on 15 geologic provinces of Alaska which includes the work of F. Barnes, R. Black, R. Chapman, G. Flint, Jr., G. Gryc, J. Hoare, D. and J. Hopkins, D. Miller, H. Powers, J. Reed and C. Wahrhaftig.

WILLIAMS, JAY P. (1888-1954)

Alaskan Adventure. Harrisburg: Stackpole, 1952. 299 pp.

"Wild Life of the Alaska National Forests," *Alaska Sportsman*, Aug., '36.

"His Majesty," *Alaska Sportsman*, June, '38.

"My Friend Buck," *Alaska Sportsman*, March, '55.

"Lituya, the Bewitcher," *Alaska Sportsman*, Feb., '38.

WILLIAMS, JOHN R.

"Observations of Freeze-up and Break-up of the Yukon River at Beaver," *J. of Glaciology*, Apr., 1955.

WILLIAMS, LLEWELLYN MORRIS (b. 1895)

Alaska Weekly, Sept., '51 (removed as secretary of state); Oct., '51 (causes of removal); Denison (biog.); Tewkesbury (biog.).

WILLIAMS, MAXCINE MORGAN (b. 1904)

Alaska Wildflower Glimpses. Juneau: Totem Press, 1953. 52 pp.

"Flowers under the Arctic Circle," *Better Homes and Gardens*, May, 1937.

"Millions of Wild Faces," *Alaska Sportsman*, Aug., '38.

"Alaska's Wild Vegetables," *Alaska Sportsman*, July, '43.

WILLIAMS, WILLIAM (b. 1862)

"Climbing Mt. St. Elias," *Scribner's*, Apr., 1889.

"Reminiscences of Mt. St. Elias," *Amer. Alpine J.*, 1942.

WILLIAMS, WILLIAM APPLEMAN

American-Russian Relations, 1781-1947. New York: Rinehart, 1952. 367 pp.

WILLIAMS, WOODBRIDGE

"King Crab: A New Fishery?" *Alaska Life*, Jan., 1945.

WILLIAMSON, HARRIET E.

"Klukwan: Home of the Chilkats," *Alaska Sportsman*, Apr., '40.

"Kodiak Grows Up," *Alaska Sportsman*, July, '41.

WILLIAMSON, HENRY

Salar, the Salmon. Boston: Houghton Mifflin, 1936. 310 pp.

WILLIAMSON, JAMES ALEXANDER (b. 1886)

Builders of the Empire. Oxford: Clarendon Press, 1942.

Cook and the Opening of the Pacific. New York: Macmillan, 1948. 251 pp.

WILLIAMSON, JOE

See Newell, Gordon.

WILLIAMSON, THAMES ROSS (b. 1894)
The Earth Told Me. New York: Simon and Schuster, 1930. 350 pp.
On the Reindeer Trail. Boston: Houghton Mifflin, 1932. 242 pp.
North After Seals. Boston: Houghton Mifflin, 1934. 266 pp.
Far North Country. New York: Duell, Sloan and Pearce, 1944. 236 pp.

WILLIWAW
See the Arctic Bibliography. See also the following: *Alaska Sportsman*, Apr., '43 (wind beaches boats); June, '43 (moves van); *National Geog.*, March, '49 (curls steel mat runway); Stuck (near Cape Thompson).

WILLOUGHBY, FLORENCE BARRETT (1892-1959)
"George Watkins Evans: Authority on Alaska Coal," *Sunset*, February, 1916.
"Woman who Nursed a Whole Alaskan Tribe: Mrs. Alice Anderson," *Sunset*, May, 1916.
" 'Chief George' Barrett: Early Alaskan Pioneer and Indian Scout and Discoverer of the Northern Coal Fields," *Sunset*, June, 1916.
"Interesting Westerners: Mrs. C.W. Hammond," *Sunset*, February, 1917.
"Oil Development in Alaska Slow," *Oil Trade J.*, May, 1917.
Where the Sun Swings North. New York: Putnam's, 1922. 355 pp. Fiction: Tlingit. From 1925 Florence Willoughby used her stepfather's name as her first, calling herself Barrett Willoughby.
"Interesting Westerners: Fr. Andrew P. Kashevaroff," *Sunset*, February, 1923.
"Interesting Westerners: Alaska's Treasurer, Walstein G. Smith," *Sunset*, April, 1923.
"A Little Alaskan Schooner was my Childhood Home," *American Magazine*, October, 1924.
Rocking Moon: A Romance of Alaska. New York: Putnam's, 1925. 360 pp. Fiction: Kodiak.
The Fur Trail Omnibus: Rocking Moon, and *Where the Sun Swings North.* N.p., 1925.
"Alexander Allan: King of the Arctic Trail," *Sunset*, February, 1921.
"King of the Arctic Trail," *American Magazine*, August, 1925.
"Challenge of the Sweepstakes Trail," *American Magazine*, July, 1926.
"Father of Pictures Captures the Spell of Alaska," *American Magazine*, January, 1926.
"The Man Who Put the Midnight Sun to Work," *American Magazine*, August, 1928. C.C. Georgeson.
Gentleman Unafraid. New York: Putnam's, 1928. 285 pp. Martin Barrett, A.M. Smith, "Scotty" Allan, George Evans, Sydney Barrington, C.C. Georgeson.
"Grand Ball at Sitka: When Alaska was Russian," *Century*, April, 1929.
The Trail Eater: A Romance of the All-Alaska Sweepstakes. New York: Putnam's, 1929. 400 pp. "Scotty" Allan.
Sitka: Portal to Romance. Boston: Houghton Mifflin, 1930. 233 pp.
Sitka: To Know Alaska One Must First Know Sitka. London: Hodder, 1930. 248 pp. London edition of *Sitka*.
"Volcanoes Packed in Ice," *Sat. Eve. Post*, Aug., '30.

"Moon Craters of Alaska," *Sat. Eve. Post*, Dec., '30.
Spawn of the North. New York: Triangle Books, 1932. 347 pp. Ketchikan. Produced as a Paramount motion picture.
Alaskans All. Boston: Houghton Mifflin, 1933. 234 pp.
Fr. Hubbard, Ben Eielson, Capt. L. Lane, Harriet Pullen, "Stroller" White.
"Lighthouse Keeper at the End of the West," *Sat. Eve. Post*, January, 1935. Ted Pedersen.
"Logs of the New Pioneers," *Sat. Eve. Post*, June, 1935.
River House. Boston: Little, Brown, 1936. 389 pp. Stikine River country, Telegraph Creek.
"I'm a Cream-puff Pioneer," *American Magazine*, June, 1937.
Sondra O'Moore. Boston: Little, Brown, 1939. 320 pp.
Alaska Holiday. Boston: Little, Brown, 1940. 295 pp. Collection of previously published stories.
"One Alaska Night: Girl Lost in the Wilderness comes upon the Deserted Cabin of a Trapper," *Reader's Digest*, February, 1943.
The Golden Totem: A Novel of Modern Alaska. Boston: Little, Brown, 1945. 315 pp. Juneau.
"The Snow Woman and Mary Hewitt," *Alaska Sportsman*, Dec., '53.
Pioneer of Alaskan Skies: The Story of Ben Eielson. New York: Ginn & Co., 1959. 179 pp.
"The Silent City," *Alaska Sportsman*, June, '59.
See also the following:
Alaska Sportsman, Nov., '59 (came to Alaska with parents from Wisconsin in 1896). Despite the laudatory and uncritical nature of her personal impressions of Alaska notables, and the romantic nature of her novels, Barrett Willoughby's works are some of the best descriptive studies of Alaska conditions in the first decades of the 20th century.

WILLOUGHBY, RICHARD G. (1832-1902)
Alaska Sportsman, Sept., '53 (photo, notes); June, '59 (by Barrett Willoughby); Badlam ("Silent City"); Bruce (Willoughby Island, mining claims); Jordan ("Silent City"); Rickard (photo); Scidmore; Wickersham; Young.

WILLSON, BECKLES
The Great Company. Toronto: Copp, Clark Co., 1899. 2v. Hudson's Bay Co.

WILMOVSKY, N. J.
The Utilization of Fishery Resources by the Arctic Alaskan Eskimos. Stanford: Stanford University Press, 1956. 8 pp.

WILSON, ALICE S.
"The Acculturation of Alaskan Natives in the Public Schools at Nome, Alaska," Unpublished master's thesis, University of Alaska, 1958.

WILSON, BRUCE
"Busy Fairbanks Sets Alaska's Pace," *National Geog.*, Oct., '49.

WILSON, CAROL GREEN
Alice Eastwood's Wonderland: Adventures of a Botanist. San Francisco: the Author, 1955. 222 pp.

WILSON, GEORGE (1842-1906)
George Turner's Betrayal of his Country. Lexington, Mo.: 1904. 4 pp. Alaska-Canada boundary dispute.

WILSON, JAMES A.
Bits of Alaska. San Francisco, 1908. 59 pp. Pacific Coast Steamship Co.

WILSON, KATHERINE
Copper-Tints: A Book of Cordova Sketches. Cordova: Cordova Times, 1923. 44 pp. Eustace Ziegler drawings.
"President is Acclaimed," *Alaskan Churchman*, Apr., 1923.

WILSON, VEAZIE (d. ca. 1895)
Glimpses of the Yukon Gold Fields and Dawson Route. Vancouver: Thomson Stationery Co., 1895. 96 pp.
Guide to the Yukon Gold Fields. Seattle: Calvert Co., 1895. 72 pp.
Glimpses of Alaska: A Collection of Views of Interior Alaska and the Klondike District. Chicago: Rand McNally, 1897. 96 pp.

WILSON, WILLIAM H.
"Alaska's Past, Alaska's Future: The Uses of Historical Interpretation," *Alaska Review*, Spring, 1970.
"The Alaskan Engineering Commission and a New Agricultural Frontier," *Agricultural History*, October, 1968.
"The Founding of Anchorage," *Pacific Northwest Quarterly*, July, 1967.

WILSON, WOODROW (1856-1924)
Hulley (election influenced by Pinchot dispute; selected the railroad route, Seward, Matanuska, Susitna); Gruening (first message to Congress favored all territorial government; beginning of sympathy for Alaska); Nichols; Wickersham.

WIMMLER, NORMAN L.
Placer Mining Methods and Costs in Alaska. Wn.DC: GPO, 1927. 236 pp. US Bur. of Mines Bulletin 259.

WINCHELL, MARY EDNA (b. ca. 1881)
Home by the Bering Sea. Caldwell: Caxton Printers, 1951. 226 pp. Jesse Lee Home at Unalaska.
Where the Wind Blows Free. Caldwell: Caxton Printers, 1954. 176 pp.

WINCHESTER, JAMES D.
Capt. J.D. Winchester's Experiences. Salem, Mass.: Newcomb & Gauss, 1900. 251 pp.

WINCHESTER, J. W.
"Dr. Cook: Faker," *Pacific Monthly*, 1911.

WINDHAM BAY
Colby (east of Admiralty Island on the mainland); Couch (post office from 1903); Rickard (Cassiar miners discovered gold here in 1869; John Muir's 1878 report stimulated prospecting by Harris and Juneau who passed over the territory); Vancouver (named Point Windham); Winslow (Max Sylva).

WINFIELD, ARTHUR M.
The Rover Boys in Alaska. New York: Grosset and Dunlap, 1914. 285 pp.

WINGERT, PAUL STOVER (b. 1900)
"Tsimshian Sculpture," in *Tsimshian: Their Arts and Music.* New York: American Ethnological Society, 1951.

WINGHAM ISLAND
Baker (near mouth of the Copper River, named by Vancouver; also called Little Kayak, and Mitchell's Island); Brooks (probably visited by Bering's men); Vancouver (named by Mr. Puget).

WINN, BESS (d. 1949)
Nine articles in *Alaska Life*:
"Philanthropist Extraordinary," Nov., '42 (Charles Switzer); "The Fighting Parson," Jan., '43 (S. Hall Young); "Edible Wild Vegetables, Sea Food, Game," Feb., '43; "Woods Wisdom," March, '43; "Priest from the Pribilofs," May, '43 (Makary Baranoff); "Alaskan Nomenclature," May, '44; "Tuberculosis in Alaska," Dec., '44; "Jewels and Jade," June, '46; "Rehabilitation," Dec., '47.
Three articles in *Alaska Sportsman*:
"Elfin Cove Fish Buyer," May, '45 (John Lowell); "The Russian's Daughter," Feb., '46 (Killisnoo); "The Stikine", Sept., '47.

WINN, ELIZABETH M.
"The Political History of Alaska, 1867-1884," unpublished master's thesis, Reed College, 1948. 122 pp. See *Alaska Weekly*, Dec., 1950.

WINSLOW, ISAAC O.
Our American Neighbors. Boston: D.C. Heath, 1921. 200 pp.

WINSLOW, KATHRYN (b. 1913)
Big Pan-out. New York: W.W. Norton, 1951. 247 pp. Biographical sketches, esp. H. Sutherland and J. Ver Mehr.
Alaska Bound. New York: Dodd, Mead, 1960. 281 pp.

WINTER and POND CO.
See T-4925 ff, and Lloyd Winter.

WINTER, JAMES M.
New York to Alaska. New York: the Author, 1943. 1900 voyage of the *Dolphin*.

WINTER, LLOYD VALENTINE (1866-1945) and
EDWIN PERCIVAL POND (d. 1943)
The Nationally known firm of Winter & Pond, Photographers, was established in the late 1890's in Juneau, closing in 1956. The two partners came north to photograph gold mining life for Underwood and Underwood. See *Alaska Sportsman*, July, '43, Sept., '43, Feb., '46 and Apr., '57.

WINTHER, OSCAR OSBURN
The Great Northwest: A History. New York: Alfred A. Knopf, 1947. 383 pp.

WINTON, HARRY N. M.
"Pacific Northwest Bibliography," *Pac. NW Q.*, April, 1941.

WIRT, LOYAL LINCOLN (1863-1961)
Alaskan Adventures: A Tale of Our Last Frontier and of "Whiskers" Gallant Leader of the First Dog Team to Cross Alaska. New York: Revell, 1937. 124 pp. Wirt was sent by Gov. John Brady to Nome in 1899. The dog journey described was from Nome to Katmai.

WIRT, SHERWOOD ELIOT
Crack Ice: A Symposium of Alaska Dementia. Juneau, 1937. 32 pp.

WISE, DANIEL
"The Territory of Alaska," *Methodist Q. Rev.,* 1881.

WISEMAN
Alaska Sportsman, see Index; Baker (tributary, middle fork of the Koyukuk); Colby; Couch (post office from 1909); Hulley; Marshall; Stuck; Underwood (large nuggets from Nolan Creek).

WISHART, ANDREW
The Behring Sea Question: The Arbitration Treaty and the Award. Edinburgh: W. Green, 1893. 54 pp.

WISHAW, LORNA
As Far As You'll Take Me. New York: Dodd Mead, 1958. 216 pp.

WISSLER, CLARK (b. 1870)
"Material Cultures of the North American Indians," *Amer. Anthrop.,* 1914.
Archaeology of the Polar Eskimo. New York: Amer. Museum of Natural History, 1918.
Harpoons and Darts in the Stefansson Collection. New York: Amer. Museum of Natural History, 1916.

WITCHCRAFT (Shamanism)
Alaska Life, Feb., '41; *Alaska Sportsman,* Dec., '37 (photo, Oktokoyuk, St. Lawrence Island); Dec., '42; Sept., '57 (revival at Angoon); March, '58 ("Witch of Killisnoo"); Aldrich; Brower (Attungowrah); Calasanz (Holy Cross); Dall; Hellenthal (a defense); Henderson; Jackson (descr.); Judge (make dead child speak); Miller (Attungowrah); Morris (Indian woman hanged for witchcraft); Petrof (*Compilation of Narratives*); Schwatka (St. Michael man prediced loss of *Jeannette*); Scidmore; Stuck; Wead; Wiedemann (doctor); Willard; Whymper; Young (reports 100 victims of witchcraft lost lives in 1878 in southeast Alaska).

WITEMAN, GEORGE
North of '62: A Story of Adventure. Buffalo, N.Y.: Foster and Stewart, Publishers, 1946. 235 pp. Chisana, Wrangell.

WITHERSPOON, DAVID COLUMBUS
Baker (topographic work on Chandalar, Koyukuk and Copper Rivers, 1899-1900; Seward Peninsula 1901-03; Tanana-Yukon, 1904-05); Brooks (area of his surveys greater than that of any other person; Mt. Witherspoon in the Chugach).

WITTEN, JAMES W.
Report on the Agricultural Prospects, Natives, Salmon Fishing, Coal Prospects and Developments, *Timber and Lumber Interests of Alaska, 1903.* Wn.DC: GPO, 1904. 98 pp.
"Fox Propagation upon Islands in Alaska," in *Report,* Dept. of Interior, 1903.

WOEWODSKI, STEPAN VASILIVICH (Manager, Russian-American Co., 1854-59)
Baker (named in his honor are Woewodski Harbor [Admiralty Is.] and Woewodski Island [Wrangel Strait]); Wickersham (his voyage in the *Nikolai,* 1839-41, descr. in Ivanshinstov's *Review of Russian Voyages*).

WOLCOTT
Gruening (joined *HMS Osprey* at Sitka, 1879); Morris (photo, at Wrangell; letter from her commander).

WOLDMAN, ALBERT A.
Lincoln and the Russians. Cleveland: World Publ. Co., 1953. 311 pp.

WOLFE, ALFRED (b. 1887)
In Alaskan Waters. Caldwell: Caxton Printers, 1942. 196 pp. Halibut fishery, BC. *Princess Sophia* disaster descr.

WOLFE, LINNIE MARSH
John of the Mountains: Unpublished Journals of John Muir. Boston: Houghton Mifflin, 1938. 459 pp.
Son of the Wilderness: Life of John Muir. New York: Alfred A. Knopf, 1945. 364 pp.

WOLFE, LOUIS
Let's Go to the Klondike Gold Rush. New York: Putnam's, 1964.

WOLFF, ERNEST
Handbook for the Alaskan Prospector. Fort Collins, Colo.: Burnt River Exploration and Development Co., 1964. 428 pp.

WOLFENDEN, MADGE and J. H. HAMILTON
"The Sitka Affair," *The Beaver,* Winter, 1955. *HMS Osprey.*

WOLVERINES
See the Arctic Bibliography.

WOLVES
See the Arctic Bibliography.

WOMAN'S BAY
Alaska Life: Nov., '41 (naval station); *Alaska Sportsman* (ice hampers operations); Baker (named by Russians about 1808); see also the US Coast Pilot.

WONDER LAKE
Colby; Franck; Wickersham (first called Alma Lake, 1903).

WOOD, CHARLES ERSKINE SCOTT (1852-1944)
"Among the Thlinkits in Alaska," *Century,* July, 1882. See *Alaska Life,* Nov., '44.

WOOD, JAMES PLAYSTED
Alaska: The Great Land. New York: Meredith Press, 1967. 181 pp.

WOOD, JOSEPH K.
Gruening (was imprisoned); Harrison; Hines (fight with Fink); Rickard; Wickersham.

WOOD, PETER
Peter Wood's 1945 Alaska Business Directory. Fairbanks: Peter Wood, 1945.
Unbelievable Years: The Truth about Alaska. Playa de Rey, Calif.: Littlepage Press, 1969. 236 pp.

WOOD, W. A.
"Icefield Ranges Research Project," *Geog. Rev.,* 1963.

WOOD, WALTER ABBOT (b. 1907)
"Wood Yukon Expedition of 1935: An Experiment in Photographic Mapping," *Geog. Rev.,* 1936.
"The Ascent of Mt. Steele," *Amer. Alpine J.,* 1936.

WOODBRIDGE, HENSLEY C., JOHN LONDON and GEORGE H. TWENEY
Jack London: A Bibliography. Georgetown, Calif.: Talisman Press, 1966. 422 pp.

WOODCHOPPER
Baker (creek is tributary to the Yukon); Broaddus (settlement); Colby (mastodon bones found here); Couch (post office 1919-23); Wiedemann.

WOODCOCK, GEORGE
Ravens and Prophets: An Account of Journeys in BC, Alberta, and Southern Alaska. London: Alan Wingate, 1952. 244 pp.

WOODEN ISLAND
Alaska Sportsman, Jan., '58; Baker (Wooden Inlet, ner Cape Ommaney); Broaddus; Vancouver (Isaac Wooden, crew member, fell overboard and was lost).

WOODMAN, ABBY JOHNSON (b. 1828)
Picturesque Alaska: A Journal. Boston: Houghton, 1889. 212 pp. 1888 on the *George W. Elder.*

WOODMAN, LYMAN L.
"The Trans-Canadian, Alaska and Western Railways," *Alaska Journal,* Autumn, 1974.

WOODRING, W. P.
"William Henry Dall," *Nat. Acad. Sci., Biog. Memoirs,* 1958.

WOODS, HENRY FITZWILLIAM and EDWARD E. P. MORGAN
God's Loaded Dice, Alaska: 1897-1930. Caldwell: Caxton Printers, 1948. 298 pp. Limited edition.

WOODWARD, FRANCES J.
Portrait of Jane: A Life of Lady Franklin. London: Hodder & Stoughton, 1951. 382 pp.

WOODWORTH, JAMES
The Kodiak Bear. Harrisburg: Stackpole, 1958. 205 pp.

WOODWORTH, RALPH W. and FRANK J. HAIGHT
See US Coast and Geodetic Survey.

WOODY ISLAND
Alaska Sportsman, Apr., '38 (Baptist orphanage); Nov., '45 (1896 visit); Jan., '56 (ice company); Baker (named by Lisianski in 1804); Dole (had 1st road in Alaska); Harriman (Burroughs); Higginson; Jackson; Petrof; Scidmore; Swineford (N. Amer. Comm. Co. post); Willoughby (Island of Rocking Moon is apparently Woody Island).

WOOLLACOTT, ARTHUR P.
Mackenzie and His Voyageurs: By Canoe to the Arctic and the Pacific, 1789-93. London: Dent, 1927. 237 pp.

WOOLLEN, WILLIAM WATSON (1838-1921)
The Inside Passage to Alaska, 1792-1920. Cleveland: Athur Clark Co., 1924. 2v. Primarily Vancouver, and Woollen in 1913.

WOOLLEY, CLIVE
See *Alaska Sportsman,* May, 1957.

WOOLLEY, MONROE
"Anchorage: Advance Agent of Alaskan Development," *Illustrated World,* 1916.

WORDEN, WILLIAM L.
"The Survey our Unknown Coast," *Sat. Eve. Post,* June, 1952.
"Every Girl's a Queen," *Sat. Eve. Post,* June, 1952.
"Alaska's Coldest College," *Sat. Eve. Post,* Sept., 1952.
"Untamed Alaska," *Holiday,* July, 1953.
"So You Want to Drive to Alaska," *Sat. Eve. Post,* Sept., 1957.
"The Town that Can't Wait for Tomorrow," *Sat. Eve. Post,* Sept., 1959.

WORK, HUBERT (Sec. of the Interior, 1923-28)
"What Future has Alaska?" in *Rept. of the Sec. of Int.,* 1925.

WORKMAN, KAREN
Alaska Archaeology: A Bibliography; see Alaska Dept. of Parks.

WORKMAN, WILLIAM
"Ahtna Archaeology: A Preliminary Statement." Paper, 9th Annual Conference, Univ. of Calgary Archaeology Assn., 1976. A superb statement available through the author at Univ. Alaska.

WORMINGTON, H. M.
Ancient Man in North America. Denver: Museum of Natural History, 1957. 322 pp.

WORONKOFSKI ISLAND
Baker (named by Russians for Lt. Woronkovski, explorer of the southern shore of the Alaska Peninsula in 1836); Broaddus; Vancouver (one of the Duke of York Islands [between Wrangel and Zarembo Islands]).

WORTHINGTON GLACIER
Alaska Sportsman, July, '56; Baker (named by Schrader, 1900); Colby.

WORTHINGTON, LAWRENCE
See the Arctic Bibliography.

WORTHYLAKE, MARY
Nika Illahee. Chicago: Melmont Publishers, 1962. 32 pp.
Moolack: Young Salmon Fisherman. Chicago: Melmont Publishers, 1963. 48 pp.

WOSNESENSKI GLACIER
Baker (named for Elias S. Wosnesenski, Russian naval officer, who made collections in the area, 1842-44, for the Acad. of Sci., St. Petersburg; near Kachemak Bay; also in the Shumagin group).

WOTTE, HERBERT
See the Arctic Bibliography.

WRAIGHT, A. JOSEPH and ELLIOTT B. ROBERTS
The Coast and Geodetic Survey, 1807-1957. Wn.DC: GPO, 1957. 89 pp. See Colbert, Sherwood, and Weber.

WRANGEL, FERDINAND, Baron von (1796-1870)
Expedition along the North Siberian Coast and the Arctic Sea. London: Caddell, 1840. 3v.
For a full listing of Wrangel's works in Russian, see the Arctic Bibliography. See also the following:
Alaska Life, Apr., '43 (C.L. Andrews); Chernenko (in Russian); Dall (member of Golovnin's second expedition to America in 1817-18; toured colonies with special attention to Nushagak; endorsed Kashavarov's reply to Golovnin); Dole (opposed Hudson's Bay on the Stikine); Harriman; Hulley (first man of distinction to govern the colonies; negotiated the Stikine River Lease [see Nichols]); Petrof; Scidmore (resumes of his work in Dall, and in Petrof); Stuck (Michael Tebenkov sent to est. Ft. St. Michael in 1833); Tompkins (Ft. Dionysius affair on the Stikine); see also the Arctic Bibliography. See also Richard Pierce.

WRANGEL ISLAND
Alaska Sportsman, March, '43 (Capt. Hammer in 1921 on the Stefansson expedition); Baker (Wrangel could not find the island in 1823 though reported by natives; first seen by Capt. Henry Kellett in 1849; seen clearly by Capt. Thomas Long of the whaling bark *Nile* in 1867 and named for Wrangel; mapped by Lt. Robert Berry on the *Rodgers* in 1881); Bartlett; Borden; Caswell; DeLong; Ellsberg; Franck (US Congressmen sought to have the island fortified); Hooper; Joerg; Melville; Muir (*Corwin*); Newcomb; Perry; Stefansson; Stuck; Wead. See also the *Jeannette.*

WRANGELL
Alaska Life, Feb., '45 (anecdotes from old court records, 1884-1904); Apr., '46 (photo); *Alaska Sportsman,* see Index; *Alaska Weekly,* Jan., '51 (Shakes Island); May, '51; Aug., '51; Sept., '51; *Alaska-Yukon Magazine,* Apr., '10; Oct., '11; Andrews (bombardment of the village; Cassiar); Atwood; Badlam; Baker (founded 1834); Ballou (descr. 1889); Bancroft; Barrow; Brooks; Bruce (pop. 1890: 100 whites, 2-300 natives); Caldwell; Cameron; Chase (Capt. Billy Moore, Cassiar); Colby; Collis; Colyer; Corser; Couch (post office: Ft. Wrangell, 1869-1902; from 1902); Dall; Davis; Denison (Wrangell Institute); DeBaets; DeVighne; Dole; Garland; Hallock; Hart; Harriman; Hayes;

Hellenthal; Higginson (founded by Lt. Zarembo; town largely destroyed by fire just before turn of the century); Hilscher (CCC rebuilt Shakes' house); Houston (see Scidmore); Hulley; Jacobin; Jackson (founding of mission, trouble with Indians); Monroe; Morris; Muir; Petrof (Dryad affair; two murders, 1869-70); Pilgrim; Rogers (Indians moved into all white Wrangell between 1880 and 1900); Rossiter; Santos; Schwatka; Scidmore; Snyder (*Alaska Mag.,* 1905); Stewart (mission); Stuck; Sundborg; Swanton (myths); Swineford; Tewkesbury; Underwood; Wardman (Indians were friendly in 1879); Webster; Willett; Willoughby (River House); Winslow; Young. See also Stikine River.

WRANGELL MOUNTAINS
Baker; Blumer (*Can. Alpine J.,* 1956); Brooks; Burnham (*Outdoor Life,* 1924); Harrer (*Amer. Alpine J.,* 1955); Moore (*Amer. Alp. J.,* 1939); Winslow (packtrain from Chisana).

WRANGELL NARROWS
Alaska Sportsman, Aug., '40 (photo); June, '41; Sept., '41; Apr., '47 (photo); July, '53; March, '56; Oct., '57; *Alaska-Yukon Mag.,* Oct., '10 (wreck of the *Colorado*); Baker; Caldwell; Cameron; Colby; Dole (first transited by steamer *Saginaw* in 1869); Higginson; Scidmore; Vancouver.

WRIGHT, BILLIE
Four Seasons North. New York: Harper & Row, 1972. 125 pp.

WRIGHT, CHARLES WILL (b. 1879)
"The 1931 Glacier Bay Expedition," *J.* Wn. Acad. of Sci., 1932. See also Baker; see also the Arctic Bibliography.

WRIGHT, FREDERIC EUGENE (b. 1877) and **CHARLES WILL WRIGHT**
The Ketchikan and Wrangell Mining Distirct. Wn.DC: GPO, 1908. 210 pp. USGS Survey Bulletin.

WRIGHT, GARETH
Alaska Sportsman, Jan., '57; June, '57; June, '58, and Index.

WRIGHT, GEORGE FREDERICK (1838-1921)
"The Muir Glacier," *Amer. J. of Sci.,* Jan., 1887.
The Muir Glacier. Sitka: Soc. of Alaskan Natural History, 1889. 22 pp.
The Ice Age in North America and Its Bearings upon the Antiquity of Man. Oberlin: Bibliotheca Sacra Co., 1911. 763 pp.

WRIGHT, GEORGE M. and BEN H. THOMPSON
Fauna of the National Parks of the US. Wn.DC: GPO, 1935. 142 pp.

WRIGHT, HELEN SAUNDERS (b. 1874)
The Great White North: The Story of Polar Exploration. New York: Macmillan, 1910. 489 pp.

WRIGHT, JULIA McNAIR (1840-1903)
Among the Alaskans. Philadelphia: Presbyterian Board of Publications, 1883. 351 pp. Est. of Presbyterian missions in Alaska.

WRIGHT, MT.
Baker (named by Reid in 1890 for Prof. G.F. Wright); Scidmore.

WRIGHT, NOEL
Quest for Franklin. London: Heinemann, 1959. 258 pp.

WRIGHT, THEON
The Big Nail: The Story of the Cook-Peary Feud. New York: John Day Co., 1970. 368 pp.

WRIGHT, WILLIAM PRESTON
The Alaska Highway. Great Falls, Mont.: the Author, 1945. 35 pp.

WRONG, HUMPHREY HUME
Sir Alexander Mackenzie: Explorer and Fur Trader. Toronto: Macmillan, 1927. 171 pp.

WROTH, LAWRENCE COUNSELMAN (b. 1884)
"The Early Cartography of the Pacific," *Papers,* Bibliog., Soc. of Amer., 1944.

WURMBRAND, DEGENHARD
See the Arctic Bibliography.

WYCLIFFE BIBLE TRANSLATORS
See the listing in T-4981 ff.

WYLLIE, P. J.
Ultramafic and Related Rocks. New York: Wiley and Sons, 1967. 464 pp.

WYMAN, GILBERT
Public Land and Mining Laws of Alaska, the Northwest Territories, and the Province of British Columbia. Fruitvale, Calif.: the Author, 1898. 776 pp.

WYTHE, W. T.
"Cook's Inlet," *Overland Monthly,* Jan., 1872.
"Kodiak and Southern Alaska," *Overland Monthly,* June, 1872.
"Southern Alaska," *Pop. Sci. Monthly,* May, 1872.

Y

YAKATAGA
Alaska Sportsman, July, '55 (photo; oil); *Alaska Weekly,* Apr., '51 (oil seepages before 1900); Baker; Couch (post office 1904-05 and from 1907; Cape Yakataga); Higginson; Thompson (*Eng. & Mining J.,* 1915).

YAKO
Wickersham (created Denali, and the Ahtna Mountains).

YAKUTAT
Alaska Sportsman, March, '38; Nov., '40; Jan., '46 (beach rescue); March, '49; June, '58 (photo from '08); *Alaska Magazine,* July, '07; *Alaska-Yukon Magazine,* Aug., '10 (photo); Baker; Barber; Brooks (beach gold, 1880); Colby (railway to Situk and Lost River); Couch (post office, 1892-95, and from 1897); Gruening (protest of fishery reserve); Higginson; Hulley; Johnson, A. (natives begged for whiskey); Potter (airfield constr.); Wickersham; Wolfe. See also de Laguna, *Under St. Elias.*

YAKUTAT BAY
Alaska Sportsman, Jan., '46; *Alaska-Yukon Magazine,* Apr., '09 (photos; coast deformed by earthquake); Baker (history: La Perouse, 1786; Portlock, 1786; Spaniards; Lisianski, 1805); Bancroft; Chevigny; Colby (Malaspina, 1791; I.C. Russell, 1890; earthquake, 1899); Harriman; Higginson (gold excitement, 1880); Rickard (Indian names); Riddell and de Laguna (19 typescript pages, library, Juneau); Tarr; Scidmore; Tompkins; Vancouver.

YAKUTAT GLACIER
Baker (between Dry and Yakutat Bays); US Coast Pilot.

YANERT, WILLIAM (1864-1952)
"A Trip to the Tanana River," *Compilation of Narratives.* With Glenn, 1898.
"From Middle Fork of Sushitna to the Talkeetna," *Compilation of Narratives.*
Yukon Breezes. Ms. University of Alaska Library.
See also the following:
Alaska Sportsman, Apr., '38 (photo); Aug., '56 (retired from Army in 1903, lived 48 years at Purgatory on the Yukon River); Baker; Broaddus; Brooks; Franck; Stuck; Washburn (first report of Broad Pass).

YANOVSKI, SEMEN IVANOVICH (Manager, Russian-American Co., 1818-20)
Andrews (tour of the colonies); Bancroft (Baranov's son-in-law); Chevigny (married Irina Baranov, returned to Russia in 1821); Higginson; Hulley; Petrof; Scidmore (Mme. Yanovski was the first hostess on the Kakoor); Tompkins (marked the beginning of naval influence at Sitka).

YARD, ROBERT STERLING
The Book of the National Parks. New York: Scribner's, 1919. 420 pp.

YARMOLINSKI, AVRAHM (b. 1890)
"Shelekhov's Voyage to Alaska: A Bibliographical Note," *Bulletin*, New York Public Library, March, 1932.
"Aleutian Manuscript Collection," *Bulletin*, New York Public Library, August, 1944. 12 pp. Jochelson.
"Kamchadal and Asiatic Eskimo Manuscript Collections," *Bulletin*, New York Public Library, 1947.

YBARRA Y BERGE, JAVIER de (b. 1913)
See the Arctic Bibliography.

YEHL (also Yeatl, Yeshl)
Higginson (Raven, beneficient spirit of the sun, moon and stars); Petrof (Tlingit deity, creator of all things); Young (story).

YEMANS, H. W.
See Cantwell.

YES BAY
Baker (Tlingit for mussel); Back (*Hunter-Trapper*, Apr., '07); Morris, F.; Scidmore (named McDonald's Bay by the Coast Survey); Vancouver.

YEVREINOV, IVAN and FEDOR LUZHIN
Bancroft (mission to the Kurile Islands, 1719-21); Golder; Muller; Hulley (lost anchors); Tompkins (geodesists).

YORK
Baker (Cape named by Beechey in 1827); Couch (post office, 1900-02); see also the Arctic Bibliography.

YORK ISLANDS
Baker (incl. Etolin, Woronkofski, Wrangel and Zarembo); Broaddus.

YORK, JOSEPH
"Minnie's Minnows," *Leatherneck*, July, 1935. Aleutians.

YOUNG, A.
"A Trip to Princess Louisa Inlet," *Mountaineer*, Dec., 1930.

YOUNG, DAVID L.
Millions Want To. Tucson: Three Flags Publ. Co., 1963. 192 pp.

YOUNG, GEORGE ORVILLE (b. 1873)
Alaskan Trophies Won and Lost. Boston: Christopher Publ. House, 1928. 248 pp.
Alaska-Yukon Trophies Won and Lost. Huntington, W. Va.: Standard Publications, 1947. 271 pp.

YOUNG GLACIER
Scidmore; Young (on naming).

YOUNG, ISOBEL NELSON
The Story of Salmon. New York: American Can Co., 1934. 48 pp.

YOUNG, SAMUEL HALL (1847-1927)
"Yukon Presbytery Redevivus: A Pioneer of '78 Plunges again into the Wilds," *Assembly Herald*, June, 1911.
Alaska Days with John Muir. New York: Revell, 1915. 226 pp. Young and Indians from Wrangell accompanied Muir in 1879 and 1880.
The Klondike Clan: A Tale of the Great Stampede. New York: Revell, 1916. 393 pp.
Adventures in Alaska. New York: Revell, 1919. 181 pp. Nome.
Hall Young of Alaska: Autobiography. New York: Revell, 1927. 448 pp.
"Kenowan the Hyda Boy," *New Era Magazine*, Fall, 1919.
See also the Arctic Bibliography; see the following: *Alaska Life*, Jan., '43; Aug., '46; Andrews (narrowly escaped death in Indian liquor battle); Brooks (Young and Mrs. McFarland deserve credit for founding Presbyterian missions in Alaska, rather than Sheldon Jackson); Colby; Davis; Hayes; Hulley; Lindsley (organized Wrangell church, 1879); Scidmore.

YOUNG, STANLEY PAUL (b. 1889)
"The Return of the Musk Ox," *Amer. Forests*, Aug., '41.

YOUNG, STANLEY PAUL and H. H. T. JACKSON
The Clever Coyote. Wn.DC: Stackpole, 1951. 411 pp.

YOUNG, STANLEY PAUL and EDWARD A. GOLDMAN
The Wolves of North America. Wn.DC: Amer. Wildlife Inst., 1944. 636 pp.

YOUTH'S COMPANION
Our Country's West. Boston: P. Mason & Co., 1897. 256 pp.

YUKOLA
Chevigny (dried salmon in the Aleutians); Henderson.

YUKON
Alaska Sportsman, Oct., '57 (Capt. Benj. Hall, first steamer on the Yukon); Calasanz (St. Michael to Koserefsky, 1888); Kitchener (Hutchinson Kohl steamer); Ogilvie (owned by Jack Parrott and others); Raymond (launched July 1, 1869); Schwatka (1883 photo); Wickersham. See Baker and Kitchener for other steamers named *Yukon*.

YUKON
Alaska Life, May, '46 (Alaska Steamship Co., wrecked near Cape Fairfield, Kenai Peninsula, February, 1946); *Alaska Sportsman*, Aug., '46 (photo).

YUKON BILL
Derby Day in the Yukon, and Other Poems on the Northland. New York: Doran, 1910. 128 pp.

YUKON CONSOLIDATED GOLD CORP.

Alaska Sportsman, July, '56; *Alaska-Yukon Magazine*, Feb., '10; Kitchener (first to start dredging, about 1906).

YUKON CROSSING

Franck (Whitehorse-Dawson road crosses on ice); Stuck (stages and stables).

YUKON FLATS

Baker (extend 200 miles from Circle); Cameron; Colby; Davis (huge lake full of islands); Hawthorne; Higginson; Hulley; Richardson; Stuck; Tompkins.

YUKON HEALTH

Alaska Sportsman, May, '57 (photo); Feb., '58 (medical service steamer was used as hotel at Fairbanks); *Alaska's Health*, June, 1951.

YUKON HISTORICAL SOCIETY

Alaska Sportsman, May, 1955.

YUKON JAKE

Wickersham (lived by himself on a sea-lion's shelf).

YUKON ORDER OF PIONEERS

Atwood (organized at Fortymile in 1893 by Jack McQuesten, Al Mayo and others); Bankson (funeral of Harry Spencer, one of the founders); Kitchener (AC Co. had negative attitude).

YUKON PRESS

Jenkins; Stuck; Wickersham (press received at mission as gift; paper published from 1 Jan. 1894 to 20 April 1899 [six numbers at Ft. Adams, 10 numbers at Circle]).

YUKON RIVER

See the Arctic Bibliography. *Alaska Life*, June, '39 (circle tour descr.); Aug., '45 (planes bomb ice-jams); *Alaska Sportsman*, see Index; *Alaska-Yukon Magazine*, Jan., '08 (descr. delta, Fr. Barnum); Nov., '08 (E.S. Harrison); March, '11 (C.L. Andrews); Allen, H.; Andrews; Baker (Russian founded Nulato in 1841; British built Ft. Yukon in 1847); Bancroft (ancient name Kwikpak, Eskimo for big river); Barnum (*Woodstock Letters*, Woodstock, Md., 1896); Beach (Barrier); Beaver; Berton; Black; Bone; Brandt; Brooks; Browne; Burg; Burke (Ft. Yukon doctor); Burpee; Calasanz; Cameron; Campbell (discovery of upper Yukon); Cantwell; Castner; Chapman (Anvik); Chase; Colby; Cole (*Weatherwise*, Aug., '52); Cook; Curtin (history); Dall; Davis; DeBaets (Seghers); DeLaguna; DeWindt; Ederer; Elliott; Franck; Fraser; Glazunov (1833-34 journey); Glenn; Goodrich (1896); Gordon, G.; Gray (power plant); Hamlin; Helmericks; Henderson (Bell first applied the name Yukon in 1846); Henry (Pac. Sci. Conf., *Proc.*, 1954); Hewitt (Army surgeon); Higginson; Hrdlicka; Hulley; Illarian; Ingersoll; Jacobsen; James (Kennicott); Kirby (prior to 1864); Kitchener (river trade; 22 towns; NC Co.); Lane; Maddren; Mason, M. (Indians); Melville (Univ. of Alaska, *Anthrop. Papers*, 1958); Menzies (*Pac. NW Q.*, Apr., '41); Morgan; Murray (Journal, 1847-48); Myers; Nelson; O'Connor; Ogilvie; Osgood (Anvik); Petitot (1870); Petrof; Pike (1892); Rainey; Raymond

(1869); Rea; Richardson (weather, 1898); Rickard; Robins; Romig; Russell; Savage; Schwatka (1883); Scull; Secretan; Sheldow; Sniffen (Indians); Spurr; Stanley; Stefansson; Stewart (1906); Stuck; Tikhmenev; Tollemache; Tompkins; Tyrrell; Underwood; VanStone; Walden; Wardle; Whymper (1865); Wickersham; Williams, J.; Winchester; Winslow; Zagoskin.

YUKON RIVER BOATS

Alaska Sportsman, see Index; *Alaska-Yukon Gold Book* (photos); *Alaska-Yukon Magazine*, Nov., '08 (photos, *Sarah*, *Tanana*); Andrews (*Yukon* sank in slough below Ft. Yukon while wintering in the late 1880's); Allen (*Yukon* and *New Racket* on the river in 1885); Bankson (*Margaret*, *John J. Healy*, *Orca*, *Gov. Stoneman*, 1898); Brooks (summary); Calasanz (4 mission boats); Cameron; Davis; Franck; Gruening (5 American companies plus one vessel enterprises in 1900 operated 41 steamers, 15 smaller vessels and 39 barges); James; Kitchener (change to oil in 1903); Ogilvie (historical notes on 11 steamers); Raymond; Richardson; Stuck; Tewkesbury; Walden; Wead (600 steamers); Wickersham; Winslow; Whymper.

YUKON STOVE

Alaska Sportsman, Dec., '48 (photo: oil drum fitted with legs and chimney and door); July, '52; Hawthorne; Kitchener (called Klondike Stove at Dawson); Henderson.

YUKON TERRITORY

See the Arctic Bibliography. *Alaska Sportsman*, see Index; *Alaska Weekly*, May, '51 (Aubrey Simmons and George Black); *Alaska-Yukon Magazine*, March, '07; Feb., '10 (on annexation to BC); Albee; Allen, A. (Seattle: Pac.Coast SS Co., 1902); Alpine Club of Canada; Anderson, J.; Armstrong, N.; Atwood, F.; Auer; Averill (S-383); Baker, R. (Arctic Bibliography); Bankson; Barger (*Ak. Sports.*, Nov., '45); Barnum (in Woodstock Letters); Barwell (*Can. Surveyor*, Oct., '26); Becker; Berton, L.; Berton, P.; Bethune (*Canada's Western Northland* [Ottawa: King's Printer, 1937]); Binning (*Royal Can. Mtd. Police Q.*, July, '41 [Indians]); Black, M.; Blackmore (*Ak. Sports.*, Nov., '38); Blanchet (*Can. Surv.*, July, '44 [Canol]); Bilis; Blount; Bompas; Bond; Booth (Arctic Biblio.); Bostock (Arctic Biblio.); Bramble; Brown, J.N.E. (*Evolution of Law and Government of the Yukon Territory*); Burpee; Cadell; Cairnes (Arctic Biblio.); Cameron; Campbell; Camsell (Arctic Biblio.); Cantwell; Case; Catto (S-1587); Clifton; Cockfield (Arctic Biblio.); Collins and Roberts (*Amer. Alpine J.*, 1958); Collins and Sumner (Arctic Biblio.); Coolidge; Correll; Cory; Coudert (Arctic Biblio. [missions]); Craig, L.; Crane; Cross (Arctic Biblio.); Cruickshank (*Royal Can. Mtd. Police J.*, Oct., '56 [summit detachment]); Curtin; Davis; Dawson, C. (*The New Northwest* [Toronto: Univ. of Toronto Press, 1947]); Dawson, G.; Day, L.; Dease; DeWindt; Dill; Dixon (Arctic Biblio.); Drury (Arctic Biblio.); Ederer; Edwards, W.; Ellis (Arctic Biblio.); Ells (*Can. Geog. J.*, March, '44 [econ. factors, Alaska Highway]); Fetherstonhaugh (*Royal Canadian Mounted Police* [New York: Carrick and Evans, 1938]); Field,W.; Finnie (Arctic Biblio.); Flint, H. (Arctic Biblio.); Franck; Franklin; Fraser; Gibb (*Can. Geog. J.*, March, '34); Gillham; Gilliat

(Arctic Biblio. [nurse]); Godsell; Gomery (Arctic Biblio.); Goodrich; Gorman (W-6767); Graham, A.; Griffin, H.; Grinnell (Arctic Biblio.); Gutsell (Arctic Biblio.); Harris, A.; Haskell; Hayne; Heilprin; Henderson; Hewetson (Arctic Biblio.); Hicks (*W. Miner*, Nov., '49); Higginson; Himes (Arctic Biblio.); Hinton and Godsell; Honigmann (*Amer. Anthrop.*, Apr., '47 [witch fear]; *Q.J., Stud. in Alcohol*, March, '45 [Indian-White community]; *Dalhousie Rev.*, Jan., '44 [soc. changes in native pop. due to econ. impact]); Hulten; Hutchison; Illingworth; Ingersoll, E.; Irving, L. (Arctic Biblio.); Jacobin; Jaques; Jenness; Jesson; Johnson, F. (Arctic Biblio.); Judd (Arctic Biblio.); Keele (Arctic Biblio.); Kennicott; Kerr (Arctic Biblio.); Kirk; Klengenberg; Knox and Pratt (Arctic Biblio.); Ladue; Laing (Arctic Biblio.); Leechman (*Can. Hist. Rev.*, Dec., '46 [Pre-hist. migration routes];] *Can. Geog.J.*, July, '48 [Old Crow's Village]; *Can. Geog. J.*, June, '50); Lingard (in C. Dawson); Lloyd, T. (*Can. Affairs*, Feb., '44); Lloyd-Owen; Longstreth (RCMP); Lynch; Lyttleton; MacBeth (Arctic Biblio.); MacBride (*Beaver*, June, '53; June, '49); McConnell; MacDonald, A.; MacDonald, M.; Macfie; McGuire; McMillion (Arctic Biblio. [history of highway proposals]); Macoun (Arctic Biblio.); Martindale; Mason, M.; Medill; Miller, M.M.; Miller, T.; Mitchell, E.A. (in C.A. Dawson [Bibliography]); Morgan, E.; Morrell; Murie (Arctic Biblio.); Murray, Q.; Neuberger (in *Alaska Life*, Dec., '43; Feb., '44; Aug., '44; Dec., '45); North Pac. Planning Proj. (Arctic Biblio.); Northern Affairs Bul. (Arctic Biblio.); O'Connor; Odell (Arctic Biblio. [Arctic Inst. Expedition]); Ogilvie; Oliver, E.; Osgood; Palmer, F.; Pearson, L. (Arctic Biblio.); Pike; Porsild; Price, C. (*Ak. Sports.*, Apr., '58); Price, J.; Quackenbush (Arctic Biblio. [mammoth expeditions]); Rainey; Rand (Arctic Biblio.); Rand McNally Co.; Raup; Reed (*Pac. Builder & Eng.*, Aug., '43); Rickard; Ridge (Arctic Biblio.); Robertson, R. (Arctic Biblio.); Robertson, W.; Robinson, J.L. (Arctic Biblio. [agriculture]); Royal Canadian Mounted Police (*Annual Report*, from 1874); Scidmore; Sealock; Secretan; Service; Sheldon; Shulman; Sola; Spindler (Arctic Biblio.); Spurr; Stanley, W.; Stansbury; Steele; Stefansson; Stewart, E.; Stone, A.; Stuck; Sturdevant; Taverner; Taylor, T. (Arctic Biblio.); Thomas, A. (W-6802); Thompson, A. (W-6804); Thomson (*Monthly Weather Rev.*, Aug., '58); Tollemache; Tompkins; Treadgold; Trelawney-Ansell; Tuttle; Tyrrell (Can. GS, 1898); Tyrrell, M. (Arctic Biblio.); Viksten; Walden; Wardle (Arctic Biblio.); Washburn; Wells, H.L.; Whelen (Arctic Biblio. [big game anthology]); White, C. (Arctic Biblio.); Wiedemnn; Williams, M.Y. (Arctic Biblio.); Williams, R.S. (Arctic Biblio.); Winslow; Wood, F.; Wood, W.A.; Wurmbrand; Young, G.; Yukon Bill; Zaccarelli.

YUKONER
Alaska Sportsman, February, 1958 (launched 1898); Curtin.

YULE, EMMA SAREPTA (b. ca. 1855)
"The Schools of Juneau," *Alaska-Yukon Magazine*, Sept., '07.
"China Joe: Story of a Juneau 'Chink,' " *Pac. Monthly*, Aug., '10.

Z

ZACCARELLI, JOHN
Zaccarelli's Pictorial Souvenir Book of the Golden Northland. Dawson: John Zaccarelli, 1908. 11 pp. 192 photos.

ZAGOSKIN, LAVRENTII ALEKSEEVICH (1808-1890)
Account of a Pedestrian Journey in the Russian Possessions in America. Typewritten translation by Antoinette Hotovitzky in the Alaska State Historical Library (1842-44). Originally published at St. Petersburg: Press of Karl Krai, 1847. 303 pp.
Lt. Zagoskin's Travels in Russian America, 1842-44: The First Ethnographic and Geographic Investigations in the Yukon and Kuskokwim Valleys of Alaska. Ed. Henry N. Michael. Toronto: University of Toronto Press, 1967. 358 pp.
See the Arctic Bibliography for a full listing of Zagoskin's works in Russian. See also the following:
Adamov; Baker; see also the Arctic Bibliography. See also extracts from the journals in Petrof.

ZAHM, JOHN AUGUSTINE (b. 1851)
Alaska: The Country and its Inhabitants. Notre Dame: Notre Dame University Press, 1886. 27 pp.

ZAIKOV, POTAP KUZMICH
Andrews (sailed from Siberia in 1772; saw Cook at Unalaska; took three vessels into Prince William Sound in 1783); Bancroft (obtained charts from Cook; was in Prince William Sound in 1779; assisted Haro at Unalaska in 1788; Vancouver visited his post in Cook Inlet); Cook; Dall (in Prince William Sound in 1781; surveyed Captain's Harbor in 1783); Tompkins (trading in Prince William Sound failed because of the fierceness of the Indians); Vancouver (visit on eastern shore was by Stepan, not Potap Zaikov). See also the Arctic Bibliography.

ZAIKOV, STEPAN KUZMICH
Bancroft (commanded the *Alexandr Nevski* in 1781; was Russian chief at Ft. St. Nicholas; brother of Potap Zaikov); Dall (with Lebedev in Cook Inlet in 1792); Vancouver (Zaikov absent when Vancouver visited his post; worked for traders distinct from Baranov). See also the Arctic Bibliography.

ZAVALISHIN, DMITRI IVANOVICH (1804-92)
See the Arctic Bibliography.

ZEUSLER, FREDERICK AUGUST (b. 1890)
"Alaskan Names," *Proc.*, US Naval Inst., Oct., 1941.
"Bogoslof Island," *Proc.*, US Naval Inst., Apr., 1942.

ZIBELL, WILFRIED
Atuutit Mumiksat. Fairbanks: Wycliffe Bible Translators, 1967. 48 pp. Eskimo Hymnal.
Inupiam Ukalhi: Eskimo Reader for the Kobuk River-Kotzebue Sound Area. Fairbanks: Summer Inst. of Linguistics, 1966. 40 pp.
Unipchaat 1.: Animal Stories of the Kobuk River Eskimos. Fairbanks: Summer Inst. of Linguistics, 1969.
Unipchaat 2.: Animal Stories of the Kobuk River Eskimos. Fairbanks: Summer Inst. of Linguistics, 1969. 26 pp.
Unipchaat 3.: Animal Stories of the Kobuk River Eskimos. Fairbanks: Summer Inst. of Linguistics, 1970.

ZIEGLER, EUSTACE PAUL (b. ca. 1887)
Alaska Sportsman, June, '55 (biog.); Chase (New England artist; Episcopal missionary at Cordova, returned to painting); Gilbert (T-1713); Kosmos (T-2511); Wilson, K.

ZIES, EMANUEL GEORGE (b. 1883)
"Hot Springs in the Valley of Ten Thousand Smokes," *J. of Geology,* May, 1924.
"The Valley of Ten Thousand Smokes," *Technical Papers,* Nat. Geog. Soc., 1929.

ZIMMERLY, ANNA
"The Discovery of Gold at Juneau," *Alaska-Yukon Magazine,* Sept., '07. Extracts from the journal of Col. Richard T. Harris.

ZIMMERMAN, HENRICH
Account of the Third Voyage of Captain Cook, 1776-80. Wellington: Alexander Turnbull Library, 1926. 49 pp.
See also the Arctic Bibliography.

ZIMOVIA STRAIT
Alaska Sportsman, Feb., '58 (photo of beach with deserted moorages); Baker (separates Wrangel Island from Etolin and Woronkofski Islands; Russian name means winter); Barrow (1952-53).

ZINN, GEORGE JOHN
"Fort Liscom, Valdez," *Alaskan Churchman,* Feb., 1917.
"Valdez and Seward," *Alaskan Churchman,* March, 1917.

ZOLLINGER, JAMES PETER
Sutter: The Man and his Empire. New York: Putnam's, 1939.

ZOLOTAREV, ALEKSANDR MIKHAILOVICH
See the Arctic Bibliography.

ZOLOTAREVSKAIA, I. A.
"Ethnographical Material from the Americas in Russian Collections," *Proc.,* 32nd International Congress of Americanists, 1956.

ZOOLOGY
See the Arctic Bibliography.

ZUBKOVA, NIKOLAI NIKOLAEVICH
See the Arctic Bibliography, and T-5040 ff.

ZUMWALT, EUGENE V.
"The Alaska Public Domain," *Journal of Forestry,* June, 1960.

The Index in the Tourville Bibliography includes the following categories:

Agriculture, General
Agriculture, Animal Husbandry
Agriculture, Homesteading
Alaska Highway
Anthologies
Artists
Atlases
Aviation
Bibliography
Biography, Collective
Biography, General
Biological Sciences, General
Biological Sciences, Botany
Biological Sciences, Entomology
Biological Sciences, Limnology
Biological Sciences, Marine
Biological Sciences, Ornithology
Biological Sciences, Physiology
Biological Sciences, Zoology
Cartography
Civic Clubs, Groups, Organizations
Commerce, General
Commerce, Fisheries
Commerce, Fur Industry
Commerce, Fur Seal and Sea Otter
Commerce, Fur Trapping, Trading, Ranches
Commerce, Insurance
Communications
Cook Books
Dogs and Dog Mushing
Economic Conditions
Education, Schools, Teachers
Education, Texts
Engineering
Ethnology, Culture
Ethnology, Legends, Tales
Ethnology, Origins
Exploration, Collective
Exploration, before 1867
Exploration, after 1867
Expositions
Fiction
Fiction, Criticism
Gold Rushes, Books Published 1862-1910
Gold Rushes, Books Published 1911-1970
Government, City and State
Government, Federal
Government, Territorial
Government, Treaties and Foreign Relations
Guidebooks
Health
History and Geography
History, Russian America
Holidays
Humor
Journals, Diaries, Letters
Juvenile, Fiction
Juvenile, Non-fiction
Juvenile, Biography
Juvenile, Eskimos and Indians
Juvenile, History and Geography

Libraries
Linguistics
Military, World War II
Mining
Mining, Laws
Mountain Climbing
Museums
Music, Songbooks
National Parks, Monuments, Wildlife Refuges
Newspapers
Numismatics
Philately
Photograph Albums and Books
Physical Sciences, General
Physical Sciences, Geodynamics
Physical Sciences, Meteorology
Physical Sciences, Oceanography
Poetry
Reference Works
Religion
Religion, Translations
Sports
Theses
Telepathy
Theatre
Transportation, Highways
Transportation, Horses
Transportation, Rail
Transportation, Water
Travel
Whaling

The Editors

Stephen W. and Betty J. Haycox

STEPHEN WALTER HAYCOX: Born in Fort Wayne, Indiana, he received his B.A. at Seattle University (summa cum laude) specializing in history and philosophy. His graduate work was accomplished at the University of Oregon where he was awarded the M.A. and Ph.D. in history. From 1970 to 1972, he served as Assistant Professor of History at Anchorage Community College. Since that time he has been on the faculty of the Senior College and the College of Arts and Sciences where he now holds the rank of Associate Professor. Haycox has served as head of the Department of History in both assignments. In addition to his courses in American Labor History, Cultural and Intellectual History, and Westward Expansion, he has offered courses in the History of Alaska. His publications include *Alaska and America: A Comparative Chronology, 1725-1973*; with Janis Burke, *Descriptive Bibliography of Historical Resource Material in the Anchorage Area*; with Barbara Sweetland Smith, *Preliminary Survey of the Archive of the Russian Orthodox Church in Alaska*; "Bicentennial Values and the Settlement of Alaska Native Claims," to be published in *Proceedings, Second Conference on Alaska History*; "Freedom, Justice and Equality: Alaska and the Bicentennial, in *Land and the Pursuit of Happiness*; and with

William Adam Jacobs, "The Role of the Local Historical Society in the Writing of History," in *Writing Alaska's History*, ed. Robert A. Frederick.

BETTY JEAN HAYCOX: Born in Seattle, she attended the University of Washington, gaining considerable research experience, and later pursued medical history while a member of the staff of King County Hospital. Her family has had long-standing ties to Alaska. In the 1890's one relative prospected for gold in the Fortymile district; two uncles, the Brightman Brothers, operated a reduction plant at Killisnoo in the 1880's; and her mother lived in Anchorage in 1918. Betty and Stephen married in 1963. They have three children, Mary, Paul and Peter.